D1565133

MELVILLE BIOGRAPHY

MELVILLE BIOGRAPHY

✣ *An Inside Narrative* ✣

HERSHEL PARKER

NORTHWESTERN UNIVERSITY PRESS

EVANSTON, ILLINOIS

Northwestern University Press
www.nupress.northwestern.edu

Printed in the United States of America

10   9   8   7   6   5   4   3   2   1

Library of Congress Cataloging-in-Publication Data

Parker, Hershel.
　　Melville biography : an inside narrative / Hershel Parker.
　　　　p. cm.
　　Includes bibliographical references and index.
　　ISBN 978-0-8101-2709-8 (cloth : alk. paper)
　　1. Parker, Hershel. 2. Melville, Herman, 1819–1891—Criticism and
interpretation—History. 3. Biography as a literary form. 4. Criticism—United States.
5. Novelists, American—19th century—Biography—History and criticism. I. Title.
PS2388.B54P37 2013
813.3—dc23

　　　　　　　　　　　　　　　　　　　　　　　　　　　　　　　　2012022480

♾ The paper used in this publication meets the minimum requirements of the
American National Standard for Information Sciences—Permanence of Paper for
Printed Library Materials, ANSI Z39.48-1992.

This book is dedicated to Heddy-Ann Richter even though on an Amtrak train heading north from Washington, D.C., on December 30, 1984, she said, "You are helping Leyda with research and you'll read all those new letters at the New York Public Library. You have a good prose style. You should write a biography. Everybody will be very grateful for it."

At the fag-end of literary criticism, when all major authors have been exhaustively analyzed, four kinds of books are being written: rare original critiques, variations of existing ideas, thinly disguised repetitions of what has already been said and sterile infatuations with structuralism and semiotics. In this decadent context a thoroughly researched biography, which is firmly based on extensive archival evidence and presents a massive quantity of new material as the basis for original interpretations, is perhaps the most valuable contribution to modern scholarship.

— Jeffrey Meyers in his chapter on
Wyndham Lewis in *The Craft of Literary Biography*

Contents

Acknowledgments

I OWE MOST TO CRITICISM from Heddy-Ann Richter, Robert A. Sandberg, and Alma MacDougall. I also thank Dennis Marnon, Scott Norsworthy, James Hime, Patricia Cline Cohen, Robert D. Madison, Paul Maher, Jr., Warren Broderick, Robert D. Hume, Mark Allen Greene, John Gretchko, and Robert E. Winslow III. For kindnesses I am indebted to Robert and Roslyn Haber, Lisa Harrow and Roger Payne, Frederick J. Kennedy and Joyce Deveau Kennedy, as well as Lottie Cain, Michael R. Clark, Chris Coughlin, Bill Deresiewicz, Mort Engstrom, Amy Puett Emmers, Joan Foster, Michael Gaynor, Athel Eugene Gibson, Brian Higgins, Stephen Hoy, Dan Lane, Alex Liddie, Edouard Marsoin, George Monteiro, Mark Niemeyer, Steven Olsen-Smith, R. B. Parrish, Noel Polk, Todd Richardson, and Paul Seydor. In the Berkshires I am indebted to Ruth Degenhardt, Kathleen Reilly, Rick Leab, Lion G. Miles, and Mandy Victor. On the Internet I am indebted to the blogger and Hawthorne reader, Nicole Perrin. At Northwestern University Press I thank Henry Lowell Carrigan, Anne Gendler, Rudy E. Faust, Marianne Jankowski, and Peter Joseph Raccuglia. I particularly thank the Melvillean Alma MacDougall in her role as copy editor.

☛ Among dates of Melville letters and reviews of his books I occasionally set down dates on which I made decisions or discoveries—not because these dates have high historical significance but because I want to remind young readers of this book that a scholar never knows in advance which day will be (as Melville says) marked with a white stone.

☛ Some of my topics need to be viewed from more than one historical vantage point and in more than one biographical context. I glance forward and later recapitulate or elaborate several times without, I trust, repeating verbatim many favorite sentences.

Preface

My topic for rumination on a September 2007 run on the beach at Morro Bay was how to get out of writing a five-hundred-page condensation of my two-volume *Herman Melville: A Biography* (Johns Hopkins, 1996 and 2002). I had told the life, in those two taut volumes—taut, I say, although each ran to more than nine hundred pages. The books were long because they were filled with old episodes freshly illuminated by new crosslights, old fragments of clues transformed into narratives by new documents, and a good many previously unheard stories which I had summoned forth from old newspapers and previously untranscribed letters. The first volume had earned a permanent slot on the Pulitzer Prize website as one of two finalists, and each volume had won the highest award from the Association of American Publishers, the first in "Literature and Language" and the second in the renamed category, "Biography and Autobiography"—the only time, I gather, that both parts of a two-volume set had won. I had done my best, and no new biography was warranted by the handful of sparkling new items I and a few others had discovered or by the belated solutions to a few vexing puzzles. Besides, if I condensed the already succinct narrative into a mere five hundred pages, who would ever again read the full rich story in the two volumes? To publish a condensed version when so much dazzling news was still not assimilated by Melville critics and general readers—why, that would be to immolate decades of heroic dedication, wouldn't it?

As always during runs along the Pacific, I surfed the recesses of my mind, this time for shapes and titles. Two years earlier after lurching queasily on the dunes I had made a quick check: no alcohol—must have been an earthquake. As I ran this time, bafflement gave way to instant exultation when a title came unsummoned in: *Melville: An Inside Narrative*—the subtitle a gift from Melville's *Billy Budd, Sailor (An Inside Narrative)*. In my diary: "What a great liberating title for the one-volume biography." The book would be a different sort of biography, its nature yet unspecified. I was nowhere near ready to start writing it, but I could work on other projects contentedly because I had a title that would draw forth the proper contents when the time came. The director of the Johns Hopkins University Press kindly gave me an amended contract for this hypothetical *Melville: An Inside Narrative*, then in May 2009 graciously released me from the contract because I wanted to place it at the same press as another book.

The actual book (as distinguished from the title) began in May 2009 as a detailed prospectus in the double-or-nothing package I offered to Northwestern University Press, this book and *The Powell Papers* (2011). I would salvage "Damned by Dollars," the final essay in the 2001 Norton Critical Edition of *Moby-Dick*, and I would speed the book along by including other heart's darlings of mine such as my 1960 MLA talk, "The Metaphysics of Indian-hating," and "The Confidence Man's Masquerade," both in the 2006 Norton Critical Edition of *The Confidence-Man*. What could be faster to put together than a collection of good old pieces? Why, it was half written already! The press offered contracts in early June, the week the Northwestern-Newberry Edition of *Published Poems* (with me as the new General Editor) was released. Intensely excited by outlining the new project, I behaved with uncharacteristic recklessness: I abandoned everything else I was working on and started writing the new book. It refused to become a collection: "Damned by Dollars" had to stay in, and another piece or two, in revisited form, but the old-favorites album would have to be delayed, or even published posthumously like the longtime Northwestern-Newberry General Editor Harrison Hayford's *Melville's Prisoners* (2003), for, it turned out, I had new things to say. The emerging contents dictated a new title.

Melville Biography: An Inside Narrative is divided into three main sections. Part 1 is autobiographical, the first four chapters dealing with my long preparation for writing a biography. Biographers like Carl Rollyson with multiple subjects (Rebecca West, Norman Mailer, Martha Gellhorn, Lillian Hellman, Marilyn Monroe, on to Amy Lowell and beyond) may gasp at my narrowness (more than half a century for a biography of only one writer!) while I marvel, in turn, that anyone can wrap up and bury a corpse one week and next week write the birth scene for a new subject. Melville research took me a long time. The last two chapters in this part describe some of the revelations and puzzlements I encountered in the actual writing and afterward.

Part 2 deals in rigorous detail with the hard turn away from factual study of Melville that literary criticism and reviewing have taken in the last sixty-odd years, a hostility to documentary facts that is, in its most extreme form, unique to Melville biography. After working on my biography in something akin to solitary confinement until midway through the first volume, I was violently assaulted. Like no other biographer of an American writer, I was the victim of a devastating preemptive strike in *American Literature*, the formerly staid scholarly journal newly seized by the forces of political correctness.

Although nothing from the great trove of Melville documents discovered in 1983 had yet been worked into any biography, this "New Melville" special issue of *American Literature* (March 1994) contained a "cease and desist" warning (115): "We already have full-scale biographies of Melville"! I persisted, only to find that no other biographer of an American writer had ever been subjected to such concerted denial of documentary evidence. In 2002 three reviewers, starting in the *New York Times*, painted me as being untrustworthy because I made two reckless surmises as if they were facts—first when I described Melville as completing a book in 1853 (something well known to Melville scholars since 1960), second when I showed him trying to publish in 1860 a book he called "Poems" (something known to everyone since 1922). The documentary evidence, of course, was visible on the pages of my biography these critics were reviewing. Melville has been and remains unique among great American writers in the quantity of recently discovered documentation and in the ferocity of the hostility to such information, even today, in newspapers, popular magazines, and academic journals (including *American Literature*, still).

In accounting for this hostility I focus on the influence of Charles N. Feidelson, Jr., the New Critic who at Yale for decades waged an unholy war against scholarship on Melville, starting with his contemptuous dismissal of Jay Leyda's *The Melville Log* in 1951. The repudiation of scholarship at Yale and elsewhere impoverished the next generations of academics, so that in the 1980s (while Feidelson still, or again, held sway over new young theorists) well-meaning critics proclaimed themselves New Historicists without knowing how to do historical research and even, a few times, tried to draw evidence from manuscript documents without first learning how to transcribe nineteenth-century handwriting. In this section I trace the lamentable politicizing of the American academy. I also expose the decades of arrogant, ignorant partisanship in the mutual-admiration cliques of the major reviewing organs, the New York City newspapers and magazines. Relentless adherence to a life-denying literary theory, the New Criticism, I decided, has had deleterious consequences not just on literary criticism and what passes as biography (as in one piece entitled "A Brief Biography" which ignores troves of new documents). Worse still, such a theory ultimately damages the character of its practitioners, because to blind yourself to Melville's aspirations and agonies, to treat him as an abstract "author figure" or "literary personality" (Feidelson's term) and not a real man, in the end leads critics to blind themselves to the aspirations and agonies of living people. Yet I am optimistic: I see the rapid systemic decline of whatever was good in reviewing in the mainstream media and academic journals as more than compensated for by the burgeoning of intelligent reviewing in personal blogs and litblogs, many of them ephemeral still, but constituting a phenomenon to be reckoned with in the evolving shapes of American publishing and reviewing.

Part 3 consists of demonstrations in the use of evidence and challenges to further research. Using episodes not fully developed in my biography or else told only in chronological fragments rather than in coherent, wide-ranging essays, I put under the microscope what goes into meticulously assembling and conscientiously interpreting documentary evidence. Starting in 1962 my days added up to years spent transcribing manuscripts and reading newspapers in microfilm or crunched over flat tables (only the blessed New-York Historical Society let me stand at a spine-friendly slanted table). Here I supplement my old discoveries by documents from recently available newspaper databases and other electronic sources. In some of these chapters I demonstrate what can be learned from the Internet beyond what we thought we knew, as when I tell a grisly story, new to me, about how the Harpers exploited the international copyright situation against Melville early in 1852. Especially in this part, I invite skeptical scrutiny from the reader and challenge young scholars to go beyond what I have done. "Young scholars," throughout this book, does not necessarily refer to those in colleges. We have entered a period when very few academics do archival research and those who do (mainly students of Melville's interest in art and in his books and the marginalia in them) are perhaps outnumbered by the small handful of imaginative and resource-full librarians and businesspeople whom I think of as divine amateurs. Melville research as never before is open to any benignly obsessive man or woman with a good computer, and the best of these researchers will find their way to the manuscripts, in time. Some of them may take up my challenge in the next-to-last chapter to harness the Internet in plotting the literary and personal interconnections among early British admirers of *Moby-Dick*, actually creating what I ignorantly wished for in the late 1980s, a database daisy-chain.

The endnotes constitute a significant fourth part of the book. Some of them do normal duty of identifying sources (with the help of the inclusive "Works Cited"). Many of the longer endnotes constitute a part that might be called "Melville and Biography" rather than "Melville Biography." Much of this book about Melville biography is autobiography, and Sidonie Smith in her Modern Language Association "Presidential Address" (2011) wants us to know that "autobiography studies, with its capacious reach, is now a site of prodigious theoretical activity" (565). Having circled back toward the realm of my *Flawed Texts and Verbal Icons* (1984), that book of textual theory, literary theory, and creativity theory, in some endnotes I relate my present enterprise to what I and others have to say about the theory and practice of autobiography and biography. While in the first three parts I keep the focus on Melville biography, in endnotes I discuss problems in Melville biography that other biographers and theorists have confronted in their work. In such notes I expatiate enough that a reader can think critically about issues while being lured on to thoughtful works by writers such as Paula R. Backscheider, Robert D. Hume, Paul Murray Kendall, Ray Monk, Stephen B. Oates, and Barbara W. Tuchman, as well as being lured back into further reflection on my own expositions on Melville biography and historiography. Heretofore, only a handful of writers on biography (notably André Maurois, Virginia Woolf, Leon Edel, Richard Holmes, and more recently Hermione Lee) have had their dicta applied, tested, and sometimes challenged by later biographers. *Melville Biography: An Inside Narrative* puts forward ideas of many biographers and theorists of biography and all sorts of life-writing in order to test them against what I have learned in working on Melville and writing my biography as well as what I have learned about autobiography and biography in writing this book.

For all my conviction that unique forces have created the modern attitude toward Melville biography, I mean *Melville Biography: An Inside Narrative* to take a seat in the same great dining hall where honorable cousins such as Richard Holmes's *Footsteps: Adventures of a Romantic Biographer* (1985) and Paula R. Backscheider's *Reflections on Biography* (2001) sit at the upper table. I mean *Melville Biography* to sit near the table occupied congenially by Paul Murray Kendall's *The Art of Biography* (1965) and collections such as Marc Pachter's *Telling Lives* (1979), Jeffrey Meyers's *The Craft of Literary Biography* (1985), Stephen B. Oates's *Biography as High Adventure* (1986), John Batchelor's *The Art of Literary Biography* (1995), Peter France and William St Clair's *Mapping Lives* (2002), and Mark Bostridge's *Lives for Sale* (2004). I see it as sitting across the room from theory-envying and theory-driven unruly, eccentric stepcousins once or twice removed like Ira Bruce Nadel's *Biography: Fiction, Fact, and Form* (1984), William H. Epstein's *Recognizing Biography* (1987) and his collection, *Contesting the Subject* (1991), and Michael Benton's deceptively innocuous *Literary Biography* (2009). In real life the Internet has brought me into contact with previously unknown stalwart double and triple Scottish-German cousins in the American South who look and act like me. Nothing so joyously fulfilling has befallen me in academic life except talking to James B. Meriwether one night in 1967, as I tell in the second chapter, but I take comfort from a number of biographers and critics of biography who have fought through to complexly challenging ideas akin to mine. With luck *Melville Biography: An Inside Narrative* can sit at a table alongside like-minded printed cousins such as William M. Murphy's piece on John Butler Yeats and Mark Holloway's piece on Norman Douglas in Meyers's *The Craft of Literary Biography*, Robert D. Hume's *Reconstructing Contexts: The Aims and Principles of Archaeo-Historicism*, and Ray Monk's "Life Without Theory: Biography as an Exemplar of Philosophical Understanding," as well as virtually seated electronic cousins such as Dan Green's *The Reading Experience 2.0*. (Confession: Being in the fourth quarter of my century, I print out pieces by the Internet blogger Green so I can mark them up.) I count on these allies to join this book in pushing one end of our table against the door so as to bar out marauders.

The fact is that despite its immense popularity literary biography is under attack from subversive interlopers, and not only theorists of biography and theorists disguised as biographers. Archival research proving arduous, would-be biographers have begun redefining archives, expanding any narrow conception of archives to include geographical location as archive and abandoning objectivist standards of truth. Instead of aiming to recover what someone wrote, one theorist now suggests transcribing manuscripts according to the critic's rhetorical agenda. Even the use of historical records is now challenged. Many critics and would-be biographers seem determined to theorize the genre of biography out of existence.[1]

These Malay pirates of literary biography, springing up, weapons drawn, from the bottom of the ship in the treacherous fashion Melville describes in *Mardi*, will not succeed. As long as libraries preserve archives such as the Gansevoort-Lansing Collection of the New York Public Library or the Melville and Morewood papers at the Berkshire Athenaeum or the Melvill-Melville papers at the Houghton Library, or the Shaw papers at the Massachusetts Historical Society, pilgrim researchers will come, even if only a dedicated few. There will always be a few literary detectives who devote months or years to the pursuit of documents in the confidence that at last they will sit at midnight in a little bare motel room in Spartanburg, South Carolina, and turn through a big shoebox full of what looks like only bills of lading until they spy a blue folded paper, clearly a letter, a letter with the signature "Really Thine, H. Melville"—a letter reassuring Melville's wife's young stepcousin Sam Savage: "Concerning the *foot-ball* part of the business, why, we are all foot-balls, more or less—& it is lucky that we are, on some accounts. It is important, however, that our balls be covered with a leather, good & tough, that will stand banging & all 'the slings & arrows of outrageous fortune.'"[2] Literary detectives will sit in dark rooms peering at their computer screens, doing their ultimately advanced searches. They will imaginatively misspell (Mellvill, Mellville, Hermann, and more) when accurate spellings turn up nothing. They will try their equivalent of "froward" and "godless" on Google every few weeks for most of a decade, as Scott Norsworthy did until he discovered a source for some of Melville's once-baffling notes in the back of his Shakespeare. They will boggle at a passage in a Melville text and find riches, as I did when I Googled "Napoleon" and "outline" and "tree" and discovered that Melville in *The Confidence-Man* was referring to a then-famous example of hidden art. There will always be a few frequenters of known archives, a few imaginative trackers of missing archives, a few librarians who recognize gaps in their institution's papers and reach out their hands for lost treasures, and a few "divine amateurs" who believe that the facts matter and that they can identify some of them from their computers or in raids on distant libraries. And for literary biography, there will always be readers who want to know about the living man or woman whose deepest being infuses the books they love.

MELVILLE BIOGRAPHY

PART I

Biographer and Biography

In the June 23, 2002, *New York Times*, Richard H. Brodhead revealed that he knew my deepest secrets, starting with this history: "Many years ago Hershel Parker set out to write the biography to end all biographies of Herman Melville" (13). Emerson said it best in "Experience": "The grossest ignorance does not disgust like this impudent knowingness."[1] The only grain of truth in what Brodhead so confidently announced was that I had started to work on Melville many years earlier. Because almost all academic critics, not just quintessential New Critics, comprehend nothing about what a scholar does, I offer in this first part of *Melville Biography: An Inside Narrative* six autobiographical chapters on what can go into the making of a biographer and a documentary biography.

When I started to work on Melville I assumed most work had been done. Why, I wondered to the co-editor, my teacher, Harrison Hayford, did we need to collate the American *Moby-Dick* against the English *The Whale* for the Norton Critical Edition—Luther S. Mansfield and Howard P. Vincent had done that in the 1940s, hadn't they, for their 1952 Hendricks House edition? The truth was that Mansfield and Vincent had made an attempt but they had not been thorough. They had missed much of the evidence, botched the story, and had not read the book for words the copyist or the American compositor had misread. The lesson in the early 1960s was stark: you have to do everything yourself if you want to know it has been done to your standards. In 1962 I began hunting reviews of Melville's books to supplement the work others had done, continued the hunt systematically for the "Historical Notes" of the Northwestern-Newberry Edition of *The Writings of Herman Melville*, published results in the Higgins-Parker *Contemporary Reviews*, and continued the hunt for my biography and for *The New Melville Log*, and beyond. Once you learn to look for full, good texts, you don't stop.

In the 1970s I fell into a new career when I saw that the most commonly taught pieces of American fiction were very seldom fine New Critical artifacts. When I edited the American Renaissance part of *The Norton Anthology of American Literature* I put in texts of Poe from the *Broadway Journal* that actually made sense, as the standard truncated texts did not always do. When you are doing the work for yourself, you think of things that ought to be known and are not available. In that collection, also, I became the first to anthologize Whitman's "Live Oak, with Moss." When you spend a career thinking things through for yourself and doing work for yourself, you are grateful when you encounter brilliant fellow-researchers with highly developed work ethics, as I have been lucky enough to do, although a curious fact is that in recent years few of them have held jobs as professors.

Some biographers write about times when they asked themselves whom they should take as their next subject. Some of them even reveal that they have accepted someone else's take-out assignment for the subject of a biography. My story is different. I have worked many months on American writers other than Melville—Emerson, Hawthorne, G. W. Harris, Thoreau, Whitman, Dickinson, Clemens, James, Stephen Crane, Fitzgerald, Faulkner, Hemingway, Mailer—and all the work I have done on these writers has been, at bottom, textual and biographical. But my first talk at a scholarly meeting, in 1960, was on Melville, my dissertation was on Melville, and except for a special issue of *Studies in the Novel* on Stephen Crane, *The Norton Anthology of American Literature*, and *Flawed Texts and Verbal Icons* all my books and collections and the majority of my articles have been on Melville. If I was going to write a biography, it would be on Melville.

As I explain in the fourth chapter, I did not set out in the early 1980s to write a biography, much less one to end all biographies. I merely wanted to help Jay Leyda expand *The Melville Log* again just as I had helped with the 1969 "Supplement." Then I would get back to my interrupted career as textual theorist and creativity theorist, for I had unfulfilled metatextual aspirations to write a book on the texts of operas, and I longed at some indefinite time to write a book about special correspondents of American newspapers before the Civil War. When Leyda was diagnosed with Parkinson's disease I had to help him full time. Now, the practical thing to do was to help him finish the *Log* and then briskly write a biography from the old and new evidence. At this point I must have believed in what I came to call the "silver platter" theory of biography, in which you write from evidence all laid out for you by someone else (even if you helped gather some of it). Leyda had certainly believed in that theory, for in his introduction to the 1951 *Log* he had declared: "In the making of this book I have tried to hold to one main aim: to give each reader the opportunity to be his own biographer of Herman Melville, by providing him with the largest possible quantity of materials to build his own approach to this complex figure" (xi). Leyda was confident that he had allowed Leon Howard to become his own biographer of Melville by presenting him with the working *Log* and joining with Hayford in "browbeating" him into writing a narrative from the documents he had been handed (as Howard said in the dedication of his biography to those two men). Others believed as passionately in the silver platter theory as Leyda had. More than one ingenuous aspirant to Boswellhood starting in the late 1980s, having found it inconvenient or downright onerous to visit a library or hard to transcribe letters, suggested that I should hand over my years of work on *The New Melville Log* to serve as his or her ready-made bio-kit.

After a few months in 1988 I had become skeptical of this silver platter theory. If you want to know what the available manuscripts say, I discovered, you have to transcribe them for yourself. In that dirtiest of all foul academic jobs, you just may discover sidelights on episodes in a writer's life or even astonishing episodes no one had ever known. By the early 1990s I knew for sure that Leyda and Hayford had been wrong—even Howard, shrewd as he was, had failed to capture the essential Melville. As I said in the preface to the first volume of my biography, I had to become my own Leyda & Company. Anyone would fail, I decided, who had not, year after year, soiled his or her own hands in devoted labor in the archives. There is no substitute for seeking documents, transcribing documents, dating them, and identifying people, places, and events referred to in them. Establish chronology first, and, if you are alert enough, you have a chance of recognizing causality and significance; listen hard enough, and you may catch elusive tones of voice. I had never taken a class from Richard Ellmann at Northwestern, when I could have, but I was the product of Jay Leyda's rigorous postgraduate training. This first part of my inside narrative traces the on-the-job training of one biographer to read and interpret evidence and to convey it in acceptable prose, a training, as it turned out (to end with Thoreau, having begun with Emerson), such as the athletes underwent.

✥ *Chapter 1* ✥

MELVILLE AND THE
FOOTSTEPS THEORY OF BIOGRAPHY

PAUL MURRAY KENDALL in *The Art of Biography* (1965) emphasizes that the modern biographer needs to be "acutely conscious of the importance of *locale*." He is sure that the "physical ambiences" of "the subject's habitat" can "enable the life-writer to tighten his grip on character, even to solve enigmas of behavior, mysterious responses to experience" (150). The biographer steeped in the subject's locales tells a better life but also develops "the life-relationship"—the unique if "indefinable" relationship between the biographer and the subject (151):

> The biographer opens himself to all that places and things will tell him, in his struggle to visualize, and to sense, his man in being. Deepest of all, the particular kind of biographer of whom I am speaking, cherishes, I believe, a conviction—call it a romantic quirk, if you will—that where the subject has trod he must tread, what the subject has seen he must see, because he thus achieves an indefinable but unmistakable kinship with his man. The winning of this kinship, more than anything else he can do, helps to annihilate the centuries, the spaces, the deceptions of change, the opacity of death.

Calling Kendall's book his "favorite work about biography" (8), Frank E. Vandiver in "Biography as an Agent of Humanism" (1983) endorses Kendall's insistence on going where the subject went, even to Louis XI's battlefield at Montlhéry, however much the terrain had changed in half a millennium (9). This notion of the "life-relationship" is enormously appealing because it exalts the biographer toward the level of the subject. What biographer would not want "to annihilate the centuries, the spaces, the deceptions of change, the opacity of death" and stand face to face with his subject, perhaps lending an elbow or a shoulder now and then?

Richard Holmes in the 1986 *Footsteps: Adventures of a Romantic Biographer* is a soul-brother to Kendall. Writing on Romantic and romantic literary figures, Holmes is himself a romantic fellow, not a hard-nosed postmodern biographer but a lover of writers, what they wrote, and where they wrote. The youthful Holmes with his grown man's pipe and his willingness to try any drink was endearing to the French, for there is nothing like sharing little pleasurable vices to foster intimacy. Of course he encountered folks who knew just whose ancestor stabled Robert Louis Stevenson's donkey! Holmes is so adept at teasing out the significances of places for him and for his nominal subjects such as Stevenson that one yearns to believe him when he describes his great early revelation:

> Have I explained myself at all? It is the simplicity of the idea, the realisation, that I am after. It was important for me, because it was probably the first time that I caught an inkling of what a process (indeed an entire vocation) called "biography" really means. I had never thought about it before. "Biography" meant a book about someone's life. Only, for me, it was to become a kind of pursuit, a tracking of the physical trail of someone's path through the past, a following of footsteps. You would never catch them; no, you would never quite catch them. But maybe, if you were lucky, you might write about the pursuit of that fleeing figure in such a way as to bring it alive in the present. (27)

This man is a Whitmanesque charmer: "Have I explained myself at all?" We surrender ourselves to his complex storytelling, becoming as interested in Holmes, for the moment, as in Stevenson. And we glorify ourselves as trackers of more than physical trails.

Even more staid biographers like me will admit that Richard Holmes's sort of direct involvement may pay off. If he had worked on Melville the ineffable Holmes would have found a way to sail on the *Charles W. Morgan* for a week or two guided by the globe-navigating Melville scholar Mary K. Bercaw Edwards, whom he, with his luck, would have found harbored, like the whaleship, at Mystic Seaport. He would have discovered a hectare in Tahiti absolutely untouched by Westerners since 1842, would have taken in all the smells of Peru, would have gnawed duff in the bowels of the *Constitution* and slept there in a hammock by special permission of the U.S. Navy and the National Park Service. And we would have loved him more for the sensual, tactile impressions he brought to us.

Holmes would never have suffered my discomfiture in 1988 when I wanted to see what Melville had seen in 1849 in Dupuytren's Museum in the School of Medicine in Paris. Even that year, as a man of middle age, and even if he had not spoken French, Holmes would not have been subjected to a thirty-minute preliminary negotiation with Mme. Thérèse. *Non, this "Herman Melville" could not have seen nothing in 1849 because the museum was founded in 1936, hein! Melville, whoever he was, could not have seen the museum because it had not existed pas!* I might if I were so minded—it was up to me—return to my hotel for Melville's journal, even printed in English, and return, and then it might be decided that I could enter into the museum, but if I did not return in fifty minutes—she used an unfamiliar expression which was not *tant pis* but some more brutal French vernacular word for "Tough!" And besides the journal I would have to have with me a guide who spoke English because I *would not understand nothing merely by looking,* and no such guide was visible. To the hotel, on the right bank, seizing merely photocopies of the journal, all I had, not the tome itself, and back. Would the tome be demanded? Mme. Thérèse nowhere visible. Isabelle, the speaker of *anglais*! Sweet Isabelle! Two-headed French babies. French babies joined at chest. French babies joined at belly. French cancers. Vats. French tumors. Many big French tumors. Vats. Heart of a French miser with a big franc stuck in aorta. Genitals and parts of genitals—nonfunctional parts of French genitals. Vats of formaldehyde. Away, flushed with victory, fifty francs well spent, in time to behold a modern marvel—French athletes in the Luxembourg Gardens vigorously smoking their Gauloises while moderately engaged in du jogging.

What good had it done me to see the two-headed French babies? In *Mardi,* written before his trips abroad in 1849 and 1856–57, Melville had described Hooloomooloo, the Isle of Cripples, and in *White-Jacket* (chap. 61) he had described the Parisian cast of the head of an elderly woman with "a hideous, crumpled horn, like that of a ram, downward growing out of the forehead."[1] Melville knew, already, of the departments of Morbid Anatomy and the Anatomical Museums of Europe, and knew he wanted to see them, for his friend Evert A. Duyckinck had been to Dupuytren's museum of monstrosities. Melville was a man who would pay to look at the grotesque. So, I persisted until I saw the miser's heart, plugged up by a franc, just as I persisted in the always closed Natural History Museum in Florence, where my wife with her UCLA Italian proclaimed the stature of her husband the professor and got us into the great room with large wax figures of pregnant women and men with bisected penises designed for students of anatomy to study and copy. Then she chatted up the attendant while I peered at the dioramas of Naples in the time of the plague. Again, I asked, what good had it done me, since I knew already that Melville was interested in monstrosities? So much for the romance of scholarship? But against such skepticism is the late-nineteenth-century vignette Scott Norsworthy found about New York City during the cholera epidemic of July 1849—a recollection by an "Old Fogy" who had ventured out and encountered Melville in company with Evert Duyckinck and Cornelius Mathews. During long moments those four men were the only New Yorkers visible in the deserted streets.[2] Also, Melville remembered being left (did he think abandoned?) in Albany in the time of the plague, 1832, when his mother and the other seven children all fled to the safety of Pittsfield, only half a year after his father had died. Melville knew what it was to be in cities in the time of the plague.

No such romantic pilgrim as Holmes, I nevertheless did my best to follow Melville, visiting and revisiting places where his feet had trod and his horses' hooves had trod in the United States and even some where his feet had trod in Europe. Almost always, I was reflecting, with lurking skepticism and a tinge of guilt, on just how valuable it really was to see what he saw, other than as a tax write-off. I went to Albany, Amsterdam, Chester, Coblenz, Cologne, Como, Edinburgh, Florence, Gansevoort, Glasgow, Glens Falls, Lansingburgh, Lenox, Liverpool, London, Nantucket, New Bedford, Paris, Pittsfield, Rome, San Francisco, Staten Island, Troy, and even Venice, where it's hard to follow footsteps. What I saw, sometimes, was pretty much what Melville saw, such as the cathedral he and Hawthorne went to in Chester. One room, the Tribuno at the Uffizi, seemed almost fixed in time, so many of the same paintings and sculptures were still there. In Florence, also, there were clear remnants of the old architecture so we could see that in Melville's time the now squared-off Caffè Doney would have looked exotic, a bit like a masonry caravanserie. Sometimes little or nothing was left. Liverpool in the 1980s was rough, left to decay with only the folly of a new "cathedral" to mock the impoverished scene. At least I got a sense of how high above the squalid dock area the once-elegant Adelphi stood, where Evert Duyckinck and then Lemuel Shaw, Jr., stayed, and saw how decrepit it had become. Not one historical postcard of Liverpool was for sale, but the Nelson statue was where Melville had seen it. (The only other strangers in town were two teenage Japanese girls looking for Strawberry Fields.) After the Blitz the narrow London streets Melville had wandered through were gone. I had to reconstitute the village of Gansevoort in my mind from the directories and the family letters.

I went through Arrowhead many times, and slept one night there. I got no frisson from prowling spirits of the Melvilles but I got what any tourist could get—a realizing sense of the power of the sight, on a good hour, of Mount

Greylock to the north from Melville's study window. Still, in her "Optical Research" in Mark Bostridge's collection *Lives for Sale* I knew just what Antonia Fraser meant: "I would never have understood the pattern of events following the murder of Riccio at Holyrood, had I not been able to go and investigate the layout of the palace myself" (113). Very much in her spirit, I climbed into the attic of the Lansingburgh house because I was pretty sure some of the boys slept up there, low headroom or not. I climbed into the attic of Broadhall because I wanted to see how the house had been altered from the time that Melville described the spot where he was working on his whaling book in August 1850. I got into the Mount Vernon Street house of Melville's father-in-law by accosting the owner with a copy of the advance proofs of my first volume. I walked round and round the Gansevoort, New York, house and made a detailed floor plan of it on the basis of dozens of references in family letters, although I did not get inside. The ineffable Holmes would have hailed a child to summon a caretaker, have been admitted, and been offered at least a cold collation and tea. I worried about the careless way one downstairs room was identified in a letter: "state" room or "slate" room? Finally, exercising one of the few powers of a biographer, I decreed that it would be the "slate" room; if a captain could "make it noon," I could "make it slate." Only after this chapter was drafted did John Gretchko present me with a room by room inventory of what was in the house after Melville's sister Frances died. What casual treasures of mahogany furniture! I made a floor chart of the Twenty-sixth Street house, based on a great range of evidence including Melville's granddaughter Frances's corrections in her copy of Lewis Mumford's biography then in the possession of Priscilla Ambrose. I identified with Melville's love of strong old elegant furniture and shared his distaste for new geegaws. It is no coincidence that my humbler but memento-filled study in Pennsylvania was photographed for the *New York Times Magazine*.[3]

But what help did I get from all my charts of preserved or lost houses, including the Manor House of the Van Rensselaers (disassembled stone by stone and transported out of the state) and Uncle Peter Gansevoort's house and the Governor's House at Sailors' Snug Harbor (which Melville frequently visited while his brother Tom was the occupant)? In an obvious way, I could contrast better the substantial unostentatious house where Elizabeth Shaw Melville grew up with what she experienced as a visitor at his mother's rented Lansingburgh house while Melville was in the Pacific and at Arrowhead. Knowing that Melville had paid for the small, rundown Arrowhead exactly what the Morewoods paid for the moldering grandeur of the Melvill estate (with much greater acreage) told me something about Melville's business sense. I knew that on a smaller scale than the Morewoods' Broadhall, Uncle Herman's Gansevoort house where Melville's mother spent her last years was furnished with fine strong colonial pieces as well as some imported furniture and that she reigned there in near-feudal splendor. I understood Melville daughter Frances's anger the better for knowing Melville as a collector and preserver of beautiful objects, however destructive he had been, at times, of his own writings and of letters that now would be worth good money to lucky descendants or other owners, such as the letter from Hawthorne in praise of *Moby-Dick*, or the manuscript of *The Isle of the Cross*. (Someone who reads this book may know just where some Melville treasures are stored.) Knowing the houses inside and out let me understand the human relationships better, sympathize responsibly with suppressed feelings, understand human weaknesses. Truly, there was value in knowing where and how the family lived, even if I never in a mystical moment caught the scent of Melville's "segar" or heard the swish of colonial gowns when they were brought down from the attic at Gansevoort for airing and possible use in ceremonies in 1876.

Melville sought out high places for superb views and reminders of satanic temptation. I knew what it felt like to live beneath mountains. During the war, when Henry J. Kaiser transported Southerners west to build ships, Mount Hood had dominated the terrain to the east on clear days. Photographs of Cavanough Mountain from my parents' eastern Oklahoma farm are hard to distinguish, sometimes, from photographs of the much higher Greylock. Some things I intuited, as when I declared that Melville experienced the sense of Vermont shouldering up behind him while he was at Lansingburgh. I was going by what I would have felt, and what I knew of his older brother Gansevoort's fur-buying expeditions into Massachusetts and Vermont. Melville would have lifted up his eyes unto the hills, from whence his help just might come. This I absolutely knew because of a religious indoctrination similar to his.[4]

Myself a lover of the Romantics, I seized the chance in Rome to wend my way down from the Baths of Caracalla to the Protestant Cemetery—by a natural progression, as Melville recorded in his journal in early 1857. The comment might be elliptical to moderns since he did not mention Shelley, but it would have been obvious to any educated person in his time, who would have expected Melville, like any tourist, to have thought of Shelley's composing parts of *Prometheus Unbound* there, perhaps to have remembered an engraving of the scene, and then naturally to have made his way down to see where Shelley's heart was buried. Did my trek down to outside the walls of Rome help? Well, as I worked my way through the torturous working-class streets from the Baths of Caracalla to the Protestant Cemetery, following

Melville following Shelley, I had time to reflect on Shelley's significance to him. The unexpected benefit was the perception that Melville, musing on Shelley, might have been blindsided by the proximity of the tomb of the lesser-known Keats. Perhaps much of the value in following the footsteps of writers lies in leaving yourself open to the indirect and unanticipated.

On the whole, I decided, it was much more important to follow Melville around the paintings and sculptures in the Tribuno in Florence than to look at Saint Mark's in Venice. Having coffee at Florian's was pleasant, but did it bring me closer to Melville? Only ironically, for a card on each of the outside tables listed notables who had sat there, Melville among them—Melville, who had been an inconspicuous, almost broken man when he was there. The grander the monument the less of it Melville could have taken in, I suspected, but I never regretted peering at a painting he had seen, or a piece of sculpture. Melville himself drew the connection between Italian paintings and English literature, noting in his Milton that the devils in *Paradise Lost* were influenced by the paintings the poet saw in Italy. I thought it was valuable to have touched the green drapery marble of the Jesuit Church in Venice that Melville had so admired and that the snobbish noncombatant William Dean Howells would soon scorn. Melville's appreciation of the marble showed me something I liked about his sense of aesthetics something for which most of the evidence lay in his marginalia.[5]

Was I able to fake what I did not see? Would readers of my biography hoot at how obvious it was that I never got to the Marquesas or Mar Saba? Did I describe Honolulu successfully on the basis of newspapers and histories and ships' logs, or has Hawaii so changed that a person born after it became a state would not know how close or how remote I was from an accurate description of what it felt like to have been there in 1843? Did I give a sense of the now-lost Greek splendor of the buildings of Sailors' Snug Harbor as you saw them from across the bay at the Battery? Did I convey the sense of what you would have encountered in the 1870s as you walked along the Hudson around the Battery and up the East River? What I learned in my researches was a revelation to me—sawmills on the Hudson; north of Coenties Slip bowsprits run in over street traffic so you could touch the figureheads; the ship-chandlery shops north of Market Street (halfway between the Battery and Corlears Hook). These last details I took thankfully from Charles H. Farnham's "A Day on the Docks" in the May 1879 *Scribner's Magazine.*

Perhaps following Melville was not as valuable as knowing what it was to live a nineteenth-century life. I survived one northern Oklahoma winter in a tent (not for fun) and lived for years without electricity and running water and some years with electricity but without running water. Therefore I knew what it meant when I belatedly discovered an advertisement proclaiming that the Fourth Avenue house Melville abandoned in October 1850 had water closets and hot water to the third floor, and I knew what it meant for Melville's wife Lizzie (Elizabeth Shaw Melville) to go from there to Arrowhead, which had a kitchen pump and no water closet or hot water. I knew how to picture the scene Melville's brother-in-law John Hoadley sketched in his March 28, 1854, letter to Melville's sister Augusta, in which he envisioned the "Arrowheads" in the evening (bereft, just then, of Maria and Fanny, who were with him in Lawrence):

> I can see you now, your face, shaded by your hand,—glowing in the ruddy light, and full of changeful expression, as the flickering fire burns brighter or subsides;—changeful, yet continuous, like the notes of an Irish melody; while Lizzie looks up at intervals from her sewing or her book, to recall by a tone and look of love, the musing wanderer from his enchanted Isles. (Parker, 2:215)

I knew about reading by firelight and the light from a coal-oil lamp, though not a whale-oil lamp.

I knew about modes of transportation. I had traveled in a wagon drawn by a team of horses I had harnessed up myself, and I had ridden horses I had saddled. I knew how to plough and build fences and milk cows. I had walked for hours at night on railroad tracks and dirt roads, without lights, so I knew what it meant for Melville to walk fifteen or twenty miles home to Lansingburgh from where he was teaching. I could imagine what it meant to Melville to have, in different decades, crossed the whole of Massachusetts in a stagecoach and then to have crossed the same parts of Massachusetts on a train. From talk about the early 1930s and from what I witnessed once in Hebbronville, Texas, I knew what it meant to go out on foot looking for work, although I never did it myself. I had traveled thousands of miles in a Model T and thousands of miles on a troop train in 1942 and many thousands of miles on trains when I was deadheading as a railroad telegrapher in the early 1950s. I had a realizing sense of the weeks of travel Melville's uncle Thomas and his family experienced in 1837, going from Pittsfield to Galena, Illinois. I understood just what the change meant to his cousin Priscilla, a decade and a half later, when she boarded a train in Manhattan and went all the way to Chicago and beyond to Galena in a few days. Perhaps no other American biographer working in the 1990s had as instinctive a sense as I did of changes in modes of transportation in the nineteenth century.

The Melvillean Warner Berthoff, whom I never met, wrote me on January 29, 1997, that he was "a sucker for various topographical details." He had been amused, he said, "by a remark about the tedious journey from Pittsfield to Albany—tedious, of course, in the 1830s before the railroad came in, but also tedious, I can imagine, to a late 20th century researcher who had to travel it oftener than he liked." That was the response I wanted (and I quote it with his permission). I had, in fact, hitchhiked from Albany to Pittsfield on a hot August day in 1962 (after a kind stranger had driven out of his way to show me Martin Van Buren's Lindenwald) and remembered the repeated undulations of the topography. I could imagine the difference between an early stagecoach ride across that stretch and, after Melville's return from the Pacific, the marvelous speed of transit on the railway cars. With Berthoff, at least, I succeeded in making use of my attempts to follow Melville's footsteps.

I was no good at ocean voyaging, but I paid attention to Melville and water within the continents. He knew waterfalls from his youth: Poesten Kill in Troy, a few miles south of the house his mother rented in Lansingburgh, and Cohoes Falls, where the Mohawk enters the Hudson. He would have known Glens Falls early. We assume he knew the falls at Kaaterskill Clove, the scene of Asher B. Durand's painting of Cole and Bryant which I used to visit at the New York Public Library. He saw Niagara, and he probably went up to see the falls of Saint Anthony, perhaps as a consolation jaunt before returning to Lansingburgh from Galena. In Melville's first book when the companions descend into the interior of the island, Toby is deterred neither by "Typees or Niagaras" (chap. 9). Melville made repeated trips to Bash Bish to see the divided waterfalls. In 1840 he may have seen the confluence of the Missouri and the Mississippi and the confluence of the Ohio and the Mississippi; later they were certainly vivid in his mind's eye. In 1849 he went to the confluence of the Moselle and the Rhine at Coblenz, the name of which, he knew, meant confluence. In 1856 he saw the confluence of the Clyde and the Leven below Dumbarton Castle. Why would he not seek out confluences of rivers, since from childhood he had walked on the Battery, seeing where the East River and the Hudson (or "North River") merged after they poured separately into the bay?

To declare that Melville was interested in bodies of water—lakes, ponds, flowing water, waterfalls, confluences of rivers, and oceans—is to announce the obvious. But there was more. Melville was fascinated by, perhaps haunted by, feelings of being subterranean, in the orlop deck, in vaults, in passages such as Giovanni Belzoni wormed his way through, in depths below depths as in the Hôtel de Cluny in Paris. He was particularly intrigued by waters that went subterranean and emerged far away. Melville learned the story of

the Arethusa fountain which he told in chapter 41 of *Moby-Dick* from his
friend Henry T. Tuckerman, apparently:[6]

> So that here, in the real living experience of living men, the prodi-
> gies related in old times of the inland Strella mountain in Portugal
> (near whose top there was said to be a lake in which the wrecks of
> ships floated up to the surface); and that still more wonderful story of
> the Arethusa fountain near Syracuse (whose waters were believed to
> have come from the Holy Land by an underground passage); these
> fabulous narrations are almost fully equalled by the realities of the
> whaleman.

The pouring in of contributory streams (*Pierre*, bk. 21) fascinated Melville
because he associated flowing water, on the surface or subterranean, with
processes of the mind and particularly with the way literary influences work
on a man engaged, as he was, in a lifelong course of self-education. Whole
ships could float, intact, up to the surface of a lake? So could memories surge
up, terrifyingly intact. Images from distant sources could suddenly, shockingly invade the conscious mind from the subconscious. In book 5 of *Pierre*
Melville pledged: "I shall follow the endless, winding way,—the flowing river
in the cave of man; careless whither I be led, reckless where I land." Rivers,
particularly subterranean rivers, flowed like the streams of thought in the
depths of the human mind. After a while, when I looked at waterfalls and
confluences he had seen I began to see them as I thought he had seen them.
(I looked at many waters but I realize now that I did not look up enough at
night in Manhattan hoping despite the ambient light to see what Melville
saw when he "strolled down to the Battery to study the stars.")[7]
    What's important for a biographer, I decided, is not visiting Niagara but
understanding that Melville, born near where both the East River and the
Hudson poured into the bay, raised on a great river near spectacular confluences and waterfalls, thought of diverse literary influences as waves at work
on him simultaneously: "Homer's old organ rolls its vast volumes under the
light frothy wave-crests of Anacreon and Hafiz; and high over my ocean,
sweet Shakespeare soars, like all the larks of the spring" (*Mardi*, chap. 119).
There Melville concludes: "And as the great Mississippi musters his watery
nations: Ohio, with all his leagued streams; Missouri, bringing down in
torrents the clans from the highlands; Arkansas, his Tartar rivers from the
plain;—so with all the past and present pouring in me, I roll down my billow
from afar." Had Melville in 1849, weeks or months after his rapt encounter with Shakespeare, felt that Milton was flowing in over the currents of

Shakespeare which were still flowing in his memory? Did Spenser, first read as soft pornography that stimulated him in early adolescence, flow in upon the current of Wordsworth about the time Melville finished *Moby-Dick*? In the spring of 1862, if he read Ruskin's *Modern Painters* then, did he think of Ruskin's words as flowing over sometimes identical words in the preface Arnold had written to his *Poems*?

Melville was particularly moved by complex literary influences such as I described in *Melville: The Making of the Poet* (183), his meditation on Arnold's tribute to Wordsworth in Wordsworth's tribute to Collins's tribute to Thomson. He knew the two earlier poems in 1862 when he was caught by the first line of Arnold's "The Youth of Nature":

> Rais'd are the dripping oars—
> Silent the boat: the lake,
> Lovely and soft as a dream,
> Swims in the sheen of the moon.
> The mountains stand at its head
> Clear as the pure June night,
> But the valleys are flooded with haze.
> Rydal and Fairfield are there;
> In the shadow Wordsworth lies dead.
> So it is, so it will be for aye.
> Nature is fresh as of old,
> Is lovely: a mortal is dead.

Melville noted, "And oft suspend the dashing oar / To bid his gentle spirit rest," and identified the words as coming from the poem by Collins on Thomson ("Ode on the Death of Thompson. The Scene on the Thames near Richmond"). Then Melville wrote, "Then let us, as we float along / For *him* suspend the dashing oar." Here Melville identified these words as Wordsworth's on Collins ("Remembrance of Collins. Composed upon the Thames near Richmond"). Melville commented, "How beautifully appropriate therefor this reminiscent prelude of Arnold concerning Wordsworth." This vividly shows Melville's sensitivity to literary echoes which for him represent a literary continuity to be treasured. As it happens, I copied the lines from Arnold from my copy of the 1856 Ticknor and Fields *Poems* which John Greenleaf Whittier had owned and which Samuel T. Pickard had annotated: "Many pages uncut. I fear thee did not read thy book through, Friend John." Now, there's a slight frisson, in concluding this paragraph, one Kendall and Holmes might have enjoyed, and an added frisson in knowing, as we do now, that Whittier and Melville were cousins, through Melville's paternal grandmother, although perhaps neither man knew of the relationship.

I did what I could, but about biography as "a tracking of the physical trail of someone's path through the past" I remain skeptical—indeed, almost an unbeliever. I was, in the 1990s, following emotional trails through family letters and Melville's prose and poetry, and most of them were harrowing and required bravery. When I was luckiest in absolutely capturing an episode, the episode usually was too painful to live with, it seemed. How many other biographers discovered one painful new episode after another in decades of their subjects' lives, with very little alleviation from new scenes of joy? Those discoveries awakened my sympathies for Melville the man. What I would have given, months on end, to have been following only physical trails, and cheerful physical trails at that, no matter how many blackflies swarmed on the slopes of Monument Mountain! Yet by looking at contributory streams, gazing at great confluences, I may have learned better to understand both Melville's sense of depth psychology and his sense of the gigantic power of literary influences, literal inflowings.

Kendall's "what the subject has seen" must be reinterpreted to include sculpture, paintings, and especially books and words in books. You see what "the subject has seen" very clearly in Melville's marginalia, where you witness his direct response to what he has just read on the page. In the long run, my lying in bed five months in 1956 reading only Shakespeare during convalescence from tuberculosis, before reading *Moby-Dick*, then my having had a seminar on Milton in 1957, and having the next year read Spenser and then Wordsworth on my own, as Melville did—all that worked to annihilate the "deceptions of change" and the "opacity of death" in the matter of Melville and me before I began to write on him. I have known some brave men. Paul Watson, the heroic captain, valiantly ate my sourdough blueberry pancakes here by the Pacific. Any of my own fantasies of high adventure as becoming a supernumerary on shipboard with Captain Watson pale against the real dangers I had confronted in following Melville's mental processes, discovering his greatest joys, sharing his high literary ambitions, suffering his greatest sorrows, calculating his financial misery, seeing him as a human being who always, always, ignored my sagest warnings that the footpaths he was taking were disastrous.

‡ *Chapter 2* ‡

Textual Editor as
Biographer in Training

The Norton Moby-Dick *and the*
Northwestern-Newberry Writings of Herman Melville

In 1952 no fortune teller would have predicted that a decade later Professor Harrison Hayford would ask me to co-edit with him a collection for W. W. Norton called *"Moby-Dick" as Doubloon*, much less that in 1963 he would ask me to co-edit the Norton Critical Edition of *Moby-Dick*, and in 1965 would make me Associate General Editor of *The Writings of Herman Melville*. In June 1952 at sixteen, the month after I finished the eleventh grade at Wister, Oklahoma, I hired out as a telegrapher on the Atchison, Topeka, and the Santa Fe Railway and later went to the Kansas City Southern. I took sick leave in 1955 with tuberculosis, but late in 1957 I went back (eight at night till four in the morning) on the Kansas City Southern in Port Arthur, Texas. By the end of the summer of 1959 I had seven years' seniority—enough, I knew, to guarantee a safe lifetime job as a telegrapher. Starting in 1953 I had patched together almost a year's worth of college credits by correspondence courses ranging from Freshman English from the University of Oklahoma to American Pragmatism from the University of California at Berkeley and Medieval French Poetry (what was I thinking?) from the University of Texas. I had taken classes at West Contra Costa Junior College in San Pablo, California. While working as the night telegrapher on the Kansas City Southern in Port Arthur, I had taken two overfull years of courses from Lamar State College of Technology in Beaumont, Texas. In August 1959 I graduated from Lamar "with highest honors," news even in Houston: I'm so old that the only time Dan Rather read my name aloud was on the radio. A few days later, I gave up the security of the railroad and entered the graduate program at Northwestern University with a Woodrow Wilson Fellowship that paid $1,800 a year and tuition.

Fresh from an intense seminar in Yeats at Lamar in August 1959 in which I fought through every sentence of *Yeats: The Man and the Masks*, I was primed, if I ever chanced to encounter the man, to set Richard Ellmann straight on his reading of a poem about a picture by Edmund Dulac. In September 1959 that same Ellmann was assigned as my advisor at Northwestern but, too shy to knock on his door, I blundered my way, unguided. From the sidelines I witnessed the turning point in modern academic literary biography, for that fall Ellmann with his biography of James Joyce single-handedly seemed to break the New Critical prohibition against literary biography. His career, and the possibilities for modern literary biography, all seemed to change. His clearing the way in 1959 helped to legitimize my interests at Northwestern in the next years and my own subsequent career, especially when I learned in 1962 how very little had changed, how powerful the forces of the New Criticism were in directing attention away from documentary research. Decades later Ellmann and I chatted amiably about a topic in academic aesthetics dear to both of us, royalties from textbooks (mine from *The Norton Anthology of American Literature*, much of his from a collaboration with the Yale professor Charles Feidelson, *The Modern Tradition*), but never about biography.

Being so shy, I did not learn that at Northwestern the Wilson Fellows got almost automatic University Fellowships the next year, so in 1960 I was already writing application letters for a teaching assistantship elsewhere when they made the awards. I got the M.A. that summer, then the next year cleared the French and German exams out of the way before I forgot all the words I had learned nights in Port Arthur. The graduate professors, I found, held to a near-uniform policy of not teaching in their seminars. They assigned reports the first day of class and by the third week, at the latest, students were conducting the classes, however ill prepared they were. Professors who did teach in seminars and especially those who taught passionately soon found themselves bound for the more hospitable department in Madison or else disappeared a year at a time as Ellmann did. I wanted to do a dissertation in the Renaissance but Virgil Heltzel curtly dismissed me because I did not know Greek and Latin. Then I thought about doing a dissertation under Zera Fink on the way the Romantic poets imitated Shakespeare in their dramas. American literature was a frivolous novelty, I had been told, not a field like railroad telegraphing, where you could keep a job, but as I bussed tables in Scott Hall I was intrigued by student gossip about the peculiar requirements of one graduate professor. The Melville expert, Harrison Hayford, students said, conducted seminars the way the older professors did, except that he would not accept a term paper. According to Hayford, a term paper was an essay you wrote, got graded on, and stuck in a drawer, like my good essays on Swift and Wordsworth the first quarter at Northwestern. Instead, Hayford insisted on a paper written to fit the interests and formal require-ments of a specific learned journal and delivered to him in an unsealed envelope addressed to that journal, the proper postage affixed. That way if he thought the paper was ready for publication he could simply lick the flap and send off the article. A very late starter, a high school dropout who had a lot of catching up to do, I made sure I got into Hayford's Melville seminar in the fall of 1960. I thought it might help that already I had read *Moby-Dick*, in 1957, and *Pierre*, in 1959, both under unusual circumstances.

I had come to Melville through Shakespeare. Getting a fresh supply of reading matter while bedridden with tuberculosis was nearly impossible, so on the first of January 1956, newly released from a sanatorium, I propped up on a pillow the one-volume Shakespeare I had bought in New Orleans in 1953, the Garden City Books edition illustrated by Rockwell Kent with a preface and little introductions to the plays by Christopher Morley. In high school I had memorized the purple passages from Shakespeare in Louis Untermeyer's *A Treasury of Great Poems English and American* and had memorized much of *Macbeth* in L. A. Sherman's bowdlerized 1899 edition (no philosophizing by the porter about alcohol and sexual dysfunction), and at Red Rock, Oklahoma, in 1952 under the meager shade of a locust tree in a pasture, cow patties all around, I had read *King Lear* for the first time in a 1947 Pocket Book of five great tragedies, memorizing some, including the bastardy speech. Starting the first day of 1956, for five months I read only Shakespeare, over and over, every day. I read all the plays, to begin with, whether I had read them before or not, reading fast, as I always did. My neat pencil notes show, just for examples, that in those months I read *Henry 6, Part 1* six times; *King John* seven times (most perplexed by the word "commodity"); *Hamlet* ten times besides listening to LPs of the play; *King Lear* nine times; *Measure for Measure*, where the well-deserved humiliations of Duke and Deputy fascinated me, seventeen times; *Coriolanus* ten times; *Cymbeline* nine times; *The Tempest* sixteen times. I read *Othello* then eleven times and played the Robeson-Hagen LP nine times.

The first time through all the plays what I understood was sometimes hit or miss. Then while reading *Romeo and Juliet* the second time through, I realized that the passage about the natural and his bauble that had baffled me was obscene, and funny. I thought about that and decided that maybe everything made sense, or was meant to make sense. I was in the acceptance phase of tuberculosis, which meant that from where I was I did not think I had to get anywhere in a hurry. That day my way of reading was transformed. Starting then, I slowed down, and would not leave a passage until I thought I understood it. That's the way I read all the plays. And that was the way I would read henceforth, all my working life. What reading this way meant was that I had learned to submit myself to the authority of the writer, to be absolutely humble in an attempt to follow meaning, which I assumed was there, so that when the meaning was violated sometimes I was paying such close attention that I was able to supply the word or a synonym of the word that should have been there. Dropout or not, I learned fast enough that while every sentence might have been supposed to make sense, some of them did not make sense, often because something had been corrupted.

For a year starting that summer of 1956 I attended West Contra College Junior College in San Pablo, waddling the first days of every week from Monday morning's pneumo-peritoneum (air pumped into the belly through a horse needle, to force the diaphragm to restrict the lungs). I rested when I could in the afternoons, exhausted from carrying the skinfull of air around school, like being always more than a little pregnant, worse early in the week than later, when some air had seeped out. Early in 1957 I spent eleven afternoons in bed reading *Moby-Dick*. I paused to look at paragraphs as long as I needed to, writing little wonder-struck comments on note cards, hardly believing what I was reading. Knowing Shakespeare then as few English professors ever do, I was astounded that a nineteenth-century American had read Shakespeare so profoundly. I was attending morning and early afternoon classes, and four times in the eleven days I was reading *Moby-Dick* I got up from my cot at night to play Cassio in *Othello*, for by then I had made my way into the Richmond Community Theatre. Since the performances were on Friday and Saturday, most of the Monday's air had seeped out of my stomach, so I didn't waddle or wobble in a sword fight. Look, or not, at Google Images. Over the 1959 Christmas break I read *Pierre* the same way, very slowly, overwhelmed again to see how Melville had absorbed Shakespeare. In the fall of 1960 I figured I could always write a non-term-paper on Melville and Shakespeare for Hayford.

By the end of the Melville seminar I understood that Hayford was one of the great Melville scholars who had worked at Yale under Stanley T. Williams in the 1940s. After writing a two-volume biography of Washington Irving, Williams had tired of all the vagueness about Melville's life and works and decided to direct his best students to Melville. In Hayford's case, that meant deterring him from working on Emerson's sermons. The great imaginative and persistent amateur scholar Jay Leyda had published a documentary life of Melville, *The Melville Log*, in 1951, and Leyda and Hayford had persuaded Leon Howard to write a narrative biography (1951) based on Leyda's *Log*. In 1952 Wilson Heflin had completed a splendidly researched dissertation at Vanderbilt, "Melville's Whaling Years." Otherwise the great new Melvilleans were students of Williams. One of the earliest, Elizabeth S. Foster, had edited *The Confidence-Man*, in which a central section deals with Indian-hating and the difficulty of finding anything but diluted Indian-haters. It was obvious to me that the Indian-hating section was an allegory in which Melville portrayed nominal Christians as diluted Indian-haters. Mistaking Christianity as one of what Melville saw as optimistic philosophies, Foster had not understood what Melville was saying about total depravity, Original Sin, and the fate of attempts to imitate Jesus absolutely. Foster was a Texan, but Episcopalian. The other Yale Melville students were great scholars and good diluted Indian-haters, too high church to understand Melville's religious absolutism. In reading about Indian-hating I had the dubious liability of being part Cherokee and part Choctaw and what I regarded as a psychological liability that turned out to be an advantage that neither Foster nor the other Melville students of the 1940s had possessed—prolonged exposure to Calvinist theology. Why, that was so long ago that Baptists believed not only in Original Sin but in separation of church and state! Southern Baptist doctrine, back then, was a perfect modern introduction to Melville's mother's Dutch Church theology. I took Melville's chapter title, "The Metaphysics of Indian-hating," for my article (not a term paper) and handed it in. The Modern Language Association was meeting in Chicago that December. The Melville Society met during MLA, and in 1960 Hayford was the program chairman and asked me to deliver my paper there. Shorn of a section showing how religious absolutism was depicted in Melville's other writings, "The Metaphysics of Indian-hating" was published in *Nineteenth-Century Fiction* (September 1963). The assembly-line collection-maker Harold Bloom reprinted it, and I still reprint it every good chance I get. It was in the table of contents when I thought this book would become a collection of favorite essays.

By the time the 1960 seminar was over I understood that several people, but not an intimidating number, had done heroic work on Melville. If you trust Hayford's memory, I decided back then that I would have a chance of joining their number. In an affidavit dated September 15, 1995, Hayford stated: "At the end of my Melville seminar at NU in 196x, you told me in your (then) shy & respectful way, in words to this effect: 'My ambition is to become a major Melville scholar.'" The speech Hayford attributed to me does not jibe with my memory of my intense diffidence, but he may have been accurate, for after that seminar there was no thought that I would work with another professor on anyone but Melville. I became a Melvillean because of William Shakespeare, John Calvin, Harrison Hayford, and Melville himself.

I planned to study for the qualifying exams in the fall of 1962 but in the spring my fellow graduate student Walker Gilmer importuned me one Friday to come out to Libertyville for the weekend to prep him for the exams by talking out answers to old essay questions and memorizing facts from his meticulously devised flash cards. Saturday evening I called Hayford and asked if I could take the exams with Walker on Monday. He shrugged off the sign-up rules and agreed. Ernest Samuels fumed but did not put up a fight about letting me take the exam, although when I answered Hayford's little throwaway Melville question humorously he observed that this was "no place for levity."

Samuels and Hayford passed both of us. Good: I would not need to study for exams in the fall and could concentrate on courses as an instructor at Northwestern for $5,500—a fortune. So when Jean Howard Hagstrum, the chairman, called me in late that week and asked me to apply for a Woodrow Wilson Dissertation Fellowship I said I couldn't. Didn't he remember that I was going to teach at Northwestern and make real money? He explained that the Ford Foundation had put the Woodrow Wilson Fellowships officers at Princeton in a bind. They could have Ford money for dissertation-year grants but only for Woodrow Wilson Fellows from one year, 1959, unless there was a prodigy from 1960 who had earned the Master's degree, passed the language exams, and passed the qualifying exams. The money was there and almost no one was eligible for it. I had met the first two requirements expeditiously and just that week, fortuitously and most fortunately, had met the third. Hagstrum assured me forcefully that rather than being required to take the instructorship at Northwestern I *would* break the agreement. I *was* going to apply, he explained. I had been looking forward so eagerly to the $5,500 that I said, "Well, I have to have $4,000." He said, "They won't give that." I was stubborn. He telephoned the Wilson office in Princeton and was told, "No, we can't do that. We'll call you back." A few minutes later they called back and told him, "The best we can do is $3,990." Trembling a little in his exasperation, Hagstrum held a ten-dollar bill out to me. I waved off the bill, but I capitulated. I can't explain this story now. I was not arrogant. I was a humble, self-abasing Southerner. I was deeply ignorant but I had been hired as an instructor, precedent-breaking for the English department at Northwestern, miraculous for me. This whole little story starting with the weekend invitation to Adlai country is something I learned not to tell graduate students who were studying for the prelims. The academic world got tougher than it had been back then.

By that time, in the spring of 1962, I knew well enough that the dominant literary approach, the New Criticism, discouraged the reader from drawing on any evidence other than that of the words of a printed novel or poem. For a teacher at Lamar I had tried to supply what he requested, "searching" critiques of poems. When I subtitled a paper on one of Thomas Wyatt's poems "A Searching Explication" he brushed off the impudent irony and said the paper really *was* searching. But I was drawn to working with historical documents and to treating novels and poems as historical documents. My use of Henry Steele Commager's *Documents of American History* in a correspondence course from the University of Oklahoma when I was depot agent at Singer, Louisiana, had marked me. Ernest De Selincourt and Helen Darbishire had marked me with their edition of parallel texts of Wordsworth's *The Prelude*, which I had bought by mail and read for private joy midnights in the cavernous Freight Office in Port Arthur early in 1959, just after the music died and mourning spread far beyond Beaumont, the home of the Big Bopper. In the first quarter at Northwestern I had written on Jonathan Swift's campaign against the Duke of Marlborough, using all the available printed documents, and on Wordsworth's early humanitarianism, using the first versions of "An Evening Walk" and "Descriptive Sketches."

At Northwestern most of the professors had been trained in the 1930s or early 1940s in historical research, in research into literary history, in biographical, biographical-textual, and bibliographical research. Already, the New Criticism was so powerful that students were arriving at graduate school with no such training, and they wanted to write critical "readings" of literary texts. By the time I received the Woodrow Wilson Dissertation Fellowship "The Metaphysics of Indian-hating" had been accepted by *Nineteenth-Century Fiction*. Documentary articles, I thought, should be even easier to place than my historical-theological explication. I could find more to publish on Melville, I thought, particularly if I worked on something historical or biographical. I chose fast enough to work on the various political milieux Melville had lived through, even if he did not actively participate in them.

In June 1962 I mailed my Melville books to General Delivery, New York City, and got a ride down to Port Arthur so I could visit my former landlady, Mrs. Lançon, a Cajun great-grandmother. After three years away, Port Arthur was a shock: the gas station where I had fueled up for my daily trips to Beaumont still had three restrooms, "White Women," "White Men," and "Colored." With my satchel and a defiantly un-Southern umbrella (accent on the first syllable, and before Totes collapsibles were invented), wearing my Baskins wash-and-wear muted gray glen plaid suit and one of my two thin ties, both with narrow blue and green stripes, one the reverse of the other, I hitchhiked east, straight to the panhandle of Florida and the River Styx, then up northward. One night I spent in Waycross, Georgia, in an old railroad dormitory as vast as the Freight House in Port Arthur. Defeated late one rainy evening at Gettysburg (ninety-nine years after my great-grandfather Costner had survived the battle there, I learned in 2011), I gave up and took a bus on into Manhattan, arriving in the middle of the night. I checked my satchel in a locker and walked across and up and down in Central Park until dawn, as innocent and invulnerable as the lady in *Comus*, which I had read in the Kansas City Southern Freight Office. After I had exhausted the accommodations suggested in my 1960 *New York on Five Dollars a Day* I telephoned Arthur Frommer. Why not? He was in the phone book. Frommer sent me to New York University Housing, where I was directed to the Penington, an old mansion on East Fifteenth Street handy to Union Square, a mind-expanding boardinghouse for pensioned or working teachers, superannuated Socialists, a would-be poet or two, motley students including a young man from Hull, a halfway house for recovering addicts, a place of refuge for hopeful Batistas, their bags kept half-packed for their return to Cuba, and now one former Baptist. Perfect. I could eat breakfast with the other lodgers and guests, work all day in the New York Public Library or the New-York Historical Society, return for dinner, then sleep in a twelve foot long by four foot wide cubicle vacated by Lavinia, a part Negro (as I would have said then) teacher who was traveling through Europe. That was room enough for reading *Clarel*, which demanded to be taken in small doses. You did not need a lot of private space in New York City. Once, I cut out of the library and joined a theater full of blue-haired ladies at a matinee to see the world's greatest Desdemona, Uta Hagen, in *Who's Afraid of Virginia Woolf?* Afterward the women and I blinked our way into sunlight, all of us equally stunned. At the Penington two Negro schoolteachers, women, sized me up for a couple of weeks then marched me off with them to Gene Frankel's production of Genet's *The Blacks* a few blocks down at St. Mark's, where the cast at one time or another included every great black actor in the country except, I think, Belafonte and Poitier. I could not talk much afterward, and for sure did not tell them about the signs I had just seen at the gas stations in Port Arthur. New York was saying in its tough way, "Welcome, Okie."

In the New York Public Library and the New-York Historical Society as I tried to piece together a story from letters and newspapers I was happier than I had ever been in my life. I exulted in finding that no one had touched the archives since the great Melvilleans had plowed through in the 1940s. Sometimes when I asked for something it was promptly handed to me although it had been withheld in whole or in part from Leyda and the Yale scholars.

When I asked to see Gansevoort Melville's 1846 London journal at the New York Public Library I was told it was on hold. For whom was it held? The great librarian Victor Paltsits. He had been dead since 1952 and none of the Yale crew had come back asking to see the diary. Merrell R. Davis, who had been granted glimpses of it and had co-edited Melville's letters in 1960 with William H. Gilman, was himself already dead, in 1961—and much mourned by Hayford. No one had come asking for Gansevoort's journal during the whole decade, 1952–62. Yes, I could edit it for the *Bulletin of the New York Public Library* and yes, later on, it could be a New York Public Library separate.[1]

Later in the summer of 1962 I found that among the Melville documents deposited in the Berkshire Athenaeum in the 1950s in the new Melville Collection were letters and other items that Melville's brother Allan's grandchildren, the Morewood sisters, had not shown to Leyda in the 1940s. They were handed over to me, the first who asked to see them. As it turned out, there was another twist: Leyda had seen some items that were not deposited later and had simply disappeared. In 1999 Paul Metcalf found a cardboard liquor box containing parts of this archive, documents loaned by Agnes Morewood before 1952 to her second cousin, Eleanor Thomas Metcalf, Melville's granddaughter and Paul's mother. In the box was Melville's 1856 letter to his brother Allan from Liverpool, known by a 1940s photocopy and long wrongly suspected of being mislaid by a highly conscientious librarian at the Athenaeum. Other documents have not reappeared: where is Gansevoort's 1834 diary? Dumped into trash in Santa Barbara decades ago, when someone disposed of Margaret Morewood's effects after she died? In 1962 the Houghton Library at Harvard and the Massachusetts Historical Society were equally hospitable, and anyone could show up and use the Boston Public Library.

Yet not all New York and Massachusetts said "Welcome." In the barrio in Hebbronville, Texas, in the late 1930s, at a time my father was jobless, I had longed to play with "the little white boy" across the dirt street. Once he led me into his dazzlingly white kitchen, but his mother shooed me out fast. When I began my dissertation I hoped that a Ph.D. would at last let me play with literature-loving white kids, whatever the actual skin color of that enviable set might be. I met two candidates for the Ph.D. at Columbia, white kids if kids ever were white (you wouldn't know their names if I told you), who were amused that Northwestern University was offering doctorates, not realizing that the Northwest Territory needed some sort of regional school. They were fascinated that I could be writing a dissertation that required going to New York City. They were dumbstruck when I told them I went to the New

York Public Library or the New-York Historical Society every day to copy out
nineteenth-century letters and diary entries about Melville and politics, or
else read nineteenth-century newspapers looking for Melville's brother Gansevoort's speeches and reviews of Melville's works and other articles about
Melville and his family. They had a great story to regale their fellow students
and Richard Chase with at Columbia, this skinny guy from the Midwest in
a wash-and-wear suit and a subdued rep tie going to the libraries every day
and looking at old newspapers and manuscripts! In 1962, a graduate student
going to the archives as if the New Criticism had never triumphed! Coming
all the way to New York to do it! They were too polite to laugh outright, but
the way they kept looking at each other showed they thought this was the
quaintest damned thing they had ever heard. It probably was. They made it
plain enough that the research required by my dissertation topic had pushed
me out of step with my sprightly contemporaries. I just didn't know how far
out of step I was.

    In New York I had gone to the Hudson wharves to say bon voyage to the
Hayfords as they sailed for Italy on the *Liberté*. Back in Evanston in Hayford's tiny dormer study in the late summer and fall of 1963 I spent three
months typing up my longhand notes on five-by-eight cards and organizing
them. I was set on writing "Melville and Politics" with only one interruption, a spring mopping-up tour through the New York and Boston libraries.
Not knowing you were supposed to apply for jobs in the fall, I assumed I
could find last-minute work at a Chicago junior college. I was so ignorant
that I resisted Hagstrum's insistence that I meet recruiters—for in those distant times, universities sent around recruiters. Before I agreed to see two
recruiters, Hagstrum had to sit me down and explain how many courses I
would be teaching as an instructor at a junior college and how little I would
be paid and how comparatively few courses I would teach and how much
more, comparatively, I would be paid at a university as an assistant professor. The great bibliographer Fredson Bowers from the University of Virginia
interviewed me in a dark green room several floors up in the Blackstone
Hotel in Chicago. The egotistical and pompous man drained the room of
oxygen, but more was going on.[2] All in all, this was a fit first meeting with
the man who for decades strove to become my personal nemesis. In the
1970s Bowers threatened to sue the Center for Scholarly Editions and perhaps the Modern Language Association if at my instigation they rescinded
the seal for the hopelessly bungled *Maggie* and threatened to sue me and
the editors of *Nineteenth-Century Fiction* for exposing the shoddiness of his
work on *The Red Badge of Courage*. Professors, as a class, are easily intimidated, Bowers knew, and he ruthlessly exploited his power, blackballing me,

blocking my publications, and lying about his actions in print. He saw to it that a monograph on Stephen Crane's *Maggie* I wrote with Brian Higgins was not published for two decades, and then in the antipodes (although in a fine journal there, the *Bulletin of the Bibliographical Society of Australia and New Zealand*). However purely he began, Bowers became the Mad Scientist of Textual Editing—a Mad Scientist who ran what may have been the world's sloppiest textual lab and promulgated varying self-serving high-sounding textual theories to cover the slovenliness. I will say more of him later.

Bowers offered an instructorship, but if I wanted to be considered for an assistant professorship I would have to fly to Charlottesville, at his expense, and give a talk. "The Metaphysics of Indian-hating" was still unpublished and therefore available, if I did not want to work something up, but I did not want to take the time for the trip, and, besides, I knew that man would choke off all independent life. Since Hayford was in Florence, out of touch, Bowers complained to his Navy buddy Walter Rideout, one of the refugees from Northwestern who had found safe harbor in Madison. Rideout called me in exasperation to say that the American literature professors had "had their eyes on me" and wanted me to go to Virginia. Deferential as always, I concealed my feelings, but I was outraged. Why couldn't they have given some indication that they had their eyes on me back when it would have made a difference, when I despaired of the quality of teaching in the English department and had to go to the German department and audit a course on Goethe by Meno Spann so I could be reassured that there were great teachers in the world, men or women who were passionate about literature and life? So people sniggered about Spann for displaying his corpulence on the Lake Michigan beach on the campus, nearly nude, surrounded by tanning reflectors? That man was alive.

The second recruiter, Bruce Harkness from the University of Illinois, had made a small splash in Bowers's 1959 *Studies in Bibliography* by playing the role of a self-consciously New Critical reader confronted with classroom texts containing not only obvious typos but also misprints which could be read as making sense, although not authorial sense. His offer of an assistant professorship was attractive because Urbana was less than two hours away from Northwestern and Hayford, who would be home in the summer. I was so naive that I accepted the job while in Urbana rather than going home and trying to bargain for more than the $6,000 Harkness offered. All I could think of was that I had a dissertation to write.

I began writing at year's end in high spirits and early in January showed Samuels the preface. He all but obliterated it with his red ink comments, the

ball point making deep grooves in the cheap yellow foolscap. The preface
was journalistic, totally unacceptable. The *tone* was all wrong, too familiar. This was no place for levity, or vivacity, any more than the qualifying
exams had been. I was demolished, mentally frozen for two weeks that icy
January, where a coffeepot full of water kept the attic cubicle habitable. I
began again, in a very subdued tone. A quarter century later I plucked up
the courage to look at the desecrated pages and was astonished to see that
the preface I had written was far better than anything in the dissertation as
finished and accepted. Samuels, out of who knows what obscure impulse
to repress or chastise, had prevented me from writing what just might have
become a book rather than a news-filled but plodding dissertation that others would plunder for *their* books. Sure, even if I had gone forward in the
original mood, I might not have been able to trick out my dissertation as a
book, since my evidence for different chapters from different decades was so
disparate, but I might have: you don't know what you can achieve when you
start off so boldly and confidently. Even now I think that if Samuels had not
beaten me down I might have found a voice in prose right away, back then.

At Urbana I continued to work on *"Moby-Dick" as Doubloon* and the
Norton Critical Edition of *Moby-Dick*, hiring the graduate student Bernard
Rosenthal to collate with me Howard P. Vincent's guillotined copy of the
first American edition against a Zehnsdorff-bound three-volume Bentley *The
Whale*—in a closed, glass cubicle in full view of the suspicious librarian. At
that time Hayford began planning a new collected edition of Melville. The
Hendricks House edition which was begun in the 1940s had been extremely
uneven and had sputtered out with one last glorious volume, Walter E.
Bezanson's 1960 *Clarel*, a copy of which I had mailed to New York City in
1962 and continued reading there. In 1965 Hayford was very late getting the
telephone call saying the Melville Project (sponsored by the Modern Language Association through the Center for Editions of American Authors, set
up in 1963) would be funded by the Department of Health, Education, and
Welfare. When he called me to say I could be Associate General Editor on
the Melville Project (to be headquartered at the Newberry Library) and an
assistant professor at Northwestern, I was waiting in an anteroom to tell the
chairman at Illinois that I would stay there another year. I am afraid I would
have, too, if I had said so, but Hayford reached the secretary in time for me to
cancel the meeting. I went back to Northwestern as assistant professor with
a salary of $9,000 a year, nominally teaching half-time and working half-
time on the Northwestern-Newberry *Writings of Herman Melville*. A former
student of Hayford's who had earned a Ph.D. at Yale before going to Wisconsin, G. Thomas Tanselle, was hired as the third member of the team,

the Bibliographical Editor. (That title proved confusing to people who did not distinguish between the words "textual" and "bibliographical." We were all three the textual editors but Tanselle had special expertise on the book as physical object.) I had been around Hayford long enough to know that "half-time" in fact meant teaching half-time (not counting teaching some of his classes) and working on the Northwestern-Newberry Edition full-time.

Hayford hired a former student of Fredson Bowers to give a summer tutorial on the master's methods of collating variant texts. The motto of the temporary office manager was "God makes mistakes. Fredson doesn't." Then Hayford fled to the East Coast, book buying for the project, and Tanselle found that he had urgent Melville business in London. *Typee* was a special case, since it was set in England from Melville's manuscript (perhaps in a sister's hand) and reset in New York from the English edition. Normally, we already knew from documentary evidence, the American editions were set from the manuscript and the English editions were set from the American proofsheets. The Bowers-trained expert sat graduate students down in the new Melville Room of the Newberry Library with an American edition of *Omoo*, say, and the English edition, the American being closer to the lost manuscript, and instructed them to write down on a tablet in pencil the page number and line number where every punctuation variant and verbal variant occurred. Day after day the students recorded punctuation variants that meant nothing and were all but inaccessible in the form they were recorded, since they were using Bowers's arcane symbols and since every item was isolated from any context. His method was inefficient to the point of being useless, a near-total waste of time (no, total, not near-total), for most of the information being recorded in that all but irretrievable form had no significance. Always irascible, the tutor became choleric when I set out to identify the copies of the books being collated.

The first thing you needed for *Omoo*, I knew from working with *Moby-Dick* and *The Whale*, was not a full collation such as Rosenthal and I had done in Urbana but a faster check for differences in wording, so we could determine whether or not any obvious authorial revisions were in the English edition, which had been set from the American proofs. (Chances seemed good that a writer would not rigorously revise punctuation without changing a lot of words.) You needed a form of the text nearest to the manuscript, one you could write on, so you could mark later variants in the margin and visualize them chronologically. We could not afford to buy copies of first editions and mark them up. Next best was a photocopy of the first American *Omoo* (made on the new miracle, a Xerox machine) for marking with the variants from the first English. What you would do, if you wanted the most important information fast, was to have the collator look only for words, the first time through, and mark the variants in the margins of the photocopy of the first edition. Then when you had most of the verbal variants you could decide whether any of them were changes Melville might have made. If he had obviously had a hand in revising a text then you could do an indefinite number of repeat collations, still looking for verbal variants but also marking the photocopy with all the punctuation variants so you could see if Melville might have revised punctuation too, particularly around passages where he was revising the words. When I tried to tell Hayford all this he turned, waving me away with his great arm. He did not want to hear me: Bowers was the great bibliographer, and his disciple was teaching us Bowers's way. The summer was over before I got Hayford's attention long enough to show him a more sensible way to proceed so we could stop wasting the time of half a dozen graduate student collators. Even then he insisted on getting Tanselle's approval before letting me make initial collations just for variant words. Frustrating servitude under a ferociously churlish misguided disciple of Bowers and absentee co-editors in the summer of 1965 had made for a hellish beginning.

Despite all the frustrations, in moments of high excitement I knew that I was absolutely, even uniquely, right for the job. I had a peculiar talent as an editor achieved during the five months I had spent in bed with Shakespeare's plays. I knew from my notes in my one-volume edition that eighteenth-century editors, men who had the new field of identifying textual cruxes in Shakespeare's plays all to themselves, had found it irresistible to display their own cleverness while testing the wit of others. I knew James Boswell's account of a non-Shakespearean test in his *Journal of a Tour to the Hebrides:* "In the 65th page of the first volume of Sir George Mackenzie, Dr. Johnson pointed out a paragraph beginning with *Aristotle,* and told me there was an error in the text, which he bade me try to discover. I was lucky enough to hit it at once. As the passage is printed, it is said that the devil answers *even* in *engines.* I corrected it to—*ever* in ænigmas. 'Sir,' said he, you are a good critick. This would have been a great thing to do in the text of an ancient authour."[3] But Johnson had merely presented Boswell with a captured crux. Conjectural emendation gets a bad name from factitious gamesmanship, the clever toying with captured cruxes, fenced in and on display. The interesting lost words are those still in the wild. What Hayford could sometimes do, and what I could do, just by reading, was identify many of those corruptions. Tanselle did not; tellingly, he did not even mention the category of conjectural emendations in his magisterial "Some Principles for Editorial Apparatus" in *Studies in Bibliography* (1972).[4]

In my 1960 seminar with Hayford I had demonstrated the value of learning to read the way I had learned in 1956, for I had stumbled at a word in *The Confidence-Man.* Describing Moredock, the Indian-hater, the American and English editions both said: "The solitary Indian that met him, died. When a murder was descried, he would either secretly pursue their track for some chance to strike at least one blow; or if, while thus engaged, he himself was discovered, he would elude them by superior skill" (chap. 27). In my experience the reader does not resort to ratiocination but simply makes the correction, changing "murder" to "number," as I did in the margin. Later on, explaining yourself, you can show that "murder" has to be an error because what is called for by the context is a word that means "several" and looks like "murder" in Melville's handwriting. The only obvious candidate in the language is "number." As it happens, Melville was following his source, James Hall, rather closely, and there the text provided belated confirmation, since the contrast there was between a "solitary red man" and "a party of the enemy." Any skeptic could be shown the word in the source with a meaning similar to that of the word that got printed. Finding such corruptions in Melville's books was one reason that Hayford chose me to be co-editor on the Norton Critical Edition of *Moby-Dick,* before the Northwestern-Newberry Edition was funded. In 1964 while working in Urbana on *Moby-Dick,* I saw that the word "argued," for example, should be "augured." My talent at conjectural emendation, or knack or whatever it was, went back to my reading of Shakespeare in 1956, after I made the decision ("life-altering decision," as they say now) to slow down and never to move past a passage until I thought I understood it.

Right away, in the first of Melville's books, *Typee,* I proved my value in a passage on Marquesan boys fearlessly climbing coconut trees (chap. 29). In the English edition, set from the manuscript, the narrator says, "What, thought I, on first witnessing one of these exhibitions, would the nervous mothers of America and England say to a similar display of hardihood in any of their children? The Lacedemonian nations might have approved of it, but most modern dames would have gone into hysterics at the sight." The first American edition differed, for someone at Wiley and Putnam's, realizing that there was only one Sparta, had changed "nations" to "nation." I did what I almost always do at such times—I absently wrote down the right word, "matrons." Once you have the word it is easy to argue rationally that the context calls for a word which applies to women: "nervous mothers of America and England," the "modern dames," must be contrasted to Spartan women; and matron is a common word for a mature woman in Melville's vocabulary. My assumption, like that of a New Critic, was that the text should make sense; I learned, starting in 1956, that often the reader was at fault when passages seemed not to make sense, and later learned not to be surprised when many words in texts did *not* in fact make sense. As an editor of Melville I read expecting his books to make sense and boggled when they didn't and stayed focused on the passage until I was sure it was right as it stood or that it wasn't. But I did not think of myself as a textual scholar reading "texts." Just as I had read Shakespeare (not the texts of Shakespeare's plays), now I was reading Melville, expecting him to make sense: I was doing biographical work, following the play of his mind.

In his 1971 "Textual Study and Literary Judgment," also in *Studies in Bibliography*, Tanselle referred to emendations "wholly dependent on literary judgment," the readings "introduced by an editor to correct what he considers erroneous readings in all extant authoritative texts" (119). He continued: "At one point in the English edition of *Typee* the phrase 'Lacedemonian nations' occurs, and in the American the same phrase in the singular; but neither 'nations' nor 'nation' makes much sense in the context, and an editor is obligated to try to discover a word meaning 'women'—as called for by the sense—which yet could have been misread in Melville's handwriting as 'nations.' Hershel Parker's solution, 'matrons,' is one of those emendations which fits all the conditions so perfectly that it must be the word originally written (or intended) by the author." When I heard Tanselle say this in a talk in Denver in 1969 I was appalled. Tanselle's rational description of the process was so far from the true cognitive process that afterward, outside in the snow, I vowed to start writing about textual matters myself. The fact was that in reading that passage I had been under no constraints at all except to understand the words, phrases, and sentences as I encountered them. In making this emendation I never once felt "obligated" to search for a word meaning "women" which could be misread as "nations." This seems illogical, but the solution to such a problem seems to come before you quite recognize that there is a problem. Perhaps the solution and the realization that there was a problem come simultaneously, or the recognition of the problem comes just before the solution, but it always *seems* to me that I get the word that makes sense, then acknowledge to myself that the word as printed must *not* have made sense, and go on. Then, typically after the passage of time, on another run-through, I say something rational like, "Oh, that word in the margin—I must have supplied what was needed, a word fitting the pattern, mothers and matrons and dames." (Ha! look what's on the cover of my offprint: "For Hershel—a Lacedemonian editor—from Tom.") Already I was focusing on psychological processes, whether Melville's as writer or mine as reader.

Later, I "hit" many other single words the same way as I had "matrons." Here's an example from *Pierre* (bk 5.5) that I noticed after the Northwestern-Newberry Edition was published:

> Well for Pierre it was, that the penciling presentiments of his mind concerning Lucy as quickly erased as painted their tormenting images. Standing half-befogged upon the mountains of his Fate, all that part of the wide panorama was wrapped in clouds to him; but anon those concealings slid aside, or rather, a quick rent was made in them; disclosing far below, half-vailed in the lower mist, the winding tranquil vale and stream of Lucy's previous happy life; through the swift cloud-rent he caught one glimpse of her expectant and angelic face peeping from the honey-suckled window of her cottage; and the next instant the stormy pinions of the clouds locked themselves over it again; and all was hidden as before; and all went confused in whirling rack and vapor as before. Only by unconscious inspiration, caught from the agencies invisible to man, had he been enabled to write that first obscurely announcing note to Lucy; wherein the collectedness, and the mildness, and the calmness, were but the natural though insidious precursors of the stunning bolts on bolts to follow.
>
> But, while thus, for the most part wrapped from his consciousness and vision, still, the condition of his Lucy, as so deeply affected now, was still more and more disentangling and defining itself from out its nearer mist, and even beneath the general upper fog. For when unfathomably stirred, the subtler elements of man do not always reveal themselves in the concocting act; but, as with all other potencies, show themselves chiefly in their ultimate resolvings and results. Strange wild work, and awfully symmetrical and reciprocal, was that now going on within the self-apparently chaotic breast of Pierre.

In this example, I absently wrote the correction in the margin (my eyes perhaps not on the hand that was writing) and only weeks later realized I had made a striking emendation.[5]

I could claim retrospectively to have been reading alertly, visualizing keenly the topographical features of Pierre's conscious and unconscious mind, watching him "half-befogged upon the mountain of his Fate," from which he caught momentary glimpses of "the winding tranquil vale and stream of Lucy's previous happy life," although the vale and stream were (rather cacophonously) "half-vailed in the lower mist." I could profess to have been shocked several lines later at the sudden alteration of the terrain,

as the condition of Lucy is "still more and more disentangling and defining itself from out its nearer mist, and even beneath the general upper fog."
I may in fact have been reading that way, but I think all I did was blink a
couple of times at "nearer" and absently write "neather" in the margin (mis-
spelling the word I meant, "nether"). Having found the right word I can
easily show that the mist is indeed "lower" while the fog is "upper," nearer to
the top of the mountain where Pierre stands, and it is reassuring to encounter the word "nether" a couple of pages on, at the end of book 5, chapter 6.
It is also easy to adduce supportive evidence from Melville's handwriting.
The copyist for *Pierre*, Melville's sister Helen, could easily have thought that
she was seeing an *r* and not an *h* since she must have known that a certain
peaked configuration could be either letter. (The *r* could have a loop at the
top of the ascender.) In Melville's hand an unclosed *a* could well resemble
several letters, including *c* and *t*.

    In the 1960s the variants that textual editors were talking about were
almost always at the verbal level, usually a dubious single word and a suggested emendation. No one was talking about textual problems involving
anything bigger (sentences, paragraphs, or more) any more than Harkness
had done in 1959 or Bowers had done in 1959 in *Textual and Literary Criticism*. In the 1970s I learned that flaws did not come only in the form of
words and phrases—that small or large passages, chapters, and even larger
sections of many commonly taught American books simply did not make
sense. I published my findings in articles through the 1970s and early 1980s
and then in *Flawed Texts and Verbal Icons* (1984). Some reviewers of that
book declared that I was an unwitting New Critic in my reading of texts. No.
The New Critics of the 1940s had made the natural universal assumption
that texts are supposed to make sense. I started with the same assumption,
but by thinking about the author and the text biographically I had come to
see that many texts did not make sense on the scale of single words, passages,
or larger hunks such as chapters.

    It would have been expected that I would continue to be a good reader
of Melville's books, but nothing in my background suggested that I could
run a shop effectively. It turned out that I could select and nurture a sharp,
disciplined team at the Newberry Library or later in the Deering Library at
Northwestern, when I had the chance. I learned how to test the competence
of graduate students at collating and proofreading, and to reward them, and
how to refuse to hire students if they could not do accurate work. You didn't
have to hurt their feelings, either: you just had to lead them out into the
vast marble entrance hall of the Newberry and tell them confidentially that
some people's minds moved too fast to do the sort of drudgery we needed

in a newly hired Bartleby. The problem was that Hayford on a given day might overrule me under the theory that part of the purpose of the project was to spread money among graduate students regardless of their level of competence, especially if they had quirky interests, such as Saroyan. I had responsibility without authority. Furthermore, it was clear that Hayford, as I had foreknown, assumed that my teaching only half-time meant that I would work full-time on the Melville project.

After a year or so a new twist began to come into play, the idea that because I was doing work for hire I should not expect to get full credit in print for my work the way the Bibliographical Editor would receive credit for what I increasingly saw as his intermittent contributions. At worst, I felt, unfairly, that he paid visits to give benign approval to the list of variants in *Israel Potter* or whatever else was there laid out for his inspection or else make useful suggestions I could apply. Anyhow, things would even out, Hayford promised, and I might get full credit for editing volumes, later on, when for whatever reason I might not have worked on them, at the last stages, as much as he and Tanselle had done. That is not what happened. I think Hayford came to feel that after I had made an independent reputation on Stephen Crane, Mark Twain, and others, and especially after I held an endowed chair, albeit not at a school as prestigious as Northwestern, I did not need the credit as much as other people did, particularly those who were at hand. Hayford's behavior was strangest in the case of the Library of America. If we let our Melville texts be used by the Library of America, Hayford's planning notes show, the "work horses," the three of us, would divide the nominal "editorship" volumes, using the Northwestern-Newberry texts and merely writing short introductions and annotations. This work horse was not assigned a volume, with the result that I wince, from time to time, like Hamlet's galled jade, when I see, say, someone like Sacvan Bercovitch citing Tanselle as the sole editor of *Moby-Dick* rather than co-editor of the Northwestern-Newberry Edition and, in the 1983 Library of America volume, introducer and annotator of the Hayford-Parker-Tanselle text. That might not have happened if I had stayed at Northwestern.

But by 1966 Northwestern was becoming progressively less tolerable, especially after the department reneged on half the promised annual $1,000 raise. Then in the winter of 1966–67 Tanselle allowed Hayford to float his name for a full professorship at Northwestern, not seriously wanting to come, I assumed, but willing to enhance his position at Madison by an offer from Evanston. In the storm box on the west side of University Hall, between the massive outer doors and the lighter inner doors, with Polar-equipped students knocking off snow as they barged in and other students bulked up with coats and books as they pushed out, I had my first face-off with Hayford. I would have continued to slave at the Newberry for him. Knowing how highly Hayford valued Tanselle's bibliographical expertise and knowing that he still could not distinguish bibliographical from textual expertise, knowing that I could not get him to focus on textual complexities that undercut Bowers's arguments, I foresaw that I would be the factotum outvoted by intermittently resident Yale men focused, often enough, on their own non-Melvillean projects. I would have to leave Northwestern sooner than I wanted to.

Before I began looking for a way out, I could take pleasure at the recoveries of Melville's words I was making but less pleasure in the big red and black books which the director and designer at Northwestern University Press had been determined to make. The text, to my eyes, was set in too thin a typeface whose letters ran into each other. Hayford, Tanselle, and I should have anticipated what might happen in design, before anything was decided. As it was, we seemed to exalt editorial lists which contained information you might use once in a year (as in letting someone know whether a compound which was hyphenated at the end of a line in our text was also hyphenated in the original text). The implication of the way we presented the lists was that every list was of the same value as the list of varying words—but then even the list of verbal variants was often not very important itself, since in several cases none or few of the variants were Melville's. The less useful lists ought to have been in smaller type (and of course in a clearer font) and the more important lists ought to have been presented more appealingly. From working on the Norton Critical Edition of *Moby-Dick* I knew by 1966 that textual lists could and should be presented in an aesthetically pleasing way. I had found the textual lists visually incomprehensible in the Norton Critical Editions I was modeling the *Moby-Dick* lists on, all laid out so that you had no idea where one item ended and another started. At Norton, John Benedict willingly tried my simple change from paragraph indentation to reverse paragraph indentation. Suddenly anyone could tell where one entry stopped and another began, and thereafter the Norton Critical Editions followed the new design. There were ways of being both scholarly and humane. Melville thought that there was an aesthetics in all things, and my experience with Norton taught me that there could be, even, an aesthetics of editorial apparatus. The 1967 Hayford-Parker *Moby-Dick* was beautiful to my eyes, clear type on strong khaki-tinted paper (in the earliest printings), a book that invited anyone to read and reread. This Norton Critical Edition became the standard classroom text for thirty-five years, until I got out the second edition to replace it in 2001, just in time for the sesquicentennial of the book's publication and shortly before Hayford's death. (Oddly, it was dated 2002.)

At Northwestern between 1965 and 1968 I haltingly began to think about the profession and the place I might take in it. That process was pushed along in 1967 when I wrote the "Historical Note" for *Redburn* after an outside critic proved unable to produce a straightforward account of the composition, publication, reception, and later critical reputation of the book. What we found, year after year, was that almost no Melville critic was able to write such a direct, reliable biographical account. They had never had to do such a thing in their academic lives: they had been trained as New Critics, not as scholars. Write an article on the unity of *Redburn*? Oh, yes. Because I was intent on writing a "Historical Note" that might become a model for later ones, and because I took it on as a workman's job, I had little ego involvement with it and could concentrate on presenting information clearly. Having found unknown reviews of *Redburn* and having become convinced that I had to talk about Melville's debt to Washington Irving's *The Sketch-Book*, I had to push for a reevaluation of the nature of the notes. They had been conceived of as assimilating earlier scholarship, not as breaking new ground. Hayford agreed to let me write the reception section from all the known evidence, including reviews I had found, and reluctantly agreed to let me make brief mention of Irving's influence, something oddly missing from the work of the Yale students of Irving's biographer, Stanley T. Williams. Today, I could produce a mass of evidence starting with Melville's brother Gansevoort's *Index Rerum* (at the Berkshire Athenaeum) to show how important *The Sketch-Book* had been in the Melville household in 1837. Back in the late 1960s every little breakthrough required humble, persistent negotiation.

Much of my frustration came because the Modern Language Association's Center for Editions of American Authors (CEAA) all but required adhering to specific editorial guidelines. Bowers had espoused W. W. Greg's "The Rationale of Copy-Text" and by his lucid explication of Greg had made it the official theory of the CEAA. Greg was perfect in the simplest cases, a small crucial improvement over the earlier bibliographer Ronald B. McKerrow, both of them talking about situations for which no authorial manuscript survived. McKerrow had said that when you find that a later edition has been revised by an author you would not set your text from the later, corrected edition because many casual changes and small errors would inevitably have been introduced into it along with corrections; you would set from the earliest text because it would retain more features of the lost manuscript, but emend it with all the verbal changes in the later, revised edition. Greg agreed to a point: when a word miscopied from the manuscript had been corrected in a later printing of a text, an editor would emend that reading into the text nearest the manuscript, but he recognized, as McKerrow had not, that many new changes would inevitably have been introduced in any resetting, so the editor should not emend into the early copy-text *all* the changes in a corrected edition, not even all the verbal changes, but only the ones you thought were the author's.

Perfect as Greg's approach was in the simplest cases where a word is printed wrong in the first edition and corrected in a later edition, it was never satisfactory for authorial revision as opposed to authorial correction. An author's belated spot revisions, I was seeing, seldom sprang from the intention that had informed the original text. Greg's rationale of copy-text could not admit the relevance of indications that authorial control over a text could ever be lost. No editor was talking about the creative process at all, but, if you pushed a CEAA editor, he would have admitted that he thought authorial control over a text never ended. We were going to have trouble with *White-Jacket*, I saw, because while Melville was carrying the Harper sheets to London he added passages plainly intended only for the British audience, in one addition attributing a meaning to the chapter impossible to assign to the chapter as it had stood in the Harper sheets he was marking up. Greg's formula did not allow for intrusive evidence from a writer's life.

Again, Hayford did not want to hear me. I had no one to talk to. Then one evening in the fall of 1967 I attended a reception for visiting textualists at the chic Near North townhouse of the director of the Newberry Library. On pale lilac carpeting in a narrow staircase I began talking about Melville's texts to a professor from the University of South Carolina, James B. Meriwether, seven years my elder, a lean Virginian who spoke a Southern dialect I had never heard, "booting" his "abouts." Soon, we were talking excitedly even as we changed positions every few minutes to allow passage for other guests. From his study of Faulkner manuscripts, typescripts, and published works Meriwether had arrived at conclusions astonishingly like those I was making from Melville's texts. Adjourning to a table in a dark bar west of the Newberry, streets I had never been into and never went into again, we talked passionately for hours about the sacredness of the creative process, about varieties of authorial revisions, about the erratic mischief of most sober second thoughts. If we had been overheard we could have been shot on the spot for heresy by two different thought-killing squads: first, the bibliographical adherents of Greg we had just left at the party, whose theory held that an author retained control (legal control and aesthetic control) over all parts of a literary work as long as he lived; second, by the hoard of surviving older and younger New Critics, who ruled out of consideration all information about the author, biographical information being irrelevant to interpretation. That night changed my life. Meriwether could have hired me at South Carolina (where some of the voices would have sounded familial, since my mother had learned to talk from Mississippians whose people had paused a few generations in the Carolinas) but I knew that I worked best if I worked slowly and alone, free to make false starts and recoveries. I wanted to be able to write Meriwether about what we were learning but not to be on departmental committees with him. It still rankled, and was ominous for the future, that Northwestern had reneged on the promised raise once the chairman thought I was safely captive (and that I ought still to be grateful that precedence had been broken by hiring me back). I was carrying far too much of the weight of the edition and getting inadequate credit for my efforts, and I was not being allowed to think with the evidence I was uncovering. Somewhere else, surely, I would find others besides Meriwether who had learned to think unconventionally about textual evidence. The next day, when I was beginning my third year as an assistant professor at Northwestern, I began looking for another job, only in California. In January 1968, with three offers in my pocket, I went to see the new chairman, Samuels. He agreed, all too belatedly, to give me the $500 of the $1,000 raise I had been promised for my second year there. When I told him David Malone and Max Schulz were ready to hire me for the fall of 1968 at the University of Southern California, he incautiously offered to give me tenure and to match the salary. When I told him that USC was offering $16,000 he swallowed, then blurted one word, "Jesus!"[6]

USC hired me despite damaging press for the CEAA. On January 18, 1968, just as I was interviewing two schools in Los Angeles, Lewis Mumford, author of the 1929 *Herman Melville*, the critical biography which relied for most of its data on Raymond Weaver's 1921 biography, attacked the CEAA edition of the Emerson journals as putting the texts "behind barbed wire," inaccessible to an eager would-be student of "The Divinity School Address" or "The Poet." Mumford published his attack in the *New York Review of Books*, the new *radical chic* organ (to use the equally new popular phrase), already the Mutual Admiration Society for self-identified New York Intellectuals, which meant selected 1930s radicals or pseudo-radicals and their docile followers. The Emerson editors had been honorably intent on letting students follow the workings of Emerson's mind; they were liberating him, not imprisoning him. By the ferocity of his attack and by the politicized forum in which he published it, Mumford cast the CEAA as the enemy of all good radical thinkers. Readers of this most influential leftist literary paper thereafter associated the Melville editors by default with enthusiasts for the war in Vietnam. No matter that some of us had kept frigid antiwar vigils. No matter, two seasons later, that the young Melville worker who had been among the first half dozen to stand in silent noontime vigil at the Rock outside University Hall arrived late at night to say good-bye to me, bruised by a nightstick and redolent of tear gas from the police riot in Lincoln Park. (I had stayed that day in Evanston, packing, preparing to fly to California the next morning.)

Then just as I was stocking bookshelves in my office at USC, Edmund Wilson in the September 26, 1968, "Special Fifth Anniversary Issue" of the *New York Review of Books* blasted the Howells, Melville, and Hawthorne editors in "The Fruits of the MLA." Wilson acknowledged there was some minimal significance in the textual and historical scholarship. He was even "prepared to acknowledge the competence of Mr. Harrison Hayford, Mr. Hershel Parker, and Mr. G. Thomas Taselle [*sic*] in the stultifying task assigned them" (9). He had heard, he said, that we three were "the constant recipients of edicts in which the management lays down to them the principles on which they must proceed in their work, and that they are sometimes as much bored and annoyed as the reviewer is by these exactions; but the project in the case of *Typee* has been so relentlessly carried out in the technical language of this species of scholarship—of 'substantives,' 'accidentals,' and 'copy-texts'—that a glossary should be provided for readers who are not registered union members—if there are any such readers—of the Modern Language Association" (10).

In December 1968, cheered on by the reprinting of "The Fruits of the MLA" in a one-dollar pamphlet, Wilson's young New Leftist followers seized control of the Modern Language Association simply by the democratic process of rounding up all like-minded people for bloc voting. They came close to killing the CEAA, as Paul Lauter snippily recalled this failure in his 1991 *Canons and Contexts*:

> In 1968, the one vote lost at the MLA convention by the coalition of radicals, leftists, and liberals concerned the Association's continuing participation in the Center for Editions of American Authors (CEAA). It was one thing to come out against the Vietnam War, racism or Mayor Daley, or even to elect a socialist as vice-president; it was quite something else to tamper with the professional interests that helped keep subsidies flowing and provided members with a sense of their social legitimacy. (143)

The passage of more than two decades had not lessened Lauter's vague but intense hostility to the CEAA. The amount of the "subsidies" flowing to the Associate General Editor of *The Writings of Herman Melville* was pathetic, and figured as an hourly rate would have been illegally low in any state with a minimum wage law.[7] Besides, there had been no glory, for Mumford and

Wilson had destroyed any "sense of social legitimacy," so that only my knowledge of the good work I had done sustained me under the attacks.

Wilson was viscerally repelled by the pedantic lists, although he did not look closely enough at the Hawthorne lists, in particular, to see the true irrationality of the design of some of them. Some of the CEAA apparatuses were far more maniacal than any outside critic knew. Some CEAA editors, especially those most closely associated with Bowers, were fanatically assembling irrelevant information and publishing it along with bits of potentially relevant information in lists impossible for a living soul to decipher. I tested: sometimes it could take me thirty-two minutes to decipher something that was not worth deciphering, when a six-second glance at a sane list (which usually meant a list showing changes in chronological order) would have given all the information a person could reasonably use. Wilson added, being an acquaintance of Bowers's, that the "great Demiurge behind all this editing seems to be Mr. Fredson Bowers," a man he was prepared to acknowledge as a great bibliographer who happened not to be "much interested in literature" (10).

Wilson's prestige was such that flatterers leapt to endorse his views without ever studying the CEAA editions for themselves. Even thirty and forty years later younger critics justified themselves to their coteries by huddling behind the corpse of Wilson as they lobbed fuzees underhanded toward scholarly editions and biographies. (As I will show in a later chapter, in 1996 the attack on the first volume of my biography in the *New York Times* by Paul Berman was a tribute to Wilson.) Instead of gratitude for worthy achievements and measured criticism for failures, we got denunciation in 1968, and it emerged that the Northwestern-Newberry *Typee* had particularly upset the old tyrant of Talcottville, who carried the black and red book around for months so as to have it handy for setting off new diatribes. His scorn of the pedantry of the presentation of the lists was deserved although he didn't know which parts were truly pedantic. The CEAA had been a nobly conceived enterprise but now it was, in fact, flawed, often deeply flawed. Intelligent, constructive criticism, just then, might have worked some good later on. Wilson and Mumford were so extreme as to be merely destructive. They were not fair, and their attacks in the intimidating *New York Review of Books* did not make life around the English departments at Northwestern and USC easier. But things were not fair in 1968, especially to hundreds of thousands of young American men.

❖ *Chapter 3* ❖

ENTANGLED BY *PIERRE*

Doing Biography Away from the Archives

IN THE "FLOWER-CURTAIN LIFTED" book (22) of *Pierre* Melville declared
that if "man must wrestle, perhaps it is well that it should be on the nakedest
possible plain." Entangled with *Pierre* for more than half a century now, my
wrestling began not in a green and golden world like that of the opening of
the book but on a naked polished linoleum kitchen floor, my back to a wall,
in a newly scrubbed empty rental unit of an Edwardian house in Point Richmond, California. There in a sustained rapturous state I read the book during
several days of the 1959 Christmas break from graduate study at Northwestern. Almost three years earlier, belly pumped up with pneumo-peritoneum,
I had read *Moby-Dick* lying in an upstairs sleeping porch, and four years earlier, isolated with bed-rest for tuberculosis in a cubicle upstairs, I had read
nothing but Shakespeare for five months. As I read *Pierre*, those earlier experiences vivid in my mind, I was ecstatic that another book could for so many
pages be as good as *Moby-Dick* (how was that possible?) and so strangely
like *Moby-Dick* in its depiction of psychological states. At the end of 1959 I
was hyperalert to Shakespearean characters and language, my memory still
strong not only for echoes of more famous plays such as *The Tempest* but also
of others such as *Coriolanus* and *The Winter's Tale*. My Southerner's familiarity with the New Testament was still strong enough to let me identify with
Pierre's impulse to obey absolutely Jesus's words to the rich young man and
to let me wince at Melville's satire in Plinlimmon's pamphlet, particularly
having just survived a course on the master ironist Jonathan Swift taught
with sustained intellectual exhilaration by Phillip Harth. Before I flew back
to Chicago on New Year's Eve of 1959 I was obsessed with *Pierre*, although I
did not know how to ask good questions about it, and for prolonged periods
ever since I have surrendered to the obsession and refined the questions.

In Los Angeles in the fall of 1968 while living with Leon Howard, the Melville biographer, in his magnificently sited 1920s Spanish house in Brentwood I had Melville work to clean up. From documents I found in 1962 and afterward, I had supplied about half of the "Supplement" to the 1969 reissue of *The Melville Log*. In Los Angeles I saw it through the press for Leyda, who was still in the East German Filmarchiv. Working with John Benedict at Norton on the Norton Critical Edition of *Moby-Dick* had been joyous, so I wanted to get the Norton *"Moby-Dick" as Doubloon* into production as soon as we could. For years during trips to New York I had been making intermittent forays into the New York Public Library Annex and the New-York Historical Society to acquire full copies of reviews excerpted in the *Log* and in Hugh W. Hetherington's *Melville's Reviewers* (1961). There and in other libraries I found dozens of unknown reviews a day because I had learned to go armed not only with Leyda's magic wand (a tight list of publication dates) but also with elaborate triple-spaced lists of newspapers known, for instance, to have reviewed, say, *Redburn* or *White-Jacket* but not known to have reviewed *Moby-Dick* or *Pierre*. My hired researchers in London had discovered a few new reviews of *The Whale*. I was determined to include full texts of all the known reviews in *Doubloon* along with a bountiful sampling of later commentary up through the Melville Revival of the 1920s and later academic criticism. On the cover and title page I reversed the names from the order in the Norton Critical Edition. The first Hayford knew that *Doubloon* was in the works was when he received his printed and bound copy in May 1970. His initial grumpy embarrassment vanished as soon as he forgot he hadn't labored long over the whole thing.

Before I left Northwestern we had startling evidence of the effects of a decade and a half of the New Criticism on simple scholarship. The critic assigned to write the Northwestern-Newberry "Historical Note" for *Pierre* (like the critic assigned to write the *Redburn* essay) proved unable to write the kind of scholarly account we needed, a straightforward history of the composition, publication, contemporary critical reception, and subsequent critical history of the book. I had written the *Redburn* essay fast, meaning it as a workmanlike job, and in 1968 Hayford decided that Leon Howard and I would divide up the *Pierre* note, Howard taking the composition and publication while I did the critical reception and later critical history. In 1969 Howard was still at UCLA and I at USC, but both in Brentwood, near enough to consult but far enough apart for us to work on our own. Then, a decade after first reading *Pierre*, I made a special hunting trip to the New York Public Library Annex and the New-York Historical Society specifically to find unknown reviews of *Pierre* for use in the "Historical Note."

Howard had a fixed idea that the least interesting and least profound part of *Pierre* was the early part, the first eight "books," he specified in the "Historical Note." The ninth book, he said, was written in a new Carlylean tone in which Melville scolded his hero even before he introduced the surprise that Pierre had been a juvenile author. "Most of the last half—and slightly more," Howard said, was "clearly written by the author of *Moby-Dick*, rather than by a potential 'Guy Winthrop'" (372), a reference to the pseudonym Melville desperately suggested in a failed attempt to gain an advance from his second London publisher, Richard Bentley, on April 16, 1852. There one of Melville's arguing points was that the book would be more valuable because it ran to "150 pages & more" than he had first described it. Howard reasonably assumed that the book as we know it was not planned out and that the Pierre-as-author section (books 17 and 18) was "most probably responsible for the greatest number" of the "unforeseen pages" (375). At my deferential suggestion, Howard acknowledged that the influence of Shakespeare had been present from the beginning of the book and allowed, also, that there had been "a vein of philosophical seriousness" in the book from the beginning (373). Edgy about his attributing Melville's open break with the Duyckincks in February 1852 to a "petulant reaction" to the review of *Moby-Dick* in the *Literary World* the previous November, I got him to put the word "delayed" before "petulant reaction" (376).

The "Historical Note" as published in the Northwestern-Newberry *Pierre* early in January 1972 (dated 1971) was not something either of us was entirely happy with. I had found many unknown reviews in time to use them in the note, including one headed "Herman Melville Crazy" which had triggered a splash of sudden hot tears into a befouled microfilm reader. Just too late I had found several more reviews I would gladly have mentioned. I turned to other projects, but I remained uneasy about *Pierre*. In the early 1970s I continued to work on "Historical Notes" for the Northwestern-Newberry Edition, writing parts of the notes on *Moby-Dick* and *The Confidence-Man*, putting the drafts away until Hayford could turn to them again. But I no longer worked only on Melville.

From the start at USC, savoring the California freedom, I contrived new graduate courses in which I tried to unite literary criticism with textual evidence, which meant biographical evidence of composition, publication, and later adventures of the author and the text. In trying to see how textual practices and critical practices could be reconciled with what I was learning about the creative process, I was following up on the ideas that I had talked to James Meriwether about in 1967. In the early 1970s, as examiner for the CEAA, I was uniquely placed to realize that the dominant textual theorists were identical to the New Critics in separating textual study from study of the creative process. My own textual approach was through biography, but W. W. Greg and Fredson Bowers, just like the New Critics W. K. Wimsatt and Monroe C. Beardsley, had outlawed biography and focused on the published product rather than the process of creation. As I brought my biographical perspective to Melville's *Pierre* (and to works by Nathaniel Hawthorne, F. Scott Fitzgerald, Stephen Crane, Mark Twain, Henry James, William Faulkner, Norman Mailer, and others), I repeatedly saw disastrous consequences from excluding biographical evidence from textual analysis and literary criticism. First my textual studies and then my writing the Melville chapter in *American Literary Scholarship* for nine years, starting in 1972, forced me to see that critics almost without exception were unthinkingly ignoring highly relevant evidence and often wasting their time on impossible assignments, such as showing Melville's "development" as a story writer without first establishing the chronology of his stories. The 1853 "Bartleby," said a critic, continued the pattern set in "The Encantadas" (1854); the 1855 *Benito Cereno*, said another, was an interesting variation on the theme of Vere in the book Melville was working on at his death in 1891. Lacking another topic, a critic could always demonstrate the unity of the splendid but maimed *Pierre*. Forced to drop out of high school at sixteen and still trying to catch up with my classmates, I was horrified by the spectacle of long stretches of human life being squandered in empty academic exercises.

Soon there was more to think with besides my evidence from Melville. Year by year the CEAA was amassing a trove of new textual evidence. Beginning in 1969, as CEAA examiner I had the opportunity to study in detail, always from a biographical point of view, the textual histories of books by Franklin, Charles Brockden Brown, Hawthorne (the posthumous romances), Mark Twain, Howells, and others. As a member of the CEAA Advisory Committee (1971–74) I got to examine others' reports on textual histories and problems. With many textual studies being published and with many facsimile editions suddenly appearing, most of them unrelated to the CEAA editions, you could learn something about many textual problems even if you were stationed far away from great libraries.

The defining moment in this part of my career began when I walked into an undergraduate class early in 1972 prepared to teach Fitzgerald's *Tender Is the Night* and found that the students (by a blunder, it turned out) had been sold the edition reordered chronologically by Malcolm Cowley. This was not truly a "revised" edition, of course, but a *reordered* edition with only tiny revisions. After an aghast moment I launched into forty-nine passionate minutes on why they had been sold a fraudulent book, showing them, for instance, that the original order was literally built into the reordered thing Cowley published, that everything in certain sections of the book they held in hand was written to follow another section, not to precede it—written so that as they progressed readers would have particular passages in mind. I enlisted the young Englishman Brian Higgins as a collaborator for a study of *Tender Is the Night*. Nobody in the CEAA had been talking about the aesthetic consequences of rearranging large hunks of prose.

In and out of the classroom through the 1970s I was working with critical approaches and assumptions and trying to relate them to textual assumptions, but the connections were difficult to push because the words (starting with "textual" and "critical") might be the same but the meanings might be different. The greatest obstacle to textual and biographical thought in the 1970s was the man who had been an innovator and liberator, Fredson Bowers. In the post-Mumford and post-Wilson climate, the ongoing torrent of his publications became a problem for anyone who cared about textual editing. Should you gloss over his increasingly subjective manipulations of the texts and his increasingly weird apparatuses so as not to give aid and comfort to the enemy? Could you criticize him at all in a way that would not undermine the whole CEAA enterprise? In March 1974 I arranged to write an article on Bowers's University of Virginia edition of *Maggie: A Girl of the Streets* for volume 5 of Joseph Katz's *Proof: The Yearbook of American Bibliographical and Textual Studies*. Bowers had leaned over backward to justify his preference for the expurgated 1896 edition over Crane's honest 1893 book. The CEAA had tied itself to the great bibliographer who had descended into fantasy biography and textual histories, no more capable of riding herd on the expenditure of significant sums of money from the federal government than he was of rounding up and riding herd on a list of variant words (for his textual apparatuses became so ill-conceived and error-ridden as to be unusable). Idealistic in those days, I wrote up my evidence with help on part of it from Brian Higgins and submitted it to the CEAA in January 1975, asking that the seal given to *Maggie* be rescinded. On June 4, 1975, the CEAA Advisory Committee refused to rescind the seal, and I was told in a letter dated June 26 that the committee felt "that it would be inappropriate for the CEAA to explain for publication its reasons for refusing to withdraw a seal already awarded to a volume." No one would back me against Fredson Bowers. The CEAA closed ranks around him, preferring to let shoddy editing carry the seal of quality rather than to further enrage him. Flush with victory, Bowers then blackballed me from the organization that succeeded the CEAA, the Center for Scholarly Editions (CSE). He later denied in print that he had done so but I have the document. (Even then, Leon Howard liked to say, everything you wrote about someone ended up on his desk.) Worse, the editor abruptly dropped the *Maggie* article from the 1975 *Proof*, then in September 1976 declined to publish it in the next *Proof* either.

In the 1970s, even after being deprived of opportunities to examine editions for the CEAA or the new CSE, I found a series of challenging textual situations which I could write about on the basis of commonly available books (some of them facsimiles) and magazines as well as photocopies of manuscripts supplied by libraries, but always putting my findings in biographical contexts. After a while I defined this part of what I was doing as "pulling rabbits out of hats"—using photocopies of Mark Twain's *Pudd'nhead Wilson* papers from the Bancroft Library (and a little from the Morgan Library), for example, or using the facsimile of the portion of the manuscript of *The Red Badge of Courage* housed in Virginia and other facsimiles, or comparing (with Bruce Bebb, at his suggestion) our pasteups of the *Esquire* version of *An American Dream* against the Dial Press version.

This was all biographical-textual work I could mostly perform without going forth to the Eastern archives and remaining there for prolonged periods (although I did, for example, go to the Morgan Library for Mark Twain and eventually gained access to Norman Mailer's storage vault and walked away with two of his working ledgers for *An American Dream* for several months). Every year I worked on several diverse projects, hopscotching, pushing one ahead, and then another. Every project came down to biographical evidence, as I kept finding as I wrote the Melville chapter for *American Literary Scholarship.* Every year I found most of the publications dismaying because, ignoring biographical evidence, critics so often argued impossibilities, the same ones, different ones. During this time I was writing portions of "Historical Notes" for Northwestern-Newberry volumes that were not published for many years. Year by year I was engaged in two or more overriding projects from which I learned lessons about textual problems not anticipated by Greg or Bowers on one side or William K. Wimsatt and Monroe C. Beardsley or E. D. Hirsch and James Thorpe on the other. Reading Shakespeare I had made myself assume that difficult sentences and scenes should make sense. Throughout the 1970s, studying and then teaching classic American texts which did *not* make sense, I resorted to biographical and textual evidence (forbidden by the New Criticism) to find out why.

In 1975 at a party where I was talking passionately about what I had been finding on several American novels, Max Schulz asked a question chairmen just don't ask: "Why don't you teach what you're doing?" As a result of that invitation, in the spring of 1976 I taught a course called, blandly, "Textual Evidence and Literary Interpretation." At the end of the semester I annotated a copy of the syllabus for Max: "I think this goes in the category of innovative courses. Despite the formidable subject matter, it was the most exciting course I have ever taught. People elsewhere felt the excitement, and courses are being devised in happy imitation of it." That was true. The students were as excited as I was, almost, and colleagues around the country were asking for the syllabus so they could construct their own variant courses. In the next years I tried for more precise titles without achieving accuracy and felicity. Textual evidence, literary criticism, creativity, aesthetics, literary theory—unequal things met and mixed in these titles. When I next taught this class nine students got eleven publications from it, two or three of them career-starting publications. I had gone as far as I could go at USC and had moved into uncharted territory. Enough of pulling rabbits out of hats. It was time to go East, to the libraries.

Looking now at this first "Textual Evidence and Literary Interpretation" syllabus I see a gap, the failure to assign anything on the creative process. It was not because I had not looked—it was because I could find almost nothing applicable to literary texts. John Dewey in *Art and Experience* was the best I could find, but his treatment was brief. As I soon found, there was very little written on the creative process that could help a textual editor make sense of a variety of literary problems. You could find dubious advice on how to make your child creative or on how creativity is allied with mental illness, but you could not find a serious study of literary creativity anywhere. I looked. Albert Rothenberg still had not published *The Emerging Goddess: The Creative Process in Art, Science, and Other Fields* (1979), which remains incomparably the best work in the field.

All this time, from 1970 until 1978, I was meticulously writing short biographies of American writers for the *Norton Anthology of American Literature* (1979), including all the major writers of the 1820–65 period except Douglass and Dickinson (much later I silently redid their author headnotes). Treating all of these small biographical headnotes as requiring serious fresh biographical research, I compared published biographies and supplemented them with research yet unassimilated by biographers and even brought fresh archival research to some of them, such as some study of the manuscript of *Walden* and prolonged work with the manuscripts of Hawthorne's uncompleted fiction, for example, or checking standard editions of lectures against the texts as reported in contemporary newspapers. In later editions of the anthology the headnotes were cut down, against my preferences, but stayed much more reliable than any other author biographies in anthologies, which almost always were lifted from previous anthologies, sometimes hilariously leaving telltale evidence of their origins.

My rededication to Melville biography did not come in one stunning moment but by stages after February 14, 1975, when I received the Summer 1974 issue of *Studies in the Novel* which contained Robert Milder's "Melville's 'Intentions' in *Pierre*." Milder began by challenging Leon Howard for saying that Melville had changed course in writing the book: "*Pierre* is an overwrought book, even a 'mad' one, but from the outset there is an unrelenting method to its madness which precludes the idea that Melville was writing a genial romance. Whatever its excesses, *Pierre* is an intensely deliberate book" (187). Milder observed that few facts "are known about Melville's life during the winter of 1851–52, the months when he wrote *Pierre*" (193), but he was not concerned with adding to those facts. As a New Critic he did not look for anything in Melville's experiences that could have affected the composition of *Pierre*, so he was not bothered by the abrupt mid-book announcement that Pierre had been a juvenile author. Rather than looking for biographical evidence or internal evidence to explain why Melville had declared abruptly that he wrote precisely as he pleased and that young Pierre, whom we knew so well, still earlier had been, all unknown to us, a poet, Milder looked for unity in ideas. A " 'new truth' " had "precipitated Melville's decline, or sense of decline"—the "perception of a moral darkness beyond Solomon" had "assailed Melville," followed by "his growing awareness of the ambiguities of the self" (195). In *Moby-Dick*, Milder argued, "Melville had shown what modern critics have since reaffirmed: that tragedy can exist with a context of metaphysical doubt, even of nihilism, as long as author and audience retain a common belief in man's potential heroism" (195–96). But Melville had come to question "precisely this potential heroism," to discover "that on the deepest level all men were hypocrites" (196). Melville's "mind had been 'overturned' by a 'sudden onset of new truth,' and, driven as always by his fierce earnestness, he set out to deliver this truth, unmitigated, to the world—to 'gospelize the world anew, and show them deeper secrets than the Apocalypse!' " (196–97).

While flaws of structure and theme in *Mardi* gave evidence of "several distinct stages of composition," Milder admitted (192), in *Pierre* there was "no evidence of such a discontinuity, and the impending tragedy of its young hero is foreshadowed from the very start." Milder was firm: "Melville was in command of his material from the very start—in command of his plot, which did not change substantially as he labored on it, and in command of his complex and ironic attitude toward Pierre, which also did not change. The book Melville published, 'loathsome' as it seemed to many of its first readers, is the book he set out to write" (192–93). Only wide and dense New Critical blinders allowed Milder to make such statement. Milder saw *Pierre* as a perfect verbal icon, unified, by definition, as almost all texts were to the

New Critics, and therefore susceptible to tidy explication. The greater the glaring anomalies in the book, I learned later, the greater the zeal of New Critics in finding and proclaiming its perfect unity.

Milder brought my uneasiness about the "Historical Note" into focus. I took the commonsense view that the Pierre-as-author sections showed that the published book certainly was *not* the book Melville set out to write. Surely, I thought, something must have happened to make Melville alter the plot with the abrupt announcement that Pierre had been a much-praised young author, unbeknownst to any careful reader of the coherent early parts of the book, those pages which since 1959 I had cherished as some of the greatest prose in American literature, as splendid as many pages of *Moby-Dick*. I agreed that Melville was in command of his plot at the outset but disagreed with the notion that the plot did not change substantially and that his attitude toward his hero did not change. I did not think that Melville had meant to write a genial romance, either, and had no quarrel with taking the book as intensely personal, although I would have defined the personal parts differently. Even "unrelenting method" and "intensely deliberate" I could agree with, but only as applied to the book up to the announcement that Pierre had been a juvenile author and intermittently beyond. For me, as for the equally obsessed critic in the November 1852 *American Whig Review*, George Washington Peck, an alcoholic and psychotic (as his 1847 review of *Omoo* and *Typee* had shown him to be), it was obvious that when Melville began the book he had not intended to make Pierre a writer:

> Just in this part of the book [the city section] it comes out sud-denly that Pierre is an author, a fact not even once hinted at in the preceding pages. Now the reader is informed, with very little circum-locution, and as if he ought to have known all about it long ago, that Mr. P. Glendinning is the author of a sonnet called the "Tropical Summer," which it seems has called forth the encomiums of the lite-rati, and induced certain proprietors of certain papers to persecute him for his portrait. All this is told in a manner that proves it very clearly to be nothing more than an afterthought of Mr. Melville's, and not contemplated in the original plan of the book, that is, if it ever had a plan. It is dragged in merely for the purpose of making Pierre a literary man, when the author had just brought him to such a state that he did not know what else to do with him.[1]

I could disagree with Peck on the reason Pierre's juvenile authorship was "dragged in" while agreeing absolutely that the Pierre-as-author section was "an afterthought," a momentously disastrous one, however brilliant some of the parts.

Starting on Valentine's Day, 1975, I began typing out on separate pages or else photocopying the known documents about the composition of the book. I had in mind an article which through the first several typescripts was haplessly entitled "The Writing of *Pierre*: Facts and Theories, Old and New." The work eventually went into an article called "Why *Pierre* Went Wrong," part of which was accepted by *Studies in the Novel* and printed in the Spring 1976 issue. The rejected part, which was about the contract for *Pierre*, went into the fifth volume of *Proof* (delayed until 1977), for which the *Maggie* article had been written. Happy enough at the time to have two publications to show the chairman of the department rather than one, I realized only belatedly that I should have pleaded to work some points about the contract into "Why *Pierre* Went Wrong."

In that July of 1975 Brian Higgins and I read the book more carefully than either of us had ever read any long piece of fiction. Our analysis went into a joint article, "The Flawed Grandeur of Melville's *Pierre*" in an Anglo-American collection called *New Perspectives on Melville* (1978) edited by Faith Pullen, a title not much brighter than the working title of my 1975 article, then (further revised) into the G. K. Hall *Critical Essays on Herman Melville's "Pierre"* (1983), and (rewritten again) into our Louisiana State University Press book, *Reading Melville's "Pierre; or, The Ambiguities"* (2006). My asking questions about the writing of *Pierre* also led, years later, to the high adventure of collaborating with Maurice Sendak on an illustrated nonce-text of the book, the Kraken Edition (1995), and writing a full introduction to it. Perhaps more than anything else besides reading *Moby-Dick*, my reading *Pierre* set me on the path toward writing a two-volume biography of Melville and ultimately to writing this book. More specifically, it was my responding to Milder's article that ultimately, after 1984, drew me back into specializing on Melville and examining episodes in his life as a biographer.

Before I tried to scrutinize my pathetic Valentine's Day inventory of documents—those "few facts," Milder had rightly called them—I put down something then-unpublishable:

> To clear the ground, I will identify a few places where I now would argue against Howard's interpretation. I don't think the evidence supports the idea that *Moby-Dick* ever was a mere whaling narrative; and while Melville may have doubted his practicality in writing it, I find it hard to believe that he ever doubted "his wisdom" in doing so. Whether or not he had *Pierre* in mind when he made his arch

comments to Mrs. Morewood around mid September on the Fates having plunged him "into certain silly thoughts and wayward spec- ulations," Melville may well have intended from the start to make *Pierre* as profound as *Moby-Dick*, merely converting a different sort of inferior literary vehicle to his purposes, the sensational romance this time instead of the whaling narrative. I don't think Melville ever meant "to address his seventh book" to feminine readers [as Howard suggests in the "Historical Note," 367]: I think he wanted to write a great book which could be accepted and bought as a mere piece of sensational women's fiction. In understanding Melville's descrip- tion of the book to Richard Bentley, his English publisher, I would say Melville was blinded to his actual performance by the magnifi- cent cogency of his first intentions rather than "blinded to his actual performance by the limited nature of his first intentions" [368]. I would argue for much stronger similarities between the first half of *Pierre* and *Moby-Dick* than Howard does. I don't see that Melville scolds Pierre anywhere in Book IX. I think the passage in chap- ter iv which looks most like scolding ("Fool and coward! Coward and fool!") must be taken as Melville's reflection of Pierre's self- accusations. (See the last paragraph of that chapter: "Impossible would it be now to tell all the confusion and confoundings in the soul of Pierre, so soon as the above absurdities in his mind presented themselves first to his combining consciousness.") Howard says that "Most of the last half—and slightly more—of *Pierre* is clearly writ- ten by the author of *Moby-Dick*, rather than by a potential 'Guy Winthrop,' and it reflects Melville's intellectual and compositional experiences of the preceding year" [372]. I would say rather that the first half—and slightly more—is clearly written by the author of *Moby-Dick*; and since "Guy Winthrop" is a desperate last-minute suggestion, a retroactive gesture, I would ignore that pseudonym, or merely say that as a whole the last 2/5ths or so of *Pierre* cannot sustain comparison with *Moby-Dick*, as the first 3/5ths can. Where Howard says "There had been a vein of philosophical seriousness in *Pierre* from the beginning" [373] (he added "philosophical" after I argued for a greater respect for the beginning books), I would say that where *Pierre* is most seriously philosophical is in those early books, not in most of the later ones. Also, rather than saying that Melville became "sardonic about his romance and serious about his preoccupation" [373], I would say that Melville changed his preoccupation.

This was a limbering-up exercise to clarify the issues for myself. Howard would undoubtedly have asked me why I had not spoken up, if I had disagreed so strongly. The truth was that I had been deferential, but I had also been inhibited because I had only impressions to offer at that time rather than worked-out opinions based on documents. One thing is clear: users of the Northwestern-Newberry "Historical Note" can justly reproach Howard for not reexamining documents already printed or taken note of, but, knowing what was available in 1969 or 1970 and what is available now, I see that no one could have written anything like a definitive account of the composition and publication.

The next day, February 15, 1975, I typed a new version of the page using the red ribbon, this time ending with a challenge to myself: "I am convinced that the first half of *Pierre* is the better, not the second half, despite the presence toward the end of such a magnificent set-piece as the vision of Enceladus. In this paper I will not elaborately argue these conclusions, though I will provide a biographical background for accepting them. What I want to suggest here most of all is that an event in Melville's life disastrously altered his composition of *Pierre*. That event was almost surely his interrupting work on the book in order to spend the week or so in New York City." (I knew the *Log* entry for January 4, 1852, in which Sarah Morewood, writing from Pittsfield, asked George Duyckinck, "Were you surprised to see Herman Melville in Town?") I did not know what "event" I was talking about (unless it was simply the act of "interrupting work" on the book), but I was convinced that "something happened." At some point in pencil I changed "event" to "a particular event" and added, "one which took place, almost surely, in January, 1852." Now, decades later, I am more than a little chagrined that I did not immediately focus on redating one piece of available evidence for that event, but I take satisfaction in having perceived that "something happened"—that some dramatic event (or events) occurred which we did not know about.

"We don't know when Melville began the book," I typed in red, setting it off from what followed in black ribbon. The first piece of evidence I had was a mid-September 1851 letter to Sarah Morewood: "the Fates have plunged me into certain silly thoughts and wayward speculations" (*Log*, 427). This may or may not have meant that Melville was already planning *Pierre*. The November 7, 1851, letter Melville wrote to Evert Duyckinck says he has his dressing gown patched up, possibly a literal or metaphorical indication that he was through with fall chores such as woodcutting and now was ready to sit down and write. I acknowledged also that while the November 17, 1851, letter to Hawthorne implies that his next book will be as much better than *Moby-Dick* as a Kraken is greater than a whale, it does not in fact identify an actual manuscript in progress. The earliest reference to *Pierre* we had was the letter Sarah Morewood wrote to George Duyckinck on December 28, 1851. Alerted by differences between the *Log* and Eleanor Metcalf's transcription in *Herman Melville: Cycle and Epicycle* (1953), I enlisted the help of the Keeper of Manuscripts at the New York Public Library, Paul Rugen, in checking the original to make slight corrections. One was the insertion of "so" in the first sentence:

> I hear that he is now so engaged in a new work as frequently not to leave his room till quite dark in the evening—when he for the first time during the whole day partakes of solid food—he must therefore write under a state of morbid excitement which will soon injure his health—I laughed at him somewhat and told him that the recluse life he was leading made his city friends think that he was slightly insane—he replied that long ago he came to the same conclusion himself—but if he left home to look after Hungary the cause in hunger would suffer.

"Hungary," we knew, was a reference to the triumphal American tour Lajos Kossuth was making. I thought Melville must have had his usual hearty breakfast, but believed Mrs. Morewood's report that he wrote straight through till dark, which came early in December in western Massachusetts. Her description (especially the word "frequently") implied a work pattern not of days but of weeks, I thought, probably throwing his work on *Pierre* back through December into November, if not earlier.

In February 1975 I thought it unlikely that when he went to New York Melville could have been much farther than halfway, if that far, given the amount of time "he later expended on the manuscript." I said that Melville "had interrupted his intensive labor on *Pierre* in order to make a two week trip to New York City, the purpose of which is unknown." I thought the trip was hastily arranged, for Sarah Morewood wrote to George Duyckinck on January 4, 1852, "Were you not surprised to see Herman Melville in Town?" (Rugen had confirmed Eleanor Metcalf's transcription that included the "not," a word Leyda had missed.) The *Log* also contained Mrs. Morewood's saying that she hoped to pass the evening of January 5 "with Mrs Herman Melville." I was surprised that Melville stayed in New York so many days, but took it as certain that his wife and new baby were with him, and presumably Malcolm, then almost three. We had the January 8, 1852, letter from Melville to Sophia Hawthorne in response to her letter praising *Moby-Dick*, so I knew he had promised not to send her again "a bowl of salt water." Instead, he said, "The next chalice I shall commend, will be a rural bowl of milk." In 1975 I wrote: "Melville is having wry fun in echoing that other Scottish nobleman, Macbeth, but a question suggests itself: why did he not say something like 'a rural bowl of milk and a city vial of cursed hebanon'?" Was he, I asked, "offering a falsely cheering and familiar contrast to his whaling book?"

The next item was the note dated only "Friday" which Melville addressed to "Dear Duyckinck": "I am engaged to go out of town tomorrow to be gone all day. So I wont' be able to see you at 11 O'clock as you propose. I will be glad to call though at some other time—not very remote in the future, either. The nut-crackers are very curious and duly valued." (The nut-crackers were evidently a New Year's Day gift, in the Dutch tradition.) Leyda had dated the letter January 9?, 1852. In the 1960 *Letters* Merrell R. Davis and William H. Gilman, Yale colleagues of Hayford's, had followed Leyda in the *Log* as dating this letter as "9?" Now as I deal with my successive attempts to assemble and grapple with documents, and to account for gaps between documents,[2] I am shaken to see that in practice I was slow to challenge authority in Melville scholarship, however independently I had begun to think about textual theory. So strong was my Southerner's respect for my elders that I did not see for years that this crucial document had been only casually and arbitrarily dated by Leyda in his *Log* and that Davis and Gilman had too readily accepted his dating. All Leyda had done was look at three successive Fridays and split the difference.

The next document we knew about was Allan Melville's January 21, 1852, letter to the Harpers which Leyda had summarized as "adjusting the details of the contract for *Pierre*": "My brother would like to have his account with your house to the 1st Feby made up and ready to render to me . . . ." In the February 14, 1975, draft I made a note in parentheses: "I have written for this letter from the Houghton Library." Remote from Eastern libraries, I was willing to make such requests of librarians I had met on their home grounds. The next piece of biographical evidence from the *Log* was Melville's Valentine's Day, 1852, letter to the "Editors of Literary World" (not addressing the Duyckincks by name), requesting that they discontinue the two copies of the paper he was paying for, his and his friend J. M. Fly's. I was baffled: "Nothing in the recent issues of the magazine seems adequate to account for this gesture." This was where Leon Howard had proposed "a petulant reaction" against the review of *Moby-Dick*, which became "a delayed petulant reaction," after my demurral. Already I had a photocopy of the Harper contract drawn up by Melville's younger lawyer-brother Allan and signed in February 1852. And we had letters from and to Richard Bentley in the early months of 1852, ending with Bentley's offer to publish a somewhat expurgated *Pierre*

at half profits and no advance, a letter to which Melville apparently did not
reply.

Unhappy because the January "9? 1852" letter was so cordial, I cast about
for an explanation: "Something had happened, and it may have happened in
Melville's inner life. Rather than supposing that the Duyckincks had somehow offended Melville in early February, it seems probable that two things
happened: (1) he became offended at them on the basis of their previous
actions, which he had tolerated at the time and (2) he found himself offending them, at least prospectively, by what he had just written in Book 17 or
what he was just deciding to write there." I was referring to his contemptuous
depiction of Evert as joint editor of the *Captain Kidd Monthly*, where he had
used Duyckinck's campaign of the previous winter to get Melville's portrait
for an engraving in *Holden's Magazine* (a campaign in which Duyckinck, as
I then could not have known, had not scrupled to enlist the powerful voice
of Melville's mother). I decided that "after the decision to ridicule Duyckinck in his manuscript, Melville could not conscientiously have kept up the
friendship." It "remains mysterious," I said weakly, not offering a third possibility: that Melville had been angered by some new behavior from at least
one of the Duyckincks.

Meantime, before Carolyn Jakeman at the Houghton Library could copy
the January 21 letter for me, what most seriously misled me was the Harper
contract as signed on February 20, 1852. It specified that the book would
contain about 360 pages. We also had the letter Melville wrote to his English publisher Richard Bentley on April 16, in which he says, "It is a larger
book, by 150 pages & more, than I thought it would be, at the date of my first
writing you about it." We did not have the letter referred to, and I assumed
(wrongly, I now know) that it was written in the first half of February 1852,
shortly before the contract gave the expected page number as "about 360
pages." I thought the contract showed that on February 20, 1852, Allan Melville expected the book would be the short book that his brother described to
Bentley at about the same time. My draft shows that Carolyn Jakeman must
have dealt with my request for a copy of Allan Melville's January 21, 1852,
letter in two stages. Before February 14, 1975, she had sent me photocopies of two scraps of paper, Allan Melville's drafts of portions of the contract,
one of which reads: "Should the number of pages in said work prove to be
any considerabl much less than 360" a "corresponding deduction shall be
made from the number of copies which is agreed will be necessary to liquidate the cost of stereotype plates and editors copies for a book of 360 pages."
Allan went back and inserted "or more" after "much less," but did not follow
through with the insertion of "or addition" after "corresponding deduction."

The contract read: "Should the number of pages in said work prove to be much less or much more than 360 it is agreed that a corresponding deduction [here "or addition" is careted in] shall be made from the number of copies which it is agreed will be necessary to liquidate the cost of stereotype plates and editors copies for a book of 360 pages." What the draft passages at the Houghton showed was that Allan was thinking that if the book varied much from 360 pages it was going to vary on the short side, not the long side. Covering the other possibility was an afterthought, even in the inscription of the contract. Everyone who had looked at the contract had assumed that this meant that the enlargement took place after the signing of the contract on February 20, 1852. Thinking so encouraged me to think, wrongly, the book was probably no more than half finished when Melville went to New York City around New Year's Day, 1852.

I thought I might help fill the gaps in January documents by looking at older and very recent reviews of *Moby-Dick* Melville might have seen, once he got to town. In *"Moby-Dick" as Doubloon* (1970), as we saw, I had printed in full all the reviews found by Leyda, Hetherington, and others, and all those I had found (including those found by London researchers I had hired), and I had found a few reviews since then. I had a mass of evidence no one before me had ever been able to lay out on a table in order. Now I offered a hypothesis, bolstered, I thought, by circumstantial evidence: "Until he went to New York City after Christmas, Melville had not paid much attention to the reviews of *Moby-Dick*." I thought he had labored through December buoyed by Hawthorne's mid-November 1851, "joy-giving and exultation-breeding letter" about *Moby-Dick*, and that what broke his exalted mood was "the sudden exposure to a large number of reviews of *Moby-Dick*, whether newly focused on reviews which had been gradually accumulated or whether in New York City he for the first time had access to a much larger number of reviews of *Moby-Dick*, at a time when he was not working intensively on his manuscript, if working on it at all, and therefore was more apt to react to them, especially in the aftermath of his abnormal work pattern, which must have left him psychologically drained." Working with all the known reviews, I focused on just what Melville was retaliating against in book 17 of *Pierre*.

Rather than assuming, as I thought we had all done, that Melville was retorting to what reviewers had said about all his books from *Typee* onward, I copied out the phrases he attributed to Pierre's reviewers, then scanned my collection of the known reviews of Melville's first books. (More than a third of a century later, I have repeated the search expeditiously on all the known reviews, in my files in my computer.) I concluded that Melville was not reacting *generally* to the reviews of his first six books so much as specifically to the earlier reviews of the latest, *Moby-Dick*. For satirical purposes the critical comments in book 17 are praise rather than blame, as when, to take one topic, young Pierre is "characterized throughout by Perfect Taste" while Melville's latest book had been condemned as containing "many violations of good taste and delicacy" and Melville had been called "reckless at times of taste and propriety" and condemned for writing "tasteless passages" and scenes which "neither good taste nor good morals can approve."

I thought, in my February 14, 1975, draft, that Melville's reaction to a batch of reviews, "probably taken as a single sustained dose," had "deflected his attention disastrously from the psychological problem he had so elaborately set up for his hero." Instead, I thought, he became fixated upon his own psychological, financial, and perhaps physical problems in pursuing a literary career while magazine or newspaper editors could offer him perfunctory and irrelevant praise or condemn him for what he knew should have entitled him to profoundest homage. In this mood he lashed out at the critics in the handiest way, in his work in progress. He began writing passages which could have relevance only to him, not to Pierre. I assumed that book 17, "Young America in Literature," where Pierre's reviews were quoted, and 18, "Pierre as a Juvenile Author, Reconsidered," were "added after the long January interruption of his work." Misled, probably, by the idea that Melville's work had been disrupted, I talked of the contradictions between Melville's assertions about Pierre in book 17 and the earlier parts of the book as if they were due to Melville's being away from the manuscript so long: "The internal evidence, in short, argues strongly that Melville had been away from his manuscript so long, and had undergone such psychological changes, that he simply forgot what he had done—and what he had done with remarkable cogency and consistency."

When I typed up the third draft on March 11, 1975, I still thought that a reasonable guess was "that Melville had written most if not quite all of the Saddle Meadows section by Christmas, and that he had not written much if any of the city section." I still did not know "why Melville interrupted his labor on the manuscript to make a trip to New York." I still thought, following the *Log*, that Lizzie was with her husband in New York. I was insistent that "the writing of Books 17 & 18 was an EVENT, at least as much as reading and reacting to EAD's review of *MD*":

> Knowing that he still could not and would not scramble for attention in the magazines, Melville now foresaw that literary titmice like Duyckinck could destroy his career; surely he had inklings enough that his manuscript contained many passages more explosive than

any in his earlier books. But the event which impelled him to cancel his subscription and his friendship with the Duyckincks may
have been less a reaction to the *Literary World* review of *Moby-Dick*
and the accumulation of unintended indignities from Duyckinck
than Melville's own action of writing Duyckinck into Book 17 as
the joint editor of the *Captain Kidd Monthly* out to pirate Pierre's
daguerreotype. Having written (or planned to write) the passage ridi-
culing Duyckinck, Melville may have felt that honesty demanded
he break the friendship. However, if this happened it can only have
puzzled the Duyckincks until they read *Pierre*. As Mr. Compson
says in *Absalom, Absalom!*, "It just does not explain." Some mystery
remains.

Slightly elaborating the earlier speculation about the Duyckincks, I was insistent but still baffled. Following this passage I noted that I still did not have
Allan's letter of January 21: "I must wait for Carolyn Jakeman to send me a
copy of the letter."

Stymied temporarily, I tried to work minutely with the chronology in
Davis and Gilman's note to the letter conjecturally dated January 9, 1852:

> Normally precise, Davis and Gilman were not proof against the
> complexities of this period in Melville's life. The Morewoods did not
> return to New York on December 29, as the editors say; they stayed
> on at Pittsfield for the New Year and returned on Monday, January 5.
> (Mr. Rugen pointed out to me that Mrs. Morewood altered the date
> of her letter to George Duyckinck from January 4 to 5. Perhaps she
> began it in Pittsfield and completed it in New York.) Mrs. Morewood
> did not expect to see Elizabeth Melville in New York on January 5,
> as Davis and Gilman say. Knowing Mrs. Morewood's need for com-
> pany, one can guess that her mention of remaining "quietly indoors"
> ever since her arrival might have taken her to midweek: probably
> the following "evening" she hoped to pass with Elizabeth was the
> eighth or ninth, which would still allow Elizabeth time to reach Bos-
> ton by the tenth. Also, it is not Elizabeth's brother who recorded her
> presence with her children in Boston, but her sister-in-law. Further-
> more, Melville's saying to Duyckinck that he was "engaged to go out
> of town tomorrow" does not mean he left for Pittsfield at the same
> time his wife went to Boston: the note specifies that he was going
> out of town only for the day. (Maybe he accompanied her and the
> boys to Boston, then returned immediately to New York.) Finally,

they "tentatively" (like Leyda, they said) dated the letter "December 9"—a most unfortunate typo for "January 9"; and January 21, 1852 fell on a Wednesday, not a Friday! Although its terseness is appealing, one had better scrap the account in the *Letters* and make do with the less concise version offered here.

My account is remarkable, I realized years later, less for the number of errors it corrects than for the number of errors it contains, all based on the best current evidence. I still boggle at my passive acceptance of "January 9" as the date assigned to the letter being discussed.

March 19, 1975, was a long day with insistent demands, but I noted in my work diary: "AM's 21 Jan. 52 letter—very imp." and the next day wrote "worked on re-doing 'The Writing of *Pierre*' to incorporate new info." Here is what Allan wrote the Harpers, blurry in the Houghton copy, a letter-press office copy (from Allan's machine, an early version of a document copier):

> My brother would like to have his account with your house to the 1st Feby made up and ready to render to me, as near that date as will be convenient to you.
>
> Respecting 'Pierre' the contract provides that if the book exceeded 360 pages a corresponding addition should be made to the number of copies required to liquidate the cost of the stereotype plates &c for a book of that size. As the book exceeds that number of pages it will of course be necessary to ascertain how many more copies are to be allowed than provided by the contract for a book of 360 pages. The retail price of the book has been also raised beyond the price fixed by the agreement, which was one dollar & of course a corresponding increase per copy should be made to the author.

First I focused on how this letter affected the timing of the composition of *Pierre*: "What looks like an afterthought in the final contract—the dawning realization that the book might run longer rather than shorter than 360 pages, merely reflects someone's failure to incorporate changes agreed to in the middle of January." ("Early January" would have been safer.) I continued: "In short, Allan's letter makes it clear that there was no sudden, inexplicable composition of roughly 150 pages of unplanned material after the contract was signed." I realized, also, that this redated the lost first letter to Bentley about *Pierre*: "Sometime between mid-January and the first week of February, most likely nearer the earlier date, Melville offered Richard Bentley a book of about the length specified to the Harpers." (Later I checked Atlantic shipping schedules to try to narrow the date; again, early January would have been a safer guess for Melville's letter to Bentley.) The letter showed that the contract, which we had dated February, in fact was drawn up and agreed to in the first days of 1852, and was copied out and signed in that form on February 20. Everything shifted, and began to fall back into place, telling a new story.

At last I began saying that Melville had gone to town to negotiate a contract for a completed book, but my chronology was still fuzzy and I failed to remind myself that Melville had never before asked for a contract from the Harpers until he had the manuscript ready to turn over to them. Worse, I still said nothing in the published form of the *Studies in the Novel* article about the punitive nature of the contract. Clipped to several pages I have a label: "Pages REJECTED by *SNNTS* and Recycled for *Proof*." In the *Proof* article I printed reproductions of the documents Carolyn Jakeman had sent me, Allan's scraps from his draft of the contract, his letter of January 21, and his copy (that is, Melville's copy) of the contract, all at the Houghton Library. Here I mentioned that the provision regarding royalty "was greatly altered from the previous contracts," being "set at 20¢ a copy after expenses rather than at half profits after expenses." I continued: "Under the old arrangement for a book priced at a dollar the Harpers would have split 50/50 with Melville after printing costs were paid, but now the publisher was taking 80¢ on the dollar." Oddly, I seemed less perturbed by this provision than by "a new and ugly item," Harpers' charging all review copies against Melville's account rather than splitting the cost, as before. I understood that "the contract was no mere incidental disappointment—it was a devastating warning." The way things were going, I said, "Melville might lose the publisher."

Although I called the contract "punitive" I did not focus on just how "devastating" it was. I must have been blinded by Leon Howard's assurance in his biography that Melville always had money in the bank in the 1850s. In the *Log* Jay Leyda had noted that on May 1, 1851, Melville borrowed $2,050 from "T. D. S." for five years at nine percent—an extraordinary sum, enough for an urban family to live modestly on for a year or two, and from an unknown lender. Leon Howard thought that Melville had borrowed the money to pay off the mortgage that Dr. Brewster held on Arrowhead. (None of that money, in fact, went to Brewster's mortgage, and before everything was settled in 1856 Melville had defaulted briefly on payments to Brewster. For how much more we know now, see the last chapter in this book, "Damned by Dollars.") I wonder now how tainted I was by the New Criticism in my failing to focus immediately on the absolute horror Melville must have felt at being offered 20 cents on the dollar when he was deeply in debt to the Harpers at 50 cents on the dollar, and when *Moby-Dick*, the book he had staked his future on (by borrowing so much money—partly to control its plating, although he ultimately stayed with Harpers) was not making him more money than all of his previous books and not, as far as he knew, exalting his literary reputation. Inflation was smothering in the 1970s and property taxes in Los Angeles (the last block before Santa Monica) were becoming confiscatory (almost a third of my annual salary!), but I still did not see the full horror of the contract for Melville.

During July 1975 when we were reading *Pierre* together day by day for "The Flawed Grandeur of Melville's *Pierre*" Brian Higgins and I went to a restaurant in LA's Chinatown. My fortune was a warning: "Guard against getting entangled in anything where you must make a decision." Various forms of the word *entangle*, we were seeing, defined Pierre's situation, and he indeed made most momentous decisions. It was too late for him, and like him I did not heed the warning, although I glued it to the flyleaf of my copy of the Northwestern-Newberry Edition of *Pierre*. When Brian left for Chicago I finished "Why *Pierre* Went Wrong" and drove to Austin to rendezvous with Noel Polk over the manuscript of *Absalom, Absalom!* In Austin, still in July, I handed the *Pierre* article to James Cox for *Studies in the Novel,* then went back to work with Polk—work so intense that even a jeweler's loupe did nothing to prevent enduring damage to my eyes. All I ever wrote on *Absalom, Absalom!* was an earlier article on how Quentin learned what he learned, which in typescript had provoked Cleanth Brooks to reread the book.[3] At least, the study of the Faulkner manuscript suffused parts of my *Flawed Texts and Verbal Icons.*

If he had asked Carolyn Jakeman for the full text of the January 21, 1852, letter, Leon Howard could have seen the letter, and she would have shown him the scraps of the draft of the contract in Allan's hand. That was an opportunity squandered. In March 1975 I had the letter but was not able to tease out its full significance. In the next decades more documents were found and either immediately or sometimes quite tardily taken account of. I learned that it is extremely hard even for the most intelligent people you know to accommodate themselves to new information. It is hard for them first to accept a new fact but much harder to adjust to how that fact affects what went before, what was going on concurrently, and what came afterward. And when what's new is not a straightforward additional fact but a more complicated revelation, an invalidation of a previously accepted belief, the location of an event or the attendees at an event, for example, or a report of a person's action which seems out of character, then acceptance of the new fact is still harder.

In "Learning in Interactive Environments: Prior Knowledge and New Experience" Jeremy Roschelle rejects the older idea that learning was "a process of accumulating information or experience." Instead, he says:

> Prior knowledge is the bane of transmission-absorption models of learning. Mere absorption cannot account for the revolutionary changes in thought that must occur. The child simply can't absorb knowledge about wool [that is, about sheep being grown for thick wool in hot climates], because prior knowledge about heat renders incoming ideas nonsensical. One can't assimilate fish schooling to a centralized mindset [because fish swimming in schools are not following a leader, as we would think]; distinct concepts for understanding decentralized systems must be developed. Jazz can't be translated into rock; one must cultivate ears for its unique organization. On the other hand, it is impossible to learn without prior knowledge. Eliminating prior understanding of heat won't explain why that sweater is still so nice in the winter, or how thick-coated sheep can be raised in the desert. The idea of decentralized systems must be built from some anchor in prior experience. (1)[4]

Biographical researchers encounter extremely subtle variations on the power and durability of prior knowledge and the mind's resistance to making either subtle or gross changes to that knowledge. Even after new information is acknowledged, prior knowledge may often spring forward, controlling memory, even though one has acknowledged it as invalid. I had a great advantage years later in expanding the *Log* with new documents into the electronic *New Melville Log*. Usually as I worked I simply transcribed and did the necessary dating and minimal identification of people named, but I did not read a new document in relation to many other documents in the computer from the previous months or the following months. Usually I was transcribing more than one document during a sitting, and moved from one to the next as soon as I could (however far away it fit in). When I was ready to write a chapter of the biography, then and then only I would read a hundred or two hundred pages of my chronology where old and new documents were indistinguishably intermingled, and then and then only, usually, would I begin to see more than the most obvious ways new documents (which were not signaled as "new") affected what we had thought we had known all along.[5]

1977. Daniel A. Wells reprinted from the January 3, 1852, *Literary World* an item the Duyckincks had based on Mrs. Morewood's news and probably had written a few days earlier.[6] The item, in facetious nautical language, contained a reference to Evert Duyckinck's own bread-and-butter gift for Melville's hospitality the previous summer, the thermometer: "Herman Melville, close-reefed in his library at Pittsfield, is doubling old Saddleback and winter, with a thermometer below zero, it is rumored on a new literary tack for the public when he next emerges in Cliff street." The Duyckincks were prepared to promote Melville's new literary experiment (always provided he had paid attention to the cautious warning about irreverence in *White-Jacket* in their *Literary World* and the somber reproach for his irreverence in *Moby-Dick*). What interested me most about the item was that it showed that the Duyckincks had not known in advance about Melville's trip to New York.

In the November 1977 *American Literature* Patricia Barber published "Two New Melville Letters"—letters which had been moved out of the main Shaw papers (at the Massachusetts Historical Society), perhaps because of their extremely personal nature, and deposited in the Social Law Library. Melville had been forced to confess to his father-in-law on May 12, 1856, that he had borrowed $2,050 from T. D. Stewart on May 1, 1851, at nine percent interest, that he had been able to make only one semiannual interest payment on the loan, in November 1851, that he had subsequently defaulted on every interest payment and now could pay neither the principal nor the interest (nor the interest upon the interest, presumably). Stewart might try to seize Arrowhead, on which Dr. Brewster still held a mortgage. "T. D. S.," it turned out, was Tertullus D. Stewart, a Lansingburgh acquaintance and a New York City friend. (In *The Confidence-Man*, in progress in mid-1856, the root of China Aster's disaster, of course, had been "a friendly loan.")

1983. In this year a great trove known as the Augusta Papers, the fragmentary remains of Melville's sister's correspondence, was found in a barn in upstate New York and almost all was acquired by the New York Public Library. In the next years nothing was published from the Augusta Papers that changed what we knew about *Pierre*.

1985. In November 1985 David Shneidman, the autograph-collecting son of the Melville lover and thanatologist Edwin H. Shneidman, published in *Melville Society Extracts* a second letter canceling Melville's subscription to the *Literary World*, dated April 16, 1852: "Editors of the Literary World:— You will please to discontinue the copy of your paper sent to me at Pittsfield." The Duyckincks had ignored Melville's February 14, 1852, request that they stop sending him the *Literary World*. Melville wrote this letter on the same day he wrote the long sales-pitch to Bentley. It might tell us something if we knew whether he wrote it before or after the letter to Bentley.

1985–87. In the mid-1980s I supplied Leyda with new documents for his expanded *Log*, and in September 1986 I took him on his last research trip, to Albany, Troy, and Lansingburgh. Parkinson's was already affecting him, and he was hospitalized most of 1987 until his death on February 15, 1988, three days after his seventy-eighth birthday. The 1986 trip made it devastatingly clear to me that I would have to carry on the *Log* myself as well as write my biography.

1988. Before Leyda's death I had worked through many of the letters in the Augusta Papers for 1850–51 in order to be sure I had all the new information we would need for the Northwestern-Newberry *Moby-Dick*. The documents clarified much about *Pierre* that had been obscure in 1975. At some point, I checked Sarah Morewood's letters again and saw that she was not hoping to visit Mrs. "Herman" Melville but Mrs. "Allan" Melville. Lizzie, Melville's wife, had been in Boston in early January 1852, recuperating from a breast infection that followed the birth of Stanwix in late October, not New York City. One dazzling new document was Augusta Melville's correspondence record for 1851 and 1852. Now we knew where everyone in the family was, month by month. Augusta did not indicate just when Elizabeth Shaw Melville went to Boston for medical treatment, but it was mid or late November, around the time of the publication of *Moby-Dick*. From the letters of Melville's mother it was clear that Malcolm was left at Arrowhead, and, according to Maria, hardly missing his mother at the end of December. Even healthy women of the Melville and Shaw class almost never resorted to traveling alone on a train, even one which went from Pittsfield straight across Massachusetts to Boston. Now we could speculate that Melville had accompanied his wife to Boston, apparently in November, rather than letting her take the train, unescorted, in great physical pain, with a hungry baby.

I learned from a December 29, 1851, letter from Melville's mother to his sister Augusta that Sarah Morewood on December 20, 1851, had attended Kossuth's speech at Tripler Hall with the Duyckinck brothers. She spoke of Kossuth at Christmas dinner from her own experience. Now it was clear from the letters that Melville had gone to New York on New Year's Eve or New Year's Day, and now it was clear that he had gone to New York to offer his manuscript to the Harpers, probably as early as New Year's Day or Friday, January 2, 1852.

I was still misled by the January 9?, 1852, letter to Duyckinck into thinking Melville could not have written book 17 on or before that date. I am astonished now to see that in "Why *Pierre* Went Wrong" as published in *Studies in the Novel* I elaborately showed what was wrong with Davis and Gilman's chronology in their note to the January 9? letter but did not challenge the dating at all. A moment's thought should have told me that the "nut-crackers" mentioned in the note were a Dutch New Yorker's New Year's gift, surely, maybe dropped off at Allan's during the traditional New Year's Day call, when Herman was out. At last, on February 2, 1988, worrying again with the old documents and many new documents, I realized that given three possible Fridays Leyda had split the difference, not thinking it would matter. It mattered. The January "9?" date helped keep me from thinking that Melville had arrived with a completed manuscript. It kept me from seeing a connection between Melville's accepting the terms of the contract and his writing book 17, in which he satirized the Duyckincks. It kept me from seeing that Melville must have kept his promise to call on Duyckinck not on January 3 but not very much later than that day.

The only way of accounting for Allan's letter of January 21, 1852, is to say that Melville began expanding the manuscript soon after the terms of the contract were agreed to. The opening of book 17 makes it almost certain that this was the first interpolation Melville made about Pierre as author, and in book 17 Melville savagely portrays Evert Duyckinck. Therefore, something happened to change the cheer of the note Melville wrote on January 2 to the fury of a few days later—some encounter, which must have involved the book which the *Literary World* so denounced on publication the next summer. The previous summer, Duyckinck had tried to persuade Melville to let Redfield publish the whaling book. Later, Duyckinck in his review of *Moby-Dick* in the *Literary World* had expressed his horror at Melville's affronts to religion in that book. Weeks later, knowing twenty cents on the dollar meant the end of his career, Melville would naturally have approached Duyckinck with the manuscript of *Pierre*, asking for help in showing it to Redfield or another publisher. Naturally, Duyckinck would have read it or much of it and have then replied honestly that he could not in good conscience recommend the book to any publisher. Already enraged at the gossip in Pittsfield that *Moby-Dick* was more than blasphemous, Melville, I decided, surrendered to new rage against his former friend. Later I was fairly sure that Melville thought he would be content with writing a book or two of satire about the New York literary scene and literature in the United States, and only later was drawn into the sulfurous, suicidal account of Pierre's literary career. In New York City something had happened between Melville and Evert Duyckinck. Knowing that Melville had completed *Pierre* in a shorter version and gotten a contract for it in the first days of 1852, I thought I knew pretty much what had happened. The factual and conjectural sequence at last made sense to me.

1991. When Maurice Sendak, urged by Joyce Deveau Kennedy, decided to illustrate *Pierre*, I persuaded him to do something reckless and outrageous, to illustrate a nonce-text, an approximation of the completed manuscript Melville carried to New York, before he heard the Harper brothers' terms and before he thought of adding anything about Pierre as an author. This text was to be a supplement to the 1852 and Northwestern-Newberry text, valuable because it would help us all think about what Melville actually did before he made such reckless additions to it. It would be an imperfect reconstruction, of course, but close enough that anyone could use it to help think about a different, completed, shorter *Pierre* which Melville had regarded as a "Kraken" book. I knew by now how hard it was to rethink anything we thought we knew, but was certain anyone who loved Melville would be willing to try the experiment of reading *Pierre* more or less as it was when Melville was first finished with it.

1995. In the "Kraken Edition," decorously illustrated by Sendak, my introduction was much better informed than the article I had written in 1975 or any subsequent publication. I tried to tell an absolutely fresh story that took account of all the known documents—many more than I had worked with in 1975. I tried a hard sell:

> In this text a reader can see the basic structure of the original *Pierre* clearly for the first time. Lucy and Glen retain the prominence in the plot Melville intended for them; the Apostles function again as ironic parallels to Pierre's own idealism; the philosopher Plinlimmon functions more clearly as foil to Mr. Falsgrave of the early Books; and the novel moves fast, as Melville meant it to, hurtling from the bafflingly high-flown opening on through Pierre's mental expansion and his unprecedented decision and on to the catastrophe, relentless, pell-mell in velocity and power. (xii)

I argued that lovers of *Moby-Dick* would "perceive its psychological stature more clearly in the light shed by the book Melville wrote next—the short version of *Pierre*, surely the finest psychological novel anyone had yet written in English" (xii).

In the Kraken Edition I announced two previously unknown meetings between Melville and Hawthorne, one at the Sedgwick house in Lenox on

November 4, 1851, another in the Wilson Hotel in Lenox (later the Curtis Hotel) just after Melville received his copies of *Moby-Dick* around the fourteenth. A few copies of *Moby-Dick* reached Pittsfield on December 18, or earlier, and word came to Melville that the locals were denouncing it as "more than Blasphemous," as his mother recorded at Christmas. Melville was angered, she said, during the week before Christmas, enraged against his neighbors. Perhaps he had been enraged for an indefinite number of weeks by the reviews he saw: I may have been at least partly wrong in thinking that much of the original version of *Pierre* had been written in the security of Hawthorne's praise.

2000. Young Pierre in the satirical book 17 is invited to lecture on "Human Destiny," a topic guaranteed to evoke fatuous platitudes. In 1998 I found that just such a lecture had been given by Orville Dewey, the Unitarian minister who was a close friend of Melville's father-in-law, Lemuel Shaw; in 1863 he baptized three of Melville's children, I found a sun-faded copy of the elegant first edition of *The Problem of Human Destiny; or, The End of Providence in the World and Man* (New York: James Miller, 1864), containing not one but twelve lectures. The year 1864 did me no good at all, but the clue to the date of the lectures was on the title page: "Lowell Lectures." In 2000 Dennis Marnon, the Administrative Officer at the Houghton Library, explained to me that "Dewey delivered 12 lectures on successive Tuesday and Thursday nights late in 1851: Oct. 21 and 23, Oct. 28 and 30, Nov. 4 and 6, November 11 and 13, Nov. 18 and 20, Nov. 25 and 28" (the last delayed because of Thanksgiving). Once I gained access to newspaper databases from the University of Delaware, I could, from Morro Bay, discover that Dewey had been going down to New Bedford to repeat the lectures all through the course. Melville may have seen notices of the lectures, which began the day before Stanwix was born, but he also may have been in Boston while they were in progress and visited family members who had attended some of the lectures. Very likely he would have seen some of the laudatory newspaper articles on them. As the *Boston Evening Transcript* said on October 3, anticipating delights: "We have no man in the country, whose reflective powers and admirable style qualify him more thoroughly for the interesting treatment of this vast subject. Dr. Dewey is a profound and independent thinker, and a consummate master of language."

Melville knew another side of Dewey, the one who spoke so confusingly in support of the Fugitive Slave Law or against it that he had to explain his talk in Pittsfield at the end of 1850 and explain his explanation. Stuck in Boston in October 1844, Melville may have seen the scathing criticism of

Dewey in the *Liberator* and in November 1851, having taken his sick wife to Boston, may have seen in the *Liberator* of October 31 this item reprinted from another antislavery paper, the *Cleveland True Democrat*:

> *The Rev. Dr. Dewey and 'The Problem of Human Destiny.'*—We learn from the Boston Post that the Rev. Dr. Dewey is about to deliver, before the Lowell Institute in that city, a course of lectures on 'The Problem of Human Destiny.' This is the same very 'liberal' Unitarian Doctor of Divinity who, in a lecture on 'The Law of Progress,' delivered by him last winter, in Boston, and we know not in how many other places, declared that, if his own mother were a refugee from slavery, he would send her back to it, to save our glorious Union. And thereupon a clerical brother of his, but not quite so 'liberal' a clergyman, said—'I believe him *this* time.' 'The Problem of Human Destiny' may be one of difficult solution; but the destiny of such a Doctor of Divinity as Dewey, supposing his last winter's zeal for the Union to continue, and the New Testament to be not a humbug, is not, we fear, so much a problem to be solved, as a 'fixed fact' to be deprecated.—

Whether or not Melville ever read an issue of the *Liberator*, he agreed with its opinion of Dewey. It is a little surprising that none of the Boston reviewers of *Pierre* condemned Melville for using the title "Human Destiny," for it would have been a slap in the face to all who had gloried in Dewey's lectures. Falsgrave and Plinlimmon, I was convinced, owed more than a little to Orville Dewey.

2001. For "Damned by Dollars," to be included in the new Parker-Hayford Norton Critical Edition of *Moby-Dick*, I took account of miserable facts which emerged in the 1990s, such as new discoveries by Lion G. Miles and Heddy Richter in the well-trodden property records in the Berkshire County Records Office. I focused also on the fact that after their December 1853 fire the Harpers had charged against Melville the cost of reprinting copies of burnt sheets that had already been charged against him. Honest men would have absorbed the loss themselves, having already charged Melville what he was obliged to pay. Melville's financial straits were far different than Leon Howard had thought, and far more miserable than Patricia Barber's discoveries had made us acknowledge. I had been very slow to look freshly at Melville's financial situation but had at last put the story together for a talk at the New Bedford Whaling Museum on June 26, 1997, then, revised a little, into the Norton Critical Edition in 2001.

I do not have an eyewitness recollection that Melville showed the manuscript of *Pierre* to Duyckinck but I have the fact of the punitive contract, I have his cheery promise to see Duyckinck soon, and I have Melville's immediately writing into his manuscript a furious personal satire against the Duyckinck brothers and later his canceling of his subscription to the *Literary World* (in a note which does not address them by name) and, after the brothers kept sending the paper, his second request to the "editors" that they cancel his subscription. I would like to have a letter or diary entry in which Duyckinck complains that Melville did not respond in a grateful way to his honest strictures about the manuscript of *Pierre*, but I don't need one. Do you? Kenneth S. Lynn didn't, for in the December 31, 1993, *Times Literary Supplement* he elaborately repeated my "educated guess" about the interview with Duyckinck and its aftermath, putting it into international circulation as received opinion if not wholly verifiable literary history.[7]

❧ Chapter 4 ❧

CREATING THE NEW MELVILLE LOG
AND WRITING THE BIOGRAPHY

JAY LEYDA'S TWO-VOLUME *The Melville Log: A Documentary Life of Herman Melville, 1819–1891* (1951) was one of the great scholarly works of the mid-twentieth century, the magnificent achievement of a filmmaker and film historian, an amateur Melvillean who at the outset simply wanted to make an accurate chronology of the writer's life for his teacher, Sergei Eisenstein. As Leyda compiled his documents in the late 1940s some of the group of Yale students who did dissertations on Melville under Stanley T. Williams, notably Harrison Hayford and William H. Gilman, shared their finds with him as early as they could without jeopardizing their degrees (which depended upon their incorporating unpublished evidence) and jobs.[1] Leyda was baffled by a few Melvilleans who hoarded their discoveries. Most notably, the Harvard psychologist Henry A. Murray reveled for decades in secret knowledge mainly gained from granddaughters of Melville's brother Allan. With letters only he knew about, Murray tantalized a few chosen highly placed professors, and hinted at eventual publication of sensational revelations. He saw Leyda as a threat to his proprietorship of information, as Clare L. Spark showed in *Hunting Captain Ahab: Psychological Warfare and the Melville Revival* (2001, e.g., 495). Spark printed much correspondence about Leyda's often-thwarted progress on the *Log* during which he was challenged by impatient publishers who imposed their notions upon him, as in forbidding him to identify the location of a document right along with the quotation from it. The full saga of Leyda's pursuit of documents and his attempts to enlist other searchers for Melville documents remains untold.

Leyda's approach "forbade an emphasis on any part" of Melville's life "to the exclusion of any other part, and forbade the neglect of material that seemed, in itself, of small importance" (xi). Nevertheless, rather than being undiscriminating, the 1951 edition was shaped by Leyda's special point of view. Few of the longer documents were reprinted in full, and Leyda made the cuts not only to shorten but also to play up some of his particular interests, not to say preferences. Not being fond of Melville's mother or his brother Gansevoort or his wife, he could deftly make three ellipsis dots satirical, and once or twice he saw what he expected to see in a letter rather than the actual word on the page. The *Log* in fact *had to be* highly selective not only because of the limits of space but simply because Leyda typically did the excerpting in uncomfortable, constraining circumstances. Living below the edge of poverty, staying in YMCAs or cadging rooms from acquaintances or their friends, he worked on the fly, unable to stay long enough in New York City to exhaust the archives in the New York Public Library, for instance. Similarly, Leyda was dependent on the courtesy of Melville's grandniece Agnes Morewood in Pittsfield as he took notes on the papers she laid out for him on a table. Unable to take time to copy out in longhand every paragraph of any long review of one of Melville's books, Leyda made on-the-spot decisions about what to copy. If he had had before him full texts of all the known reviews he would have excerpted differently, so as to acknowledge influences more sharply or to brand plagiarism or to highlight different themes as the most salient. If he had held photocopies of all sides of a correspondence represented by letters at Harvard, say, and others at the New York Public Library, he would surely have made different excerpts. As it was, his uncanny ability to seize on significant passages in a document and his phenomenal memory infused the pages with heart-wrenching significance and apparent coherence.

The Melville Log was accepted as impressively monumental and useful for scholars but not of any obvious significance for literary critics. William Braswell in the May 1952 *American Literature* called the *Log* and Leon Howard's biography both "notable achievements," but his wording was tepid (245): "The Melville that one becomes acquainted with in these pages will probably be rather different from the man he had in mind. Here, minus the legends, is the man as he acted, as he appeared, and, so far as the nonfictional documents reveal, as he thought. For one who likes his facts neat the book makes fascinating reading from beginning to end." More imaginative critics, of course, would not like "their facts neat" but diluted (with what— soda, bitters?) and would not find the *Log* fascinating. In *American Quarterly* (Spring 1953) Carlos Baker was far from enthusiastic (78): "Being, perforce, a patchwork of snippets from family letters, ships' records, and other similar data, as well as autobiographical reminiscences culled from Melville's own writings, *The Melville Log* makes disappointing reading." So went other reviews, for *The Melville Log* was published just as the New Criticism (which saw biographical research as irrelevant to interpretation) was triumphing in one American university after another as the postwar generation of professors assumed power.

Over the long term, the single most virulent and influential enemy of the *Log* was Charles Feidelson, ironically the man promoted by Yale in the early 1950s to "replace" Stanley T. Williams. Paul Lauter recorded the shock to students when the old bibliographical, biographical, and historical notes from Williams's classes had to be junked in the new order at Yale embodied by the new authority at the podium.[2] An early convert to the New Criticism and a lifelong proselytizer for it, Feidelson dismissed the *Log* in the December 1951 *Yale Review* as wayward, a "mere accumulation of data," much of it "rather dreary stuff" (298) and as a "welter of disconnected and often trivial data" (299) irrelevant to literary criticism. Feidelson depicted Leyda, Leon Howard, and Gilman (author of the 1951 *Melville's Early Life and "Redburn"*) as representing the "earth-bound" historical school of Melvilleans in contrast to "intuitional, or high-flying, school of Melville studies" (298). Leyda was earth-bound when he included "even such items as the fact that on July 21, 1836, Melville's sisters received awards at the Albany Female Academy" (298). This was the only "sort of truth" (299) the *Log* offered. Unless "our interests are merely anecdotal," the welter of trivial data "would seem to demand an even greater exercise of imagination than any for which earlier biographers can be reproached" (299). Feidelson knew for sure that in the new Yale and the new American university system any "exercise of imagination" (299) upon such dreary data would be misplaced: "While earlier biographers made the error of treating their images as objective facts of Melville's life, the new school" (of Leyda and Howard, and of course of the pedestrian students of his own pedestrian predecessor at Yale) was "in danger of reducing Melville to the simplistic terms of an external chronicle" (300). The hapless Leyda and Howard had tried to resolve "the Melville problem" by "an appeal to fact" (300) when what is needed is enriched speculative interpretation. How often during the more than third of a century until 1988 did Feidelson inveigh or rant against that compendium of dreary facts, *The Melville Log*?[3] Year after year, when he came to Melville in his courses? It seemed so, to judge from the publications of his more notable students who continue to reveal their disdain for mere facts even into the new century.[4]

Adequate praise came at last in a reconsideration in the Winter 1955 *Hudson Review* when George Barbarow dismissed an unnamed reviewer's contempt for the " 'tag-ends and jots and tittles' " in the *Log* (585). For Barbarow, the "minutiae tend to reinforce the illusion of authenticity, upon which the book leans heavily for its effect, and to provide a continuing measure of contrast between Melville's imaginative flights and his routine business

of living" (585–86). Perceiving that the *Log* proceeded "by contrasts, strikingly appropriate to its subject" (590), Barbarow insisted: "The significance
of any one piece of evidence is found in its difference from those before and
those after; no detail is absolutely trivial, as the angry reviewer [the 'tag-ends'
carper] implied, it is only more or less trivial than its fellows, or, to speak in
a more favorable tone, more or less tremendous" (590). This response to the
Log ranks with that of Maurice Sendak, who confided to me that he had
edited it all with an old-time moviola in his own mind. Sendak's experience
suggests forcefully that Leyda's "cutting" needs to be seen in relation to his
experiences in film editing. Minutiae reinforce authenticity, as Barbarow
said, but they do more, I found, when I worked with old documents freshly
and worked with new Melville material, notably the surviving remnant of the
comprehensive archive of Melville's sister (the Augusta Papers). I agreed with
Leyda on the doctrine of inclusiveness because I learned that you never know
what detail may prove to be of dazzling relevance. The devil was always in
the details, but, Barbarow knew, so were the angels. Responsible high-flying
imagination, responsible literary criticism, I found by the early 1990s, *always*
had to be built from data that included tag-ends and jots and tittles.

Leyda was at the East German Film Archive when he began preparing the
"Supplement" for the reissue of the *Log* by Gordian Press in the mid-1960s. I
had loved the *Log* since 1962. I had bought the two volumes when I decided
to do a dissertation on Melville under Harrison Hayford. Living high and
saving money on $265 a month from the Woodrow Wilson Foundation, I
had carried the *Log* to the New York Public Library, the New-York Historical
Society, the Berkshire Athenaeum, the Massachusetts Historical Society, the
Boston Public Library, and the Houghton Library, annotating it as I went,
making a few corrections and adding in the margins what I might need from
parts of documents Leyda had omitted. Nothing much on Melville had been
found in the 1960s to rival the work of the 1940s (although I kept up my
review hunting). When Hayford passed over to me some of the items for the
new "Supplement" which Leyda had sent him, I made corrections, such as
the year Thomas Melvill's family moved from Pittsfield to Galena. It turned
out that the reason Leyda had the year wrong was that he had not seen all
the letters I had seen. The documents had been deposited in libraries after
Leyda had seen them in private hands, and sometimes the owner had deposited documents he had not seen. In 1967 I wasn't always sure that Leyda's
not quoting a document meant he hadn't seen it, but I xeroxed a bulky stack
of my notes—typed from my longhand transcriptions (mine had been one of
the last pre-Xerox dissertations), along with the reviews I had found. Northwestern University paid to ship my packet behind the Iron Curtain. Late in

1968 while I was living with Leon Howard in Los Angeles (as it seemed that half the academic population of California had done, one time or another) I read proofs for the Gordian Press "Supplement," about half of which I had supplied. (Leyda's acknowledgment for my "generous help" was written long before I made the bulk of my contributions: *he* was always the generous one.)

Back on this continent in 1969, Leyda became Pinewood Professor at New York University in 1973, the year he protested in *The Chief Glory of Every People*, edited by Matthew J. Bruccoli, against the dreariness of most recent criticism and the neglect of biographical research: "With so much left to be known, how can we allow the present state of our knowledge to freeze and become permanently acceptable? Perhaps we have become too content with the biographical materials already at our disposal" (164). Yet in the year *The Chief Glory* was published, Patricia Barber, against the criti-cal tide, added the information that Melville had almost bought a house in Brooklyn in 1857. My contribution consisted of more contemporary reviews, but I had new documentary evidence about *Pierre* in articles published in 1976 ("Why *Pierre* Went Wrong"), in 1977, and later. As it turned out, within a few years some old hands, among them Henry A. Murray, Wilson Heflin, and Merton M. Sealts, Jr., joined younger people in making important Mel-ville discoveries (or revealing old information), not big caches of documents but single documents or little caches often of significance quite dispropor-tionate to their size. It seemed, a few years after Leyda's lament, that all hell might be breaking loose in Melville biography again, as it had in the 1940s. In the late 1970s, while almost all critics were still focused on displaying unity of literary works in their New Critical readings, a few people made remarkable discoveries. Among the new people were Patricia Barber, Hans Bergmann, Stanton Garner, David Jaffe, very notably Joyce Deveau Ken-nedy and Frederick J. Kennedy, Alice P. Kenney, Kathleen E. Kier, Walter D. Kring and Jonathan S. Carey, George Monteiro, Amy Puett, John P. Run-den, and David K. Titus.

During the nine years I wrote the Melville chapter in *American Literary Scholarship* I called attention to new documentary articles, as in the long paragraph I gave to the 1976 discovery of the Melvilles' marital crisis of 1867, news from Walter D. Kring, minister of the Unitarian Church of All Souls, New York, assisted by Jonathan S. Carey. There I served notice that the Mel-ville Society was preparing a booklet to be introduced by Dr. Kring. The booklet was delayed as Donald Yannella and I solicited and then coaxed comments, particularly from old Melville hands who had met Melville's daughter, Frances Thomas, and his two older granddaughters and might have valuable information to put on record. The booklet was published at last in 1981 (with a title that was my collaborator's surprise to me), *The End-less, Winding Way in Melville: New Charts by Kring and Carey.* The Melville Society sent copies to all members and to many libraries, for free. Thirteen years later Yannella and I were staggered by being accused in Cathy David-son's "New Melville" issue of *American Literature* of trying to suppress the information we had worked so hard to publicize.

The next year, 1977, Amy Puett Emmers published a letter from Mel-ville's uncle Thomas to Lemuel Shaw about two women who turned up at the Green Street house in Boston with claims against Herman's father's share of old Thomas Melvill's estate. The histrionic tone of the letter sug-gested, wrongly, it turned out, that the younger of the women might have been an illegitimate daughter of Melville's father—news that roiled a few people for many years and is discussed in chapter 5 in this book. In 1977 also Patricia Barber found two Melville letters in the Shaw Papers in the Social Law Library in Boston, not with the bulk of the papers at the Massachu-setts Historical Society, which showed the extremity of Melville's financial plight dating from May 1851. It took decades for scholars to absorb the full horror of Patricia Barber's news and to eke out the story from other records. (See the second volume of my biography and particularly my last chap-ter here, "Damned by Dollars.") In 1977 T. Walter Herbert, Jr., as Alice P. Kenney had done, returned to the Gansevoort-Lansing Collection that the 1940s generation had mined and pioneered study of Maria Melville's Dutch Reform worship. In 1977, also, Frederick J. and Joyce Deveau Kennedy, answering Leyda's plea, began publishing additions to *The Melville Log.* In 1978 the Kennedys published what they had found from descendants of the Savages, the family of Mrs. Melville's stepmother, notably a wonderful letter Melville wrote to young Samuel Savage. (The Kennedys' research continued in an extraordinarily detailed masterpiece on Melville's very early admirer, Archibald MacMechan, published in 1999.) In 1978 Donald and Kathleen Malone Yannella published Evert A. Duyckinck's diary for part of 1847, lav-ishly footnoted, but never followed up on this extremely important source, and no one else has followed them. That year Walker Cowen sampled part of his 1965 dissertation on Melville's marginalia by printing Melville's anno-tations in his copies of books by and about Hawthorne. In the next years the Kennedys and Stanton Garner, who was working on Melville's Civil War and Custom House years, were joined by others who made surprising discov-eries—among them Hans Bergmann and Thomas F. Heffernan.

Despite the importance of the discoveries by Barber, Kring, the Kennedys, and others, youngish academics in the 1970s and early 1980s very seldom took account of biographical evidence, either the evidence long available or more recently discovered, and almost never tried to find new evidence. We were in the long wake of Deconstructionist criticism as it was co-opted, institutionalized, and formularized, as Henry Sussman had argued in *Glyph* 4 (1978). The brightest of the new crowd, as Jay Martin announced in a 1981 review in *American Literature*, were playing word games for themselves and their coteries, ignoring historical evidence (and biographical and textual evidence). As the 1970s ended and the 1980s began, no one emerged to analyze significant new documents with strong, sophisticated critical powers.

In 1977 Jay Leyda had asked me to undertake a second expansion of *The Melville Log*. I refused, for many good reasons—the overpowering one being that although a few other scholars contributed to it in the 1940s and I had contributed to the 1969 "Supplement" it was quintessentially Leyda's in concept and execution. I did have suggestions. From writing the annual Melville chapter in *American Literary Scholarship* I knew that people were not using the 1969 *Log*. Critics who cited the *Log* continued to cite the 1951 edition and those who used the 1969 plainly found it hard to flip back and forth to integrate the items in the "Supplement" into their proper place in a re-envisioned chronology. I urged Leyda not to do another edition unless he could integrate the items in the "Supplement" and all new items into a new sequence—otherwise people would not use the third edition. Starting in the summer of 1979 I was in Delaware, not Los Angeles, and able to go to New York to make suggestions directly. Leyda agreed to try. Then in 1982 Francis E. Plumeau discovered the greatest trove of all in a barn in upstate New York, a portion of the papers of Melville's sister Augusta. I emphasize this because Leyda solemnly laid on me the responsibility of giving Plumeau (who died in January 1985) full credit as the true discoverer of the Augusta Melville Papers which the New York Public Library acquired in 1983 (or acquired almost all of, to be precise). The news was well publicized in the national press, and soon it was understood that the New York Public Library had acquired the bulk of the papers.

Public interest in the Augusta Papers was so high that it seemed as if we might be entering a new era of biographical scholarship, especially when the New York Public Library made it clear that the documents would be available to all qualified researchers (despite a quick attempt at a power grab by those who thought they could emulate Leon Edel and gain exclusive access).[5] In 1983 I was making another career, I thought, as textual theorist ready to move from fiction to opera, and would let the dust settle down from the initial excitement. Besides, I was a Southerner, and Southerners do not scramble for a place at the high table. The dust around Forty-second Street and Fifth Avenue had settled fast. After a while there were few comers to see the new additions to the Gansevoort-Lansing Collection, even among the surviving members of the older pre–New Critical generation.

The acquisition of the surviving papers of Augusta Melville by the New York Public Library made a new *Log* not merely desirable but essential.[6] In 1983 I was writing *Flawed Texts and Verbal Icons* on a computer,[7] so I tried to tell Leyda what the modern way of working should be, but he was unable to handle the complexities of enlisting someone at New York University with computer skills to help him on the *Log*. Instead, he started by retyping all the "Supplement" himself (rather than photocopying it and Magic Tape-ing it together), and then spliced that in with his typescript of new items from the discoveries made in the 1970s and others from the early 1980s, including reviews I had continued to send him, as well as new items from the Augusta Melville Papers. Out of his own pocket Leyda paid a professor to do work that was never done and hired the "designer" to have the entries from the "Supplement" and the new items printed up in type like that of the original *Log*, and then paid him to cut apart two copies of the 1951 *Log* and paste in the newly printed items upon wide base sheets. While I began gathering material for a narrative biography I kept Leyda supplied with my discoveries in the form of printouts on fan-fold paper. A wry note in his shaky hand: "Hershel is a faucet." In his review in the *New Republic* (30) James Wood mocked my "self-congratulation" in quoting this line in the first volume of my biography. I was "a connoisseur of facts," so "superstitious about facts" that I threw "them about like salt," trying to "drive out the devil of interpretation." Leyda and I understood that no archangel of interpretation could fly high and powerfully unless set aloft from a grounding in fact. Leyda's passion that I write the biography became intense—more intense, perhaps, than his hopes for *The New Melville Log*. Neither of us quite understood how inextricably the research on the *Log* would relate to the biography. Four decades earlier, Leyda and Hayford had naively assumed that Leon Howard could write a reliable biography from Leyda's documents, and in the early 1980s I still did not understand that it was impossible to work responsibly from someone else's compilation of data.

Soon after Leyda began making serious arrangements for the third edition his doctor confirmed the diagnosis of Parkinson's disease. As it turned out, the disease made Leyda unable to work with the manuscripts in a sustained way. That I discovered when I took him on his last research trip, to Albany and Lansingburgh in September 1986. Late that year I saw that I had to give up almost everything else to help him. I perforce took up what we agreed to call *The New Melville Log*, and on April 16, 1987, after Leyda was in the hospital, I took home from his New York University apartment two cardboard boxes on Amtrak. I had to stash the boxes in the unheated back storm box in Wilmington until I got rid of the cockroaches and their eggs, for the New York University apartments were—well, Village apartments. The boxes contained photocopies of the Augusta Papers, miscellaneous correspondence, and Leyda's "proofs"—an enlargement of the *Log* which the designer had printed after inserting Leyda's additions, including the 1969 "Supplement." The fact that the new type was just a hair different from the original was a benefit for my work because I could tell at a glance what was new, but it would have been a distraction to ordinary readers.

During 1987 I stopped thinking of the 1951 and 1969 editions as *The Melville Log*; instead, the *Log* was the designer's proofs. Onto these pages I taped my additions in the form of printout. The unexamined assumption, in mid-1987, was that somehow the designer could incorporate my essential additions by dropping an equivalent number of spaces, and photo-offsetting the whole. Late in the year that was more a wistful hope than an assumption. I was slow to see how serious the problems were. The proofs for Melville's first years looked pretty good because Leyda had added little to them, but as soon as I got to the 1830s the entries began looking jumbled and others plainly were self-contradictory, so there was no point going on until these few pages were straightened out.

Early that summer of 1987 I got out Julia Maria Melvill's letters from Leyda's New York Public Library photocopies of the Augusta Melville Papers and set to work. It took me three weeks, toward the end of which I went to Pittsfield to check the vital records to be sure whether the minister Ballard was married in June and when the first snowstorms came and when the Cattle Show and Fair was held in particular years. Finally I had all Julia's letters dated pretty closely, and to my baffled, irritated joy I even knew the answer to a puzzle that had teased Leyda and William H. Gilman and Merton M. Sealts, Jr., and the rest of us for decades. In his memoir of his uncle Melville recalled having spent the "greater portion of" a year in Pittsfield, *with* his uncle. Which year? we wondered. It was a bad riddle. In 1837 Melville spent the greater portion of a year in Pittsfield, but his uncle had left Herman in charge of the farm when he departed for Galena, Illinois. Writing thirty-odd years after the fact, Melville had conflated his memories of haying with his uncle one August and sitting with his uncle by the fire another October and had superimposed his uncle's presence upon his memories of the months when he was the man of the house (or the farm) in the absence of his uncle and his slightly older cousin Robert, also in Galena. This was big news to a few living people, but the practical result was that I was working with a snipped apart and re-xeroxed and newly retaped set of proofs for the 1830s, not expanded much beyond the length Leyda had created but still a mess for the designer to have new headings printed for and then to recut and rephotograph. I might as well have been revising a stereotyped book, I felt so constrained to keep any corrections or revisions the same length the entries occupied in the proofs, and I had to work on the assumption that every absolutely essential new item would have to displace an equivalent number of lines already in the proofs, so as not to disturb long stretches of the pagination. I showed the rearranged 1830s proofs (bloodied, bescissored, and beflagged) to Leyda in the hospital and told him the riddle, to his delight. We both confidently expected that these pages would be the only ones that had to be totally recut.

The first of September 1987 I went to work with my new assistant Mark Niemeyer to straighten out the rest of the *Log* in two or three weeks. That turned out not to be enough time. By then I had glimpsed the disastrous consequences of the method Leyda had chosen for expanding the *Log*. Visualize what happened: whenever you cut up a thousand pages into several thousand pieces so you can splice in hundreds of new pieces of paper, new items are going to get put in the wrong places, and new and old slivers of paper are going to get lost, half a page here, a page there. Every horror you can imagine had happened, and worse. One small oversight had disastrous consequences. The practice in 1951 was to name the location only when the location changed. If you had twelve New York City items in a row, only the first was headed "New York." No one had anticipated what would happen when, say, a Pittsfield item was spliced into the middle of a New York sequence without redoing the next item to start "New York." *Hundreds* of locations were thrown off, and given the technology being used these places were uncorrectable, since to splice in a new location would require resetting of type and re-cutting the rest of the heading (what if the four-letter Bath needed to be changed to the endless Canandaigua?) and perhaps moving a few words down to the next line (and in a heading running several lines that would mean that all the lines would have to be reset, printed, and recut).

In trying to correct old errors, errors that were in the original *Log*, I was frustrated by the knowledge that every change we called for would require "typesetting," then cutting and splicing on top of all the other changes. I had a copy of the *Log* in which a former assistant, Jim Hutchisson, had proofed for me all the quotations from reviews against photocopies of the original reviews, marking corrections I had laid up against the day Leyda would do a third edition, but now I felt I could call only for corrections of actual words, not spelling or other minor details. Even so, the pages of the "proofs" for the years Melville's books were being reviewed were littered, the correct "pleasingly" replacing "pleasantly," "definitively" replacing "definitely," "It is" replacing "His," and so on. Then as weeks went on we accepted the fact that we would have to verify every new item against the manuscripts, since the Parkinson's had advanced much faster than Leyda himself knew. This meticulous and saintly man could always forgive any rogue almost any lapse if he was a competent document-transcribing malefactor. Leyda's fate was that as that insidious disease progressed he had not always been able to transcribe accurately any more. In my study I had a large number of photocopies of documents, from routine political recommendations to extraordinary letters from Sophia Hawthorne (Melville had talked about the "sunny haze" of Hawthorne's face, not his "sunny hair," as the 1969 "Supplement" and the new "proofs" had it), and sometimes (we would keep a rough count) Niemeyer would spring up fifty or sixty times a day (if I was weighted down by my lapboard full of proofs) to pull down a book or package of photocopies, and after work he might stop off at the library to check half a dozen items: that's what the task demanded on the simple level of physical agility, and Leyda's physical agility had faded away.[8]

Throughout the fall of 1987 I identified or re-identified correspondents ("Nilly" [Cornelia], not "Milly" Van Rensselaer Thayer), relocated cities (often taking two Baths a year, one in Maine and one in the wilds of western New York), and straightened out sequences of letters (or parts of the same letters). Hayford was being pressured by Northwestern University Press to submit *Moby-Dick*, and in turn he was pressuring me to write my part of the "Historical Note," but my duty seemed clear as long as there was any hope of getting the *Log* out before Leyda died, and as the weeks passed I got up and worked on the *Log* from one to three hours in the middle of the night and I started every morning with Niemeyer by saying, "There is nothing in the world I would rather be doing today than working on Jay Leyda's *The Melville Log*." I was grim about the mouth at times, but I meant what I said, and Niemeyer began saying it too, and meaning it.[9]

Once we found that pages and parts of pages of the original *Log* had been lost from the "proofs," we no longer operated under the constraint of trying to make every correction take up the same amount of space as the erroneous text it was replacing. Just as well, for about that time I took up an unused pile of letters from Priscilla Melvill. Leyda had included other letters by Cousin Priscilla, but even in those he had sometimes been baffled by her signature, as when she signed herself "Tousin 'Cilla"—baby talk. Try translating baby talk to a world-wandering scholar with no children. Leyda agreed (once again, *of course* he agreed—he had no vanity) that we had to use more of Priscilla's letters. The most painful change I made was redoing July and August

1850. After the first edition of the *Log* appeared Leyda had decided that Melville started the essay on Hawthorne before he met the author of *Mosses from an Old Manse* (as the putative speaker, the "Virginian," asserted), and signaled that change in the 1969 "Supplement." This was a conscious decision made in good health, not a decision made while enfeebled by disease, but the evidence, including some Leyda had not used, all went the other way. Once I had gone through all the pertinent letters in the Augusta trove I saw that Harrison Hayford and Leon Howard long ago had been almost exactly right about the composition of the essay, and I called Hayford and Sealts to describe how the new documents either confirmed or very slightly modified what Leon Howard had said in his 1951 biography. Both told me to go with the evidence. It took three days to redo three pages, with four-aspirin headaches every day from guilt, and I never told Leyda about it.

I *did* go up to tell Leyda what I had found in Priscilla's letters about the outcome of Melville's letters in 1852 in which he first urged Hawthorne to write a story based on the history of the forsaken wife, Agatha Hatch, which he had been told that summer, then at last declaring that he would write the story himself. In his index to the 1884 *Hawthorne and His Wife* Julian Hawthorne listed an "Agatha letter," and printed it, explaining that Melville "had suggested a story to Hawthorne; but Mr. Melville recently informed the present writer that it was a tragic story, and that Hawthorne had not seemed to take to it" (quoted in Parker, 1:475). In this undated letter from Boston, not Pittsfield, Melville mentioned Hawthorne's having urged *him* to write the story and that he had decided to do so, and therefore besought a "fair wind" on him for the voyage. That letter I date to about December 12, 1852, after Melville's visit to the Hawthornes in Concord. In 1929 S. E. Morison printed the first known letter in this sequence, an August 13, 1852, letter in which Melville explained that during his recent visit to Nantucket he had met a lawyer who talked "of the great patience, & endurance, & resignedness of the women of the island in submitting so uncomplainingly to the long, long absences of their sailor husbands." The man cited a legal case that he had handled a few years earlier; as Melville did not say to Hawthorne, he was John H. Clifford, the state attorney general (Parker, 2:113–15). Clifford kept his word to send to Melville documents about Agatha Hatch, who at Pembroke, Massachusetts, had rescued a wrecked sailor named Robertson. He married her and abandoned her when she was pregnant. Seventeen years later he reappeared with money and gifts. Suspecting that he had committed bigamy, Agatha kept silent. After his death it emerged that "Robertson" had been married twice more. Melville thought that the story was one Hawthorne could write. In "The Significance of Melville's 'Agatha' Letters" (1946),

Harrison Hayford published yet a third of Melville's letters to Hawthorne about the story, one dated October 25, 1852. The biographical significance of the letters, to Hayford, was that they exposed "serious errors in the theory now generally held," that "Melville, in despair and defiance at the reception" of *Moby-Dick*, had written *Pierre* "with no expectation that it would succeed with the public; he expected it to be his last book; and he took up the pen again, toward the middle of 1853, only because no other means of making a living were possible" (305). This "plausible theory," Hayford argued, was "substantially refuted by the 'Agatha' letters" (306) and other evidence that Melville did not mean *Pierre* to be his last book and that after completing it he still had intentions of writing. He concluded: "What ill wind, prevailing over the fair breeze he had besought, prevented him from writing—or at any rate from publishing—the story of Agatha, is a matter upon which at present one can only speculate" (309). I mention elsewhere Hayford's last footnote (310): "A letter of his mother, dated April 20, 1853, indicates that he [Melville] had become absorbed in a 'new work' during the Winter and had it 'nearly ready for the press' by that date. What work it was is not clear." Leon Howard so strongly suspected Maria Melville of prevaricating in her claim that he would not bother to refute it directly (203–4). Why Hayford did not understand that this "new work" was the one Melville determined to write in the letter to Hawthorne from Boston I do not understand. I never asked him. In 1960, Merrell R. Davis and William H. Gilman in their edition of Melville's *Letters* showed that in his November 24, 1853, letter to the Harpers Melville mentioned still having possession of the book which he had offered the Harper brothers earlier, around June, when he had been "prevented" from printing it. In 1987, transcribing Cousin Priscilla's letters, I learned that Melville had completed a book called *The Isle of the Cross* on or near May 22, 1853. As Paula R. Backscheider says (xvi), "there are moments of triumph so intense that time seems to stop and the pen shakes in the biographer's hand"—or the telephone shakes as he calls the scholar who had worked hardest on the "Agatha" story in the 1940s, Harrison Hayford, and then Merton M. Sealts, Jr. I took Priscilla's revelations as proof that Melville had indeed begun the book in mid-December 1852, had it almost ready on April 20, and had finished it on or right around May 22. Hayford and Sealts read the evidence just as I did. The title I took as proof that Melville had written the Agatha story or something that story had become as he worked on it. *The Isle of the Cross*, of course, could have been a different book, but in any case it was the one in process in April, surely, and the one completed in late May, and offered to the Harpers, I learned, in early June. (By that time, Clifford was governor of the state of Massachusetts.) In consequence, I told Leyda, I was chopping up the early 1853 pages to make a new story.

My new evidence from the Augusta Papers shone a spotlight on other old items: suddenly Pittsfield couldn't be where Richard Lathers (Allan Melville's wealthy brother-in-law) gave Melville those Irving volumes, it was New Rochelle (just look at the inscription in Sealts's *Melville's Reading*), and Melville was there at Lathers's estate, Winyah, probably after he had dropped *The Isle of the Cross* off at the Harpers and before it was clear that he was going to be "prevented" from publishing it. Here a lifeless and slightly inaccurate set of entries suddenly made terrible sense, and once we knew why Melville had gone to town we could heighten the drama by altering some of the quotations Leyda was making from sister-in-law Sophia's letters in the Augusta trove. Working as I was doing, eyes on the task at hand, I did not think every day about whether or not what I was finding could be incorporated into the third edition, but when I paused from what I was doing it was clear that the more missing pages and parts of pages we put back into the proofs and the more mislocated items we spotted and hauled into place and the more new items we discovered, then it was less and less within the realm of possibility to correct the *Log* under the reset, print, cut in, re-photograph, and photo-offset system. Before Thanksgiving I changed the morning chant to this: "All right, it may never be published. I'll use it myself and deposit a set in the Newberry Library." After Thanksgiving I relied on the novelist Louis Zara to pass encouraging news on to Leyda, who by then wanted to see the finished volumes.[10]

At the end of 1987 while my brother was nursing my dying father in eastern Oklahoma I flew every week to Fort Smith, Arkansas, and slept on the floor of my mother's room in Sparks Hospital to nurse her after a second hip replacement. Meanwhile, Jay Leyda, this man of delicately refined tastes in music, dance, theater, and literature, was lying in the Rusk Institute of Rehabilitation Medicine where his roommate of the moment kept the television blaring hour after hour, every sit-com, every commercial. There was no dignity: I was the only one who ever cut his toenails there. Leyda died on February 15, 1988, after thirteen months in the Institute of Rehabilitation. On March 14, 1988, a month after Leyda died, I was so frantic that I wrote in the wrong diary space, for March 21: "At everyone's command—no rest since Sept. 1, no command over my time or chance to stay in good physical shape." Working in the middle of the night every night was not the wisest thing to do; my immune system became so compromised that I had recurrent post-surgical infections. The next day the proofs of the "Historical Note" arrived. Fine: page proofs on the composition of *Moby-Dick* that looked beautifully authoritative, until you looked at the content. Hayford had been so deter-mined to get the *Moby-Dick* volume out in the Northwestern-Newberry Edition that he began drafting the "Historical Note" from Evanston, without consulting the Augusta documents. What followed was high-level diplomacy as I called Hayford, then Tom Tanselle and Alma MacDougall ("editorial coordinator" at this point for several of the volumes). My diary: "But as I wkd wi [NN] proofs I got more & more concerned about how much I will have to do *myself* to get proportion & sequence better than what's there in page proofs now. Very upsetting. . . . Deciding I can supply pages in what HH now has & wait & see what to do about what is not yet written at all." On March 21 it was decided: "I can work on his part already in proofs while he works on the new parts. OK—I can still go on to Providence." I had promised to talk at the Northeast Modern Language Association meeting in Providence on "A Hard Year for an Old Man," how Thomas Powell and Herman Melville had pained Washington Irving in 1849–50. Powell was the British forger, a lifelong torment to Robert Browning, who burst onto the New York literary world in 1849 and caused a multitude of problems for Charles Dickens and Cornelius Mathews and caused grief to Washington Irving and then Mel-ville. Tracking down Powell had led me to wholly unexpected discoveries, such as a toned down version of what the indignant Irving had said when he read Melville's insults in the pseudonymous "Hawthorne and His *Mosses*."

In Providence on March 24, 1988, a small, intense crowd welcomed my news about Irving and remained attentive to what I had to say about the state of *The New Melville Log*. I started with a promise: I was not going to tell then maudlin stories of my deep intimacy with Jay Leyda and my uncanny ability to revise the *Log* just as he would have done and the near-mystical way I had been entering his mind just as Tom Jenks about that time was boasting of fus-ing his consciousness with Ernest Hemingway's to edit *The Garden of Eden*. As I explained, neither I nor anyone else seemed to know more than a small arc of that global man. I gave them hot news. The eighth book Melville com-pleted wasn't *Israel Potter*—he had finished the "Agatha" story under the title *The Isle of the Cross*.

In Providence I brandished a few pages of Leyda's new "proofs" of the *Log* and alluded to there being problems, but I didn't say that for weeks it had looked as if the *Log* was simply unpublishable. I did not mention what I had been working on all the way up on Amtrak—an outline for thirty or fifty pages of the *Moby-Dick* "Historical Note" that had to be transformed into some-thing like prose before May for Northwestern University Press to publish it, as it needed to do, in the current fiscal year. If the *Log* seemed unpublish-able, the "Historical Note" under the circumstances seemed uncompletable.

For the audience at Providence I recited a bit of a speech from the opening of *Macbeth*, for I felt like that bloody sergeant whose plight made it obvious that he could report the latest state of the battle. David Hirsch, the editor of *Modern Language Studies*, was excited about my news and wanted more, so I wrote up an interim report on the *Log* which he printed in the Winter 1990 issue. I reprint much of it in the remainder of this chapter with slight changes because it captures my "knowledge of the broil" as I felt it through most of 1987 and all through the next years.

On March 24, 1988, south of Trenton, 6:30 p.m., I paused my revising on my new sixteen-pound laptop (Gordo, we called it, from Gordian) and wrote on paper: "Is there anyone who could help me in the next week besides Mark? Can't be any established scholar—there is none. I guess I just have to do it. I can do it. I can do it. I can do it. I have to do it." In fact, a few other graduate students rallied round with Mark to run trips to the library. I worked day and night. Mark worked every day, it seemed. We worked so hard we became careless. On April 15 someone re-formatted the hard drive. Hot tears dashed down on the sidewalk as Hayford watched from the door as I comforted the stricken worker. Well, we had a recent printout of the "Historical Note." Not all was lost. Mark to the rescue, bringing Rich Duggan, the University of Delaware tech man, to Wilmington. He recovered almost everything though some files ever after were like Swiss cheese. At five I said to the crew: "And I whipped up a soufflé." Alma (in residence, for who knew how long), wonderfully ironic: "When *did* you find time?" Mark and I stayed up all night in the kitchen, writing. "Abt 4 or 430 I said to hell with prose, let's try for English. We got 9 or 10 pages printed out"; Alma was "printing off and on all night on 3rd floor." At dawn we drove Hayford to the Philadelphia airport. I found that I could work fast on the remaining parts of the "Historical Note" because, months earlier, I had inched so slowly and carefully through the Augusta Melville papers and other old and new documents for 1850–51. Strangely enough, it was a new story, but painful to write because so many people in the ideal audience were dead, those who would have cried, "I never saw that!" or "Where did Hershel get *that*?" No question, some of the fun of telling a new story was gone: I had to *imagine* Leon Howard's grousing, testy pleasure rather than witness it.

A few weeks later I arranged to go up to New York to turn what had become of the proofs over to Roger Texier at Gordian Press. Let *him* take over the problem of thinking about how to salvage the *Log*. I went off to Europe to follow Melville and talk about Ernest Hemingway at Schruns.[11] Having incautiously promised Bobbs-Merrill a *Billy Budd* book for a series, I planned it all out on a nine-by-twelve manila envelope on a train out of

Strasbourg (a place where I could not follow Melville) on June 27, 1988. "When can I write this? . . . Not till after New Orleans then California? Probably,—maybe August—w/out Mark." [In August I had no assistant.] "I want to do it at a stretch. I want to do it in 21 days. That's 21 into 135 [the limit for the series]. *6 pages a day average. That's your goal.*" I was determined to meet my obligation to Bobbs-Merrill, but I was thinking as a biographer. I hoped by my experiment to understand the consequences of writing at such speed as Melville did in the summer of 1849: did the books become blurs to him? did he forget what was in them? By writing the *Billy Budd* book so fast I might know better how Melville remembered *Redburn* and *White-Jacket.*

As soon as I got home I went as a spouse to New Orleans where my wife was attending a librarians' Rare Book and Manuscript conference. Weak, having recurrent infections, while changing planes at Nashville I called the doctor in Wilmington to arrange for an antibiotic to be waiting in New Orleans so I could work through the trip. I went to the Howard-Tilton Library to see "hard copy" of the *Picayune* because I was looking for a quotation from a New Orleans paper that Perry Miller had not footnoted and that I hadn't seen when I scanned microfilm of that paper as the most likely source (the microfilm images were like specks under a film of milk). Since the unreadable microfilm was available, the librarians would not let me see hard copy of the *Picayune*, wife in the trade or not. When I thought I heard the word "Yankee" I considered identifying myself as the depot agent and telegrapher of the Kansas City Southern Railway at Singer, Louisiana, and other metropoli in Beauregard Parish as well as Calcasieu Parish, starting in 1952, but I kept my mouth shut. Not wanting to waste my research opportunity, I looked in the card catalog and came upon the *New Orleans Commercial Bulletin*, a title some might have slighted but which I found alluring because I knew there were literary reviews in the *New York Commercial Advertiser.* The librarians were slow bringing out the bound volumes because they were using their book carts to wheel in bottles of booze, and several hours later, after I had settled down to work at last, they threw me out to have their cocktail party for my wife and her colleagues. This wasn't even Mardi Gras; this was midsummer.

I started in on the inch-wide Scotch-taped pages of the *Commercial Bulletin* for 1848 and soon saw that there was an interesting regular letter from a special correspondent in New York City who first signed himself "Gotham," then (discovering that a competitor was using that same pseudonym) "Croton," from the pure water that had so enhanced life in Manhattan. (During our stay in New Orleans salt water was marching relentlessly up the Mississippi.) Still hankering for the *Picayune,* a few yards away, beyond the carts of booze, but untouchable, I saw that the correspondent, a lawyer, was interested in literature. Before long it became clear that he knew Cornelius Mathews very well and was a friend of Evert Duyckinck. He knew the absolute inside dope on why *Yankee Doodle* had failed. He had inside information about Herman Melville we had never known, including what plainly passed in the Duyckinck circle as simple truth—Melville had written *White-Jacket* in "a score of sittings." My diary that night: "News about HM—wrote WJ in a score of sittings!" (I swear what I wrote in a previous paragraph about planning to do the *Billy Budd* book in twenty-one days is true.) Thinking a while about what "Croton" said, I saw that "a score" could be literally true, if, say, Melville had found and organized sources one day, surveyed them carefully the next, and written like hell the third. That day I had experienced my only hallucination during the decades of working on the biography, the vision out of the corner of my right eye of an old man in a limp blue raincoat: "Spirit of Jay standing right beside me as I pulled out (longhand) plum after plum.—Intensely exciting day—great items for *Log* & for *Powell Papers* & misc items. . . . then Cafe du Monde." Even if the antibiotics brought on the visitation from Leyda, New Orleans was already, and still, a city of ghosts for me, the wandering Kansas City Southern teenage telegrapher, buying a one-volume Shakespeare, standing outside jazz clubs, now still trying to tap out messages and hoping someone was reading me.

I knew of only one lawyer with a New Orleans connection who was that intimate with Mathews and Duyckinck and who knew Melville—Jedediah B. Auld. Assuming that the writer had to be Auld, I ordered microfilm of the *Commercial Bulletin* after I got home, the maximum five rolls at a time, and my new assistant, Donald Blume, photocopied all of the "Croton" letters as well as those of the replacement "Hans Yorkel," who said interesting things about *Moby-Dick* and *Pierre.* I finally discovered that the editor of the *Commercial Bulletin* in an 1854 farewell note identified "Gotham," "Croton," and "Hans Yorkel" as the same man, A. Oakey Hall, not Auld at all. Hall was even better—a contributor of New Orleans sketches to the Duyckincks' *Literary World* and later mayor of New York, brought down during the Tweed scandal, and with a personal connection: he had read law with one of Peter Gansevoort's brothers-in-law, and later as mayor worked with Melville's brother Thomas (the governor of Sailors' Snug Harbor). Here was a huge trove of letters (enough to make a book of many hundreds of pages) written from the midst of the Duyckinck circle over a period of years crucial to Melville's career. Hall had great things to say about my rogue Thomas Powell, and plenty of plums for the *Log.* Leyda was right—documents are

out there waiting for us to lift a hand toward them, even if we are just traveling as a spouse, along for the ride. So Tulane would not let a Yankee see the
Picayune: I found a little gold mine instead, laced with nuggets for the *Log*.

Back from New Orleans, brooding over the gossip in the Duyckinck circle that Melville had written *White-Jacket* in a score of sittings, I faced up to
my European fantasy of writing a book in twenty-one days. As it turned out,
I wrote the book between July 13 and August 24 and printed it and mailed
it on August 25, 1988. The first long weekend, Mark Niemeyer came out of
retirement and worked with me (expecting, he told me much later, that he
would have to write off all his August vacation), then I slogged on through
nineteen consecutive days at over ninety degrees and no air conditioning.
The computer went all gummy, as I did.

While I was writing the *Billy Budd* book Texier was finding a solution to
solve our problems with *The New Melville Log*—optical scanning. Since we
had the scanning company do the "Supplement" first, I copied hunks of it as
needed onto diskettes of the 1951 *Log* as they arrived, then moved them to
the proper sequence (saving the cleaning up process for a later stage). Luckily I had gotten off WordStar in 1987 and learned the wonderfully humane
and reliable WordPerfect, the same word processing program the scanning
operator was using. There were serious problems with the procedure, for it
lost features which I had to restore "by hand." We lost all italics, for instance,
and had to reinsert them, since the feeling was that Harcourt, Brace with
Leyda's help had worked out a brilliant design which we should happily follow. (Other scanning programs may already have been able to read italics,
for all I knew, but I could live with such limitations of the program Texier was using.) The type font of the *Log*, especially italics, proved hard to
scan, and odd things happened—"Brodhead" would appear as "Brodbead";
"Duyckinck" in almost a dozen forms (even when spelled right in the *Log*);
and "Hawthorne" appeared as anything from "Hamthorne" to "Hawtborne"
to "Hawtliorne" to "Hawthoine." Before editing any file I had to use the
search and replace function to clean up errors such as occurrences of "I" that
needed to be changed back to "1." Except for the fact that corrections were
easier to make, it was like working with a typescript made by an overpaid
and incompetent typist in 1971 when I was in a hip cast. Cleaning up the
diskettes took up many weeks, but it was finite. I just had to plan on serious
old-fashioned proofreadings at the final stages—by any good people I could
conscript for the chore.

And of course in the scanning process we lost all the work that had gone
into making a sequential new *Log*: we lost all Leyda's additions except those
in the "Supplement," *all* the post-1969 items that Leyda typed up and had

reset and cut and pasted into the original sequence—many dozens of pages. I had a massive amount of new inputting to do just to get Leyda's additions back in, but at least I could do much of it from the proofs that Mark and I corrected in the fall of 1987 and early 1988. I could enter these additions of Leyda's with the correct town and correct date (even if they were wrong in the proofs) and when I reordered (to get entries or parts of entries in proper sequence), I could enter the item right the first time. This stage too was finite, a matter of many days or a few weeks. And there was more good news: whatever lengthy item I had taped onto the margins of those proofs in 1987 was in the form of printout, and I still had all those additions on diskette, so I could slip these already proofread items into place (and shape them later just as I would do to any other entries). I added all the items on my diskettes sys-tematically, of course—everything has to be done by meticulous stages, one thing at a time all the way through so I would not be distracted. But I confess that I could not resist slipping an April 1848 letter from Priscilla to Augusta into place before any other item, a letter about Herman Melville's previously unknown visit to Pittsfield in which Priscilla called Uncle Thomas's farm Melville's "first love," a phrase I would have paid a lot for in the early 1980s when I was first trying to sell to skeptics the idea of the psychological impor-tance of the Berkshires to Melville.

Now I could correct any error I knew of or learned about—all the words and all the punctuation and spelling in any review, for instance, going back to Hutchisson's marked copy of the *Log* (or to the original reviews) rather than to the proofs we marked in 1987. I could do something much more drastic: I could move all the "July" reviews, for example, to the start of any July rather than the end of the month. Monthly periodicals dated July nor-mally came out sometime after the middle of June, and often I knew within a day or two of the publication date because newspapers noted the arrival of the new issues. In the 1951 *Log* any letter written in July about a July review or any newspaper appearing in July with comments on a July review would be talking about something the reader had not yet seen. Putting all monthly reviews at the start of the month was still hit or miss, but if I knew for sure that a periodical was late (or delayed in shipment, as the *Southern Quarterly Review* might be), I could place it about when it reached New York. Hayford had supplied me with copies of new Melville letters and better transcrip-tions of old letters as well as hundreds of corrections his team and Howard C. Horsford had made in the passages Leyda quoted from Melville's jour-nals, all of which could be whipped into the text. And there were several categories I wanted to expand. I wanted to include more examples of family rhetoric than Leyda did—more of Uncle Thomas's political invective in the

Pittsfield Sun, more quotations from student essays written by members of the family, more of brother Gansevoort's political oratory, more of Lemuel Shaw's rhetoric in his well-publicized legal decisions. I could include any document I saw where a member of the family called attention to anyone's word usage, whether it was "as the Irish say" or "as Gan says" (Gan being one of several family nicknames we never knew) or "as Herman says." I could fill out some of the documents that show the weaker sides of the character of Melville's father and Uncle Thomas, particularly, but also others, even Peter Gansevoort.

Leyda had been dealing with documents still held in private hands, sometimes, and was being discreet, but he also practiced the forbearance of a man who had dealt so often with unpredictable fathers that he wore his blue raincoat indoors so he could shrug out of it and hold it as he walked backward. I added much from a cache of Morewood family wills and inventories of possessions that Leyda never saw, although he was delighted I had seen them and would quote from them. I added a few notes Allan Melville made to his second wife on newspapers that came to the house during the Civil War, papers I drove to Gettysburg to see. I added anything I knew about that I thought I should add, constrained by the nature and proportions of the entries that Leyda established in the 1951 edition and also by the need to stay within three volumes. (My notion, one I tried out on Leyda, was that the three volumes would be about equal if we start the second on October 11, 1849, and the third on October 11, 1856, days when Melville sailed east from New York.)[12]

By the time I got around to writing the article for Hirsch in the spring of 1989 things were easier for me. Harrison Hayford, G. Thomas Tanselle, and I, with much help from Alma MacDougall and Mark Niemeyer, had gotten the "Historical Note" and the rest of *Moby-Dick* together and it had been published in August 1988. In January 1989, thanks to my ally on the 1967 Norton Critical Edition of *Moby-Dick*, John Benedict, I had signed a contract with W. W. Norton for a big (six–seven-hundred page) biography of Melville to be finished, if not published, in the centennial of Melville's death, 1991. In January and February 1989 from Roger Texier of Gordian Press I had received diskettes of the 1969 "Supplement," first, then diskettes for the entire 1951 *Log*, the product of optical scanning. *The New Melville Log* by Jay Leyda and Hershel Parker (or the other way around, if the *Log* pile grew very much) was at last feasible, at the cost of jettisoning the labor of the "designer," as I will explain.

In 1988 and 1989 I had advantages Leyda never had in the 1940s and never had or else could never profit from in the 1980s, although nothing can compensate wholly for my not having the power of Leyda's memory in those early years and his cinematic elegance at cutting from item to item. Leyda had discovered reviews thick and fast in the big newspaper collections using what Hetherington later called the magic Leyda wand, a calling-card sized listing of publication dates of Melville's works. He copied quotations (in longhand, of course) as he encountered the reviews, and rarely copied *all* of a review. Therefore, as I have already indicated, he did not necessarily have at hand the best evidence that one reviewer was plagiarizing and that another was double-dipping, and he was sometimes ill-equipped to judge what the most important early tendencies were in a given reception: so much depended on which reviews he found first. He never had before him a set of photocopies of all the known reviews until I provided him one (with the help of Brian Higgins), when it was too late for him to rethink his quotations. There is something of a hit-or-miss quality in the reviews in the 1951 edition, and even more so in the "Supplement" and in Leyda's choices to add to the third edition, where there are too many items taken from unrepresentative sources merely because they were recently discovered. As I pruned and sometimes expanded in the process of rethinking the quotations from the contemporary reviews, I had to remember that new items tended to get more space than they would have had if they had been discovered in the 1940s. The great photographer Leyda had taught Margaret Bourke-White how to use a sixteen-millimeter camera. Now I rethought all the problems of the reviews under an amateurish photograph of Leyda I had taken on his last research trip, in September 1986, in the musty basement of the Troy Public Library. In the picture he was reading the review of *Moby-Dick* in the *Troy Budget* I had just discovered using the version of the Leyda magic wand in the back of the Mailloux-Parker *Checklist of Melville Reviews.* With the great volume open in front of him on a massive blue-and-white oilcloth-covered table, surrounded by foxed and crumbling volumes of local newspapers, damaged by Parkinson's disease already, Jay Leyda was happy—happier, he declared, than if he were sitting in the Pierpont Morgan Library. You see why I loved that man.

Just as Leyda never had been able to draw his quotations from all the known reviews, he never had in front of him two sides or three sides of a major correspondence. Allan Melvill's letter was in this library, Peter Gansevoort's answer was in another, and Thomas Melvill, Jr.'s comment might be somewhere else. At the Houghton Leyda might copy a letter, then weeks or months later see at the New York Public Library the letter it was written in response to. There was no way he could know in advance what would be the most pertinent passage to choose to play off against the original letter or the next one in the interchange. He saw items together only as he made a rough mounting for his first edition of the *Log*, and by that time even he had sometimes lost (if he ever had possessed) a good sense of what was most significant about a given letter. Three and a half decades later, for the new *Log* he chose quotations from the Augusta Melville papers without re-consulting much material already in the archives, in New York or elsewhere.

I was in a better position, even in 1989, for the new weighty laptop was a wonder to me: on its hard drive I could carry with me on research trips the entire working copy of the third edition of the *Log*. In a library I could put a letter right into place, properly styled, and I could put in much more than I expected to print, knowing that I could trim down after I had before me a full or nearly full record of, for instance, a complicated three-sided correspondence. When Sergei Eisenstein entrusted him with the only complete copy of *The Battleship Potemkin*, Leyda of course preserved the movie intact. Entrusted with the *Log*, I had to choose which parts to add from documents Leyda did not know about, and I often had to recut the documents in the 1951 *Log* differently because many more connections and different sorts of connections were now visible. Beyond any question, many documents that were in the 1951 *Log* and the "Supplement" would make fuller sense in the third edition because we would know better what the overt and covert messages were and could point up the significances by slight alterations in the italic lead-ins, those apparently neutral devices that Leyda could make ineffably judgmental.

The *Log* became a new entity in my computer which after a year or two had grown to twice, then three times, its former length, old and new documents in a single sequence, in chronological order. What emerged, year by year on my screen, was the fact that the new discoveries, once they were seamlessly worked into place, played the very hell with many documents in the original *Log*. Late in 1989 I was ecstatic from the realization that some of the most challenging and rewarding phases were upon me, right along with the tedious searching for arabic "1" that the scanner read as "I." Now entries would take on personalities. Cute little "Early September" might all but throw a tantrum and demand to play leapfrog with stolid "mid-December." Items dated by season, such as "Fall" or "Spring," started jumping up and down like a broken tail of a "y" on the screen of a Hinman Collator (that huge invaluable machine for looking for variants in copies of books supposedly from the same edition) crying "Move me, move me!" Once I shifted such items others slid into different places, and all at once fuzzy words were infused with strenuous human motivations. As I made additions to the *Log* month by month it became clear that newly understood family members and

other people would throng *The New Melville Log*, and I could guarantee that
it would be a shock to see them making familiar with our old friends. Poor
Julia Maria Melvill stepped out of the shadows to become a major voice of
the 1830s, a witness to complex family comings and goings. Her older half
sister Priscilla first emerged in Julia's letters then in the next two decades
stepped forward in her own words, in a voice that at times sounds uncannily
like Melville's own or like Isabel's in *Pierre*, even though her most Isabel-
like letters that survive are written after that book was published. Melville's
brothers and sisters took on shades of personality we never had an inkling of,
so that in the newly added or merely revised biographical paragraphs at the
beginning of the *Log* I could have been able to give tiny character sketches
of them as no one could have done before 1983.[13] I had dozens of titles of
books and articles Gansevoort read between 1837 and his death, a major
addition to Sealts's *Melville's Reading*, and with the computer I could whisk
out the Gansevoort items for 1837–46 and study his whereabouts. I could
do the same for all the brothers and sisters and have all the known evidence
before me when I tried to characterize sister Kate or sister Fanny, for example, two of the figures who had been shadowy. Melville himself was strikingly
illuminated—for now I had many more of the words he spoke and many
more of his physical gestures, as well as many more comments on him. I
could hope to put into the *Log* every word of his known marginalia—not all
the markings, of course, but all the words.

I ended the article Hirsch had commissioned for *Modern Language Studies*, "*The New Melville Log*: A Progress Report and an Appeal" (Winter 1990),
with some specific appeals for help in providing transcriptions of Melville's
marginalia, for example, or in tracking down unknown correspondence.
Augusta Melville's correspondence log, which survived for the years around
Moby-Dick, showed that she wrote to members of old established families
in the land, like the Van Rensselaers, whose papers might have survived. I
hoped that people living near an archive might be willing to check printouts
of my transcriptions against the originals. None of that happened. I was making deep financial sacrifices for the *Log* and had no shame:

> *How can you help?* Jay Leyda slept in the cheapest hotels and Ys and
> cadged beds from Melvilleans town to town. I'm too old for that, but
> not too proud to suggest you let me house-sit in New York or Bos-
> ton a few days at a time while you go on a carefree vacation. *MWM,
> mid-fifties, avid jogger, professional, non-smoker, big but tidy. Happy
> to water small nonaggressive plants but does not walk dogs or cats.*
> (65–66)

The great generation of Yale students of Stanley T. Williams helped Leyda, and so did Leon Howard, Wilson Heflin, and many others. Now was the time for another pooling of resources, for at last the *Log* was rolling, or at least scrolling up and down my screen, not just being salvaged but being freely augmented and burnished beyond anything I had dared to hope.

As it turned out, few academics wanted to help me even when I presented myself as a little red hen. The greatest benefactors of the *Log* besides librarians were book dealers, notably the magnanimous William Reese, but the ad in *Modern Language Studies* evoked a welcome from the quintessential Manhattanites Robert and Roslyn Haber. While staying with the Habers I worked methodically at the tasks I had laid out for myself at the New York Public Library, then yielded to temptation, giving myself fifteen minutes to treasure-hunt in a folder with an alluring title, "Undated Letters or Unidentified Correspondents." Soon I saw familiar handwriting—what has become known as Melville's "D. D." letter to Duyckinck, in which he declined to review a book. I have quoted Backscheider on the triumph so intense that the pen shakes in the biographer's hand. Now I was so nervous I shakily rubbed the back of the librarian as she leaned over to look at the document. She took away the document and did not return, although she sent someone out with a photocopy. Did she understand that I was trembling from excitement at finding the letter? It did not matter that the letter was of no great obvious importance—what mattered was the way a few minutes of self-indulgent kicking over the traces had paid off, for once.

Still febrile, I shared the new letter with the Habers but did not report to them the phantasmagorical nature of my walk in Manhattan that night. Two Costner brothers from northern Mississippi, sons of a Confederate soldier who had gotten as far north as Gettysburg, had homesteaded in the panhandle of Oklahoma Territory, my grandfather Edgar Lugene and Moses Amariah (Uncle Mode, in my mother's stories). Near the Habers' apartment one of Uncle Mode's great-grandsons stood on a billboard, looking down, his left jeans-clad leg straight, the right crossed over it at the shin. Who was living a fantasy? Was this Guymon, O.T., or Gotham, N.Y.?

On the first of February 1989 I refused to cut eighty-eight pages of the *Billy Budd* book down to fifteen and asked Bobbs-Merrill to return the manuscript. Diary: "I could not have showed more restraint—No big deal—I will find a publisher—left msg for Jonathan [Brent] at NU Press." Norton had given a large advance to a writer for a biography of Melville (not, I clarify, Geoffrey Wolff, who just then was also thinking about doing a biography of Melville). The would-be biographer had counting on my supplying him with all my additions to the *Log* and when I politely declined to share he stiffed Norton for the advance (I was told) when he gave up the project. That had cleared the way for Norton to offer a contract to me. The contract came on February 2, "advance in the works." The same day, I sent the *Billy Budd* book off to Northwestern.

Most of my working hours from 1986 into the early 1990s were taken up not by writing but by transcribing documents. In 1989, 1990, and 1991 I spent more effort than ever on the *Log*, doing systematic additions from my 1963 dissertation and from my annotated volumes of the 1951 *Log*, for instance, but also systematically adding new reviews to the *Log* and correcting the 1951 and 1969 texts against photocopies or fresh transcriptions of the original reviews. That's dog's work, although intermittently exhilarating. With the help of Ruth Degenhardt I looked at items in the vault at the Berkshire Athenaeum, most significantly Gansevoort Melville's copies of the *Index Rerum*, which Mert Sealts had overlooked despite their relevance to Herman Melville's reading. I worked on the Northwestern-Newberry *Clarel* and the G. K. Hall Higgins-Parker volume of essays on *Moby-Dick*, but I worked primarily on *The New Melville Log* (lighted magnifier to the right of my monitor, perpetual calendar ready at my left), creating an engorged working file containing almost all of the Augusta Papers in full, for instance, and all the known reviews of Melville's books, in full, rather than excerpts of them. The results at first made the *Log* anomalous—old documents excerpted except when I had replaced them with full texts, new documents in full texts. I didn't have much choice. I had to transcribe new documents in full because every one I added might help me date another document or identify a person referred to in still another. It was while doing yeoman's work on the *Log*, transcribing new documents into it (in the process, dating or redating many of them) and making new sense of surrounding old documents, that I solved many biographical tangles,[14] most of which I was unaware of until I found myself snared in them. Time went into making lists which I never used, at least in full—every word Melville was on record as speaking, every article of clothing he is known to have worn (think of that fancy waistcoat that impressed Duyckinck), every gift Melville is known to have presented to anyone, every place Melville is known to have revisited, every poem he is known to have quoted. These were warming-up exercises.

In August 1988 I had been as gummy and sick as the computer, and on December 21, 1988, I got some medical results: "Shocks—'Severely diminished lung capacity (no resilience)'—'bad enzyme activity in liver (not *serious*) & heart blockage'—'Abnormal' EKG—aortic valve blockage." I knew there was old lung damage from tuberculosis in the mid-1950s (and later found damage to the thyroid gland from too many too-careless x-rays), but I had been running daily for almost eleven years and abstaining from alcohol for two (after realizing that I would have to do the *Log* as well as the biography). The doctor cheerfully told me I could fall dead running but I could keep on running if I wanted to, so I did. Within a few days I was getting up to work in the middle of the night as usual. But the troubles were not over. In the mid-1980s I had become suddenly and violently allergic to tobacco and perfumes during a night of pub-crawling about Chicago with Brian Higgins, and was being exposed to tobacco smoke every time I went to the university. In 1989 I began protesting against cigarette smoke in Memorial Hall at the University of Delaware, hoping to gain a smoke-free workplace because the smoke kept triggering infections. By April 1989 smokers (including one graduate student who had broken a whisky bottle on his forehead) were threatening me with physical violence, all aside from the assaults with smoke. I thought wrongly that the chairman was keeping a paper record of incidents as I reported them. He did not want threats of violence on a graduate student's record, he later admitted. He knew who was important.

Then in July 1989 on jury duty in Wilmington I was exposed to thick clouds of cigarette smoke inside the courthouse and in the toilet adjacent to the jury room. By the third day pain had localized to eruptions above the right eye. It was misdiagnosed as a sinus infection but after an agonizing weekend it was recognized as shingles and at the hospital I offered the information that I had collapsed after massive assaults from tobacco smoke. The admitting doctors chuckled at my blaming tobacco, for they had just been warned to look for Kaposi's sarcomas on the bodies of middle-aged blue-eyed men with shingles. They did not find the sarcomas, but the older doctor scooted close to the head of the bed and observed confidentially, "Heavily into anal, eh?" The "eh?" was priceless. Long before Eve Kosofsky Sedgwick invented "homosexual panic" (see a later chapter!), the younger doctor used a cleaver on my forehead when he took a tiny culture of the sore. The good part was that their diagnosis got me into isolation, a private room with a view of the Washington Street Bridge over the Brandywine, and got me morphine for hours until I made the mistake of mentioning how much the drip was helping the pain. The scar on the forehead was permanent, as it was meant to be, but after a few years it faded in among evidences of general deterioration.

Weakened as I was by old damage and by working so long in the middle of the night on the *Log*, I needed to start if I was going to write the biography. Robert Skidelsky in "Confessions of a Long-Distance Biographer" says (17): "My serious learning started in the King's College, Cambridge library in 1977. Some diary entries from that summer capture the terror, excitement and pitfalls of research: '*12 July:* To Hershel Road to see Richard and Anne

Keynes. I was dreading it, but they were very friendly, and offered me several large sherries. He suddenly said: "I want you to see Maynard's letters to Lydia"—so I arranged to start reading them next week.'" With my diary entries that follow I take a greater risk than Skidelsky because I incorporate my struggle to achieve a smoke-free workplace even as I endeavor to give a sense of the difficulty of carrying on any sort of professional obligations other than writing the biography. Concerning anything like a personal life I choose to be silent. While quoting a good deal on the fight for a nontoxic workplace, I minimize in my excerpts from the diary deaths in the family, extreme pain before and for months after two rotator cuff surgeries, a move from Wilmington, Delaware, to Landenberg, Pennsylvania, and other significant disruptions. What biographer working for years with masses of archival material does not experience devastating events?

On December 20, 1989, is this diary entry:

3:44 pm 20th *started writing Biography.* Woke up rested & cheerful Happy mg—dancing around the job of starting to draft some pp of the *Biography*—Read Sandberg on "B[urgundy] Club"—incl new "The House of the Tragic Poet"—28° and wcf of 0° but *not* very windy so Ran 4½. Reckless—after gg around Tower crossed frozen Brandywine over Swinging Bridge with no floorboards. Taking a big chance—so went home & started writing last chapter my key being decline of Hawthorne in ct to *his* decline Never mind that I only did a page plus—I started. Lay down 20 mins, maybe 5 min deep sleep.[15]

21 December Wed night-Thurs mg. Restless night 15° up to 25° before going down *precipitously* Thurs night—Wk on HM Biography—in a confused state, o/c—*no tone established,* & no sense of selectivity yet. Assembling material from various files—apparently I destroyed all the *MD* ["Historical Note" WordStar] files!! But be resolute—this o/c=a necessary stage.

22 December. Wkg on start of *Pierre* why Mamma had more time to be on Herman's case.

23 December Did not write *any* on biography (want to do s/t every day).

24 December Trying *Pierre*—see I can't present all the evidence—have to give conclusions & blaze ahead not strewing page with "the evidence is" or *probably* or *very likely*—A new technique.

27 December At 7 am actually began the biography—"Pulled Hither & Thither"—on sale of NYC house and readjustment of expectations—doing a story. BEGAN (ie getting *tone & proportion* & strategies) working on early 1851.

28 December 1989 Up working on biog 2–3:30 & slept rest of night till 6 up there in 3rd floor.

30 December *Haunted*—the Haunting by the Family has begun–Some work on Aug 1851. Sat Morning 30th—the problem starts—being haunted by a throng of characters—The sisters, Mamma, EAD, NH, Robert so I have to live with them for the next year and a half and have to find strategies for making this nocturnal haunting useful, focused.[16]

1 January 1990 Melville biography absorbing all energy—awake at 1 am with the thronging, clamoring characters—result (immediately) of adding some parts of EAD letters not in *Log*.

5 January 1990 Decided to start with *Redburn*, backing up to get a running start—& after a little confusion it went great & I got on to WJ before 5 pm—So extremely busy [with other demands including *Reading "Billy Budd"* and the *Checklist of Melville Reviews* and "The Powell Papers" and the G K Hall book on MD]—& seeing that I will succeed if I just keep myself in the chair in front of the screen.

6 January 1990 Some work on WJ period.

7 January Up early & off (60 dollars each) to Wash DC Natl Gallery East Wing for a terrifically spaced 49 ptg F E Church show incl one Kate [Gansevoort Lansing] gave to Albany Institute of History & Art—wow!

8 January Called John Benedict about [probable size of] biog—he was not scared abt it.

9 January Awake at 1:30 & up till 4:30 wkg on *BB* then jarred awake by alarm & bk to *BB* at nearly noon trying hard to keep my focus as I plow on thru the chapter-by-chapter section—aware of the need to keep an intensity going until I am done—& then to be vigilant as I revise on the screen—*Exalted* but fearful— exalted by the fact that almost all of it is good, fearful that I will not make all the needed final revisions.

10 January up on BB 3 am–5 am then slept till 8:45.

15 January Did not get to write—Trying to keep perspective on interruptions— part of the business of living.[17]

22 January 1990 I am starting on getting Shak editions into biog summer 1850 section—HM & what was on his mind as he went to Pittsfield, aesthetic/historical problems.

23 Progressed on 1850 into Idyl in good day's work. Worked 11–1 am[—] Realized EAD decided to stay till 12th on Wed or early Thurs (Maria *knew*)—Have to change LOG.

24 January—Almost prodigious day of pushing on through Aug 9–12.

25 January Up 1:30–3:30 on Aug 12–15 1850. Rain when I looked out at 3:30 am. 11 am that tension of not wanting to lose the momentum yet knowing that hours have to pass before I get down late Aug—WI[rving], Sophia, NH, Augusta—*the retelling in sequence*—[On Run, at Water Tower:] Bummed paper & pencil [from a stranger] at Sam Francis [DuPont] statue & made excellent notes on Sophia & Tappan & other *motivations* from Sept 50—coming alive—pushed on till 4:10 no nap. About here the 25th I said, "I put it in the book already"—used the term "the book"—

26 January *Tired* but soldiered on thru the day—inching up to purchase of Arrowhead *& febrile* about discoveries—Realized how very *pissed* Leon would have been at what I've done in the last days—me the *father pleaser.*

29 January 1990 Mumford died Friday January 26 at 94.

2 February 1990 Up at 4 am needing to get down stoicism →recklessness & *Mardi* to EAD Feb 50—why HM cd let go.

7 February 1990—Slave labor up at 4:30 am pausing at 5:30 pm—Drove thru Isle of the Cross & Office-Seeker.

9 February 1990—Resigned from NCL & SAF & Review and other editorial boards—No time for them. [Painful to have to resign from NCL, where my 1960 Indian-hater speech was published, in 1963, and where I first proposed restoring *The Red Badge of Courage.*]

15 February 1990—Jay Leyda dead 2 years—and today Willard Thorp died—Walking home, exhausted, umbrella—attacked in Plaza Parking lot by 8–10 black men (some teenagers)—hit with brick in left buttock—("You got a problem," I heard—as I was trying to get away)—Then chased them but in Earth Shoes—no help [from anyone]

16 February 1990—Work on [writing of] Typee trying not to lose momentum but wiped out from classes, [chairman's] insistence that his secretary can smoke under my cubicle, and gang attack—very perturbing, making me more wary than ever—

26 February 1990 Copy of Mod Lang Studies (Winter 1990) with *Log* article came and Isle of the Cross offprints came from AL

NYC 2 March 1990 NYPL Got the Hoadley—Got Powell refs in EAD to GLD—Corrected some of the Picnic [on Monument Mountain] letters & got more refs to picnic 1850 then before noon in folder of undated & unidentified discovered HM letter to EAD—*Ecstatic* trembled—DISCOVERED A MEL-VILLE LETTER.

12 March 1990 Stunning letter from Nina Murray—AM to HM 17 Oct 1844 [Henry Murray had owned it for decades].

18 March 1990 Holland PA almost to Trenton Fascinating Anna Morewood 84 years old, widow of Henry (Larry) Gansevoort "The only Melville or Gansevoort that counts is the one standing in my own shoes." [Anna was the daughter-in-law of Milie, born 1849. Yes, daughter-in-law of the child born just after Malcolm.] Locket February 1872 [each girl got a Tiffany mourning locket charged to the estate; I already had the bill]. AM to Florence, Flo to Agnes—carte de visite photo of Allan. Gold—gorgeous Tiffany locket—Big, great photo of Allan in field north of Arrowhead—Took it off with me to have it copied [She had Lathers's copper humidor].

31 March 1990 Serious cleaning up—adding & moving about (of marginalia) Before getting out of bed the fine idea of saying *"one 'decision'"* [M made] was to take NH along on the journey [in *Clarel*].

March 1990—[Battling post-surgical infections all month and regularly sickened by tobacco smoke at the university. Enlisted OSHA, who on March 30 said it was the dean's call—not true, I am sure—and the dean smokes—Among other things trying to figure out how to use Bezanson's 1960 introduction for NN *Clarel* and yet get it updated.] Big confrontation 2–3 April 1990 everyone against me [on smoking] except Robinson.

2 April 1990—At 12 after enlisting CER confrontation with sun-burnt [chairman] in hall [His secretary's office was directly below my cubicle and smoke went straight up and collected there]. Said: "R is an elderly woman with an addiction and I will not ask her to go outside to smoke." I told him, loudly & distinctly, that his first duty was to provide a workplace that did not endanger my health & that my health took priority over her addictions. Called Robin Elliott [OSHA] and relayed *this* info before class. At 930 got Carol H who today early will talk to Vice President Maxine Colm, in charge of Personnel (Salaried staff) . . .

3 April 1990 I . . . must have a workplace that does not make me sick. R says she will not smoke any more [directly under my cubicle] . . . But the [chairman] still sd she could smoke when I was not expected down to my office (Jesus) & I said that was not the terms of the deal by which I came down— . . . He still worries about *R's* rights & does not see the damage he was doing to my health . . . Taught very well anyhow.

5 April 1990 Call to HH about more HAM [Murray] letters to Jay re Oct 44 Wilson [Heflin] knew [something] about the letter Nina [Murray] sent me [Murray had recently been toying with HH and Wilson, longer with Jay].

9 April 1990—Left letter to [chairman]. Turned in copy for . . . [dean] The letter is in effect . . . a notification of what I expect of him—no less than a reversal of position [on smoking in Memorial Hall].

10 April 1990—At 2 recognized the infection—Could not heal [these weeks] because of the stress caused by . . . attack. So a really miserable day except when I got into teaching & thought of why HM was able to write about the process of the mind in [*Pierre*]—having watched himself write *Moby-Dick*.

11 April 1990—Talked to s/o in VP's office about a memo to supervisors on duties to protect non smokers.

15 April 1990 Carvel's death in NY Times. [Carvel Collins, the great accumulator of Faulkner documents, who figures later in this book.]

16 April 1990—No unpleasant encounters—smoke free Memorial Hall— Really a triumph—my contrib to Earth Day 22 April.

17 April 1990—Good class on Bartleby & Paradise & Tartarus on what new ways we must think of them [after knowing that Melville completed *The Isle of the Cross*].

10 May 1990—Felt very upset in mg before talking to woman in Employee Relations—better now that I have determined to push a little more on . . . treatment of me—no wonder I have not recovered.

11 May 1990—The thing is in motion—Want some good out of it—a no nonsense ruling that "smokers' rights" are not to be considered.

In 2nd half 1990—Bitter departmental struggles over "Smokers' Rights"—[Joined with other] senior professors protesting to dean the chairman's leveling us down— Work on the "Historical Supplement" for *Clarel*—Work on *Checklist of Melville Reviews*—Work on "Domesticity" article for G. K. Hall book—Looking over the *Billy Budd* printout; page proofs 13 September 1990—Much work on *Log*.[18]

Arrowhead 6 June 1990—Worked through Anna Morewood's astonishing donation—May 1851 letter Augusta to Allan, Florence on her country house, Milie's school autobiography, much Morewood stuff incl Lizzie to Willie.

18–23 June 1990—Back in Pittsfield all week Inputting on laptop rather than photocopying.

9 July 1990 Request that I review a long article by [a biographer-to-be of Melville] proving that Melville wrote *Redburn* in 1839–1840!!!!!!! Oh good God.

10 July 1990 up 12:30 to 2 am on Checklist; deciding to write biog chapter nearest *Clarel* as a way of not wasting the *Clarel* momentum

23 July 1990 John Benedict died.

August—work on microfilms of Shaw Papers at Hagley

29 August 1990—Regular smoking in men's room on 2nd floor—Call from Cicely Harmon saying VP Maxine Colm is handling my case with the Academic Senate—Decided to declare "university service" for all this struggle to have a smoke-free working environment! [Fat chance of getting {annual service} credit for it!]

1 September 1990 [Shingles aftermath] post herpetic neuralgia on scalp—but I will get a smoke free work place—I *will* change UD to that extent.

4 September 1990 Maxine Colm called—She had summoned the [chairman] over . . . So I get to work thru Hayward Brock & they'll get me protected except from passing strangers.

7 September 1990—Hayward toured Memorial Hall with Joe Miller of OSHA looking for ashtrays, etc. New signs going up [they were regularly torn down for the next years]—The chairman is left totally out of the loop—Hayward is committed to making the building smoke free.

12 September 1990 [Chairman] determined to offer the [endowed] chair to [an older male] from Princeton instead of Lois Potter—My contribution, aloud: "He smokes, she doesn't." To myself, "No way in Hell!" [Chairman, in meeting, publicly] reviewed the new no-smoking policy smoothly, butter not melting etc

17 September 1990—Called Hayward's office about smoking cleaning women.

8 October 1990—For me to start writing I need peace. I don't want to retreat into writing as escape from misery.

9 October 1990 So today I have to start writing—Started writing with flight from NYC after Malcolm's funeral—not good, but a start.

15 October 1990—Bad smoke. RW—she and others will stop, by God.

16 October 1990. [President of Norton] Lamm says he'll check my biog manuscript for style & his assistant who did an undergrad or MA thesis on HM will ck it for factual accuracy—*I did not say anything.*

25 October 1990—RW smoking away—I got very sick because I did not notice it soon enough—Left word for Hayward Brock.

5 November 1990—Mailed letters to Hayward and Maxine—want violations on record—Someone has been smoking in the dome, even.

7 November 1990—Wrote the Director of Libraries after she refused to move ashtray urns from the entrances: "If I as part Choctaw and part Cherokee complained that the only way I could get into Morris Library was to walk past signs where the urns read: 'THE ONLY GOOD INDIAN IS A DEAD INDIAN' you would find the authority, fast, to remove the signs. I don't see that a psychological assault such as a racist sign should be regarded as necessarily more dangerous than a direct physical assault, which is what anyone allergic to tobacco smoke now suffers in order to enter the library." I added parenthetically: "the users of Smoking Room 323 [in Morris Library] cannot sit in their own smoke: they often prop open the door to let smoke go out into the stacks." I continued: "I am sending a copy of this letter and (with your permission) a copy of your letter to Ronald Whittington, Maxine Colm, Robin Elliott, and Dean Edith Anderson as a way of raising consciousness about the need to see anyone's objection to smoking by an entrance to a building of the University of Delaware strictly as an *access* issue. We build ramps for people confined to wheelchairs. We can find ways of preventing unnecessary damage to the health of people who are still mobile but already damaged by tobacco smoke." [The urns and the smokers stayed, and the door to Smoking Room 323 continued to be open to the stacks much of the time. I retired early in large part because I never could gain smoke-free access to the library.]

12 November 1990—Smokers in lobby—Big blue No Smoking sign torn down—No sign even in men's room—Left word at Dean's office.

20 November 1990—Very depressed by RW and other violators and vandalizing of signs.

25 November 1990—Started 1839 instead of 1842—Got 9 pp or so, into Liverpool.

26 November 1990—realized that Leon's saying HM was a growing boy in the summer of 1839 was not just because he was still *thinking* of 1837 but probably because he had it in typescript before he heard of Bill Gilman's discovery of the year Melville sailed to Liverpool.

29 November 1990 [Work on "Deconstructing *The Art of the Novel* and Liberating James's Prefaces"] The manic joy of discovery is still with me, this dark, dark cold November morning—The joy of following HJ's mind for the great adventure he was on [in the Prefaces and the revisions].

30 November 1990—Excited about HJ's Prefaces and the emerging story.

17 December 1990 5 copies of *Reading BILLY BUDD* paperbacks came.

30 December 1990—Chicago: Melville Society Meeting: "Into the Lions' Den."[19]

1991 [Infections and frequent] antibiotics—one general anesthesia. Work on LOG, article on G W Harris, POWELL, GK Hall, NAAL.

11 October 1991—Battle for a smoke free teaching environment—taking over everything—Mysterious sickening smoke flowing into amphitheater by my podium starting at stroke of noon [so I wobbled at every peroration]—Students claimed not to smell it. Finally CER found that every day a janitor was rushing into a nearby closet when the noon bells rang and lighting up.

13 April 1991—gave a great HJ speech for Soc for Textual Studies prelim form of Deconstructing speech, worked on the expansion—

18 May 1991 Maurice Sendak said he would do the cover for my biography dust jacket.

18 June 1991 started on biog for first time since November of 1990—Connected to old part of 1839 and got thru 1840 early 27 June 91.

27 June 1991—got thru 1840.

24 September 1991 at NYPL Melville meeting HH noted that I was not asked to be on the program and identified me as "the most distinguished Melvillean of his generation," then went on firmly: "which is not my generation." MS [Maurice Sendak] said he felt like a star-fucker [a reversal of his usual experience].

25 October 1991—College Lit article on diversity recd.

2 December 1991 AHI article and copies of *Editors' Notes* [an essay long suppressed because it exposed Fredson Bowers's folly in editing *Pragmatism*].

24 December 1991—The Checklist of M Reviews came.

[December 1991 to January 1992—Moved from Wilmington, Delaware, to Landenberg, Pennsylvania, four miles and three states from University of Delaware. Now Google Earth shows it as the last house, the very last house, in southeast Pennsylvania. From it you walk out in the woods to where the three states come together.]

20 Jan 92—accident on ice—shoulder torn.

Much work on LOG as of 10 March 92.

3 April 92 in Buffalo on HM as sex symbol.

18 April 92—Julia Reidhead agreed to print *Live Oak, with Moss* in NAAL [First time this gay love sequence was printed in an American literature anthology: I still believe printing it was the most important thing I ever did for the profession.]

3 May 92 told Sendak what Jack Stillinger says, that my idea that genuine art is coherent is extremely dubious. MS repeats slowly, absorbs it, and says, "Thank God I'm not long for this world."

5 June 1992 Donald Lamm—demanding NAAL work instead of work on biog ("yelling" at me).

22 July 1992 Got thru July 1852—Saddest line in bk—after this day he could never in the rest of his life even pretend to be happy.

23 July 1992—[Melville's inscription in the guest register in Naushon: "Blue sky—blue sea–& almost every thing blue but our spirits."] Every thing blue but our spirits—the last day when he could even pretend to be happy—A profoundly disturbing effect on me—But pushing.

24 July 1992—Nothing to write in diary because all I did was write. Heavy emotions because of realization about HM's never being happy again.

26 July 1991—Piling up pages, anyhow—wishing I could magically jump about to happier episodes but knowing I can't.

28 July 1992—Pushed on & on tempted to look for an easier softer chapter to do. I have 80+ new pages since 2 July integrated with 20 or so old pages on Sept 51–June 1853, awk though some passages are.

30 July 1992—So—moments of triumph—hours of focusing, moving, selecting, shaping—Thank God for the computer.

31 July 1992—Worked on 1853 in night & finished it early after getting back up—Then faced the awkwardness of 1854 & at last decided on narrative plus sections on long term CHANGES set in motion—Extremely difficult to isolate—leaving HM & Augusta & Lizzie & Composition to be told as narrative *Did not write at all*—worked at organizing.

2 August 1992 1854=HARD—but I am writing & it only gets better.

3 August 1992—So some progress on 1854, organizing thematically the section to go after the Wedding in January—before the year as it relates to HM & Lizzie & poor Augusta.

11 August 1992 [after trip to Gansevoort, NY and Pittsfield] Putting stuff in LOG and putting little touches in biography—surprising how much I brought back, including the clipping on Hoadley that gave me my key to Kate—At a novelistic phase—keys to character—Hoadley's low confidential whisper.[20]

10 October 1992—More work on 1859—313 pages done since 2 July 92.

28 October 1992 Asked Tommo [Thomas Osmond, research assistant] to go to Library where he found answer to my question "Did JQA write an epic" Yes, Dermot MacMorrough High excitement He called from Morris—I gave him the fragments from Dante flyleaf Silence—then "No"—So I went to Morris—NUC got citation Poems of Religion & Society 1848—last hope? I already had this in computer Biog 1860 but see now there may be a pattern—[HM] may have scanned a lot of early national (US) epics to see what the poetic tradition was, like the Fredoniad May have been looking at U S epics like the Columbiad.

5 December 1992—Pushed through 1867 to juncture of 1990's 1867–69. The Golden Spike at 7:15 pm at 941 pages—Jesus I hope no one else ever has to suffer as much as I did today over Malcolm's death—Dissolved in tears from [watching a] few minutes at end of Cousin Kevin's *Field of Dreams* then bawling about Malcolm—Nose streaming for hours after that bit of *F of Dreams*—[Surreal:] Deer in back fading into White Clay Creek Preserve just like ballplayers disappearing into green corn. This is my *Field of Dreams* [Landenberg, on promontory above the 1,700-acre nature preserve].

4 January 1993—up 2–4 am on 1835–36—Finished 1836 & first half of 1837 & hooked up to start of 1991 June draft (June 1837) by 4 pm—So I have 1084 or so pages—all but some years in the 1840s drafted.

5 January 1993—Awake at 4, up before 5 working on 1842 first half—Working on Home front 1842—got 9 pages.

6 January 1993—Awake at 4 again, up at 5 again to press onward. Started writing HM in early 1842 but didn't get too far before Tommo came.

7 January 1993—To Hagley—Saw nothing on [Allan's] wedding in Phila Public Ledger & Daily Transcript April & Early May 1860 To Hist Soc of DE but NO Phila file there.

8 January 1993 — Up at 630 after a bad night — Ideas about Cannibalism, Greek myth, Pollard, Allan Melvill. HH says he wants to go to NYC with Tommo. Fine! What's my research assistant for? Great exposure for Tommo.

9 January 1993 — Took much of the day but I pushed on into unsatisfactory Typee section.

12 January 1993 Work on *Omoo* using Rita Gollin and Wilson Heflin — Pushed mostly thru Tahiti draft I spent 2 hours on microfilm of Boston Post 1872 again not finding what Mert says he saw [We — HH, I, Mark, Steven Olsen-Smith, others — spent many days looking for an article on Allan's crooked dealings which Mert said he saw; I have never found it even after many newspapers are digitized].

13 January 1993 — Envy Tommo the trip — young knight off on a quest.

14 January 1993 — Tommo off to New Haven & Boston — Good call from Tommo in NH after his visit to 409 Temple St. Bill Reese charming as always — may have some better readings of the erased words in the Dante flyleaf — Good Knight errant.

22 January 1993 — Long day — HH read several years starting 1851 last quarter — Hard to gauge his opinions except he wants to leave in all the sex references that HAR wanted me to take out.

23 January 1993 — HH pushing on, fairly fast, commenting — reminding — but not despairing.

24 January 1993 — HH wkg thru 1863 as I left him at 11 pm — In mid day I protested about my doubts & he made another declaration, this time saying that "my generation" qualification in Sept 1991 was just, saying I had *surpassed* him, & saying (awkwardly holding my hand) directly — "I love you, Hershel" — So the torch can still be held & passed bk & forth — but it's mine for as long as I live — He actually thought some (early 63) was ready — sd I was rolling there — HH says I am rolling in 63 — [that part] doesn't need revising.

25 January 1993 — Up at 1 am stirred up by HH's praise, by my [shoulder] pain & by dread of surgery — Got HH off to NYC.

26 January 1993 Getting ready to revise in *printout* instead of just on screen. I had *never read any of it*, really, after writing it — except passages worked over for a talk or the G K Hall piece.

28 January 1993 [Rotator cuff surgery] Dr A happy, stoked with himself [for improvising a double-headed fish hook for my shoulder when he found how bad

the tears were] — Morphine [Very long hard recovery, sleeping on floor for weeks with arm over my head, perpendicular, or straight out away from body.]

2 February 1993 — Call from Bill Reese — Told him about Edinburgh Rev 1810 [as source for HM's annotations in HM's copy of Hazlitt *Lectures* which Reese had bought]. He is UPSing me his LECTURES tomorrow. [That is, Reese sent me Melville's own copy.] — HH's plan OK with him — to have a section of non-marginalia notes in books — Call to HH but got him at dinner & he will call back tomorrow. REESE the Generous — Bad night changed into 3 different slings but better than Monday night.

3 February 1993 — Tommo by at 3 unexpectedly to bring books incl Modern British Essayists which I asked for on phone. Great, [they were] at Morris Library. — So HM did not have to go to 1810 *ER* — cd have used reprint in Jeffrey volume. Expands evidence.

4 February 1993 — Bulk and quality of new evidence partly from Hazlitt & partly from *Modern British Essayists* — Told Bill Reese about it — that HM may have gotten (probably did get) the Alfieri there — Great guy: "No one else deserved such free use of the Hazlitt" — He will keep eye out for HM's *Mod Brit Essayists*. [This was what it was like before Bookfinder and Amazon.]

2 April 1993 — Aware of my conspicuous character defect — that I want the respect of people I am properly contemptuous of.

2 July 1993 — Anniversary of my starting work in 1992 so I must start writing today — Did a trifle but mainly wkd in Hawaii — Used "Kermit" to access Delcat — Went to UD worked 2–3 hours in Special Collections inputting on disk which I took home — Found SF attack on HM — Checked out a pile of books incl Wilkes' Exploring Expedition — Have several good contemporary descriptions of Hawaii — Rain all night — awake 3–5:45 should have worked.

4 July 1993 — Got all of Lahaina drafted and at 4:30 ended by understanding Leon's error in his contemptuous generalization about Dr Judd at Lahaina — EAD mis-remembered, that's all — So, plugging along I'm on my way.

5 July 1993 — Work on 1843 in Honolulu pretty steadily till 3:30 — bleary now — Into the pattern, slogging on getting a first draft using Olmsted & Wilkes and other travel writers — So I am embarked on last phase of this draft — much to do in 1840s still.

12 July 1993 — Brilliant hour at 2 — putting Charlotte's 1944 comment [on HM being resentful of Harpers all his life] to use — Imagination such as Leon didn't have though he had great intelligence. REVERSED Saunders and Nichols, put Saunders first—months to let bitterness grow—*So much better a story than Leon's.*

14 July 1993—1199 pages at 11:45pm.

1994: Revising more than writing.

31 December 1994—Ended year with full 849 page draft of Vol 1— & starting to polish instead of to write or to revise.

After the December 1989 start I wrote most of the first draft of the biography not consulting books at all, only consulting my files in the working text of *The New Melville Log,* identifying phrases and sentences I wanted to quote and copying them whenever I could so as to avoid rekeying passages and introducing new errors. I wrote the second half of Melville's life first, for reasons having to do with my own physiology, psychology, and the nature of some of the new documents: I was afraid if I waited until I had written the first half I would not be strong enough to tell such a sad story in a way that would engage readers. Think about it: a biographer of Emerson in the last few pages can become defensive as the great mind fades away, a biographer of Mark Twain for a few pages can become exasperated at the depiction of grandiosity, laziness, and self-indulgence, but even a biographer of Hemingway, however wearied of alcoholic posturing and the ludicrousness of the "daughter" fantasies, does not have to transmute four decades of sustained misery into a narrative that will not plunge a reader into profound depression.[21] Keeping the second volume from being full of groans, moans, and subterranean shrieks—keeping it somehow enjoyable though being heartbreaking—was the hardest intellectual, emotional, and aesthetic feat I ever accomplished. After I finished that part of the draft I put it aside and went back to Melville's early years.

The worst blow to work on the biography was the death of John Benedict, my beloved editor of the Norton Critical Edition of the 1967 *Moby-Dick,* who had smoked defiantly after surgery for throat cancer, but not for very long. Benedict's death left my biography an orphan. The president of Norton, deciding to edit the biography himself, set himself to allay all my concerns by reassuring me (as noted in my diary) that his secretary had taken a class on Melville and would be his fact-checker (since of course everything could be checked in books). Oh. No one could check my facts without spending months in the New York Public Library, months in the Berkshire Athenaeum, weeks at the New-York Historical Society, weeks at the Massachusetts Historical Society, days in the Newberry Library, days at the Houghton Library, days in the Library of Congress, days in many other libraries. And because

I had much more highly relevant information than anyone had ever had (including much more about the period of *Moby-Dick*), the book was not going to be confined to the standard Pulitzer-sized five-hundred pages which Norton, all reasonably, wanted to publish.[22] Barbara Tuchman in "Biography as a Prism of History" in *Biography as High Adventure* elegantly complained that "biography has lately been overtaken by a school that has abandoned the selective in favor of the all-inclusive" (102). That was not my school: I had previously unknown masses of information before I began the rigorous process of selection. Robert Caro, writing about Lyndon B. Johnson, may already have been facing what I faced, but no modern biographer of a great American writer had in hand such a mass of new information that demanded not only to be told in new stories but also to be employed so as to re-slant almost every episode that had previously been known. No one else was ever going to amass such documentation and see how to put it into story form. What could I do?

After complex negotiations in which Hayford egged me on to tell the full story, whatever the length, in August 1995 I abrogated the contract with Norton and proposed to return the advances (although I was not legally obligated to). The new Norton editor advised me on the phone that I should "shit can" my letter. If I approached another press, he muttered darkly, I was "in a bad way." In fact, when word got out that I was writing a biography, I had begun receiving inquiries. When I received one from Eric Halperin at that Deconstructionist haven Johns Hopkins University Press, I was amused enough to reply tersely, "Do you know what kind of work I do?" On August 18, 1995, just as I broke with Norton, the National Endowment for the Humanities (NEH) asked me to recommend Skip Gates (whom John Benedict had adored) for still yet another million-dollar-plus NEH grant. Stuck for several days with no publisher for my near-decade's worth of a privately financed do-it-yourself Politically Incorrect Unfit-for-NEH-Funding biography of a dead white man, I reveled in an hour of miserable jealousy before running the megrims off in White Clay Creek. That was a low point. Running that day, in one or another of three states on my route, I remembered Eric Halperin. He was away and by design unreachable. Lindsay Waters at Harvard University Press, his priorities in good order, kept a weekend play-date at the Cape, as I understood it, instead of seizing the chance to read my sample chapters. Monday? Too late. Other presses offered contracts sight unseen. Halperin returned, leaving Johns Hopkins but replaced by Willis G. Regier, who drove up to my house, contract and cash at hand (the cash to pay off Norton). The Johns Hopkins book was beautiful—a new drawing by Maurice Sendak on the cover. The critics, of course, would be as happy as I was.

Never able to gain smoke-free access to Morris Library at the University of Delaware, I retired at sixty-two in 1998 so I could transform my rough draft into the second half of the biography. In Morro Bay, California, we bought a Spanish Colonial fantasy house on a steep grade. A Pride of Madeira bush flourished near the street but the slopes on either side of the house were bare. Behind, uphill, there were no stairs to the tiny high rectangle of dirt yard. Started on spec on a plot with ocean and Morro Rock views, the house had been far along before the aerospace collapse hit California. The bones were strong but the final details from toilets to faucets and light fixtures were cheap. The house had outlets for cable television in every room but not a single bookshelf. The kitchen had a small sink and a tiny electric cooktop with a rim so high that a soup-pot could not be seated on a burner. The room was dominated by an eight-foot-long banco eighteen inches high, perfect for a row of docile toddlers who would never grow taller. Big enough but impossibly configured, the kitchen would not work over the long haul, so we had to start thinking and negotiating about how we could transform the space, as we did, ourselves, in 2002 and 2003. I claimed the narrow floor over the garage, but even after the computer was set up it had to be swathed in tarps and blankets for months while I hauled concrete blocks and freshly mixed cement through the room to build what I humorously called a whale-watching parapet, from which, in fact, I have viewed whales. I bought a big table saw and an electric tile saw, allowing time for masonry and carpentry projects rather than writing the biography. How hard could a kitchen remodel be? After all, a cabinet was just a box, wasn't it? How hard could it be to cut tile for an inside corner? I had described in the first volume how long it took for Melville to establish a work routine when he moved to Arrowhead in 1850, so none of the disruption to the biography occasioned by a transcontinental move and house renovations should have been surprising. Most of the disruptions did not come as surprises, but they were frequent and damaging to prolonged, intense concentration.

I got back to work on the biography intermittently in 1999, but at the end of the year Norton wanted a new edition of *Moby-Dick*. The 1967 edition was still selling, but it was a third of a century old. Furthermore, it was time to revise the *Norton Anthology of American Literature* for the sixth edition. I fought to continue on the biography but surrendered on February 3, 2000: "So I have a lot to do on NCE & will just set to." I would do both Norton projects first even if it was by no means certain I could finish the biography, for I was pausing in a series of surgeries, getting as much done as I could before the next. I had warnings in the failure of mentors. Merton M. Sealts, Jr., was in too much pain to talk on the telephone for long. Harrison Hayford was increasingly silent. I wanted to let Hayford hold a copy of a new edition of the Norton Critical Edition *Moby-Dick* while he could and I wanted to let Norton market a sparkling Sesquicentennial Edition. I prepared the study for work on the Norton Critical Edition "with better light & seating arrangement." Always, a new project requires stowing down and cleaning up in a constricted space: the devil is in retrieving documents when it's time to remount the stream of composition on a forsaken project. I began weeks of writing footnotes for *Moby-Dick*, which we had very lightly annotated in the 1967 edition. Focusing on one task at a time, I was slow to realize how much remained to be done in the whole volume.

The recurrent terror was that I might not have the energy to take up the biography after pushing myself for many months on other projects. After all my research, I might not complete the biography. In *Clarel* young Clarel muses: "No incompletion's heaven ordained" (1.19.43). But Melville was haunted by lines from Wordsworth's "Malham Cove"—"Things incomplete, and purposes betrayed,/Make sadder transits o'er Truth's mystic glass,/Than noblest objects utterly decayed"—lines he read in 1861 in Henry Taylor's *Notes from Life in Seven Essays*. Late in life, apparently, as he struggled to complete old and new projects and get them into print, Melville quoted "purposes betrayed" in his "Rip Van Winkle's Lilacs."[23] Despite my fears, I had made a bargain, and repeatedly reconfirmed it. I would do the Norton Critical Edition with absolute good cheer for as long as it took, whatever the consequences. I would do the *Norton Anthology of American Literature* revisions when the time came, giving all my attention to the jobs joyously. Yet that unrealistic decision was repeatedly challenged, as on April 5, 2000: "trouble sleeping b/c of crush of NCE work. . . . anxious about time being consumed by NCE." I fought to keep such thoughts in abeyance, as on May 4: "Pride in doing a good job for the next generation of NCE users" and June 12: "Proud of achievement." Amid irregular disruptions for household labor and a series of traumas from deaths of friends and family, I "finished" the Norton Critical Edition on June 13. I noted: "Pride—just not the good thing I most wanted to be doing." The Norton Critical Edition, I knew, might even be exceptionally attractive, for Carol Bemis, the editor, had passed on to the designer my picture of the woodcut of the self-portrait of Tupai Cupa, the original of Queequeg. Then I stowed down and cleaned up in preparation for work on the *Norton Anthology of American Literature*. On June 15, 2000, I noted: "Exhausted from the long NCE haul—NCE took 5½ months." That was not looking ahead to the many weeks of proofreading the next year, 2001. I turned back to the biography and finished another full draft on December 10, but at a price: "7 November—Scary level of exhaustion—beyond self-pity—despair & fear that I may die in next weeks of the NCE and V2 even before BH [Brian Higgins] comes to work on *Pierre* and I have to work on the NAAL 6. Utter exhaustion."[24]

In January and February 2001 I worked on the *Norton Anthology of American Literature*, then on the twenty-sixth began proofing *Moby-Dick*, Heddy Richter reading aloud from a photocopy of the first edition, commas, caps, and all, while I held the new proofs. In March I wrote a foreword for a Northwestern University trade paperback of *Moby-Dick*. Proofing the Norton Critical text of *Moby-Dick* took weeks. Intermittently in May I rewired lamps for later installation and did other household chores and moved out of the way of a hired painter. In early June I mailed off the *Moby-Dick* and on July 11 mailed the anthology and by July 13 was back to work on the biography. In August I undertook a stringent cutting of the second volume in which, with the help of the copy editor, Alma MacDougall, I got it down from forty-three chapters to forty, like the first volume, and to a page length only slightly longer than the first. Then on August 14 the *New York Times* reported disturbing news: William Manchester could not hope to finish his trilogy on Churchill.[25] For many months I had been living with the fear that I was sacrificing the biography to the Norton Critical Edition and other projects. Well, now the biography was in shape good enough to be published. I would not, after all, suffer the fate of some writers of multivolume works.

On August 21 the gorgeous cover of the new Norton Critical Edition of *Moby-Dick* arrived, and the first copy of the book came on September 10, the day before 9/11. Any other time, I would have reveled in the splendor of Tupai Cupa tattooed in cobalt and gold. I kept working. On September 29 I mailed the disks for volume 2 to Johns Hopkins and the next day turned to work on the bibliographies for the anthology. On October 7, 2001: "This year—a blur—work, work, NCE, V2, NAAL—pushing, pushing." Good people had died during this labor. Merton M. Sealts, Jr.—Mert—died on June 4, 2000. On March 22, 2001, Andrew Costner, my uncle, died. On May 15, Essie Rogers Jones, my last part-Indian great-aunt, died at the age of one hundred, having, as I liked to say, lived in three centuries, but not very long in two of them. On June 4 Jeanne Shneidman died, the thanatologist Edwin Shneidman's wife, and on October 5, Lou Zara, who had befriended Leyda. On December 10 Harrison Hayford died. Holding the new Norton Critical Edition of *Moby-Dick* he had said to his son Charles, "A mountain of work."

Early in 2002 *Herman Melville: A Biography, 1851–1891* had to be proofread. For the cover Maurice Sendak drew a portrait of Melville partially shrouded by vines. Tony Kushner gave this account in his survey of Sendak's drawings for other people's books: "Among these are the two loving portraits of Melville, as a young man and in oppressive late middle age, that Sendak provided for Hershel Parker's giant two-volume biography. Sendak promised the portraits at the Melville conference at which he met Parker, in May 1991, five years before the first volume and eleven years before the second were ready for publication; when the books were ready, Sendak delivered. 'A man of his word,' says Parker" (188). I had in fact said just that in an e-mail to Kushner, and Sendak had done more than he promised in 1991—he had drawn two pictures, not the one I thought would be required, the second powerfully mysterious and evocative. Again, I was satisfied. Who would not like such a beautiful book filled with news about Melville?

✢ Chapter 5 ✢

FACTS THAT DO NOT SPEAK FOR THEMSELVES

In the December 1996 *New Criterion*, James W. Tuttleton pronounced me "innocent of a 'theory of biography,'" because I had not fitted events in Melville's life "to any Procrustean thesis about 'childhood development' or 'the nature of personality'" (26). He sternly exposed my blithe stumblebum excursion onto the rarefied terrain of literary biography: "Parker seems content to present the facts and let them, as it were, speak for themselves." Just as well, he decided: "This is all the more remarkable to me, and commendable, since Melville and his work have regularly been stove-in by a battering ram of Freudians, Jungians, Ericksonians, Lacanians, etc., looking for (and finding!) Oedipus complexes, world-class archetypes, signs of family incest, tropes of the omphalos, regressions to savagery, intimations of homosexuality, hints of heterosexuality, and, of all things, *symbolic* cannibalism" (26). The truth is that once word got out that I was going to write a biography, friends, acquaintances, and strangers thrust theories of biography on me. The world's greatest thanatologist, Edwin H. Shneidman, a Melvillean, confidentially asked which of two approaches I was going to take—Freudian or Jungian. I replied politely, for I loved Ed, but I had just fought my way free from an attractive but constrictive wrong-headed literary theory, the New Criticism, and an attractive but constrictive wrong-headed textual theory, W. W. Greg's rationale of copy-text, and was not about to put on a new set of blinders. I would, as always, accumulate as much evidence as I could and then see what story it told. Isn't that what real biographers did? But if Tuttleton is right, during the twelve years I wrote the biography I absolutely did not know what I was doing. Even now, I can't identify a single page where I let "the" facts, "as it were," or as it weren't, speak for themselves.[1] Tuttleton's sweeping accusation is worth looking at in some detail, for I thought that my process always was to identify facts before I could conceive of an episode and give it a new voice.

I would think that no biographer ever has "*the facts*." Even when an event is documented by several witnesses (as Melville's first meeting with Hawthorne was) we have only a fraction of "the" facts which the witnesses all could have put on record, if they had known or cared that what they were writing would be of high literary historical interest centuries later. A dozen or more other people who saw Melville and Hawthorne that day could have obliged by writing elaborate descriptions in diaries and letters all of which could have survived to be properly archived and made accessible. What I would give for their contributions toward the "facts"! Cornelius Mathews, caught up in his pride in his own reading of William C. Bryant's poem to the company and joy in escape from the city, promptly published his account of the day in the *Literary World* but said nothing about any time Melville and Hawthorne spent together. Years after Hawthorne's death in 1864 some other witnesses began to catch on that something momentous had occurred there in Hawthorne's life (if not Melville's). In 1871, two decades after the event, James T. Fields published his account of Hawthorne in the Berkshires in the February 1871 *Atlantic Monthly* (in time to be reprinted in the *New York Tribune* on January 18, 1871, and elsewhere), then he republished it early the next year in *Yesterdays with Authors* (Boston: James R. Osgood, 1872). Harry Sedgwick (who had seemed so young in 1850) in *Century Magazine* (August 1895) made his belated contribution to the accounts of that day, by that time recognized as memorable, especially for Hawthorne biography. The first to put Melville and Hawthorne alone together for a time on Monument Mountain was Melville's first biographer, J. E. A. Smith, in the articles he published in the *Pittsfield Sun* a few months after Melville's death. He had not attended the picnic himself and doubted what someone had told him, that Oliver Wendell Holmes was there, but he had the story that on a Berkshire excursion Melville and Hawthorne "were driven by a sudden summer shower under the shelter of a rock shelf on the west side of Bryant's Monument mountain, thoroughly wet. Thus baptized, they were brought into close communion." It is Smith's account which decades later burgeoned into legend, as you see in Merton M. Sealts, Jr.'s 1974 *Early Lives of Melville* (133).[2] Any biographer will tell you that he or she could not present all the facts and also tell you that the recovery of even the smallest of facts will often redirect a story.[3]

Tuttleton might have known that far too often what the biographer takes as established fact may be untrustworthy. In the 1930s Luther Mansfield's transcription of a holograph letter made Evert Duyckinck say that on the way up the mountain Hawthorne had looked "mildly" about for the Great Carbuncle of one of his stories. Mansfield's and every subsequent retelling of the Melville-Hawthorne meeting from Willard Thorp in 1938 on to the present has been tainted. Melville, we knew, had been performing acrobatics, climbing out onto an overhanging rock as if it were a bowsprit, almost ready, it seemed to some recent writers, to lasso the Devil's Pulpit and hand-walk the rope over to it. We did not know just how Hawthorne had behaved during the actual meeting. Only after my first volume was published did I transcribe the manuscript of Duyckinck's letter for myself and see that Hawthorne had *not* been looking "mildly" about for his Great Carbuncle. Instead, he had been hamming it up, looking "wildly" about in the crevices of rocks and roots of trees for the jewel he had written about long before—a story he took for granted that his companions knew. I noted my correction of the old misreading in the "Documentation" for the second volume of my biography, the best start I could make on publicizing it, although I have continued the campaign elsewhere.[4]

I and other biographers of Melville and Hawthorne had surmounted the problem of Hawthorne's only looking "mildly" about, for we knew that Hawthorne had written Horatio Bridge that he liked Melville "so much" that he had invited him to spend a few days with him, since Melville was only vacationing in the region. By itself, that invitation was extraordinary enough to alert us to Hawthorne's enthusiasm for Melville. We also had Fields's 1871 recollections of Hawthorne's manic behavior later that day in the Icy-Glen. Most of us managed to insist, partly against the evidence of "mildly," that Hawthorne had admired Melville almost as much as Melville was excited about meeting him, but we did not know how just how extravagantly (and uncharacteristically) Hawthorne had behaved when the two men first met. I am glad to see that in my biography I stressed that the attraction between Melville and Hawthorne was mutual, but I would have written the account differently if I had possessed the right word which was revealed by a powerful little "fact," my seeing a *w* instead of an *m*. To my knowledge, no biographer of Hawthorne or Melville has yet worked the correct reading into an account of the meeting, not Brenda Wineapple in her Knopf book on Hawthorne (2003) nor Andrew Delbanco in his Knopf book on Melville (2005), even though the correction was available in the 2002 second volume of my biography. It makes a tremendous difference, the reading of that one wobbly letter. I avoided many other little embarrassments and a few near disasters by making my own transcriptions, very often, even when the documents were in *The Melville Log* or quoted in other documentary works. When, I ask myself, does a biographer learn not to take *any* transcription on faith? No biographer has all the facts, *and the facts do not speak for themselves.*

Tuttleton did not understand that for every episode a biographer (I mean one who is writing from documents, not from other biographies) has to search facts out, try to verify them, then select them, organize them, and finally decide how to emphasize them. Facts are never able to speak "for themselves." They gain a voice only when they are used in a narrative. Many

times new facts and old facts collide so as to reveal an unknown shock to
Melville's inner life and an unknown episode in his outer life. Sometimes
they merely tease. Did Melville make an excursion to West Point to uncramp
his muscles after his first few winter months of work on his whaling book?
As a biographer I spotted a comment about such an excursion which might
have implied that Melville was the one who made it, since the writer thought
that whoever did make the excursion might make a good story of it. A luck-
ier or more industrious biographer may muster eyewitness testimony and
other exhibits until he or she has in hand what looks like a preponderance
of evidence that Melville went on that outing, or may discover clear and
convincing evidence of Melville's outing, or may even bring forth evidence
beyond a reasonable doubt such as records of Melville's visit in the diaries of
three Southern cadets, all respectful toward the acquaintance of Fayaway.[5]

   *Facts never speak for themselves but are given voice by the responsible imag-
ination of the biographer.* The term "responsible imagination" is not current
where you would expect it: I do not find it in the archives of the journal *Biography*. It does not recur in New Critical or New Historicist criticism. Rather,
it is applied now to present social needs, as in *Common Fire: Lives of Commitment in a Complex World* (edited by Laurent A. Parks Daloz, Cheryl H.
Keen, James P. Keen, and Sharon Daloz Parks), where it refers to "the sort
of imagination practiced by people 'committed to the common good'"—
by people who "appear to compare reality in a manner that can take into
account calls to help, catalyze, dream, work hard, think hard, and love well.
They practice an imagination that resists prejudice and its distancing tendencies on the one hand, and avoids messianic aspirations and their engulfing
tendencies on the other" (151). "Responsible imagination" is thus a religious
term, a self-help and socially conscious term. In a blurb for *Theology and
Literature: Rethinking Reader Responsibility* (edited by Clara A. B. Joseph
and Gayle Williams Ortiz), S. Brent Plate says: "Theology needs the literary
imagination and, indeed, will not survive without it. However, a responsible
imagination is never imagination for imagination's sake, for it is connected
to the gendered, ethnic, class, national, and postcolonial realities of identity,
of real people living in the world." In the examples that follow, I use it to
mean imagination that is based on and restrained by facts.

*A letter (apparently written around 1833) by Thomas Melvill, Jr. (Herman's
uncle), about two women who called at his parents' house in 1832, making
claims.* One benefit of working on my biography for a decade and a half
was that by the time the first volume was ready for print I or someone else
had solved most of the problems that had gnawed at me for months or years.

In this category goes the speculation about the two women who called at the home of Thomas Melvill, Sr., at some time between the deaths of Allan Melvill (Herman's father) in January 1832 and the senior Thomas Melvill in September 1832. Thomas Melvill, Jr.'s letter followed two or more which Lemuel Shaw, the executor of old Thomas Melvill's estate, had written about "Mrs. A. M. A.," and Thomas had replied, in a missing letter explaining (as he reiterated): "I feel confident that my good father *never saw,*—or at least *never knew,* or *conversed,* either with *her,* or *Mrs. B.*" They had called twice, seeing only Mrs. Melvill and her daughter Helen (Herman's aunt). Thereafter Thomas Junior had called on them and had succeeded "in dispelling the erroneous ideas they had formed of *claims,*" on his father based on something they were apparently owed by the late Allan Melvill, for they had formed erroneous ideas concerning the condition of his financial affairs. Thomas Junior had paid Mrs. B. something. The younger woman, Mrs. A. M. A., had later appealed to Shaw as executor in words that Thomas rejected:

> Mrs. A. M. A.—must be mistaken in stating that I *"gave her some encouragement".*—On what foundation could I give her encourage-ment? I had no means of my own. My brother left none—and I had strong reasons to think, that it would not be done, by those members of my own family who might have means, should the case be made known to them;—All of whom, except Helen, are to this day, as I presume, ignorant of her existence—
>
> From the little I saw of her, I thought her quite an interesting young person,—that it was most unfortunate she had not been brought up different—and I most deeply regret that she too, has been called to feel the disappointments & sorrows, so generally attending our earthly sojourn.—

This is undeniably mysterious. Thomas is at pains to say his father probably never heard of the two women's calling at the house and making requests. *Thomas,* the only surviving son, had been informed, presumably by both his mother and his sister Helen. If the matter were a mere business debt, keeping the news from the elder Melvill would hardly seem to have been required, since he knew he had allowed his son Allan to run through the whole of what would have been a great inheritance. Just possibly, however, the old man was so disturbed by his daughter-in-law Maria's being left penni-less with eight children that he could not bear to face his own folly in making advance after advance to his son. The most puzzling section of the letter is Thomas's comment on the way the "interesting" younger woman had been brought up, imperfectly provided for or imperfectly trained, it would seem, and certainly sorrowing.

Who knows what critics and scholars would have said if Melville had not written *Pierre*? But because Melville wrote *Pierre*, in which the hero learns that his father may have begotten an illegitimate daughter, Melvilleans leapt to the conclusion that *Pierre* was far more autobiographical than we had known—as autobiographical, say, as *Redburn*, if not *Omoo*. Amy Puett, who first published the letter from Thomas Melvill, Jr., took it as revealing that Melville's father had begotten an illegitimate daughter. Henry A. Murray, it emerged, had long ago come to the same conclusion as Puett. It was with this letter in mind (for he knew about it for decades) that Murray had seized on Mabel C. Weaks's report that Melville had written in an album, "Tell truth and shame the dead" (as I discuss later in this chapter). Others, including Philip Young, bought into the lurid story (Young being abetted by my obligingly sending him my printouts of Melville's cousin Priscilla's letters).[6] In "Allan Melvill's By-blow" Henry Murray (and his collaborators) identified the two women accurately as Ann Bent and her niece Ann Middleton Allen, importers of English and French goods, and found a telling connection between Allan Melvill and Ann Bent: "a letter from Allan Melvill to his father, dated December 23, 1823, instructing Major Melvill to pay a number of debts, one of which was to Ann Bent, in the amount of $7774" (4). However, Hayford in *Melville's Prisoners* (166–68) pointed out that the document in question involves $77.74, not $7774.00, and it asks the major to *collect* the money from Ann Bent, not to pay it to her. Hayford at last painstakingly demolished the theories, one seemingly well documented claim after another, in the process giving a detailed account of interchanges between and among a few Melville critics and scholars about their speculations and publications.[7] Hayford concluded: "It is uncritically imaginative literary biographers, not women like these [callers at the Melvill house], who seek and find satisfaction in such dubious revelations" (170). The melodramatic story had satisfied "a psychological need of unduly imaginative biographers." For that reason, people will believe the lurid story, perhaps even if the rest of the Melvill-Shaw correspondence is found. The need "for a good story," Hayford said, "will not be assuaged by any rational appeal to relative plausibilities." The best Hayford could do, he realized, was to persuade some readers "to classify this case as one more quandary in Melville biography" without, however, removing all mystery from Thomas Melvill, Jr.'s melodramatic tone (170).

Melville's trip to Illinois in 1840. Since 1985, thanks to Stanton Garner, we had an appalling newly recovered anecdote about Thomas Melvill, Jr., in

Galena, an early twentieth-century account of Melville's uncle being caught stealing from the till of his employer, Hezekiah Gear:

THOMAS MELVILL JR: "Oh, Captain, spare me."

HEZEKIAH GEAR: "You must make some restitution."

THOMAS MELVILL JR: "I can't, for the money is spent. It's been going on for years."

HEZEKIAH GEAR: "There is nothing to do. I could send you to prison for life, but that would not bring back the money. [He pauses for a moment then continues.] Major, for the sake of your good family and for the sake of your gray hair, I'll not punish you, but I never want to lay eyes on you again."[8]

Garner dated the incident to the early 1840s when Herman was in the Pacific, a time when it had minimal significance for Melville biography. Not working on the biography at the moment but simply wanting to put the document in the right year in the *Log*, I inched through unpublished letters in the Shaw Papers I had first looked through in 1962. There I discovered that Thomas Melvill acknowledged to Shaw that he had become suddenly unemployed early in 1840, although of course he did not reveal the true circumstances to Shaw. He never had a job in a store in Galena again, so this evidence ties the melodramatic story to early 1840. We knew that in early July Melville along with his friend Eli Fly, who had just resigned as the law clerk of Melville's uncle Peter, had arrived in Galena for a surprise visit, hoping to rise in the West with the help of his uncle, Major Melvill. If his uncle had been successful in Galena and the town had been flourishing, perhaps Herman would have stayed there indefinitely. Whether or not Herman learned his uncle had been caught stealing, I knew now that on his arrival the major was unemployed and unable to help even himself and his children, and certainly not his nephew. It takes almost no imagination to picture Melville's disappointment, although we do not know just what ingredients went into the bitter mix. Much sooner than Leon Howard had thought, Melville returned home, with consequences for literature—his signing on a whaling voyage.

What Melville did when he returned from Illinois. In a very damaged but still *just* decipherable letter in the Augusta Papers, Elizabeth Gansevoort, from Bath, New York, on September 2, 1840, pleaded with her cousin Augusta to visit her: "you have a Brother that I *know has nothing else to do*, and would be willing to come with you." This was a letter so pale that I had to gird myself up to struggle with it. Once I read it, I did a survey of the family and decided that the brother had to be Herman, home already from Galena, and home for some time, unlike what Leon Howard had thought. At some point I made the connection to "Loomings," where Ishmael explains that when he goes to sea as a simple sailor the officers order him about in a way that is "unpleasant enough." He goes on: "It touches one's sense of honor, particularly if you come of an old established family in the land, the Van Rensselaers, or Randolphs, or Hardicanutes. And more than all, if just previous to putting your hand into the tar-pot, you have been lording it as a country schoolmaster, making the tallest boys stand in awe of you. The transition is a keen one, I assure you, from a schoolmaster to a sailor." Knowing that Melville had returned from Galena much earlier than we had thought, I decided that in late 1840 Melville, like Ishmael, might have gone more or less directly from schoolmaster to whaler. In the first volume I ventured a guess: "Late that summer, for all we know, he may very well have looked for another job teaching school around Lansingburgh" (179). In 1999 a new document emerged from the liquor box in Paul Metcalf's house—papers loaned to his mother by her second cousin, Agnes Morewood. Gansevoort had written to Allan on October 6, 1840: "I am very glad that Herman has taken a school so near home." From the documents available to anyone at the Massachusetts Historical Society I had discovered a story of a hopeful trip to Illinois and a poignant disappointment. What I cautiously proposed about school-teaching was only an educated guess, phrased as such ("for all we know"), one happily verified three years after the volume was published.

"Only an educated guess," I just admitted. That warrants a comment about Leon Howard, a shrewd, responsible scholar, browbeaten, as he said, into working from Leyda's yet-unpublished *Log* rather than spending years himself in the archives. Howard was not a years-in-the-archives man. He was the sort of scholar who would chat up the director of a library, look over a famous manuscript with him (male in those years), and come to reasonable conclusions about it that more pedestrian workers might plod away for a long time without perceiving. On Melville Howard made many educated guesses which by my tally were without exception wrong. The problem was that given two or more choices the would-be rational Howard always pushed Melville into taking the sensible one. Informed, or I might say *beaten down* by a much greater mass of evidence, I became predisposed to accept irregular, illogical behavior from Melville. After a time I was never surprised when he ran headlong away from the course that his mother and I thought represented his own best interests. On the matter of what Melville did after returning from Galena and before trying to find work in New York City then signing on a whaler, I merely considered what he would naturally have done once he was back in Lansingburgh. In instances where evidence has later emerged, my record with educated guesses is, I think, perfect, and I would not be surprised to learn that other biographers who have toiled in the archives would bet serious money on their own best educated guesses. We are far from infallible, but when we are forced to guess, we may bring an imposing array of evidence to the topic, even if our reasons have to be dragged up from a murky level of consciousness and even if, as in this instance, they involve taking some of the details in a piece of fiction like "Loomings" as possibly autobiographical.[9]

Cousin John's report on Maria Melville's shopping list. In the Augusta Papers is a charming letter to Maria Melville in Lansingburgh from Cousin John in Troy dated Monday morning, August 30. Humorously headed "(Commercial.)," the letter is a report on John's efforts to supply the items on Maria's shopping list: "Pine apples are out of season; not *one* in market. Smoked Salmon—*none* to be found to-day. . . . Cocoa nut cakes, sugar plums & almonds, the 'pair' selected on Saturday as a present, and 2 pounds Lemon powder, accompany this."[10] On July 31, 1988, by using a perpetual calendar I saw that the possible Lansingburgh years were 1841 and 1847. Because of Maria's extremely straitened circumstances, 1841 was out of the question so the year had to be 1847. (I later identified the writer as Herman's second cousin John Van Schaick, who had briefly been engaged to Augusta, and found another letter corroborating the year.) Biographers forget that famous writers and their families sometimes celebrate happy occasions just as normal people do. We knew Melville took Lizzie to Canada for their honeymoon. It never occurred to us that Maria would give a party for the newlyweds after they arrived in Lansingburgh on August 27. She had not had a party in two decades, but her impoverished life seemed about to take a turn for the better, and she sent out invitations on both sides of the Hudson. I phrase that extravagantly on the basis of a single surviving note from across the river declining the invitation, but Guert Gansevoort's mother would have been invited from Waterford (the best I can tell, they were still there) and Peter Gansevoort and his family from Albany. When I discovered the nature of the party I was so overjoyed for the long-suffering Maria that it took me several days to get around to being happy for Herman and Lizzie. Again, this shopping list did not "speak for itself" until I dated it and realized what the party was for and how much giving it ("throwing it," I want to say) meant to Maria Gansevoort Melville, who had been trained to behave grandly and had suffered much for many years.

Why Melville started Redburn *when he did.* On July 23, 1989, I transcribed the start of a diary by Thomas Melville (Herman's younger brother) on the

Navigator which had been dated "[1860?]" by the New York Public Library. According to the diary, the ship left the pier at the foot of Maiden Lane on Monday, May 28, and anchored off the Battery for three days. My perpetual calendar told me that the possible years were 1849 and 1855. Tom had been a whaler for years, but that experience did not count in a merchant ship. He was still a "boy" in rank, according to the diary, but I knew from letters in the early 1850s that his rank would have been higher in 1855. The year was 1849, easy to confirm by going to a newspaper. The May 28 "Marine Journal" of the *New York Tribune* listed the *Navigator* with Captain Putnam (Tom wrote Putman) as cleared for Canton. On May 31 Herman along with Henry Thurston (the young brother-in-law of Herman's brother Allan) went aboard the *Navigator* to see Tom off. On April 5 Melville had written to his friend Evert Duyckinck about his ambition to write a still greater book than *Mardi*: "But live & push—tho' we put one leg forward ten miles—its no reason the other must lag behind—no, *that* must again distance the other—& so on we go till we get the cramp & die." He had also expressed a contradictory fantasy: "I bought a set of Bayle's Dictionary the other day, & on my return to New York intend to lay the great old folios side by side & go to sleep on them thro' the summer, with the Phaedon in one hand & Tom Brown in the other." Yet on June 5, he wrote to Richard Bentley:

> I have now in preparation a thing of a widely different cast from "Mardi":—a plain, straightforward, amusing narrative of personal experience—the son of a gentleman on his first voyage to sea as a sailor—no metaphysics, no conic-sections, nothing but cakes & ale. I have shifted my ground from the South Seas to a different quarter of the globe—nearer home—and what I write I have almost wholly picked up by my own observation under comical circumstances. In size the book will be perhaps a fraction smaller than "Typee"; will be printed here by the Harpers, & ready for them two or three months hence, or before. I value the English Copyright at one hundred & fifty pounds.

Those are facts. By a day or two or three or four after Tom sailed, Melville had in hand *Redburn*, whatever he was calling it then—a book he dedicated in due course to his "younger brother, Thomas Melville, Now a Sailor on a Voyage to China."

Now was time to visualize the scenes, particularly Herman's going aboard the *Navigator*. The oldest brother, Gansevoort, dead in 1846, had seen Herman off for Liverpool in 1839, almost exactly ten years earlier, and Tom was ten and a half years younger than Herman. In 1849 Tom looked uncannily like Herman had looked in 1839, and now Herman was playing Gansevoort's role. I knew that Melville characteristically responded in a powerful way when something momentous happened in a place where something else of high significance to him had occurred. Loving Tom as he did (concerned enough in 1846 to go to Westport, Massachusetts, to see him off on a whaling voyage), he was stirred by Tom's departing on the *Navigator* on such a long and, he knew better than anyone else in the family, dangerous voyage. What were the odds that Tom would return safely, if at all? I assumed that Herman was moved by memories of Gansevoort and himself in 1839. Seeing Tom off, I thought, would hurl him back into memories of the poverty that had driven him to sea at nineteen, just before he was twenty. I assumed that the psychological effects of seeing Tom off were stunning if not downright hallucinatory: for Herman, looking at Tom must always have been a little bewildering, like looking in a slightly flattering mirror and seeing his younger self. I assumed all this on my detailed knowledge of a powerful recurrent phenomenon in Melville's life and works, as I explain in chapter 18.

I assumed that it was seeing Tom off that made Melville think of starting, just then, a fictionalized version of his own first voyage. Melville must have thought that this was a brilliant idea for a simple job. He could dash the book off mainly from memory and redeem himself from the two years spent on the failing *Mardi*. I also assumed that, as it turned out, writing semi-autobiographically proved much more dangerous than Melville had thought. John Sturrock in "The New Model Autobiographer," contrasts "the old kind of autobiography" (such as the guarded kind I present to you in the chapter on *The New Melville Log*, for instance) with the "higher degree of candor" which is reached "when the autobiographer sets off in pursuit of the unlit portions of his past rather than the lit ones and produces revelations that were revelations to himself too" (62). Melville may have done something this daring as he approached and continued the writing of *Clarel*. I would adapt Sturrock's words for *Redburn* to say that Melville did not set off in pursuit of those unlit portions but blundered into them, his reckless exploitation of his childhood opening him to rapid psychological growth which made possible the strongest parts of *White-Jacket*. Melville started writing *Moby-Dick* eight months after starting *Redburn*, knowing by then that the pursuit of both lit and unlit portions of his past would produce new revelations. Then, all aware, late in 1851 he continued his pursuit, more recklessly than ever, in *Pierre*.

Tom's 1849 diary entries did not speak for themselves, but I made a strong story out of the bare facts. I do not have a document in Melville's hand which says, all coolly, "the reason I started *Redburn* when I did was that Tom was just then sailing for China and my seeing him off reminded me strongly of Gansevoort's seeing me off on my first voyage. That in turn led to some curiously powerful memories." Some critics who had never set foot in the Melville archives would demand an affidavit. Such Lady Catherine de Bourgh critics make themselves feel good by revealing how scrupulous *they* would have been if ever *they* had confronted biographical evidence: *they* would have been great proficients.[11]

    I come back to Tom's bit of a diary in other chapters, for like the revolving Drummond Light that P. T. Barnum installed on Broadway, its implications ray "away from itself all round it" so that other episodes are "lit by it" (*The Confidence-Man*, chap. 44).

Melville's hope to make a Grand Tour in 1849–50. Because we know that Melville was back at home in New York City at the beginning of February 1850, we have always discounted newspaper reports from the time of his departure that he planned to be gone for a year. Those papers back in October 1849 must have been wrong, we assumed. We knew how joyously enthusiastic he was on the *Southampton* when planning itineraries, as in the October 15 journal entry: "This afternoon Dr Taylor & I sketched a plan for going down the Danube from Vienna to Constantinople; thence to Athens in the steamer; to Beyroot & Jerusalem—Alexandria & the Pyramids. . . . I am full (just now) of this glorious *Eastern* jaunt. Think of it!—Jerusalem & the Pyramids—Constantinople, the Egean, & old Athens!" We also knew how philosophical he sounded in his diary for November 17 when he finally accepted the fact that he could not afford to go on his own Grand Tour: "Bad news enough—I shall not see Rome—I'm floored—appetite unimpaired however—so down to the Edinburgh Castle & paid my compliments to a chop." Naively, we took him at his word. Once I focused on the journal entries and saw that Melville had indeed hoped to stay away many months if he could, gathering material for his books in the company of a cousin of the younger travel-writer Bayard Taylor, I concluded that Melville seldom wanted anything so much as he wanted to travel for many months or even an entire year when he left New York in October 1849. I imagined his failure to sell *White-Jacket* fast enough at a high enough price was a profound disappointment. I decided, with no explicit statement to back me up, that Melville in the course of early and mid-1850 came to feel that in returning to the United States so soon he had behaved in an exemplary fashion. By then he had forgiven himself for spending too long on the unpopular *Mardi* (hadn't he paid for that by writing two books in one summer?) and as he worked on the whaling book became increasingly resentful at having been so very good in abandoning his plans for a Grand Tour. I think his desire to move to the Berkshires and be near Hawthorne was involved with his sense that he had made a major renunciation and deserved to do something that he now wanted, whatever his wife, mother, and sisters thought of leaving a Manhattan house with flush toilets and hot water running up to the third floor. Did I invent the disappointment over abandoning the fantasy of the Grand Tour? Had I become such a connoisseur of Melville's painful disappointments that would I invent new ones in my nineteenth-century misery memoir?

Then in 2010 William Reese shared with me the letter to Melville's British publisher, Richard Bentley, on November 10, 1849, in which Melville hoped that Bentley could return from Brighton in time to see him on the twelfth. In any case, he wrote, "I trust that at a more genial season—in the Spring—I shall return, & that we shall then become pleasantly acquainted." Melville expected still to sell *White-Jacket* for enough to pay for months of frugal travel in Europe and the Levant which would then be repaid by the books he would write about his new travels. Already from the evidence at hand in the 1990s I had decided just how miserably disappointed Melville had been and how reconciling himself to the disappointment had affected him in the next many months. The newspaper accounts were accurate.

How Melville's essay on Hawthorne pained Washington Irving. Here is something that had been lying around for a hundred and twenty years. Through my pursuit of that English crook Thomas Powell, I picked up the modern scholarly edition of Irving's *Life of Goldsmith* which quoted from Pierre M. Irving's *The Life and Letters of Washington Irving* (1864). The nephew of the author recalled Powell's slurs of the great writer and also the insult from another contemporary who called Irving a self-acknowledged imitator of Goldsmith. Shocked, I realized the modern editor had not recognized the phrase as coming from Melville's anonymous 1850 essay on "Hawthorne and His *Mosses*" in the *Literary World*. Ever since 1864 there had been in print evidence that Melville's reference to Irving had hurt the old man, so badly that years later his nephew-biographer Pierre was still furious and still putting the best face on things in his bland account in the biography. We don't use our imaginations: *we* bleed when someone prints something nasty about us, but we expect that *Irving* would have been superior to that sort of pain. Here is Pierre Irving's account of things:

It was some months after this [the attacks by Thomas Powell] that I mentioned to him an article I had been reading in a weekly periodical, in which the writer, evidently alluding to his [Irving's] preface in his biography of Goldsmith, styles him, in an invidious spirit, "a self-acknowledged imitator of that author." At the close of that preface, the reader may remember he addresses Goldsmith in the language of Dante's apostrophe to Virgil. . . . He smiled; said he meant only to express his affectionate admiration of Goldsmith, but it would never do for an author to acknowledge anything. Was never conscious of an attempt to write after any model. No man of genius ever did. From his earliest attempts, everything fell naturally from him. His style, he believed, was as much his own as though Goldsmith had never written—as much his own as his voice.

This was not the language of self-eulogy, but of quiet self-vindication. He had never meant to warrant such perversion of his quotation, any more than Dante meant to confess himself an imitator of Virgil. There were undoubtedly qualities of style as well as mental and moral characteristics in which he resembled both Goldsmith and Addison, the two with whom he is most frequently compared, while in others it would be impossible to confound them. (Parker, *The Powell Papers*, 214)

I know just how much Irving was hurt and how outraged Pierre was because in the Berg Collection of the New York Public Library is a note about this in Pierre's hand: "Using his words against him." What hurt the most was that the anonymous author in the *Literary World* had used Irving's own words against him, perverting them, both Irvings thought.

We had known some of the story. Irving had treated Gansevoort Melville graciously in London in 1846 (where Gansevoort was secretary of the American legation) and had become the godfather to the American edition of *Typee* by recommending that George Putnam accept it. Then, surely, when Minister Louis McLane next saw Irving he must have denounced Gansevoort to him, for he had been trying for months to persuade James Buchanan to remove him from the legation. As far as we know, Irving, the consummate good old boy, never spoke or wrote Herman Melville's name again. Questions remain. Did Pierre Irving and his uncle know who wrote the essay on Hawthorne's *Mosses*? They could easily have found out, and the wonder is that Duyckinck, as editor of the *Literary World*, did not censor the insult no matter how rushed he was to get the praise of Hawthorne into print. In some bookstore or other did Melville read this passage from the biography in 1864, and realize how much pain he had inflicted on the man whose influence had been so strong, as late as *Redburn* and even long afterward?

Eli Fly's dying message to Herman Melville. On March 4, 1854, Maria Melville wrote to her daughter Augusta from Longwood, near Boston:

> The next morning Miss Titmarsh called . . . Lizzie, the Judge & I were alone in the room, & Mrs Shaw very much engaged. So we had all her conversation. The subject happened to be about Hingham. In one of the pauses I enquired if she knew Mr Fly. Oh yes the most interesting man she had ever seen. She did not wonder, that notwithstanding his bad health Miss Hinkley had married him. I then enquired about his death. Mr Fly had left a message to Herman said Mrs Titmarsh, looking at the Judge & something about a Cloake, Sir, I believe which Mr Melville had given him? A post mortem examination had taken place, one lung was entirely gone, of the other but half remained. The widow was inconsolable.

The deathbed scene is Dickensian, and Thackeray used the pen name "Michael Angeleo Titmarsh," but this real Mary T. Tidmarsh lived in Hingham all through the 1850s. I was haunted by the scene, inexplicably moved by Fly's dying message to Herman Melville. Who would not be intrigued by "something about a Cloake" which Herman had given him? Perhaps this was a most mundane fact, but it was what you could fairly describe as a deathbed message, and it just may not be mundane.

In the liquor box which Paul Metcalf opened in 1999 was a letter from Gansevoort to Allan on January 14, 1841, after Herman had sailed on the *Acushnet*:

> Fly called to see me on Sunday last and dined at Bradford's. He manages to scrape along on the slender salary which he receives from Mr Edwards. He is very attentive to his duties, & steady & regular in his habits. In the end he will doubtless succeed. Herman sent to Fly as a parting souvenir his vest & pantaloons. The coat was exchanged at New Bedford for duck shirts &c. At sea shore toggery is of no use to a sailor.

Is it possible that Fly, knowing he was dying, wanted to remind Herman that in 1841 if not longer he had dressed in the vest and pantaloons

of an impoverished young whaleman who later became one of the greatest American writers? Possible. Dickens, with what Melville thought was his
over-plotting, would have made this so. I would not put it in a biography as
fact, but I like the story I imagine. *Something about a vest and pantaloons . . .*

Melville's inscription in an autograph album in the 1850s. In the 1940s
someone showed Mabel C. Weaks at the New York Public Library an 1850s
autograph album that someone had carried about the Berkshires gathering
signatures of celebrities. Weaks later told Henry A. Murray that Melville
had written in it, "Tell truth and shame the dead." Murray applied this news
to his reading of *Pierre* as Melville's willful shaming of his father (because,
Murray thought, he had begotten an illegitimate daughter). When Murray
first told me of the inscription in this album I knew nothing of the letter
on which Murray based his belief, but I knew Shakespeare. I thought, but
did not say out loud, something like, "Ah, what a bitter play on Hotspur's
speech." Then, on reflecting, I realized that Melville had not been playing
on Hotspur's words at all—he had been quoting them: "Tell truth and shame
the devil." Melville habitually spelled that last word "devel," and in his hand
"devel" could look like "dead." I tried this out on Hayford, as I usually did,
and Sealts, then diffidently suggested it to Murray, who, it turned out, had
not recognized the quotation as coming from *Henry IV, Part 1.*
    On October 13, 1971, Murray wrote me with his usual gentlemanly com-
plimentary disdain, for he knew there was a great gulf fixed between his
imaginative self and plodding pedants (and Hayford and others were guilty of
encouraging him to think so):

> All the work that you have done and are doing is of intense interest
> to me, and, as I told Jack [Putnam], I look up to you as 100 per cent
> dependable ever since you persuaded me that one of my readings of
> HM's hand-writing was probably wrong. "Tell the truth and shame
> the dead" ("devil" was your guess), although by telling the truth about
> his dead father, HM believed that he *had* shamed him, even though,
> let us say, that hive of moralistic dicta, Benjamin Franklin, was widely
> venerated despite his illegitimate children, one of whom became
> Governor of New Jersey. Someday that album containing short state-
> ments by famous men will probably be re-discovered—maybe by
> you—and your reading will be confirmed, in which case the question
> (which you might consider more often than you do) will arise: what
> significance, if any, does it have? Was HM, for instance, admonishing
> himself for telling so many lies (and thus honoring the devil)?

We do not have the actual album. We have the "fact" of Weaks's telling Murray what she read in it. We have Murray's use of what she told him. He did not know Melville's actual words, I thought, though neither of us had seen the album. We have my attempt in the biography to put the presumed inscription briefly in the context of Melville's allegorizing his own sufferings of the mid-1850s in "I and My Chimney," where he was acting as an allegorical Come-Outer, about the same time that he allegorically portrayed the Devil as offering satanic assurance that nothing is amiss in America at the time, say, of Bleeding Kansas. I concluded: "Melville signed the autograph book with a resolute determination not to surrender, not . . . to allow his chimney to be razed: 'Tell Truth, and shame the Devel'" (2:261). Weaks's fact did not speak clearly for itself, I was sure. Does it speak, in my biography, and again here?

The fact of the death of Lemuel Shaw in 1861. Biographers had done nothing with the death of Melville's father-in-law, even though with that death Melville had lost the last man in Boston who genuinely loved him. Knowing it had to have been big news, with Shaw as chief justice of the Massachusetts Supreme Court, even at the end of March and the start of April 1861, with the nation divided and almost at war, I determined to fill in the record in the *Log* and see what I could learn for the biography. I went to a dozen or so Boston papers in one of my favorite haunts, the Boston Public Library. In several of the papers I found long reports on the funeral, which was literally a state, or commonwealth, funeral, under the direction of the Bar Association's "Committee of Arrangements" rather than the family, with elaborate sequences of taking seats and prescribed areas of seating. Because of an extraordinary late-winter storm, not everything went as planned. Some people who had expected to be there could not brave the storm. (One was Clifford, the former governor who had told Melville the story of Agatha Hatch.) There may be more facts to be brought forward about Melville and the others at the funeral, but none of this solemn occasion had been part of Melville biography before I retrieved many facts from the newspapers. For now, no one besides me has thought and imagined much of anything about this momentous occasion, one of the most solemn in Melville's life. Do other documented episodes in Melville's life lie waiting to be discovered and brought to life—first by our research and later by our responsible imaginations? Or first by a low order of imagination—just by realizing that there has to be evidence surviving, then looking for it and interpreting it?

As so often happens, I reached out for one thing and found at least two. The Boston papers gave long quotations from the funeral oration delivered by

Shaw's friend Orville Dewey, the man who had baptized the three younger Melville children. I had much evidence from Melville's writings that helped me see how a man taught Dutch Church Calvinism by his mother would have regarded the quasi-religious beliefs of a company of Boston and New York Unitarians. After Melville's friend Dr. John Wakefield Francis in 1819 helped find a forum for the first Boston Unitarian to preach in Manhattan, a man approached him with the furious accusation that he had "permitted heresy to come in among us, and have countenanced its approach" by furnishing accommodations "for the devil's disciples." Knowing of Dewey's high-sounding and much-applauded recent lecture series, Melville early in 1852 had satirically given young Pierre an invitation to lecture on the same fatuously exalted topic. Now Melville listened as Dewey, an intimate friend of William C. Bryant, ended the sermon with a quotation from "Thanatopsis." What was Melville thinking?

Lizzie's poem on steadfastness. Jay Leyda printed in the *Log* for May 8, 1869, a poem Lizzie wrote which was suggested, her note said, by a sermon by Henry W. Bellows at All Souls Church. It begins: "'Hold on,' my soul, with courage for the 'fight'/'Hold out' my feet, the weary 'course' to run." This does not seem like a very significant fact. Luckily, at some point Merton M. Sealts, Jr., sent me a photocopy of it, and, years later, on June 12, 1999, I looked at it to check the transcription for the *Log* and saw that, yes, there was a tiny loop at the end of last number in the year, but the number was 7, not 9 — 1867. The poem was dated some time after Lizzie had consulted Henry Bellows about her unhappiness with Melville and about her half brothers' offer to let her return to 49 Mount Vernon Street, leaving her husband in New York City. Taking time from his plans for a tour of the Holy Land, Bellows had suggested a lurid fake kidnapping which Samuel Shaw had rejected in a letter dated May 6. Bellows may have called on Lizzie for a consoling visit after he received Sam's letter and before Lizzie wrote her poem. (On May 18 he called before boarding the *Ville de France*, but missed her; she wrote him on the twentieth not realizing he had sailed.)

Lizzie retained her poem as her private record of her decision not to yield to her Boston family's officious advice that she might leave her husband. This "fact" did not speak fully for itself to Leyda when he prepared the *Log* and would not have spoken even if he had dated it correctly, since he did not know about the letters Donald Kring published from the Bellows Papers in the 1975 *Proceedings of the Massachusetts Historical Society.* When I received the photocopy from Sealts I thought only that Lizzie's misery and resolution had stretched two years beyond the crisis Kring had discovered.

The *fact* of the poem did not speak powerfully until the moment that I dated it correctly: as so often, this episode of biography emerged from grub work on the *Log*. Sealts for whatever reason had sent me a photocopy so of course I must sooner or later check it against Leyda's transcription. I respected Elizabeth Shaw Melville more than ever because I knew the immediate context in which she drew on a sermon of Bellows's (possibly the one on May 5, 1867) in recording her resolution to endure her marriage.

Melville's flight to Staten Island in 1872. The *Log* for June 2, 1872, prints this from Catherine (Kate) Gansevoort's diary while she was in Staten Island at the mansion occupied by the governor of Sailors' Snug Harbor, Melville's youngest brother, Thomas: "Cousin Herman & Lizzie are staying here." Other entries that summer show Melville in New York, you would think at home on Twenty-sixth Street as usual, but a letter from Thomas and his wife dated August 4 says this: "Herman & Lizzie left here yesterday for Pittsfield where they will stay some days & then go to Gansevoort." Telling events of 1872 badly out of order, Leon Howard skipped over these clues. After Melville's brother Allan's death in February 1872 Maria Gansevoort Melville failed rapidly and died at the Governor's Mansion in April. Lizzie soon took her daughters to Boston but Herman (and Stanwix) stayed in Staten Island, Herman commuting to work by the ferry. Leaving the girls in Boston, Lizzie returned not to Twenty-sixth Street but joined Herman in Staten Island. They were there when Stanwix left for Kansas. They stayed on all summer, until Herman's vacation in August, and afterward went back to Staten Island. Herman and Lizzie did not return to Twenty-sixth Street until late October or early November.

This flight from Twenty-sixth Street had never been remarked on. I decided that Herman and Lizzie were so broken by the two latest deaths in the family that they took refuge in the great Governor's Mansion while weeks turned into months, half a year in all. Tom and his wife, Katie, were hospitable—all the easier because they had many rooms and a full staff of servants. During early July, especially, while dozens of Manhattanites were dying of heat, Lizzie rejoiced at being in cooler Staten Island. Herman at least got to enjoy the cooler nights though he commuted to work as usual by ferry. There were immediate benefits and long-term literary consequences. As I said in the biography (2:744), that summer "was Melville's best chance to improve his acquaintance with the more notable of the four hundred or so pensioners at the Sailors' Snug Harbor." An obvious possibility, overlooked by critics, is that some of what Melville experienced in 1872 may have gone into his late prose and poetry about sailors, particularly superannuated sailors. Melville lived on Staten Island for half a year—a long enough time for us to try to visualize what living there meant to him.

March 26, 1885, the day Melville's wife and his cousin Catherine (Kate) Gansevoort Lansing went shopping (allowing me to re-create one scene from a shopping list and another from notes on a shopping expedition). This is an entry from Cousin Kate's diary which I transcribed in 1998: "Lizzie Melville called while I was eating breakfast. Went out to-gether—to *Kropman.* 5 E. 17*th* St. *Brentano's* ordered magazine The Contemporary for Sept. 1884." The women, both swathed entirely in black, we know from other evidence, although that fact is not in the diary entry, went to Brentano's to order a back issue of a London magazine, the *Contemporary Review,* which (the diary entry does *not* say), they knew contained W. Clark Russell's article in which Melville was praised very highly—where the sayings of the men in the forecastle scene in *Moby-Dick* were compared to the language of "some giant mind of the Shakespearean era." Soon after Kate's copy of the magazine arrived in this country some members of the family for the first time took Herman Melville seriously as an important writer. Some of them began reading *Moby-Dick.* This shopping expedition was of the utmost importance, for no one in the family except his daughter Frances was ever disrespectful of Melville's writing again. Thrilled, almost overwhelmed at the revelation in Kate's entry, at first I envisioned sympathetic weather, a blustery winter day, black skirts whipped about, but in sober fact by noon it was around forty degrees and the Signal Service Bureau accurately indicated fair, warmer weather, following March 25, which had been a day of "sunshine and mellowing weather" on which the dying President Grant could be taken outdoors. I did the weather when writing this chapter, using Delaware's database for the *New York Times,* having failed with the American Historical Newspapers database. Cousin Kate's little record still clutches my heart when I read it. In my mind it is still one of the most heart-stirring scenes in the biography. It's the *dryness* that stirs me most, the noncommittal matter-of-fact item in a rich woman's list of a day's errands in lower Manhattan. And it reminds me that we have not exhausted the Gansevoort-Lansing Collection of the New York Public Library after all these decades of dipping into it. If I found this item when I was using an Amtrak commuter ticket to look at all the documents I could before retiring from Delaware and moving far away (if the house in Landenberg, Pennsylvania, sold), what else is still there, undiscovered, in that collection?

Herman Melville himself said that he stood for the heart, not the head. I stand for the fact which stirs the biographer to responsible imagination. Here

I quote (and will quote it later) Emory Elliott's modernist house-cleaning in the *Columbia Literary History of the United States*, where he rejects "the old records, diaries, letters, newspapers, official firsthand documents, or statistical figures examined by the historian." Elliott declares that "the historian is not a truthteller but a storyteller, who succeeds in convincing readers that a certain rendition of the past is 'true' not by facts but by persuasive rhetoric and narrative skill" (xvii). As much as I aspire to "persuasive rhetoric and narrative skill," I always begin with "the old records, diaries, letters, newspapers, official firsthand documents, or statistical figures," the nearest I can get to the "facts." My most profound emotions and highest imagination were evoked and engaged as I lived year after year with "the old records, diaries, letters, newspapers," and other documents from Melville's life. The emotions and the imagination always were restrained and disciplined by the facts, but the emotions and the imagination always suffused the stories that emerged from the facts, facts which never once spoke to me for themselves.

✢ *Chapter 6* ✢

DESIDERATA AND NEW DISCOVERIES IN TRADITIONAL ARCHIVES AND DATABASES

THE BRILLIANT, COVETOUS, MANIPULATIVE, generous, secretive psychologist Henry Murray liked to hoard Melville documents, and he lived long enough to hoard some of them for more than half a century. Toward the end of his life he toyed with a few Melville scholars by alluding tantalizingly to what he thought he knew about Melville's "imaginary sister" and about Melville's homecoming from the Pacific. After he died, Murray's widow came upon an extraordinary document, the letter Allan Melville wrote to his brother Herman on October 16, 1844, after Herman had notified him of his arrival in Boston. That letter, once Nina Murray sent me a copy, led me to identify the long-puzzling handwriting on the October 1844 note in the *Log* announcing Herman's return and a companion note in his brother Allan's hand (in the Augusta Papers), also announcing Herman's imminent arrival in Lansingburgh. I saw that the note in the *Log* was in Herman's own hand, in a setup for surprising his mother. Now, two or three of the handful of active Melville researchers like to sit on their discoveries just until they have tied up the episode neatly, but electronic databases have made even brief sitting on documents riskier than ever before: sit too long (unless you have a unique document in your pocket) and you get scooped. Dennis Marnon, Geoffrey Sanborn, George Monteiro, Scott Norsworthy, and I have all been scooped. We are in an era of simultaneous discovery unlike any since the day in the 1940s when Jay Leyda and Wilson Heflin collided in the National Archives, having both filled out call slips for the log of the USF *United States*.[1] To make great Internet discoveries you don't have to be a lifelong Melville researcher like Monteiro or me, either. You can have a Ph.D. in medieval literature and a non-academic day job and be an Internet surfer and archive raider like Scott Norsworthy—but then you would also need his exceptionally keen nose for the highest class of buried Melvillean truffles.

The most notoriously missing Melville items are some of his letters to Hawthorne. At first, the Hawthorne family regarded the letters as essential material for describing the poorly documented Lenox interlude, and later, but not too late for Julian (Hawthorne's son, like Murray, long-lived), they were of monetary value, too valuable for the Hawthorne descendants to destroy. I long suspected that Murray in the 1920s had bought some of these letters, for he was one of the few Melville fanatics who had ample money and means of access to the Hawthorne descendants. Before Nina Murray sold the Francis Street house in Cambridge I diplomatically suggested that she might look for a wall safe in the study behind the boards that Murray had torn off the barn at Arrowhead. Possibly thinking I was a mad Jamesian biographer instead of a dogged Melvillean, she declined to wreck a perfectly good wall. If the new owners rent a metal detector or simply take up a crowbar will they find a safe behind the siding, and in it some letters to Hawthorne? These missing letters to Hawthorne go high in any list of desiderata, but the highest place of all will always be accorded to a letter we have to assume Melville himself destroyed, Hawthorne's letter in praise of *Moby-Dick*. Imagine the auction value, especially if Melville made on it any notes for his reply!

The texts of the letters to Hawthorne are known (although those known only in transcriptions may contain errors). Unless there are still more letters the Hawthorne descendants have left unpublished, startling new revelations are not to be expected. However, we might see Melville's place in the New York literary world somewhat differently if we had the full text of Melville's splendidly intimate letter to Nathaniel Parker Willis from London which Willis excerpted in the January 12, 1850, *Home Journal* ("I very much doubt whether Gabriel enters the portals of Heaven without a fee to Peter the porter—so impossible is it to travel without money. . . ."). Decades later Jay Leyda had forgotten why he chose in his 1951 "Biographical Notes" to refer to the Willis "documents thus far opened for general use" (xxxiv). I took Leyda's subtleties of language very seriously. It was his elliptical account of Thomas Powell in the "Biographical Notes" that set me off on decades of research, at last reported in *The Powell Papers*, the title of which was taken from another of Melville's letters written from London late in 1849. Hoping Leyda's wording reflected special knowledge of Willis's papers that had to be kept secret in the mid-twentieth century, I sent out not dozens but hundreds of letters to libraries without finding the master-trove Leyda may have heard about. Ever since 1922, when Meade Minnigerode printed many documents by and about Melville from the Duyckinck Collection in the New York Public Library, we have fixated on Melville as a member of the Duyckinck circle. Perhaps nothing we might find in a trove of Willis documents would destroy that idea, but it is entirely possible that Melville moved in and out of other literary "circles," on familiar terms with more literary men and journalists in New York in the late 1840s than we know about. When William Porter of the *Spirit of the Times* referred to him as "our friend Melville," was he using a journalist convention or speaking from more or less intimate personal acquaintance?

I wanted more letters from Melville to Willis for many reasons. One was that I wanted evidence about how he behaved among other men who had knocked about the world. I wished I could have overheard him telling stories to a group of men at sea, on the *Charles and Henry* and on the *United States,* trying out tall tales about some maiden he was perhaps calling something like "Faaua" (not the last-minute marketing inspiration, Fayaway). Or were the best of those stories preserved in his first two books, almost intact? Before he got home was he telling about his naked son?—the story that turned on the tailor's practice of dressing the male genitals to the left or right pants leg?[2] Some of the time, at least, Melville hinted, teased, bragged, but undercut the sexual boasting, turning the stories comically against himself. When I started working on Melville I was young and inhibited. Now I'd like to hear what his contemporaries called "racy." I'd like to hear the stories he told that shocked Evert Duyckinck. I think he would have talked more frankly to Nathaniel Parker Willis, who said this in the *Home Journal* on October 13, 1849: "*Conversational literature,* or books written as agreeable people talk, is the present fashion with authors and passion with readers. Herman Melville, with his cigar and his Spanish eyes, *talks* Typee and Omoo, just as you find the flow of his delightful mind on paper. Those who have only read his books know the man—those who have only seen the man have a fair idea of his books." Just before he died, Melville's brother Gansevoort met Willis in London, as he recorded in his diary: "We had a long, friendly & I may almost say intimate conversation" (*Gansevoort Melville's 1846 London Journal,* 18). After that, Gansevoort acted as Willis's brother-in-law's groomsman. Willis had been something of a Lothario, at least before and between marriages, according to his own assertion in the *Tribune* on October 18, 1849 (in a curious denial that he was a profligate): "That, in my first residence abroad, and when a single man, I saw freely every manner of life which, by general usage, a gentleman may see, I will not deny." The fragments of Melville's letter to Willis that survive are among the glories of his still youthful exuberance. What if we had a dozen such letters, and his to Melville, instead of comments on Melville by Evert A. Duyckinck? We have some of Willis's reviews of Melville's books, but that's not the same thing.

I still don't know Melville as a man among men. At times I fantasized imaginary conversations for him (never with me)—fantasized his being deep in talk with people I knew he would have relished. Melville met General

Grant in Virginia, and they may have talked about Galena or other interesting topics, but I wished that he could have sat down with the great Southern guerrilla John Mosby (who eludes capture in a *Battle-Pieces* poem, "The Scout Toward Aldie") in cozy confabulation about Sir Walter Scott and that arrogant young murderer of Mosby's men, George Armstrong Custer.

Besides the great documents which may yet exist, there are pieces of paper I would love to see simply to appease my antiquarian longings. On October 17, 1843, the *Albany Argus* picked up news from the *Bennington (Vt.) Gazette:*

> Repeal speeches of Gansevoort Melville, esq., of New York, are printed in handbills, and hawked about the streets of Dublin and other towns in Ireland. It is also stated that one of the carriers who was selling them in the city of Wessex, was taken up by the police. His papers were taken from him, and copies were immediately sent to the British Government at London, because the magistrates considered them "dangerous and inflammatory."

Are any of these incendiary documents preserved in British archives? I don't covet original documents, but I would be delighted to pin up on the wall a giclée of one of these dangerous pieces of paper next to a giclée of one of the handbills that Gansevoort wrote to William Cramer about on July 8, 1844, from Honesdale, Pennsylvania:

> I consented to remain over a day—Handbills were immediately struck off & riders sent to post them up on all public places within a circuit of 20 or 25 miles—there's democratic energy for you! This m^g I walked about the village & found my name conspicuous on every corner in letters an inch long & heralded in terms that would make Demosthenes blush and made me smile.[3]

If one had wall space enough, what fun to contrast advertisements of Gansevoort Melville's speeches with advertisements of Herman Melville's books in the 1840s! So much for desiderata.

When the first volume of my biography was printed in 1996 I was still bothered by scenes for which I did not have enough evidence or else had very unsatisfying evidence. In 2002 in the "Documentation" to the second volume I pointed out two puzzles that had been solved. One was the matter of what Melville had done after returning from Galena in 1840 (and returning much earlier than Leon Howard had thought). As I said earlier, my guess

that he might have taught school again near Lansingburgh had been verified (vindicated, I thought) by a letter Paul Metcalf found in a liquor box.
My Romantic colleagues having let me down, I had been unable to identify the painter who had been a friend of Shelley and Byron and who three
decades later was a frequent guest at Dr. Francis's along with Melville, Evert
Duyckinck, Rufus Griswold, and Henry Tuckerman. After my first volume
was published I bought and read Tuckerman's *Book of the Artists* and learned
from it that the painter was William E. West, who sang for his supper with
enthralling stories, such as the one about Shelley's unexpected arrival during
one of Byron's sittings for a portrait.

In 2009 a new puzzlement capped a story first published in the 1996 volume. We had long known this passage in the manuscript "Recollections of
Frederick Saunders":

> Mr. Herman Melville sent to this publishing house the manuscript
> of "Typee". Mr. Saunders read the same with great interest and gave
> his opinion that "this work if not as good as Robinson Crusoe seems
> to me to be not far behind it." A council was held, and it was decided
> to object to the acceptance and publication of the manuscript, on
> the ground that "it was impossible that it could be true and therefore
> was without real value."

Literally from his deathbed Jay Leyda directed me to letters by Melville's
niece Charlotte Hoadley in the New-York Historical Society. Writing to Victor Hugo Paltsits of the New York Public Library on February 14, 1944, she
made this comment about Melville and *Typee*: "One thing I do know, the
Harpers refusing it calling it a second 'Robinson Crusoe' embittered his
whole life." In establishing a sequence for events of 1845 I was able to put
Saunders's and Charlotte Hoadley's comments together with Melville's note
on the cover of the draft manuscript of *Typee*—the cover that survived in the
1983 Augusta Papers along with only fifteen leaves of the draft. (This made
sixteen known leaves, since one had long been held in the New York Public
Library.) Melville had labeled the draft for Augusta: "Begun in New York in
the winter of that year [1844–45]/Written in the Spring of 1845/. . . finished
in Lansingburgh in the early part of the summer [1845]—After which much
was added & altered."[4]

I took what Charlotte wrote as simple truth because as a child Lottie (as
I knew her from the letters) had been a good listener when her mother, her
aunts, and her grandmother Melville talked, and later a good listener to
her father when he talked about *Clarel*. All Melville's family knew just how

crushed he had been by the Harpers' rejection. Home from whaling, he had spent several months writing out his adventures in the Marquesas only to have it flatly rejected by the leading American publishing house. Another man might have carried the manuscript to a second publisher the day the Harpers rejected it, but Melville was not always resilient after a rebuff and was never good at any sort of financial negotiation. Taking the Harpers' rejection to mean that the manuscript was unpublishable, he stored it in the law office of his brothers Gansevoort and Allan. If the book was without value, unpublishable, he would lose not only the career he had been projecting, he would also have no means of supporting any woman he might want to propose to. What could he do, start teaching school again near home, where schools had a way of dying under him, leaving him, in at least one case, due several dollars? Gansevoort had become a famous (and infamous) Democratic orator, but in the early summer of 1845 he was, like Herman, downcast, waiting for an appointment from James K. Polk, the new president whom he had done so much to elect. Melville would have remembered, all his life, that or many days or even for several weeks, the two brothers, for all Gansevoort's successes, were companions in misery, unrewarded for their spectacular efforts, the one very public, the other very private. Charlotte's letter had allowed me to put Melville's subsequent long connection with the Harpers in a new light.

Melville's career might have been over before it started, but by the greatest of good luck a Democratic friend of Gansevoort's and Allan's, Thomas Low Nichols, the chief organizer of the "Great Torch Light Procession" in 1844, came by the office on Wall Street to congratulate Gansevoort on his tardy appointment as secretary of legation to the American embassy in London. This had to be after July 10, 1845, when the *Evening Post* noted the news. Nichols had offered his congratulations (and condoled with Gansevoort on the poor salary attached to the appointment) when Allan, officious and presumptive, told him that their brother Herman had been "'a little wild'" and had sailed on a whaler:

> "He got home a few months ago," said the young lawyer, "and has been writing something about his adventures among the cannibals. Would you like to look at it?" I had a couple of hours to spare, and took the package of the sailor boy's writing. It was the manuscript of "Typee" . . . .

In this account in his 1864 *Forty Years of American Life* Nichols described what followed, emphasizing his role in making Melville's reputation: "I read 'Typee' at one sitting, and had, of course, no doubt of its success; but the better to assure it, I advised the diplomatic brother to take a copy to London, and have it issued there simultaneously with its publication in New York. I felt sure that the reviews of the English press would make its American success, and I was not at all sure that the process could be reversed" (1:345). I had no evidence to confirm this account, but I had no reason to doubt it, and it fit with what I knew had to be a hasty attempt to get "the" manuscript ready for Gansevoort to pack away for his voyage.

That is what we knew until late in 2009, when the historian Patricia Cline Cohen discovered that Nichols in 1846 was writing two or three letters a week as the New York correspondent of the *Charleston Evening News*, signing himself "Observer." The researcher she hired in South Carolina, Kendall Spillman, found treasures, starting with this letter printed in the July 13, 1846, *Evening News*, after reports of Gansevoort's death had reached the United States and during the high excitement in the newspapers over the "resurrection" of Toby, Melville's companion in the Marquesas:

I wrote to you something of the beautiful narrative of "Typee," written by my friend Melville, a younger brother of our lately deceased, and deeply lamented Secretary of Legation at London. Perhaps I take more interest from the work than I should have done otherwise, from the circumstances of my knowing the author and his family, and of the work having been submitted to me in manuscript. I read it through at two sittings, and after conversation with the author, suggested the addition of certain incidents, which he related in the course of conversation, and advised the late Gansevoort Melville to take a copy to London, that it might appear in England simultaneously with its publication here, or [so] that the author might reap the benefit of a copyright in both countries; an advantage, for which he is indebted to the superior liberality of the British Government in literary matters. My advice was taken, and I am gratified to see that the work excited great interest in Europe, which assisted very much its reception and sale in this country.

Our wise critics here, though, compelled to confess the great merit of the book, set it down as a place [piece] of pure romancing, while I had every possible reliance upon its entire truth. As a romance, it placed its author beside Defoe, but as a true narrative, it is a work of far greater importance than any literary reputation it might confer.

From these circumstances you may judge of my gratification of the news that "Toby," the companion of Melville, in the "Typee Valley," has turned up at Buffalo. He confirms Mr. Melville's narrative

in every particular; carries the scar upon his head, from the wound
inflicted by the Happers, and while he supposed his companion to
be still in the Marquesas, if alive, he induced his sister to name her
child Melville. Is not this very nice?

This is more specific than the much later account in *Forty Years*. Writing
about the events of the year before, Nichols makes it clear that after reading
the manuscript (in *two* sittings!) he had met Herman, who perhaps had been
staying in town, or perhaps was back down to see Gansevoort off. Herman
had told him episodes from his adventures which were not in the manuscript and Nichols had recommended that he add them, which he did, either
before Gansevoort left or afterward, for we know he sent additional sections
to England. All this was indeed "very nice."

This was, in fact, great news to me as biographer, but Kendall Spillman
found still more on Melville, incidental to her research for Professor Cohen.
On December 14, 1846, the *Charleston Evening News* published this from
Nichols, still writing as "Observer":

> Your readers will be pleased to learn that Mr. Melville, author of
> "Typee," has a new work ready for the press. I have no doubt that it
> is worthy of its author's reputation, so suddenly acquired. I had the
> pleasure of reading the former work in manuscript, and am prom-
> ised a similar gratification in regard to the present today, so that in
> my next I shall be able to speak more particularly about its merits.
> It is certain that for a man not much [more], I think, than twenty-
> six years old, the best years of whose life have been spent upon the
> ocean, Mr. Herman Melville is a very remarkable character.

Some day in the second week of December Nichols presumably received
the manuscript of *Omoo*. Papers reached the South fairly fast by steamboat.
The *Charleston Southern Patriot* on Wednesday, April 1, 1846, noted that
the only New York paper that came that day was the *Herald* "of Sunday last"
while it had Washington papers "up to Monday morning." (A letter from
"Observer" would not have been sent by telegraph.)

Whether Nichols read *Omoo* before Evert Duyckinck did is not clear.
Duyckinck wrote to his brother George on December 15:

> Melville is in town with new MSS agitating the conscience of John
> Wiley and tempting the pockets of the Harpers. I have read it. His
> further adventures in the South Seas after leaving Typee. He owes a

sailor's grudge to the Missionaries & pays it off at Tahiti. His account
of the church building there is very much in the spirit of Dickens
humorous handling of sacred things in Italy.

There is a little enigma within the puzzlements of these days late in 1846: a
woman who lived "uptown" had the manuscript of *Omoo* before Duyckinck
did. On December 8, 1846, Melville wrote to Duyckinck that on his brief
Thanksgiving visit to New York he had left the manuscript of *Omoo* "with a
particular lady acquaintance" of his, adding, that the "lady resides up town."
Uptown in 1846 was a fluid term. Greenwich Village had been "uptown"
during the cholera epidemics of the 1820s. In 1850 Twenty-second Street was
so far uptown that a male visitor to Edwin Forrest's wife when the actor was
away on one of his tours might very well think himself unavoidably stranded
overnight if he had become so involved in conversation that he did not notice
the passage of time. A resident of Bond Street, Sophia Thurston, engaged to
Allan Melville, that month referred to Allan as having moved uptown, nearer
to her, so he could call on her four nights a week. The lady who had the
manuscript was not Sophia, who told Augusta that she had been busy reading Prescott on Mexico. The lady could have been Alexander Bradford's wife,
Marianne, who had been Gansevoort's friend and patron. We simply don't
know anything like the full range of Melville's "particular" acquaintances,
but we can be sure his involvement with the lady was innocent: he had been
engaged since the previous summer, Lizzie had just visited Lansingburgh in
October, and he had paid a post-Thanksgiving visit to Boston.

In the letter printed in Charleston on December 16 Nichols preceded the
news that he had read the new book with a reminder to his readers:

> If I remember rightly, I gave you some months in advance of its
> publication, a notice of "Typee," a most extraordinary and high[ly]
> successful work, by Herman Melville. I had the pleasure of reading
> "Typee" in manuscript . . . . I have just been favored with the perusal
> of another MSS. Volume of South Seas Rovings, by Mr. Melville,
> and it is from no impulse of personal friendship that I predict for it a
> greater success than that which attended the publication of Typhee
> [Typee]. Mr. Murray having made a very liberal offer for the English
> copyright, this work will soon be published simultaneously in Lon-
> don and New York.

The news that Nichols wrote to the Charleston paper about *Typee* before it
was published is extraordinary.

The occasion, presumably, was after Herman received word from Gansevoort that John Murray would publish the book. Any time after late
November 1845 Herman knew that the book was under strong consideration,
from the letter Gansevoort wrote him on November 3 for the steamer of the
fourth. The *Britannia* steamed from Liverpool on the fourth for Boston and
arrived there on the twentieth. By late November Melville seems already
to have sent some additions to Gansevoort, perhaps some of the sections
Nichols had suggested that he write up (if he had not added them before
Gansevoort sailed). Then, Nichols would have had occasion to brag about
his connection with the author and the secretary of legation. In all likelihood
Nichols's early notice of *Typee* reached Charleston in late November or early
or mid-December 1845, *the first published mention of Melville as the author
of a book.* Imagine the substance of what Nichols told his Southern audience: "I read this young man's book in manuscript in July and recommended
that his brother take it to London and look what has come of that! John Murray has agreed to publish it!" If the *News* survives for November–December
1845 we will be in luck, thanks to Patricia Cohen and her assistant, Kendall
Spillman, and thanks to the vogue of special correspondents, that great force
for unification of the country amid contrary forces pulling it apart. And it is
always possible that this mention of Melville as the author of a book may survive in another newspaper's reprint of Nichols's letter.

Most of the time in writing my biography I confessed any biographical
puzzlements on the page, as I did for young Thomas Melville's sailing from
Westport, Massachusetts, in 1846. I had no evidence that Herman Melville
went to Westport except my sense of the workings of fraternal love: "Perhaps no one in the family was there to stay with young Tom 'till the last,'
but Herman's involvement in the composition of his second book and in
the reception of the first was intense indeed if it kept him from accompanying Tom to Westport as Gansevoort had accompanied *him* to New Bedford"
(1:410). I covered myself in the first volume with this construction (my "till
the last" being a reference to the way Gansevoort had stayed with Herman at
New Bedford and Fairhaven). As it turned out, Tom sailed in April then put
back in port briefly before finally sailing on May 5, 1846. Herman was there
for the first sailing, at least, for a copy of *Typee* has turned up with an inscription to "Captain Ball" dated "Westport April 18th 1846." It never hurts for a
biographer to assume that loving brothers act like loving brothers, even when
one has just become something of a celebrity. I'm not wholly proud of my
"if" clause, but what should I have done, without evidence?

In the 1882 *Frank Leslie's Sunday Magazine* Scott Norsworthy found a
vignette in "Reminiscences of an Old Fogy" about a July Sunday in 1849,

during the cholera epidemic, when sensible people were indoors, out of the
way of infection:

> I shall never forget one Sunday in July, 1849, when the cholera was
> raging in the city. It was a tremendously hot day. I had been asked to
> dine with a friend, and on my way to his house, I met three well-known
> New Yorkers. One was Herman Melville, the famous novelist; another
> was Cornelius Mathews, one of the most original of our authors, and
> the third was Evert A. Duyckinck, a most admirable critic.
>
> As we strolled down Broadway under the shade of the trees, we
> were struck by the air of utter desolation that reigned. We looked
> up toward Union Square—we were standing near Eighth Street—
> not a living being was visible. We looked down toward the Battery.
> The same solitude prevailed. As we advanced a few blocks, a soli-
> tary pedestrian emerged out of Howard Street and crossed Broadway.
> The spell was broken. Humanity once more came on the scene.

This man, his account shows, had been "actively engaged in mercantile
business" with both store and office on Broad Street. He lived near Union
Square and took the Broadway stagecoach to and from his office. He was a
personal friend of General William Worth, who died in 1849. Perhaps, like
Worth, he was a Mason and an Episcopalian (but he went to hear Methodist
ministers). He was familiar with many journalists (including Thomas Powell) and theatrical people (including Allan's friend James Hackett), especially
opera singers and their managers. He was a Columbia graduate. Stephen
Hoy thinks he was a Schermerhorn, probably John. I puzzle less about the
identity of the acquaintance than what the experience meant to Melville.
Did he remember that vacant Manhattan when he wrote in "Bartleby" that
Wall Street on Sundays was as deserted as Petra? In 1857 in Florence when
Melville saw the wax figures depicting "Naples in the Time of the Plague" he
must have remembered Albany and Manhattan in the Times of the Plague.[5]
     I did not puzzle enough about the staffing of the populous Fourth Avenue
house where the Melvilles lived before moving to western Massachusetts,
although I found a reference to a servant in a letter from Lemuel Shaw, Jr.
I should have checked the census for 1850 in time to say that four foreign
servants were living in: Eliza Brown, Mary Lynch, Margaret McGuire, and
Eliza Whittendale, information John Gretchko later sent to me, long before
Ancestry.com changed our lives. In 2009, using one of the new newspaper
databases, I found different advertisements which Allan Melville placed
in late 1850 and early 1851, offering the house for sale or rent. The house

consisted of three floors plus attic, fourteen rooms, with a Dewitt hot air furnace, a Beebe's range (such Beebe's advertisements are on the Internet as I
write this chapter), Croton water, a copper boiler, hot and cold water to the
third floor, water closets (plural), a bath, drain. In the face of all that comfort,
Melville prevailed and took six grown women (at times, seven) and a child
into a small cold rural house with one pump for cold water in the make-
shift kitchen and, I would bet, even more chamber pots in the bedrooms
and upstairs study than there were shield-like milk pans in the barn. If I had
known how modern the Fourth Avenue house was, I could have made an
even bigger story than I did about Melville's compulsion to escape from New
York and become a neighbor of Hawthorne's.

I found in the 1980s that the artist Felix Darley had made his arduous
way to Arrowhead in 1853 or 1854, asking directions (stuttering nervously
according to his habit?), finally directed through bog and through bush
by locals who thought they were Puckish. Did he meet Melville through
Henry Tuckerman? or at Dr. John Francis's? Melville must have seen Darley's illustrations of Irving after he had proclaimed his own declaration of
independence from Irving in the essay on Hawthorne. Did these illustrations
affect Melville's repentant homage to the old man in "The Paradise of Bachelors and the Tartarus of Maids" and still later "Rip Van Winkle's Lilac"?
Darley must have talked to Melville about his friend Poe. He was good to
be around, genuinely sweet, quietly humorous, almost as gorgeous as Hawthorne had been, the age of Melville's younger brother Allan—and until the
Augusta Papers we never knew they were friends. As far as we know, Melville never visited Darley's Owl's Nest in Claymont, Delaware, but Charles
Dickens did. So did I, once, while it was being renovated, the plaster down
and some of the lath torn off, and holes in the floor you could drop an easel
through, if you folded it up. I thought about buying it, to save it, but it was
cynically overpriced. The whole area was run down, what you'd expect from
an area adjacent to the south edge of Chester, Pennsylvania, that industrial
dump where Wilmingtonians went to shoot up, in my time. Dickens could
see the Delaware River from Owl's Nest, but in the 1980s you couldn't see
the river for the trees, anymore. Darley cared about Melville, yet he never
illustrated anything of his, just for fun? No luscious drawings of scenes from
the South Sea stories? How I wish I had a dozen letters from him to Melville
and Melville to him! Not a word about Melville in any Darley papers left in
libraries in Delaware, either, not that I could find, not even in the Historical
Society. Will this paragraph be enough to evoke new documents?

In 1962 in the lower depths of the New-York Historical Society I saw a
remarkably large tooth on which was a long inscription:

> Ship Swift New Bedford/Capt Worth/30 Months out "On the Line"
> June 17 1860/This day took an 80 barrel "Sperm Whale"/from
> whose jaw this tooth was taken/Presented by Capt Worth to Her-
> man Melville/Author of "Typee" and "Omoo" & by him to E. S.
> Doolittle Jan 1867—

A few years later while I was sending Jay Leyda new items for the "Supplement" to his 1951 *The Melville Log* I told him about the tooth, and he
published a full-page photograph of it in the 1969 Gordian Press edition
(opposite p. 948). Four years later, declaring that completely "unforeseen
things turned up," he credited me: "It was Hershel Parker who saw that
tooth."[6] In writing the second volume of my biography I was unable to find
a person named "E. S. Doolittle" and wondered if Melville might have been
following James Fenimore Cooper in making fun of busy-acting Yankees as
veritable Doolittles. After all, in 1850 he had referred to his hapless cousin
Robert Melvill as Mr. Doolittle. I was worried about a report of Melville's
speaking sarcastically to his wife, belittling her, and wondered if he could be
commenting on E. S. Melville, who had attended a party in the Berkshires
as "Cypherina Donothing." Happily, on July 4, 2006, in the era of Google,
Scott Norsworthy informed me that the recipient was the Albany artist Edwin
Stafford Doolittle (1843–79), who in 1867 had a studio in New York City. He
was only one of who knows how many artists Melville knew personally.

Then on February 18, 2010, in the fultonhistory.com database (while
looking for something else)[7] I found a June 1, 1887, article by S. S. Stafford,
Doolittle's heir, written for the *Albany Journal*, headed "A SPERM WHALE'S
CAPTURE/THE LIVES OF THREE MEN AND SIX HOURS' WORK REQUIRED./A True
Story of the Pacific—A Captain who Hunted and Finally Captured a Whale
Roving the Seas Bristling with Harpoons, Trophies of Former Fights—A
Strange Tale of the Sea." This is the first paragraph:

> Lying on my desk and used as a paper weight is the tooth of a
> "Cachelot" or sperm whale. This mass of solid ivory, nine inches
> long by three wide and weighing 33 ounces, was one of the teeth
> that "aided in [*sic*] the mighty sea Leviathan to live." On its surface
> is written the following: "Ship Swift of New Bedford, Capt. Worth.
> Out 30 months. June 17, 1860, 'On the Line,' Pacific Ocean. This
> day captured an 80-barrel sperm whale from whose jaw this tooth
> was taken. Presented by Capt. Worth to Herman Melville, author
> of 'Typee and Omoo,' and by him given to Ed. Stafford Doolittle
> of Albany, N. Y." This tooth has a history which was told me by a

participant in the capture of the monster who was killed after a protracted and bloody fight of six hours during which the lives of three
men were sacrificed and two whale boats destroyed.

Stafford had the story from "Thomas Brown one of the crew of Capt. Worth's
boat." On June 16, 1860, the *Swift* had encountered a Sag Harbor sperm
whaler who had "three of her boats stove by a big 'sog head,' as they called
a sperm whale, whose back bristled with harpoons to which were attached
fathoms of whale line, the trophies of former fights." Thereupon Worth
"ordered a bright lookout" for the whale, promising "ten dollars' reward to
the man who first sighted the whale." Brown claimed the prize. Melville
himself would not have been ashamed to put his name to the description
which followed of the encounter with the injured and angry whale. Sections
were called "An Angry Whale's Movements," "A Second Revengeful Dash,"
and "The Whale Crunches a Boat." No wonder Captain Francis S. Worth
found Melville and bestowed the tooth on him. When? How did he find
Melville? Was it when Worth was in the United States from early December
1861 until mid-October 1862? How long did Melville keep it?

The story gets better. Google on February 22, 2010, rewarded me with a
picture of Captain Worth's gravestone in Nantucket, but it was Yahoo! which
came through most gratifyingly.[8] Worth was the son of a Starbuck mother
and the husband of Adaline Chase, daughter of Owen Chase, the captain of
the *Essex* in 1820 when it was sunk by a whale and the author of the *Narrative*, a copy of which was treasured by Melville. All Worth had to do was read
Moby-Dick to know of Melville's profound interest in his family—both sides,
but he may have talked to his brother-in-law, the son of Owen Chase, who
had loaned Melville a copy of his father's book in the Pacific. Perhaps Worth
told Melville something of the interesting family genealogy beyond Owen
Chase's and Elizabeth Starbuck Worth's generation.

E. S. Doolittle is not a famous name now, but Melville may have known
Albert Bierstadt, Frederic Church, and others whose fame is high. On February 24, 1865, Bayard Taylor wrote him: "On Monday evening next, the
27th, 'The Travellers' meet here, and it would give me great pleasure to see
you among the guests of the Club. Many of the members are no doubt old
friends of yours—Darley, Church, Bierstadt, Gottschalk, Cyrus Field, Hunt,
Bellows and Townsend Harris. We simply meet to talk, winding up our evenings with a cigar and frugal refreshments." "Here" was 139 East Eighth
Street, not the rooms taken later in the year by the newly formed "Travellers
Club" at No. 1 Fourteenth Street. Was Taylor's group different from the later
Travellers? Did Melville go down to Eighth Street to talk, smoke, and eat

with these men? Or did he avoid this invitation and others? This is tantalizing. Melville's uncle Peter Gansevoort owned Bierstadts. He and his circle of
Albany friends seemed to own half the best Hudson River paintings in existence, buying them as they were painted. Melville collected prints because
he could not afford superb American oil paintings. He saw Richard Lathers's
very expensive but often mediocre European oil paintings and surely did not
want many of them whatever they cost.

For my second volume one of the most extraordinary documents I used
was Lizzie's letter to Augusta on June 29, 1863, about her new sister-in-law
(Allan's second wife), Jane Dempsey Randolph Melville, a divorced woman
with a living ex-husband, all but unbelievably selfish and imperious and
very wealthy, just then well along in training to become quintessentially the
wicked stepmother:

> The last report from the farm [Arrowhead] was, that Jenny got very
> much disgusted with a "cold spell" of weather, and took Milie and
> went down to New York, for a few days I suppose. The rest were
> left "out in the cold"—But they have four servants to take care of
> them, and now it is warm again. I <u>must</u> relieve my feelings—<u>Great
> fool!</u>—say it—or "bust," like "Greel[e]y & the nigger"—

I was confident that the language sounded more racist than it would in context. The best I could do was guess it was "a current anecdote," the "point of
which was that even the most self-suppressed of people would burst under
extreme provocation, like a steam boiler" (2:538). On June 18, 2008, I
learned that the Alexander Street Press had opened wide, temporarily, *The
American Civil War Online.* Hurray! Five minutes after logging on I had in
front of me the April 5, 1862, *Harper's Weekly* cartoon in which "Old Mother
Greeley" in a dress marked "TRIBUNE" is "On the Rampage after General
McClellan," standing behind him demanding "SAY NIGGER OR I'LL BUST!!!"
while he is at a desk holding a paper. Either McClellan will sign an immediate emancipation order or Horace Greeley will burst from frustration at the
delays in ensuring the freedom of the blacks.

Once we know what Lizzie was referring to we can focus on matters other
than the racist language and see that she was recalling a year-old cartoon with
perfect confidence that Augusta (and others at Gansevoort) had seen it in
Harper's Weekly and remembered it, probably from passing around the issues
we know Melville was receiving. Already it was clear to me just how much
Lizzie felt herself one of the sisters from the intimacy with Helen and her visits to Lansingburgh while Herman was in the Pacific, and afterward. She felt

perfectly free to express herself to them. Everyone knew how appalling Jenny was, and in the next decades only poor vulnerable Kate Gansevoort Lansing was taken in by her, to the point of harshly misjudging Allan's and Sophia's daughters. It is a new world for certain types of research, and the Alexander Street Press earned my thanks for its generosity. Leaving the source for Lizzie's "Greel[e]y and the nigger" unidentified had, truly, gnawed at me for years. I worried about it more than anything except what I discuss below, Perry Miller's date of 1850 for the article about Melville as a taciturn man until warmed-up.

I took some stories as true, however unlikely, even though I was not able to pursue them beyond a single document. Charles Hemstreet, born in 1866, given Melville's reputation in 1903 would have had no reason to dress up his *Literary New York* with an anecdote about Melville and a mention of the current address of Melville's widow. We have to assume that he was accurate in his depiction of Melville's performance at one of the regular Sunday-evening gatherings at the home of the fairly close neighbors, Alice and Phoebe Cary:

> Herman Melville was invited to the [53 East] Twentieth Street house at the time when he was at work on his *Battle Pieces*, and could look back on years of adventure by land and by sea, and on the hardships that had supplied him with the material from which to write so much that was odd and interesting. At one of these Sunday-night receptions, at which Alice Cary introduced him first, Melville told the company, and told it far better than he had ever written anything (at least so one of his hearers has recorded), the story of that life of trial and adventure. (224–25)

According to Hemstreet, Melville "began at the beginning, telling of his boyhood in New York, of his shipping as a common sailor, and of his youthful wanderings in London and Liverpool." Melville went on in "true sailor fashion, and with picturesque detail" to tell the story of "his eighteen months' cruise to the sperm fisheries in the Pacific" and his captivity among cannibals (225). The detail ("eighteen months") is specific enough to suggest that Hemstreet was using a printed source written by one of Melville's "hearers," the one he says recorded the event ("fifteen months out," Melville says in *Typee*).

Melville's name is not in Mary Clemmer Ames's *Memorial of Alice and Phœbe Cary*, although she gives a very large list of guests. Melville would not have been out of place, for Ames comments on the openness of the sisters, quoting a "merely fashionable woman" as exclaiming, "What queer

people you do see at the Carys'! It is as good as a show!" (61). No one has yet
found anything "recorded" in a newspaper or magazine. Hemstreet raises
the possibility that Melville really told of "his youthful wanderings in London and Liverpool," which if true would excite those who believe Melville,
like Redburn, saw London on his voyage to Liverpool. Would our Melville
tell a yarn as if were the veritable truth? Hemstreet's account is also fascinating because it describes Melville in full tide of talk, halfway between what
Sophia Hawthorne (May 7, 1851) called the "growing man" who dashed "his
tumultuous waves of thought up against Mr Hawthorne's great, genial, com-
prehending silences" and the late-in-life ranter against politicians as "damn
fools." As for dating, was it early 1866, after the sisters noticed the poems
appearing in *Harper's New Monthly Magazine,* but before the publication
of *Battle-Pieces*? As more and more newspapers are usably made available in
databases, Hemstreet's source (if it was a published record) may be found.

An unsolved mystery is the identity of the book "D. D." The fun is in
how I found the reference to it, as I have mentioned. On March 2, 1990, at
the New York Public Library I was checking Evert A. Duyckinck's letters to
his brother George about Thomas Powell, the forger, and correcting some
of the letters about the hike up Monument Mountain when Melville and
Hawthorne met. I was pushed hard for time, as always, but when I saw a
folder marked "Undated Letters & Unidentified Correspondents" I yielded
to temptation. Soon I was trembling from excitement, for there was a note in
Melville's hand:

Monday P.M.

Dear Duyckinck:

    I return with my thanks D. D. which you were so kind as to pro-
cure for me.

    I can not stop in this evening, but will be happy to do so ere long.

    By-the-bye-, you should read, or at least look over D. D. It is well
worth any one's reading. It is the last leaf out of the <u>Omnium Gath-
erum</u> of miscellaneous opinion touching the indeterminate Ethics
of our time.

    With which Johnsonian sentence, I conclude.

H. M.

"D. D." has not yet been identified (there are proponents of *Daniel Deronda*),
but because the note is on paper Melville used in 1876 I am going through
databases looking at the books listed under "New Publications" for that year.
This will take many hours. Someday, someone will find a "D. D." book so

plausible in date and content that all living Melvilleans will accept it as the veritable "D. D." The moral for students in the archives: Do what you came to do, focusing sharply because there is never enough time. If you are in newspaper files, avert your eyes from "Lurid Murder," skip "Breach of Promise Suit," and speed past "Man Spun into Rug by Roller." Yet, dear student, once in a while, like the diluted Indian-hater, rush headlong "towards the first smoke," into the perilous zone of the undated and unidentified.

I wish I had known before 2002 about the interview of the journalist George Alfred Townsend ("Gath") with the former Collector of the Port of New York, Chester Alan Arthur, in 1879 which Dennis Marnon found or Townsend's different 1881 interview with Arthur which Scott Norsworthy found.[9] Around 1874 (according to the 1881 account) Arthur told Townsend that Herman Melville's novels had given him much delight and that he was glad to keep Melville "in a comfortable clerkship." In the 1879 interview Arthur is quoted as casually saying, "The shark is only an angel well governed," then explicating the passage from *Moby-Dick* to the baffled Gath. Doing so required him to tell about his early admiration for Melville and his surprise, when he was an associate officer in the Customs House, at seeing the name "Herman Melville" in a list of men "doomed to be decapitated," and saving his job. He added: "Then when I became Collector of the Port I kept him in my eye and protected him again, though I never spoke to him." In 1879 Gath added: "After such a life of adventure and of literary prominence, it is strange to see Melville doomed by politicians to lose his clerkship, and only saved by the youthful remembrance of Gen. Arthur." When Arthur became a candidate for vice president and later became president, did he ever again mention Melville in an interview? Is Melville mentioned in the presidential papers? As far as we know, neither of these articles by Gath was reprinted in a New York City paper where it would likely have come to Melville's attention. He may never have known that for several years, starting while he was working on *Clarel*, he had a guardian angel, a man with a Lansingburgh connection who later became president of the United States. When you think about it, it is to Chester Alan Arthur that we owe Melville's ability to continue his epic poem to completion and to publish it. Perhaps historians will remember his presidency for his support of the Pendleton Civil Service Reform Act, but nothing in his presidency is as important to American literature as his saving *Clarel* for us.

One piece of evidence tormented me for years. This document flew in the face of what I thought I knew about Melville. It kept me awake some nights and it cost me hundreds of dollars including a hunting trip to New Orleans. Perry Miller in *The Raven and the Whale* with his usual contempt for documentation printed several lines he attributed to a "New Orleans reporter" describing Dr. John Wakefield Francis's "capacious house at 1 Bond Street" in 1850:

> Of an evening one may drop in, and find a genial gathering, surrounded by the smoke of their own cigars. One is at home here—and so is the Doctor, if not professionally engaged. Tuckerman keeps his classicality for his Addisonian books, and is full of anecdote and humor; Griswold, fiery, sarcastic, and captious; Duyckinck critical; Melville (when in town) taciturn, but genial, and when warmed-up, capitally racy and pungent. (18)

Miller was skeptical and disdainful: "That Herman Melville was an intimate of the Doctor's may be doubted, but the figure of Francis looms so large on the scene where Melville learned how to be a writer that we must suppose it part of his instruction" (18). Miller was arrogantly ignorant in thinking Melville was too far outclassed by Dr. Francis for them to be intimate friends.[10] In fact, Dr. Francis and Melville had cherished a very warm mutual admiration and affection.

What worried me was not Miller's condescension toward Melville but the year, 1850. I knew Melville, and Melville was not taciturn then (although he told Sophia Hawthorne he was complained of for being too silent [*Log*, 925]) and did not need to be warmed up around men. Possibly, I thought, in February through May or June 1850, he may have been so deeply absorbed in his new book on whaling that he was avoiding social occasions and might have been lost in his thoughts if he ventured out. "When in town" was a mystery too, unless that referred to his absence abroad between October 1849 and the beginning of February 1850, or the few weeks he was away in August, or the time after his move to the Berkshires in early October 1850. "When in town" plainly, I thought, ought to apply to years after 1850, after Melville was living in Pittsfield, and making only occasional trips to the city. Melville would have been "in town" occasionally from 1851 up until Dr. Francis's death a decade later. Yet nothing in the report was absolutely impossible in my mind except the description of Melville as so "taciturn" that he had to be warmed up before he would hold forth. After 1852, when Melville had been crushed by reviews of *Pierre* and for several years was quite hopelessly in debt, he became taciturn, or worse, the "most silent man" Maunsell B. Field had ever known—until he "never chanced to hear better talking" in his life than a conversation between Melville and Oliver Wendell Holmes on East India religions and mythologies (*Memories of Many Men and of Some Women*, 202).

Determined to find the article Miller quoted, in July 1988 I went to New Orleans to look through the 1850 papers, starting with the *Picayune*, which I thought the most likely. I have told how the librarians at Tulane would not let me handle the paper copy of the *Picayune* so that I was forced to settle for the *New Orleans Commercial Bulletin*, where I found the treasure-trove of Oakey Hall's letters. Home, I used the microfilm of the *Commercial Bulletin* to print out all the letters from the late 1840s through the end of 1854, although a new correspondent was writing the letters the last several weeks. I kept looking. Eventually, back in Delaware, I discovered that Miller had taken the quotation from Henry T. Tuckerman's introduction to his reissue of Dr. Francis's *Old New York* (1866), putting names to the initials Tuckerman printed there. With his usual sloppiness, Miller had misrepresented the item, for Tuckerman made it clear that the reporter was writing *from* New York City to New Orleans. The discovery of Miller's source was sour for me because it made 1850 more plausible than ever: Melville's friend Tuckerman ought to have gotten the year right. Nevertheless, I did not believe Tuckerman any more than I had believed Perry Miller.

Now when I look at what I did in the first volume I find that I evaded the problem. I quoted the passage from Tuckerman in a chapter on the time of *Mardi*, earlier than 1850, but did not say a word, as far as I see now, about "taciturn." This was burying evidence because I was convinced it was wrong (as in fact it was)—the only time I succumbed to that temptation. Then a few years ago Scott Norsworthy, using Google, located the article on Dr. Francis as printed in the *New York Times* for January 24, 1855, along with the information that it was taken from the *New Orleans Commercial Bulletin*. I e-mailed Norsworthy that I was going down to my garage. There in the box of photocopies I had possessed for two decades was the original of the article I had spent so much time searching for, since I had copied several weeks' worth of letters written by Hall's replacement and had not read all those letters from the end of the year. There were slight variants, as when the New York text contained words modified so as not to offend the churlish local resident Griswold. This is the original text, from the *New Orleans Commercial Bulletin* of November 24, 1854, misspellings intact:

> One is at home here—and so is the Doctor if not professionally engaged. Tuckerman keeps his classicallity for his Addisonian books, and is full of anecdote and humor; Griswold, fiery, sarcastic and captious; Duykinck cynical; Melville (when in town) taciturn, but genial, and when warmed-up capitally racy and pungent—painters

and sculptors, men of deeds, not words, and among them, rarely seen abroad, the friend of Shelly and Byron.

This is the corrected and revised text in the January 24, 1855, *New York Times:*

> One is at home here—and so is the doctor, if not professionally engaged. TUCKERMAN keeps his classicality for his ADDISONIAN books, and is full of anecdote and humor, GRISWOLD, anthological and captious; DUYCKINCK, critical, MELVILLE (when in town,) taciturn, but genial, and, when warmed up, capitally racy and pungent;—painters and sculptors, men of deeds, not words, and among them, rarely seen abroad, the friend of SHELLEY and BYRON.

In the *Times* version are corrections that only an author would make. What was printed in New Orleans about Duyckinck could be corrected ("cynical" had to have been a misreading) and what could be said in New Orleans about the irascible Griswold would be better suppressed in Manhattan.

I assumed the author was Tuckerman, since he used the *Commercial Bulletin* text in his introduction to the 1866 reissue of Dr. Francis's *Old New York,* making the obvious correction about Duyckinck. I was wrong. In 2011 Scott Norsworthy discovered that the corrected *Commercial Bulletin* version had been reprinted in the *Knickerbocker* in August 1858 and ascribed to Dr. Augustus K. Gardner, who was a longtime acquaintance of Melville's, and that the article on Dr. Francis was followed by "The Doctor," a poem by "H. T. T." which Tuckerman reprinted in *Old New York* following the vignette about the four notable guests. All Tuckerman needed was his copy of the *Knickerbocker,* not either newspaper version. So the successor as New York correspondent for the *Commercial Bulletin* was Dr. Gardner, who like Tuckerman frequently made extra money as a special correspondent. That's interesting, too, and more proof that in our digital age all the *Commercial Bulletin* letters from New York ought to be put online as a great resource for historians.

Although I had mistakenly thought Tuckerman wrote the piece, I felt vindicated, for Gardner wrote it long after the catastrophic reception of *Pierre* changed Melville's characteristic behavior. In late 1854, taciturn until warmed-up was fine. As I review all this I am proud of knowing the document was wrong, even though Tuckerman repeated the year as 1850, but not proud of the way I handled it. I should have confessed my uneasiness in the text of the first volume rather than gliding over the problem. Privately,

I worried more about this item than anything else in either volume, for if 1850 was the date, I did not know my man. It was *such* a puzzlement to me! Will other biographers reading this instantly rush forward with stories of their rightly refusing to accept authoritative-looking evidence? Or their shame at not directly confronting evidence they do not believe?[11]

While I was in the East I should have assembled a list of known guests who frequented Dr. Francis's and should have read dozens of New York City papers (and of course there were dozens) and two or three dozen out-of-town papers that printed regular letters from their New York City correspondents, looking for mentions of the men who came to New York. I could have maximized my efforts by starting when a foreign celebrity was in town, and then I should have looked at their letters and diaries. There have to be records still—diaries or letters of men who attended and described how Melville talked, once he were warmed up with the liquor. A biographer should be omnivorous, omnipresent, immortal, and strong as a horse. I couldn't do everything. I'm apologizing. With new databases a superannuated Melvillean can initiate an investigation from a village on the central coast of California but real research would have to be conducted in archives all over the East, and beyond.

PART II

Critics vs. Biographical Scholarship

CRITICS AND REVIEWERS regularly resist or outright deny new (and even old) documentary evidence about Melville biography, far beyond any resistance to information about any other American writer. There are historical reasons for this. In the case of every other "major" nineteenth-century American writer, even Thoreau, even Whitman, there was high continuous interest in the author's lifetime and books written about the writer during life or soon after death. Even Emily Dickinson, once her poetry began to be published, never faded out of public awareness for any decade. Usually intimates of the writers prepared biographies and collections of letters soon after the authors' deaths. The lack of such reliable studies is what prompted Stanley T. Williams to put his best 1940s Yale students to work on Melville. When the New Criticism swept American colleges in the 1950s, scholarship on Emerson, for instance, seemed set, for no great caches of biographical material were expected to emerge on major writers.[1] Melville was unique in that the basic chronological documentary source, *The Melville Log*, was not published until 1951, after the rise of the New Criticism, so that Charles Feidelson and others set out to discredit it. Four and five decades later, Melville was unique because of the mass of new information from the 1983 treasure trove of family documents which I worked into the first (1996) and second (2002) volumes of my biography. Reviewers lay in wait to discredit my biography as Feidelson had lain in wait to discredit the *Log*. Critics also lay in wait, unwilling to change their minds about what they thought they knew and determined to declare their freedom to ignore new documentary evidence if they just wanted to write criticism. Melville was also unique in that the self-constituted band of "New York Intellectuals" had political reasons for diminishing him. Even in the twenty-first century, they show their political bias in championing the *New York Review of Books* attacks on the

Northwestern-Newberry Edition of Melville and connect that to their championing (for political and sexual reasons) the "critical biography" of Newton
Arvin, a book that contained fine readings of some of Melville's works but
which as biography was not only derivative but missing major episodes. Ever
since the 1980s these Intellectuals have seen Arvin as a martyr because he
had been a communist and was a homosexual, and have followed him in
depicting a truncated Melville.

The resistance to new scholarship on Melville was such that no other biographer of an American writer was ever subjected, as I was, to the demolishing
preemptive strike in *American Literature* which I quoted in the preface: "We
already have full-scale biographies of Melville"! No other biographer of an
American writer has been subjected to such concerted denial of documentary evidence and outright assassination of my reputation as a scholar. Some
part of the attacks must be anomalous, I told myself, the result of the history
of Melville literary criticism and scholarship in the American academy and
the special and even unique history of Melville biography. Puzzling over the
motivation of New York City reviewers and critics, at last I saw political and
personal motivations for attacks on the first volume, but at least it was a Pulitzer finalist. Later, the effect of several reviewers' branding me as a fantasist,
not a reliable researcher, was to knock the second volume out of contention for a Pulitzer and other New York prizes. Surely if I won a Pulitzer in
2003, or was a finalist again, jurors a year or two hence would hesitate to give
the award to another book on Melville or even on another mid-nineteenth-
century American writer. Here was a twist on the specter of the loathed
"Rival" deplored by Frances Wilson, Claire Tomalin, and Jane Ridley:[2] In
2000 and 2001 I had not dreamed I was in contention with a future biographer of Hawthorne as well as a future biographer of Melville. It's time, now,
to tell this story in *Melville Biography: An Inside Narrative*. After all, I am
the only one who can tell it comprehensively and with hard-won judicious
objectivity.

❧ *Chapter 7* ❧

AGENDA-DRIVEN REVIEWERS

Melville in the Insular New York Newspapers and Magazines vs.
Global Loomings from "Ragtag Bloggers" and Litblogs

IN THE OCTOBER 1959 *Harper's* Elizabeth Hardwick inveighed against "The Decline of Book Reviewing," especially "the unaccountable sluggishness of the *New York Times* and *Herald Tribune* Sunday book-review sections" (139). Seeing only "sweet, bland commendations," a "universal, if somewhat lobotomized, accommodation," she longed for "the brine of hostile criticism" (139). Abysmal as the quality of the reviewing was, the "truly dismaying" aspect of those newspapers was "the quality of the editing" (141). During the New York City newspaper strike of 1962 Hardwick and several of her cohorts, in what has been told and retold in Homeric terms, seized the opportunity to create their own paper, the *New York Review of Books*. Half a century later, the *New York Review of Books*, on the high authority of *Esquire*, extols itself on its website as "the premier literary-intellectual magazine in the English language" and boasts that throughout these decades it "has posed the questions in the debate on American life, culture, and politics." Idealism has long fled the *New York Review of Books*, leaving vanity in charge. As I explain in chapter 11, Hardwick herself rose in high Kentucky dudgeon yet again toward the end of her life to protest a less than sweet, bland commendation of her booklet on Melville and to threaten unnamed but dire retaliation against the *New York Times* if it ever again hired the honest reviewer. The *Tribune* is long defunct, and the book-review section of the *New York Times*, supine, on life-support, may die any year now with hardly anyone's noticing. The reviewing on Melville in the *New York Review of Books* has without exception been partisan, self-serving, or (at best) merely ignorant. As far as I know, not once in this half century has *any* New York magazine or newspaper assigned a Melville biography to a reviewer who knew the principal scholarly books on

Melville (say, a reviewer who had read *The Melville Log*) and who had dirt-
ied even one of his or her hands with a little archival research on Melville.

As I discuss in chapter 11, New York City editors and reviewers alike have
united to present a limited Melville derived from Newton Arvin's 1950 book
and from the Arvin-influenced May 10, 1982, *New Yorker* article by John
Updike, "Melville's Withdrawal." Their amputated manikin of a Melville
had no interest in painting and sculpture, no interest in poetics or what he
called aesthetics (despite his proclaiming that there is an aesthetics in all
things). Their Melville is a condensed version, a man who did not complete
a prose book the year after *Pierre* was published, a man who did not complete
in 1860 a book he wanted to call *Poems*, and a man whose *Clarel* is hardly
worth reading. All the New York City mainstream print media, newspapers
and magazines alike, have united to present this cut-down Melville. Even
the most frequent reviewer, Andrew Delbanco, in his *Melville: His World
and Work* (2005), truncates Melville, only glancingly mentioning *The Isle
of the Cross* and *Poems*, having denied their existence in 2002. After reviewing me numerous times it had become clear that Delbanco had not read at
all carefully the books he was paid to review and that if he had ever looked
at the 1951 *Melville Log* he no longer remembered what he had seen in it.
You have to assume that level of ignorance or else you have to acknowledge
the unthinkable, that in his review of my second volume he knew better
but deliberately denied, for instance, the long-known fact that Melville left
Poems for publication when he sailed to San Francisco in 1860.

Mentioning the frequency with which Delbanco has reviewed biographical books on Melville focuses attention on how very few critics—and no
scholars—the New York City newspapers and magazines have tapped to
review biographical books on Melville. In 1992 Delbanco published in
American Literary History his "haphazard tour" of recent publications, "Melville in the '80s," where he identified what he called (710) "the pressing issue
for most critics": whether or not Melville "was able to think outside the con-
stricting categories of his own culture"—a nod to John Updike's formulation
in the *New Yorker*. Defining "the labor of contextualization" as "the most
valuable ambition of the Melville industry" (713), before alluding vaguely
to "the steady output of the Northwestern-Newberry editors" Delbanco surveyed the field (713):

> Each year sees new enlargements in our awareness of the specific
> details that constituted the mental world through which Melville
> moved: we have lately been informed about contemporary expla-
> nations for body spasms following hanging (McElroy); prevailing

definitions of monomania (McCarthy); popular anxiety over the specter of slave revolt (Sundquist); and Melville's views of the Sabbatarian controversy (Marsh).

Significantly, Delbanco did not say one word about any work with manuscripts such as the monograph-length "Historical Note" in the 1988 Northwestern-Newberry *Moby-Dick*—a study that might, I thought, have been mentioned as a labor of "contextualization."

In his *American Literary History* article Delbanco described how he had scrutinized me in the New York Public Library in 1991 as I listened to Harrison Hayford: "During Hayford's talk Hershel Parker could be seen sitting intent in the audience, a portrait of the biographer facing a long march between credulity and skepticism. Some of the juiciest Melville stories, he knows, are unprovable, and the 40 years since Leon Howard's biography provide evidence that Melville's is a devilishly hard life to write" (709–10). This impudent knowingness spooked me, but largely by virtue of having made this survey, Delbanco acquired a reputation as a writer on Melville. From then on he wrote on Melville not by doing research on Melville's life and the backgrounds of his books but by writing reviews, primarily, it pains me to remember, of my books, and attributing to me, as time went on, lickerish feelings that recalled his use of "juiciest" here. Leeringly intrusive, voyeuristically describing my thought processes, Delbanco made me feel stalked by a pornographer who was progressively revealing something of himself, not of me. In 1996 while photographing me for the *New York Times Magazine* Lizzie Hummel announced herself as a friend of "Andy" at Columbia; when I kept a blank face, she explained, "He does what you do. Melville." "Not hardly," I thought, "not hardly." Delbanco, it was clear, had read dozens of critics, but in 1996 (or even 2002) he still, as I will persist in pointing out, had not ever read or did not remember major episodes in the 1951 *Melville Log*, much less ever transcribed an unknown Melville document, or read carefully anything I had been publishing.

Maurice Sendak and I met at the Pittsfield Melville conference in May 1991. The second day, glassy from speeches, I encountered him in the men's room of the Berkshire Athenaeum as I prepared to flee the critics. He fled with me and my companion to Stockbridge Bowl, where we walked around the replica of the Hawthorne cottage and talked about *The Melville Log*. When he confided that he had made a moviola of it in his mind, I lured him on with highlights of my recent discoveries in the archives. I lured him, as it turned out, into something of a publishing disaster, for I believed passionately still in the capacity of Melville critics to learn. I laid out all the old and new evidence about what happened after Melville brought the completed *Pierre* to New York at the start of 1852, for it was clear that the unplanned enlargement started very early in January, almost as soon as the punitive terms of the contract were agreed to. At home I took up a copy of the book and cut out all of Melville's late additions about Pierre as a writer—something easier said than done, but what I arrived at was an approximation of the short version of *Pierre* which Melville had thought of as his "Kraken" book. I presented Sendak with this rough-and-ready text and he agreed for HarperCollins to draw illustrations only for this short book, not the published book with the Pierre-as-author pages. HarperCollins published this "Kraken Edition" late in 1995. All along I thought of it as an occasion for Sendak to illustrate a unique, challenging nonce-book, a one-time-only text, a fascinating curiosity. Mainly, I hoped that readers would think biographically and aesthetically, so that they could imagine a *Pierre* very much as Melville wrote it, before he suffered the annihilating session or sessions with the almost unbelievably mercenary Harpers. Surely, I thought, everyone would want to read something very close to the book which Melville completed next after *Moby-Dick*, especially if they could feast tired eyes on Sendak's sure-to-be-charming illustrations.

Unlike Delbanco, Richard H. Brodhead, another repeat reviewer of Melville books, at least started with the reputation as a critic of Melville, based on his quintessentially conventional New Critical 1976 *Hawthorne, Melville, and the Novel*. In the "Young America in Literature" section of *Pierre*, he observed there, "Melville shifts to topical satire" (182). In the course of explaining "why Melville tells his story as he does" Brodhead was unperturbed that "the second half of the book has little to do" with the "literary endeavor" of the first half (181). He also was unperturbed that "the structure" of Melville's "narrative becomes looser" (181). Brodhead patted the author on the head (182): "Melville was wise not to let a foolish consistency keep him from exploring the subjects and methods he does in these chapters; they are among the most interesting in *Pierre*. But their inclusion has a curious effect on the book's narration." In this reading, Melville's failures were aesthetic, but the laudable result of the failures was that they provided Brodhead with "interesting" chapters for New Critical explication, however much looser they were than the earlier chapters.

When I read this I reacted to Brodhead's coolness with visceral horror: here was the bloodless New Criticism blandly, smugly indicting itself. In *Flawed Texts and Verbal Icons* (1984) I summarized biographical evidence for the "two very different and imperfectly combined creative processes" that went into *Pierre*, "the second one destructive of part of the achievement of the first." Then in a footnote I took up Brodhead (28–29):

While most critics find unity at all costs even in books known to have a strange compositional history, now and again a critic of the post-New Criticism generation (like a good many first generation American Literature scholars such as Leon Howard) is content to place less stock in formal perfection. Richard Brodhead, in particular, has displayed a remarkable tolerance toward Melville's altering the direction of *Pierre* half way through the book as we know it. Brodhead observes, as Leon Howard and many others had done, that the second half of *Pierre* has little to do with the first, then with mild benignity decides that "Melville was wise not to let a foolish consistency keep him from exploring the subjects and methods he does" . . . even though the inclusion of new material "has a curious effect on the book's narration." Brodhead knows the book is split in two. Rather than demanding a verbal icon, however, he makes the best of a bad situation, finding interest where he can—but at the cost of closing his eyes to the agony that lay behind Melville's decision to record his rage against his reviewers and his fears about the death of his career as a writer, even if doing so meant wrecking what might well have been the most tightly unified work he had yet written.

"Closing his eyes to the agony" still sums up for me the bloodlessness of modern literary criticism written by academics trained in the New Criticism by students of the original New Critics like Charles Feidelson or their descendants. They have been trained not to think of biography as even potentially relevant to literary criticism, so that "Melville" is an intellectual construction, an abstraction, not a real person. Melville is dehumanized.

You can see this explicitly, although also couched benignly, in Bruce L. Grenberg's *Some Other World to Find* (2):

> I make virtually no effort to define Melville's "personal" beliefs, attitudes, and convictions, and devote little space to the oft-rehearsed external events of Melville's life and times.[1] Although some critics find it irresistible to identify Melville the man with the artist-Melville, I am persuaded by the simple, persuasive truth of Charles Feidelson's assertion that "the Melville (1819–91) remains largely unknown, so that all attempts to identify the omnipresent voice of the novels with Melville as he lived and breathed have been self-defeating." The "Melville" that I refer to in the following pages, therefore, is Feidelson's "literary personality, a created figure who inhabits a created world," and when I write of "Melville's" attitudes or changing

perspectives I am referring ultimately to the artist-Melville, who is
defined, and can only be defined, by the works themselves.

Once you make Melville a "literary personality, a created figure" you can
do with him as you will, disregarding human feelings (disregarding agony, as
Brodhead did).

As long ago as 1970 William V. Spanos looked back at the results of the
New Criticism ("Modern Literary Criticism," 87):

> We have, in fact, despite theoretical insistence to the contrary, disso-
> ciated literature from life in a radical way and established a critical
> frame of reference that reduces the original encounter with the liter-
> ary work to something perilously like intellectual exercise expressed
> in a counter language that does violence to the full existential expe-
> rience. We are beginning to see at this late date that the principle
> of autonomy is sharply narrowing the boundaries and, in the pro-
> cess, dehumanizing the critical enterprise; indeed, that behind the
> strategy of the New Criticism lies the impulse to disengage literature
> from the defiling contingencies of life in historical time.

"Dehumanizing the critical enterprise" involves dehumanizing the author as
merely the putative source of texts that a critic can exercise his or her talents
on. After being indoctrinated to ignore the author and to treat the literary
work as an autonomous artifact anyone is free to practice criticism upon,
even a critic whose disposition in childhood and adolescence had been
genial enough, even the most generous, loving young person will develop a
hardness of heart toward the author.

In the January 7, 1996, *New York Times Book Review* Richard H. Brodhead, by then the A. Bartlett Giamatti Professor of English at Yale University
and dean of Yale College, wrote the "Bookend" (35) entitled "The Book
That Ruined Melville." Brodhead did not try to get the facts straight, for he
informed the readers of the *New York Times* that *The Confidence-Man* was
"first published in 1856"; that the Harpers had slashed Melville's royalties
rate "in half" for Pierre; that Melville had "finally" agreed to the contract on
Pierre, not almost at once. Brodhead allowed for a possibility: "It's a thrilling
prospect, the chance to be among the first people in history to read 'Pierre'
as Melville may 'really' have written it." I had been sure that readers would
want to know, as nearly as they could, what Melville had at least early in his
work on it thought of his Kraken book, grander than *The Whale*. But Brodhead was not up for such an aesthetic thrill: "Since when did readers feel

they should have access to every stage of a work's evolution?" The prospect was "thrilling," but Brodhead, smug in his New Critical certainties, strained for a contemptuous demotic idiom and found one: "Thanks but no thanks." Brodhead was secure in his refusal to learn anything new about the "evolution" of this novel I found almost uniquely tantalizing.[2]

I glance ahead in my analysis here to look hard at the way the New Criticism seduces its practitioners into dehumanizing both writers like Melville and writers on him. When the second volume of my biography was published Brodhead damned me in the *New York Times* (June 23, 2002) as a "demon researcher" (13) with a "single-mindedness worthy of a Melville hero," a hero such as Ahab, who also ended in wreck. Can this have nothing to do with the Yale professor Feidelson's calling Melville "a prime example of the demonic writer" (*Symbolism and American Literature*, 163)? I was a demon researcher but I could not be trusted because I had passed off private surmises as fact, Brodhead declared. According to Brodhead there was no evidence that Melville had finished a book called *Poems* in 1860. In fact, all scholars had known about *Poems* since 1922. According to Brodhead it was merely a surmise of mine that Melville had completed a book in 1853. In fact, all scholars had known about this book since 1960, and I had published the title, *The Isle of the Cross*, in 1990. In accusing me of making unfounded surmises Brodhead (as I discuss in a later chapter) had erased the existence of the grand array of Melville scholars who had preceded me. Most immediately and most painfully to me, he had erased the existence of three men, all dead by 2002, who had rejoiced at my discovery of the title in 1987—Leyda, Hayford, and Sealts. Brodhead's false accusations about me must be in some way a consequence of his New Critical training and practice, I decided. In sober truth, if your training leads you to dehumanize Melville, to be blind to his agony, how can you *not* carry your training over to the way you treat real living people, at least people unlike you, such as a fanatic, demonic researcher? This is worth re-emphasizing: If you think that facts about authors are not real and authors are not real, then you may come to see living people outside your own private circle as unreal. Cut them and they will not bleed, or if they do bleed their suffering can never be of the significance of your own discomforts or the discomforts of your class. Let me offer a maxim: *The kind of literary criticism you learn to write and continue to write all your life affects all the rest of your behavior.* Some of the behavior of Melville critics who refuse to look at documentary evidence is innate in their character, I assume, but some of their actions, I would think, must be a consequence of lifelong practice of a dehumanizing literary approach, the New Criticism. Their nature is subdued to what it works in, like the dyer's hand.

Google supplies a great many studies of the psychology of cruelty, with particular emphasis on dehumanization. Recent work includes David Livingston Smith's *Less Than Human: Why We Demean, Enslave, and Exterminate Others* (2011). Albert Bandura in "Moral Disengagement in the Perpetration of Inhumanities" (1999) describes how "social practices that divide people into ingroup and outgroup members produce human estrangement that fosters dehumanization" (200). Brodhead and later other reviewers who falsely accused me of surmising or fantasizing the 1860 *Poems* did not "enslave" or "exterminate" me, to echo the title of Smith's book, but they demeaned me at what should have been the height of my career and they went as far as they could go toward exterminating my reputation as a careful scholar. They denied me both recognition and tangible rewards.[3]

After attending Sean Wilentz's November 1995 Princeton celebration of the centennial of Edmund Wilson's birth, Andrew Delbanco (the Columbia professor) and another attendee, Paul Berman (a Columbia graduate), seem to have gone away determined to honor Wilson's memory by renewing the attack on whichever Northwestern-Newberry editor first showed himself, Hayford, Tanselle, or me. Chances were that I would win, what with the HarperCollins *Pierre* already announced and with the first volume of my biography promised for 1996. Hitting the big time, Delbanco got the privilege of reviewing the Sendak *Pierre* in the April 4, 1996, *New York Review of Books*. Still not having become familiar with *The Melville Log*, either 1951 or the 1969 edition with a "Supplement," I remind you, Delbanco made careless errors. In fact, *Moby-Dick* had *already* been "fully transferred from brain to paper" when Melville asked Sarah Morewood not to buy it or read it (42). Sarah Morewood did not say that Melville had begun *Pierre* "under a state of morbid excitement which will soon injure his health" (42). Delbanco had Melville getting "to work in earnest" on *Pierre* by January 8, 1852, which was about the time he began enlarging the completed short form for which he had already negotiated a contract (42). The setting of *Pierre*, Delbanco said confidently (43), is upstate New York—reasonable but more than Melville tells us. Delbanco's description of the additions was askew. I never said that sections "were tacked on in the last weeks before publication" (42). They were written in January and some of February, not late June. For Delbanco my evidence was merely "extraneous biographical information" (43), extraneous as all biographical evidence is to a child of the New Criticism. Delbanco, as blind to Melville's agony as Brodhead in 1976, said I claimed "that Melville was in a pique when he threw in the sections about Pierre as a frustrated writer" (43). A "pique"? Melville the popinjay? Melville the pipsqueak? Melville, whose Ahab had been in a pique against Moby Dick?

Delbanco envisioned passages not as having been composed over bitter, wry, or miserable minutes or hours or days but as coming pre-formed, so they can be thrown in, as a lump. It is as if Delbanco could not visualize Melville in the process of writing sardonic passages out of nearly-suicidal pain. Then Delbanco continued with a lengthy New Critical reading of the original *Pierre*, having, like Brodhead, declined the opportunity to try to experience what Melville was doing in the last several weeks of 1851 and to wonder at what he thought he was doing, then and later.

In four interminable pages of the *London Review of Books* (October 3, 1996), Richard Poirier spewed forth (here I co-opt his own words) "an exceptional degree of self-infatuated portentousness" about the "Kraken" edition of *Pierre*. He had absorbed a good deal of my new information, especially some of the redatings, but could not understand that twenty cents on the dollar was punitive when Melville was already in debt to the Harpers at fifty cents on the dollar. Seriously overpaid at Rutgers, he shrugged comfortably: "A disappointment of that sort is common enough among writers"! There would have been no point in Poirier's trying to read something very close to what Melville first wrote. In the mood of Weaver and Mumford, Poirier declared: "From beginning to end, in every crevice, and in whatever version, *Pierre* is an allegory of Melville's thwarted career as a novelist. It is a totally self-absorbed performance wherein failure is attributed to the nature of literature itself and to language as a necessary betrayer." This was also a rapturous tribute to the New Criticism, half a century after its first popularity: unity had to be there in *Pierre* from beginning to end, in every crevice.

On the contrary, glorious powers are ardently on display in the first half and more of *Pierre*, as Brian Higgins and I showed in our patient 2006 reading, and those pages have nothing to do with a "thwarted career as a novelist." Part way through the writing of *Pierre* Melville did learn that *The Whale* had been printed without the epilogue and that he was being criticized on the grounds that a first-person narrator has to survive, but his career was not truly thwarted until early January 1852. Months after the publication of *Pierre*, from mid-December 1852 until late May 1853, he wrote another book, *The Isle of the Cross*. To judge from his letters to Hawthorne in 1852, Melville was intensely concerned with appropriate language and had no thought of failure in the nature of literature and no thought that language in the hands of a master need be a "betrayer."

Speaking at the Princeton celebration honoring Edmund Wilson apparently left Paul Berman certain there would be no surer way of demonstrating his fealty to the man who had savaged the Northwestern-Newberry *Typee* in the *New York Review of Books* than to pick up Wilson's lash and cudgel. In the 1997 *Edmund Wilson: Centennial Reflections*, edited by Lewis M. Dabney from the Princeton conference, Berman in his phone-booth-sized article, "Wilson and Our Non-Wilsonian Age," redefined himself as a throwback to the grand old-fashioned "public intellectuals" of Wilson's generation (270). Ready to emerge from the article as Supercritic, Berman pledged to hold himself to the standards of the giants or at least "to give it a try" (275). Wilson, whatever his faults, had been a learned man. Berman, getting into the Melville reviewing business without knowing much about Melville or Melville scholarship, hastily, as he said, "signed on to write a review" of Laurie Robertson-Lorant's biography of Melville for the online *Slate* (July 10, 1996). Elsewhere I point to Carl Rollyson's observation that reviewers make a habit of lifting information from biographies they are reviewing and repeating it as theirs.[4] Delbanco, Brodhead, and Poirier are all masters of this trick. Not yet having mastered it, Berman guilelessly let Robertson-Lorant "remind" him of commonplaces, rising only to disagree with her about one of Melville's short poems, "The House-top."

The *New York Times Magazine* on December 15, 1996, printed an article by Philip Weiss, "Herman-Neutics," that opened to a slightly more than full-page color picture of me in my study at Landenberg, Pennsylvania.[5] On a corkboard behind me was an array of my favorite snapshots but by very bad luck the only photograph of my mother up there was blocked by my head. I protected myself by not reading the whole article, having recognized in the reporter a covert Melville-as-homosexual-wife-beater agenda, but I kept a copy of that issue and have looked at the picture at least a dozen times over the years. All hell broke loose on Saturday the fourteenth, when copies of the Sunday paper became available, phone calls, an instant surge on Amazon's ranking, that upstart measure of popularity.

Sporting his new electronic street creds, Berman gained the great privilege of reviewing my first volume for the December 22, 1996, *New York Times Book Review* (12–13), which was available on the sixteenth, the Monday after the "Herman-Neutics" article. Berman had done Edmund Wilson proud, devoting more than a tenth of his review to mocking Wilson's bête noir, the Northwestern-Newberry Edition, not to discussing my biography. The other ninety percent was also annihilating. My "fanaticism for exactitude" was such that I gave "not just the tiniest details, but the details about the details." "Whole forests among these details are new," Berman averred, and "of the million fresh facts" he was most struck with those revealing the business dealings of Melville's father. Most of those particular facts were not in fact new. "'Tis new to thee," as Prospero says. Savagery lurked amid apparent approval: "To make your way through the intricacies of Mr. Parker's

account has some of the charm of going into bankruptcy yourself." Yet for all
my facts I had not done enough work to please Berman:

> You wade through Mr. Parker's gigantic leaf-drifts of petty facts
> regarding letter writing, cousins, sisters, rentals, sales, architecture,
> debts, billings and contested wills—reassuring yourself all the while
> that, at least, everything you could possibly wish to know about Her-
> man Melville will eventually turn up. But that is not the case. About
> the Polynesians and their charmingly idiosyncratic notions of sex
> and meat, for instance, Mr. Parker tells us hardly more than can
> be learned in Leon Howard's "Herman Melville: A Biography" of
> 1951.

(Why had I ignored the readers of the printout who had begged for more
about "the Polynesians and their charmingly idiosyncratic notions of sex and
meat"?) On "Melville's special insights into colonialism and race" and "his
warm, economically dependent and politically awkward relations with his
father-in-law," there was "more in the one-volume, slightly jargony study by
Laurie Robertson-Lorant" Berman had reviewed for *Slate*. For illustrations I
had only Sendak's new portrait of Melville: I had not even printed a diagram
of a whaleship!

As for the last meeting between Melville and Hawthorne in the Berkshires, it was "vivid" enough to make Berman eager for more: "I wonder
how Volume 2 will begin, and what other tiny jewels of research will sparkle among the tons of material that Mr. Parker has surely exhumed." The
gleeful minimizing of "tiny" was Berman's attempt to capture the sarcasm of
Edmund Wilson, who said that Hayford, "Taselle" and I did well enough in
the "stultifying task" assigned us, but "tiny" also points to something different between the master and the man. There was about Wilson a profound
love of literature and literary relationships. However much he was appalled
by pedantry (and there was, in the apparatus of the Northwestern-Newberry
Typee, formulaic pedantry), he would have understood the grandeur of spirit
that infuses the last scene of my first volume. Wilson himself was not a small
man. And Berman? "Stuff by a small man," Melville said of a critic, remembering Carlyle, who called the triumph of a small reviewer the triumph of a
fool. Harrison Hayford (whose Yale dissertation was on Hawthorne and Melville) understood: "A real DIAMOND of a find." No consolation at the time:
when Berman's review hit the bookstores the day after the *New York Times
Magazine* had appeared with that formidable color photograph, my book
died. Bookstores returned boxes unopened.

Early in his review of my first volume in the *New Republic* (March 17, 1997), James Wood declared that language "is pressed and consoled" in *Moby-Dick* "with Shakespearean agility: "No other novelist of that age could swim in the poetry of 'the warmly cool, clear, ringing, perfumed, overflowing, redundant days'" (29). There's a canker in this rose. You can't tell it here, but the canker poisons everything Wood says about Melville's style, for Wood did not understand "redundant." In his *New Republic* review of Delbanco's *Melville: His World and Work* (December 26, 2005–January 9, 2006), Wood elaborated his essay on Melville's language in *Moby-Dick*:

> Melville's words muster their associations, their deep histories, on every page. There are scores of allusions to the King James Bible. Adjectives and adverbs are placed in glorious, loaded convoy: "The warmly cool, clear, ringing, perfumed, overflowing, redundant days, were as crystal goblets of Persian sherbet, heaped up, flaked up, with rose water snow." With a tiny smirk of irony, Melville saves the word "redundant" for the last place in that gorgeous list: as if to say, "I dare you to find any of these multiple adjectives . . . *redundant!*" ("God's Dictionary," 28)

The first thing you think of, if you know even a shallow history of Melville's words, is that he cannot be using "redundant" to mean "duplicative." He must be using it in a Latin sense, one easy enough to establish with a dictionary if you don't know Latin. If you know Melville, whether or not you know Latin, you know that he takes many latinate words from John Milton. It takes only a moment on Google to locate a couple of likely analogues in *Paradise Lost* and in *Samson Agonistes*. As it happens, the use of "redundant" in *Paradise Lost* is in a description of Satan as serpent which Melville was very familiar with: "his head / Crested aloft, and carbuncle his eyes; / With burnish'd neck of verdant gold, erect / Amidst his circling spires, that on the grass / Floated redundant: pleasing was his shape, / And lovely." Melville used the passage in *The Confidence-Man*, for example. Or look at this passage in *Samson Agonistes* where the fallen hero laments his condition: "to visitants a gaze, / Or pitied object, these redundant locks / Robustious to no purpose clust'ring down, / Vain monument of strength" (lines 567–70).

When Melville's two-volume Milton (Boston: Hilliard, Gray, 1836) first came into view in 1983 in the Phillips Gallery I got a glimpse of it, and when it came up for auction again at Sotheby's in 1989 I was equipped with a copy of the same set, onto which one cloudy Manhattan day I inscribed all Melville's marks and annotations I could see. Now I open my surrogate for Melville's own Milton and see that Melville did some underlining and marking of the page opposite "Floated redundant" and that in the *Samson Agonistes* he drew a line along all of lines 559–74, with another, shorter line along 567–69, three of the lines I just quoted, including "these redundant locks / Robustious." It apparently did not occur to Wood that "redundant" did not mean something like "duplicative." If he had been sensitive to Melville's language enough to know the word had to be Miltonic (or most likely was Miltonic), he could have consulted *Melville and Milton* (2004), edited by Robin Grey, which reprints from *Leviathan* (March and October 2002) the transcription of Melville's marginalia in his Milton by Grey and Douglas Robillard, in consultation with me. But that would have meant being scholarly instead of a smirking, superior critic. Wood does not understand the nobility of Melville's literary ancestry and the towering grandeur of Melville's spirit. Now that Wood brings it up, I see that I simply don't associate with people who smirk, any more than with people who smoke. Life's too short.

You can't tell from his review of my first volume what Wood thought "redundant" showed about Melville's smirking, but what you can tell is that he was reviewing my book as a platform for what I saw as shaky theological bloviations. My factual narrative distressed Wood: "Melville is tied down by Parker's Lilliputian facts," though at times my "dribbling data" could be useful (30, 33). Wood frankly misrepresented the way I said I had composed the book (30):

> Parker has spent his life in Melville-devotions. He is not a critic, he is a connoisseur of facts. He tells us in his introduction that he has spent many years working on the *New Melville Log*, a documentary account of Melville's movements, and that in writing this biography he simply moved chunks of the *Log* from one computer file to the other.

This is false. The only "chunks" that remained in the biography were quotations I did not want to risk rekeying. However little a true critic like Wood could appreciate it, my struggle for years was to discover, select, condense, and shape, always shaping facts into narrative. What's distressing about Wood to a biographer is his cynical double self-promotion: a review is an occasion for a lengthy essay on some topic which interests him (such as ravishment by metaphor). The end in view is not an honest, conscientious review of the book he is paid to read and reflect on but a chapter for a collection of essays.

Seizing, like Wood, on my description of my expansion of *The Melville Log*, Delbanco in the *New York Review of Books* (May 15, 1997) implied that

I had transferred too much of the "digitized log into a biography of the traditional paper and cloth variety" (18). I did this, of course, without selecting,
condensing, or shaping. Then, I hated "the void," Delbanco said (18, and
said again later on 18) and tried to find a document to populate it. Of course!
I did exactly that. One day, all belatedly, I realized that Gansevoort, being
Gansevoort, could not have remained silent after returning to New York in
1844 from his great Western speaking tour. He had to have spoken in New
York City, and Herman would have been back down from Lansingburgh
for his triumph. Delaware had four or five 1844 New York City newspapers,
and in the *Herald* I found my treasure—Gansevoort's magnificent speech in
Newark, New Jersey, one which I decided was echoed in *Moby-Dick*. For the
second volume I realized there was a void for Judge Shaw's funeral and once
I got to the Boston Public Library I found one of the most powerful scenes in
Melville's life. If a biographer does not first perceive a void, though no earlier
biographer had perceived it, and then imagine where to look for documentary evidence that might fill it, that biographer is little worth. I do hate voids.[6]
What's crucial here is that the good biographer who works from original documents and not from other biographies learns very early to put out his or her
hand. Put out your hand, I told my students, and over the decades not one
of them ever came back empty-handed—surprised, chagrined, befouled perhaps, but never empty-handed. Even now, weekly, I can put out my hand on
my computer and find something absolutely new, such as the description of
how Melville and Charles Van Loon jointly dominated the meetings of the
Philo Logos society. Never a researcher, a professor who wrote his 2005 biography of Melville from Higgins's and my collection of contemporary reviews
and from the two volumes of my biography (even quoting snippets from my
quotations), from Arvin and other books, Delbanco just did not understand.
Say it yet again: I am a biographer and I do hate voids!

    Not having much if any experience as a researcher in the archives
(repelled after once playing the tourist at the Houghton Library, to judge
from his 2005 account and from his lack of notes to archival evidence), Delbanco did not understand how documentary evidence can be deployed, as
when he says that on Melville's return to Boston "Parker's engine of invention remains at full throttle" in the depiction of Melville's acquaintance with
Elizabeth Shaw (19). Accusing a documentary biographer of fantasizing, of
course, is the ultimate damnation. I refer the reader to the chapter in this
book on Melville's courtship of Elizabeth Shaw. I did debate with myself
about inserting perhapses and maybes into the biography, but the evidence
was compelling. One problem with a multiplicity of evidence is that to tell
a story and justify it at every phase is all but impossible. The chapter on the

courtship in this book is not narrative; it is a demonstration of how to weigh the evidence that you accumulate and how you muster it into narrative.

Curiously, Delbanco found that I trivialized Melville by finding "no grand theme," but "only a reductive and overdetermining one: at the root of every mood and motivation Parker finds sexual craving" (19). In turn, I was shocked at Delbanco's assumption that Melville's father would not have suffered sexual deprivation in Maria's absence, not when there was "a large population of prostitutes in antebellum New York" (19). I'm shocked now at copying these words. Allan and Maria, the documents show, and the pregnancies show, were a sexually active couple who frankly missed each other during their separations. Their letters make this plain. Look at Maria's description of Herman as very restless and ill at ease without his intended (her letter to Augusta on May 30, 1847) and you see a woman with Regency sexual sophistication, not a cringing Victorian. Delbanco quite misrepresented me (19): "When Herman reaches adulthood, the sex theme takes charge, and we get a portrait of a randy young man strutting through what Frederick Crews has called 'the age of the draped piano leg.'" A randy strutting young man? Reading those words I see that I have wandered in on someone else's pornographic fantasy, not mine: it was Delbanco, after all, who in 1992 had projected "juicy," lubricious, stories upon me, claiming to have read them in my mind. My discovery that Melville was the first American literary sex symbol surprised me, too, when I discovered it and worked the news into my first volume. But there is no "waggish leering" (20) in my biography. That's simply not in my character. In my chapter on Fayaway I recur to this passage, for Delbanco was not through with it himself.

I reject the twist Delbanco gives the topic: "It is one of the signal failures of Parker's book that with all its talk about sex, it takes small account of how much Melville was haunted by the 'visitations' of sin" (20). I simply don't think Melville spent his days searching his conscience for sins past, present, or future, the way many a child of Calvinism does. Melville could worry himself about the biblical and Miltonic themes that Hawthorne summarized, and he thought that to make sense of the world you had to throw in something like the concept of Original Sin, but he was not worrying about his own sins. His broodings were philosophical, "metaphysical," not tormented introspection into his motives and actions. It's clear from his 2005 book that Delbanco follows Arvin in minimizing Melville's broodings about both philosophical and aesthetic issues. Dig there! In reflecting on Andrew Delbanco's review I have to remind myself and you (once again) that although Delbanco had read books (by Mumford and Arvin, for sure) and articles (by Updike, for sure) he *still* had not read (or did not remember major scenes in)

The Melville Log (either the first edition, 1951, or the one with the "Supplement," 1969). Although he had played the tourist in at least two libraries, he made no quotations from original documents in his 2005 book. Snippets of quotations from the Augusta Papers taken from my own longer quotations from the original documents do not count as research, since he never knew the contexts from which I had made my own selection. This basic ignorance of Melville documents, published as well as unpublished, may lie behind Delbanco's bewildered disdain of what is new to him.

Berman, Wood, and Delbanco all had more or less transparent agendas, although not announced up front. Berman and Delbanco were continuing the Mumford-Wilson attacks on the Center for Editions of American Authors and the Northwestern-Newberry *Writings of Herman Melville*. Coincidentally, Berman might have pleased the editor of his *A Tale of Two Utopias*, the same man who had taken great pride in the prospect of editing my biography for W. W. Norton, the one who had declared that he would "shit can" my letter in which I formally abrogated the contract because the terms had been broken but in which I offered to repay the advances, which I could legally have kept. Who had gotten young Berman the honor of reviewing my biography in the *New York Times Book Review*? Aside from ingratiating himself with the Wilson-revering *New York Review of Books* crowd, Delbanco had a pretty clear agenda. He could establish himself as an authority on Melville the easy way, not by doing research on Melville but by reviewing what I published, then what I published next, and then what I published after that. Thereafter, plundering the Higgins-Parker collection of reviews and my two volumes of the biography, he could emerge with a biography of his own, even if he did not get around to learning some basic episodes in Melville's life until after 2002 and even if in 2005 he omitted whole years of Melville's creative life and much of his intellectual and aesthetic life. Wood was using reviewing as an occasion for largely irrelevant essayistic flights which could be collected in a book. These reviewers indulged in personal insults, but there were outshone by John Sutherland in the London *Sunday Times* (January 5, 1997): "Reading this biography is the most dreary and stultifying experience imaginable. Rolling peanuts up hills with your nose or counting traffic on the M25 is fun by comparison." When Sutherland published his my-bottom-was-lower-than-your-bottom saga of his alcoholism in 2001 I did a quick count and figured he was some fourteen years sober when he imagined rolling those peanuts. Well, I've known alcoholics who kept themselves on a raging dry drunk longer than that.[7]

What had Berman said—"gigantic leaf-drifts of petty facts"? For Wood I was "not a critic" but only "a connoisseur of facts." Delbanco deplored the "promiscuous detail" (18). The best commentary I have seen on biographical facts is Ray Monk's in "Life Without Theory: Biography as an Exemplar of Philosophical Understanding," in the section on "The New Biography: The Importance of a Point of View." There Monk quotes Lytton Strachey on "two duties of the biographer": "a becoming brevity—a brevity that excludes everything that is redundant and nothing that is significant" and the duty "to maintain his own freedom of spirit" (537–38). Strachey was intensely concerned that the biographer "lay bare the facts of the case, as he understands them" (538). Monk reminds us of Strachey's definition of the qualities that make a historian, which to my mind are the same as make a biographer: "a capacity for absorbing facts, a capacity for stating them, and a point of view" (538). History, Strachey went on, "is not the accumulation of facts, but the relation of them. . . . Facts relating to the past, when they are collected without art, are compilations; and compilations, no doubt, are useful; but they are no more History than butter, eggs, salt and herbs are an omlette" (538–39). Nothing is wrong with compilations, but discrimination is needed. *The Melville Log* is a compilation? Yes, but with artful ellipses in what meets the eye and artful selection in what is not on the page at all. Strachey, as Monk lucidly portrays him, would have understood: "He believed . . . that the arts of history and of biography (and he was vehement in his insistence that both were arts) consisted not only in the discovery of facts but also, and more crucially, in the *interpretation* of them, but he regarded the two processes, discovery and interpretation, as quite separate from one another" (539).[8]

Monk traces Strachey's "characterization of Victorian biographies as 'two fat volumes . . . with their ill-digested masses of material, their slipshod style, their tone of tedious panegyric, their lamentable lack of selection, of detachment, of design'" (537). Lazy reviewers used their secondhand impressions of Strachey to condemn my volumes without reading Strachey carefully and without reading my biography, often revealing their witlessness in variations of "exhaustive and exhausting." Another phrase much in vogue with slovenly reviewers, "mind-numbing detail," suggests that their minds came to their assigned task pre-numbed. Reviewers who dismissively pat a biographer on the head as "indefatigable" reveal that they have never devoted much effort to any intellectual or aesthetic enterprise, certainly not to the creation of something monumental in difficulty and size. Having particular reviewers in mind, I wrote sympathetically in my biography (2:688) that while writing *Clarel* Melville "was fatigable, and often desperately fatigued, but he persisted; 'indefatigable' is offered as perfunctory praise only by superficial critics who have no idea what real work is." Such reviewers never glimpsed that I am totally in agreement with Strachey. I simply found so much new

material, so many facts to take account of, that it would have been dishonest to write a trim little biography and pass it off as all that was needed. I left
Norton, giving back $50,000 I was not obligated to repay, just to have my
freedom to tell (with my interpretation) the whole new story. And outside of
New York City, many reviewers rejoiced at that story.

Harold Beaver in the January 10, 1997, *Times Literary Supplement* read
the book which Sutherland had failed to read:

> The linking of so much material into a continually engaging narra-
> tive is a magnificent achievement; and it is fitting that the author of a
> whale of a *Whale* should be the subject of this whale of a biography.
> Hershel Parker's *magnum opus* is a magisterial work of retrieval and
> unflagging scholarship, whose sheer diversity of detail adds human
> complexity to what earlier often seemed no more than an inert
> chronicle. It caps all previous endeavours. Whatever new discoveries
> are made (and there may be some surprises yet) will have to be built
> on his meticulous groundwork. He not only clarifies all known facts
> but demythologizes the fiction, carefully distinguishing biographical
> references from much spurious self-reference which deceived earlier
> commentators.

Long before, Beaver had ravaged the Hayford-Parker textual section of
the 1967 Norton Critical Edition of *Moby-Dick* for his Penguin edition
("Hayford-Parker Readings Adopted" became "Other Emendations Adopted"
and "Hayford-Parker Readings Considered" became "Other Emendations
Considered"). After Norton decided not to sue, I consoled myself that if I
had been English my work would have earned me a promotion to "Reader of
American literature" at the University of Warwick. Beaver's late atonement
was timely. In London as guests of Lisa Harrow and Roger Payne in order to
do research in the British Library, particularly the Colindale newspapers, we
used the current *Times Literary Supplement*, available at every WHSmith, to
expedite our way through the gates.

There were reviews of the sort I was sure I had deserved. On December
15, 1996, Robert Faggen in the *Los Angeles Times* said, "Parker's study is
an awesome achievement, indispensable for all serious Melvilleans, with the
vividness of a great Victorian novel and the precision of the finest historical
scholarship." On January 26, 1997, William W. Starr in the *State* (Columbia,
S.C.) began by saying, "Like Leon Edel's massive multi-volume biography of
Henry James, Parker's work seems certain to stand for generations as a monument to Melville biographical research and interpretation." The biography,

he concluded, "breathes new life into one of the great American writers, and its narrative expanse—if perhaps more than many readers will require—is an unrivaled resource in giving us a deeper understanding and appreciation of Herman Melville." (I am not flattered by the comparison to the idiosyncratic Edel.) Douglas Sealy in the *Irish Times* (February 8, 1997) saw in the volume "a Balzacian richness of detail." Brian Kiernan in the *Sydney Morning Herald* (June 14, 1997) declared it "a monument to American literary biography," like Richard Ellmann's *James Joyce* and Leon Edel's *Henry James*, and elaborated:

> Parker's meticulous, often day-by-day accounts of Melville's interactions with this literary community during the writing of *Moby-Dick* is freshly informed and absorbing. When it reaches this stage, Parker's narrative soars above dutiful documentation—and if, during the long approach to it, readers might feel somewhat overwhelmed by detail, they can always skip ahead, confident that the excellent index will allow backtracking and checking. The ending is a triumph.

In the *Richmond (Va.) Times-Dispatch* (September 14, 1997) Welford D. Taylor saw the volume as "far and away, the best informed biography of Melville ever written, deriving as it does from Parker's vast yet easy grasp of the mountain of secondary studies and from literally thousands of unpublished documents." Taylor continued: "But Parker's work is more than authoritative. Its learning never calls attention to itself, nor does he, as story-teller, intrude. Rather, by establishing an up-close perspective, from which we view the everyday Melville in his numerous milieus, Parker creates a living sense of the man."

The only review by a Melville scholar (as distinguished from critic) was that by Stanton Garner in *Melville Society Extracts* (March 1998). Garner complained about "the inadequacy of the documentation" in which the lack of documentation made it impossible to "check, or profit from, Parker's discoveries" (28–29). I found this perturbing, since my intention was to have *everything* attributed: newspapers were identified by date, reviews of Melville's books were to the Higgins-Parker collection (unless they were recently discovered), letters to and from Melville were to the *Correspondence* (unless they also were specified as new). I included a lengthy chart of correspondents which made it possible to see the repositories in which the manuscripts were held (and even to tell from the chart when a particular document was held apart from most of that person's letters). *Everything*, I thought, was documented, discreetly and efficiently. The mistake about documentation stayed in my memory but I had all but forgotten until now that Garner liked the book (28):

> If you want to understand a life, read a proper biography. I mean, read a work such as Parker's, in which one's sense of the defensible and justifiable is never offended, even though the outer limits of our knowledge of Melville are pushed far beyond our expectations. As an editor of the Northwestern-Newberry edition of Melville's works, Parker has long been close to what is, collaterally, a large biographical project.

That insight into the biographical basis of editing is one which only a scholar would appreciate (indeed, an influential school of editors does not acknowledge it). I emphasize the relation between editing and biography by the title of the second chapter of this book. More from Garner, who was gracious about my correcting him once (28):

> The experience also seems to have schooled him in the techniques of discovering material where it lies hidden and developed in him a sense of what may remain to be discovered if only one persists. Nor has Parker been reticent in obtaining the assistance of others, thus extending his reach beyond scholarly arm's length.
>
>   The result is stunning. What in the past has been no more than a hint, a reference, or a brief note in [Leon] Howard becomes an illuminating account of an incident in Melville's life, and what was an error (in this case, a date in my own report on Uncle Thomas's disgrace in Galena, Illinois), is corrected, uncloaking a new insight into Melville's early search for a career and thus into his motive for voyaging aboard the *Acushnet*. If this is a large volume, it is also one in which questions are answered, misapprehensions set aright, and whole briskets of knowledge added to our hoarded heaps.

All this went into the hands of the right people, members of the Melville Society (28–29):

> This is not only a thorough biography, but also a sensitively conceived and artfully executed one, in which the prose is competent at least and stirring at best. . . . In our time, it is rare for a scholar to dedicate so much of his inner resources for so long to what our profession selfishly demands, achievement without hope of compensation in

kind; and Parker still has the second volume and the *Log* to complete. Of what we have so far, we could ask for little more, for this is a task large in conception and deft in execution. When completed, it will be a standard by which other scholars will have to measure their own aspirations and intentions. In short, it is a masterwork with which Leyda's confidence has been well repaid.

This came, of course, many months after the annihilating reviews in the New York newspapers and magazines, and although it went to a select audience, that audience was unfortunately small, and as far as I know no one ever mentioned Garner's review. Reading it now, I see something quite missing from the New York reviews—a largeness of spirit in envisioning Melville (28): "One can hardly read the closing pages, in which one senses a world gathered around a nearly empty dining room in a Lenox hotel to observe the author of one of the great works of all time handing a copy to another great author, to whom it was dedicated, without the sense that there never was, nor ever will be, another such moment."

Looking back from October 28, 1999, Trevor Butterworth in a piece in *NewsWatch* noted that in "Ireland and Britain," the winner of the 1997 Pulitzer Prize for biography, Frank McCourt's *Angela's Ashes*, was honestly marketed as fiction. It was too bad that the "Pulitzer biography jury in 1997, which included the historian and biographer Doris Kearns Goodwin, gave 'Angela's Ashes' the prize over competition from 'Herman Melville: A Biography, Volume 1, 1819–1851' by Hershel Parker—a serious work of history."[9] But even with this welcome attempt at vindication from Butterworth, the damage to my reputation by the misreadings and misunderstandings of Delbanco and the others just described was accomplished. It even spread out, as vilest rumor always does, as when Alan Helms after reading Delbanco's slurs decided that I was a "slippery fish" (414) with evidence—a baseless secondhand accusation that keeps popping up on the Internet.[10]

Ian Hamilton in his *How to Do Biography: A Primer* (2008, 333) offers this short paragraph: "Let me dispel the gloom, however. Telling someone's story well may be the most life-affirming thing you'll ever do!" I had thought so until Berman's *New York Times* review came out and I saw what I was facing. Was continuing on the biography worth it, after all the labor of writing and all the damage to my health and peace of mind? On October 1, 2000, I copied Gutzon Borglum's ungraceful but powerful declaration into the back end-pages of the first volume of my biography, what his granddaughter Robin Carter describes as his "philosophy on creating": "The reason for building any work of art can only be for the purpose of fixing in some durable form a great emotion, or a great idea, of the individual, or the people."[11] I wasn't thinking about Melville, although it could have applied to him in the composition of *Moby-Dick* or *Clarel*. I was thinking of myself, isolated from professional Melville critics and defamed by New York City critics of my first volume while I struggled to achieve a state of grace and remain in that state for as many months as it took to finish the second volume of the biography. I understood then what Melville experienced when *Moby-Dick* was trashed — too many too-powerful commentators had trashed my first volume without reading it. Melville fought to stay in a state of grace, and succeeded, almost all the way through his work on *Pierre*. But then he was caught off guard by the contract the Harpers offered, twenty cents on the dollar instead of fifty, and he exploded in what he inserted into the completed *Pierre*. I would not explode.

If I had not held myself in that state of grace, that "zone" athletes talk about, I could not have finished the second volume. Was it heroic? Well, writing the biography was the great adventure of my life, outdoing my five months of doing nothing but reading Shakespeare. Put it this humble way: at my lowest moments, when I felt that no one could carry on Jay Leyda's work while writing his own narrative biography, I played a tape of the group Forebitter in my Bronco II, the "Harbo and Samuelson" song about the hearty young Norwegian oystermen who set out to row across the Atlantic, west to east. *"They were not only brave, but by God they could row!"* I listened and blubbered in the Bronco then went back to work. And of course if I had not been my own Leyda I could not have written a biography filled with new episodes and new understanding of my vastly larger cast of characters. At the simplest level, I found episodes when I dated documents. How many of my cherished stories started with transcribing and dating?

After 1996 and 1997 I ought to have known what to expect but I was off guard in 2002 when the second volume was savaged much more cruelly than the first. In the May 20, 2002, *Nation* Brenda Wineapple (whose vulgar ignorance of Melville and desecration of the Lamb of God I look at elsewhere in this book) declared that I was as secure in my fantasy biography "as Edmund Morris is in his imaginary *Dutch: A Memoir of Ronald Reagan*" (39). Brodhead in the June 23, 2002, *New York Times* implied that I had invented *The Isle of the Cross* (1853) and *Poems* (1860) out of thin air (13). In the *New Republic* (September 30, 2002) the look-ma-no-hands biographer-to-be Delbanco said I couldn't be trusted at all on anything because I had merely surmised the existence of those lost books (34). He had, of course, not read all of the book he was reviewing, for the evidence about the books is on the pages. And Elizabeth Schultz in the *Common Review* (Winter 2002) echoed those two critics about the merely "putative" existence of those lost books (45). If Wineapple in the *Nation* had not done it already, these reviews, one coming from a named professor at Columbia, the home of the Pulitzer Prizes, knocked me totally out of the running for any New York prize. In 1997 a letter from George Rupp had come to "Hirshel Parker": "Though the 1997 Pulitzer Prize in Biography was won by Frank McCourt, I hope you will be pleased to learn that you were among the jury's nominees, a rare distinction." In 2003 there was no such letter, name spelled right or wrong. There was, however, for the second time the highest award from the Association of American Publishers' Professional/Scholarly Publishing Division, in the new, more appropriate category of "Biography and Autobiography" while the first volume won in "Literature and Language."

Several reviewers of Delbanco's 2005 *Melville: His World and Work* bought into his self-serving claim that for Melville as for Bartleby "no materials exist for a full and satisfactory biography of this man." Because there survives so little detail, he proclaimed, "any conventional biography of Melville is a business bound to fail" (xxi). Bound to fail "for sheer lack of material," William Grimes echoed in the *New York Times* (October 5, 2005). In the London *Independent* (January 15, 2006) Tom Rosenthal turned the disclaimer into a compliment, "Andrew Delbanco is modest enough to admit that, while there is no end to the biographing of Melville, there are few new facts about him." Jay Parini in the London *Guardian* (November 4, 2005: "Jay Parini hails the first proper life of the elusive author") agreed that "Melville left few traces of himself." He had good news: "Unlike Parker, Delbanco knows when to shut up." Very strangely, on June 11, 2009, I received an e-mail purportedly from a Jay Parini who wanted to be "in touch" with me and let me know that he knew how much work and skill had gone into my "magnificent" biography, which he was rereading closely and with great admiration. This ventriloquist hacker, as it must have been, invited me to stop by "his" old farmhouse on a hilltop overlooking the Green Mountains. Imagine the shock to the real Parini had I dropped by, if indeed a veritable Parini inhabited such a farmhouse! No one challenged Delbanco for ignoring "details" about Melville's life or for following Mumford and Arvin in ignoring whole episodes of Melville's life and many of his prolonged intellectual and aesthetic engagements. Even the skeptical Vivian Gornick in the *Nation* declared, "*Melville: His World and Work* is a full and faithful account of all that is already known and recorded of the writer's personal life" (45), unaware of how many episodes of Melville's life and how many of his artistic interests had been truncated or totally ignored.

Frederick Crews, as far as I know, never struggled through complex American textual puzzles far enough to formulate textual theory and never grappled with complex evidence from American archival sources to the point of discovering new episodes of the life of a writer like Melville. Had he done so (for he is the best critic of his generation) in the *New York Review of Books* (December 1, 2005), he would not have bought into Delbanco's image (xxi) of a Bartleby-like Melville for whom "no materials exist for a full and satisfactory biography." He would not so readily have bought into the Mumford-Delbanco idea that Melville's creativity had been snuffed out before he became a poet. He might not have praised Delbanco for going against the academic grain when in fact he went in lockstep with Newton Arvin. Delbanco all but ignored Melville's preoccupation with painting, sculpture, and architecture and his engagement with ideas about aesthetics. He slighted Melville's experiences in Europe and the Levant and slighted the evidence of his marginalia in Vasari and other art historians and critics. Going only from the book he was reviewing, Crews clearly had no idea that Delbanco's biography was as truncated as Arvin's in its dismissal of the importance of foreign travel, the importance of Melville's aesthetic grapplings, the significance of the months Melville worked on *The Isle of the Cross* and of the two or three years he worked on the book he wanted to call *Poems*, the book that Delbanco had expressed such skepticism about in 2002. Had Crews read my biography and recent writings by Robert K. Wallace and others on Melville and art he might have used Brodhead's street-talk, "Thanks, but no thanks," when asked to review Delbanco's *Melville: His World and Work* (in which on page 208 Delbanco does echo Brodhead's "Thanks, but no thanks" in the January 7, 1996, "Bookend"). As it was, the incomparable Crews was hamstrung so that he made pronouncements on the Delbanco "Mini-Melville" as if it were a comprehensive, rounded life showing the full if thwarted trajectory of Melville's career.

Late in 2006, focusing on what Brodhead, by then president of Duke University, was doing and saying about the admirable lacrosse coach Michael Pressler and the obviously innocent lacrosse players, I decided I had to put on record how similarly he had trashed my own reputation. As I had so presciently said in 1984, Brodhead was indeed blind to human agony: he refused even to look at exculpatory evidence the agonized parents of lacrosse players pleaded to show him (one ATM videotape would have cleared one of the endangered players instantly). I wrote what was published in the June 2007 *Nineteenth-Century Literature* (out in July) as "*The Isle of the Cross* and *Poems*: Lost Melville Books and the Indefinite Afterlife of Error." In June 2007 I began setting the record straight on the Internet, before the

Nineteenth-Century Literature article appeared. Later, in the introduction to *Melville: The Making of the Poet* (2008) I commented on how Brodhead, Delbanco, and Schultz and other critics had distorted the trajectory of Melville's career by denying or minimizing Melville's lost works. A version of the book went into the capacious Northwestern-Newberry Edition of *Published Poems* in 2009. Although I had not slept one night in peace in the five years from June 2002, after June 7, 2007, I have never lost sleep over Wineapple, Brodhead, Delbanco, and Schultz. Suffering in silence is a killer. The reviewers' false statements about *The Isle of the Cross* and *Poems* survive in print and on the Internet, of course. The afterlife of error is indeed indefinite.

Because of my unique ability to put Brodhead's shocking behavior at Duke in a long, rich New Critical context, I became a "blog hooligan" (the contemptuous term invented by Cathy Davidson) and intermittently an Internet columnist, flogging myself into the new century. Then in January 2011 I started my blog (http://fragmentsfromawritingdesk.blogspot.com/), where I can lay out the truth about reviewers. I reproduce, for example, the lengthy index entry on marginalia along with Robert Milder's strange rebuke of me for ignoring that rich resource.[12] As I finish *Melville Biography: An Inside Narrative* it seems possible that a pack of New York City reviewers can never annihilate any well-researched book as totally as they could do in 2002. The usually innocuous *New York Times Book Review* survives, in diminished state, as does the often rabid *New York Review of Books*, and they are read, still. Yet never again will pompous, error-filled articles in the *New Yorker* or self-serving misrepresentations and outright lies in the *Nation* or the *New York Times* or the *New York Review of Books* or the *New Republic* hold place on the Internet unchallenged for years.

When John Palattella in the *Nation* (June 2, 2010) lamented "The Death and Life of the Book Review" (arguing that book review sections should not be judged by whether they turn a profit) "TheBigAl" posted this comment on the *Nation* website: "You don't seem aware of the breadth of quality literary blogs on the Internet. As an editor, we find these days that we often have more luck getting attention from persuasive and prestigious blogs than from newspaper book review sections, where editors have their own agendas." A blogger posted: "Beyond Barnes & Noble Review there are actually a number of websites that provide quality books coverage," among them "The Complete Review" and "Berfrois." Daniel Green, one of the heroes of Internet reviewing, quoted Palattella's claim that although we "are in the throes of another newspaper crisis" nothing has appeared in print or online the way newspaper strikes brought forth the *New York Review of Books* and the *London Review of Books*. On June 3, 2010, Green objected: "This is manifestly

not the case. Just two examples: The Quarterly Conversation (http://www.
quarterlyconversation.com/) and Open Letters Monthly (http://www
.openlettersmonthly.com/). You might have more honestly said, 'Nothing
comparable to the *NYRB* or the *LRB* written and edited by recognized, mainstream literary journalists, preferably based in New York, has emerged.'"

Rain Taxi in the Summer 2005 issue (that early) contained Scott Esposito's survey, "Litblogs Provide a New Alternative for Readers." A writer on the
topic of litblogs was sometimes lucky if a link to a brilliant litblog or personal
literary blog outlasted a recommendation. Nevertheless, the situation is sta-
bilizing, Esposito made clear:

> One trait shared by virtually all litbloggers is their enthusiasm for
> defying mainstream opinion, and because of this willingness to offer
> a countervailing point of view the litblogging community has man-
> aged to attract a substantial audience in a relatively short period
> of time. The highest-trafficked blogs get thousands of hits per day
> (sometimes tens of thousands if they're in the news), and the pub-
> lishing industry has taken note. Many litbloggers regularly get galleys
> from publishers ranging from Random House to Copper Canyon
> Press to the Dalkey Archive, and anecdotal evidence indicates that
> their coverage has helped sell books and prop up emerging authors
> . . . . Several well-regarded midlist authors . . . have done interviews
> with litbloggers, and some publicists are beginning to develop lasting
> relationships with favored litbloggers.

After intelligent reviews of my 2008 *Melville: The Making of the Poet* appeared
in litblogs and individual blogs, I arranged that review copies of *The Powell
Papers* (2011) be sent to some of the bloggers. I expect that presses, more
and more, will send review copies to litblogs and pre-tested bloggers (the
"veteran" bloggers of the future), where the best reviewers consistently write
more intelligently than the average *New York Review of Books* pontificator.

Of course there is resistance to Internet reviewing. On his Reading Experience 2.0 site (October 23, 2007) Daniel Green hilariously surveys the
motives of the blog-bashers: "The disdain for literary blogs and other 'non-
traditional' sources of literary discussion that drips from the pens of Gail Pool
and Richard Schickel and Michael Dirda must rise from a mounting fear
that their sense of separation from mere 'amateurs' is at risk: If you can't look
down on bloggers, after all, who can you look down on?" The hacks and the
occasional admirable mainstream media reviewers will not soon be driven

out by "ragtag bloggers" (although newspaper book review sections are dying month by month), but authors may have multiple chances to be heard in the new Internet age. We will see what happens when *Melville Biography: An Inside Narrative* is ready for reviewing.

✢ *Chapter 8* ✣

LITTLE JACK HORNERS AND ARCHIVOPHOBICS

THE NEW CRITICAL CONQUEST of Yale and other universities imposed a devastating disruption of the study of American literary history and its relation to American history as a whole. From the 1950s on graduate students were trained only as New Critics, not in the handling of scholarly evidence, and few of them made any effort later on to master for themselves the scholarly training their generation had been denied. As if to demonstrate how triumphant the New Criticism had been all along, despite the string of nominally new literary approaches with new names, in the late 1970s and early 1980s Charles Feidelson, the vilifier of Jay Leyda's *The Melville Log*, experienced what Barbara Foley in "From New Criticism to Deconstruction: The Example of Charles Feidelson's *Symbolism and American Literature*" described as "a remarkable resurgence of popularity" (47). In a close analysis Foley linked the deficiencies of Feidelson's theories to the deficiencies of the new Deconstructionists. She showed that "New Criticism and deconstruction jointly enshrine nonrationality and self-reflexivity in literature and criticism" because they both "conceive of the historical world as lacking in inherent structure or meaning" (58). She continued with a detailed analysis of how Feidelson's contempt for facts fits with Deconstructionist contempt for material reality, "facts" (58):

> The New Critical designation of scientific language as inferior to poetic language suggests that the "facts" of the material world are inert and fragmented data, possessing no capacity to illuminate the complexity of human experience. As Feidelson puts it . . . there is a profound epistemological abyss between the realm embodied in the symbolic imagination, that of the "thinking ego," and the realm of "brute fact."

Foley went on with an analysis directly relevant to my concerns in this chapter: "The root cause besetting New Criticism and deconstruction as theories of literature and methods of reading is, I propose, their common elimination of history from the lexicon of literary study" (60–61). History and, of course, biography.

Ironically, just as Feidelson's views were enjoying a late efflorescence, some professors, primarily younger ones, displayed what perhaps ought to have embarrassed them, an urge to have something to do with enterprises which sounded downright scholarly—the creation of new histories of American literature. The standard literary histories had been published in the late 1940s, in a last hurrah before the dominance of the New Criticism. Although professors in the early 1980s were untrained in research into history and literary history (and biography), two bands of them enthusiastically decided to turn their hand to literary history while there was still time, before they turned forty-five or fifty or fifty-five, in many cases. After three decades of the New Criticism, surely something scholarly would look good on their résumés, as long as it did not demand much historical and biographical research and as long as it did not require them to make a public recantation of their allegiance to the New Criticism.

Rather than trying to educate themselves in the alien fields, the new New Historicists proceeded to write history and literary history as if research had all been done long before, once and for all, prior to, say, around 1940. The General Editor of the *Columbia Literary History of the United States,* Emory Elliott, blandly rationalized his contributors' failure to do research. They were doing something better than poring over musty old documents in pursuit of an impossible goal of telling the truth about literary history. Elliott proclaimed the new order of things in the introduction:

> The old records, diaries, letters, newspapers, official firsthand documents, or statistical figures examined by the historian are no longer thought of as reflecting "the" past; rather, there is no past except what can be construed from these documents as they are filtered through the perceptions and special interests of the historian who is using them. Thus the historian is not a truthteller but a storyteller, who succeeds in convincing readers that a certain rendition of the past is "true" not by facts but by persuasive rhetoric and narrative skill. (xvii)

A similar disregard for new historical research marked the competing *Cambridge History of American Literature,* the General Editor of which, Sacvan Bercovitch, in a *Times Literary Supplement* review (January 9, 1987) placed one of his contributors, Michael T. Gilmore, "at the forefront of a new generation of critics who are . . . reshaping our ways of thinking about literature and culture" (40). Yet in the book being reviewed, *American Romanticism and the Marketplace*, Gilmore avoided archival research into contracts and promotion tactics and distribution systems and sales figures while instead proceeding as if William Charvat had long ago done all the research that ever needed to be done (in his 1968 *Profession of Authorship in America: 1800–1870*). These new authors of literary history were writing literary history the fast easy way, without new facts, taking a Hawthornesque Celestial Railroad to the *Columbia Literary History of the United States* and to the *Cambridge History of American Literature*.

Elliott was right: the contributors to these new literary histories were not such fools as to hope to tell the truth: there was no such thing as truth. They were, as he promised, storytellers, and were to be judged on their narrative verve, not on anything like discovery of and adherence to facts. In the prevailing spirit of the entire *Columbia Literary History*, the author of the Melville chapter, Robert Milder, did not even refer to the great trove of new biographical material available at the New York Public Library since 1983. So much for facts! Instead of looking at biographical documents, Milder made a biographical argument about fullness and organic unity: "Reading Herman Melville in his fullness means attending to the peremptory inward development that impelled his most ambitious books, strained the confines of his literary forms, and gave his career an organic unity that subsumes and transcends the cumulative achievement of his works" (429). In *Reading "Billy Budd"* (1990) I protested against Milder's extrapolating the old New Critical version of organic unity to apply not only to literary works but to Melville's life, never mind that some of Melville's own compositional processes were disrupted and never mind that his writing career "suffered violent truncation rather than anything that obviously resembles an organic progression" (93). Milder was displaying New Criticism run amok—the literary approach that had banned biographical information now forcibly, even procrusteanly, imposed not upon literature but upon a writer's life.[1]

Milder talked in biographical terms but did not think in human terms, as genuine biographers must do. It seems not to have occurred to him, for instance, to talk about Melville as a writer who completed at least two books that he could never publish. "Reading Herman Melville in his fullness" for Milder, oddly enough, did not mean thinking about the months Melville had spent on the lost book Davis and Gilman had shown he had completed in 1853 or on the volume he called *Poems* which he finished in 1860. Let's talk straight. If Milder had written two or three books he had been prevented from publishing, would he omit all mention of them and still reflect on the fullness and organic unity of his career? Would he think of his own thwarted career as having had anything like a "fullness and organic unity?" Is Herman Melville less a human being than Robert Milder or me? Speaking for myself, I know that having a monograph-length essay (on Fredson Bowers's edition of Stephen Crane's *Maggie*) suppressed for two decades, under threats of lawsuits, absolutely wrecked the possibility that I could think of my career as having an organic unity. Many people read that essay in the 1970s but did not comment on it out of fear of Bowers. There was, all those two decades, an absence of commentary on the long article just when it would have evoked much discussion and might even have changed policies at the National Endowment for the Humanities and the Modern Language Association. When it was finally published, it was as true as ever but the circumstances had so changed that it had no practical impact. Now the article is in my list of publications (and Brian Higgins's, for his part of it), but its failure to be published in the 1970s wrecked the fullness and unity of my career. What is true of a scholar like me, I submit, is immeasurably more powerfully true of a great writer whose book between *Pierre* and "Bartleby" we will (barring a miracle) never be able to read. Critics like Milder objectify great writers, in this case crushing Melville into a formula devised for criticizing poetry. Cleanth Brooks, Robert Penn Warren, and the other original New Critics never meant their theories to transmogrify, in the hands of a disciple, into a theory of human biography in which a great writer can be mangled worse than Procrustes ever did to his guests — in fact can be pulverized into a factitious unified smoothness like processed cheese food.

In the early1980s Richard Brodhead, like others of his generation, decided to branch out from criticism to engage in literary history without first learning how to do historical research.[2] The result was the 1986 *The School of Hawthorne*. I did not think Melville had ever been a student of Hawthorne's and questioned his presence in the book, especially since Brodhead did nothing new to justify his inclusion. At Yale, Brodhead had not been trained in writing literary history. The New Criticism, embodied by Yale's Charles Feidelson, had scorned biographical-historical research for decades. A scholar would have worked his or her way through dozens of nineteenth-century American novels lying neglected in Sterling Memorial Library before thinking of writing a book called *The School of Hawthorne*. I had a good idea of what the research should have involved, for in 1961, after I had decided to work on Melville with Harrison Hayford at Northwestern, I arranged to take my only graduate independent reading course. I went through all the literary histories of American literature making lists of nineteenth-century American novels pointed out by one critic or another as interesting although neglected. I read or skimmed thoughtfully two hundred or so books and made little two- or three-page reports on them. Among the best surprises for me were Harriet Beecher Stowe's New England novels. Nobody wrote more authoritatively about the New England theology of the Young Republic than Stowe. What I learned served me extremely well in classes later on, and came into play when I looked at *The School of Hawthorne*.

Brodhead had elected to write a contribution to the history of the novel in the United States without reading very widely in the novels written in the United States. Through most of the book he was attempting to show Hawthorne's influence on American novelists of the second half of the nineteenth century—without having any idea how pervasive that influence was. When I began looking for novelists other than the dead white men in his book I did not find them. How, I asked, backing away to an earlier decade, can Brodhead have mentioned Harriet Beecher Stowe several times without knowing that Hawthorne's influence can be traced in her New England novels, very obviously, the title should tell you, in *The Pearl of Orr's Island*? Then, I found this remarkably invidious comment (8): "Thomas Bailey Aldrich, a once-admired poet more forgotten now than even the word 'limbo' can suggest, found his poetical vocation while reading Longfellow." As someone who knows firsthand just how much pain Brodhead's snide innuendo can inflict (for I remember my baffled agony at his vicious accusation in the *New York Times* that I, alone in my "black hole," had fantasized Melville's *Poems*), I wince at the contempt in this sentence as I retype it. Here, as in his review of my biography, his elitist contempt masks Brodhead's own ignorance. Aldrich is farther out of reach even than "limbo"? What about the nearby shelves of the Sterling Library? Brodhead should have harrowed Hell itself if necessary in reading through novels of the nineteenth and early twentieth century looking for followers of Hawthorne. How can you write a book about *The School of Hawthorne* and mention Thomas Bailey Aldrich with such disdain as a forgotten poet and not discuss, not mention at all, his popular *The Stillwater Tragedy*, which opens with an extended passage written in loving homage to Hawthorne's set piece in *The House of the Seven Gables* on the passage of the night and the morning while a corpse awaits discovery? Brodhead singled out Aldrich because he had seen his name but had not read him. What of all the other nineteenth-century writers he had heard little or nothing about? Brodhead, like Milder, exemplifies the folly of practicing the New Historicism without historical research.

What can be said about Brodhead's treatment of Melville in this *School* book? Let me just point out that Brodhead grounds a theory of creativity and of Hawthorne's influence on Melville on his reading of one of the most famous passages in Melville's letters: "What I feel most moved to write, that is banned,—it will not pay. Yet, altogether, write the *other* way I cannot. So the product is a final hash, and all my books are botches." This, of course, is from the letter to Hawthorne long dated June 1?, 1851, but which I redated in my first volume to around mid-May, as explained in another chapter. Three times, Brodhead cites this passage (always without using Melville's emphasis on the word "other"), first on page 20: "Hawthorne's influence on Melville takes the form first of a personal interaction, then of a literary relation. But both of these form part of a larger story too: the story of how (in Melville's term) an 'other way' of authorship got established as an artistic possibility, in America in the 1850s." On page 24 Brodhead says: "Melville's state in the year after *Mardi* is that of a writer for whom writing has become, quite suddenly and unexpectedly, the focus of powerful new drives and ambitions. . . . He now learned in hard practice what he had airily accepted in theory: that if he was going to write in that self-delighting 'other way,' he would jeopardize the income his growing family depended on, and forfeit too the sort of public approval that had emboldened him to experiment in the first place." Then on page 33: "Writing *Moby-Dick* did indeed take fortitude . . . . And it was his ability to believe that his self-willed, publicly unsupported writing efforts had the exalted value this concept promised, I would claim, that gave him the courage to write 'the other way.'"

Why single out these passages rather than tote up a long list of errors? Because Brodhead's reading of this passage so damningly gets something important not just slightly askew but flat out backwards. Melville was lamenting to Hawthorne, as all scholars have known for many years, that what he most wanted to write, what would have given him highest pleasure, was banned because it would not pay. (Argue if you want to that he ought to have taken highest joy in *Moby-Dick*; perhaps he rightly did, but perhaps he at some profound level wished to have done something else or to have done parts of that book differently. Certainly he wished he had been able to focus on it longer and more consistently!) Melville cannot write what he is most moved to write yet he cannot wholly suppress himself and write the *other* popular way, say even more popular variants of *Typee* and *Omoo*. So the product, specifically *Moby-Dick*, is a mixed-up affair, partly what he is most moved to write, partly what he thinks will sell best. There: that's a simple explication. Intent on his grand fanciful argument about Hawthorne helping Melville "realize himself as a writer," Brodhead fails the first test of a New Critic, to pay attention to the words of his texts.[3]

Focused so narrowly while I taught classes, worked on Melville, and dealt with a succession of illnesses and deaths besides Leyda's, I was probably of all Melvilleans the one least aware that traditional archival research was being

repudiated by almost every American literary critic, particularly those writing on Melville. Then in the late 1980s a would-be rising star of "criticism,"
the author of one of the new books on a "crisis" in education who hoped
to secure a niche for himself by linking "criticism" and the "profession,"
reviewed my *Flawed Texts and Verbal Icons*.[4] What he said was fuzzy to the
point of irrelevance, although I knew that a former student of mine had tried
hard to give him basic tutoring in the relation of literary theory to textual and
creativity theory, matters that remained utterly alien to him. At a conference
early in 1987 after my talk this critic came up to me, flustered, suppressing
his outrage that I had mentioned that Michael T. Gilmore, the author of
American Romanticism and the Marketplace, ought to have consulted a mass
of archival material highly relevant to his topic. Did I *"really think,"* he sputtered, that *"there really could be unused information"* that his friend might
have found, if he had thought to look? I jotted down those words as soon as I
could, and that night in my diary I commented: "Breaks my heart—*no* sense
of what it is to be a scholar."

Making some fragmentary satirical notes about the "New Ignorants" who
were getting mid-level and upper-level jobs in Ivy League schools, I hastily
elaborated a theory of the economics of literary theory to account for yup-
pies of the arbitrage generation who did not themselves produce anything
of value but who merely traded in preexistent products. They were growing
rich, comparatively, without producing a worthy product, I decided. From
my point of view they were inhumane because they showed no awareness of
the historical labor force, the genuine scholars who had toiled in the known
archives in previous decades and who sometimes had discovered new caches
of documents. My appalled "New Ignorants" was a recollection of a review
by Jay Martin in the January 1981 *American Literature*.

Today, groused Martin, "our scholars" (he should have said critics) "go to
Paris to deconstruct their American educations, and then to behave scandal-
ously at home" (654). As he thought about the situation he worked himself
up to this denunciation (654–55):

> In order to write about the nineteenth-century American imag-
> ination of authority and genealogy, would it be necessary or even
> desirable to become acquainted with the major American intellec-
> tual historians of the period, or to know accurately the character and
> condition of family life, or law, or social relations on the East coast,
> or to become acquainted with the sociologists of American commu-
> nity and the anthropological investigations of American mores? *Ach
> du lieber! C'est une idée très nouvelle!* What must be called nothing

less than the new ignorance is fully displayed in Eric J. Sundquist's *Home As Found: Authority and Genealogy in Nineteenth-Century American Literature*. Anyone who reads this book seriously must be dazzled by the extraordinary display of intelligence and the dexterity of imaginative insight evident in it. . . . What a shame, then, to see him willingly giving over his capacity to fashion.

While playing this fashionable game, Martin continued (655), Sundquist had claimed that "Melville centrally embodies 'the nightmare of self-generation . . . in a bizarre [parodic and patricidal] incest fantasy'"—a claim Martin dismissed as a caricature dashed off "not only unhesitatingly but with completely unreflexive self-assurance," where the Frenchified critic was fusing "insight with blindness."[5]

Along with the sociologists and the anthropologists Martin mentions, the scholar-critic might have started with knowing the history of the composition and publication of the Melville texts he cited, and might even have gone far, back beyond the published American authorities into the Gansevoort-Lansing Collection in the New York Public Library or the Shaw Papers in the Massachusetts Historical Society. Martin brilliantly identified what was wrong with what turned out to be an academic generation but he did not see that a turn to textual scholarship and biographical scholarship might have led to true breakthroughs for these critics who so wasted their brilliance and thrived while wasting it. In the next years as I witnessed egregious examples of this New Ignorance in many of the latest publications on Melville I came to see the writers more and more as like the money-changers in the Temple, taking their cut as they transferred a transformed version of history into the New Historicism but contributed nothing new to the stock of knowledge.

The writers of the new literary histories had seldom done research at all comparable to that of the writers of the 1940s literary histories, who had read as widely as they could rather than reading to assemble politically correct candidates for canonicity. Nevertheless, a few young academics, notably Neal L. Tolchin, actually went to the archives. Tolchin worked his findings into his 1988 *Mourning, Gender, and Creativity in the Art of Herman Melville*. In 1992 Andrew Delbanco, a contemporary who had *not* worked in the archives, offered this praise (711):

> Another substantial book, Neal L. Tolchin's *Mourning, Gender, and Creativity in the Art of Herman Melville*, uses psychoanalytic categories to propose a different way in which antebellum American culture was constricting and oppressive. Here we learn that Americans,

especially women, were subject to a pathology of chronic grieving that placed them in "a double bind . . . which at once prolonged the process of mourning and blocked the expression of feeling in bereavement."

While employing his "psychoanalytic categories," Tolchin (xv) declared that he had essayed "a radical revision of the biographical text" which located "Maria Melville's hitherto marginalized influence at the center of the tensions in Melville's art."

In achieving this revolutionary view, Tolchin had ventured into the New York Public Library to look at some of the letters in the Augusta Papers and had traveled to Pittsfield to look at family letters in the Berkshire Athenaeum. Tolchin did not recognize that he was having trouble, particularly with Melville's mother's letters. Maria Gansevoort Melville's handwriting is usually clear, after you transcribe several dozen of her letters—an observation that almost guarantees that I will blunder when I quote her in this or another chapter. Tolchin printed some very strange transcriptions, and his biographical conclusions on the basis of some of the mistakes are breathtaking. For instance, Tolchin declared that Melville's mother "spoke with gratification of his [Melville's] aggressive behavior" after he had "shipped out to Liverpool, in 1839": "I have just written Herman a few lines, his conduct delights me." How Herman would have known to look for a letter in Liverpool (and how it could have pursued him reliably) is not clear, but luckily the letter was sent to Pittsfield, since it was written on September 25, 1837 (not 1839), while Herman was managing the Melvill farm and just before he had begun teaching near there.[6]

Here is Tolchin (16) on a letter by Maria that he dates September 18?, 1841:

> In another letter to Augusta, Maria further elucidates her version of Calvinism. For exercise, she suggests "walking, riding, & jumping, when nobody is looking on, for I hold that running, & jumping, when in the country together with ——, singing, laughter, are conducive to health." In her own youth, Maria had attended balls and studied the piano.

I date the letter September 16, 1841, and read the passage this way (not correcting "runing"):

> improve your time, by taking exercise, of every kind, walking, riding and jumping, when nobody is looking on, for I hold that runing, &

jumping, when in the country together with hearty, loud, ringing laughter, are conducive to health, therefore will positively conduce to longevity.

In this I see nothing at all about Calvinism. Augusta was visiting Gansevoort cousins in Bath, New York, sufficiently rural, the urban-born Maria was sure, to allow Augusta to exercise freely to strengthen her body. She may well have had a theory about vigorous exercise helping the internal organs to settle into proper position: she had ideas about the body and mind. This passage has nothing to do with attending balls and studying the piano.

Any transcription, any dating in Tolchin is suspect, even any recipient. Maria's letter of March 4, 1854, that he refers to on page 174, for example, is not to Sam Shaw (she was staying in the Shaw house in Boston and Sam was at home) but to her daughter Augusta. Maria had prevailed upon the Unitarian Sam to take her to a church where she would hear a sermon nearer the Calvinism of her Dutch Church. Her goal was the Congregationalist church on Ashburton Place on Beacon Hill because of its proximity to the Shaw house on Mount Vernon Street, although the weather worsened during the sermon and she and Sam had to walk home on icy streets. Maria very likely knew the minister, Edward N. Kirk, who had been a notable Presbyterian leader in Albany when she was there in the 1830s but was now heading the Mount Vernon Congregationalist Church. (On a given day, a Congregationalist might think of himself as more earnestly Calvinistic than a Presbyterian, but their beliefs were so similar that many members attended the one or the other depending on what was available where they lived.) Tolchin says that Kirk "chastised the influence of 'a pleasant novel' and 'showed the necessity of Teachers to give direction to the minds of most hearers.'" Maria wrote this: "We had an excellent sermon. He compared the society of the world generally to drift wood, having no power to direct their course, to day influenced by a pleasant novel, tomorrow, reading a religious work & partially influenced by its teachings, & so on from day to day, going on its purposeless way, doing nothing." In Maria's account, Kirk said nothing at all about "Teachers" but "shewed the necessity of Preachers to give direction to the minds of most hearers & to fix it rightly &c." Tolchin did not tease out the significances of Maria's going to hear Kirk, which showed that she was comfortable asserting her needs for Calvinistic sustenance even in a Unitarian household. Furthermore, she was not afraid to hear a controversial minister. Kirk had become an antislavery minister on his path to greater radicalism, for a little later he heard the freed Anthony Burns address a crowd and decided, daringly, that Burns was more of a man than he had supposed. Well-meaning and industrious but haplessly amateurish, Tolchin had become a modern Little Jack Horner who sat in libraries and stuck in his thumb over and over, almost every time pulling out not a plum but an apple of Sodom such as Melville alludes to in *Typee*. Yet these apples of Sodom are still current, still part of a much praised and widely quoted book on Melville.

Tolchin's difficulties with transcribing and understanding are most prominently displayed in the first paragraph of his second chapter, "The Liminality of Grief: Mourning Ritual in *Typee*." Here Tolchin's misreadings are so serious as to undermine not just a single chapter (built upon these misreadings) but his entire book:

> In a letter of February 7, 1846, a puzzled Maria Melville comments on her son's recently published first novel, *Typee*, "his book which none of us understand, so contradictory in its information." One wonders if Mrs. Melville associated her son Gansevoort's leg ailment with the mysterious leg injury that the narrative persona, Tommo, suffers and which causes him to be carried about on a native's back. Writing on March 5, 1839, Melville's mother describes how "Gansevoort has still to be carried to the fire and is unable to bear his weight." One further wonders whether the cause of Tommo's disability, his exposure to "death-like coldness" during a rainy night spent in a ravine, triggered for Mrs. Melville a memory of her husband's fatal exposure. To explore the social text of Tommo's leg wound and how it relates to Maria Melville's sense of *Typee*'s contradictions, I examine the novel's conflicting types and peeps, as it links the pain inscribed in Tommo's body to Melville's frozen grief for his father.

(Tolchin's arch "types and peeps" is of course a play on *Typee: A Peep at Polynesian Life*.) Tolchin's reading is remarkable as "a radical revision of the biographical text," but it rests upon a transcription of a document in the Augusta Papers by a New Historicist not trained in working with manuscripts.

To begin with, the letter Tolchin purports to quote is not dated February 7, 1846, but February 28, 1846. In it Maria explains a complex situation to her daughter Augusta, then visiting the Van Rensselaer cousins in Albany:

> Herman left us last monday Eveg for Troy on his way to New York by the early Cars—he receiv'd a letter from Allan in the morning regarding his book which none of us understood, so contradictory in its information. Herman was very desirous of having it come out in Wiley & Putnams "Library of Choice Reading," and from Allans

letter, the thing was not determined, and indeed the arrival of the
Book itself by the Cambria by the reading of Allans letter was more
than uncertain. If the book was not got out by the first of March he
would lose the Copy right in America, so Gansevoort wrote. Herman
had no Idea of that you may suppose, to have the copy right was all to
Herman—so he concluded to go to New York, altho Gansevoort particularly requested him to remain here—but too much was at stake
and he went down—to assure himself that all was safe.

Tolchin had constructed his chapter on an absolutely false basis. Maria, of
course, does not say that the whole family was puzzled by *Typee*. No, they
were puzzled by Allan's letter about *Typee*. In actual biographical fact Maria
Melville nowhere manifested any "sense of *Typee*'s contradictions," if such
contradictions existed. On the contrary, good mother that she was, she perfectly understood how important preserving the American copyright for his
book was to Herman. In a later chapter I reemphasize that Maria meant just
what she said: the copyright really was "all to Herman." Critics can invent
and magnify "contradictions" but in the real world money matters.

    After wildly misquoting the letter, Tolchin explained that he would build
his elaborate theory on the basis of "the social text of Tommo's leg wound
and how it relates to Maria Melville's sense of *Typee*'s contradictions"—how
the social text relates to a sense of contradictions that Maria Melville never,
in fact, experienced. For any New Critic, of course, the opening of a chapter
or a larger work carries in it the plan of the whole. Well-trained critic that he
is, Tolchin recurred to his powerful opening as he constructed the rest of the
chapter. He began a new section of the chapter with a reminder that some
of Tommo's actions and "the contradictory peeps at Marquesan life" must
"have been in large part responsible for the bafflement with which Melville's
family read *Typee*." To reemphasize, Herman and Maria, at least, were puzzled by Allan's muddy letter, but not about the meaning of *Typee*. And of
course, good critic that he is, Tolchin in the last sentence of the chapter tied
the whole back to the first paragraph: "Tommo mirrors back to Maria Melville the 'contradictory . . . information' of her own unresolved grief as it has
been transmuted into and energized her son's fictive mourning rite."

    The first readers, you think, would have done a little spot-verifying of Tol-
chin's transcriptions and then would have hooted the book out of libraries?
That did not happen. No one at Yale University Press (Yale, just as Feidelson was retiring from the English department), no reader for the press, no
reviewer or critic (conspicuously not Andrew Delbanco) checked any of Tolchin's transcriptions from manuscripts. It did not matter at all that Tolchin

had built a whole chapter on a fantastic misreading of Maria Melville's hand-writing, and that, of course, according to the theory of organic unity he had to argue that the falsely conceived chapter was built into and affected the entire book.

I called the mistranscription in Maria Melville's February 28, 1846, letter to the attention of Brian Higgins so he could mention it in *American Literary Scholarship: An Annual / 1988* (55), but apparently no critic took that warning to heart. Tolchin's book has been cited favorably dozens of times. In the *American Historical Review* (April 1990) Karen Halttunen declared that "Tolchin convincingly demonstrates that Melville's work abounds with images of blocked bereavement and with thinly veiled references to the death of his father." Furthermore, Tolchin "offers a compelling synthesis of the body of Melville's work" (577). Bryan Collier Short in *Cast by Means of Figures: Herman Melville's Rhetorical Development* (1992) cites Tolchin as successfully exploring "relationships between Melville's writings and larger cultural issues such as gender, politics, and empire" (177) in distinction to his own study, a "rhetorical biography." Karen Elizabeth Smythe in *Figuring Grief: Gallant, Munro, and the Poetics of Elegy* (1992) cites Tolchin's book as "a biographical study" (9). Robert Milder quotes with apparent agreement: "For Neal L. Tolchin, the failure of the Melvill(e) family and the culture at large to provide adequate outlets for grief left Melville with a 'lifelong inability to finish mourning for his father" (*Exiled Royalties*, 270 n. 37). Julia A. Stern, in *The Plight of Feeling: Sympathy and Dissent in the Early American Novel* (1997), offers this praise (241):

> Much of my thinking about the relationship between the feeling that characterizes sentimentality and the pathological disturbance of mourning that takes shape in melancholia is inspired by Mitchell R. Breitwieser's remark that, in a recent work on Melville and mourning in antebellum America, Neal L. Tolchin has identified the centrality of a blocking and channeling of mourning in genteel culture, and the consequent production of an underground melancholia. Tolchin's extensive and perspicacious investigation of Melville's America suggests to me that sentimentalism is a reappearance of the Puritan sublimation of mourning. (241)

It is "an important study" (166), says Peter Balaam in *Misery's Mathematics: Mourning, Composition, and Reality in Antebellum American Literature* (2009). As dozens of favorable citations show, Tolchin's book has entered into common knowledge among writers interested in histories of emotion, in grief, misery, gender, death, and even the making of the middle-class family. Not one of the critics who have praised its insights and have incorporated its findings has seen that the second chapter is built upon a grotesque error which taints many other passages and the design of the whole book. A critic who takes this flawed book as "substantial," as "a compelling synthesis of the body of Melville's work" is deluded, and insofar as the critic incorporates Tolchin's findings into his or her own work, that work is tainted.

The Little Jack Horner syndrome also occurs when the academic sticks a thumb into published books rather than actual archives. Wai-chee Dimock's *Empire for Liberty* (1989), an early contribution to the New Historicism, was blurbed by Sacvan Bercovitch as giving "a model of a new kind of historical scholarship that has absorbed (as distinct from imitated) 'European theory' and whose historicism is a form of sophisticated multidisciplinary analysis." This is from her second paragraph (3–4):

> Far from being a liability, territorial expansion had come to be seen, by the 1830s, as a basic requirement for the nation's well-being, so basic that it became practically an alimentary need. Major Davezac, a speaker at the 1844 New Jersey Democratic State Convention, proceeded from just that premise when he alluded to America's "pasture grounds"—invoking, in his zeal, if not the "mighty bulk" of the whale, then something almost as bulky: "Make way, I say, for the young American Buffalo—he has not yet got land enough; he wants more land as his cool shelter in summer—he wants more land for his beautiful pasture grounds. I tell you, we will give him Oregon for his summer shade, and the region of Texas as his winter pasture. (Applause.) Like all of his race, he wants salt, too. Well, he shall have the use of two oceans—the mighty Pacific and the turbulent Atlantic shall be his."

Melville, Dimock declared, "could not have known about a speech at the New Jersey convention," but he and Davezac, "the enshrined writer and the forgotten speaker," together inhabited "a historical moment" (4). Davezac was worth recalling, "obscure as he once was and discredited as he has since become" (5).

Dimock gave no evidence that Davezac had become discredited except by her personally stringent standards of political correctness in which anyone is evil who advocated expansion. Her "historicism" had not driven her to find even the first name of this man who was anything but obscure. Auguste Davezac had led a remarkable life. Born in Santo Domingo in 1770, he was studying in France during the great uprising of 1791 in which two of his brothers were killed. The surviving members of the family fled to the new United States, settling in Louisiana, where Davezac rejoined them and studied law with Edward Livingston, of the prominent New York family, who became his brother-in-law. The great adventure of his life was being aide-de-camp to Andrew Jackson at the Battle of New Orleans, and every American in the 1840s knew that whatever credit some precisionists gave to the Treaty of Ghent the war was really won at New Orleans on January 8, 1815. Jackson had sent Davezac to The Hague for much of the 1830s as chargé d'affaires. As Jackson became more feeble and made fewer appearances even in Tennessee, Davezac was, by the 1840s, after his removal to New York, the living Manhattan connection to that still-recent battle which Americans cherished as ending the Second War for American Independence. At the dinner table in the Manhattan of the 1840s, with yet another war with England seeming imminent, over Oregon, that pasture ground for the bipedal American Buffalo, Davezac could tell intimate tales of Jackson and even tell about the legendary Jean Lafite (or "Lafitte"). Davezac was also a prominent literary man, capable of writing learnedly on Froissart's *Chronicles* in the November 1843 *United States Magazine and Democratic Review*, one of his favorite places to publish. His contemporaries would have hooted at the idea that he was obscure. To be sure, Whigs could attribute his fame to his publicizing himself, as when Thurlow Weed in his *Albany Evening Journal* on November 12, 1844, referred to him as "glorification DAVEZAC, who by his endless parrot songs of Jackson and the Battle of New Orleans" had "sickened and disgusted both friends and foes." (Everybody knew everybody: Melville gave Weed a copy of the Revised Edition of *Typee* in August 1846.)

Melville, Dimock was sure, "could not have known" about a particular 1844 speech of Davezac's. But how far-fetched is it to think that Melville may have known a good deal about Major Davezac, and perhaps might even have read some of his speeches, perhaps even that particular one? Melville's older brother Gansevoort in his instant-retrieval *Index Rerum* (now in the Berkshire Athenaeum) which he used in 1840 and 1842 noted a speech by Major Davezac "of New Orleans" and just where to find it ("the whole speech is contained in Bell's New Era for February 29, 1840"). In the 1840 election, while Herman was in the United States, Gansevoort had campaigned with Davezac, according to what Davezac wrote to Robert J. Walker, the secretary of the treasury, on April 11, 1845: "Soon after my arrival in the State of New-York, I became acquainted with Mr. G. Melville, by being fellow labourers in the cause of Democracy, in the canvass of 1840. Young as he then was, he gave indications of talents, as a popular orator, which his mature exertions, in the last memorable contest, have proved not to have been fallacious" (letter in the National Archives). As reported in the *New York Tribune* of June 15, 1843, on the previous day Davezac and Gansevoort both championed the dissolution of the union between Ireland and Great Britain at a great Repeal meeting, Davezac speaking at length as one of the stars and young Gansevoort speaking more briefly. During the final days of the 1844 campaign Herman was in New York with Gansevoort and Allan, the next younger Melville brother, and would have been aware of his older brother's association with a hero of the Battle of New Orleans. During that campaign Allan had saved in a "bushell" basket dozens of thin newspapers containing Gansevoort's speeches, and might well have saved some of Davezac's along with his brother's, since the two were political allies.

When Davezac rode in the great Democratic torchlight procession in Manhattan on November 1, 1844, in which Gansevoort and Allan Melville also took part, and which Herman almost surely witnessed, he carried a banner and a flag, the banner proclaiming "THIS FLAG WAS AT THE BATTLE OF NEW ORLEANS 8TH JANUARY, 1815: MAJOR A. DAVEZAC." For all Democrats he was a national hero. Early in 1845, while Melville was writing *Typee* in Manhattan, Davezac was everywhere in the press. The *Democratic Review* in February, out in late January, carried an article on him accompanied by "a Portrait on Steel," and the article was reprinted in the *Broadway Journal* and the *New World* and perhaps elsewhere. Davezac in the April 11, 1845, letter to Walker championed Gansevoort Melville for an appointment from President Polk on the basis of his great services in 1844. For a time Gansevoort had possession of the strong letter of support which Davezac wrote for him, and typically would have shown it to Allan. Herman might have been in Lansingburgh by then, but he might have heard of the letter from Gansevoort or Allan if he did not actually hold it in his hands and read it. Certainly to Melville there was nothing obscure and nothing discredited about Auguste Davezac. A historian judging by modern standards of political correctness might well find grounds on which to disapprove of Davezac, as when he worried, after Mexico decided that blacks could not be enslaved, that New Orleans slaves would run off along the coast of Texas and take refuge in the newly independent country. Dimock, however, seems arbitrarily to have declared Davezac discredited because he believed, half a decade before the admission of California to the Union, that the United States should expand to the Pacific. Harboring in Morro Bay, California, as I do, I feel more than a little distressed at Dimock's implicit condemnation of California's having been brought into the Union. Can Californians ever redeem themselves to her level of politically correct purity?

What Dimock practiced in *Empire for Liberty*, and what many of her New Critical and New Historicist peers practiced, was historicism without historical research. Names of historical figures? pieces to be used as decorations. Yet she traveled to libraries: "I would like to acknowledge my indebtedness to the Melville Collection at the Newberry Library, which has compiled the nineteenth-century reviews" (228 n. 16). "Which" is revealing: the impersonal "Collection" had compiled "the" reviews. She had the thrill of discovery by opening a drawer and finding reviews compiled by the "Collection"! She could not visualize my compiling the files during repeated trips to the New York Public Library Annex, the New-York Historical Society, and many other repositories. The "Collection" had compiled "the" reviews—meaning all the reviews that existed? I was engaged in an ongoing compilation of reviews but it plainly never occurred to her that she could have joined in the hunt, perhaps in papers especially apt to take a political slant congenial to her. "Which has compiled" reveals her failure to visualize real scholars doing productive work in her own time. Similarly, she is thrilled by dipping into books written by people who have gone to libraries more remote even than faraway Chicago and have handled expensive books with their own hands. She cites a book by R. W. Van Alstyne for the source of her quotation from a 1776 book, not just any old book but "a rare book in the Huntington Library"—'way out in California, near the City of Angels (217)! Dimock breathlessly flirts with the trappings of scholarship.

Dimock had absorbed without question her New Critical and New Historicist training. For her there were no living researchers engaged in ongoing archival scholarship, and there never had been living writers engaged in ongoing creative projects. For her (223), the "standard critique of the notion of 'creativity' is Pierre Macherey, *A Theory of Literary Production*" (which she cites in a late translation). She cites approvingly Jerome McGann, a follower of James Thorpe's theory of the socialized text (which denigrates the creative process), and cites Paul Feyerabend's 1987 "Creativity—A Dangerous Myth" (223). In that article Feyerabend declares that "the view that culture needs individual creativity" is "not only absurd but also dangerous" (701). The creative author is a myth (the *reader*, trendy academics had known since the 1970s, creates meaning, not the writer) and the idea of individual creativity is dangerous, at least to current critical theory. As Joel Myerson said in *Text* (1993), McGann suggested "an almost Marxist, collective ownership of the text among the authors and other participants in its creation: the 'workers' of the text have indeed united" (115). Dimock does not cite the great 1979 book by Albert Rothenberg, *The Emerging Goddess*, which she ought to have known as the "standard" book on the creative process, and does not cite exciting new work done on creativity and in the cognitive sciences in the 1980s, particularly on perception and memory.[7] She apparently had no practical information about the creative process and no idea at all about what real scholars do, no idea that real scholars compile evidence exhaustively before daring to try to interpret it. No wonder she typically takes her quotations at second hand, from people who have quoted passages from other books: picking her quotations from other books distances her from real scholars working with real documents. As Robert D. Hume says in *Reconstructing Contexts*, among New Historicists literary criticism becomes "an elaborate game played for the self-glorification of the participants" (190).[8]

It is typical that Dimock takes the item about Davezac "as quoted in" (215) Albert Weinberg's *Manifest Destiny: A Study of Nationalistic Expansion in American History* (1935), the way, as I show elsewhere, that Andrew Delbanco picks up phrases "as quoted in" my biography of Melville. Dimock and Delbanco violate the basic tenets of historiography. Dimock's New Critical teachers apparently did not tell her that a real scholar tries hard to avoid citing something as "quoted in" another book. At Harvard did Alan Heimert not teach students to try not to take a quotation secondhand? (I don't see any "quoted ins" in his 1963 essay on political allegory in *Moby-Dick*, discussed later.) A scholar goes to the book or to the manuscript, for who knows what else, preciously relevant, might be in the document right beside the morsel the earlier historian or biographer picked out to quote? Even if the words are quoted accurately, one cannot know the contexts from which they were quoted.[9] Also, it is curious that so much of the scholarship Dimock relies on was published before the New Criticism. It seems as if the decade of the rise of that long-dominant approach to literature somehow gives the American New Historicists a cutoff decade, the early 1940s, beyond which histories such as Weinberg's can be taken as sacred texts. Critics such as Dimock, however much they are praised as models "of a new kind of historical scholarship," are not in fact doing historical research, and they learn nothing from the archives about Melville any more than about Major Auguste Davezac. You stick a thumb in a 1930s history and pull out what may be a veritable truth and may be an earnest attempt at truth which has been supplemented over the decades and perhaps even superseded by other real historians.

Even older scholars, it turned out, had lost some of their archival skills during the long dominance of the New Criticism. In 1992 Hennig Cohen and Donald Yannella published in *Herman Melville's Malcolm Letter* the best Melville letter in the Augusta Papers, the one to Allan about the birth of his first child, Malcolm. Tolchin-like, they took the occasion to relate the 1849 letter to paternalism, authoritarianism, and attitudes toward death displayed in the Melville and associated families. Cohen and Yannella confuse family members, as in quoting Maria's letter to her brother, Peter Gansevoort, and his wife about the care being given to Peter and Maria's mother. Peter had no wife at the time of the letter, and the "Sister Mary" thanked for "her kindness & attentions to Mamma" is really Mary Chandonette Gansevoort, Guert Gansevoort's mother (143–44). Cohen and Yannella quote Maria Melville's letter to her niece Kate Gansevoort, Peter's daughter, about the death of Dr. Howard Townsend (142) without realizing that Mrs. Townsend, Justine (whose name they give as Justina on 145), was known in the Melville family as Cousin Teny, a Van Rensselaer, the sister of Augusta's dear friend Nilly Van Rensselaer Thayer. As you would expect from older Melville hands, their transcriptions were conscientious, although they misread one important word in the "Malcolm" letter itself (preferring the "robust" over "valiant"—"as valiant as Julius Cesear") and made heavy weather of a good many words they call "undeciphered," including the three they quote on page 189 that were clear to me.[10]

Like anyone who dips in here and there in different years in an archive, Cohen and Yannella make some snap judgments on slight evidence. They are particularly harsh toward Helen Maria Melville, Herman's older sister, describing her as "superficial and conventional" (213). After quoting her preference for "solid reading, really enlarging and cultivating the mind" over a slight novel or even history romantically written (213), they ask: "How could the creative, imaginative, intellectually, and artistically gifted Herman have responded to such observations that so clearly flew in the face of his own theory of fiction? Our suspicion is that her remarks, which were not untypical of popular thinking, would have been yet another reason for his turning inward" after Malcolm's death (213–14). They scold her: "Such views from one's own sister carried greater weight by virtue of their very source: a family member, a sister, with whom he had shared their parents' roof and whom he had also helped provide a roof for when he was first married" (214). When Yannella at the May 17, 1991, Berkshire Athenaeum panel on biography described Helen as "the least capable, intellectual, of the brothers and sisters," I am recorded as crying, "Oh no . . . Oh no!" (Bryant and Milder, 239).

Helen was brilliant, verbally inventive, the intellectual equal of Gansevoort and Herman, I would think, the first three children getting the most attention and thriving from it, despite later deprivations, or perhaps just innately superior. Herman loved writing to her more than any other family member because he knew she would understand his humor. Here (from the NYPL-GL Additions, the Augusta Papers) is Helen on June 20? 1854, telling Augusta about her settling into a new house (see Parker, 2:194–95):

You ask about the wardrobe—two able-bodied, but by no means Samsonic looking men, carried it up stairs, without much apparent effort; but I thought it my duty to restore their expended strength by a glass of wine after the feat was performed. Tell Herman (for Mama's edification) that they gulped it down at one swallow, and did not stop "to sip and taste the flavor as gentlemen do who are accustomed to drink wine daily,"—I quote from the maternal—perhaps they did wisely, considering the quality of the liquid, our vintner cheated us in that last pipe.

I am truly sorry that Demosthenes broke his back—his neck I mean—in trying to assist its descent—but never mind—you shall have a marble bust of Judge George Griggs on the same pedestal one of these days.

Here is Helen on January 14, 1855 (quoted in *Correspondence*, 274):

Herman's letter with the spirited etching as a vignette at the close, afforded us much amusement, George is well acquainted with the unfortunate individual left in the Cimmerian darkness of the depot, but until Herman's letter arrived, had no idea that his more happy brother, about to leave it for the opening realms of day, had conde-scended to bid adieu to the last sojourner in the confines of gloom. He fully reciprocates the love, or respects, whichever sentiment he intended for him, and looking upon him (Herman) as a glorious leader, has followed his illustrious footsteps even to the counter of the Ship-Bread-Baker, where he purchased a half-barrel of the self same flinty abomination; which three times a day, he essays to bite, break, soak, or otherwise subdue its innate hardness of nature, and crunches, and munches, the vile concentrated essense of bread-stuff, with so much apparent gusto, that my teeth stand on edge, and my throat feels dry and husky, in pure sympathy with what I imagine to be the state of his chewing & swallowing apparatus. In mercy to his elbows (the cloth ones, I mean) and his hands, please get from Herman a full, true, minute, and succinct account of the process of breaking these adamantine biscuits. George proposes that I shall say masticating instead of chewing—deglutinating instead of swallowing—take your choice . . .

Herman's drawing has been lost (Parker, 2:242), but the evidence of the lov-ing badinage of brother and sister has emerged in the Augusta Papers. Helen

had been under a financial cloud in the early 1840s when she might otherwise have profited by being sheltered in the house of Chief Justice Lemuel
Shaw for so many months. Her husband, George Griggs, was a gruff man
even when younger, and was not a young man when he finally proposed to
Helen. By then she was so far past her youth that the boy she carried almost to
full term died in her womb. Yes, she could express herself conventionally on
occasion, but she was much brighter than her other sisters, and treasured by
Herman (and probably, although little evidence survives, by Gansevoort). She
should have been the wife of a splendid man like John Hoadley, the engineer-
poet, whom her anxious, precisionist younger sister Kate did not deserve.

Like so many Melvilleans since Raymond Weaver, Cohen and Yannella
proved unable to judge Maria Melville fairly. Weaver and Lewis Mumford
were so over-the-top in their denunciations of the woman that even the rational Leon Howard was infected with their horrified disdain for her, as when
he assumed she was prevaricating in April 1853 when she said Herman had
a new book almost ready for the press. Cohen and Yannella devote a remarkable analysis to one letter to her niece Kate Gansevoort, now married to
Abraham Lansing:

> For Maria there was a poignancy that more strongly suggests the
> profound sense of family and continuity. She wrote Kate in Febru-
> ary 1872 and reflected, "How well we all remembered the evening
> when the ring came for my father." So in making this gesture, Henry
> [Gansevoort] and Kate who carried out his [Peter's] request, were
> maintaining a Victorian memorializing tradition. Her aunt contin-
> ues, "He opened it at the dinner table—and was so much pleased
> with it. He wore it, all during his illness . . . and it was only on the
> morning of the day he died that I took it off his hand . . . by his desire
> and have had it ever since. Mama says that I am to keep it now. With
> that ring which I cannot too highly prize with its double associations,
> I have now the beautiful gift from Cousin Henry. How beautiful it
> is—how I wish my father could have seen it" (225).

They comment on "the confusion in generations" (230 n. 23):

> Maria is clearly talking about the ring received by her father from
> her grandfather, but her mother had been dead for more than forty
> years at the time this letter to Kate was penned. Perhaps the explana-
> tion is that she was merely confused or flustered. It should be noted
> that the letter is in her hand and signed "Maria G. Melville."

In fact, the letter is *not* in the hand of Melville's mother, Maria G. Melville, but it is altogether characteristic of the hand of the person who wrote it, Maria G. Melville, Allan's first daughter, born the month Malcolm was born in 1849. She is talking about a mourning ring for the late Henry Gansevoort which Henry and Kate's father (Peter) had wanted sent to Allan, who had cherished it till he died. Maria had then taken it, with the permission of "Mama," her stepmother, Jane Dempsey Melville, and now a new gift has arrived from Kate. The willingness to assume that Melville's mother was physically strong enough to write but mentally doddering is perfect evidence of how the 1920s maligning of this woman has persisted. At the time the letter was written Melville's mother was dying, absolutely devastated by the death of her son Allan in February 1872, but she was not out of her mind, not grotesquely confused or flustered as Cohen and Yannella assumed.

At that 1991 centennial meeting Yannella alluded to Melville's neighbor Sarah Morewood's improper fascination with George L. Duyckinck, the shy, devoutly Episcopalian younger brother of Evert Duyckinck and co-editor of the *Literary World*. We all shouted him down, I declaring, "She was a religious woman!" (Bryant and Milder, 237). Yannella had read Sarah's letters in the Duyckinck Collection and none of the rest of us had. I thought I knew her through the letters in the Augusta Papers and in the *Log*, but I knew only part of the story, and in fact had not known what to make of one fragment of a letter about a servant sent with a midnight message across the hill from Broadhall to Arrowhead. Later, Lion Gardiner Miles, a Berkshire researcher, went to Yale for me to look in the Gardiner papers (his family's papers), where he found a dumbfounding letter about Sarah's notorious pursuit of the young brother-in-law of President Tyler two summers before Melville's idyll in the Berkshires (Parker, 2:42–43). I was still naive in 1991, slow to learn that minor members of my cast of characters might be much more complex than I was giving them credit for being. I thank Lion Miles and apologize here to Yannella for simplifying a very complicated woman and wrongly challenging him in public. I was right about Helen when I challenged him that day in 1991, but embarrassingly wrong about Sarah Morewood.

I was delighted to take part in that panel discussion at the Berkshire Athenaeum in 1991 since I got to tell several new stories in advance of the biography. Over the next years John Bryant gave me the chance to correct the transcriptions of what I said (what in my Southern accent made it hard for others to hear the word "uncircumcised"?), and I was content that I would be quoted correctly in his and Robert Milder's strangely titled *Melville's Evermoving Dawn: Centennial Essays*. When the book came in 1997 I was appalled at two or three dozen errors in Bryant's notes to the panel discussion (252–58). Melville's aunt Mary D'Wolf had given him a copy of Hawthorne's *Mosses*—no, it was Aunt Mary Melvill (253). Allan Melville's first child, Maria Gansevoort Melville, was born in 1848, Bryant said; no, 1849, just after Malcolm was born (254). Kate Gansevoort Lansing was not Elizabeth Melville's sister-in-law but her husband's first cousin (254). Melville's uncle Leonard Gansevoort was long dead in the 1860s, not just settling into Glens Falls (255). Melville's sister Kate indeed married John Hoadley, but it was not their daughter, "Melville's niece Maria," who "married Herman's neighbors John and Sarah Morewood's son" (255). That son, Willie Morewood, married Allan's daughter Maria Gansevoort Melville, not the Hoadleys' daughter Maria. In response to my protestations Bryant seemed unfazed, more than a little surprised that I thought three dozen or so dubious little points mattered. Why should I feel humiliated? The answer was simple: I cared for these people. At the time the panel discussion took place, five years before my first volume was published and six years before the Bryant-Milder collection was published, I knew the Melvilles more intimately than anyone at the Pittsfield conference because I had been living with them for years, learning their secrets, being, at times, haunted by their needs and longings and deservings. It matters to a biographer, a biographer who works from documents, that Aunt Mary Melvill, Uncle Thomas's widow, then taking her last chance to revisit the old home, gave Melville the copy of *Mosses*, not Aunt Mary D'Wolf.

When Laurie Robertson-Lorant's *Melville: A Biography* was published in 1996 before my first volume, I itemized to the publisher some of what I had found in a several-hour scan of her book in preparation for mentioning her in my revisions to the preface. Eager but inexperienced, she had related incidents reminiscent of Raymond Weaver, Lewis Mumford, and the contrivances of New York University professor Edwin H. Miller in his biography of Melville (1975). In her book (but not mine) a fourteen-year-old Herman had been caught boozing in a Schenectady barroom (60). Hun or Hunn Gansevoort was Herman's first cousin, son of Peter and Mary Gansevoort, she revealed (89). It mattered to me when Robertson-Lorant wrote about a nonexistent cousin, "Millie Van Rensselaer Thayer," instead of Cornelia (Nilly!) Van Rensselaer who married Nathaniel Thayer in 1846, not 1845 (137), and whom Melville visited in 1846, after he had finished *Omoo*, not before *Typee* was published. Ruthlessly she had killed off Cousin Stanwix Gansevoort decades early (89). She had assigned Maria Gansevoort Melvill (as the name was still spelled) a nephew, "Henry Gansevoort," in the 1820s (26). Robertson-Lorant informed the reader that "boys—and perhaps even a few rebellious girls—shed their clothes" and swam together in the "Hudson's many streams or tributaries" (45). A biographer who thinks someone like Helen Maria Melville might have swum naked in the Hudson simply does not comprehend American class distinctions. Decades later gentlemen and ladies taking the ferry boat to Staten Island were sometimes aghast at the state of undress of Irishwomen on the beaches, but gentlewomen like the daughters of Maria Gansevoort Melville did not "skinny-dip." I cringed when Robertson-Lorant luridly asserted that the intensely religious Augusta Melville liked "being escorted around Albany and Lansingburgh by Stephen Van Rensselaer, until it dawned on her that his reckless driving hinted at qualities undesirable in a marriage prospect" (130). Stephen Van Rensselaer, the mature and securely married pillar of the Albany Dutch Church, Augusta's spiritual mentor, far more akin to her in religious matters than, say, Helen and Herman—Stephen Van Rensselaer, the father of Cornelia (Nilly, not Milly!) Van Rensselaer Thayer!

In my biography Sister Fanny does not visit Black Rock, New Jersey (182); instead, she accompanies Allan and Sophia Melville to the scenic Black Rock near Niagara Falls. Herman Melville buys his father's own copy of *The Anatomy of Melancholy* at a famous Manhattan bookstore in my biography, not in Pittsfield (625). I had thought I was aware of things sexual, but Robertson-Lorant outdid me not only with Augusta's thoughts about Stephen Van Rensselaer but with her teasing description of a Herman who in 1847, safely out of sight in Washington City, put the moves on a girl from Bond Street (155) at a time when he was engaged to Elizabeth Shaw. No, he had not been flirting "a bit with 'one of the sweetest of our Bond Street girls.'" The flirting was wholly Robertson-Lorant's invention and the girl referred to was Sophia Thurston, whom Allan Melville married later in the year. Herman at the end of July 1850 did not go "to New York to bring his mother and sisters to Pittsfield" (243); Maria Melville went there first in June and others followed. In Robertson-Lorant's book, but not mine, Melville and Sophia Hawthorne sat cramped together "on the verandah of the red cottage overlooking Stockbridge Bowl" (253). In fact, the cottage lacked that architectural feature and in my book the two sit more grandly on the verandah of the higher situated Tappan house—painted brown (hence, "Chateau Brun"). It was Helen who had the special friendship with Mrs. Ives and Augusta who had the special friendship with Cornelia (Nilly) Van Rensselaer Thayer. In my biography Augusta has poignant reason for being at Arrowhead in June 1851, Helen for being in Manhattan and Brooklyn; in Robertson-Lorant's account they change places (272), with no reason given. Melville, we are told by Robertson-Lorant, "burned his love letters to Lizzie" (618), those which his daughter Bessie possessed in the early twentieth century.

Robertson-Lorant had gone to many archives and tried hard, but she was like Tolchin in finding some handwriting too hard to read. She had availed herself of the new bounty of information in the Northwestern-Newberry volumes such as the 1993 *Correspondence* and in my publications and speeches, but she simply had not gotten well acquainted with the throng of men and women who made up the family of Herman Melville. Such misconstruing, I reassured the publisher, was so pervasive that no one should feel safe in quoting from Robertson-Lorant's book, any more than from Weaver's.

One reviewer scathingly reproached me for saying that Robertson-Lorant had made "vigorous forays" into the archives, which he assumed she had plundered fully and correctly, but as far as I know, not a single person mentioned any factual disagreement between me and Robertson-Lorant. Everyone behaved the way Robert Milder did in *Nineteenth-Century Literature* (March 1998) when he declared her book "up-to-date in its scholarship" (538) or as Elizabeth Hardwick did in 2000 when she offered this assurance: "She has the large family under her thumb—everything is here, picnics, headaches, housekeeping in the midst of the book after book written by the subject" (160–61). No one went to the archives to double-check her and see if "everything" was not only there but was accurately depicted.

In the few pages on Melville in her *Hawthorne: A Life* (2003) Brenda Wineapple stuffed together an astonishing number of errors, sentence by sentence. The "Pittsfield farm owned by Melville's cousin" (222) was not owned by Robert Melvill, ever, and in any case had already been sold to the Morewoods, although they did not take possession for many months. "August 5, a day soon to be promoted as an American *Déjeuner sur l'Herbe* (without the scandal)" was not in fact soon promoted that way, not through the 1850s and 1860s or still later, and certainly not celebrated mainly as the day Melville and Hawthorne met. The promotion of the day as significant in American literary history was a phenomenon of the 1930s or later, as I say elsewhere. She published after I had revealed in my second volume that on the climb Hawthorne was excited, not phlegmatic, uncharacteristically hamming it up, looking *wildly* about for his Great Carbuncle, not *mildly*. This is so important a correction that every biographer should use it, but she does not. She has James Fields slipping in his patent leather shoes, but no one says that. Presumably his patent leather shoes had regular soles. She says, "Herman Melville is the daredevil who sprints from rock to jutting rock" (222). Duyckinck in a letter to his wife says that Melville, "the boldest of all," seated himself "astride a projecting bow sprit of rock" (*Log*, 384). Fields in the February 1871 *Atlantic* (251) says Melville bestrode a peaked rock, which ran out like a bowsprit, but not that he ran or leaped. Who says he sprinted (or leapt) from rock to jutting rock? In reference to the Monument Mountain–Icy Glen party, Wineapple says, "Of the group, Melville captured Sophia's fancy" (222). What group? The only ones Sophia Hawthorne saw that day were Dudley Field (and Mrs. Field?), who called for Hawthorne in a comfortable "chariott and two"—two horses. Now, she saw some others later, including Melville. But Sophia never was exposed to "the group" who had made such a day of August 5, 1850. Wineapple failed to visualize the scenes. Then she calls *Redburn* "autobiographical" without qualification (223). She calls Melville "the bushy-bearded young man" (223) when there is no source for his being bushy-bearded on August 5, 1850. This is Wineapple: "Melville was the coxswain, not a dry-docked Custom House inspector, come back to tell all, striding off the gangplank into a garret where he could dip his pen into the inkpot and be, of all things, a writer" (223). Here we have Wineapple in her romantic fiction mode, with a lapse into Prufrock ("come back to tell you all"). Melville had not been a coxswain, as far as we know, had he? So he claims to Bentley to have been a harpooneer! Melville may have stridden (strode?) off a gangplank or walked slowly off one or he may have left the *United States* by a rope ladder for all we know. He never wrote in a garret (can you imagine the problem of lighting one?). This is cheap fiction.

Wineapple says that when Duyckinck went home to New York City "he carried the first installment of Melville's review of *Mosses from an Old Manse*" (224). No, he carried the whole review. (I comment elsewhere about her saying "it's not clear when Melville began the review.") Wineapple has Melville (or his Virginian) reading Hawthorne "while lying on the new-mown clover near the barn" (224). Melville puts himself inside the barn, "the hillside breeze blowing over me through the wide barn door"—another of her characteristic failures to visualize. There are other errors, delivered in lurid, irrational prose such as this: "Melville pictured Hawthorne as a mate bobbling like him on the troubled seas of publishing, recognition, and posterity" (225). The speculation that Melville "likely" burned Hawthorne's letters "at Hawthorne's behest" is absurd (228). All these errors and vulgarities, and more, are in a twenty-first-century biography. Others of Wineapple's errors, including the worst, perhaps the grossest, most ignorant error made about Melville in any biography, her desecration of Melville's reference to the Lamb of God, I merely mention here but have more to say later: when Melville says that after writing a wicked book, *Moby-Dick*, he feels as spotless as the lamb, she prints the wrong article ("a" lamb), as if Melville had in mind a spiffy-clean Berkshire County South Down or Romney Marsh ruminant (243).[11]

I hoped that *Herman Melville: A Biography, 1819–1851* would set off excursions to the archives to see if I should be challenged and corrected. As far as I know, the only person to take issue with an episode in the biography and to go on to shed light on a different episode was Randall Cluff. When he was a graduate student at the University of Tennessee he had helped me assemble documents on Gansevoort Melville's great speech in Nashville in 1844 and particularly to answer the question, "Had Jackson addressed the mass meeting?" His answer was no, although Gansevoort would have let his Eastern crowds think the answer was yes. Then Cluff went on to identify the reviewer of *Typee* in the April 9 *New York Evangelist* as Henry Cheever, who wrote from inside knowledge: "We are sorry that such a volume should have been allowed a place in the 'Library of American Books.' It can only have been without reading it beforehand, and from deference to the publisher on the other side." John Wiley was repudiating much of the book his partner George Putnam had accepted. What Wiley required of Melville was the ruthless excision of some sexual passages and all criticism of the American missionaries in the South Seas. I was grateful for Cluff but disappointed at the general disinclination of others to rush to explore topics that plainly ought to reward a little more digging. There have been isolated findings in the last two decades (including the identification by Geoffrey Sanborn and Scott Norsworthy of Melville's sources for his notoriously controversial notes in the back of his Shakespeare). Only Scott Norsworthy, Warren Broderick, Richard E. Winslow III, and George Monteiro have regularly been finding unknown contemporary reviews of Melville and only a very few people, notably the librarian Dennis Marnon and Norsworthy, regularly have been discovering new sidelights to episodes in Melville's life, or even new episodes. And Warren Broderick and John Gretchko still retrieve valuable documents from the public archives.

Naively, I had thought that if anyone disagreed with me or simply was intrigued by something I had described, that critic could lay out all the evidence and see if I needed to be corrected or supplemented. In his very long review in the *New York Review of Books* Andrew Delbanco repeatedly accused me of misreading the evidence, but he never once tested what I had said against the archival evidence I was citing. His accusations were powerful enough to be used against me by Alan Helms, who called me a "slippery fish" on the authority of Delbanco. In his own 2005 biography (xxiii) Delbanco reveals uncontrollable revulsion and terror at the very idea of scholarly research. Its roots may go back to New Critical indoctrination, but the manifestation suggests a pathology beyond my investigation here. I refer to his depiction in *Melville: His World and Work* of the horror he experienced in the Houghton Library when confronted with the possibility of pursuing archival research: "I felt that I was eavesdropping, like a tourist in a church who comes upon a worshipper kneeling in prayer" (45). Being so sensitive, Delbanco naturally assumed the worst of me because I had brutishly transcribed hundreds of intimate private letters, coldly violating Melville's privacy decade after unsavory decade in my pursuit of material for a biography. However, by depending on Higgins's and my *Herman Melville: The Contemporary Reviews* Delbanco deprived himself of the chance to learn something about the world of nineteenth-century newspapers by searching through them for reviews, and by depending on my biography for snippets from Melville family letters not in *The Melville Log* he deprived himself of knowledge of the letters in their entirety, from which I had quoted small, and perhaps unrepresentative, portions in order to enforce particular points. There is no substitute for getting one's hands dirty if one wants to understand the world and the work of a writer, and Delbanco's hands stayed clean, as they did the day he, figuratively at least, tore off the library's white gloves and fled the Houghton, never, to judge from his book, to return. He is a true archivophobic.

I thought I had invented the word archivophobic to describe what so rackingly afflicted Delbanco that day in the Houghton Library, but a search of the word on Google turns up its use in the February 1977 *Journal of Southern History* by Virginia Cardwell Purdy, Women's History Specialist for the National Archives and Records Service. According to Edwin A. Miles (1977), Purdy told a gathering that "the malady of Archivophobia" was what "caused the federal archives to be underutilized or neglected entirely by historians in general as well as those interested in women's history" (79). A tip of the hat to Virginia Cardwell Purdy!

In this chapter I have assumed that Tolchin and others all intended to transcribe what the letter writers wrote, but I acknowledge that it is no longer safe to assume that people working with Melville's manuscripts are determined to recover precisely what he wrote. In *The Fluid Text* (2002) one of the 1990 Pittsfield panelists, John Bryant, recalled that where I read a word in the double handful of draft pages of *Typee* as "peroration" he read "promotion." He then announced a new policy on the transcription of Melville's handwriting: "The scribble we both 'see' is the same" but the "readings we give to it vary with our differing rhetorical agendas" (19).[12] I would have thought the readings varied with our familiarity with Melville's hand and vocabulary, with the acuity of vision (however assisted by jewelers' loupes and flex-armed lighted magnifiers), and, when necessary, by prolonged and repeated inspections, in different moods and different lights, but not so. Bryant's goal no longer was absolute determination to capture what Melville wrote but in cases of any doubt to pick a reading that fit a rhetorical agenda. I had recognized even in my hero, Jay Leyda, instances where a word was inadvertently mistranscribed because it fit a prejudice against someone in Melville's family, so I knew that our expectations could make us inadvertently see a word wrong. Naively, as a transcriber of manuscripts I had wanted to find the right reading, whatever it was. Are we in a new place where textual Sganarelles will boast that they have discarded all the old aims and methods of scholarship? Where there is no such thing as a misreading?

Still worse, we are in fact witnessing the emergence of a new biographical terrain where life-writers are beginning to redefine the idea of "archives" out of existence, so that they can boldly go beyond traditional documentary evidence, not even pausing there. In *Archivaria* 23 (Winter 1986–87), Pamela Banting was ahead of her time, as her title shows: "The Archive as a Literary Genre: Some Theoretical Speculations." Vinay Lal in *Biography* (Summer 2004) offered no opposition at all to Antoinette Burton's earlier *Dwelling in the Archive: Women Writing House, Home, and History in Late Colonial India* (2003). Indeed, Emory Elliott's throwing-out-the-baby introduction to the *Columbia History* is recalled in Lal's phrasing: "At one time the notion of archives brought to mind political history, state documents, property ownership deeds, and tax records, but Burton suggests that the archive can be rendered, if one may use a term that evokes its own sexual politics, infinitely more fecund as a site of other histories. It is commonly imagined that archives yield public and political histories, and that such archives have little room for private memories; but Burton's intent is to fragment the opposition of public and private, of history and memory, and in particular, of history as the site of masculinist thinking and grand narratives, and of memory as the site of feminine desire and domesticated ruminations" (673). Burton asks, says Lal, "What histories do domestic interiors yield? What are the architectural idioms of history? How can a home be the foundation of history? Why do the metaphors of home and house occupy such a prominent place in history and memory? What is the relationship of women to the archive?" (673–74). Perhaps we should be grateful that none of the Melville critics mentioned in this chapter has followed contributors to Burton's *Archive Stories: Facts, Fictions, and the Writing of History* (2005) to the extreme of redefining "archive."[13] No critics of Melville have yet followed Wendy M. Duff and Verne Harris (in a 2002 piece in *Archival Science*) toward what sounds almost like archive as Facebook: "We need descriptive architectures that allow our users to speak to and in them. Architectures, for instance, which invite genealogists, historians, students, and other users to annotate the finding aids or to add their own descriptions would encourage the leaking of power," since those of us "who are on the inside of the information structures must create holes in our structures through which the power can leak" (279).

Mark Allen Greene set forth his position in his abstract for the 2002 "The Power of Meaning: The Archival Mission in the Postmodern Age": "Some archivists at the forefront of writing about the complexities of electronic materials have challenged the traditional U.S. definitions of 'records,' 'archives,' and 'archivists.' Where once those terms were broad enough to encompass virtually all forms of documentary material, these writers, exemplified by Richard Cox and Luciana Duranti, have urged on our profession a narrower conception of records and archives. This challenge threatens to undermine the important socio-cultural *meaning* of archives and archival material. It is vital that archivists reclaim and reaffirm a broad conception of their professional purpose and an equally broad definition of what constitutes archival material. To do otherwise is to accept a truncated and sterile vision of our profession" (42).[14]

To do otherwise than as Greene says is to risk the loss of irreplaceable human records, the stuff of biography. During the early triumph of the New Criticism some of its practitioners made no move to resist the destruction of old bound volumes of American newspapers. Who would want to read newspapers when all that was needed was a literary text? Now the postmodern conquest of libraries is undermining the archival bases of traditional biography. When anything is an archive, who needs to go to the library? Who needs what we used to call an archive? Not an archivophobic, certainly, but not even a bold Little Jack Horner. If writers like Burton succeed, it looks as if the New Historicist game of dipping for decorative embellishments into really old books (1930s books, say, and some of them in faraway libraries and in bound volumes which are not always "previewed" in Google Books) and dipping daringly into manuscript collections for a vivid phrase or a quaint name to use as a one-of-a-kind garnish—it looks as if this game will lose its cachet once the old definition of archive is redefined out of existence.[15] Meanwhile, who teaches transcription of nineteenth-century American handwriting? What's happening is not pretty.

❖ Chapter 9 ❖

BIOGRAPHICAL SCHOLARS AND
RECIDIVIST CRITICS

In 1973 Jay Leyda protested in *The Chief Glory of Every People* against the dreariness of most recent criticism and the neglect of biographical research: "With so much left to be known, how can we allow the present state of our knowledge to freeze and become permanently acceptable? Perhaps we have become too content with the biographical materials already at our disposal" ("Herman Melville, 1972," 164). Leyda's *The Melville Log* had come to seem so monumental yet (as Charles Feidelson said in 1951) so trivia-filled that a belated New Critical generation saw no reason to search very long in it, much less go behind it and beyond it. The meek young critics of the 1970s who had grown up near libraries, if not in them, tended not to challenge scholarship but simply to ignore it. They did not dispute, say, the conjectural dates that Leyda and Gilman and Hayford had given to some letters, forgetful that Jay and Bill and Harry were young men working in libraries when they assigned dates which had become "traditional." When they mentioned the letters they followed those dates because it saved them from having to rethink biographical evidence or (appalling thought) to look for additional evidence. The critics Leyda was talking about had been brainwashed at Yale and other great schools into thinking that archival research was always inimical to literary criticism and that, anyhow, nothing was left to be discovered.[1]

To some extent all modern Melville critics may have been intimidated by several decades in which confusions, misconceptions, and outright mistakes about Melville and his works had sprung up and persisted. Melville wrote some books which purported to be autobiographical but contained fictional sections and others which were taken as autobiographical although they were in large part fictional. Melville got dates of events in his life wrong even when he was trying to be accurate. He seems to have destroyed many of the documents his biographers would most eagerly have availed themselves of, such as Nathaniel Hawthorne's letter praising *Moby-Dick*. During Melville's last decades, when he had passed into obscurity, new errors came into print and were repeated, such as the assertion that he had voyaged around the globe in 1860. At his death the lack of reliable documentation weakened biographical statements by obituary-writers and even by his Berkshire friend Joseph E. A. Smith in the series of articles he published in the Pittsfield *Sun* in late 1891 and early 1892, the first attempt at a full biography.

The first twentieth-century biographer, Raymond Weaver, who fueled the Melville Revival in the United States with his *Herman Melville: Mariner and Mystic* (1921), did not have enough solid information to permit him to systematically establish dates and facts about Melville's early life, even if he had been temperamentally inclined to devote such attention to detail. Lacking information and moved by personal biases, he declared (60) that Melville's mother was remembered "in such terms as 'cold,' 'worldly,' 'formal,' 'haughty' and 'proper'; as putting the highest premium upon appearances; as frigidly contemptuous of Melville's domestic economy, and of the home-made clothes of his four children." Worse, Weaver went on (62), it "seems not altogether fantastic to contend that the Gorgon face that Melville bore in his heart; the goading impalpable image that made his whole life a pilgrimage of despair; that was the cold beautiful face of his mother, Maria Gansevoort." In his 1929 critical biography, which relied on Weaver for information, Lewis Mumford was blunter: "Both Melville's father and his mother were monsters" (15). Weaver's and Mumford's disdain toward Maria Melville infected not only subsequent critics but also some of the next generation of scholarly researchers.

Lacking documentation, Weaver guessed that Melville, despairing after the hostile reception of *Moby-Dick*, coiled "down into the night of his soul" and wrote *Pierre* expecting it to be his last book (341). In his critical biography based upon Weaver's, Mumford elaborated on some of Weaver's formulations about Melville's literary career. William Braswell in 1936 held that "Melville expected *Pierre* to be his final publication. In this novel he was having his last fling. He was satirizing his own too idealistic self, and he was giving a parting blow to a world that had struck him many a blow" (427). This "plausible theory," Hayford argued in 1946, was "substantially refuted by the 'Agatha' letters" which Melville wrote to Nathaniel Hawthorne in 1853, "especially," he pointed out, when they are read in conjunction with Melville's letters to the English publisher Richard Bentley during the negotiations over *Pierre* in 1852 (306). In his last footnote (310) Hayford cited a letter from Maria Melville of April 20, 1853, saying Melville had become so absorbed in a new work that it was now "nearly ready for the press."[2] Five years later, Leon Howard in his biography apparently took Melville's mother's letter as prevarication and concluded that whether Melville "bogged down or simply gave out in his efforts, the 'new work' seems not to have been 'made ready for the press'; and, in April, its author fell in with the family's plans to get him a political job" (202).[3] In 1960 Merrell R. Davis and William H. Gilman demolished the "last fling" theory of Melville as author in *The Letters of Herman Melville*—merely by printing the November 24, 1853, letter from Melville to the Harpers which made it clear that he still possessed the 1853 book he had been "prevented from publishing" earlier in the year. This was by itself enough to refute the Weaver-Mumford theory of Melville's willful abandonment of fiction. Then William Charvat in *The Profession of Authorship in America, 1800–1870* (1968) reviewed the evidence that Melville had actually worked on the Agatha story (256).

The Weaver-Mumford theory of *Pierre* is far from dead even in the twenty-first century. The notion that Melville renounced fiction after (take your pick) *Moby-Dick* or *Pierre* is still current among critics, largely because of Nina Baym's 1979 spin on an old myth, "Melville's Quarrel with Fiction." With the appearance of the article in the prestigious *PMLA*, with her succinct and arresting title, and with her two-fisted arguments, Baym appealed to younger critics just learning to be New Historicists. She paid no attention to the work of Hayford, Davis, and Gilman, and selectively ignored pages by Charvat. Now, slightly recast, "Melville's Quarrel with Fiction" flourishes on the Internet, although its basic tenets, obviously wrong at first publication to anyone who knew the *Letters*, have been exposed as invalid on documentary grounds ever since 1990, when my article on *The Isle of the Cross* was published in *American Literature*. The best refutation of Baym on aesthetic grounds is Shirley M. Dettlaff's "Melville's Aesthetics."[4]

Nor have biography and criticism recovered from Weaver's huddling all of Melville's life after *The Confidence-Man* into "The Long Quietus," the last of his seventeen chapters. Weaver's disproportionate treatment of Melville's later life was followed by subsequent biographers. Lewis Mumford (1929) homogenized the last decades: "The days pass and one day is like another: there is comfort in monotony. The sixties have passed; the seventies have come" (326).[5] That bland pronouncement mocked me from the top rim of my computer's monitor for many months during which I struggled with a mass of complex documentary evidence on Melville's last decades! As late as 2005 Andrew Delbanco varied Weaver's elegant "The Long Quietus" as "The Quiet End" (288).

In 1922, the year after Weaver's biography, Meade Minnigerode in *Some Personal Letters of Herman Melville and a Bibliography* printed documents from the New York Public Library Duyckinck Collection. These documents, all unknown to Weaver, included several letters about Melville's early career, manuscripts of reviews he published in the *Literary World*, among them the one for Melville's essay on Hawthorne's *Mosses from an Old Manse*, and letters about his attempt to publish a volume called *Poems* in 1860. No other such massive and significant scholarly discovery followed in the next two decades. In the 1930s, the decade after the Melville Revival, Robert S. Forsythe, Willard Thorp, Charles Roberts Anderson, and a few others began to establish facts and to sort truth from previous errors, one episode at a time. Having finished his two-volume life of Washington Irving (1935), the Yale professor Stanley T. Williams conceived the plan of directing a number of dissertations on particular periods of Melville's life, particular works by Melville, or literary influences on him. Writers of some of these dissertations were Elizabeth S. Foster (1941), Merton M. Sealts, Jr. (1942), Walter E. Bezanson (1943), Harrison Hayford (1945), Merrell R. Davis (1947), William H. Gilman (1947), Nathalia Wright (1949), and Edward Fiess (1951). The task assigned them and others of Williams's students was to test Weaver's use of documentary evidence and adduce fresh evidence as well as to reexamine what Mumford and later critics had done with Weaver's information and his conclusions. Equal to the great Yale Ph.D. researchers of the 1940s was Wilson Heflin, whose 1952 Vanderbilt dissertation on Melville's whaling years was based on massive archival research. With the notable exception of Bezanson, these scholars focused on Melville's prose. Their efforts were known and appreciated in a small circle of scholars, but writers on Melville in academic publications and in journalistic outlets were slow to take account of new evidence brought forward by Forsythe, Anderson, Thorp, the Yale students of Williams, Heflin, and Leyda. Jay Leyda in his 1951 *The Melville Log* seemed to place the capstone on the decade and more of new research. Yet a "critical biography" (a term meaning a literary study strung on a biographical chronology), Newton Arvin's *Herman Melville* (1950), became at once more influential among certain classes of Melville admirers than the work of genuine scholars, and has remained so.

Many questions had been answered between 1922 and 1951. Gilman, for example, had discovered what year Melville sailed for Liverpool (1839) and had reasoned about whether or not he visited London on that trip (probably not). Forsythe, Anderson, and Hayford had concluded that Melville could not have spent much more than three weeks with the natives in the Typee valley, certainly not the four months which he claimed.[6] Hayford and Heflin had worked out how long (if ever) Melville served as a harpooneer on a whaleship (probably not at all). Hayford kept emphasizing what year

Melville last saw Nathaniel Hawthorne (1857, not 1856). Establishing facts about Melville's life accelerated in the late 1980s when I began transcribing into the electronic *New Melville Log* hundreds, ultimately thousands, of documents from newspapers and from many manuscript archives. In this process I dated many dozens of undated or misdated items, especially letters in the Augusta Papers, and with those letters dated or redated other, already known documents. I answered such questions as how long Melville stayed in the Mississippi valley in 1840 (days or weeks, not months), what he did next after returning East (he taught near Lansingburgh before going to New York City), what year after his return from the Pacific he first returned to the Berkshires (1848, at the latest), whether or not he wrote the *Mosses* essay before meeting Hawthorne (he met Hawthorne first), how often he saw Hawthorne in the Berkshires (I added one meeting from the Augusta Papers and one from the *Windsor* [*Vt.*] *Journal*), when the final contract for *Pierre* was agreed to (early January 1852), and what book he next wrote after *Pierre* (*The Isle of the Cross*). Given the extreme resistance to factual information, it should not be surprising that even when errors have been corrected, critics and even biographers still carelessly repeat old misinformation from Weaver or from other obdurate sources of errors.

The fateful Melville Society meeting in December 1990, described in chapter 4, had made it clear that the sane old rules of evidence had been overturned, and "facts" no longer mattered.[7] That would have been the time to abandon my politically incorrect biography about a dead white man, for its reception had been vividly foretold. I kept working on my biography, despite that warning and many others. The most ferocious assault while I was still writing came in Cathy Davidson's March 1994 "New Melville" issue of *American Literature*, which had been, when I was on the advisory board, a respectable refereed journal. The message, which I obsessively repeat, was staggeringly hostile, immeasurably ignorant, and absolutely unambiguous: "*We already have full-scale biographies of Melville.*" The standard journal in the field, the journal of record, had been surrendered to the forces of political correctness. Only a fool, I suppose Davidson thought in 1994, would continue working on *The New Melville Log* and the biography after her "New Melville" was published. I went out for a spring run to calm myself and fell on the last patch of ice in Maryland, breaking my right wrist so that I had a small outward manifestation of almost unbearable inward pain.

By the publication of my second volume many (but far from all) old gaps in basic knowledge had been filled and many often-repeated errors had been corrected. In my biography I resisted the impulse to flag an episode with

"Watch me set Weaver Straight Again!" or *"Heads Up Now—New Portion of Old Episode Starts Here!"* or even *"Be Alert Now—Previously Unknown Episode Coming Up!"* In the preface to the first volume I explained:

> The abundance of new documentation affords me the extraordinary—almost unique—luxury of telling my new story without reference to other biographers, after these prefatory pages. The alternative would have been to choke the pages with modifications, corrections, and rebuttals, some significant, some quite trivial. . . . I never correct any biographer in the body of this book, and I have resisted coming down emphatically when I am quoting a document that someone else had mistranscribed or misdated. (1:xvi)

Who would have thought that anyone wanted extraneous gloating?

Yet James W. Tuttleton, in the December 1996 *New Criterion*, was deeply vexed at my "deliberate refusal to engage with previous biographers" (26):[8]

> Such an attitude, in my view, is really an impediment to Melville studies and an obstacle to learning itself, which is cumulative and aggregative and which proceeds, among other ways, by the careful documentation and elimination of error. Parker's method presupposes that his life is the really accurate one, that only his need be consulted, that it displaces all previous work, and in all this we have to take him at his word. Such a viewpoint discourages collation of information, the comparison of various biographical accounts, and the verification of fact. I have the greatest respect for Parker's work on Melville. And I am convinced that he knows more about Melville's life and books than anyone else in the world. This will be the standard biography for years to come. But he has tried to close the door to comparative analysis and it won't do. (27)

The last thing I wanted was to be "an impediment to Melville studies and an obstacle to learning itself."[9] Far from meaning my biography to close the door to investigation, I had hoped earnestly to encourage careful scrutiny of the evidence. The reader certainly did not need to take me on faith: my intention was to document everything. If I quoted a letter, I dated it and named the archive where it was held. I was *encouraging* anyone to check my work. I *expected* that my biography would send dozens of young academics to the libraries wanting to see why I said what I did and find that still more needed to be explored and presented to the world.

Yes, much (but not all) learning is "cumulative and aggregative," as Tuttleton said, and almost everything I had ever written on Melville had built upon the work of Jay Leyda, Wilson Heflin, Harrison Hayford, Merton M. Sealts, William H. Gilman, Merrell Davis, Elizabeth Foster, and other students of Stanley T. Williams and occasional later contributors such as Frederick J. and Joyce Deveau Kennedy. The glory, for me, in finding the title *The Isle of the Cross* was precisely the fact that I was building upon the work of Hayford and Sealts, both then still alive to rejoice at my telephone calls, and on the work of men who would have rejoiced with them if they had been alive, Gilman and Davis, and William Charvat. (As I have said, Jay Leyda rejoiced from his bed at the Rusk Institute of Rehabilitation Medicine when I took Amtrak up to tell him.) But to stop the narrative in the biography in order to weigh what Hayford said or almost said in 1946 about what Melville was writing in the winter of 1852–53, what he and Davis did in 1949 and what Davis and Gilman added in 1960 and what Charvat added in 1968 and then to triumphantly proclaim the title, *The Isle of the Cross*—that would have been to blur the news. I was writing a biography, not a history of Melville scholarship, as I do in parts of *Melville Biography: An Inside Narrative*. Nor was I writing a narrative of my private adventures in the archives as I do in some of these chapters.

Harrison Hayford and Jay Leyda knew just how strongly I acknowledged—and celebrated—scholarship as "cumulative and aggregative." Anyone reading the chapter in this book on Melville and Hawthorne's last dinner in the Berkshires will see a demonstration of scholarship as cumulative and aggregative, and scholarship as lovingly respectful of those who went before. We add our grains of sand; a few times, if we are lucky, we pile on a handful of sand all at once. Think for a moment what it meant to Hayford in 1987 when I told him that the Agatha story which he had written about in the mid-1940s, when he was a lad of thirty, had been finished in late May 1853 and that the title was *The Isle of the Cross*.

Like Tuttleton, again, I find the idea of tracing the history of scholarship enthralling, and do it repeatedly in *Melville Biography: An Inside Narrative*, which is not a narrative biography, but he had no idea of the sheer number of places where I got on with my story only by ignoring small and large errors in previous biographies. Would Tuttleton have wanted me to set straight everyone who had ever argued that Melville had written his essay on *Mosses from an Old Manse* before meeting Hawthorne? The time to engage other biographers would have been if the evidence was inconclusive and there was real reason for uncertainty. That just did not happen. Leon Howard thought Melville had money in the bank in the first half of the 1850s. Once we began to learn how deeply in debt Melville was, there was no point talking about what Howard thought. I would have been fatuous to try to counter biographical fantasies such as Edwin H. Miller's lurid claim in his critical biography that "something occurred" in the relationship between Melville and Hawthorne in September 1850, "possibly during Sophia's three-week absence from Lenox" (247). Previously, Hawthorne had "kept Melville at a distance a great deal of the time," but now Hawthorne wrote to Sophia of "our trouble" and said that "we shall never be comfortable in Lenox again." The "younger man must have introduced the subject of male friendship, not once but many times," Miller asserted (249). Then, according to Miller, Melville had "maniacally indulged himself in wild capers, like signing a letter 'his X mark,' visiting Hawthorne in a Spanish cavalier's costume, and cavorting in the company of the Duyckinck brothers during an August day that included a visit to a Shaker village" (250). Not knowing of the meetings in early and mid-November, Miller speculated that Hawthorne in his letter of mid-November "may have informed Melville for the first time of his departure" (250). How many paragraphs would it have taken to explain to the reader's satisfaction that Melville did not, *really did not*, dress up in a Spanish cavalier's costume but merely called out something on the order of "Buenos días, señor" or "Hola, señor"? Miller's vivid fantasizing would have taken dozens of pages to correct. The only responsible thing to do was to ignore Miller.

I shared Tuttleton's feelings much more than he could have realized, but I was haunted by the memory of a long evening in Los Angeles in the late 1970s when Carvel Collins, who had promised a William Faulkner biography for many years, had fascinated and appalled me, Regina Fadiman, Michael Millgate, Meta Carpenter Wilde, and others with his stories of how he was correcting Joseph Blotner's biography of Faulkner one line at a time. Might he have finished his biography before he died if he had simply written it without correcting Joe? Michael, already an aspiring biographer, observed to me cautiously that Carvel was "an accumulator." I was not yet an aspiring biographer, and far from being a hoarder was still at the stage of hastening to share anything I found, usually by publishing it as fast as I could, in the Melville Society newsletter, as I did with "Herman Melville Crazy" (January 1973). I had not yet gone down the pages of the biography by Leon Howard, whom I loved like an uncle, putting "No" "No" "No" in the margins, but even in the 1970s I understood the lesson about fixating on someone else's errors rather than telling your own story. Fredson Bowers had already cost me too many days and nights identifying his errors and trying to sort out his convoluted truculencies, a period I remembered from the late 1970s as an expense of spirit in a waste of shame—and futility, since the *Maggie* exposé I had done with Brian Higgins was still unpublished and, it seemed, apt to be unpublishable for the rest of my life.

In the early 1990s I was determined not to go Carvel Collins's way. For me madness lay in approaching a biography by focusing on earlier biographers' errors. Besides, to have done what Tuttleton wanted would have meant doubling the length of the book, at least, while turning it into a relentless ongoing celebration of my superiority to previous benighted tellers. No, I told myself, to correct other people's errors is to march into a Great Dismal Swamp from which no biographer and no narrative has ever emerged. I was writing a biography from documents, not from other biographies, as Lewis Mumford, Newton Arvin, and Edwin H. Miller had done and Andrew Delbanco was to do, so I would not profit from reading other biographers' outdated stories. Once I began writing, I never read any chapter of an earlier biography (and later found nothing in Laurie Robertson-Lorant's 1996 volume that met the test of being both accurate and new to me).[10] My reason for leaving biographies aside was not just to save space that discussing old interpretations would have required. My massive labor of the late 1980s and early 1990s, especially, was to put all the old and all the new documents together in a sequence. In every period of Melville's life my new documents, when intermixed in sequence with the previously known documents, dictated a very different story than anyone had told. Finally, I reached the point of having what seemed a sufficiency of documents incorporated and only partially assimilated because I had not yet read through the new expanded sequences. I began experiencing keen psychological urgency, anxiety, in fact, to see what the documents meant so I could start writing. Enough of the gathering phase—at least for a time! The trick you have to master is to know when you have really done enough gathering. Collins had fixated at the state of accumulating documents and correcting Joe Blotner, and understandably so, for to go on and begin to write a biography is terrifying, or ought to be, if the writer is serious. Nevertheless, if the biographer persists long enough, the imperative to stop accumulating and start writing ultimately becomes still more powerful, as I tried to convey by quoting "When Lilacs Last in the Dooryard Bloom'd" in a note in chapter 4. Resolved to start, I cleared my mind of preconceptions and began to read a stretch of documents, new ones all intermixed with old ones (often old ones in a corrected order). I read on until I saw a chapter-length story emerge, and then tried to blaze ahead getting the story told.

Mark Kinkead-Weekes in "Writing Lives Forwards" eloquently makes a case for working chronologically:

> Why did the authors of the Cambridge biography of Lawrence
> choose not only an old-fashioned chronological approach but a strict
> one, following his life forwards, miming the way that it was lived,
> and banning all hindsight? Of course biographers who have been
> researching for years do already know the general shape of the story
> they have to tell and how it will end, before they write the first word;
> and of course a life could not be written week by week, let alone
> day by day, even if enough data were available, without insufferable
> tedium. What is possible, however, at the crucial first-draft stage,
> when a general sense of things begins to develop into an organized
> story, is to work on, and then narrate in, time-spans small enough to
> allow all the evidence to be freshly commanded at once, with noth-
> ing but space ahead. This approach brings immediate advantages.
> Misconceptions show up, puzzles can be clarified, unexpected
> connections appear, simply through careful attention to the exact
> sequence and context of events. (236–37)

This is precisely right: any time you create a chronology consisting of long-
known documents and new documents, you will find yourself inserting a new
document into place without rereading the whole chronology to see how it
may affect what was already there. When you read a section of an enlarged
chronology afresh (after you have been conflating old documents with newly
discovered documents), *then* you see connections that were not necessarily
clear during the weeks or months you were enlarging your files by interpolating a new document here and another there. One joy of reading the new
chronology is that old documents in part or whole spring to new life, vivified
by a new document and also clarified, often enough, enlightened, by parts
of other old documents which also suddenly spring to new life as a result of
some new sidelight. All through the next "time-span" you work with, and the
next, little or large discoveries reverberate, perhaps keep reverberating to the
end of the life. I have remarked on the test of intelligence of a reader, the
ability, once you are confronted with a new document, to conceive how new
information affects what was already known and to be comfortable with a
new version of an old story or with an almost totally new episode. The biographer working through a greatly enlarged chronology *always* will experience
shocks of understanding, electrical insights, and out of the accumulation of
insights a new narrative defines itself, demanding to be told.[11]

For all my celebration of chronology, in my biography, I did not, after all,
start with Melville's birth, but at eleven years old, the day he and his father
packed up the last bits of papers and other possessions from an empty house

and fled to the *Swiftsure*, which was neither swift nor sure but moored all during a stormy night at the Courtland Street dock, where Allan Melvill's creditors might at any time have seized him. At the opening of the Leon Levy Center for Biography at the City University of New York in December 2008,[12] John T. Matteson read that first paragraph aloud after these comments:

> The opening paragraph of a biography should reflect the character of that subject, in the way that perhaps the music of a great aria fits the mood of the words that are being sung. . . . Hershel Parker . . . gives us, I think, a sense of darkness very much in keeping with the work of Melville himself. As I read this paragraph I hope you will listen with me for the notes of guilt, menace, and human dread that were to be sounded in much fuller force in Melville's works—*Pierre*, *Moby-Dick*, and *Benito Cereno*.

This scene was the last time we know that Melville was alone with his father, alone in shared present danger, the future ominous. After that "eloquent beginning" (to use the title of the CUNY session) I turned back to chronology, and stayed with it through the two volumes, the first of which, some pages later, is rounded out with the joyous scene in which Melville is again alone with a man supremely important to him—alone with Nathaniel Hawthorne in Lenox to give him a good-bye present, one of the first copies of *Moby-Dick*.

My biography was new to the point that not a single episode could be told as an earlier biography had told it. Yet even if I laid out a complicated new (or partially old) story with great clarity, I could not make reviewers pay attention to it. Reviewers! Resisting the temptation to write an eighteenth-century "character" sketch of the reviewer, I lace my comments here with several phrases from Paula R. Backscheider's *Reflections on Biography* (2001) and Carl Rollyson's *Biography: A User's Guide* (2008). Newspaper and magazine reviewers are parasitical, eking out their livings on other people's blood and brains. People who write several reviews a year tend to be constitutionally lazy, or else they would be writing something of their own. The fact that both "reviewers and their editors are lazy," says Rollyson, shows in reviewers' padding their pieces by summary of the biography. Routinely, Rollyson says, reviewers "exercise their own authority over the subject even though much of that authority is gained from reading the biographies they are reviewing" (275). Typically, these reviewers open their review by parading more-or-less accurate knowledge which they have just picked up from the book under review. Backscheider phrases this neatly: "Biographers . . . discover their best

new material recited as though the reviewer just happened to know it" (xiv).
Often, reviewers get more wrong than they get right. Rather too benignly,
Rollyson says, "organs such as the *New York Times* often choose reviewers
who are ignorant of the subject and of biography, or are obviously hostile
to the genre itself and regard reviewing biography as a chore" (275, 276).
Backscheider complains justly, "I have turned away from review after review
of my *Daniel Defoe: His Life* that narrate pieces of Defoe's exciting life and
never engage questions of selection, organization, or presentation" (xiv). I
would add that reviewers almost never describe the sort of original research,
if any, that went into the biography, and how accurately any archival material is conveyed. Worse yet, editors choose reviewers with malign personal
and political agendas; alternatively, reviewers who are enemies of the subject
or the biographer finagle the chance to review books they intend to trash.
The personal agendas of many reviewers (here I would include James Wood)
override any possibility that they will focus fairly on the book being reviewed.
There's a saving six percent of honorable New York City reviewers, I have
been told, but I have not encountered any of them writing on Melville.[13]
In the 1990s you could find responsible reviewers writing for newspapers in
smaller capitals such as Richmond, Virginia, and Columbia, South Carolina, or even in Boston, Los Angeles, Sydney, and sometimes London, but
their reviews seldom appeared on the Internet. Now, book review sections in
newspapers that survive in towns of any size are shrinking or disappearing. As
I said in chapter 7 the best hope is Internet reviewing, the litblogs or individual bloggers, or honest reviewing on Amazon.[14]

You would hope for better from literary critics, after the dust has settled.
However, like reviewers, many literary critics continue to act according to
their natures, which is to ignore facts and particularly to ignore the conscious correction of mistakes. (Of course, a reviewer like Brodhead or Milder
may also play critic in a given year.) Jay Leyda had taken the Virginian of
the *Mosses* essay as speaking for Melville when he declared he had never
met Hawthorne. When I worked through the 1850 Augusta Papers for the
1988 Northwestern-Newberry *Moby-Dick* Historical Note I constructed,
mainly from Maria Melville's letters, a day-by-day account of the first two
weeks of August 1850. I had then far more evidence than anyone else had
worked with and felt no joy at all in discovering that Jay Leyda had been
wrong. Once a detailed narrative of early August 1850 was in print in the
1988 Northwestern-Newberry *Moby-Dick,* in my 1996 biography, and in the
2001 Norton *Moby-Dick,* I assumed that critics would take note of these latest findings. In my view, to take one example, Brenda Wineapple in her 2003
biography of Hawthorne had an obligation to work through the evidence and

clarify or supplement it. Instead, she declared: "Though it's not clear when Melville began the review, whether before or after meeting Hawthorne, it's obvious that Melville was smitten with Hawthorne and his work" (224). The Harlequin Romance vulgarity of "smitten" aside,[15] it's worth pointing out that accuracy here makes a difference for Hawthorne biography as well as Melville biography, and any biographer writing about the meeting of the two men and the composition of the essay has a duty to acknowledge the facts. It is perfectly clear that Melville met Hawthorne before starting to write the *Mosses* essay. Wineapple simply did not do her homework about Melville's writing of the *Mosses* essay. She thwarts the goal of all real scholars, which is to make an advance in knowledge that others will build on.

Even writers who try to take some note of new information can set understanding back instead of advancing it. Robert K. Martin and Leland S. Person in 2000 devoted more than a page in their "Missing Letters: Hawthorne, Melville, and Scholarly Desire" to my account of Melville's long morning's work on the *Mosses* essay on August 9, 1850. I had been explicit about the sexual component in Melville's words and behavior. If I had needed authority, I could have pointed to what Albert Rothenberg in *The Emerging Goddess* says about the erotic arousal that accompanies phases of high creativity.[16] I said this, about Melville:

> Writing so intimately about Hawthorne's power to arouse his literary aspirations had left him more than a little febrile—excited intellectually, emotionally, and sexually—sexual arousal being for Melville an integral part of such intensely creative phases. In this state of intense and undirected arousal Melville acted out an extraordinary display of deflected sexuality. Lacking someone more appropriate to lavish an excess of esteem upon, Melville abducted a younger man's bride. . . . Unacquainted with [William A.] Butler's new wife, . . . Melville . . . "whisked" her out of the car and into his buggy, then whirled away with her "behind a black pony of very questionable build, gait and behavior." . . . Except in the light of the aroused sexuality and literary ambitions of his morning's work, Melville's dangerous skylarking is incomprehensible. . . . By the time the Butlers escaped, some of the tension may have drained out of Melville's system, but at night he dressed to fit his aroused state—as a Turk. In the popular imagination a Turk was not only sexually strange but also sexually formidable, the very pattern of an exotic predatory infidel. . . . Melville this evening bedecked himself or allowed the women to bedeck him as a figure society saw as sexually vigorous and threatening, turbaned and fitted

> with a make-do dagger or scimitar, or else a real sword left over from
> his uncle's noncombatant service in the War of 1812. (1:760–61)

My analysis was explicit: Melville had been sexually aroused by writing the
essay on Hawthorne and, unable or unwilling to analyze his feelings, had
nevertheless acted out in ways that deflected his homoerotic arousal into
what looked like nothing but predatory heterosexuality.

I described what Turks meant to Melville ("sexually vigorous and threatening"), but I see now that I failed to cite the passage from "Leaf 16" of
the fragment of the draft of *Typee* that turned up in 1983 and is housed in
the New York Public Library Gansevoort-Lansing Additions. There Melville
adapted the opening lines of the concluding song from John Gay's *The Beg-
gar's Opera*: "With Captain Macheath in the opera I could have sung, 'Thus
I lay like a Turk with my doxies around.'" Lining this through, Melville elaborated a comparison of himself to an "effeminate ottoman" surrounded by
"houris" in his "ser[a]glio"; then he added: "Sardanapalus might have experienced such sensations—but I dout whether any of the Sultans ever did"
(Parker, 1:365). How few times do we know of Melville's imaging himself as
another person, real or fictional? In one letter he saw himself as Lord Byron,
whose *Sardanapalus* he recalls here. I should have mentioned this in the
biography to clarify what dressing like a Turk meant.

Rightly or not, I assumed that on August 9, 1850, Melville had not
reached the cool, ironic, and downright amused understanding of his own
sexuality which he revealed in passages in *Clarel* two decades and more later.
Astonishingly, Martin and Person accused me of *not* paying "considerable
attention to the Hawthorne and Melville encounter," of displaying "relatively
little interest in the matter." Here I had located high comedy in Melville's
ignorance, just then, of his own sexual feelings, and displayed high interest
in the ways in which he deflected his own attention from that arousal, but
Martin and Person were not impressed:

> While certainly acknowledging the erotic feelings that Haw-
> thorne aroused in Melville, Parker goes to some length to displace
> those feelings from Hawthorne to other, more conventional love
> objects. . . . Parker's language reveals a great deal about the scholarly
> desire he brings to the Melville-Hawthorne relationship—acknowl-
> edging Melville's sexual "arousal," but then calling it "undirected"
> and displacing it to a heterosexual encounter. This move is a per-
> fect illustration of the triangulation of male-male relationships and
> the homosexual panic that Eve Kosofsky Sedgwick has studied in

> *Between Men* and *Epistemology of the Closet.* But it could be Parker
> rather than Melville who panics and attributes to Mary Butler's
> husband a different kind of panic that backhandedly compliments
> Melville's heterosexual prowess. . . . Parker stops just short in these
> pages of analyzing the connection between Melville's arousal and
> his relationship with Hawthorne. (106–7)[17]

This, of course, rests on the absurd notion that only overt practitioners of
queer theory or gay criticism can understand how homoerotic arousal can be
deflected into heterosexual high jinks. In my experience with such practitioners I see a kind of recurring arrogance, as if they think they own the topic of
male sexuality. They also (I am thinking of Alan Helms's grim desire to read
even a factitious poetic sequence, rather than Whitman's "Live Oak, with
Moss," if it can be packaged as homophobic) tend to repress any sense of
humor which might have lightened their lives. Far from being panicked in a
"perfect illustration" of Sedgwick, I was writing an episode which modulated
from my tribute to Melville's high literary creativity to depiction of hilarious sex farce. Martin and Person, being professionals at their game, were
haplessly sure I could not possibly have meant what I was explicitly saying
about Melville, and they had to appeal to the ultimate authority, Eve Kosofsky Sedgwick, however little she knew of Melville.

Martin and Person at least seized on my new information, although they
were sure I did not understand it. More often critics do not rise to their level
of discussing new factual evidence. One of Melville's most quoted pieces of
writing is the "dollars damn me" letter to Hawthorne. This letter Jay Leyda
tentatively dated June 1?, 1851, and Davis and Gilman followed him in
1960. After the Northwestern-Newberry *Correspondence* volume was published, I transcribed Augusta Melville's letter to Allan on May 16, 1851, then
recently donated to Arrowhead by Anna Morewood. The details in it, including a reference to "a flying visit from Herman," allowed me to redate the
letter to early May as part of a new thick chronology of early 1851. Hayford looked over the evidence and approved. I still did not have a precise
date, but the whole story of hiring a typesetter for *The Whale* was altered,
pushed earlier by Augusta's letter. In his 2004 *Monumental Melville: The
Formation of a Literary Career*, Edgar A. Dryden referred repeatedly to the
"June 1?, 1851" letter, without mentioning my redating (11, 202, 213). In
his *Exiled Royalties: Melville and the Life We Imagine* (2006), Robert Milder
took what he called "the letter of [June 1?] 1851" as the "particular donnée"
of his book (xii). In his 1999 *Melville's Anatomies* Samuel Otter made this
letter of Melville's the alpha and omega, starting the acknowledgments (xi)

with "In a famous 1851 letter to Hawthorne" and ending the last note with "Herman Melville to Nathaniel Hawthorne, [June 1?], 1851, in *Correspondence*, 191." Yet on page 7 Otter refers to "the famous letter Melville wrote to Hawthorne in May or early June 1851" and on page 265 says: "Traditionally, the letter has been dated around June 1, 1851. Recently, Parker has argued for a date in early May." There Otter leaves the matter, as if a critic has no duty to examine the evidence. This sort of statement evades responsibility. A difference of three weeks or so just might matter. Even a critic needs to realize what a word like "traditionally" amounts to, as I have said: it means that Leyda and others did their best, given what they had to triangulate with, and succeeded in getting pretty close. There is nothing sacred about a conventional dating, but there *is* something sacred about the search for something closer to the truth of Melville's life. A critic or biographer is free to challenge my dating but only if he or she will work through the evidence. How can a critic justify using a disputed date without assessing the evidence? Because critics are as lazy as reviewers, or because they regard the search for accuracy as something other people concern themselves with?[18]

In the introduction to *The Cambridge Companion to Herman Melville* (1998) Robert S. Levine divided writers on Melville into "bookworms" and "creative readers." "Bookworms" were "those critics" (I would say "scholars") who "practice an accretionary, author-based approach committed to recovering Melville's intentions by paying close attention to what is known about his biography, reading habits, compositional methods, and so on" (4–5). The "creative readers" were those "who pay a bit less heed to the ascertainable facts in order to explore from more theoretical and speculative perspectives the cultural discourses, logics, and concerns informing Melville's texts" (5). A *"bit less heed,"* as it turned out, came down to almost no heed at all. Although Levine asserted that his *Companion* was "conceived with the notion that it would be salutary for Melville studies" if bookworms and creative readers "were more responsive to each other's work" (6), he did not include any "bookworms" in the collection. Even Cindy Weinstein, the professor cited proudly for making a study of "Melville's critical reception" (7), blithely proceeded without using the basic tool, another Cambridge book, the Higgins-Parker *Melville: The Contemporary Reviews*, and of course without supplementing that collection by fresh hunts in old newspapers and new databases.[19] Levine's creative contributors disregarded far more "ascertainable facts" than they paid heed to, and the bookworm nowhere reared a lowly head. The mindset exalting imagination over traditional scholarship continued, as in the September 2009 *American Literature* review by Hugh Egan of my *Melville: The Making of the Poet* and *Frederick Douglass and*

Herman Melville: Essays in Relation, edited by Robert S. Levine and Samuel Otter. According to Egan, the "contrasting modes of critical engagement" in the two books "remind us of the fault lines separating traditional archival scholarship and more theoretical, speculative investigations" (623).[20]

The one place you would expect to see meticulous attention to detail is a chronology, but recent attempts to work with the chronology of Melville's life have tended not to take much account of new discoveries. In *Herman Melville A to Z: The Essential Reference to His Life and Work* (2001) Carl Rollyson and Lisa Paddock did not prepare themselves for such a massive work, not even Rollyson, a professional biographer. Errors come thick. In the "Chronology" (ix–xxiv), Melville is working on his uncle Thomas's farm in 1834–35; Melville visits St. Louis in 1840 and spends Christmas with his family in Lansingburgh; he publishes his *Mosses* essay on August 5, 1850; the authors call *The Isle of the Cross* "a novella"; Melville is the last to see Evert Duyckinck alive; there is nothing in 1860 about *Poems*. Later, Helen "as a child" attends Elizabeth "Sedgewick's" (Sedgwick's) school and she undergoes an operation on her foot in 1854 (74); *The Isle of the Cross* is merely a "proposed long work" (74); the Spouter Inn is transported to Nantucket (188); Melville goes to New York in July 1847 to meet Charles F. Hoffman (221). There are strange omissions, such as "Maramma" (the much discussed home of the High Pontiff in chap. 105 of *Mardi*), and wondrous inclusions, such as "unparticipating man, the." The point of "the essential reference" book is to be inclusive and accurate.

Giles Gunn's *A Historical Guide to Herman Melville* (2005) belies the name. The chronology is appalling. According to Gunn, Melville worked on his uncle's farm in 1845; Melville began *Typee* in Lansingburgh; Gansevoort Melville's "political career blossoms" in 1846; Melville began *The Whale* in October 1850; Melville begins *Billy Budd* in 1888. *The Isle of the Cross* is not listed under 1852 or 1853. Gunn asserted that "an early draft of *Typee* has recently turned up" (228)—an error probably caused by John Bryant's frequent misleading references to "the draft of *Typee*" when no such thing is known to be extant. (I repeat because the misinformation is so widespread: only fifteen leaves were discovered in the Augusta Papers to supplement the leaf long kept in the Gansevoort-Lansing Collection of the New York Public Library. Sixteen leaves are known.) Gunn corrected none of his contributor Milder's errors, such as referring (50) to Lemuel Shaw, Jr., as Elizabeth Shaw Melville's stepbrother (he was her half brother and she treated him simply as her brother).

In "A Brief Biography" in Gunn's *Historical Guide*, Robert Milder mentioned the money from Melville's contributions to *Harper's* and *Putnam's* as helping "to sustain him as a working author while he recovered from the psychological ordeal of writing *Pierre* and the critical ordeal of having published it" (36). Only then, out of order, did Milder continue with a mention of what should have come between *Pierre* and the magazine pieces: "In 1852–1853 Melville evidently wrote and 'was prevented from printing' . . . a narrative entitled 'The Isle of the Cross' based on the history of a Nantucket woman named Agatha Hatch Robertson" (36). "Evidently," he says, not quite able to acknowledge its shape as a real novel but as a "narrative," something to be a little doubtful about. In the Gunn collection Milder admitted daringly (risking the wrath of Brodhead, Delbanco, and Schultz, as explained later in this chapter) that Melville had completed a book he called *Poems* in 1860, though he mistakenly amplified the title by calling it "the simply titled 'Poems by Herman Melville'" (43) and dismissed it as not containing anything but pieces by "a fledgling poet" (57).

In his "brief biography" Milder counted out Melville's production in "the first decade or so" of his "forty-five-year development of mind, character, and art" (18):

> *Typee* (1846), *Omoo* (1847), *Mardi* (1849), *Redburn* (1849), and *White-Jacket* (1850); then *Moby-Dick* (1851), followed immediately and as if by some interior urgency by the disastrous *Pierre* (1852); then the philosophical retrenchment (but aesthetic mastery) of the magazine pieces (1853–1856) and the comic/pathetic *Israel Potter* (1855), the vertiginous ironies of *The Confidence-Man* (1857), and finally silence.

The "eleven-year parabola of Melville's rise and putative fall covers only the first act of his career," Milder went on to say, for there was a "distinguished second act" that included *Battle-Pieces* (1866), and *Clarel* (1876), and "a fertile, if abbreviated third act beginning with his retirement from the New York Customs House in 1885" (18).

For Milder, "successful biography is a labor of integrating the outer life and the inner life" (19). Despite "the richness" of the merely external, factual Melville "family archive" there is little, Milder said, in the way of "testimonies to the interior life," the truly valuable materials "from which the biographer must reconstruct or imagine or invent a 'Melville'" (19). It seems never to have occurred to Milder that there was anything to be *reconstructed* or *imagined* or *invented* from the fact that Melville spent many months during the "parabola" writing *The Isle of the Cross* and (if the parabola were extended beyond a decade) perhaps as much as three years writing *Poems*. Milder missed the chance to rethink Melville's career in the light of all the

books and shorter pieces he is known to have written, missed the chance to
glimpse the full arc of a "parabola" of Melville's "development"—where the
word "development" implies an attention to successive stages in the process
or progress. Even if a critic declares himself a devotee of the life which he
"imagines" rather than the life which a scholar retrieves from the archives
and interprets, such a critic has an obligation to imagine as much of Melville's "development" as is known. A responsible critic would exercise his
reconstruction or *imagining* or *inventing* (to repeat Milder's own powerful and
appealing words) on a "Melville" who produced *Typee, Omoo, Mardi, Redburn, White-Jacket, Moby-Dick, Pierre, The Isle of the Cross*, some "magazine
pieces" (including more tortoise material than was ever published), *Israel
Potter* (serialized before book publication), one unpublished magazine diptych, *The Piazza Tales* (including the introduction, never a magazine piece),
The Confidence-Man, three unpublished lectures, *Poems*, and *Battle-Pieces*
and *Clarel*, as well as the post-retirement publications and uncompleted writings (some of both of which probably date from the late 1850s). For Milder
to write about Melville's "development" (18) in the Gunn collection without mentioning *The Isle of the Cross* and *Poems* is to stand at the doorway to
biography, not to enter the room even briefly, and to shout into the room,
like the satanic red-bearded stranger at the Chicago Melville Society meeting in 1990, described in a note in chapter 4, "THE FACTS DON'T MATTER." In
this instance, the facts beg for imaginative understanding which Milder, the
author of "A Brief Biography," was incapable of summoning up. Brevity in a
"biography" is no excuse for omitting huge hunks of a writer's working life.[21]

For Milder, a contributor to the Levine collection as well as Gunn's 2005
collection, it was a very short step from his chapter in the 1988 *Columbia
Literary History of the United States* (where he extended New Criticism from
artifact to biography, treating Melville's life as if it had the unity of a perfect literary work) to his 2006 book, *Exiled Royalties: Melville and the Life
We Imagine*. In the 2006 preface Milder declared that the two volumes of
my biography had made available "more than any reasonable person would
want to know about the outward particulars of Melville's life while leaving
room for new imaginative uses of its material" (xii). In practice, what Milder
did is disastrously *unreasonable* and *unimaginative*. Still contemptuous of
mere fact, Milder proclaimed his success in making "new imaginative uses"
of all the "material" of "Melville's life" (xii). But because he had relegated
so much of the material into the category of "*more than any reasonable person would want to know*" Milder simply could not make himself aware of
all the "material" which might repay imaginative attention. In consequence,
the sum of what he regarded as "material" was diminished by whatever facts

he had dismissed. The book subtitled *Melville and the Life We Imagine* is necessarily limited to the fragments of material Milder chose to exercise his imagination upon. In this instance, the facts beg for imaginative understanding which Milder, the author of "A Brief Biography," was incapable of summoning up. "Reading Herman Melville in his fullness" means attending to *all* of his books, even if some of them are lost books that cannot be held in the hand: all the more need for responsible imagination.

Milder knows that I am "evidently" right in saying Melville completed *The Isle of the Cross* in 1853, but in his *Exiled Royalties* (144) he mentions Melville's visit to Hawthorne at Concord yet strangely omits the obvious purpose of the meeting. Melville's letter to Hawthorne from Boston in mid-December makes it clear that he went to Concord to talk about the Agatha story, to try to persuade Hawthorne to write it, and, hearing flatly that this friend could not write it, had decided that he would, after all, write it himself. Merely to mention Melville's saying he enjoyed the visit is not to write scrupulously, and to write about Melville's fascination with the Agatha story, as Milder does, without mentioning *The Isle of the Cross* is intellectually deplorable. Neither *The Isle of the Cross* nor *Poems* is in the 2006 index. Milder simply could not "imagine" the two lost books as taking places in the "parabola" of Melville's "development." Yet Melville brooded for months over the true story on which he based *The Isle of the Cross* then toiled on it from mid-December 1852 until around the end of the third week of May 1853, perhaps May 22 precisely. He wrote poems exclusively (except for lectures) between sometime late in 1857, apparently, all through 1858, 1859, and the first months of 1860. These long stretches of struggle and, I would say, triumph, deserve to take their place in any believable account of Melville's "forty-five-year development." Responsible imagination begins with facts.

The great damage from recidivist critics occurs when a huge part of the trajectory of Melville's career is falsely described, as in Delbanco's 2005 inability and Milder's 2006 inability to take account of *The Isle of the Cross* and *Poems* as requiring many months of Melville's working life.[22] The word "trajectory" in relation to biography has been belabored in recent theorizing. Backscheider says that William Epstein in *Recognizing Biography* "has located the demand for the 'myth' of the 'straight line' in the nineteenth century and associated it with the modern conception of a career, 'an organized trajectory of individual advancement'" (105).[23] An organized trajectory is only as good as its component parts, and an individual's trajectory is not always an advance. Milder, like several critics and biographers discussed in a later chapter, chooses in *Exiled Royalties* to write about part of Melville's trajectory as if it were the full trajectory as currently described (170). To some extent, at least, Milder is under the influence of Nina Baym's 1979 "Melville's Quarrel with Fiction," which he quotes without challenge to the basic argument. Other critics, some still less scrupulous, seem to have fallen powerfully under Baym's influence in reinstating the old Weaver theory. I have occasion again to mention three such critics, Richard Brodhead, Andrew Delbanco, and Elizabeth Schultz, who in 2002 expressed their high-minded doubts as to the existence of *The Isle of the Cross* in 1853 and a volume Melville called *Poems* in 1860. I had merely surmised that Melville completed a book in 1853, said Brodhead, by then the dean of Yale College, in the June 23, 2002, *New York Times*. My surmises went on: "Parker is also convinced that Melville prepared a volume of poems in 1860 that failed to be published. If this is so, a stretch that had seemed empty of literary strivings was instead a time of new effort and new failure—a black hole Parker alone has the instruments to detect" (13). Andrew Delbanco, the Levi Professor in the Humanities at Columbia University, known to be a biographer-in-waiting, in the *New Republic* (September 2002) declared that I was "amazingly certain" (34) of my own conclusions, such as Melville's completion of a book in 1853 (merely a surmise, he said) and *Poems* in 1860 (it "was never published—and it is a surmise that Melville ever wrote it"). Delbanco warned that my certainty of my conclusions meant that the second volume, like the first, "must be used with caution" (34). Elizabeth Schultz in the *Common Review* (Winter 2002) gave a further punitive twist to the accusations: "Parker also reads betrayal and despair into the disappearance of two manuscripts, which he contends Melville completed—a novel, putatively titled *The Isle of the Cross*, and his first collection of poems" (45). As Backscheider says, "For an academic to be accused of 'making up things' . . . is the most serious charge that can be levelled against him or her and may discredit that person forever" (xix). I may die still widely discredited and shamed in print and on the Internet by the false accusations of these three Melville critics, but starting in 2007 I have been trying to make the truth known, even at the cost of some barely perceptible repetitions.

In dismissing me as the sole adventurer to bring back a report from that "black hole," Brodhead was dismissing three quarters of a century of scholarship. To be blunt, Brodhead was acting as if the scholars from Minnigerode on had never labored in the archives, never published their discoveries, never rejoiced when later workers added their supplementary findings. I alone "had the instruments to detect" *Poems*, so I had fantasized it. I was an unreliable biographer, and the scholars I had revered and built upon had never existed. I have talked about Brodhead's blindness to human agony. He, Delbanco, and Schultz also display here something worse: blindness to human existence, blindness to the working lives of remarkable scholars.

They dismiss scholars like Thorp and Hayford as if they had never existed. I emphasize this again to make clear the wreckage Charles N. Feidelson made of scholarship at Yale and other Ivy League universities and the contempt for human beings which his principles encouraged.

Does such slander in the mainstream media matter, except to the person whose reputation is being damaged and to the children and grandchildren of the now-dead scholars whose memories are erased? Yes, for such false proclamations still confuse the innocent critic who reads the slanderers but not the scholarship. Apparently influenced by one or more of these critics, Edgar A. Dryden in 2004 (207 n. 2) said, "Hershel Parker argues convincingly that Melville tried unsuccessfully to publish a book of poems in 1860." No, no! In my biography there is *no such argument.* Why would I argue something everyone knew? Instead, I merely make a fresh presentation of the long-familiar evidence that when Melville sailed from Boston with his brother in 1860 he left behind in manuscript a volume of poetry which he expected to be published in New York in his absence. I had new things to say about his reading epics on the voyage and other matters, but not much new about the volume of poems except some attention to the evidence of its length.

What's at stake with the denial of *The Isle of the Cross* and *Poems* is a true sense of the trajectory of Melville's career, in which *The Isle of the Cross* comes between *Pierre* and the first stories and in which the lectures precede *Poems* and *Battle-Pieces* follows it. A responsible critic would have dismissed Baym's efforts to keep something like Weaver's unsupported theories before new generations of critics. A responsible critic would have been open to ways that *Pierre* as a psychological novel grows out of the examinations of the workings of the mind in *Moby-Dick.* Such a critic might have looked at ways in which Melville's suggestions to Hawthorne about the Agatha Hatch material might seem to continue or develop beyond his techniques in *Pierre.* Instead of writing about "Bartleby" as if it followed *Pierre,* such a critic would use all the available evidence to speculate responsibly about how Melville might have grown, in style, psychology, and intellect, in the process of brooding about the Agatha Hatch story in the fall of 1852 and of writing the lost *The Isle of the Cross* from mid-December 1852 till late May 1853. Similarly, a responsible critic would take account of how Melville might have grown as a poet in the process of writing the lost *Poems* from 1857 or 1858 until May 1860. No one can think responsibly about *Battle-Pieces* (1866), *John Marr* (1888), and *Timoleon* (1891), or about the 1876 *Clarel,* without taking into account the book of poetry which Melville was not able to print in 1860.

Criticism cannot be valid, for instance, if, denying the actuality of the lost *Poems* (1860), or simply not visualizing the book as something that ever existed, critics distort the trajectory of Melville's poetic labors by referring to *Battle-Pieces* as Melville's "first collection of poetry" (as Edgar Dryden does) instead of his first *published* book of poetry. Criticism is vitiated, if not invalidated, when anything poetically "unconventional" in *Battle-Pieces* is ascribed to Melville's turning directly, however belatedly, from prose to his Civil War poetry. Some critics, in fact, still write as if *Battle-Pieces* followed *The Confidence-Man* (1857) without any intermediate literary work, or, at best, as if it followed next after the composition of his three lectures in the late 1850s. In the March 2010 *American Literature* Cody Marrs engaged in verbal gymnastics to avoid treating *Poems* as a real part of Melville's career. Marrs said not a word about the disappointment Melville might have felt about having Harpers refuse two of the poems (as they seem to have done) and about having at least two publishers reject *Poems*, so that it, like his *The Isle of the Cross*, went unpublished and lost, at least as a collection. Marrs's minimization started in this summary, which claims to be a review of "facts" (91):

> Let us begin with the facts: upon completing the *Piazza Tales* (1856) and *The Confidence-Man* (1857), Melville plunged himself into verse, studying the poetry of Dante, Friedrich Schiller, Heinrich Heine, John Milton, Matthew Arnold, and John Keats, among others. He began experimenting with his own poems, producing a slim volume in 1860 that did not find a publisher; and then, in 1866, one year after the fall of Richmond, Virginia, he published his first book of verse, *Battle-Pieces and Aspects of the War*.

"Slim volume" may be true but we do not know it for a fact. The mention of *The Piazza Tales* is strange, since only the introductory sketch dates from 1856, and the mention of *The Confidence-Man* seems not as important to Melville as the financial disaster of May 1856 and the long trip to Scotland, England, the Mediterranean, and back to England—a trip during which Melville had time to reflect on his future. Instead of writing more fiction, he began late in 1857 an abortive career as a lecturer, delivering the last of the third lectures early in 1860.

Marrs elaborated a theory of Melville's turning to poetry in which the chronology is wildly altered, in which the shift to poetry takes place during the Civil War (94):

> Melville understood poetry first and foremost as a mode and medium of worldly engagement. As such, we should grasp the birth of his poetic career not as a withdrawal but as a politico-aesthetic

realignment—and as a profoundly situated one at that. One of the most glaring shortcomings of [William C.] Spengemann's and Parker's counternarratives is that neither one acknowledges the degree to which the Civil War reshaped Melville's career, despite the fact that his first book of published poems is not about imaginary islands or sailors in the Pacific but about America's descent into "Nature's dark side," that "conflict of convictions" which brought about unprecedented national bloodletting. The fact that Melville's inaugural public verses are war lyrics is indispensable to our understanding of his shift from prose fiction. . . . What we discover in the structures and meanings of *Battle-Pieces* is nothing less than an immanent account of Melville's poetic turn, an inside narrative revealing that Melville's adoption of verse originates in his experience and understanding of the Civil War as a historical event.

To begin at the end of this quotation: No, Melville's adoption of verse originated in the years *before* the Civil War when he was apparently preoccupied with the Risorgimento in Italy (particularly as it had entered poetry in English), preoccupied with classical literature and classical values, and constantly steeping himself in the finest poets working in the English language, among them contemporary poets including Tennyson and the Brownings. The honorific word "inaugural" itself seems selected precisely to deflect attention from the lost but very real *Poems*, the book on which Melville labored for at least two years, very likely for at least two and a half years. To call *Battle-Pieces* "Melville's inaugural public verses" is sleight-of-hand that deflects attention from *Poems*, which Melville meant to be his "inaugural public verses" and which he thought for months had indeed been published as his "inaugural public verses." Only the rejection of *Poems* by publishers kept it from marking the "birth" of Melville's "poetic career." What went into making Melville a poet had taken place before May 1860.

What would it take to stimulate Melville critics to take account of the simple fact that he thought he was a poet by the late 1850s and in 1860 was ready to face the world as a poet? Marrs refers (93) to my "meticulous account of Melville's reading and writing habits" but pays no attention to what I said about the damage done by the failure of critics to visualize his lost books as real, as products of months or years of his working life. Let me quote Jay Leyda again ("Herman Melville, 1972," 164): "With so much left to be known, how can we allow the present state of our knowledge to freeze and become permanently acceptable? Perhaps we have become too content with the biographical materials already at our disposal."[24] The situation is far worse than Leyda described. Critics are more and more denying the existence of "biographical materials already at our disposal." What will it take to encourage a critic like Marrs to think about Melville as a human being with a lived life, a human being as real as he is, as real as Brodhead, Delbanco, and Schultz? The answer probably is a total apocalyptic rejection of the New Criticism, for Brodhead's New Critical denial of the existence of Minnigerode, Thorp, Howard, Hayford, and many others was presaged in his 1976 critical book, *Hawthorne, Melville, and the Novel,* just as Delbanco's was in his "Melville in the '80s" (1992).

✢ *Chapter 10* ✢

Presentism in Melville Biography

Half a century ago "presentism" was strictly a theological term identifying the belief that biblical prophecy, especially that in the book of Revelation, was then in the course of fulfillment. By 1974 in "Purposes and Ends in History: Presentism and the New Left" Howard Schonberger marked a change, identifying a New Leftist meaning for "presentism," that history had become "a key to reshaping programs and actions in the present" (449). Now an article on the Science Encyclopedia website explains that presentism "takes issue with the proposition that historical knowledge of the past should be pursued for its own sake, and offers instead the call for interpretations of the past that contribute to morally responsible critical perspectives on the present age."[1] Yet as late as November 3, 1997, in another online site, Word Spy, Paul McFedries treated the word as a neologism when he quoted William Safire: "In the midst of this millennial miasma, another word has come along to stir up historians: *presentism*. 'It's when a historian sees events in the past through the prism of present-day standards,' the lawyer-historian [Annette Gordon-Reed] tells me. 'For example, Thomas Jefferson is often judged harshly as a sexist even though the notion of complete equality between the sexes was almost unthinkable in his era.' Gordon-Reed calls it the 'why wasn't Jefferson like Alan Alda' question."

In her May 2002 president's column of the American Historical Association's journal *Perspectives on History*, "Against Presentism," Lynn Hunt argued that, at its worst, presentism "encourages a kind of moral complacency and self-congratulation. Interpreting the past in terms of present concerns usually leads us to find ourselves morally superior; the Greeks had slavery, even David Hume was a racist, and European women endorsed imperial ventures. Our for[e]bears constantly fail to measure up to our present-day standards." A little later John Shedd raised two objections in his *History Teacher* review of an avowedly presentist 2003 book by Douglas Selwyn and Jan Maher: "Presentism limits what we may discover about the past

251

because it puts so much stress on how history influences today that it screens out parts of the story that do not look immediately relevant to us. It hinders us from seeking to utilize the perspectives of past times in our analysis and thus works against a fuller understanding of people who lived before us."[2]

On December 4, 2009, on Google I got no hits for "presentism in biography," "presentist biography," "presentism and biography," "biographer as presentist," "presentism in American biography," or "American biographer and presentism," "presentist biography," or "American biographers and presentism." Nor did I find "presentism" or "presentist" in the index of any of my two or three dozen recent books on biography. In showing its presence in Melville criticism I begin with a glance back at Andrew Delbanco's 1992 survey, "Melville in the '80s," in which he identifies "the leading American studies scholars" and their topics: "Ann Douglas on the enervating sentimentality of antebellum culture (of which Melville was a bitter critic); Sacvan Bercovitch on its millenarian arrogance (which Melville both decried and abetted); Richard Slotkin on violence as a constituent part of the American self (of which Melville was an eloquent witness)." Delbanco continued, "With chilling prescience, these scholars rendered antebellum culture as a prefiguration of the complacencies of the Reagan decade" (711). But were these scholars (or critics?) working presciently if they read America in the middle of the nineteenth century as prefiguring "the Reagan decade"? Or were they reading backward, seeing antebellum America in the light of their own judgments of the 1980s? Delbanco here prefigured the presentist weaknesses that undermine his 2005 biography.[3] Yet even if the topic is poorly identified and illogically applied, the recent biographies of Melville by Laurie Robertson-Lorant (1996) and Andrew Delbanco (2005) both celebrate presentism and exemplify its faults.

First Robertson-Lorant. In *Slate* (July 10, 1996) Paul Berman ventured into Melville territory by reviewing Robertson-Lorant:

> The book tells us relatively little about the theological and philosophical notions that pressed on Melville's imagination, which is a pity. But we do learn something about politics. The views of the biographer herself, as they emerge in the book, are those of a good-hearted and slightly simple-minded modern liberal. Robertson-Lorant is a foe of genocide, racism, and of the Republican Party, except when Lincoln was its leader. She feels that it is always necessary, when mentioning such 19th-century marvels as the Brooklyn Bridge, to remind her readers that many an oppressed immigrant worker died in its construction. She is admirable, and predictable, and her only

error is to project those instincts onto Melville, who railed against imperialism, racism, missionaries in the South Seas, and other bad things, yet was not always admirable, and never predictable. Melville was a brooding metaphysician, and Robertson-Lorant is merely an indignant idealist. And so she reads too much into certain of his writings. In his poem "The House-top," for instance—about the New York draft riots of 1863—she sees a protest against "poverty, class conflict, and race hatred."

The poem, he announces, "contains nothing of the sort. By reading too much in, she reads too much out, and we are presented with a Melville who is nine-tenths topical and one-tenth profound."

The fullest analysis of Robertson-Lorant's biography as a presentist document is in the December 1996 *New Criterion* review by James W. Tuttleton, who, though critical, was seemingly compelled to defend her as a product of his own university. "Ms. Robertson-Lorant," he said, "took her doctorate from New York University and acknowledges the inspiration of the eminent Americanists Gay Wilson Allen and William Gibson" (25). This is the Allen who decade after decade hoped against hope that Walt Whitman was *not* a degenerate, a homosexual—who hoped, oh hoped (*The Solitary Singer*, 424) that "actual perversion" (homosexual love-making) was, oh heavenly powers, not likely! This is the Gibson, a lovely, sweet man, who as the inspector for Fredson Bowers's now notoriously misconceived and error-ridden Virginia Edition of Crane's *Maggie* gave this endorsement (in a copy in my possession): "As always, Professor Bowers' texts and apparatus are impeccable." Tuttleton observed that the Melville biographer Edwin H. Miller "might very well have been another of her teachers at NYU, although she scants his work" (25). This was the Miller who in his 1975 *Melville: A Biography* fantasized for Melville "a Spanish cavalier's costume" (250) for his "wild caper" of making sexual advances which Hawthorne rebuffed and because of which (Miller said) Hawthorne fled the Berkshires. In most regards Tuttleton, a fierce New York University loyalist, saw Robertson-Lorant's performance not in the light of her tangible biography of Melville but in the light of the inspiration and superb training which by definition she had received and absorbed at New York University: "She was taught to plumb the archives and secure the facts" (28).

Yet even while focused on defending a New York University Ph.D. as the product of rigorous training in scholarly methods, Tuttleton acknowledged that "inundating detail that is marginal to Melville's life" obscured "the historical context" in Robertson-Lorant's treatment (27):

Long paragraphs or even pages are given to discussion of extra-
literary events. We learn more than we need to know about how sex
was repressed in Melville's day (though he and Lizzie managed to
produce four children, and six or eight were not uncommon at the
time). We also hear about how blacks were enslaved and American
Indians were discriminated against. The domestic situation of women
and the laws that governed property loom large in the Robertson-
Lorant account. In case anybody is interested (and we aren't), she
repeatedly flourishes her radical *bona fides* by constantly faulting the
market economy, and we hear a great deal about the despoliation
of nature by westering America. She is so hopelessly PC that she
makes me want to go out and get the bumper sticker "NUKE THE
WHALES."

Robertson-Lorant's life is an instance of the abysmal New Historicism, which authorizes anyone to jerry-rig her own political
prejudices into a so-called context for a historical biography. She is
thin, thin, thin, on Melville's political views and so comes very close
to seriously misrepresenting his fundamental social conservatism. . . .

In short, for Robertson-Lorant a biography is an occasion for
didactic homily, and she never misses a chance to demonstrate her
superior morality, often in the most risible ways. An instance: "Having recently learned that ACLS supported teachers and artists who
were blacklisted during the McCarthy reign of terror in the 1950s, I
was doubly proud to have been a recipient of an ACLS fellowship."
Imagine being proud of a link with Communist teachers and artists
who wanted nothing less than the overthrow of our constitutional
liberties and the violent wreckage of our elective government! Poor
woman, she hasn't the faintest clue about what a "reign of terror"
is. . . . Evidently Dr. Robertson-Lorant is one of those parlor Marxists
in the educational world for whom "the new market capitalism and
industrialization" can be blamed for Melville's and even America's
ills. Adolescents should be protected from her.

From this diatribe Tuttleton moved on to a long treatment of Robertson-
Lorant on homosexuality and her conclusion that Melville "'undoubtedly'
experienced some form of homosexual activity." For this claim, he said,
"there is zero evidence and every reason to doubt it" (30).

In the March 1998 *Nineteenth-Century Literature* Robert Milder supplemented these analyses. Robertson-Lorant's biography was "not a book for
professional Americanists, much less for knowledgeable Melvilleans" (537):[4]

Robertson-Lorant evidently aims to give us a Melville for the 1990s. In practice this means a Melville meritoriously liberal in his writing on the touchstone issues of the time (more *our* time, perhaps, than his own) but not above tyrannizing over his household with the combined force of the Victorian paterfamilias and the frustrated man of genius. Her main themes—"Melville's sexuality, his relationship with his wife and children, and the degree of responsibility he bears for his older son's suicide" (Robertson-Lorant, p. xv)—are important additions to the emphases of older biographies, but rather than complement established concerns they have been allowed to displace them.

As Berman, Tuttleton, and Milder indicate, Robertson-Lorant makes Melville into an exponent of political correctness. For her, "The 'Gees" is a satire on "scientific racism." "The Bell-Tower," as everyone should have known, indubitably shows how "the Union could be destroyed by slavery." Ignoring the religious allegory in *The Confidence-Man*, Robertson-Lorant identifies "the Indian-hater" with "the modern Rambo" (365). How did it happen that in my dining room in Morro Bay the creator of Rambo managed to eat chicken without remarking on the resemblance of his world-famous character to an Indian-hater, a figure he knew to be of high interest to his host?

Tuttleton had drawn the line at quoting the passage in *Melville: A Biography* where Robertson-Lorant explains what *Moby-Dick* "is," but I resolutely quote it (280):

> *Moby-Dick* draws from a deep reservoir of Native American folklore and myth. It is a vision quest, a narrative sweat lodge or purification ritual, and a Ghost Dance mourning the closing of ancient spiritual frontiers. It is Melville's lament for the extermination of the Indians by white settlers and the importation of Africans as slaves, both of which sowed seeds of sin and death in the New World Garden. It is an apocalyptic vision of industrialization and imperialism, an elegy for the medicine man supplanted by the gunslinger.

However deeply Robertson-Lorant "was taught to plumb the archives and secure the facts," what she announces so confidently is astonishingly reductive. This is *not* what *Moby-Dick* "is." And part "Native American" is not what I am. I am *part Indian*, Cherokee and Choctaw, *not* part "Native American," that condescending neologism invented, employed, and forced upon others by politically correct whites. This paragraph and much of what

Robertson-Lorant says on politics is offensive on many levels—racial, political, intellectual, aesthetic.

For Robertson-Lorant's presentism in another extreme form, consider her treatment of "Norfolk Isle and the Chola Widow," Sketch Eighth of "The Encantadas," first published in the May 1854 *Putnam's New Monthly Magazine* and reprinted in *The Piazza Tales* (1856). The sketch is introduced by apposite quotations from Spenser (about a woman sorrowing by a shore) and Chatterton (about a woman grieving for her dead lover, "gone to his deathbed"), with a quotation added in the book version, a stanza from Collins's "dirge in Cymbeline."[5] The narrator (in what is offered as a personal experience) announces at the outset that Norfolk Isle has been made sacred "by the strongest trials of humanity," trials suffered there by Hunilla, a "Chola, or half-breed Indian woman of Payta in Peru," a "human being" whom he and his shipmates rescued from her isolation there long after her husband and brother drowned offshore, in her sight. In the long interval between isolation and rescue she had suffered what Melville as narrator cannot bring himself to name—"two unnamed events" perpetrated by men who ought to have rescued her. Drawing the lesson that "out of treachery" Hunilla had nevertheless invoked trust, he announces: "Humanity, thou strong thing, I worship thee, not in the laurelled victor, but in this vanquished one." He and his shipmates offer her not indignity but "silent reverence of respect."

Charles F. Briggs censored the ending before publication in *Putnam's*, leaving it this way: "The last seen of lone Hunilla she was passing into Payta town, riding upon a small gray ass; and before her on the ass's shoulders, she eyed the jointed workings of the beast's armorial cross." In a letter to Melville on May 12, 1854, Briggs apologized "for making a slight alteration in the last paragraph of the Chola Widow, which I thought would be improved by the omission of a few words"—perhaps an explicit reference to Jesus's entering Jerusalem on an ass. As proof that he "did not injure the idea" or "mutilate the touching figure," Briggs told Melville that James Russell Lowell had written him "that the figure of the cross in the ass' neck, brought tears into his eyes, and he thought it the finest touch of genius he had seen in prose." What haunts the narrator still is not only Hunilla as an emblem of suffering and yet enduring humanity but the problem of whether or not it is wise to put on record the worst that human beings are capable of. He declares, in exasperation, "Events, not books, should be forbid," but he does not spell out what Hunilla has suffered. Robertson-Lorant reduces the story to this (339): "Melville raises a woman of color to heroic stature while portraying colonialism as an earthly hell."

In Melville's story Hunilla is emblematic of "humanity," not of Chola half-breeds and other non-Caucasian women, and the story has nothing to do with colonialism, as an earthly hell or otherwise. Granted, Melville had winced when his straightforward assessment of colonialism was censored out of the American edition of *Typee*. Far from abandoning the subject, he recurred to it in *Omoo* and later books, including *Moby-Dick*, and nearby, in Sketch Ninth of "The Encantadas," he refers to "adventurous spirits" who "lead colonists into distant regions and assume political pre-eminence over them." Nothing in Sketch Eighth puts Hunilla's story in the context of colonialism. For Hunilla, "misery's mathematics" has nothing to do with her being an anachronistic "woman of color" any more than it has to do with colonialism. Under the flag of irrelevant automatic political correctness Robertson-Lorant diminishes and distorts the powerful, memorable sketch, where living hells may be created by Nature or by other human beings. As Robert Milder said in 1998, this is "a Melville for the 1990s" (537).

Bad luck plagued Melville's "Benito Cereno" long before "presentism" acquired the meaning Gordon-Reed defined. In April 1855 the publisher's reader for *Putnam's Monthly* deplored the "dreary documents" at the end and delayed the first installment until October. Just after the first of three installments came out, the *New York Evening Post* identified Melville's source as "Particulars of the Capture of the Spanish Ship Tryal, at the island of St. Maria; with the Documents relating to that affair," a chapter in the Massachusetts seal-hunter Amasa Delano's *Voyages and Travels* (Boston, 1817). Fine, but the *Post* then gave away the plot, with two installments of a masterpiece of suspense still unpublished. The real Delano (a miserable, churlish man, although blood kin to the great charmer, Franklin Delano Roosevelt) printed the terse account from his ship's log before telling the rest of what happened when, in 1800, as captain of the *Perseverance*, he boarded a drifting Spanish ship off the coast of Chile. Thirsty and hungry, the "captain, mate, people and slaves" all crowded around him, so pitiable that Delano at first ignored breaches of discipline. As a lesson to his readers, Delano rejoiced that in the ensuing crisis his "good wholesome floggings" had paid off in the behavior of his crew. Throughout, he kept his "policy of insurance" inviolate—another lesson to his readers. The Spanish captain, Benito Cereno, proving treacherous, Delano sued in a Peruvian court. Most of his chapter consisted of translations of depositions and other documents dealing with his legal efforts to gain his promised reward.

Sextupling the length of the original narrative, Melville imbued it with powerful emblems, tableaux, and symbolic actions. The stern-piece of the Spanish ship (renamed the *San Dominick*) is "medallioned about by groups of mythological or symbolical devices," the center figure "a dark satyr in a mask, holding his foot on the prostrate neck of a writhing figure, likewise masked" (49).[6] On an elevated poop deck six black hatchet-polishers seemingly exemplify "the peculiar love in negroes of uniting industry with pastime" (50). A "carved balustrade" on an "abandoned Venetian-looking" water-balcony gives way like charcoal before Delano (74, 73). A "large, misshapen arm-chair" resembles "some grotesque, middle-age engine of torment" (82–83). A flag with the Spanish castle and lion serves as a barber cloth. Repeatedly, the imagery suggests European aristocracy in decay.

Reconceiving the real Delano's unpleasant character, Melville made his "American" (as he repeatedly identifies him) healthy, blunt, capable, confident, rational, forgiving, naive, "a person of a singularly undistrustful good nature, not liable, except on extraordinary and repeated incentives, and hardly then, to indulge in personal alarms, any way involving the imputation of malign evil in man." The wise reader, Melville emphasized, could judge whether such trustfulness displayed "more than ordinary quickness and accuracy of intellectual perception" (47). Melville's Delano, embodying white stereotypes about blacks (although the morality of accepting stereotypes is not an issue in the story), cannot see what is before him, and stands bewildered: "Trying to break one charm, he was but becharmed anew. Though upon the wide sea, he seemed in some far inland country; prisoner in some deserted château, left to stare at empty grounds, and peer out at vague roads, where never wagon or wayfarer passed" (74). Forced against his will into suspicions, Delano reassures himself, but remains trustful for shorter and shorter periods. Foreboding tales force their way into his consciousness. In one, Malay pirates rise up from seemingly empty decks to slaughter their victims. Melville's Delano does not credit these tales: "He had heard of them—and now, as stories, they recurred" (68). Trusting in a Providence above (in a cosmology where there is no Satan below), Delano inhabits a Deistic universe (or a Unitarian one, as Melville's Boston family did). After harrowing suspense, the prolonged and intermittently terrifying ambiguity is resolved in lightning-bolt revelation and bloody action. Not wisdom but obliviousness saves Delano, this time.

Some hasty critics still assume, as Leon Howard did (221–22) that Melville, inept or weary, stuffed his pages with the legal depositions as printed in *Voyages*. In truth, Melville composed half that section so painstakingly that the added passages are (one could dare to say) seamlessly integrated into passages from the original. If not seamlessly, at least no critic has ever claimed to have been able to identify infallibly, simply by reading the story, what in the depositions was Delano's and what was Melville's. In his *Voyages* Delano had printed multiple versions of the story without concern for their effects, but Melville in only two tellings explores and exploits the primitive delight and reassurance that even sophisticated readers experience in hearing a compelling story told over again, the same yet different. In Melville's coda, Delano and Cereno reflect on the events. Delano dismisses the memory: "the past is passed; why moralize upon it? Forget it" (116). Melville's American survives at the cost of not being aware of evil, not being fully human. The weaker, wiser Spaniard (the European) is destroyed by knowledge of evil.

The bad luck that marked the story before and just after publication now persists as biographers twist the story to the ends of political correctness, sure that because it was written during the crisis over slavery it must contain partisan wisdom which we can apply to the present. Melville said in the "Supplement" to *Battle-Pieces* that he had always abhorred slavery "as an atheistical iniquity," so this must be a story "about" American slavery and must fit a presentist's agenda. Robertson-Lorant declared (349) that the story is "an indictment of 'benign' racism." In 2005 Andrew Delbanco wrote (242): "Today, one recognizes in *Benito Cereno* a prophetic vision of what Benjamin Barber calls 'American innocence so opaque in the face of evil that it seems equally insensible to slavery and the rebellion against slavery'—the kind of moral opacity that seems still to afflict America as it lumbers through the world creating enemies whose enmity it does not begin to understand." Reading "Benito Cereno" is almost intolerably suspenseful. Pondering over it is downright disturbing for what it suggests about the American national character. But it does not depict an America which "lumbers through the world creating enemies whose enmity it does not begin to understand." Delano does not truly understand those he befriends, but he does not create enemies. Indeed, Melville could itemize national sins. He did so in *Clarel* (1876), as in "The Shepherds' Dale" (4.9), but in "Benito Cereno" he did not indict: he identified an American archetype, a good man habitually blind to evil.[7]

Delbanco walked a tightrope in applying post 9/11 presentism to *Moby-Dick* (12–13):

> Since he "arrived" in the mid-twentieth century, there has been a steady stream of new Melvilles, all of whom seem somehow able to keep up with the preoccupations of the moment: myth-and-symbol Melville, countercultural Melville, anti-war Melville, environmentalist Melville, gay or bisexual Melville, multicultural Melville, global Melville. As for how he will fare in our "postmodern" (or is it already post-postmodern?) age, the early signs suggest that he remains as current as ever. In the immediate aftermath of that terrible day now known as 9/11, Captain Ahab was suddenly everywhere.

For some, he was a symbol of America's obsession with hunting down bin Laden.

Here Delbanco quoted others, including Edward Said ("collective passions are being funneled into a drive for war that uncannily resembles Captain Ahab in pursuit of Moby Dick"), but did not himself take clear responsibility for comparing "President George W. Bush to Ahab in his determination to attack Iraq" (13).

Delbanco had it both ways (165): "In spite of its author's relative political aloofness, *Moby-Dick* became a book about politics—or at least a book that lent itself to political interpretation." He continued (165): "Ahab has proven to be a prophetic mirror in which every generation of new readers has seen reflected the political demagogues of its own times—as when, in the 1940s, Ahab seemed to predict Adolf Hitler's monomaniacal rantings against the Jews, or, more recently, he is invoked as anticipating George W. Bush's obsession with hunting down first Osama bin Laden, then Saddam Hussein." In a note (327) Delbanco quoted a question by a Chilean writer, Ariel Dorfman: "what if 'Saddam might be the whale and . . . George Bush might in fact be an Ahab whose search for the monster in the oceans of sand and oil could end up with the ruin, not of the monster, but of those who were bent on its extermination?'" What indeed!

In 1992 Delbanco after describing Toni Morrison's view of *Moby-Dick* (722) said, "I find myself (for more, I think, than filiopietistic reasons) better persuaded by Heimert's version of Ahab as Calhoun"—Alan Heimert being his teacher at Harvard. Heimert found it inconceivable that Melville could be a decent respectable citizen in Massachusetts in 1850 and 1851 and not be obsessed with ending slavery. Heimert and others convinced themselves, with presentist common sense if not truth on their side, that no great writer could ignore the most important political question of his lifetime. Three critics in short order between 1960 and 1963 brought Melville into accord with current racial attitudes in their still imperfect democracy, after *Brown v. Board of Education* and, in one case, after the first Freedom Rides. All three of the well-meaning allegorizers shared from the same fund of wishful thinking and the same willingness to fudge what evidence there was and to twist arguments when the evidence was lacking so that Melville could be celebrated as a true patriot. Willie T. Weathers made Melville promise "ultimate triumph for America's constitutional guarantees of liberty and justice, and thereby safety for the hope of a free world" (276).[8] Charles H. Foster made Melville turn *Moby-Dick* into "a democratic, an anti-slavery fable" (279). Alan Heimert allowed that "Melville was not alone in his visceral democracy, nor was he in

1850 the only patriot who loved the Union," but he was one of the "few" who understood how profoundly the Compromise was a victory for manufacturing interests and for the slave states (317). In the 1970 *"Moby-Dick" as Doubloon* I decided the only way to handle these equally passionate allegoricists was to quote them at length, one by one, straight-faced, and let their arguments cancel each other's out. All of them were making detailed (if strained and contradictory) arguments about the historical contexts of 1850–51 but all three were presentists at heart, determined to salvage Melville as a man whose ideals were conformable to the latest, best, evolving ideals of liberal, patriotic whites in the Kennedy years. As I say in a later chapter, if you read enough articles in 1850–51 Whig papers and Democratic papers in the Boston Public Library, as I did in 1962, you acknowledge that in 1850 and 1851 the opposing parties sounded very much alike on the Fugitive Slave Law and sounded exactly alike on the horrible illegality of rescuing of fugitive slaves.

Delbanco tried to cloak himself from the extremes of presentism yet the effect of his writing was to excite just that in sympathetic reviewers. *Publishers Weekly* (July 18, 2005) said: "Even now, Delbanco observes, Melville's uniquely American myth of Ahab and the white whale has been recognized in President Bush's pursuit of Osama bin Laden." The *New Yorker* said approvingly (quoted from the publisher's reviews in Amazon): "Melville's very 'dissidence in his own time,' Delbanco writes, makes him seem at home in ours." In "Orphan in the Storm," posted in *Books & Culture: A Christian Review* on September 1, 2005, Roger Lundin wrote: "With his own eye cast on the politics of our post-9/11 world, Delbanco notes that in the years leading up to the Civil War, Melville repeatedly assailed his nation's political culture for a 'kind of moral opacity that seems still to afflict America as it lumbers through the world creating enemies whose enmity it does not begin to understand.'" Most reviewers—unfamiliar with the past and unwilling to try to understand the past—seized on Delbanco's book as displaying Melville's relevance to the post 9/11 world and praised it the higher for its presentism. They seized on his suggestive and tendentious nods toward presentism as if he had overtly endorsed the opinions he quoted.

On October 16, 2005, in the *Los Angeles Times*, "Beyond Melville the Literary Legend," Robert Faggen objected that "Melville is far too distant from politics, and his books are much too psychologically complex and multivocal to sustain a one-dimensional political interpretation." He agreed with Delbanco part way: "Delbanco is surely correct when he points out that the masterful short story 'Benito Cereno' reveals in the naiveté of its protagonist, Capt. Amasa Delano, 'the kind of moral opacity that seems still to afflict America as it lumbers through the world creating enemies whose enmity it does not begin to understand.'" Faggen was willing to accept Delbanco's moral of the story as Melville's, but he continued with a caution. Delbanco was "a little too eager to turn Melville into a finger-wagging liberal warning of the evils of totalitarianism and American imperialism."

In the Spring 2006 *Claremont Review of Books* Cheryl Miller declared that "Delbanco is not so much concerned with the historical Melville as with the Melville who 'keeps up with the preoccupations of the moment,' who 'remains as current as ever.' His biography aims less to illuminate Melville's life than our own." She elaborated her argument more than any other reviewer had done:

> Delbanco's approach inadvertently suggests that Melville still matters to us not because of the genius of his work but rather because we can attach to him the fashionable opinions of the time. The ease with which we can read into the novels our own opinions appears to be evidence of Melville's continued relevance. . . . In one of the book's more humorous remarks—the humor being apparently unintentional—Delbanco welcomes to the "community of Melville critics" the actor Richard Gere and former Senator Gary Hart, each of whom compared President Bush's decision to invade Iraq with Ahab's mad chase after Moby Dick. Later he writes that "Benito Cereno," that tale of a mutiny on a slave ship, is the "most salient of Melville's work" for us "in our time of terror and torture," warning against "the kind of moral opacity that seems still to afflict America as it lumbers through the world creating enemies whose enmity it does not begin to understand." This isn't literary criticism but second-rate punditry and polemicism.

Without explicitly committing himself as a presentist, Delbanco managed to convey to Cheryl Miller that he was nothing but one. He tried to protect himself, yet Miller tellingly concludes that he allowed for any interpretation to be possible in "the literary equivalent of those 'Choose Your Own Adventure' books: you need only pick which Melville you like best and turn the page." Is the United States "a ship of state sailing toward disaster under lunatic leadership as it tries to conquer the world"? Or is it not?

Cheryl Miller continued with a detailed analysis of Delbanco's method of refusing to commit himself to an interpretation:

> Some critics have commended Delbanco for refusing to give pat answers, but after hundreds of pages of "maybe, maybe not," you

want someone, *anyone*, to exercise some judgment. Delbanco is by no means unwilling to descend into the mud, but he does so in the style of a reporter too fastidious to report directly on the scandal but more than happy to report on the "rumors" going around. This above-the-fray attitude can be maddening as when Delbanco tells us, "The quest for the private Melville has usually led to a dead end, and we are not likely to fare better by speculating about his tastes in bed or bunk." Sensible enough, one thinks—or would think, if the preceding 30 pages hadn't been spent in fervid analysis of such momentous questions as whether while on ship Melville "availed himself of male partners, or relieved himself in as much privacy as he could find . . . or waited for the next contact with island women."

Part of the motive behind this approach seems to be the desire to sell books, which leads Delbanco to try to be trendy. We are told that *Pierre* "anticipates" Freud's study of sexual desire, that *Moby Dick* "anticipated" the modernist prose of Woolf and Joyce and is "the work of a twentieth-century imagination." Numerous works win praise for their "postmodern" qualities. Delbanco litters his text with pop culture references (Stanley Kubrick, Donald Trump, and Tiny Tim all make an appearance). He even tries to spice things up with some amateur psychoanalyzing of Melville, especially on the subject of sex. It's not that Delbanco's interest in the prurient is completely unfounded. He is surely right to say that the environment in *Typee* is "sex-drenched," what with its wind that blows like a "woman roused." But to say that the way the plot of "Benito Cereno" unfolds is like being sexually teased? Or that the chimney in Ishmael's dream is phallic? Or that Isabel's ear in *Pierre* is vaginal? Delbanco seems particularly fond of Freud, but unfortunately he hasn't learned that sometimes a cigar is just a cigar.

Melville, she concluded, is left as "merely the tutelary divinity of all our little pet projects and preferences."

In the *New England Quarterly* (June 2006) John Bryant responded to Delbanco's "success at bringing Melville's antebellum world in contact with modern and postmodern views" (335):

After all, the readers who made Melville the nation's subversive culture-hero are we, the survivors of a Civil War, two world wars, the sexual revolution, the Holocaust, and other ethnic cleansings. The contemporizing that Delbanco performs is as refreshing as it is necessary given the ineluctable applicability of Melville's words, thought, and art to modernism. With wit and insight, he brings to life the antebellum Melville situated among his New England and New York friends, and yet gives him equal presence among such moderns as Friedrich Nietzsche, W. H. Auden, and C. L.R. James.

As for "Benito Cereno," Delbanco's reading, Bryant said approvingly, explores "current conversations involving gender, homosexuality, race, and racism." Similarly, Matthew Forrest Lowe in *Literature and Theology* (September 2006) was sure that Melville's "thought seems not only more relevant today" than ever but also versatile — "his reflections on obsessive quests, national destinies and religious ambition can be hoisted, aimed and thrown at political targets as readily as any whaling harpoon" (335). He continued: "A sampling of such thrusts, ranging from early comments on Melville and *Moby-Dick* to recent observations on the Ahab-like crusades of the Bush administration, serves to open Andrew Delbanco's biography of Melville" (336).[9]

Despite Delbanco's attempts to distance himself from himself, his readers saw and for the most part approved of the presentism in his book. In chapter 10 of *The Confidence-Man* a "somewhat elderly person, in the quaker dress, had quietly passed through the cabin," handing about odes "which, for the most part, after a cursory glance, had been disrespectfully tossed aside," so that they litter the floor "as if fluttered down from a balloon." Now already even the names of the friends and celebrity critics Delbanco strewed about on his pages are less recognizable. The downside for Delbanco, as for Robertson-Lorant, is that the shelf life of presentist books is short, so that hers is already a book of the 1990s, as Milder said, and Delbanco's is even more securely identified with the era of the second Bush.

Chapter 11

THE LATE TWENTIETH-CENTURY MINI-MELVILLE:

New York Intellectuals Without Information

WHILE ASSEMBLING MATERIAL for this chapter I broke off to read James Wood's *New Republic* (January 23, 2006) review of Andrew Delbanco's *Melville: His World and Work*. In chapter 7 I dealt with what I thought was Wood's off-base theological bullying and a vulgar mistake about Melville's smirking over "redundant," which is used in *Moby-Dick* in a Miltonic sense, not to mean "duplicative," as Wood thought. I wrote up my findings about "redundant" while I was still more than a little outraged. After worrying for a few minutes about the likelihood of getting my protest into print, I realized that aged biographers can maneuver around the tragic possibility of leaving wise words to be lost forever or at best to be published posthumously. I posted what I had written on Amazon as a review of Wood's *The Broken Estate*—fittingly, I thought, since rather than reviewing the books that came his way Wood used them as springboards for his theological bloviations, as I said on Amazon. Later I added a comment about Wood's review of my first volume that was the pretext for the essay on theology and Melville in *The Broken Estate*.

Instant gratification achieved, I continued gathering recent newspaper and magazine documents, lined up all biographies from Weaver and Mumford onward, and focused on what was missing in Wood and missing in many other critics. The missing ingredient was *information*. In his commentaries on books on Melville, Wood regularly displayed a high intelligence running amok for lack of information and what looked like lack of interest in the history and the sources of information. Hopping as opportunity dictated, from the *London Review of Books* and the *Guardian* to the *New Republic*, Wood had blurred his nationality so that by the time he moved to the *New Yorker* he was acknowledged as the newest but most powerful living New York Intellectual, although residing then in Massachusetts. He had written disrespectfully of one of the middle New York Intellectuals, John Updike, and had flattered the oldest, Elizabeth Hardwick, but he had become very much like Updike (and Andrew Delbanco) and a good deal worse than Elizabeth Hardwick in turning his back on information about Melville. All the New York Intellectuals display in common not just disregard of relevant information but in varying ways outright hostility (sometimes ferocious hostility) to factual information about Melville.

The older members of the New York Intellectuals all had political reasons for wanting to ignore or dismiss information about Melville. With the younger members, including Andrew Delbanco (just as much as his Yale-nurtured colleague Richard H. Brodhead, who was implicated in some of Delbanco's biographical errors about Melville), there is a further twist, for they were trained from early youth by first- and second-generation New Critics. This meant, for their adult years, that younger New York Intellectuals still reflexively dismissed biographical evidence as irrelevant to interpretation and, in any case (they are sure) as all but impossible to ascertain for reliable use (even if the evidence is clearly presented to them). Starting in their early professional lives, they avoided archival work. Brodhead, a kind of big buddy mentor for Delbanco (it emerged in 2002) could publish a book titled *The School of Hawthorne* in 1986 dealing, as I have said, only with what was common knowledge about still fairly well known dead white men, ignoring important early "students" such as Harriet Beecher Stowe and Thomas Bailey Aldrich. Brodhead had been trained to pay attention to the text, at least, if not all the books in the American Literature section, but he was not well taught, for, as I have pointed out, *three times* he got backward Melville's famous distinction between what he was most moved to write and what he felt obliged to write, this in the course of basing a crucial argument on Melville's lament (20, 24, 33). Brodhead and Delbanco, as late as 2002, both putting themselves forward as authorities on Melville, could demonstrate, to put the best light on what they said then, that at most they had merely dipped into *The Melville Log*, the *Letters*, or the later *Correspondence* or any of a dozen other standard sources, and did not always know how to interpret what they encountered there, and did not read what was on the pages they were reviewing (such as Melville's twelve-point memorandum to Allan on the publication of *Poems*). Can anyone tell me how could they have read Melville's memorandum and then expressed such skepticism about Melville's finishing the book he called *Poems*?

Having never hunted out manuscript letters or even nineteenth-century newspaper articles about Melville themselves, New York Intellectuals have recently found themselves helpless and hapless in criticizing genuine archival work. Emerson said, "Men have come to speak of the revelation as somewhat long ago given and done, as if God were dead." The Intellectuals act as if revelation or discovery in the archives is all over and done. Sometimes the Intellectuals are even willing in public to deny evidence commonly known for decades, as Brodhead and Delbanco did in 2002, when they thought the risk of public exposure was slight enough that they could safely accuse me of fantasy in discussing the volume called *Poems*, which Melville completed in 1860. Sometimes they acknowledge the existence of documentary evidence (as when Hardwick acknowledged my first volume but selectively ignored parts which were particularly relevant to her discussions). Hardwick even pleaded a senior citizen's winsome personal preference for disregarding documentary evidence: "Scholars, deciphering the messy manuscript, have decided that Melville's final title was *Billy Budd, Sailor*. I have kept *Foretopman* out of a sentimental affection for the old title under which most of us first read the story" (142).

The recent New York Intellectuals revere Lewis Mumford not just for his early association with Edmund Wilson but for what he did three decades later—his excoriating of the Center for Editions of American Authors editors of Emerson at the start of 1968 in the then-young *New York Review of Books* (of which Hardwick was a founder), months before Wilson's horsewhipping of the Melville editors in the same periodical. Mumford cruelly damaged the reputations of the editors of Emerson's journals and miscellaneous notebooks. One of them, I know, died before he could recover any peace of mind, long before his labor in transcribing Emerson's handwriting was praised. Wilson became obsessed about *Typee*. Substantiated reports confirmed as fact that he continued to rail about the pedantry of Hayford, Taselle (as he spelled Tanselle), and Parker for many months before his death in 1972.[1]

For adolescent and post-adolescent would-be public Intellectuals of the 1970s and 1980s, the youthful aspirants to the ranks of Mumford and Wilson, this comparatively recent 1968 pairing had exalted the astonishingly up-to-date Mumford into the Olympian company of the somewhat junior *Partisan Review* veterans, and his longevity kept him in their minds. Old friends of Wilson and younger idolaters were assembled by Sean Wilentz at Princeton late in 1995, the year Wilson would have been one hundred. From that conference came Lewis M. Dabney's *Edmund Wilson: Centennial Reflections* (1997), which featured comments by three from the *New York Review of Books* (Jason Epstein, Barbara Epstein, and Elizabeth Hardwick) as well as two others from their generation who appear briefly in this chapter, Alfred Kazin, who had recommended the publication of Jay Leyda's *The Melville Log*, however little he later profited from it, and Daniel Aaron,

who as a Smith College colleague had read all of Newton Arvin's book on
Melville before publication (as Arvin says in his acknowledgments, xii–xiii).
It also included articles by Paul Berman and Andrew Delbanco, who play
major parts here. In his *Reflections* article Berman provocatively asked (266),
"Has the American culture that could once generate an Edmund Wilson
become incapable of generating anyone similar today? Has a fundamental
habit of mind changed in American life, and is the age of critics-in-general
(and readers-in-general) behind us?" The Princeton audience, of course,
hearing or reading this challenge, knew the answer was "No," or in a Melvillean spirit "NO! in thunder." In this self-promoting and mutually promoting
talk Berman was celebrating himself, Delbanco, Wilentz, and perhaps others in the room, as the high embodiments of the new generation of "public
intellectuals" or "literary intellectuals." Unsurprisingly, Delbanco cozily
quoted and elaborated on Berman in at least the printed version of *his* contribution (247–48). Their method, Berman declared, was to be magnanimous
and rigorous in their pledge "to stop scorning the intellectuals from earlier generations; to take the best of them as models and to hold ourselves
to their standards" (275). In practice, this too often meant fawning over the
older New York Intellectuals and carrying on their old battles (such as those
against the Center for Editions of American Authors) without understanding
why the battle lines had been drawn or where they *could* have been drawn
more intelligently.

The Melville of the self-identified New York Intellectuals of the 1930s
through the 1980s, as well as newer members of the coterie as reconstituted
at Princeton in 1995, derived in part from the Melville of the 1921 biography by Raymond Weaver (a professor at Columbia, like Delbanco). Weaver
had cobbled his biography together as best he could, deriving many pages
by inserting long sections from Melville's books as autobiography, as when
he devoted several pages to Jackson, in *Redburn*, seeing him as "a fit rival
to Conrad's Nigger of the Narcissus" (93).[2] Weaver quoted at length some
of Melville's then-known letters and the 1849 journal without establishing
their contexts and quoted lavishly from histories of the whale fishery so as to
recapitulate the history of Pacific exploration and settlement by Europeans.
He was a magpie, copying out vivid pronouncements from earlier critics of
Melville and all too frequently omitting the writers' names as he ran their
distinctive phrases into his book in what now looks like, well, plagiarism. He
leapt years, linking Hawthorne's departure from Lenox in 1851 directly to the
censored journal entries Sophia Hawthorne published about Melville's visit
to him in Liverpool in 1856, supplemented by Julian Hawthorne's account.
Then Weaver skipped back into a discussion of *Pierre*. He transcribed and

printed several pages from the 1849 journal, enough to give a sense of Melville's happiness in talking metaphysics and drinking on the voyage out as well as his walking part way from Deal to Canterbury and days of sightseeing in London and trying to sell *White-Jacket*. He gave a good account of a dinner at John Murray's.

Weaver put Melville in the National Gallery once (292) but not seeing paintings and had him in Bentley's "fine old room hung round with paintings" against dark walls (302), but what's missing, when you look, is any sense of Melville as an eager viewer of painting and sculpture in London or during his days on the Continent. Weaver described the 1856–57 journal as "a staccato jotting down of impressions, chiefly interesting . . . as another evidence of Melville's scope of curiosity and keenness of observation" (353), and he represented it by three pages from Melville's dazzlingly vivid description of Constantinople, including a visit to Santa Sophia, but no mention of museum going anywhere on the trip . He offered, I should say, a sadly imperfect but heroic transcription (not, it emerged, his own but based on the transcription of his student, Gerald M. Crona).[3] Weaver signed off with "The Long Quietus" (a compression of decades into a few pages) after dealing with Melville's friendship with Hawthorne. He knew nothing of *The Isle of the Cross* (1853) or *Poems* (1860) and said almost nothing about *Battle-Pieces*, *Clarel*, and Melville's other published poetry. He also said almost nothing about Melville and art. It's hard to be sure in Weaver, since he is so disorganized, but I don't see him ever showing Melville looking at a painting in a museum.

In defining who could be cherished as models, the junior New York Intellectuals of the late 1990s like Weaver mined Melville's early books as if they were autobiographical, but they could have picked that up from Mumford's 1929 book along with disdain for Melville's parents. Weaver's obvious literary faults such as the amateurish lack of order may have repelled the Intellectuals. Then, not having been overtly penalized at Columbia for his homosexuality, Weaver was not useful as a symbol of political oppression. All of the New York Intellectuals read backward from the fate of Newton Arvin, persecuted for his homosexuality (and, they were sure, his having been a Communist): anything Weaver had suffered must have been a mere inconvenience in comparison. But perhaps the strongest reason they ignored Weaver is, as Diana Trilling remembered, long after her husband's death, and long after his forgiveness of Weaver and their reconciliation, that Weaver had tried to block young Lionel Trilling's appointment at Columbia.[4] Despite her husband's forgiving Weaver, vengeance was hers, after all?

The younger New York Intellectuals derived more of their image of Melville from the more coherently arranged critical biography which stands at one remove from Weaver's book, the 1929 study by Lewis Mumford, who wrote from Weaver's book with a little help from Melville's oldest grand-daughter, Eleanor Thomas Metcalf, and with some new information, the biggest cache of which was what Meade Minnigerode published in 1922 about Melville and Evert A. and George Duyckinck, in which was the doc-umentation for Melville's 1860 volume he wanted to call *Poems*. Frances Melville Thomas, Melville's surviving daughter and Eleanor's mother, gave permission for Mumford to glance through her father's journals (hard to decipher, yet not as "messy" as the *Billy Budd* manuscript), but transcrib-ing them would have been more work than he wanted to do. He committed Weaver's sin of taking Melville's early books as straight autobiography, as in his recounting of the Launcelott's-Hey scenes in *Redburn*: "Melville came upon a motionless figure of a woman, with a dead baby at her breasts, and two blue-skinned children clinging to her . . . with not a soul except Mel-ville to offer succour" (34). Surprisingly, he even took as real Redburn's trip to London: "Mr. Weaver has cast doubts on this adventure in London: he regards it as one of the few wide inventions Melville made in Redburn: but to me its very vagueness and mysteriousness smells of reality" (35). Partly because of his association with their master critic Edmund Wilson in the early 1930s (as the two dreamed of Americanizing Communism), Mumford was easier for the later New York Intellectuals to take as a model. Relying on Melville's books for his biography persists up through Elizabeth Hardwick and still taints Delbanco's treatment of *Redburn* in 2005, where he says: "In describing the boy's distress, Melville was surely recalling his own feelings as a boy of twenty" (29). Of course, "boy of twenty" shows little awareness of how fast a youth might have become a man in hard times.

Mumford was not so much hostile to new information as careless with what information there was. Take this about the year 1850: "In the spring, he left New York and went up to Broadhall with his family—the old homestead that his Grand-Uncle Thomas had sold when he emigrated to Ohio, had now been converted into an inn: his grandfather's old desk was still mildewing in the barn, and Melville brought it to light, cleaned it up for his own use, and sat down to it" (135). It would take pages to straighten out the errors and misconceptions in these few lines. There are other faults throughout, such as Mumford's slighting the poetry, especially *Clarel*. Like Weaver, Mumford glossed over whole years in Melville's life, as in what I quoted earlier: "The days pass and one day is like another: there is comfort in monotony" (326). My early discoveries about Melville's life after *Moby-Dick* revealed an abun-dance of overwhelmingly sad news, new episode after new episode, so sad that I decided, as I have explained, that since I was approaching sixty years old I had better draft the latter part of his life first, while I was healthier than I would be two or three years later in reaching that section if I started with the birth and went forward.

Donald L. Miller in *Lewis Mumford: A Life* posed a question and gave a retort to it: "The real question we ought to ask ourselves is not how Mumford could have made so many mistakes in the book, but how he could have written so convincing an interpretation of Herman Melville, given his scanty research and the amazingly short period of time it took him to complete the book. And the answer . . . is that Mumford was not writing about Melville primarily, but about himself" (275). Miller is right. Much of the genuine power that infused the book came from Mumford's intense engagement with his subject. In the winter of 1928–29, while he was writing the book, Mumford himself was a momentous man already, profoundly fascinated by a still more momentous man, and for all its flaws his book did not diminish Melville. He left great blank spaces in the canvas, but the part of the portrait he filled in did not diminish his subject.

Melville scholars have dismissed Newton Arvin from mind for half a century because he performed no original research and was not in any useful sense a biographer, but the New York Intellectual establishment has revered him.[5] First, he was a Communist in the 1930s when it was chic to be a Communist, writing for *Partisan Review* while it was Stalinist, in 1935, then later wooed by Philip Rahv and Frederick Dupee to return to the magazine in its new Trotskyite phase. Besides that, the Intellectuals have protected him as a homosexual who suffered for his sexuality. In 1960 the Massachusetts state police anti-pornography unit arrested Arvin and charged him with felony possession of obscene materials for sale, exhibition, loan, or circulation, and being a lewd and lascivious person in speech and behavior. (Google Images shows that the cache of "pornography" which cost Arvin his reputation was by modern standards PG or at worst PG13.) Overlooking his craven betrayal of his friends to the anti-pornography unit, the New York Intellectuals (as Barry Werth shows in *The Scarlet Professor*, 218–19) saw Arvin's arrest as punishment for his lifetime of leftist activities, the punishment for homosexuality coming as a delayed retribution for his political alliances after it was no longer fashionable to prosecute such seemingly harmless former Communist Party members. Lionel Trilling, his colleague Daniel Aaron, and, most powerfully, Edmund Wilson stood by him; Jason Epstein, soon to be a founder of the *New York Review of Books*, tried to facilitate his return to literary work. Years later Andrew Delbanco oddly felt compelled to link sexuality and critical insight when he identified Arvin as "the secretly gay critic Newton Arvin" (*Melville: His World and Work*, 203) who thought Melville "could only venture the prolix hint" about brother-sister incest in *Pierre* as his way (Delbanco explains, 203) of confessing to homosexual feelings.

Like Weaver and Mumford, Arvin took the character Redburn pretty much as a self-portrait of Melville, and like Weaver (more than Mumford) he focused on the frightening Jackson in *Redburn*, a conventional Gothic villain, I had thought, fun for Melville to sketch out. Arvin treated *Pierre* seriously, as Mumford had done, though he gave his followers their excuse to minimize the book by exclaiming memorably that it was "four-fifth claptrap, and sickly claptrap to boot" (226). Later writers could quote that dismissal and ignore the genuine criticism Arvin had performed on *Pierre*. Much more than Weaver and Mumford, Arvin grappled with *Clarel* and tried to convey some of its power. Yet it was Arvin, not Weaver and Mumford, who set the limits of what the New York Intellectuals permitted themselves to know about Melville. Arvin did this most firmly in his treatment of Melville's 1849 trip to London and the Continent and his 1856–57 trip to Scotland and England, the Levant, and Europe.

For his section on the 1849 trip Weaver had made a preliminary transcription of parts of Melville's journal and quoted several pages from it, and Mumford, rather than summarize Weaver or try his own sequential account, had created a speeded-up dramatized version of the experiences that was a narrative tour de force (119–31). Arvin was cavalier: "Melville thrust the manuscript of *White-Jacket* into his carpetbag and set out for England," he announced abruptly (131). No, the *sheets*, not the manuscript, and the "carpetbag" is a little too closely derived from Ishmael. Rather than suggesting something of the possible richness of Melville's aesthetic and intellectual experiences, Arvin did his best to cut off all thought (132):

> The trip had no very profound effect on Melville's development: it was too late in the day for that. But it was not a bad thing for his self-regard to land in England again, after ten years, not now as a shabby unknown, but (as he said with a certain grimace) as the "author of 'Peedee' 'Hullabaloo' & 'Pog-Dog'." . . . He was treated with consideration and even hospitality everywhere; he met no very great celebrities, but he dipped a little into London society, literary and otherwise.

Why did Arvin want to obliterate Melville's experiences in London and Paris? For years I thought that Arvin's saying the trip "had no very profound effect on Melville's development" was inexplicable, but I found the answer in Werth's book. Soon after he went abroad in 1929 Arvin wrote home from

London that he was a "bad traveler" who was tempted to "take a boat home" right away. After London he spent twenty-five days in Paris "suffocating in the heat," Werth says (50), before sailing back to the United States. Since London and Paris had meant so little to *him*, Arvin decreed that they had meant equally little to Melville. Any biographer will wince sympathetically: how many of us have had to resist projecting our personal frailties, crotchets, obsessions, and prejudices onto our subjects?

This is all Arvin says of art (132–33): Melville "was indefatigable in making the rounds of churches and museums, castles and fortresses, theaters and zoos." Arvin did acknowledge that Melville was affected profoundly by his visit to the Hôtel de Cluny in Paris, especially the "ruinous Roman baths below it," and that in Coblenz "he was stirred by the magnificent pile of the fortress of Ehrenbreitstein across the Rhine" (133). According to Arvin, Melville had felt a powerful emotion while visiting precisely one example of antique architecture and another when viewing a fortress on a superb natural height. Astonishingly, Arvin seizes on a few unrepresentative words from Melville's journal in order to *minimize* the impact of Europe on Melville, not to acknowledge or magnify it: "the river Rhine is not the Hudson" (133).

Arvin's treatment of the 1856–57 trip included a brief quotation from Hawthorne's notebooks about Melville's saying he had "pretty much made up his mind to be annihilated" and Hawthorne's reflection on how strange it was that Melville persisted "in wandering to and fro over these deserts, as dismal and monotonous as the sandhills amid which we were sitting" (209). Otherwise, Arvin made only disconnected mention of Melville's "journey to Palestine"; he identified it again as the "journey to Palestine" and then mentions the "return from Palestine" without naming sites other than Liverpool. Arvin, that is, showed absolutely no interest in Melville's exposure to the natural splendors and the aesthetic treasures of the Levant and Europe in 1856–57, any more than he had in his treatment of Melville's time in England and Europe in 1849. Strangely, the younger New York Intellectuals followed his example. We all know the story which goes round in studies of animal intelligence. While being boarded on a ship single file, some sheep needed to jump over an obstacle. One of the herders noticed and removed the obstacle but the next few sheep, having seen those before them jump at a certain spot, jumped at that spot though there was no longer anything to jump over. Almost unbelievable but true: the powerful New York Intellectuals imitated the action of the sheep. Having learned from Arvin that these two trips *"had no very profound effect on Melville's development: it was too late in the day for that,"* they all leapt over Melville's experiences in England and the Continent in 1849 and then leapt over most of his longer, wider 1856–57 trip.

Arvin's hand is heavy on John Updike, the Pennsylvanian who by his long connection with the *New Yorker* and the *New York Review of Books* became accepted as a New York Intellectual in the vacuum left by Wilson at his death in 1972. Famous himself before he got round to reading any of Melville, early in 1982 Updike tried out "Melville's Withdrawal" as a lecture at the Rochester Public Library, having structured it on a series of surprises. By that time, two decades after *Rabbit, Run*, Updike's solipsistic self-esteem was such that he was talking about his own surprises in discovering one commonplace after another (Surprise No. 1: Melville was young when he wrote *Moby-Dick*! Surprise, surprise!). In his blog *Mondoweiss* (June 17, 2009) Philip Weiss quoted Updike's infamous opening comment of the lecture, casting it as a command, not a polite request: "All Melville scholars leave the room." Weiss went on: "He was about to take his crack at an important literary question (Melville's withdrawal from the world in his 30s) and didn't want to be confused by the facts." Perhaps no Melville scholar was there in Rochester, but if Howard Horsford, the professor at the University of Rochester who was editing Melville's journals and had discovered a great number of facts, was there and stayed on, ignoring the speaker's command, he would have suffered from Updike's conspicuous silence about those journals.

Apparently no scholar, at Rochester or elsewhere, straightened out Updike on anything factual before he went into print in the May 10, 1982, *New Yorker*. A scholar would stumble over dozens of rubbish piles in Updike's pages, just as in Mumford's book. Melville did not work on *Redburn* and *White-Jacket* for five months (120); the farm in Pittsfield was not Cousin Robert's (120); in 1850 Melville did not go to the farm ahead of others in his family (120); we do not know that Melville "thoroughly revised the whaling story" after meeting Hawthorne—finishing it is not the same as revising it (120); Amos Nourse was not Elizabeth Shaw Melville's doctor (124). Updike got Melville's tortoise book in the wrong year (130); ignores the fact that Melville tried to publish *Poems* in 1860; and blithely declares that *Billy Budd* was left completed (145). Updike was no more accurate than Mumford was, but with less excuse for inaccuracies, after the publication of *The Melville Log* (1951), *Letters* (1960), and Bezanson's 1960 edition of *Clarel* (which *ought* to have been acknowledged on 142). Also, "Melville scholars" by the early 1980s knew about Melville's borrowing a huge sum from T. D. Stewart in 1851 and not being able to pay the interest on it for several years or to pay the principal when it came due, but Updike seems to have heard nothing of this. He toted up box scores on reviews (120–22, 140) as if all were of equal impact (three positive! only two negative! why, the reviews were favorable!). Any novelist knows, as Updike himself surely knew, that one or two well-placed negative reviews can poison the well. What reviews hurt Melville the most? How did he respond to them? Does not a writer bleed? Updike himself, who wrote "At War with My Skin" for the September 2, 1985, *New Yorker*, bled from hostile reviews. Both Melville and his wife in their old age suffered from skin problems, but Updike saw Melville as an unsuffering phlegmatic, of a broad-shouldered make, like Ishmael in "The Ship," off whom criticism bounced. Melville, in fact, would have been a stoic, if only he had not been in such pain. This seeming heartlessness came because Updike's Melville was an abstraction which he was using to prove something about nineteenth-century America, not about someone who had been a living writer. Updike systematically reduced Melville in this program-matic statement: "Something is wrong . . . with being a writer in America; one of Melville's biographers, Newton Arvin, calls his subject's treatment by the public 'the heaviest count in our literary annals against the American mind'" (120).

Updike was contemptuous of *Pierre* without trying to account for Mel-ville's ambitions for it. He ignored Mumford's and Arvin's attempts to understand the book even while profiting from Mumford's view of it as "an abortive complement" to *Moby-Dick* and Arvin's reiterated "claptrap." In turn, Updike's hand proved heavy on Delbanco (*Melville: His World and Work*, 179–80): "It was a performance at once furious and feeble, and of all Melville's works is the one whose tone is hardest to get hold of—a book, as John Updike has remarked, that 'runs a constant fever' and whose charac-ters are 'jerked to and fro by some unexplained rage of the author's.'" Like everyone then, Updike was ignorant of the title of the book Melville wrote after *Pierre*, but he might have seen in the *Letters* (1960) that Melville had finished a book in the spring of 1853. The 1982 Updike article in the *New Yorker* was smugly arrogant, ignorant, self-satisfied, riddled with factual errors and dogmatic assertions, fatuous. Updike condescendingly patted Melville on the head: "Melville was right to withdraw when he did, from a battle that had become a losing battle" (147). Updike should have come to terms privately about how he was surprised by what he had learned, and then he should have looked at what scholars had found (Arvin was no scholar) rather than publishing his amateurish reflections in a major national magazine.

Delbanco, the most persistent aspirant to the mantle of Edmund Wil-son, in 2005 honored Updike's views again in the depiction of Melville's "withdrawal" and in Updike's later sardonic mockery of Melville for what Weaver had called his "Long Quietus." Here is Delbanco on the "long silence" (288): "This version of his career has become so well known that when John Updike's fictional author Henry Bech wins the 'Melville Medal, awarded every five years to that American author who has maintained the most meaningful silence,' Updike had no reason to doubt that readers would get the joke." Like Weaver, Mumford, and Updike, Delbanco shortchanged the poetry, including *Clarel*, and wrapped things up in a section echoing Weaver, "The Quiet End." In his *Artistes sans Oeuvres: I would prefer not to* (1997) Jean-Yves Jouannais invented an author whose idea of literature was so lofty that his works were all imaginary. This is very like what the New York Intellectuals make of the later Melville.

Mumford got much wrong but presented Melville as a noble figure. Arvin grappled honorably with the theme of religious absolutism in *Pierre* and even decided that in *Clarel* Melville's "linguistic and compositional powers were passing through a kind of autumnal rejuvenescence" (271). The citing of Arvin by a New York Intellectual on a historical (not critical) argument is usually suspect, the sign of an unspoken agenda, sometimes political, more often sexual. Because he suffered public shame for his sexuality, the Intellectuals continued to honor Arvin for his emphasis upon homosexuality in Melville (as if he had monopolized the theme that others had treated, notably A. A. Brill and W. Somerset Maugham); and they never mention that he tried to spare himself by sacrificing friends to the state police anti-pornography unit. Updike was interested both in the homosexuality theme and in Arvin's analysis of the way America mistreated Melville. Unlike Updike, Arvin had been sensitive to Melville's pain: "it is impossible not to imagine that, with his strongly neurotic capacity for suffering, he had undergone real anguish over the revilement of *Pierre*. Given, indeed, the insecurity of his emotional equilibrium, the curve that his literary career had described could hardly have been more unfortunate than it was; no other American writer—and very few writers anywhere—have undergone Melville's particular ordeal" (201). Updike coolly saw Melville as collaborating "in his own ever profounder obscurity" (140) during his years in the Custom House; how could he not have, Updike thought, in an America so hard on her writers? What Arvin and Updike say about the American mind being unreceptive to writers is ludicrous without a detailed examination of the biggest obstacle to making a career as a writer in America in Melville's time: the lack of an international copyright law. In the third section of this book I devote two chapters to this much-mentioned but insufficiently scrutinized topic.

There is a good deal of truth in a statement Updike made about Melville and "greatness" (147): "By mid-life, though not yet forty, he had come to care only about greatness, in the sense that Dante and Shakespeare possessed it, and that Hawthorne—cool, slight Hawthorne—had once represented it to his fervent impressionable prime." Yet Updike did not proceed with an account of Melville's relation to great Continental writers, ancient, Renaissance, and modern, or to great English writers such as Spenser, Shakespeare, and Milton, or to Pope, Byron, and Wordsworth. In 1982 not enough of Melville's marginalia was available for anyone to have documented Melville's quest for an aesthetic credo in 1862, as I managed to do in the early 1990s, but Updike could have displayed a Melville actively engaged throughout his life with great dramatists, poets, essayists, and critics of England, Scotland, and the Continent. To display Melville as the man who continued to search for the requisites of greatness, long after he had first achieved it himself, would have blown apart Updike's theory of the oppressive power over him of the American mind.

Furthermore, Updike wholly left out Melville's passionate and discriminating interest in painting, sculpture, and architecture. Early exposed to art, for historically valuable paintings were in both the Melvill and Gansevoort family houses, Melville had developed his interest in art in the late 1840s, when his portrait was first painted in Lansingburgh and when he went to galleries in New York and became friends with artists, perhaps most intimately with Felix Darley (a friendship not widely known in 1982). That interest was deeply nourished on the trips abroad in 1849 and again in 1856–57. On his return from Europe in 1857, Melville's first lecture was on statuary in Rome — and he began borrowing books on art, including Vasari's *Lives* (which he was able to buy in 1862). He continued to go to galleries in New York City once he returned there in 1863, and he associated, still, with some artists and, late in life, with the great architect and theorist of architecture Alexander Jackson Davis. He continued reading essays which inculcated literary principles, as many of the writers attempted to do in the early *Edinburgh Review*. Classic essays from the *Edinburgh Review* and other great quarterlies were available in the set he purchased in 1849, *Modern British Essayists*, among them Francis Jeffrey's reviews of almost all the great volumes of Romantic poetry. To the end of his life Melville pondered aesthetic treatises in books and in current magazines, arguing with them, supplementing them, and incorporating ideas about them into his ongoing writings. You could make the argument that Melville's mind was constantly *expanding* rather than withdrawing, even on through the 1870s and into the 1880s or even till the end of his life. Yet Updike said nothing about Melville's trip in 1849 to London and the Continent. He passed over the 1856–57 trip as a "restorative voyage to the Holy Land" which happened to occasion Hawthorne's record of Melville's saying he had "pretty much made up his mind to be annihilated." Updike did not say a word about Melville's saturation in art and architecture (and landscapes) on these voyages. He wrote before Robert K. Wallace publicized the portfolios of Melville's engravings in the Berkshire Athenaeum, but he could have examined the evidence already available that Melville became a serious student of aesthetics as well as a knowledgeable collector of all he could afford, prints of paintings. This omission is peculiarly strange, given Updike's own interest in painting.

Updike congratulated Melville on withdrawing "when he did, from a battle that had become a losing battle." Quoting Melville's declaration to Hawthorne that his powers had developed swiftly, during a five-year period or so, and that "the flower must fall to the mould," Updike commented: "By bowing to that organic fall, and abstaining from a forced productivity, and turning to public silence and private poetry, Melville preserved his communion with greatness, and enhanced with the dignity of a measured abstention the communion we enjoy with him" (147). Here Updike rejoiced, in his quiet way, at the silencing of a Titan.

The next chance for a follower of Edmund Wilson to take on Melville came when the first volume of my biography was published in 1996. Somehow Paul Berman, who had published nothing I have ever seen on Melville except his recent online review of Robertson-Lorant, gained the privilege of reviewing it for the *New York Times Book Review* (December 22, 1996). Berman was still stoked from the November 1995 gathering of old New York Intellectuals and younger would-be New York Intellectuals at Princeton. His speech there was still unpublished, forthcoming in Dabney's collection, so he was in a curious state of suspension, between having declared himself a successor to Edmund Wilson in front of a select leftist and neo-leftist group at Princeton in 1995 and the fervently anticipated future moment when he would (with *A Tale of Two Utopias: The Political Journey of the Generation of 1968*) emblazon his status as a successor to Wilson to the world at large. Berman had changed into Supercritic garb in private but not yet did anyone outside the select group of Wilsonites know that he was a new self-designated public intellectual. Much rode on his performance in the *New York Times*. Rather than focusing on my book, Berman seized the occasion to attack me and the other editors of the Northwestern-Newberry Edition of *The Writings of Herman Melville*, making it the *New York Review of Books'* glory year 1968 all over again (12–13):

> The spirit behind Mr. Parker's biography has a good deal in common with another of his Melvillean projects, the 13 volumes (so far) of the Northwestern-Newberry edition of Melville, of which Mr. Parker is associate general editor. The labor that has gone into those volumes is Pharaonic. The Northwestern-Newberry "Moby-Dick" took

23 years to edit and contains nearly 500 pages of commentary about the book's publishing history, comparisons between the English and American versions and a list of every single word that was hyphenated at the right margin in Melville's original text. On the other hand, to the earnest "Moby-Dick" reader who stumbles across one of the many obscure references and would like to flip to the back pages to find a brief explanation of what Melville had in mind—to that unhappy person, the Northwestern-Newberry "Moby-Dick" offers very little help. There is not even the diagram of a ship. The 23 years of drudge labor appear to have addled the editors' minds, until literature has slipped from view and antiquarianism alone remains. And that same combination of microscopic detail and macroscopic lack of judgment reappears in Mr. Parker's enormous biography.

My wounds, unhealed from Wilson's lashing in 1968, were crisscrossed with new slashes from this out-of-the-grave whipping. Anyone who remembered 1968 knew as he read this passage that Berman had dug up the corpse and was rolling obsequiously before the bones of the corpulent churl of Talcottville. How better to prove his worthiness than by demolishing anyone identified by Wilson as representative of the Center for Editions of American Authors?

Berman's review stunned me. I had hoped, all naively, that someone would weigh my book against earlier biographies to see what new information I had discovered and employed, what stories of wholly new episodes I had told, and upon what evidence. If I had been deluded in writing for my imaginary audience, it may have been because (excepting only *The Tale of a Tub* and *Gulliver's Travels*, taught by the incomparable Phillip Harth) I had been supremely lucky never to have read a difficult book as a class assignment but only for myself, on my own time, at my own pace, and here I had a magnificent story with absolutely unknown episodes and space to tell them in. I had thought there ought to have been enough to talk about without resurrecting Wilson and rearticulating the bones of his right hand long enough for a reviewer to hold them together to wallop and claw me again. I had even thought that someone might say "Thank you."

What interests me in retrospect is Berman's attitudes toward new information about Herman Melville's life. In his fourth column Berman gets round, again a little inexactly, to what is new in my biography (12):

The book is some 900 pages long, and even so counts merely as Volume I, with Melville 32 years old at the end, fondling the first

printed copies [of *Moby-Dick*]. Mr. Parker is a professor of English
at the University of Delaware, and his fanaticism for exactitude is
such that he gives us not just the tiniest details, but the details about
the details. He quotes a precise description of Melville by Nathaniel
Hawthorne's wife, Sophia—"His nose is straight & rather handsome,
his mouth expressive of sensibility & emotion," and so forth for half a
page—and then he doubles the precision by telling us that Sophia's
account "is by all odds the fullest such description of Melville known
to exist."

My comment (1:773) had clarified the true significance of Sophia's
description: "All this was written on the basis of her personal observations
(supplemented by any reading she had done in his books), for his identity as
the Virginian remained unrevealed. It is by all odds the fullest such description of Melville known to exist." I make no apology: my fresh transcription
of the letter propelled my story forward, and any rational reader, I still think,
would have been intrigued by everything Sophia said, especially when the
surprise came, later on, that Melville was the Virginian she had rhapsodized
about. I was telling a story.

Berman went on, relentlessly (12): "Whole forests among these details are
new, and of the million fresh facts, the most striking, as I judge them, reveal
the commercial dealings of Melville's father. . . . To make your way through
the intricacies of Mr. Parker's account has some of the charm of going into
bankruptcy yourself." I would have thought the most striking of fresh facts
would have come from those that revealed new episodes in Melville's life.
What about the revelation that Melville arrived in Galena, Illinois, in 1840
at the worst possible time for help in his finding his fortune in the West? The
account of Melville's adventures in Tahiti and Eimeo which incorporated
never-before-used sources? The account of Melville's surprise homecoming
to Lansingburgh, with the astonishing solution to the decades-long mystery
about the handwriting on the shorter note announcing Herman's imminent
arrival? What about the guided tour of Melville in the act of preparing a
manuscript, based on a handful of newly discovered leaves from the first
draft of *Typee*? Or the account of what stunning experience caused Melville
to start *Redburn* just when he did, and the psychological consequences of
that act? What of the final clearing up of the circumstances under which
Melville wrote his essay on Hawthorne and the revelation of unsuspected
influences on it from Maurice Mangann and Thomas Powell? Or the telling of what an encumbrance the Fourth Avenue house had become by early
1851 and Melville's folly in borrowing a huge sum on the strength of his

faith in his whaling book? Or the drastic revision of the dating for Melville's taking the manuscript of that book to New York City to be set into type, and revision of the date of the letter to Hawthorne ascribed to June 1?, 1851? Many times, new facts among those in the "whole forests" had revealed new episodes. Berman might have considered that even the smallest piece of evidence could have high dramatic significance.

Except to complain when I did not quote as many anthropological sources on Polynesia as Weaver had, Berman showed no interest at all in the history of scholarship, and what he knew of it was apparently what he had gained from skimming Robertson-Lorant. He was not at all interested in the scholarship at hand (13): "You wade through Mr. Parker's gigantic leaf-drifts of petty facts regarding letter writing, cousins, sisters, rentals, sales, architecture, debts, billings and contested wills—reassuring yourself all the while that, at least, everything you could possibly wish to know about Herman Melville will eventually turn up." He might also, I thought, have specified *Index Rerum* in honor of Gansevoort's notes or "shopping list" in honor of Cousin John.[6] Berman continued (13): "But that is not the case. About the Polynesians and their charmingly idiosyncratic notions of sex and meat, for instance, Mr. Parker tells us hardly more than can be learned in Leon Howard's 'Herman Melville: A Biography' of 1951." That was strong. It got worse (13):

> Mr. Parker tells us almost nothing about Melville's special insights into colonialism and race, and very little about his warm, economically dependent and politically awkward relations with his father-in-law, the chief justice of Massachusetts, who kept sending escaped slaves back to bondage in the South. On these delicate topics, there is more in the one-volume, slightly jargony study by Laurie Robertson-Lorant, "Melville: A Biography," which came out a few months ago, than in Mr. Parker's mass of details. I don't even mention the majesties of Melville's vocabulary, his odd relation to Shakespeare, the Platonist and Calvinist ideas that bear so crucially on his sea beast, his miraculous ability to convey the feeling of motion, his ferocity, the richness of his images—in a word, Melville's genius. On topics like those the reader is better off looking up Newton Arvin's "Herman Melville" of 1950 or Charles Olson's "Call Me Ishmael" of 1947.

This was, as it was meant to be, demolishing, and the final sentence was annihilating (13): "I wonder how Volume 2 will begin, and what other tiny jewels of research will sparkle among the tons of material that Mr. Parker has surely exhumed." Tiny jewels, tiny character?

As I have said, sales of my book had been soaring on Monday morning, December 16, 1996, on the basis of the article by Philip Weiss in the *New York Times Magazine* the day before, "Herman-Neutics." Sales died that day after the early copies of the *Book Review* were received in bookstores around the country. Many bookstores promptly began returning books. Berman had not reviewed my biography, but he had done well the job he set for himself. The bones of the tyrannical curmudgeon of Talcottville could settle back, appeased for the moment. Berman's fellow-Wilsonite Delbanco, who had let it be known that he would write a biography of Melville, that Monday must have found his way much clearer than it had seemed the day before, when the slightly more than full-page color photograph of me in my study at Landenberg, Pennsylvania, had presided over the opening of Weiss's article, which began with the identification of me as "the dean of Melville schol-ars." Well, something came of that—a novelist I had read about in an earlier *New York Times Magazine* telephoned me a few days later. Not having read modern fiction after Faulkner, I had to ask, "Are you the Texas horses man?" I needed to go to Colindale to look for reviews of Melville's books in Eng-land and Scotland? He had, it turned out, formidably hospitable friends in Clapham Common, the whaleman Roger Payne and the actress Lisa Harrow.

As I have mentioned, James Wood reviewed my first volume in the March 17, 1997, *New Republic* and republished the piece, somewhat revised, in *The Broken Estate* (1999). In the *New Republic* he began with a gratuitously insulting neologism: mine was a "semi-biography"—not because it was half fiction or half essay but because it was the first volume (30). And I was "not a critic" but merely "a connoisseur of facts" (30). According to Wood, I had confessed that in writing this "biography" (or "semi-biography"?) I had assembled documents chronologically in my computer then "simply moved chunks of the *Log* from one computer file to the other," not bothering to construct a single sentence of prose of my own. This is false, as I have said.

Then Wood charged that I quoted "from almost every published contem-porary review of Melville's novels" (30). That of course is also false. I take some pride in having searched for many months, all told, since 1962, for unknown reviews, crouching into microfilm readers, painfully straining to turn pages on low tables, happiest at the New-York Historical Society, where I could stand at high slanted newspaper reading tables. I was relieved to have published, with Brian Higgins, most of the known reviews in the Cam-bridge University Press *Herman Melville: The Contemporary Reviews*, but I had been selective in quoting in the biography. Wood complained that I had filled "twelve pages with reviews of *Omoo*" but had almost neglected to describe or interpret the book. To my mind the reviews of *Omoo* that came to the attention of Melville, his publishers, and his friends and family were important—indeed, they were crucial. If the reviews had not been favorable, he and Elizabeth Shaw could not have announced their engagement and proceeded with plans for marriage, and Melville could not have confidently embarked on *Mardi*. Then, the reviews by Horace Greeley and G. W. Peck came just in time to sour the mood of the wedding. Finally, in 1849 Richard Bentley would not have taken a chance on *Mardi* if the English reviews of *Omoo* had not been favorable. I could not tell the story without the reviews.

As for not describing the book, in chapter 12, "Beachcomber and Whaler, 1842–1843," I had told what was known of Melville on Tahiti and Eimeo, drawing on old sources and two previously unpublished sources, one found and transcribed by Wilson Heflin and one Rita Gollin had found in the 1878 *Shaker Manifesto*, neither yet used in a biography. In chapter 23, "Winning Elizabeth Shaw and Winning the Harpers," I had reviewed what scholars had shown about the sourcebooks for *Omoo*, focusing on the way he "used, misused, and downright abused his sources." Now I see that, behaving almost as if I fancied myself a critic, I had devoted a substantial paragraph to one "of the characteristics of his mature style," Melville's "powerful portrayal of images from different times and places which alternate rapidly in the mind, merge with each other, and (in later examples) disentangle again. In *Pierre* and in *Clarel*, he made profound use of this psychological phenomenon, but it appears in most of its essentials in *Omoo*" (1:454).

I see that I had also devoted most of a page to describing "Melville's new command of language, particularly in the way his descriptions of events and actions were now saturated with the Scriptures" (1:454). You would have thought that Wood would have liked that paragraph on Melville's use of the Bible, since in 2006 he wrote in his review of Delbanco what I quoted earlier: "There are scores of allusions to the King James Bible." Indeed, there are scores of allusions to the King James Bible in *Moby-Dick*. Therefore I would have thought that Wood might have been intrigued by my concluding that *Omoo* was "saturated with the Scriptures" (1:454) and citing chapter and verse for more than a dozen examples (1:454–55). He ought to have liked my conclusion that some readers would enjoy the evidence that Melville's brain was "Bible-soaked" even while his use of the Bible would offend "many pious people who kept a wary eye out for the use of God's word in vain, and who would find such submerged allusions blasphemous" (1:455). After all, in the theological center of his nominal review Wood had declared that Melville was "soaked in theology" (34). Well, what I said was "Bible-soaked." One would almost think that Wood turns tetchy when anyone one else dares to talk about religion, that he feels he has the modern monopoly on monotheism, and polytheism too? Melville was taking a risk, I said, with his biblical language.

Two decades after writing it, I look at my concluding paragraph on the composition of *Omoo* with delight and pride. I had been delicately humorous about the sexuality in *Omoo*, demonstrating Melville's own adeptness at sexual innuendo in describing how a stranger in Tahiti should have his knife in readiness and his caster slung. In a parenthetical exclamation (*Omoo*, chap. 78), Melville had identified Mr. Bell, the husband of the infinitely desirable Mrs. Bell, as a "happy dog!" That term was loaded. Melville had passed on to the publisher John Wiley the review in which the *Times* of London had said this about him: "Enviable Herman! A happier dog it is impossible to imagine than Herman in the Typee Valley." I laugh aloud now, in reading, after this space of time, my summation of the successful author and lover (1:459): "Meanwhile, his knife in readiness and his caster slung, there were hours when it was impossible to imagine a happier dog than Herman in the Hudson Valley." At the moment I wrote that, I must have been in my modest way a "happy dog." I did well by *Omoo*, take it all in all.

Melville, Wood charged, was "tied down by Parker's Lilliputian facts." Nevertheless, it was "at least a fine family chronicle" (30). Then Wood abandoned my "semi-biography" for rhapsodical excursions of his own. Midway, he recollected me long enough to slap me into the dirt before snatching me halfway up, a mighty fist clutching my shirt: "His [Melville's] reading, which had been eager but arbitrary, now took on a systematic wildness. Here, Parker, with his dribbling data, is useful." He slapped me down with "dribbling," jerked me up with "useful," then dropped me hard (33). My data would in fact have been useful, if one paid a little attention to it, but my dates of Melville's reading, for instance, got mixed up in Wood's mind. Far, far into theological rhapsodies in the *New Republic*, Wood remembered me again: "Parker is right to call *Moby-Dick* 'the most daring and prolonged aesthetic adventure that had ever been conducted in the hemisphere in the English language'" (35). Then Wood was swept up and away with his metaphysical flights. Well, what was the *New Republic* paying him for? Not for reviewing a book fairly and conscientiously but for writing a dazzling critical essay which he could collect in *The Broken Estate*? On information Wood was clear: he accepted that a certain bit of information could possibly be "useful" but no data was necessary for his eccentric theological effusions none of which he connected to the book supposedly under review.

Andrew Delbanco took up the attack on my first volume in the May 15, 1997, *New York Review of Books*, elaborating on Wood. No matter if the details were new, Delbanco wanted to be screened from them, but he objected that my "big book" was "unfortunately without annotation" (19). What? There are no footnotes, but every letter not already published in an accurate text in *Correspondence* is cited by writer and recipient to an archive, every citation from a newspaper or magazine is dated, and most reviews are in the Higgins-Parker *Herman Melville: Contemporary Reviews*. In his extremely long denunciation of the book for being overly speculative and self-assured (the "certainties are alarming") Delbanco mentioned not a single new episode which I discovered and described. Instead, he cast himself as a bibliographical Hercule Poirot (18):

> There is in this promiscuous detail a certain desperation, and a clue to how the book was composed. Nearly fifty years ago, the pioneer Melville scholar Jay Leyda assembled a chronological compendium, *The Melville Log*, of every document then known to shed light on Melville's daily activities. Realizing that the *Log* would never be finished (an enlarged edition was published in 1969), Leyda liked to call it *Melville: The Endless Study*. [Not to my knowledge—only a section.] As Leyda's scholarly heir, Parker agreed to take over the work for further expansion, and by the late 1980s he had transferred it onto his software, where it became an "ever-varying and digitized *Log*" that could be "corrected and augmented from day to day." In turning this digitized log into a biography of the traditional paper and cloth variety, Parker should have left more of it in his computer.

Like Wood, Delbanco was determined to describe my biography as consisting of pure hunks from the *Log*, not stirring or at least conscientious narrative created from hints in many old and new documents, episode after episode. Of course the book Delbanco was reviewing had been, until the last moment, itself a digitized thing. The documents in the *Log* and the narrative in the biography had been equally digitized, although the latter was in my own prose voice, such as it was. Before Delbanco went into print with his review, the Pulitzer Prize jury at his own Columbia University had reported that the first volume contained "great passages of exciting writing."[7] The prize for biography went to an early misery memoir marketed in Ireland and Britain as fiction, according to the indignant Trevor Butterworth, whom I quoted in chapter 7, but, hey, at least they put me on the Pulitzer site forever, despite Berman, Delbanco, and the other New York reviewers.

Following the sexual emphasis of Arvin, Delbanco paid homage to Robert K. Martin for his claim that "every positive depiction of sexuality in Melville is a depiction of male masturbation, frequently mutual"—a practice which Delbanco (earnestly determined to be helpful) declared to have been "distinguished in Melville's day from sodomy, a term generally reserved for anal or oral penetration" (20). Oh. Without naming them, Delbanco paid tribute to his seniors (Weaver, Mumford, Arvin, Updike) in referring to Melville as speaking "in the voice of young Redburn" and in stressing the portrait of Jackson as a "proto-Ahab" (21). Delbanco's piety was such that in the review he could not write his single sentence on *Pierre* all on his own: "But with *Moby-Dick*'s bitter sequel, *Pierre* (1852), whose style has been aptly described by John Updike as 'abrasive and latently aggressive,' the pace of invention starts to slow" (21). He staked out political ground presumably pleasing to the former wife of Robert Lowell by asserting that in *Benito Cereno* "a smug New Englander is held to account for his obtuseness in the face of slavery's horror" (22). Melville was not allowed to be himself, but he could be used as weapon in modern culture wars. At the end of "Loomings" "two and two" there floated into Ishmael's inmost soul endless processions of the whale. Anyone who falls asleep after reflecting on the influence of Newton Arvin may see spectral and living New York Intellectuals leap sheeplike over a vacancy one by one and round again, one by one, all because the 1929 trip to London and Paris had no very profound effect on Arvin's development (132): *"it was too late in the day for that."*

❧ *Chapter 12* ❧

THE EARLY TWENTY-FIRST-CENTURY MINI-MELVILLE

New York Intellectuals Without Information

EVERT DUYCKINCK, CORNELIUS MATHEWS, and other members of the 1840s New York literary group who tried to exalt the young United States into world culture were satirized by their enemies as the Mutual Admiration Society. Yes, they were parochial in touting Mathews as their own American equivalent of Dickens rather than celebrating their own American Melville in all his complexity or, a few years later, recognizing the grandeur of Walt Whitman, but they started high with Dickens as a model, and they wanted to flourish in as bright a literary society as the London literati. Duyckinck delighted in the sailor Melville even when he proved to be a sailor who read old books, but he disciplined the irreverent thinker and stylistic genius. The twenty-first-century Mutual Admiration Society of New York Intellectuals[1] patriotically has canonized Melville, or roughly half of him, the autobiographical former sailor part that Duyckinck was comfortable with. These current New York Intellectuals, however, exalt a homosexually obsessed Melville and a failed Melville (crushed by society). They slight any mention of Melville's saturation in British and Continental literature. They minimize Melville's love of art and his fascination with histories of art and aesthetics. They still treat Melville's serious study and composition of poetry very much as Alfred Kazin did at Barnes and Noble in Union Square with me and Paul Metcalf in 1997, when he brusquely growled that poetry was only a sideline with Melville and something he was never very good at.[2] (Good or not, it was, I pointed out, what Melville wrote for a third of a century.) The assault of the New York Intellectuals on Melville's complexity of mind and nobility of character is pervasive, and it begins with their assault on his biography, for they ignore long stretches of his working life. In this they were one with their era's quintessential New York Intellectual, Susan Sontag. As Carl Rollyson pointed out in "'Fascinating Fascism' Revisited: An Exercise in Biographical Criticism" (2009), "Unused to the rigor and discipline of biography, Sontag cannot countenance new evidence" (8).

When James Wood was putting together his reviews to make up *The Broken Estate*, I was not surprised to see, he revised his review of my first volume so as to make his Melville chapter even more frankly a theological treatise. The early reader Elizabeth Hardwick supplied high praise for the front flap of the dust jacket: "In these essays a very bold intelligence illuminates literature and culture with dashing fluency." The next year for her *Herman Melville: A Penguin Life* (2000) she seized on the riches being offered (*Time* [May 28, 2000] said the advances ranged from $50,000 to $100,000, and she would not have started at the lower end of any scale) as a chance to disinter an old piece on "Bartleby" (undistinguished, but much praised by her coterie), to present a long appreciation of *Moby-Dick*, and to push her fascination with what she saw as homosexuality throughout Melville's works. As a "biography," even as a "short life," her book is an embarrassment. In a child, being unconscious of one's limitations is not necessarily a fault, and when an adult writer has escaped critical scrutiny for many years he or she may enter a second childhood of misplaced confidence. More aware of the existence of evidence than Wood, and more receptive to it at her best, she nonetheless was not able to take proper pains by, say, checking a date in the *Log*. Errors leapt out of many of the pages. William Charles Macready made his escape from the Astor Place with the help of John Jacob Astor and Washington Irving (60)? There were witnesses to "the actual destruction of the *Pequod* by Moby Dick" (76)? Repeatedly, she said that Melville was thirteen when his father died (16, 25—an error she may have picked up from Weaver, 54), and, perplexingly (given the distance between the start of January and the start of August) that he was not quite twenty-two when he sailed on the *Acushnet* (34). She dated an important letter about poetry fifteen years off, following Mumford (149). Curiously, she was pleased with her idea that while he was writing Melville could have used or abused "a young male amanuensis or literary admirer" (50, presumably an imaginary white lad of pleasing shape and countenance), but she arbitrarily (and without any authority in *Typee*) decided that his bearer and pallet-mate Kory-Kory was "quite ugly to begin with," even before his "atrocious choice of tattoos" (38). She wasted time on nearly pointless quotations from her great *Partisan Review* friends and other well-known writers: Auden, Hart Crane, Mark Twain, Mrs. Trollope, Rahv, Rimbaud, Tolstoy, D. H. Lawrence, Updike (on his theme of

Melville's "withdrawal"), Matthiessen, Blackmur, Arvin, Arvin again, Law-rence again, Daniel Hoffman, Matthiessen again, Howells, Aaron, Wood, Wood again. She misquoted in ways that vulgarized Melville's language (even in a hastily written letter he would never have said that *Redburn* was "'written for tobacco'" [20]). She congratulated herself on her magnanimity that had allowed her to read my first volume, even while she dropped in an adverb, "actually," which branded me as alien: "With a firm commitment and persistence, this biography is actually a pleasure to read. I have used it and offer the all-knowing scholar my gratitude" (160). She was gracious to me, actually, but she did not use my biography very carefully. I intuitively understand Hardwick: all that stands between Oklahoma and Kentucky is Arkansas (or will be, once Arkansas reclaims that stolen bootheel from Missouri).

Like Weaver and Mumford, Hardwick took some of Melville's early books as straight autobiography: "In the midst of young Redburn's good manners and proper upbringing, his being the son of a Melville and a Gansevoort is a grotesque irrelevance" (23). She mused evocatively: "Nothing in Melville is more beautifully expressed than the mood of early sorrow in the forlorn pas-sage at the opening of *Redburn*" (22). When you take any of Melville's books as straight autobiography you close your eyes to all the psychological, cre-ative, and intellectual complexities that lie between and among experience, recalled experience, imagined experience, and aesthetically formulated experience. You minimize the human being. For all her sympathy, she mini-mizes Melville's humanity: "When the Civil War arrived, Melville followed it with some distress of spirit about the slaughter" (28). "Some distress of spirit" over what Melville called the 300,000 Union dead, to say nothing of the Southern dead?

Hardwick, like Updike, followed Arvin in minimizing Melville's trip to London and the Continent in 1849 and his 1856–57 trip to Scotland, Eng-land, the Mediterranean, then Italy and other European countries, and back to England. For 1849 she relied on a quick itinerary: "Paris, Bruges, Brus-sels, Cologne—a sort of Grand Tour by a very eager student" (62). No: a Grand Tour was just what Melville was forced to deny himself, I had shown. But wait! Bruges? Bruges? a place down on a map, to be sure, and therefore by Melville's definition not a true place, and certainly a place not known to be visited by Melville. Was Hardwick nostalgic for Bruges? Then for the later trip she listed "Constantinople, Cairo, Greece, Palestine, Rome, Flor-ence, Venice, and Naples" (148)—Naples after Venice? For the 1849 trip she was silent about art Melville may have seen (and wrongly says *White-Jacket* was published "while he was there" [62] in London). For the 1856–57 trip

she made a list: "Streets, palaces, cathedrals, pyramids, mosques, each painting, statue, campanile and hospitable café" (148). She said not a word about
Melville as an appreciator of art and a would-be collector of art, not a word
about Melville's prolonged course of study of art history and aesthetics. As
I said earlier, Arvin's trip to London and Paris in 1929 had been so miserable that he dismissed Melville's 1849 trip as equally miserable, and Updike,
sheeplike, had jumped over that quite momentous phase of Melville's life.
Hardwick jumped with equal mindlessness, not over an imaginary hurdle,
like those sheep of the researchers in animal intelligence, but over historical,
aesthetic, emotional, and literary treasures, Melville's profound responses to
England and a bit of the Continent in 1849, and his more still more profound responses in 1856 and 1857.

Hardwick knew of Melville's aristocratic background but was fixated on
what she saw as his social awkwardness. Straining hard, she quoted Macaulay on Fielding, who, according to Macaulay, "was sometimes glad to obtain
by pawning his best coat, the means of dining on tripe at a cookshop underground, where he could wipe his hands, after a greasy meal, on the back
of a Newfoundland dog" (6). She applied this by saying that while writing in New York City and then in Pittsfield Melville "might in his obscure
and never quite assimilated nature, have preferred life in the underground
cookshop with the Newfoundland dog" (6). Is this an attempt to distance
herself from this crude upstart, however high his birth? On the next page she
declared that "*poor* Melville seems to come to mind when we think of this
profligate benefactor of our literature" (7, her italics). You can dress Melville in a "suit and tie" (37) but he will always have just crawled out of the
forecastle. While Hawthorne's classmates were Henry Longfellow and Franklin Pierce, "Melville's mates were drunken, venereal, negligent, brutalized
wastrels one would hurry past on the street. We note that Hawthorne would
hold the position of Consul in Liverpool but that his previous recommendation for a similar post for Melville came to nothing. Apparently Melville did
not appear to be quite suitable" (67). Hawthorne, she thinks, saw through to
Melville's unsuitable qualities (she did not intend her pun?), though "he was
in his garments as a gentleman" (67). You can dress him as a gentleman, but
he will always be a "Grub Street journeyman" wiping his greasy hands on his
Newfoundland dog? She simply could not think of Melville as being from a
social class as high, say, as a Lowell—and yet he was, and higher still, akin to
Scottish nobility, the lords of Leven and Melville.

In putting the book together Hardwick seemed most driven to show that
Melville wrote mainly about homosexuality: "Obsession and a compulsive
need for *confession*; homoerotic intrusions came into his writing again and

again with an unknown intention; subliminal matter, unconscious or boldly aware? Perhaps he is as blind as his readers, unacquainted with the naming of irregular impulses." (125) She reveled in Queequeg and queerness, and she expatiated for many pages on homosexuality (125–41), strangely making me her partner: "Parker suggests that Melville came to understand the folly of what he had written [about Redburn and Harry Bolton], came to acknowledge that he had revealed homosexual longings or even homosexual experience."

I am staggered by her distorting what I said about the Come-Outers so as to make it apply, possibly, to members of this group "announcing themselves as homosexual" (138). In making me complicit in her desire to see Melville as obsessed with homosexuality she skipped over my account of Tom's sailing for China in 1849 and its significance for Melville's development as a great writer. Perhaps I should, after all, have flagged passages in my biography which I knew were absolutely fresh and important: such a passage could bear a warning: "Here Be Monsters." Because mine was a chronological biography, I could not do what I do in a later chapter in this book—that is, expatiate on the phenomenon in Melville of what we now call morphing. In May 1849, I was sure, seeing off to China the brother who looked so much like him, now just ten years after Gansevoort had seen him off to Liverpool, had triggered powerful, even hallucinatory images and had pushed Melville into starting a book about his first voyage. This is how I left Melville's decision to write *Redburn* in the immediate aftermath of seeing Tom off for China (Parker 1:639, 645):

> For Melville there was . . . danger in writing fluently about the bitterness of youth ("never again can such blights be made good; they strike in too deep, and leave such a scar that the air of Paradise might not erase it"). That danger was not uppermost in his mind as he wrote, for he was writing too fast to let himself think much about what feelings he was stirring up. . . . Only a young and still naive man could have thought that he could write a kind of psychological autobiography . . . without suffering any consequences. By the next year or year and a half, the act of writing the early quasi-autobiographical chapters of *Redburn* had caught up with him, changing him profoundly. Melville knew about the Come-Outers, the sect whose members followed Paul's injunction in II Corinthians 6:17 ("Wherefore come out from among them, and be ye separate"). William Lloyd Garrison had headlined the term in the *Liberator* while Melville was in Boston in October 1844, and later Melville punned on the name of the

sect, relishing its metaphorical significance, in *The Confidence-Man:* come-outers were people who came out publicly with information about themselves that should have been kept private. In the summer of 1849 Melville was working too hard to notice that he had unwittingly joined the psychological equivalent of this new American religious sect; in mythological terms, he had opened Pandora's box when he thought he was merely describing the lid. (1:639, 645)

Here I was suggesting, as I have elsewhere in this book, that we should take the consequences of writing *Redburn* much more seriously than anyone had done. This book which Melville knew he could get into and out of fast, drawing mainly on his own recollections or books already familiar, for a change, stirred up potent if still submerged memories that began to emerge in the next weeks, in *White-Jacket*, and that aggressively made their way to consciousness in *Moby-Dick* and *Pierre*. *Redburn*, I thought, made possible the psychological depths of those books. Melville must have thought he had distanced himself enough from his early life to risk basing a narrative on it. Hardwick looked at the passage in my book on *Redburn* but missed the psychological import. As biographer I provided the information. It was her obligation as critic to get past her preconceptions about *Redburn* as a portrait of the young Melville and see the book in a new light, after what I showed about its impulse—as a reckless book undertaken by a hardworking novelist without heeding the danger. No one writes something close to an autobiography, particularly an autobiographical account of traumatic childhood, writes it under pressure of time, and then emerges unchanged, even if such a person dusts himself off and goes about his daily life for a while, seemingly having remained just the same man.

For decades the New York Intellectuals had fawningly reviewed each other's books, as Edmund Wilson and Newton Arvin were doing even as Arvin was dying, and since they infiltrated and often dominated the few important reviewing organs in the country their mutual flattery was often taken as disinterested criticism. If the New York Intellectuals had been at all sensitive to the grotesqueness of their public mutual admiration, the *New York Review of Books* would not have published John Leonard's slavering "The Wise Woman and the Whale" in the July 20, 2000, issue:

Elizabeth Hardwick and the whale: although it is very dark inside the whiteness, she will read her way by oil lamp to Melville, "the most bookish of writers, a tireless midnight student." Thigh-high in ambergris and spermaceti, she makes herself as much at home as on the prison ship, or the cannibal islands, or the Berkshire farm where Herman wrote in twelve-hour shifts, or inside the Manhattan townhouse down whose stairs he may have tossed his wife. Wherever and whatever—novels, letters, and biographies; marriage and derangement; carnival or crypt—Hardwick always moves in with her subject. And before she entertains, she will have picked the locks, ransacked the closets, let the madwomen out of the attic, brought up bodies from the basement, and bounced on the double bed like Goldilocks or Freud. About this brilliant domesticity, there is also a jujitsu.

Mainly, the jujitsu involved Hardwick on Melville's "sex life." Leonard quoted her on the "homoerotic intrusions" that came into Melville's writing "again and again," and insisted that "Melville-and-sexuality seems to be what everyone is interested in except James Wood in *The Broken Estate*, who prefers Melville-and-Calvin." Leonard's praise was shameless: "Hardwick has always had the shaman's gift of disappearing into writers she loves, speaking in their voices, seeing through their eyes. Almost alone among our serious critics of literature, she makes us *need* to read the books she has chosen to care about." Attributing precise knowledge about Melville to Hardwick, he made repeated blunders himself. Accurate information was not in request here: worship was, and worship was supplied.

Worship is pretty much what Hardwick got on July 26, 2000, from Maria Russo in *Salon*. Repeating Hardwick's error about Melville's age at his father's death, Russo brilliantly devised a way of praising the incoherencies of the book: "Like most great critics, she has an eclectic method that's difficult to pin down." Whew! That sentence kept Russo out of trouble. Most of Russo's piece concerns Hardwick on "the question of Melville's homoeroticism," which she reinforces rather more vulgarly than Hardwick did in saying that the year in which Melville wrote *Moby-Dick* "was also the year Melville fell hard for his Berkshires neighbor, Nathaniel Hawthorne." (Why make a point of outdoing men in vulgarity, the way Brenda Wineapple does later [224] in declaring Melville as "smitten" with Hawthorne?) In July 2000 the *Library Journal* confirmed such appreciations as Leonard's and Russo's: "Highly recommended as an excellent introductory guide to Melville's choppy seas and craggy shores."

In the *New York Times* on July 30, 2000, Erica Da Costa was not worshipful: "Elizabeth Hardwick's biography of Melville is not a scholarly chronicle but a literary critique couched in terms of a life. . . . That Melville is a great writer hardly need be said, but to explain why he is a great writer requires a perception less adoring and more attentive to the knotty nature of greatness."

Hardwick's 'Herman Melville' is long on adoration and short on critical attention." Heresy may have been allowed to voice itself more freely under the Spanish Inquisition than in New York City under the reign of the New York Intellectuals. In a letter in the August 20 *New York Times* almost as long as Da Costa's review, Hardwick protested against being charged with being "'short on critical attention.'" Writing in genuinely high dudgeon, Hardwick took at Da Costa what begs to be called umbrage:

> My book studies all of Melville's writings, especially "Redburn" and "The Confidence Man" as well as the shorter works, "Bartleby," "Billy Budd" and "Benito Cereno," none of which is mentioned by the reviewer. I do not find Erica Da Costa sufficiently informed about Melville's many writings and the general critical opinion about them to be a proper reviewer for yet another book on the subject.

What Hardwick meant by the last sentence is ambiguous, but I take it as intimidation—a warning that the *Times* must never again hire Da Costa as a reviewer, certainly not for the next book on Melville. If they hired her again, Hardwick might blast them for disrespecting her. After all, older hands at the *Times* were still reeling from her onslaught in *Harper's*, forty-one years earlier, on the mediocre *Book Review* section of the *Times*: "Everyone is found to have 'filled a need' and is to be 'thanked' for something and to be excused for 'minor faults in an otherwise excellent work' by a 'thoroughly mature artist'" (139).What was required in 2000 was what John Leonard supplied, in heaping measure—abject fawning over members of the in-crowd. And in 2000 what Hardwick had accused the *New York Times* of in 1959 was now true not only of the *New York Times* (despite Da Costa's anomalous review) but also true, all too regularly, of the *New York Review of Books*, the *Nation*, the *New Republic*, and the *New Yorker*.[3]

Andrew Delbanco's review of my second volume in the *New Republic* (September 30, 2002) proceeded with the usual New York Intellectual evocation of the mighty—Lewis Mumford, Newton Arvin, Elizabeth Hardwick, Saul Bellow (and Walker Percy). Delbanco had not become more careful with facts. He claimed that Edmund Wilson once referred to a "'chastening'" of Melville's prose style; in fact, Wilson in his title of a chapter in *Patriotic Gore* was not commenting specifically and only on Melville (35). Like Hardwick, Delbanco made sloppy errors, as when he reduced Melville's "The Metaphysics of Indian-hating" to a stark backwoods phenomenon, wholly missing the Calvinistic allegory which is Melville's point (36). This time Delbanco swung two ways on information: "We know little with assurance about

Melville's private life," he affirmed, yet this volume, like my first, was "an avalanche of undifferentiated facts" (34). The second volume was "an incomparable sourcebook that will be plundered for years by anyone who wants to try to correlate this great writer's life with his work"; yet we do not need "its density of impertinent detail" (34). There was in volume 2 a "glut of information"—this despite the fact that there is a "paucity of records documenting Melville's life" (35, 36). Delbanco shows no comprehension of any value in the new information I was condensing and attempting to convey in sparkling narrative. He made a strange accusation: "Parker too rarely turns to the work" (36). My turning to commentary, as Mumford, Arvin, Updike, Wood, Hardwick, and Delbanco himself do (and often commentary that pushes Melville toward modern political correctness), would have indefinitely expanded the volumes at the expense of new information and actual new episodes. I was writing biography (including biographies of Melville's books), not primarily literary criticism. To be sure, I was absolutely convinced that valid criticism would have to be built from scratch on what could be learned from biography, in this case my biography, but I kept that conviction private.

The strangest thing of all is what Delbanco reveals about his ignorance of Melville's life. You have to believe that he reviewed me three times (counting the review of the Sendak-Parker Kraken Edition of *Pierre*), always annihilatingly, without ever having paid much attention to basic texts such as *The Melville Log*, Leon Howard's biography, the Davis-Gilman *Letters*, and the later Northwestern-Newberry *Correspondence*, or to the documents quoted in my books which he was supposedly reviewing. There is an alternate possibility. If you believe that Delbanco had to have been familiar with the basic books of Melville scholarship in 1996, 1997, and 2002, when he was reviewing authoritatively, and believe that he read my books before reviewing them, then you have to believe that he deliberately lied about the state of scholarship in order to brand me a biographer guilty of irresponsible surmises about something so important as Melville's lost books.

Here is Delbanco's giant "NO TRUST IN PARKER" warning to the reader (34), in the spirit of the barber's "NO TRUST" sign in *The Confidence-Man*:

> Like the first volume . . . it must be used with caution. For one thing, Parker is amazingly certain of his own conclusions. . . . He is sure that immediately after completing *Pierre*, Melville wrote an unpublished novel (Parker implies that after failing to find a publisher, Melville burned it) inspired by a story he had heard about a sailor who disappears for thirty years, then returns to the wife for whom he has become a distant memory.

Now, I did not say "immediately after finishing *Pierre*"; most of a year intervened, as I make clear; and Delbanco's summary of what we have known as
the "Agatha story" leaves very much to be desired. The evidence is all laid out
in my biography—the correct date, to within a few days of mid-December
1852, of Melville's beginning to write the story based on the experience of
Agatha Hatch; the assertion of his mother that he was nearing the end of
work on it in April 1853; the letters Cousin Priscilla Melvill wrote to Augusta
in May and June 1853 which I transcribed from the 1983 New York Public Library trove, from which I learned the title, *The Isle of the Cross*, and
the exact or closely approximate date of completion, May 22, 1853; and the
November 1853 letter published in 1960 by Davis and Gilman in which
Melville refers to the book he had been prevented from publishing. All this
I recounted in the biography with my usual generous quotations. Melville
scholars such as Leyda, then ill, and Hayford and Sealts, then healthy and
alert, had rejoiced in 1987 at my discovery of the title *The Isle of the Cross*
and the date of completion. I had published the information in *American
Literature* (March 1990), since it deserved wide and immediate dissemi-
nation rather than lying in my computer until I could publish the second
volume.[4]

I am relieved now to see that I devoted a whole chapter to *"The Isle of
the Cross:* September 1852–June 1853." I could hardly have been clearer
(2:154–55):

> When Maria wrote Peter on 20 April that Herman had composed a
> "new work, now nearly ready for the press," she was, as usual, speak-
> ing the exact truth. [This wording was my private way of handling
> the fact that Leon Howard has accused her of prevaricating without
> getting into an argument with Leon.] On 6 April from Arrowhead
> Augusta had written to her Cousin Priscilla, still slaving in the
> female academy in Canandaigua—the first letter she had written to
> her since the previous October, when she had sent bad news about
> the little "Brown Cottage" [the one Priscilla hoped to occupy]. Now
> she told her cousin the title of Melville's manuscript: "The Isle of the
> Cross." Not thinking of the necessary lag in time between the near-
> completion of a manuscript and its publication, Priscilla Melvill
> in late April through part of May kept watch for any public men-
> tion of the new story. . . . At Arrowhead, Elizabeth (Bessie) Melville
> was born on 22 May, and on the same day, from Canandaigua, Pris-
> cilla Melvill coincidentally wrote to Augusta: "When will the 'Isle
> of the Cross' make its appearance? I am constantly looking in the

journals [meaning newspapers] & magazines that come in my way, for notices of it." The letter arrived at Arrowhead on 26 May, and four days later Augusta replied to Priscilla, telling her of the birth of Bessie and also that Melville had completed *The Isle of the Cross* (on or about the day Bessie was born). . . .

On 12 June Priscilla wrote to Augusta: "I am glad to hear such a favorable report of *Lizzie*—she is really gathering quite a little family around her & Arrowhead Mansion will hardly be spacious enough—the 'Isle of the Cross' is almost a twin sister of the little one & I think she should be nam'd for the heroine—if there *is* such a personage—the advent of the two are singularly near together."

What is the truth here? That Delbanco had not seen any earlier comment on *The Isle of the Cross*? That he had not been competent to read my account in the chapter he was reviewing? And was his decision never to use the title of the book a way of denying its reality?

Delbanco was not finished with his warning that my second volume, like the first, "must be used with caution" (34):

He [Parker] is sure that when Melville traveled by slow boat to San Francisco in 1860, he expected to find waiting for him a finished copy of a book of poems that he had entrusted in manuscript to his brother for transmission to his publishers before leaving the East. (Such a book was never published—and it is a surmise that Melville ever wrote it.) . . . . In short, Parker trusts his own intuition completely, and, presenting inferences as facts, he expects his readers to trust it, too.

"*Such a book was never published—and it is a surmise that Melville ever wrote it.*" This is even stranger than Delbanco's warning about *The Isle of the Cross*. Once again, I need to review the facts, since Delbanco's stated ignorance of them is so baffling. Raymond Weaver in 1921 did not know about *Poems* (1860), the volume Melville left for publication when he sailed with his brother Thomas on the *Meteor*. Weaver had not known of Melville's association with Evert A. Duyckinck and had not consulted anything in the Duyckinck Collection of the New York Public Library. As I need to point out again, the next year, 1922, Meade Minnigerode in *Some Personal Letters of Herman Melville and a Bibliography* published a cache of letters about the volume of poetry, including Melville's twelve-point "Memoranda for Allan concerning the publication of my verses." The document is memorably expressed: "Don't have the Harpers. . . . For God's sake don't have *By the author of 'Typee,' 'Piddledee,' &c* on the title-page. . . . Let the title-page be simply Poems/by/Herman Melville. . . . Don't have any clap-trap announcements and 'sensation' puffs—nor any extracts published previous to publication of the book." In 1951 Leyda added one document in the *Log*, Charles Scribner's rejection of the collection, but other than that Minnigerode in 1922 had published almost all the known evidence. And everyone knew it, every critic from Willard Thorp, who made much of the information in his 1938 *Representative Selections*, and every biographer from Howard onward. Lewis Mumford used the new evidence while correcting one of Minnigerode's hasty conclusions, and even Newton Arvin, also much honored by the New York Intellectuals, knew about the volume, though he said little except that the "failure of these poems to find a publisher had not disheartened Melville enough to silence him." (Arvin peculiarly says the poems in *Battle-Pieces* were "for the most part better ones"—better than the ones in the 1860 volume most or all of which we have never seen?) Melville's twelve-point memoranda is quoted in the *Log*, of course, and reprinted in full in *Letters* and *Correspondence* and quoted in many other places, including my second volume. Is it possible that the man who took it upon himself to denounce my biography in the *New York Review of Books* and the *New Republic* in fact knew so little about Melville's world and his work? If he did know what a reviewer should have known, then did he choose to lie about *Poems*, assuming no reviewer would challenge him, a few years later? When he said my biography would be plundered, was he thinking of the use he was in fact to make of it in his own biography which he had already promised?

So according to Delbanco in the *New Republic* I must be treated as irre-sponsible because I merely surmised the existence of *The Isle of the Cross* and *Poems*. Is this character assassination from obdurate ignorance, foremost, or does some of it spring from jealousy of me for gathering and weighing archi-val evidence that no one else had bothered to hunt for or known how to hunt for (or, in the case of the famous Augusta Papers, had bothered to look at)? Or could there be a still stranger explanation. Did he assume that another professor, about his age, another product of the New Criticism only belatedly come to social consciousness, knew more about Melville than he did, and more than I did, or did they coordinate their stories? For on June 23, 2002, in the *New York Times* Richard Brodhead, who held an endowed chair at Yale and was dean of Yale College, had formulated the same accusation about what he called my "surmises about works Melville never published that did not survive." Brodhead had deemed one particular "surmise" dubious: "He makes the case that in 1852–53 Melville wrote a novel based on materials he shared with Hawthorne about a sailor who deserted his wife. If this is true, then the theory that Melville renounced writing after 'Pierre' is just wrong" (13). I had made "the case" about the Agatha story (not named as *The Isle of the Cross* by Brodhead, just as not named by Delbanco)—but had I made it convincingly? Was it a "true" case? "The stories," I had said, "take on a new light now that we know that Melville wrote an entire book between *Pierre* and the first of the stories" (Parker, 2:164). The "challenge for readers" was "to imagine how writing it allowed Melville to grow from *Pierre* to 'Bartleby.'" If I was, after all, right, then "the mysterious leap from 'Pierre' to the work he [Melville] published after a silence, the very different 'Bartleby the Scrivener,' can be explained in a new way," Brodhead perceived (13). My judgment had been cast as literary criticism, so Brodhead appropriated it as if it were by rights his. I saw it all differently. Having mugged me, Brodhead then had deftly robbed me. I quote again the "black hole" accusation that another "surmise" of mine was really an outright fabrication: "Parker is also convinced that Melville prepared a volume of poems in 1860 that failed to be published. If this is so, a stretch that had seemed empty of literary strivings was instead a time of new effort and new failure—a black hole Parker alone has the instruments to detect."

According to Brodhead (who shared Delbanco's baseless skepticism), I had convinced myself that Melville had prepared a volume of poems—I and no one else, for this was merely a "surmise." Enjoying his formula, "If this is true," "If this is so," Brodhead made a very strange charge. If Melville completed a volume of poems, then a stretch in which we knew of no literary work by Melville "was instead a time of new effort and new failure—a black hole Parker alone has the instruments to detect." I alone? Well, starting with Meade Minnigerode in 1922, continuing strongly with Willard Thorp in 1938, blasting forward with Jay Leyda in 1951—and so on, as the troops were augmented, down to Merton M. Sealts, Jr. It was not a case of "Parker alone"—I was in agreement with all these scholars. Brodhead, and later Delbanco, in their failure to acknowledge scholarship about *The Isle of the Cross* and *Poems*, did permanent damage to my reputation. The stress I suffered from their unwarranted, utterly unfounded attacks did horrific damage to my health during the rest of 2002 and for the next five years, until I began speaking out in June 2007.

Now that I have begun defending myself, I realize how important it is to reiterate my defense of several very great scholars, for in slandering me Brodhead and Delbanco had denied the existence of all the men upon whose labors I had built, especially Hayford, then Davis and Gilman, and then Sealts (who had worked on the chronology of Melville's writing in the 1850s), for they had prepared me to understand what I was reading when I came to Cousin Priscilla's letters about *The Isle of the Cross*. In the normal course of work, discovery often builds upon previous discovery. Brodhead and Delbanco seem not to realize that the mighty contributions of heroic scholars such as Hayford and Sealts should mean anything to them as modern Intellectuals. Yet disregarding the history of scholarship, as Brodhead and Delbanco do, is a matter of morality, and their ignorance, feigned or real, is culpable. That is, Brodhead and Delbanco reveal, at best, ignorance of three quarters of a century of scholarship, or, at worst, a willful erasing of the life-work of a several great scholars, including Thorp and Leyda. Let me say this again because critics in very recent years have explicitly argued against it: *disregarding or distorting the history of scholarship is a violation of morality*.

Elizabeth Schultz committed the same sins against scholarship in her slightly later review of my second volume in the *Common Review* (Winter 2002):

> Parker also reads betrayal and despair into the disappearance of two manuscripts, which he contends Melville completed—a novel, putatively titled *The Isle of the Cross*, and his first collection of poems. Throughout ["Throughout," really?] his biography, Parker bemoans the loss of *The Isle of the Cross*'s ghostly manuscript, imagining Melville's regret at never having found a publisher for it. Although there is only tentative evidence for the manuscript's existence and submission to a publisher, its ostensible rejection leads Parker to view his heroic author as victimized: "masterful as he could be, [Melville] had a way now, after the failure of *Moby-Dick* and *Pierre*, of seeing himself as passive victim to whom things were done." (45)

The influence of Brodhead and Delbanco, if not Schultz, is such that they continue to mislead the ignorant who are all too willing to buy into the rhetoric of journalistic disdain. You can see this in Alan Helms, who as a professional queer-criticism practitioner insisted on finding homophobia in a poem of Whitman's where it does not exist, and railed at me with ammunition from Delbanco. For Helms, whom Edmund White hailed as "the most famous piece of ass" of his (White's) generation, I was "a slippery fish, as anyone familiar with the new first volume of his two-volume biography of Melville can attest—an exhaustive, exhausting book in which conjecture repeatedly turns into 'fact' without so much as a nod to evidence of any kind."[5] What was Helms's authority for calling me "a slippery fish"? Why, it was this, I emphasize again: "Andrew Delbanco takes Parker to task for this misleading habit"—the habit of turning conjecture into fact. In this book I mention Helms's second-hand slander in different places because I want to suggest the way it has spread on the Internet, his slander feeding on Delbanco's slander while gullible quoters of Helms have no idea of how flimsy *his* great authority was.

By 2005, when he published *Melville: His World and Work*, Delbanco had somehow learned about the existence of the two lost books he had assured the readers of the *New Republic* I had merely "surmised." Casually mentioning Melville's having offered the story of Agatha Hatch to Hawthorne, he continued cheekily (208):

> When Hawthorne replied, in effect, thanks but no thanks, Melville decided after all to take a crack at the story himself. The result was a novel-length manuscript, now lost, submitted the following spring to Harpers under the title *The Isle of the Cross* and promptly rejected, possibly because the Harpers anticipated a legal dispute involving descendants of Agatha and her bigamous husband. Melville later made cryptic reference to having been "prevented from printing" it.

"Thanks but no thanks," of course, had already been used with equal cheekiness by Brodhead in his January 7, 1996, *New York Times Book Review* "Bookend" dismissing the Kraken Edition of *Pierre* (35). "Taking a crack at the story" of course demeans the whole brave enterprise. Oddly, Delbanco's only citation here was to *Correspondence* for "prevented from printing," not to a source for the title of the book (364). Later Delbanco also belatedly recognized the existence of a collection of poems: "Exactly when Melville started writing verse is unknown, but by the spring of 1860 he had accumulated enough poems to fill a small manuscript, and while in New York waiting to board the *Meteor*, he asked his brother Allan to place it with a publisher" (266–67). Delbanco continued, with more errors to match the ones just quoted (the manuscript may have been large rather than small, and Melville was not in New York waiting to board the *Meteor* when he wrote to Allan—he was in Pittsfield, and he boarded the *Meteor* in Boston, not New York). There is no note explaining the source of Delbanco's sudden, if inexact, knowledge of *Poems*, and once again he did not give Melville's title for the volume. This sort of near-miss, fair approximation, sort-of-near-right was about the level of any biographical passage in Delbanco. Even at the end of the book he had Melville seeing "the gilded statue of naked Diana"

(318) from his second-floor windows (windows, plural? sight line verified?),
although the goddess as copper weathervane was hoisted atop the Madison
Square Garden tower after Melville was buried in Woodlawn. Be blunt: in
his whole book Delbanco never for the length of any longish paragraph demonstrated command of documentary evidence about Melville's material
world or literary works.

In the preliminary comments on his "Notes" in the bound "uncorrected
proofs" of his 2005 book (319), Delbanco averred: "Though I have tried
to give some sense here of what I owe to previous scholars, anyone writing about Melville incurs a debt too large to be fully enumerated." He gave
this sense of what he owed by citing John Bryant's *A Companion to Melville Studies* (1986) and Robert Levine's *Cambridge Companion to Herman
Melville* (1998), a comically unequal pairing. The 1986 book is a massive
compilation with many authoritative chapters, crowned by Tanselle's classic
"Melville and the World of Books." Nothing like that graces Levine's little
collection of essays the political correctness of which all but guarantees they
will have short shelf-lives. In the acknowledgments at the end of these uncorrected proofs Delbanco wrote (383): "I hope that my debt to the community
of Melville scholars is at least hinted at in the notes, but I must add particular
thanks to Samuel Otter for sharing his unpublished work on the reception
history of *Moby-Dick*, and to Robert K. Wallace for helping me track down
some elusive materials."

Something happened. My guess is that someone who knew a little about
Melville pulled Delbanco aside and whispered these words or words very
like them:

> Well, Andy, I see you are not apologizing in the book for accusing
> Parker of making up *The Isle of the Cross* and *Poems* and then say-
> ing that he was untrustworthy all the way through both volumes. I
> also see that you give no source in the notes when you now men-
> tion the existence of *The Isle of the Cross* and *Poems*. You have
> decided to treat them not as famous like *Moby-Dick* but as gener-
> ally known, like *Israel Potter*, even though you professed not to know
> about them in 2002? That's just a bit strong, you know. And you
> don't mention Parker anywhere as a source although you are quoting
> from his and Higgins's volume of contemporary reviews throughout
> and even picking bits out of his quotations from family letters rather
> than going down to Forty-second Street and reading the entire letters
> yourself. That's raw. Maybe you had better do something magnani-
> mous, like listing him with people who have provided you incidental

advice? Then you will look all shiny, except to people who know what you said about Parker in 1997 and 2002.

Apparently someone, perhaps Gary Fisketjon, his agent, got to him, and instead of the silence of the uncorrected proofs the book contains this altered version (387): "I hope that my debt to the community of Melville scholars is at least hinted at in the notes. Like all students of Melville, I am keenly aware of, and especially grateful for, the prodigious scholarship of Hershel Parker, whose discoveries have immeasurably deepened our knowledge of Melville's life. I must also add particular thanks to Samuel Otter for sharing his unpublished work on the reception history of *Moby-Dick*, and to Robert K. Wallace for helping me track down some elusive materials." That of course made everything right with all the reviewers, none of whom pointed out that Delbanco had vehemently denied the existence of two books of Melville's in 2002 then mysteriously had learned so much about Melville in the succeeding weeks that he alluded to their existence in 2005, although only to one of them by title.

A phrenologist feeling the bumps on Delbanco's head would pronounce the Organ of Veneration abnormally developed. In 1992, Delbanco had openly flattered Updike as "the most limber prose stylist of our own time" (720), and his reviews are laced with such backpatting and manly shoulder-hugging. Vivian Gornick tried to define this habit of Delbanco's in "The Scrivener and the Whale," her review in the *Nation* (December 5, 2005). *Melville: His World and Work*, she said, was "saturated in quotations" (45):

> On every other page—or so it seems—Lewis Mumford notes, Elizabeth Hardwick observes, Harold Bloom remarks. A rudimentary list of those quoted includes Edward Said, Walker Percy, E. M. Forster, Newton Arvin, Edmund Wilson, W. H. Auden, John Updike, along with lesser known but influential academics such as Frank Lentricchia, Richard Slotkin and Dominick LaCapra. The odd thing here is that much of what these scholars and writers say can be said without the invocation of their illustrious names (45–46).

It is a travesty of scholarship to drop names of people who never added anything significant to knowledge about Melville even while rigorously avoiding engagement with the archival work and speculations of scholars such as Meade Minnigerode, Willard Thorp, Elizabeth Foster, Walter Bezanson, Wilson Heflin, Jay Leyda, William H. Gilman, Merrell R. Davis, Merton M. Sealts, Jr.—names which do *not* pepper Delbanco's pages. In his 1992 survey of work on Melville in the 1980s Delbanco had ignored the "Historical Note" in the Northwestern-Newberry Edition of *Moby-Dick* and the remarkable Northwestern-Newberry *Journals* in favor of sympathetic attention to critics with strong social agendas. In 2005 he summoned back much the same cast of characters to be flatteringly quoted, and often illogically and disruptively quoted. To be a scholar was to be shunned in *Melville: His World and Work*. In what Gornick quotes, Delbanco's compulsive stroking of his friends is obvious. I have quoted him on his self-damaging filiopietistic deference to Alan Heimert and elaborate those comments below. I understand the feeling, for I am profoundly filiopietistic toward Jay Leyda and Harrison Hayford, but I have corrected them living (except once, when Jay was too weak to understand) and corrected them dead, and when they were alive and strong they rejoiced every time, for what counted for them and for me was adding a grain to truth.

Gornick, in the passage I just hijacked for a high purpose, took up Delbanco's account of his uneasiness in the Houghton Library, his feeling that he was "eavesdropping, like a tourist in a church who comes upon a worshipper kneeling in prayer" (45). She comments: "Now we know we are in the presence of adoration; and sure enough, the preface ends: 'Anyone who reads Melville's words will know what Emerson meant when he wrote in his journal that, while reading Shakespeare, "I actually shade my eyes."'" These sentences, Gornick adds, made her "desperately uncomfortable." What, she wondered, "can follow from such a beginning except hagiography, pure and simple?" Hagiography, she decides, "though not pure and simple" (45). She means hagiography of Melville, but she might have made a more serious point: the veneration Delbanco displays is not toward Melville so much as toward his older cultural heroes and toward fellow New York Intellectuals. The name-dropping (which very frequently is simply mindless massaging of egos) shows that when Delbanco was not writing with Arvin in hand (or within easy reach) he was writing with books of other New York Intellectuals and their allies open before him—not writing from nineteenth-century documents. Delbanco fills his pages with the names of critics because he does not write from a core of knowledge that creates self-reliance. In Emersonian terms, instead of saying, "I think" or "I am," Delbanco quotes some Politically Correct saint or some Self-Identified Public Intellectual sage. Naturally, this reflexive reliance on his authorities leads to his inadvertently exposing his and their mutual ignorance or fatuity. Here is his comment on Melville's presence in Boston in October 1844: "He may have spent a few days 'lingering or malingering' (Elizabeth Hardwick's nicely inconclusive phrase) and possibly a few nights lodging at the home of Judge Lemuel Shaw"

(62). Delbanco had no business honoring Hardwick by this inconclusiveness, for "malingering" is the last thing Melville would then have been guilty of. In order to continue as Hardwick's follower after her death he validates her self-indulgent and quite wrongheaded jingle. (And did he remember his contemptuous condemnation of my fantasy that Melville spent time with Judge Shaw and his family?)

A biographer experiences topgallant delight from moments of discovery during research, whether it is the title of a lost book or a revelation about a sister's character or the realization of what it meant that a portrait was on a certain wall on a certain day. What sustains a biographer is that joy. When the biography is of a great writer, what also sustains the biographer is joy in demonstrating in fresh ways what the writer achieved and how he achieved it. There is very little joy at Melville's artistic achievements in Delbanco's book. By nature, a New Critic like Delbanco can never experience the thrill of a documentary discovery that sheds light on interpretation of a book of Melville's since he wrote his biography from other books, not from documents. Delbanco also shows very little intense aesthetic engagement with the literary works. For instance, the value of "Benito Cereno" for Delbanco is as "our best evidence that during his years of personal withdrawal from the intellectual circle to which he had once belonged, Melville had kept his eye on the gathering storm" (231). What he says about Melville's masterful creation and manipulation of tension is tawdry adolescent vulgarity: "Reading *Benito Cereno* is something like being teased with a promise of sexual relief but having it continually deferred" (237). The only time that his treatment of the story picks up is where he quotes Lewis Mumford, paraphrases "the notable black writers Sterling Brown and Ralph Ellison," quotes Benjamin Butler, who had "recently" written about "'blindness to evil,'" and quotes Russell Banks, the "author of a historically informed novel about that avenging terrorist John Brown" (231). He is happy quoting, notably when he is paying irrelevant homage to Elizabeth Hardwick (62) or elaborating (86) her peculiar depiction of the louche Melville, or the "flâneur," as Delbanco prefers. His greatest joy is not in Melville but in the wit with which he nods to his real or his fantasy friends, like this high cleverness about Melville's "'long silence,'" the anecdote about Updike's character Henry Bech who wins the "Melville Medal" for maintaining "the most meaningful silence" (288). Delbanco seems desperate that the friends whom he compulsively quotes get the joke, especially any delightful in-joke that only a select few can share. The deepest aesthetic and physiological and psychological response to a literary work comes first always in solitude, it seems to me, as it was for Melville and *The Faerie Queene*, and Pierre and *The Faerie Queene*, and Melville and

Shakespeare. Delbanco is never alone with *White-Jacket* or *Moby-Dick* or "Benito Cereno": he may hold a book in his hands but he is always nodding to this friend, quoting that acquaintance, alluding to that mentor, smiling, winking, leering, nudging, back-slapping, assuring himself of his place in his hall of right-minded politically correct Intellectuals.[6] In paragraph after paragraph in *Melville: His World and Work* nothing can be valid unless it is vouched for or shared with Delbanco's real or fantasy coterie. (Contrast the grandeur of spirit displayed by Stanton Garner in the passage I quoted in chapter 7 about the sanctity of those moments in the hotel in Lenox.)

Delbanco goes perhaps farthest askew in his deference to his teacher Alan Heimert, who had faced a problem I faced about the same time in work on my 1963 dissertation, "Melville and Politics": how could Melville (being a good humane fellow like, say, me or Heimert, at the start of the civil rights sit-ins) *not* have worked into his whaling book something of the tensions over the Fugitive Slave Law of 1850 and early 1851? Heimert, knowing only what was public knowledge in 1963, which means knowing only a rough, imperfect sequence of events in Melville's life during the composition of *Moby-Dick*, convinced himself that *Moby-Dick* was indeed a political allegory in which Ahab was John Calhoun. In Boston Melville's father-in-law, Chief Justice Lemuel Shaw was prominently involved in the "Shadrach" case of February 1851 when abolitionists stormed the courtroom and escorted the black man off to Cambridge, from which some of them saw him on to safety. Young Richard Henry Dana, by this time an abolitionist, had volunteered to defend Shadrach and rejoiced at his escape. Shaw's old friend Daniel Webster, the secretary of state, called the rescue "a case of treason." Then early in April the fugitive Thomas Sims was arrested in Boston and was remanded into slavery and shipped south on April 12. On the Shadrach case the very liberal, almost radical *Boston Investigator* declared that "it is better to obey even a bad law, than resist by physical force its execution." (On April 8, 1846, the *Boston Investigator* had approvingly quoted from *Typee* Melville's exposé of the way the wives of the missionaries flogged the Hawaiians hooked to their equipages—a passage soon dropped from the Revised Edition.)

In 1962 I read dozens of papers in the Boston Public Library on both the Shadrach and the Sims cases before concluding that *all* "respectable" Americans, represented by all the Whig as well as all the Democratic newspapers in Boston (and elsewhere), united in defending the Compromise of 1850, which included the Fugitive Slave Law. Only wild-eyed extremists like William Lloyd Garrison denounced it. John C. Hoadley, later Melville's brother-in-law and still later a Republican and an ardent abolitionist, rejoiced at the late December 1850 Pittsfield celebration of the passage of the Compromise (Parker, 1:801). Of course, within a few years public opinion in Massachusetts changed, as a result of efforts by what had seemed, in a twentieth-century term, the lunatic fringe, so that an illegal personal liberty law, forbidding remanding of escaped slaves, was passed in defiance of federal law. (The rapidity of that change gave me many a great moment as a teacher of Thoreau—and Paul Watson—in the next decades.) But in 1850 and 1851 it was still possible for Melville, a young man trying to make up for lost time, to absorb himself in personal problems and an almost unacknowledgeable ambition—to complete the book which he perceived, month by month, to be the most exalted literary creation ever put on paper in his imperfectly conceived and precariously Compromised country.

Between Shadrach's arrest and the remanding of Sims, Melville had bewildered his city friend Evert Duyckinck by refusing to be daguerreotyped for an engraving in *Holden's Magazine.* He had begun to think of "Fame" differently, now that he was sure that his whaling book was attaining Shakespearean grandeur. He had hired laborers to build, in the dead of winter, a piazza on the north side, below his study window, and to make other alterations to his house. He had reluctantly accepted unfavorable terms for the sale of the "indenture of lease" on the Manhattan house, which had been sitting empty. He had made a foray to Lenox and stayed overnight in order to take Hawthorne and Una home with him so he could smoke and talk books with Hawthorne in the study and the barn and make at least one mildly funny joke about the title of Thoreau's only book as "A Week on a Work-Bench in a Barn." He had escorted his invalid friend Eli Fly all the way to Springfield and returned alone. He had met his mother at the depot on her return from New York on April 9 and loaded up her vast array of purchases for the garden she would plant, supplies for papering walls and covering furniture, as well as "sugars" and a "demijohn of brandy." Then on April 11 Melville saved the Hawthornes a trip to the metropolis of Pittsfield by carrying items to them. His reward was an inscribed copy of *The House of the Seven Gables,* which he read (instead of writing protests about the plight of Thomas Sims) and which he privately praised in his letter to Hawthorne on April 16 (to be read as if published in the "*Pittsfield Secret Review*"). Besides, he had set himself to doing all the spring chores, and was finishing his book, getting rebuffed when he asked the Harpers for an advance, then seriously considering the step he took on May 1, borrowing an enormous sum of money, a friendly loan from Tertullus S. Stewart, of Lansingburgh and New York.

In the early 1990s Anna Morewood, a daughter-in-law of Melville's niece Milie, deposited at Arrowhead Augusta's letter to Allan of May 16, 1851, in which she refers to Allan's mention of a "flying visit" from Herman to New

York, preliminary to "the longer one." The important letter to Hawthorne
long dated "June 1?" was still dated so as recently as the Northwestern-
Newberry *Correspondence* volume; only later, from Augusta's letter of May
16, did I move it to early May, as I have discussed. Melville was using part
of what he borrowed to pay for the typesetting of the whaling book, we now
know. Melville kept on adding shanties of chapters and essays to the book,
and, possibly, wrote the last chapters last; in his June 29 letter to Hawthorne
the tail was "not yet cooked"—perhaps written but not yet set in type. Whatever he did, Melville did not at the last minute transform *Moby-Dick* into a
political allegory. The book was too far along when Sims was remanded for
Melville to have worked the fugitive slave crisis all through it coherently,
even if he had wanted to. "Who aint a slave?" was his question.

In 2005 Delbanco's organ of veneration forced him to resurrect Heimert's
1963 allegorizing of Ahab as Calhoun so that he could claim that "in spite
of its author's relative political aloofness, *Moby-Dick* became a book about
politics—or at least a book that lent itself to political interpretation" (165).
That is, Delbanco paid homage with a flat assertion then weaseled out of
an improbability with an "at least" construction. This is playing out private
loyalty at the expense of the reader. Delbanco went farther, taking Ahab
as "a prophetic mirror in which every generation of new readers has seen
reflected the political demagogues of its own times" then evoking "George
W. Bush's obsession with hunting down first Osama bin Laden, then Saddam Hussein" (165). Like the other New York Intellectuals, Delbanco tamed
Melville, diminishing him toward his own limitations, making political use
of him in modern issues at the cost of not seeing what roles he played in his
own nineteenth-century world.

With even less distancing of himself than from Heimert, Delbanco paid
homage to the senior New York Intellectuals, committing himself to their
practices that repeatedly minimized Melville. He followed Arvin, Updike,
and Hardwick in collapsing Melville's last years and slighting all the poetry
(even though he was now admitting the existence of the 1860 volume,
although not acknowledging its title). He also minimized Melville's experiences and his mental growth. Just as Arvin (and Updike and Hardwick)
had glossed over Melville's travels in England and the Continent in 1849
and in 1856–57, so did Delbanco. His treatment of the 1849 trip was even
stranger than any of theirs, for he referred to it in a chapter entitled "Escape
to New York" (not "Escape *from* New York"). This was peculiar in two ways.
First, it is ludicrous to skip over a major episode in Melville's life, his adventures in England and the Continent, treating the period in a chapter weirdly
mistitled. Second, my evidence showed me that in 1848 and 1849 Melville

was conspicuously *not* escaping *to* New York but already working toward a declaration of independence from his New York acquaintances. Recognizing this, in my drafts I entitled a chapter "Escape from the Cannibal Island"— that is, escape *from* New York, but changed the title before publication to "Hiding Out in the Cannibal Island" and applied it to early 1850 (when Melville's friends among the literati were sniping viciously at each other), before his eventual escape to Pittsfield. By calling his chapter "Escape to New York" Delbanco showed political solidarity with Arvin at the cost of depicting a Melville isolated from European culture, very much in line with David Reynolds's *Beneath the American Renaissance*, the classic attempt to situate great American writers in American (not British or European) literary contexts. Delbanco was minimizing Melville into a New Yorker like the Duyckincks—an intelligent enough fellow, but definitely not a New York Intellectual, and he was falsifying Melville's changing attitude toward the Manhattan literary milieu. It would not do to show a great writer turning his back on the petty sniping of the New York Intellectuals of his time.

Here is how Delbanco handled Melville's 1849 experiences abroad while what he was really doing, according to Delbanco, was "escaping" to New York (120):

> One extended absence was a four months' journey to London and the Continent in the fall and winter of 1849–50, undertaken mainly for the purpose of placing *White-Jacket* with an English publisher. He had become, by then, a city creature. In his London diary, we get a glimpse of his "vagabonding thro' the courts & lanes" (including the red-light districts), book buying, bar-hopping, theater- and museum-going, a man at ease with every aspect of urban life from the private gentlemen's clubs to the spectacle of a public execution. "The mob was brutish," he wrote in his journal about the howling crowd at a public hanging. (Charles Dickens was present, too, though the two men were unaware of each other.)

Given the lubricious pattern of references it is not surprising that Delbanco gave more space in his sentence to "including the red-light districts" than to "theater- and museum-going." That is all: nothing about Paris or Cologne, nothing about a painting or a sculpture or a curious example of architecture Melville may have seen, nothing about any geographical features that might have caught his eye, though he does at the start of the next chapter have a paragraph on galleries in which Melville might have seen nautical paintings that influenced *Moby-Dick*. All but unbelievable: because Newton Arvin loathed his weeks in London and Paris in 1929 Updike, Hardwick, and Delbanco, jumping sheeplike, deprived Melville of one of his most momentous experiences. Such are the consequences of writing biographies from biographies and other books rather than the original documents. "Escape to New York" gets the emphasis absolutely backward.

For the 1856–57 trip Delbanco focused on Hawthorne's journal more than Melville's journals, as did his predecessors among the New York Intellectuals, but he did a little more than most of them with the rest of the trip. He at least listed Constantinople and Cairo, and spent more than a full page on Palestine. Then he said: "From January till April, he [Melville] continued to write almost daily journal entries as he made his way back to England via Lebanon, Cyprus, Greece, Italy, and Switzerland. . . . One effect of the trip was to confirm Melville's sense that the Bible was a collection of improbable fictions . . . . Melville's journal is a document of spiritual exhaustion" (265–57). Of Italy Delbanco said only that Melville "savored his meals and snacks in Florence and in the charming village of Fiesole" (257). Disregarding sequence, like Hardwick, he quoted Melville while sick in Rome: "This day saw nothing, learned nothing, enjoyed nothing, but suffered something" (257). This is almost as dogmatic as Arvin's saying there were no consequences for Melville from the London trip—he was too old for anything to have affected him. In Delbanco's version, Melville "saw nothing" in Rome when in fact he had been an assiduous gallery-goer and had even sought out artists in their studios. The only art Delbanco mentions, even obliquely, is that Melville in London visited Madame Tussaud's and that in Oxford "he felt at last an 'amity of art & nature' in the college gardens" (257).

You could almost excuse Hardwick. What is wrong with writing a 150-or-so-page short semi-biography and leaving out two intense, months-long exposures to extraordinary people and great art and historical places? She needed the space for the wise words she wanted to repeat from an earlier essay and to elaborate her musings on homosexuality. But Delbanco's book was called *Melville: His World and Work*. Anyone who buys the book would expect to learn a good deal about all the known episodes of his life. Melville's experiences in the Pacific branded him, leaving him thenceforth with highly personal views of colonialism, of Christianizing native peoples around the world, of comparative religions, of cultural relativism. Berman said I did not treat this part of Melville. I did treat it, even in the first volume, although I saved my best formulation for the peroration of a long paragraph in the first chapter of the second volume, so I could apply it to the published *Moby-Dick* (2:6):

Better than any other American of his generation, Melville knew geopolitics as a humble but reflective observer and as a pondering autodidact. This man who now saw the world in terms of "linked analogies" . . . had known, as early as 1848, and believed passionately in 1850 and 1851, that literary greatness was there for the seizing as much as the Marquesas Islands and California had been just a few years earlier. American literary greatness had been a Loose-Fish that Melville in his whaling book had made a Fast-Fish forever.

Just as Melville is unthinkable without the Pacific, to any scholar he is also unthinkable without European art, architecture, geography, and history. Arvin, Updike, Hardwick, and Delbanco all denied us even a glimpse of that side of Melville, and not one of them gave us a glimpse of the Melville who set himself to be a student of art history and aesthetics (as applied to literature as well as to art), the one who combed his way through Giorgio Vasari's *Lives of the Most Eminent Painters, Sculptors, and Architects* at least twice; the careful student of John Ruskin's *Modern Painters*; the man who put himself to the trouble of recording and analyzing Francis Jeffrey's depiction of the working habits and rhetorical strategies of Victor Alfieri, whose autobiography Melville read in order to weigh his own manner of writing against the Italian's; the man who in 1862 set himself a course of reading in English and European literature and criticism in a quest for a satisfactory personal aesthetic credo. Later, Melville made a thorough study of Thomas Warton's massive *History of English Poetry*. On this side of Melville I have done some work which is distilled in *Melville: The Making of the Poet* (2008).

Delbanco's 1992 article in *American Literary History* nominally covered the 1980s, but he might later, before 2005, have looked at the 1991 *Savage Eye: Melville and the Visual Arts*, edited by Christopher Sten, particularly at Sten's "Melville and the Visual Arts: An Overview." Sten's main title for the book, *Savage Eye*, gains attention while sacrificing truth, for even if Melville was a naif early on he became a connoisseur later on, no longer a backwoods savage. Bad title aside, Sten's own chapter is a remarkably comprehensive guide to Melville's "engagement with the arts" (3). Sten celebrates the Melville who was an admirer of architectural wonders and engineering feats of the past and present, an enthusiastic appreciator of "panoramic views of buildings and monuments," an admirer of sculpture who sought out sculptors in their studios, a faithful peerer at engravings loose and in books, a conscientious gallery-goer and would-be collector who was constrained to engravings only by his lack of funds for oil paintings. This Melville has been well described by several scholars such as Christopher Sten, Dennis Berthold, Gail Coffler,

Douglas Robillard, and Robert K. Wallace, all represented in *Savage Eye*. Even better than Sten as a guide to Melville as a museum-goer in Europe and the Levant is Howard C. Horsford in the Northwestern-Newberry *Journals* (1989—but oddly ignored by Delbanco in his survey of "Melville in the '80s"). In 2005 Delbanco went out of his way to thank Robert K. Wallace for supplying him some material, but he apparently did not bother to read what Wallace had been writing about Melville and art: there is no "Wallace" in the index, no more than Horsford or Sten.

Building on the work of others as well as his own pioneering researches, Robert K. Wallace in "'Unlike Things Must Meet and Mate': Melville and the Visual Arts" (2006) sketches an important case succinctly (342):

> Melville's interest in the visual arts began in the family home in New York City in the 1820s, grew as he became a reader of illustrated books in Albany in the 1830s, diversified on his voyages to Liverpool and the South Seas in 1839 and the early 1840s, found expression in his novels of the later 1840s, reached an epiphany during his voyage to London and the Continent in 1849, and achieved artistic and psychological integration in *Moby-Dick* in 1851, at the age of thirty-two. During the remaining forty years of Melville's life . . . his interest in the visual arts continued to grow. This was particularly so after the voyage to the Mediterranean in 1856–57 that introduced him to artistic monuments ranging from the pyramids of Egypt to the minarets of Istanbul, the temples of Greece, and the paintings and sculpture of Italy. The extended epiphanies of this extensive voyage, coinciding with the winding down of his career as a writer of fiction, opened two new areas of artistic satisfaction for the rest of his life—as a writer of poetry and as a collector of art.

The substance of this paragraph was meant to be recapitulative, not original. Wallace was pulling together what others would agree with—me, Douglas Robillard, Dennis Marnon, Dennis Berthold, Christopher Sten, Scott Norsworthy, and more. He would agree if I added to the last sentence my point about Melville becoming a student of art history and of aesthetics as applied to both art and literature. But in Delbanco's index there is no Bierstadt, no Church, no Darley, no Gifford, no Doolittle, no Vedder, or for that matter no Ruskin and no Vasari.

Delbanco's Melville is pretty much a self-made writer. Yes, Delbanco mentions Shakespeare and Milton, and there is a passage on a course of reading, but the index tells the story: the focus is on Melville as home-grown, in alliance with David Reynolds's arguments in *Beneath the American Renaissance*. In Reynolds's index Spenser is not mentioned at all; Scott and Byron are mentioned once, in the same list; Shelley once; and Wordsworth, Coleridge, Keats, and Leigh Hunt, for example, are omitted altogether. Similarly, Delbanco's index shows Spenser not at all, Scott not at all, Byron not at all, Shelley once, Wordsworth twice (once in a short list), Coleridge three times (once with Wordsworth, another time in a list, once to quote "motiveless malignity"), Keats twice (once in a casual comparison and once to quote the de rigueur "negative capability"), Hunt not at all. By contrast, my index to *Melville: The Making of the Poet*, in order to accommodate the specific references to specific poems, devotes almost an entire column, in small type, to Byron.

Melville knew Spenser from adolescence long before rereading him in the mid-1850s; he knew high points of Shakespeare and Milton long before his careful reading of them in 1849; he knew Restoration and eighteenth-century poets and essayists from adolescence onward; he knew much of Wordsworth at latest from 1849. Melville's marginalia, very seldom mentioned by Delbanco, shows that he carried in his brain formidable swatches of British poetry, ready to note on a page of poetry what he recalled as an influence or a borrowing. Yes, *Redburn* owes much to Washington Irving's *Sketch-Book*, although Delbanco does not mention that debt, and yes, Melville argued with Emerson on the pages of the essays, and knew other American writers, most notably Hawthorne, and read even Whitman, by late in life, but he was the product of an education using British books in cheap American reprints, including great textbooks such as Lord Kames's *Elements of Criticism*. By midlife he was familiar with works of Dante, Goethe, and Schiller and other European writers in translation. He was so steeped in British poetry and criticism (and even fiction) that a discussion of his writing is vitiated if it ignores any of two or even three dozen British writers from Dryden to Pope to Scott to both Brownings. Some omissions, of course, are more serious than others. Omitting Byron or Scott from a book on Melville is like omitting William Faulkner from a book on Cormac McCarthy. The writer Delbanco depicts is indeed a "poor" creature, as Hardwick said in another context.

Something else is at work with Delbanco besides a need to deny Melville's achievement in poetry and to obscure his knowledge of British and Continental literature and his dedicated pursuit of knowledge about art and aesthetics. Something else is at work even besides his ignorance of basic scholarship on Melville—Delbanco's uncontrollable revulsion and terror at the very idea of scholarly research as revealed in his account of "eavesdropping" in the Houghton Library.

Delbanco's book gathered almost nothing but praise in New York City and London. In the *New York Observer* (September 26, 2005), Ted Widmer called Delbanco's the "finest biography ever written of this essential American." Jay Parini in the London *Guardian* (November 5, 2005) said: "Unlike Parker, Delbanco knows when to shut up. . . . One can hardly imagine a more artful or succinct biography." Over the years Frederick Crews as a critic had thought about as far as anyone could be expected to think who had not soiled his hands and expanded his mind in either textual or archival research, but in the *New York Review of Books* (December 1, 2005) he said: "If any one volume stands a chance of satisfying the lay public without oversimplifying the current state of knowledge, Delbanco's *Melville: His World and Work* is that book." As I showed in chapter 7, Crews disastrously took for granted that Delbanco's book must have given proportional coverage of all episodes of Melville's life and to all of his intellectual preoccupations. In the Manchester *Observer* on November 13, 2005, Aniti Sethi applauded the political relevance: "Delbanco powerfully expounds its [*Moby-Dick's*] contemporary renaissance of resonance in George W. Bush's obsession with hunting down bin Laden and Saddam Hussein." In the *New Republic* (January 23, 2006) James Wood declared, "Delbanco is a fine historian as well as a fine critic." In a blurb Ted Solotaroff of the *New American Review* offered the ultimate accolade: Delbanco "has placed himself in the company of Edmund Wilson, Alfred Kazin and Richard Chase as a trustee of our literature." No one complained that Delbanco's Melville was a sorely diminished writer. With Delbanco's book in 2005, the New York Intellectuals had triumphantly brought Melville biography down to the level of a quintessentially American mid-twentieth-century art form, the Classic Comic, decked out for the Age of Bush II.

PART III

The Biographer in the Workshop:
Demonstrations and Challenges

ONE OF MY RATIONALES for this third part, where I reconsider passages in my two-volume biography and adduce new material about Melville's life, is well stated by Paula R. Backscheider (86): "Whenever an especially original, complex argument had to be made, as about Defoe's first arrest for seditious libel, the consequences of interrupting the story of the life for an extended period had to be carefully weighed." I could not play off Melville as the idol of heterosexual males because of *Typee* and *Omoo* in the 1840s (in volume 1) against the chapter in the second volume on his revival, which gathered force in the 1880s led, very often, by homosexual males. A narrative could have been constructed on sexual responses to *Typee* and *Omoo*, since they are so near in time, but such a study could not have been part of a narrative biography. Because the "Melville Revival" was less concentrated in time, there was no hope of inserting an entire chapter on the revival into my second volume. Here I can play the two chapters against each other, even though other chapters intervene. In the biography I could not halt the story of Melville's courtship or his last meeting with Hawthorne in the Berkshires in order to muster all the evidence I had gathered, but here I can write chapters demonstrating to any young aspirant just what went into my research and my biographical decisions, much of which could not show in the published narrative. In the biography I gave attention to the lack of an international copyright law, based on my research in newspapers, magazines, and histories, but here, aided by new newspaper databases, I have been able to tell a more detailed story of the first part of Melville's career and to tell a horrific new episode in 1852, one I learned from databases while writing this book. I could not, in the biography, write a separate essay on the way Melville himself experienced and also wrote about the physiological and psychological phenomenon of morphing between scenes, events, and people—apparently dissimilar yet overlappingly identical before separating again. I mention that phenomenon early in this book and devote more space to it in the chapter on Melville's taking Hawthorne along as he wrote *Clarel*. Just as there was no way of treating copyright adequately in a chronological narrative biography, especially if I had known what I know now, there was no way of treating the consequences of Melville's borrowing $2,050 from Tertullus D. Stewart, for they were apparent every day of the next four decades of Melville's life, as I suggest in the final chapter. Here then are biographical chapters that could not fit into a chronological biography.

Seven chapters in this part are demonstrations of a biographer at work with traditional archives as well as new resources such as electronic databases. They all can, of course, be supplemented. The next to last chapter, the one on the British admirers of Melville, is different: the product of old-fashioned research under pressure of a deadline in 1988, it is offered as a challenge to scholars who will avail themselves of the resources of the Internet, particularly electronic databases, and will also search out documents in many unexplored British paper archives. Dig there, I say, and you will find a great story.

❖ Chapter 13 ❖

MELVILLE AS THE "MODERN BOCCACCIO"

The Fascinations of Fayaway

IN A LETTER TO HAWTHORNE written in early May 1851 Melville lamented what he foresaw as his fate:

> What "reputation" H. M. has is horrible. Think of it! To go down to posterity is bad enough, any way; but to go down as a "man who lived among the cannibals"! When I speak of posterity, in reference to myself, I only mean the babies who will probably be born in the moment immediately ensuing upon my giving up the ghost. I shall go down to some of them, in all likelihood. "Typee" will be given to them, perhaps, with their gingerbread.

Without seeking permission, Julian Hawthorne published this now-missing letter in his *Nathaniel Hawthorne and His Wife* (1884), where the Melville family and thousands of others saw it. Thereafter this passage was requoted so often as to become instantly recognizable. Very much as Melville predicted, in a letter printed in the *New York Times* on May 21, 1904, Charles Welsh suggested adding *Typee* and other books to a previous listing of "Books for Boys." In 1906 the Chicago Public Library included *Typee* and *Omoo* in a "Selected List of Books for Boys" of twelve to eighteen. The library of the University of California in 1911 included *Typee* in its "One Thousand Books for Children" compiled by Penrhyn W. Coussens. It may have been Melville's own well-known reference to children and their gingerbread that led editors to print *Typee* (and sometimes *Omoo*) in early twentieth-century compilations of children's books.

None of Melville's contemporaries treated *Typee* as a book for children or juveniles and none of the travelers who tried to verify his stories and none of his admirers who followed him to the South Seas treated it so. The first English edition, *Narrative of a Four Months' Residence in a Valley of the Marquesas; or, A Peep at Polynesian Life*, was published by John Murray early in 1846. Augmented before the end of the year with "The Story of Toby" (news about the fate of Melville's companion in the Marquesas) and given Melville's preferred main title, *Typee*, this book made Melville the subject of immediate intense heterosexual speculation in England, and a little later around the globe, for the book went out to the whole sphere of British influence as part of Murray's Home and Colonial Library. All through the nineteenth century the English edition, unlike the American one, which was ruthlessly expurgated a few months after publication in the so-called Revised Edition, retained Melville's exposé of the South Sea missionaries and their wives for abuse of Polynesian natives and his pro-British and anti-French depiction of the colonial powers in action in the South Seas. The Murray edition retained also Melville's depictions of other scenes that could be regarded as vulgar, including the Falstaffian pun on catastrophe, and scenes which were sexually explicit as well as frequently suggestive.

All sailors in the Pacific knew what happened when ships arrived in the Marquesas: native women swam out to offer themselves to the sailors, very much as Melville described as something that occurred on his fictional ship, the *Dolly*:

> What a sight for us bachelor sailors! how avoid so dire a temptation? For who could think of tumbling these artless creatures overboard, when they had swam miles to welcome us? . . . The 'Dolly' was fairly captured; and never I will say was vessel carried before by such a dashing and irresistible party of boarders! The ship taken, we could not do otherwise than yield ourselves prisoners, and for the whole period that she remained in the bay, the 'Dolly,' as well as her crew, were completely in the hands of the mermaids. . . . These females are passionately fond of dancing, and in the wild grace and spirit of their style excel everything that I have ever seen. The varied dances of the Marquesan girls are beautiful in the extreme, but there is an abandoned voluptuousness in their character which I dare not attempt to describe. Our ship was now wholly given up to every species of riot and debauchery. Not the feeblest barrier was interposed between the unholy passions of the crew and their unlimited gratification. The grossest licentiousness and the most shameful inebriety prevailed, with occasional and but short-lived interruptions, through the whole period of her stay. (chap. 2)

The first American edition, rushed into print to forestall piracy from any imported copies of the British edition, was only slightly censored, but it omitted the sentences at the beginning of the quotation ("What a sight for us bachelor sailors!" down through "swam miles to welcome us?") and later this sentence: "Not the feeblest barrier was interposed between the unholy passions of the crew and their unlimited gratification." Standing aloof, a good Christian bystander, Melville implied, he had witnessed the orgy on shipboard, the same sort of orgy described by earlier voyagers.

The veracity of Melville's depiction of Marquesan sexual habits was clear to reviewers familiar with missionary and naval accounts of arriving in the harbor at Nukuheva. In London *John Bull* delicately observed that a few passages were liable "to the same censure which was bestowed upon Dr. Hawkesworth for his account of Otaheite, in Cook's Voyages" (March 7, 1846). In January 1848, belatedly, the *New Haven New Englander* brushed past the *Narrative of the United States Exploring Expedition* (1844), where Captain Charles Wilkes had described women swimming out to ships, in order to quote "a single passage from Darwin's 'Voyage of a Naturalist,' the modesty of whose opinions, with the enlightened character of the observer, strongly commends it to the impartial reader."

Whatever the truth about how he had conducted himself in the face of that temptation, subsequently Melville had done what few sailors had done—he had gone ashore and lived with the sexually generous natives. In *Typee* Melville depicted sexually charged scenes he claimed to have witnessed and experienced in the interior of the island, many of them featuring the beautiful and often naked maiden Fayaway. No wonder that after a while, perhaps soon after his rescue in August 1842, if what happened was a genuine rescue, he began saying he had lived with the natives longer than he had. By the time he wrote *Typee*, three weeks (the most he could have spent with the inland Marquesans) had become four months, an increase designed, in part, to multiply not only the possibilities for anthropological research but also sexual observations and experiences. By then, also, Melville had refined his narrative strategy of depicting his role ambiguously—as prim, shocked observer and as very possibly a happy participant in sexual liberty.

In Melville's lifetime the Murray edition was the only unexpurgated edition available. Once John Wiley looked at what he had too-hastily published and began to hear from members of missionary churches such as the Presbyterians and Congregationalists, he was alarmed. His own reputation was damaged, and such criticism could affect contributions even as it blackened the fame of men devoted to bringing Christianity to the heathen. In mid-1846 Wiley demanded that Melville cut all the criticism of the missionaries and political sections as well as still more of the sexual statements and sexual implications. Anxious to keep his new career, Melville agreed to everything with only a lament about expurgation as an "odious" word to suggest how he felt (in a July 1846 letter to Evert Duyckinck). Wiley was frugal as well as pious. If someone guiding the expurgating printer fixed his eyes on a naked female breast, the printer cut it out of the plates if he conveniently could, but this was an expensive overhaul, and by no means were all of the sensuous passages removed. Thereafter this expurgated text, the one taken over by the Harpers in mid-1849, was the only edition sold in new copies in the United States.

In both the first English and first American edition Fayaway was indeed depicted as intimate with Tommo, as Melville called his alter-ego narrator. Once Tommo overcomes the taboo that keeps Fayaway from a canoe, three of them go sailing, Kory-Kory (the man Friday) rowing while Tommo and Fayaway recline "in the stern of the canoe, on the very best terms possible with one another" (chap. 18)—about as suggestive as the teasing narrator could be without breaking into obscene boasting. Then one day the narrator disembarks Kory-Kory and paddles to the windward side of the lake:

> As I turned the canoe, Fayaway, who was with me, seemed all at once to be struck with some happy idea. With a wild exclamation of delight, she disentangled from her person the ample robe of tappa which was knotted over her shoulder (for the purpose of shielding her from the sun), and spreading it out like a sail, stood erect with upraised arms in the head of the canoe. We American sailors pride ourselves upon our straight clean spars, but a prettier little mast than Fayaway made was never shipped a-board of any craft. In a moment the tappa was distended by the breeze—the long brown tresses of Fayaway streamed in the air—and the canoe glided rapidly through the water, and shot towards the shore. Seated in the stern, I directed its course with my paddle until it dashed up the soft sloping bank, and Fayaway, with a light spring, alighted on the ground; whilst Kory-Kory, who had watched our manœuvres with admiration, now clapped his hands in transport, and shouted like a madman. Many a time afterwards was this feat repeated. (chap. 18)

Melville continued with his characteristic teasing: "If the reader have not observed ere this that I was the declared admirer of Miss Fayaway, all I can say is that he is little conversant with affairs of the heart, and I certainly shall not trouble myself to enlighten him any farther." What he had just described, of course, was a beautiful South Sea girl who used her only article of clothing as a sail to catch the wind while Melville (no one reading in 1846 thought a fictional "Tommo" was the narrator) watched from the stern, occupied not with strenuous paddling but merely with directing the course of the canoe. She was entirely naked, this girl with whom the narrator was "on the very best terms possible with one another." This scene, which men and women readers remembered powerfully, was, another traveler announced a few years later, fictional, there being no lake where Melville placed one, but no one paid much attention to the wretched spoil-sport.

Most of the first reviewers of the English edition and the first American edition took a tolerant, worldly tone toward the sex in *Typee*. In the *Salem Advertiser* (March 25, 1846), Nathaniel Hawthorne wrote:

> The author's descriptions of the native girls are voluptuously colored, yet not more so than the exigencies of the subject appear to require. He has that freedom of view—it would be too harsh to call it laxity of principle—which renders him tolerant of codes of morals that may be little in accordance with our own; a spirit proper enough to a young and adventurous sailor, and which makes his book the more wholesome to our staid landsmen.

The reviewer in the London *Times* (April 6, 1846) was frankly envious:

> Mr. Melville, after all his troubles, is most agreeably surprised and sumptuously entertained. He is provided with provisions and attendants, a home is given to him, and the houris of whom he had dreamt on board the Dolly—but lovelier far than even his excited imagination had pictured them—hover around him, eager to enhance his bliss. Enviable Herman! A happier dog it is impossible to imagine than Herman in the *Typee* Valley.

Relishing the "happy dog" comparison, Melville in his next book, *Omoo* (1847), exploited its erotic implications as he regarded the husband of a beautiful white woman in Tahiti: "Mr. Bell (happy dog)" (chap. 78).

The reviewer in the London *Examiner* (March 7, 1846) took delight in Melville's assurance that the women and Fayaway in particular were less fully tattooed than the men: "These 'gentle ones' among the Typees, let us observe, are less tattooed than the lords of creation,—Herman's Armida having only 'three minute dots no bigger than pin heads' on either lip, and a tasteful 'undress epaulette' on each shoulder"—the quoted words emphasizing Melville's pun on military dress uniform. In particular he celebrated "the graceful, winning, irresistible, beauty, Fayaway" and was delighted that all "the young ladies" wore "the summer costume of Paradise." A week later the London *Critic* printed Melville's description of "the beauteous Fayaway" as being "so graphic and full of colour, that to overpass it would be unpardonable." The writer in the *New York Evening Mirror* (May 9, 1846) rhapsodized: "The inhabitants sleep sixteen hours out of the twenty-four, and feast and make love the other eight. It is difficult to realize, but it is so. It is unfair to class Mr. Melville with Sir John Mandeville, because he has had the good luck to live with Fayaway in Typee, while other mortals have grown wizen over anthracite in New York."

The London *Spectator* (February 28, 1846) praised as "too natural to be invented by the author" the section in chapter 18 which it called "The Bath of the Nymphs," a scene which "but requires us to call the savages celestials, to suppose Mr. Melville to have dropped from the clouds instead of 'bolting' from the skipper Vangs, and to fancy some Ovidian graces added to the narrative, in order to become a scene of classical mythology." Numerous reviewers in both countries chose their extracts from *Typee* passages in which Marquesan women were unclothed, quoting, as did the *Wilmington (Del.) Gazette*, descriptions of the bathing nymphs. The *New York Subterranean* chose for an extract what it called "Description of a *Typee* Beauty." The London *Atlas* (March 28, 1846) chose as a "very pretty cabinet picture" the description quoted above of Fayaway using her tappa as a windsail. Charles Fenno Hoffman quoted the same scene in the *New York Gazette and Times* (March 30, 1846), introducing it by saying: "With this wood Nymph *Fayaway* by name, and a Man Friday called *Kory-Kory*, our American Crusoe revelled in all sorts of out-of-doors felicities." Wiley & Putnam's editor, Evert Duyckinck, writing in the *New York Morning News* (March 21, 1846 and in the weekly edition on March 28), was so caught up in Melville's story that he rewrote it more sensuously, making Fayaway sleep next to Melville—a mistake with some considerable significance, given his recurrent disapproval of the man who became a friend:

> . . . the gentle Fayaway, a beautiful nymph, slept at night by his side. In the valley there was nothing to do but eat, drink and sleep. Not an inch of ground was under cultivation—there were no roads, banks, days of the week or other civilized impertinences, but baths, dances, refreshing fruits, gossiping warriors, susceptible damsels, in garlands of roses and perpetual siestas.

This was picked up blithely by the *Hill's New-Hampshire Patriot* (Concord, April 30): "And the gentle Fayaway, a beautiful nymph, slept at night by his side. In the valley there was nothing to do but eat, drink and sleep." In fact, at different times Melville says that Toby and Kory-Kory slept by Tommo's side, but the reviewers and not Melville put Fayaway beside him.

The power of Melville's eroticism emerged at times very strangely. William Oland Bourne's review of *Typee* in the *Christian Parlor Magazine* (July 1846) was meant to warn all decent people away from the book. He mocked Melville's eroticism and gluttony: "The charming Fayaway—the simple-hearted trustful maiden whom he left weeping on the lone island shore—no doubt waits his return with tearful eye: and besides this allurement, a score of Typeean gourmands are also waiting, in the shade of lofty cocoa-trees, for their noon-day meal. How can Mr. Melville resist such temptations?" Then in the midst of the stern review is interpolated an astonishing paragraph:

> Come, oh yearning soul of the angelic FAYAWAY! let me henceforth be the chosen partner of thy tabued pleasures! let me bask beneath the mild ray of thine azure eye, and repose on the swelling oval of thy graceful form! No lingering love for the griefs of a civilized home shall tempt *me* to leave thy presence! no profane desires for the pains and miseries of these pent-up cities and sin-cursed streets, and fashion-worshipping crowds, shall distract my sighing heart, and cause me to leave thee weeping amid the dashing waters of thine entrancing abode. With thee let me sport on the mirror-surface of thy sacred waters, and ramble beneath the refreshing shades of the cocoa and the palm! No recreant will I be to thy matchless love—no reckless fugitive from thy twining arms! So let me rest, and no palaces of earth, or lands of other names and customs more refined, shall tempt me to flee thy loved abodes!

Then with no transition, as if a spirit-writer had exemplified Melville's insidious power to lure decorous men into lascivious thinkings by interpolating this paragraph without its entering into his mind as he wrote it down, Bourne fell back into his condemnations.[1] Many other reviewers agreed about *Typee*, and later about *Omoo*. The reviewer of *Omoo* in the *Boston Post* (May 5) declared that the "Tahitian girls are sprites of fun, softness and beauty." Wanting more personal sexual details, the reviewer deplored Melville's strategy of describing his friend Long Ghost as having all the sexual fun: "One wishes that Mr Melville had not been quite so chary of relating his own adventures with the fair Tahitians."

For slightly belated readers, the Revised Edition left Melville and Fayaway reclining in the stern of the canoe, no longer "on the very best possible terms possible with one another," but it retained Fayaway's use of her robe as a sail. Elsewhere the Revised Edition contained scenes which readers found sexually provocative, for the expurgator left descriptions of polyandry and scenes of bathing and anointing. Melville's teasing rhetoric was part of the fabric of the book that survived, so much so that the writer in the *Boston Christian Observatory* observed in May 1847, "the attempts at wit are so constant, and so laborious, that they are far from pleasing to a chaste mind." Several commentators saw what the writer in the January 1848 *New Englander* saw—that Melville had been slyly lascivious—in his second book, *Omoo*, as well as his first: "The unfinished records of the love scenes of our modern Boccaccio, which leave the reader in a state of not very uncertain surmise as to the secret incidents, we commend to the conscience of their author." After *Omoo* appeared in 1847 but before it rounded the Horn, the *Honolulu Friend* (June 1, 1847) acknowledged that Wiley & Putnam had done well to suppress Melville's criticisms of the missionaries in the Revised Edition (discussed below), but wished the sensual passages had been as thoroughly excised:

> If the author had erased other passages, we think he would have shown good judgment and exhibited "a sober second thought." Such a course would certainly have led him to suppress some of those glaring facts respecting his habits of gross and shameless familiarity not to say unblushing licentiousness, with a tribe of debased and filthy savages of Marquesas. In chapter XIII, *revised* edition, he refers to an anointing process, performed every evening, when the girls gathered about him on the mats. "I used," he remarks, "to hail with delight the daily recurrence of this luxurious operation, in which I forgot all my troubles, and buried for the time every feeling of sorrow!" In Chapter XVII, revised edition, there is the following remark, "Bathing in the company of troops of girls formed one of my chief amusements!!"— Scores, aye, hundreds of passages might be quoted, showing that the writer sunk lower than the debased people among whom he took up his temporary abode.

This writer for the *Friend* went farther than the religious press had originally gone: after the criticism of the missionaries was removed and after the most grossly offensive passages had been trimmed it was easy to see what else should have been expurgated. Similarly, the tardy Horace Greeley in the *Tribune* for June 26, 1847, declared that *Typee* and *Omoo* were *both* "unmistakably

defective, if not positively diseased in moral tone, and will very fairly be condemned as dangerous reading for those of immature intellects and unsettled
principles. Not that you can put your finger on a passage positively offensive;
but the *tone* is bad." George Washington Peck in the *Whig Review* for July
1847 followed with an extraordinarily long analysis of the precise character of
Melville's (or, it became clear, Peck's own) sexual perversity.

The early reviewers and subsequent writers responded to Melville's depiction of sexuality in the Marquesas according to their own natures—envying
him, reproaching him, denouncing him. Reviewers had a way of projecting
onto Melville their own fantasies (Fayaway sleeping by his side) and unnam-
able perversities such as roiled in Peck. Often they were so caught up in
the story that they longed for a continuation. Melville's romantic portrait of
Fayaway provoked the reviewer in the London *Gentleman's Magazine* (July
1846) to exclaim: "Ah! thou gentle and too enchanting *Fayaway*, what has
become of thee?" That was a question that echoed through the century.
Within two years travelers to the Marquesas had begun checking up on Melville and reporting on their attempts to identify Fayaway and even Melville's
presumed offspring by her. In 1848 Lieutenant Henry A. Wise did on-the-
spot research:

> I made enquiries at Nukeheva . . . about [Melville's] former associ-
> ates, and without in the least designing to sully the romance of his
> *Typee* love—I saw a damsel named Fayaway from that valley—who
> was maid of all work to a French Commissary of the garrison—she
> was attired in a gaudy yellow gown, ironing the Crapeau's trows-
> ers—heu-nefos! heui! There was also a diminutive young "oui oui"
> tumbling about the floor—so I judged she had become childish of
> late—yet the proof is not strong, for it is quite as much in vogue in
> these heathen groups to change names . . . and it may not be the
> genuine Fayaway after all.

Unsurprisingly, the announcement of Melville's wedding provoked raucous
humor in the newspapers, some of which the family must have seen, such as
this squib in Horace Greeley's *New York Tribune* (August 7, 1847): "BREACH
OF PROMISE SUIT EXPECTED,—MR. HERMAN TYPEE OMOO MELVILLE has
recently been united in lawful wedlock to a young lady of Boston. The fair
forsaken FAYAWAY will doubtless console herself by sueing him for breach of
promise."

Everyone knew that Elizabeth Shaw was marrying the man who had
deserted Fayaway—so that in a peculiar way she stood in Fayaway's shadow,

and as the wedding day approached, out of fear of fans or what we would call groupies Elizabeth abandoned her plan of being married in the New South Church, as she wrote her stepcousin Sam Savage in September (Parker, 1:541):

> At first I had some idea of being married in church and ordinarily I think it the most appropriate place for such a solemn ceremony—but we all thought if it were to get about previously that *"Typee"* was to be seen on such a day, a great crowd might rush out of mere curiosity to see "the author" who would have no personal interest in us whatsoever, and make it very unpleasant for us both—So I determined to have it in the house, as privately as possible inviting only our relatives, and a very few intimate friends.

After Melville's marriage, an editorial in the *Honolulu Friend* made this lickerish suggestion: "We would earnestly recommend the dashing Melville, who has won such laurels among the literati of the old and new world, to take a trip with his young bride to scenes of earlier days—it may be, the gentle Fayaway would stand upon the beach to extend a cordial welcome."

By pretty clear statement and by subtler implication Melville let men, and some women, conclude that he had been happily and guiltlessly a sexual athlete despite his dubious lameness. An overexcited English visitor to New York, Ellen Oxenham, wrote Augusta in October 1846 of her hopes that "a small ray of Typeeian felicity" might fall on her from Tommo's bright eyes. Even more decorous women also saw him in terms of his sexuality, as when Catherine Dix, the wife of John A. Dix, in February 1847 was very much interested in even Melville's conventional brother Allan "from his connections with Typee, and the lovely Fayaway," and in 1850, after Sophia Hawthorne met him she wrote her sister Elizabeth Peabody (August 8, 1850) that she saw "Fayaway in his face." "Maherbal," a young man reporting to the *Windsor (Vt.) Journal* from Lenox on January 10, 1852, referred to Melville as "one whose name often lingers now in terms of adulation upon many rosy lips."[2] Melville on the *Southampton* in 1849 was amused at a young woman reading *Omoo*: "Now & then she would look up at me, as if comparing notes" (as he recorded in his October 14 journal entry). Recently women, some with rosy lips, have made it clear that being treated as a sex object or as a sex symbol can seem demeaning and even dehumanizing. When Melville lamented to Hawthorne in 1851 that he was famous as the man who had lived among the cannibals, he was being euphemistic: his reputation more specifically was that of the man who performed many sex acts with Fayaway, and had done God only knew what with other Polynesian nymphs, and had been touched very intimately by Kory-Kory.[3]

Later commentators continued to worry about Melville's abandonment of the beautiful girl. In reviewing *Moby-Dick* on November 17, 1851, the *Springfield Daily Republican* complained: "There is one painful thought connected with the tale. There is no Fayaway in it. Alas! fickle and forgetful Melville, that thou shouldst ever forget the gentle native who gave herself to thee in her far-off, savage home, and take to wantoning with 'the monsters of the bubbling deep!'" In 1856 the *New York Spirit of the Times* in a piece on "Dottings About Island Coasts" reported that one of Fayaway's friends had told the author she never "got over" Melville's desertion. Nothing changed in the next decades, except that the references to *Typee* alone became a little less frequent and people toward the end of Melville's life tended to think of him as the author of *Typee* and *Omoo*. The reviewer of Melville's lecture on Roman statuary in the *Cincinnati Enquirer* of February 3, 1858, declared: "'Fayaway' is the most attractive and best-known character Mr. M. has drawn, and there are few who do not have sentimental recollections of the fair, lithe, graceful Indian girl, with all the instinctive delicacy and refinement and cha[r]mfulness, which the highest circles of society often fail to exhibit."

Throughout Melville's lifetime his most famous character was not Ahab or the White Whale—it was the beautiful, delicately tattooed Marquesan maiden Fayaway, and it was his depiction of his behavior with her (particularly in the robe-as-windsail scene) that made him a heterosexual sex symbol to many of his contemporaries. Reviewers gushed over her, poets (including Thoreau's friend Ellery Channing) celebrated her in verse, Bostonians compared her favorably to Elizabeth Shaw, travelers to the Marquesas tried to identify her, and artists depicted her. Shipowners named vessels for her, including a schooner out of Monterey, California, which was in the waters nearby when Melville sailed into San Francisco in 1860. Fayaway entered British racing history in a succession of avatars throughout Melville's lifetime. The Gale database of British newspapers is a good source, now, for the racing fillies. Perhaps having learned of the use of the name during one of her trips to England, Melville's neighbor Sarah Morewood named a fine filly Fayaway in 1860.

Throughout Melville's lifetime *Typee* was his most famous book just as his most famous character was Fayaway. From his description she was visualized by readers as naked. The artist John La Farge hoped, he said in 1890 (*Log*, 825), to see "a Fayaway sail her boat" in one or another of the South Sea islands, and he illustrated that scene from *Typee* with a girl standing naked in the prow of a canoe catching the wind with her tappa robe spread out as a sail. Despite many excisions, it remained erotic in ways that pleasantly aroused many male readers and that incited other male readers into twisted, pathological analyses of the way Melville's sexual suggestiveness had belatedly insinuated itself into their previously pure minds. Modern readers who come first to *Moby-Dick* and *Billy Budd, Sailor,* or perhaps to "Bartleby the Scrivener" and "Benito Cereno," find it very hard to understand that some of Melville's contemporaries could think of Melville the way we think of priapic young male movie stars.

While reading the contemporary reviews and transcribing documents in the Augusta Papers I realized that *Typee* had made Melville the closest we had to an American Byron, the first American literary sex symbol. I boldly said so in a talk at Buffalo in 1992, converting the host of the meeting, Kenneth Dauber, who confessed he had been skeptical. I said so again in the first volume of my biography. One critic, Andrew Delbanco, early in 1997 was disdainful, as I mention elsewhere (19):

> When Herman reaches adulthood, the sex theme takes charge, and we get a portrait of a randy young man strutting through what Frederick Crews has called "the age of the draped piano leg." Nicknamed "Typee" by friends, Melville, according to Parker, attracted the nineteenth-century equivalent of a rock star's groupies, and was "the first American author to become a sex symbol." He was "a man whose experiences fueled diverse sexual fantasies of many men and some women" (a fact Parker infers chiefly from a phrase in one woman's fan letter—"Typee, you dear creature, I want to see you so amazingly"); and so when Sophia Hawthorne, wife of Melville's great contemporary, remarked upon first meeting him in 1850, that "she saw Fayaway in his face," Parker decides that what she chiefly saw was "a man unlike her husband, a man with a history of sexual conquests."

Delbanco's vulgar tone was all wrong for the context, and he revealed a dubious understanding of Victorian mores. Why cite Crews? This recourse to a critic as authority looks forward to Delbanco's 2005 book, which was written from other books rather than from primary documents. In any case, what Delbanco ineptly cited from Crews seems to have been a joke in the nineteenth century, according to the exposé by Matthew Sweet in his 2001 *Inventing the Victorians,* not an actual practice among the excessively delicate populace. I had, of course, drawn my conclusion from many diverse pieces of evidence, not from "a phrase in one woman's fan letter." And nothing could be farther from the truth than the assertion that I had depicted Herman Melville in his late twenties as a randy, strutting hunk. Melville teasingly wrote the scenes on which readers made their conclusions, but as far as I know in person he made no effort to live up to the sexual imaginings of his readers, and I never depicted him as randy and strutting.

Weirdly, in his 2005 biography (64) Delbanco describes Melville as "the randy young globe-trotter up in the attic reliving his escapades" (though why he thought Melville would have written in the attic of the Lansingburgh house is beyond me, and I have been up there to check out that low dark space). In 1997 when I read Delbanco's review I felt I had wandered into someone else's pornographic fantasy. Having reproached me in 1997 for calling Melville our first literary sex symbol and paying too much attention to one letter, Delbanco in 2005 says: "With its lubricious accounts of oil rubs and orgies, *Typee* gave its author a measure of fame and even attracted to him the nineteenth-century equivalent of a rock star's groupies: 'You dear creature,' one woman beseeched him in a feverish fan letter, 'I want to see you so amazingly'" (71). Is there a technical term in rhetoric, poetics, or jurisprudence for what Delbanco has achieved here in the reuse of material, mine and his?

Delbanco's accusation unfairly blackened his readers' view of me. All my life, because of my Southern upbringing, I have avoided randy strutting men, young or older. While Norman Mailer might display himself as randy and strutting, when I probed his treatment of male sexuality in *An American Dream* I found a fearful honest complexity at work in the original magazine version. Never telling sexual jokes, I tend to let deadpan humor carry my meaning, as Phoebe-Lou Adams pointed out in her January 1997 *Atlantic* review of my first volume. Such humor is regularly misunderstood by critics (particularly, I notice, by practitioners of "queer theory," who think Eve Kosofsky Sedgwick is the ultimate if not sole sexual authority), and certainly lost on Delbanco. It was also lost on Philip Weiss in the June 18, 2002, *New York Observer*: "Hershel Parker . . . speculates that Melville's sexual adventures may have occurred at sea and in foreign ports, then adds, 'Surely he had done nothing reprehensible in the United States.'" Weiss added solemnly, "Well, no one can be sure of such a thing." Melville himself was the master of the subtle throwaway comment, such as the comparison in *White-Jacket* of the Portuguese sailors to "young bridegrooms, three months after marriage, completely satisfied with their bargains, after testing them." That was young and male and joyous, akin to G. W. Harris's depiction of Wat Mastin, and I was trying to be at least as delicate, although, alluding to *Omoo* and a review of *Typee*, I permitted myself this sentence on Herman during his engagement which I quote in another chapter: "Meanwhile, his knife in readiness and his caster slung, there were hours when it was impossible to imagine a happier dog than Herman in the Hudson Valley" (1:459).

By now my realization that Melville was the first American literary sex symbol has made its way into academic criticism and into general guidebooks. The view entered the journal *American Literature* (September 2000) in Maurice S. Lee's "Melville's Subversive Political Philosophy: 'Benito Cereno' and the Fate of Speech": "*Typee* . . . marked him for intensified scrutiny when he, in the words of Hershel Parker, became a 'literary sex symbol'" (512; reiterated in Lee's 2005 *Slavery, Philosophy, and American Literature, 1830–1860*, 157). Not mentioning me, Nick Selby in *Herman Melville, "Moby-Dick"* (1999) said flatly of Melville: "As a young man, a sailor turned author of romantic sea-faring fictions, he was a literary sex-symbol" (14). In *A Routledge Literary Sourcebook on Herman Melville's "Moby-Dick"* (2003) Michael J. Davey, also without mentioning me, observed that Melville's essay on Hawthorne's *Mosses* "sheds much light on how Melville's conception of his art had evolved since the heady days of *Typee* and his initial fame as a literary sex symbol" (1). Similarly, Raychel Haugrud Reiff in *Herman Melville: "Moby-Dick" and Other Works* (2008) said casually that *Typee* "pushed Melville into the national spotlight as a sex symbol" (15). When you stop being acknowledged for your biographical formulation, you have won your point. Melville as literary sex symbol is part of popular culture, something everyone has always taken for granted.

❧ Chapter 14 ❧

MELVILLE'S COURTSHIP OF ELIZABETH SHAW

IN THE DECADES AFTER the late 1940s, when New Criticism drove out scholarship, very few professors of literature spent many hours toiling in the archives. Even now, professors of American literature (a field which scarcely existed in the late 1940s, then gained ground within departments only slowly), critics usually, not scholars, tend to share a strange skepticism about documentary evidence. Having never worked in the archives, their idea of being scholarly means reading literary criticism by other professors, and they don't really believe anyone can find a new document that significantly changes what was known about an episode in Melville's life, much less one that reveals a wholly new episode. Yet, very oddly, they may want a biographer to produce an affidavit for even the most minute fresh assertion. Nowadays people who know the least about research are apt to set the highest standards for people who are doing the work of retrieving archival information.

Here I look at the documentary evidence for what led up to the so-far undisputed fact of Herman Melville's marriage to Elizabeth Shaw on August 4, 1847. How the couple came to marry, as told by the groom's biographers, contains some curious notions of mid-nineteenth-century courtship and matrimony. Raymond Weaver in 1921 brought Melville back from the Pacific to Boston, accurately enough, but did not mention Elizabeth Shaw at that point. Instead, he was deflected into a fantasy of dendrological, olfactible, and vocal stasis: "The identical trees in the Boston Common blotted out the same patterns against the New England stars; none of the streets had swerved from off their prim and angular respectability. His mother he found living in Lansingburg, just out from Albany, N. Y. There was the same starched calico smell to his sister's dresses, the same clang-tint to his mother's voice" (521). In Weaver's book, Herman had arrived in Boston and headed straight for Lansingburg (without the final *h*) to sniff at a sister's dresses (Helen's? Augusta's? not young Fanny's or Kate's?) and listen to his mother's "clang-tint" voice. Then Weaver lurched forward (257): "Melville had dedi-cated *Typee* to Chief Justice Lemuel Shaw of Massachusetts. The Shaws and the Melvilles were friends of years' standing. . . . Shaw had been engaged to Melville's aunt, Nancy." On the next page Weaver quoted from Melville's March 19, 1846, letter to Shaw from "Lansingburg": "Remember me most warmly to Mrs. Shaw & Miss Elizabeth, and to all your family, & tell them I shall not soon forget that agreeable visit to Boston." Weaver then elaborated: "The Miss Elizabeth of the letter, the only daughter of Chief Justice Shaw, and Melville were married on August 4, 1847."

Melville's father, Allan Melvill, had gone into marriage with eyes open, Weaver was sure: "On the evidence of surviving records, Melville's father had resigned himself to the institution of marriage as to one of the established con-veniences of Christendom. Allan was a practical man, and he soberly saw that he gained more than he lost by generously sharing his bed and the fireside zone with a competent accessory to his domestic comforts" (258–59). Weaver decided that Herman Melville, in his own approach to marriage, "showed none of the prosaic circumspection of his father." No: "From his idealisation of the proud cold purity of Maria, Melville had built up a haloed image of the wonder and mystery of sanctified womanhood: without blemish, unclouded, snow-white, terrible, yet serene" (259). Weaver evoked the "Blessed Mother," the "Virgin Mother of the Son of God," and Fayaway (from *Typee*) before deciding that "Melville transferred his idealisation of his mother" to Eliza-beth Shaw (260). Far from resigning "himself to the institution of marriage" as an established convenience of Christendom, Herman had been extrava-gantly idealistic, Weaver assumed, quoting words from *Pierre*: "During his courtship of Elizabeth Shaw, it seems that 'the audacious immortalities of divinest love'" were in Melville (260). He concluded: "None of Melville's letters of courtship survive. There are more direct evidences of the fruits of his love, than of its early bloom" (260)—presumably an allusion to the subse-quent procreation of Malcolm, Stanwix, Elizabeth, and Frances.

In 1929 Lewis Mumford landed Melville at Boston in 1844 and got him rapidly to New York City, where he found that his family "was in the process of growth and change" (66)—family perhaps meaning the three brothers, although Tom had not lived in New York since 1830. Still vaguely, Mum-ford sent Gansevoort off to England before Herman started writing a book and had Herman visiting relatives and Boston connections before starting to write: "After a little visiting among his relatives and with Chief Justice Lemuel Shaw of Massachusetts, an old friend of the family with a marriage-able daughter, Melville settled down for a while in Lansingburgh: he had decided to write an account of his adventures" (67). (The writing had in fact taken place in New York and Lansingburgh in 1844–45, Gansevoort had carried the manuscript of Herman's book to England in 1845, and settling down with Elizabeth Shaw did not occur until after their marriage in 1847.) Suddenly, in Mumford, Melville "was twenty-eight years old" and "the friendship or the affection between him and Judge Shaw's daughter, Elizabeth, deepened, and in August, 1847, they were married" (86). Lacking evidence which the Massachusetts Historical Society could have provided, Mumford could "only dimly speculate upon what manner of girl Elizabeth Shaw was," but he was sure of Melville's feelings:

> Melville probably worshipped Elizabeth at first, and idolized her beyond all reason; for he loved romantically, and romantic courtship is a heightened and extravagant season even for men of less imagination and hot impulse than Melville. He who wishes to keep that original and etherealized image of his lady should run away from her: when he breaks it, he will feel, Melville later declared, like Pluto snatching his Proserpine, and once the image is broken every fragment will be a reproach. It is the romanticized Circe, and not her victim, who under the spell of marriage turns into an animal . . . . (86–87)

After "an arduous honeymoon," Mumford explained blandly, "and a brief sojourn with Herman's mother at Lansingburgh, they settled down at 103 Fourth Avenue, New York, in company with Melville's brother Allan and a swarm of sisters," four constituting a sororal swarm (87).

In 1950 Newton Arvin frankly confessed that Melville's "marriage was a step not wholly easy to account for or understand" (125), since it had followed after no courtship:

> After apparently living for the better part of three years at home in Lansingburgh, Melville, in the summer of 1847, had married and removed to New York. . . . Melville's interest in Elizabeth Shaw may well have been deepened by his need of Judge Shaw's paternal presence. Herman and Lizzie had doubtless been friends from childhood, and there was something almost cousinly in the marriage, something extremely expressive of Melville's emotional dependence on his near relations, his deep-seated diffidence toward outsiders, especially of the other sex.

In fact, Elizabeth knew members of the Boston Melvill family. On August 25, 1830, the day his nomination to be chief justice was announced in the newspapers, Shaw wrote to his wife: "We are all well. My mother, Oakes Elizabeth & self all dined at Mr. Melvill's today." That is, Elizabeth, born in 1823, all her life would have remembered old Major Melvill; when she solicited a copy of the poem about the old major from the very aged Oliver Wendell Holmes after her husband's death, she remembered the "Last Leaf" himself and surely had known the poem from childhood. She knew some of the Melvill sisters very well, especially Melville's aunt Lucy Clark, for she had passed a long summer visit in 1839 with her in Hallowell, Maine, after Lucy's second marriage, to Amos Nourse. In Herman's absence Elizabeth had become an intimate friend of his sister Helen and had visited Lansingburgh, but the notion of Herman and Lizzie as childhood friends (playmates?) is Arvin's invention. His further fantasy of "cousinly" feelings has at least the justification that Melville knew that Shaw might have become his uncle. Cousinly for Arvin was not intimate enough to explain the marriage. He decided that cousinly feelings had grown even more intimate: "For Melville himself, there was doubtless, in his feeling for Lizzie, a very large strain of the brotherly, even of the filial" (127). There was, of course, no component of normal heterosexual arousal toward Lizzie in "Melville himself."

Leon Howard in 1951 had the advantage of working with Jay Leyda's files of The Melville Log and the disadvantage of not performing archival research himself, any more than the previous biographers had done. Howard explained that on the arrival of the United States in Boston, Herman was among the members of the crew whose term of enlistment was not up and were required to wait several days for the secretary of the navy to authorize their discharge. Knowing from the Log that a first cousin of Melville's was in the Navy Yard, and guided by Leyda's assumption that an unsigned note the family saved ("Herman has arrived & you may expect him every moment") was likely in this cousin's hand, Howard stated this as fact: "Lieutenant Guert Gansevoort, however, was stationed on the receiving ship Ohio while recovering from the strain of his court-martial for the hanging of Philip Spencer" (88). Here "while recovering" was Howard's somewhat awkward way of working in an informative reference to the notorious Somers case of alleged mutiny and hangings, of almost two years earlier, at the cost of prolonging Gansevoort's recuperation. The "Melville family," Howard went on, "was able to get word that Herman had arrived and might be expected home at any moment." The phrasing "was able to get word" allowed Howard to allude to the word "moment" which survived in the mysterious note and yet not to claim outright that the handwriting on the note was Guert's (a look at his letters in the New York Public Library would have proved it wasn't). Trying to make normal sense of a baffling scrap of information, Howard missent

Melville directly to "his home in the familiar village of Lansingburgh." (Later a remarkably similar unsigned note surfaced in the Augusta Papers, in Allan's hand, dated New York, not Boston, "Monday Evening October 21, 1844": "Herman has arrived & you may expect him every hour after tomorrow.")

It was in the middle of the night on April 5, 1990, while teasing out a minute chronology of Herman's whereabouts in October 1844, that I recognized the handwriting on the unsigned note. After laughing at myself and slapping my head—what fools we mortals be!—I slid a note under the door of my houseguest, Harrison Hayford, along with a copy of a page from a contemporary document, the scraps from the first draft of *Typee* with Xs drawn in two strokes, like a backwards small *c* and then a regular small *c*, touching, and small *r*'s with a looped ascender, and with other words used in the note circled in the draft pages. Unmistakably the note Leon Howard thought was Guert's was in Herman's handwriting and the two notes together revealed the story of a young man's homecoming to Lansingburgh, a dramatic surprise for Maria Melville. We had not recognized the handwriting as Melville's because we had nothing in his hand from the previous years and very little in the next year, and the 1845 and 1846 documents were not available in handy facsimile. If we had been shrewder and cleverer, we could have looked at the draft leaf from *Typee* which we had photographically reproduced in the Northwestern-Newberry Edition in 1968 (presumably, it now appears, a gift from Augusta to her younger cousin Catherine Gansevoort Lansing). It was my familiarity with the fifteen additional leaves of the first draft of *Typee* preserved in the Augusta Papers that allowed me, on returning to the October 1844 handwriting, to see at once, at last, that no one else in the family did an *x* with two strokes the way Herman did and no one else looped his *r* so distinctively.

How this evidence emerged is curious and more than a little dismaying. Dr. Henry A. Murray was fixated on Guert as the writer of the shorter note, but, like Leyda, had not compared the handwriting to that of Guert's letters in the New York Public Library. In Leyda's time, carrying around a photocopied sample of cousins' handwriting or even the handwriting of brothers and sisters was not feasible. But it was not just ignorance of the handwriting that allowed Dr. Murray to amuse himself and tantalize Harrison Hayford and Wilson Heflin for years. It was also the failure to pay attention to Allan's note after it surfaced in the Augusta Papers. Before recognizing Herman's hand I had created a more minutely detailed sequence of Herman's and Gansevoort's movements than Leyda had in the *Log* (determined to see where they met each other after Herman's return from the Pacific) so I was focused on Herman's need to keep secret his return to the country. Just the way critics fixate on passages of a text without asking how the text reached the state they are holding, scholars fixate on documents without imagining them in human contexts. As a teenaged railroad agent-telegrapher I had deadheaded across country and appeared before my mother without warning, after not seeing her for a year or two. Herman, I realized, had been more considerate of his mother: he had worked out an early warning system, planning to pass Allan's note on to one or more of the sisters to show his mother, then to have his own note passed to her. She, of course, knew his handwriting, most recently, it seems, from a letter from Hawaii, and she would have stormed toward the door to find him. The notes got separated, but they were both preserved because they reminded the archivists Allan and Augusta of one of the happiest days in the lives of the Melvilles. Maybe it is not imagination we need so much as experience, to allow us to make sense of how families behave and how boyish a young man of twenty-five can be.

Howard did not speculate about what Herman had done in Boston other than to contact Guert and "probably" (93) see his uncle, Captain John D'Wolf, the great traveler across Siberia, in Dorchester. Howard knew that in Melville's absence his sister Helen "had become intimate with the Shaws in Boston" and that she was greatly admired by "the judge's only daughter, Elizabeth, who had begun to visit regularly in the Melville household in Lansingburgh," although he could not define "regularly" (89). Howard did not speculate about Herman's seeing the Shaws and did not mention Herman's Boston aunts. (He did not know about their estrangement from Maria and her children after the death of her father-in-law in 1832.) Howard then mistakenly had Melville living in New York City in February 1846 and had him taking a vacation from New York late in the month and going to Lansingburgh, "vacation" being a peculiar word to use of an unemployed man (97). He declared that Melville "had prolonged his vacation" by spending eight days in March 1846 with the Shaws in Boston (98):

> Helen was visiting and . . . Herman could appear, for the first time since his childhood days, with an air of assurance. As an author who was soon to become a public figure, he had acknowledged, both at home and abroad, his family's indebtedness to Judge Shaw by dedicating the book to his brother's most consistent benefactor; and his new self-confidence was a revelation both to the judge and to his daughter, Elizabeth, who was then twenty-three and had probably been curious for several years about Helen's wandering brother.

Howard's "probably" covers ignorance: Elizabeth had not only been curious; she had had her curiosity satisfied, the Augusta Papers show: before Herman arrived in Boston in 1844 she had read his letter or letters from Hawaii, so she knew already of his adventures with the Typees as well as much more—*more than we know*. This needs to be emphasized: in early October 1844 Lizzie knew many details about Herman's adventures that no scholar has ever known. Only if Herman's letters from the Atlantic and Pacific show up will we know what she knew, and perhaps not even then, for she may have seen reports in newspapers that we know nothing about. Howard says that "the arrival of Elizabeth Shaw on the last day of August [1846] for a two-months' visit enlivened the [Lansingburgh] household and gave Herman someone new to impress" (100). In Howard, Herman leaves in late November 1846 "for a ten-day visit with the Shaws," and "if he did not become formally engaged to her during this [November–December 1846] visit his intentions were almost certainly known by the time of his next trip to Boston in early March [1847]" (103). Howard assumed that Herman and Allan together would be able to buy a house in New York City "large enough for themselves and their brides and for their mother and four sisters" (104). Howard concluded: "The young author had definite plans, if not a regular job, when he arrived in Boston on the first of June [1847] to settle the date of his wedding" (104).

In 1975 Edwin Haviland Miller concentrated his discussion in a few sentences:

> In 1846 Herman began to court Elizabeth Knapp Shaw, who was a close friend of his sister Helen Maria. Elizabeth was three years younger than Herman. . . . The mother did not survive the birth of her child, whom the Judge baptized with the mother's name. With the best of intentions Shaw paid what he no doubt considered a tribute to his wife's memory, but his legal mind did not perceive the burden of guilt that he was placing upon the child. Fortunately, when she was five years old her father married Hope Savage, who proved to be an unusually generous stepmother. The courtship continued for approximately eighteen months. Elizabeth spent about two months in Lansingburgh in the fall of 1846, and in March 1847 Herman was in Boston for a week or two. On June 1 [1847] . . . he returned to Boston once again, this time to propose. (138)

Miller had an idea of Shaw's munificence: Herman and Allan "were able to purchase the house after Judge Shaw advanced $2,000."

For my account I had, like Howard and Miller, *The Melville Log* (with its documents from sources in the United States and around the world), but I also had many previously unused documents I had transcribed from manuscripts in the Berkshire Athenaeum, the Massachusetts Historical Society, and the New York Public Library (particularly from the Augusta Papers). I had William H. Gilman's dissertation notes from many libraries and, most helpfully, his notes from the New York City Book of Conveyances on the indenture of lease (a twenty-year lease) for the Fourth Avenue house. From the New-York Historical Society I had Charlotte Hoadley's 1944 letter about the Harpers' rejection of *Typee*. I had taken notes on many newspaper articles in the Boston Public Library, the New York Public Library Annex, and elsewhere. I had Joyce Deveau Kennedy and Frederick J. Kennedy's discoveries in the Savage papers (that is, papers of the family of Lemuel Shaw's second wife, Hope Savage Shaw). I had, also, the October 16, 1844, letter of Allan Melville's (discussed in chap. 7) that had once been in the files of his Morewood granddaughters, a reply to a letter Herman had written from Boston.[1]

From old and new documents I had worked out a detailed new chronology of Herman's movements between his arrival in Boston and his reaching New York and Lansingburgh, and I had filled in the gaps with my best speculations, based primarily on the new documents.[2] I knew far more than anyone else, but despite my new array of evidence the critic Andrew Delbanco in the *New York Review of Books* (May 15, 1997) denounced my account of the courtship (19):

> When the story reaches Melville's return to Boston harbor, Parker's engine of invention remains at full throttle. Finding no contemporary record of what Melville did during his first days in town, he presumes that "the only reasonable thing for Herman to do" was to visit Judge Lemuel Shaw. . . . Herman, Parker guesses, "may have been invited to stay at the Shaws'," and the guess turns quickly into an assertion: "In exchange for her stories of his family, Herman told some of his wondrous adventures."

Delbanco showed a pattern of condemning my cake as unfit for rational consumption, then freeze-drying it and serving up pieces of it himself later, as in his 2005 observation that in Boston on his return from the Pacific Melville "may have spent a few days . . . and possibly a few nights lodging at the home of Judge Lemuel Shaw, Chief Justice of the Supreme Judicial Court of Massachusetts" (62).

How much of what I wrote was invention? My engine of researching, ordering, and interpreting had been running full throttle, I would have thought, rather than my engine of invention. I remember thinking of throwing in "perhaps" and "it is likely" a few times, or phrasing the story more this way: "If they met and she told him stories of his family, did he tell her some of his wondrous adventures?" I decided that the evidence was strong enough to support my telling the Boston meeting as fact. You decide, after reading this chapter. After all the to-do, I still am chary of perhapses for this story.

What I Knew About Melville's Thoughts and Actions in Boston in October 1844

I knew he read newspapers. Like anyone arriving home after a long time away, Melville on his arrival in Boston scanned as many newspapers as he could lay hand on, which meant, to start with, a selection from the dozen or so local daily papers. Before and after his discharge, Herman caught up on international, national, and local news. He put on record in the "Appendix" to *Typee* just where he discovered how the American press had purveyed a piece of history that he himself had witnessed, Lord George Paulet's brief seizure of Hawaii for Great Britain in February 1843 and Rear-Admiral Richard Thomas's ending the occupation on July 31, 1843: "[G]reat was the author's astonishment on his arrival at Boston, in the autumn of 1844, to read the distorted accounts and fabrications which had produced in the United States so violent an outbreak of indignation against the English." You could hardly pick up a paper in October 1844 without seeing the name of Gansevoort Melville, the great Democratic orator, for reports were coming in daily of his campaigning for Polk and Dallas in Ohio and then in western New York. The brother who had seen him off on his voyage to the Pacific was a famous man, extolled by the Democrats and reviled by the Whigs. After Herman had looked at current or recent papers that came to hand, he had reason to do more research into his brother's role in the political history of the late spring. It looks to me as if he may have dropped into a reading room ashore and turned through back files of papers, for when he wrote Allan from Boston he mentioned Gansevoort's great June 4 triumph, not something he might normally have found in the papers brought on board for the crew to peruse. We are sure he read this because Allan in his October 16 reply wrote that Gansevoort's "first appearance since the nomination of M^r. Polk was at the ratification meeting to which you refer as having seen an a/c [account]." Furthermore, on October 12 Gansevoort Melville asked William E. Cramer to send Shaw a copy of the *Albany Argus* welcoming him home to the Empire State, so at least one issue of the familiar hometown newspaper was probably on a table at the Shaw house on Mount Vernon Street.

The ship on which Melville arrived, the *United States,* itself was written up in the Boston papers because the purser's slave, Robert T. Lucas, had asked for freedom on the basis of his having been carried into a free state.[3] On October 11, before Herman was discharged, Chief Justice Shaw ruled on the case, which was reported as the "Discharge of a Slave from service on Board an U. States vessel." The sailors on board witnessed the calm way the purser, a gentlemanly Virginian, accepted the decision. For some hours Herman, in sight of the State House, was still living under the Articles of War, while the former slave was a free man in Massachusetts. The astounding fact was that two newsmakers were his brother and a close friend of his father's, the man who would have married his aunt, Nancy Melvill, had she lived. Almost equally astounding was his having been an eyewitness to history in the Hawaiian Islands, so that now he was in a position to testify in elaborate and lively detail about what had occurred there in 1843.

I knew that Melville intended to surprise his mother, and did surprise her. In his now lost letter to Allan written October 13 (if he dated it correctly) and mailed three days later, he must have told Allan not to tell their mother, because in his reply Allan emphasized that he would not write to her until he heard further from Herman. Herman did in fact prevent anyone from writing to tell his mother he had returned from the Pacific. Whatever specific plan he had in mind may have been modified when he and Allan conferred in New York, but the upshot was that he simply appeared at the door of the house in Lansingburgh heralded by no formal letter at all. Watching to catch the eye of one of the sisters, as I speculate, he would first have passed in the note in Allan's hand, and then after whatever dramatic delay he would pass in the note in his own hand, for it was, unmistakably, his hand that Leyda had thought might be Guert's. Was that not a great surprise? And had he disregarded the instructions of Gansevoort, hastily sent to Allan, that he shave his nautical beard and make himself presentable before showing himself to his mother?

   This may be hard to understand for critics who have grown up with a BlackBerry attached to one ear and a hand curved around a Kindle or iPad, even harder for younger people with implanted microchips giving their GPS coordinates, but there really was a time when young men simply showed up unannounced having come hundreds or thousands of miles, as Herman showed up in Galena in 1840, expecting to rise in the world with the help of his uncle, Thomas Melvill. Many tables were big enough so that you could pull up one more chair than there had been the previous meal and blend in with your brothers and see how long it would take your mother to realize there was one more diner at the table than at the previous meal. Few mothers ever died of shock in such situations, and, for decorous young men who had been away on a long adventure, happily surprising your mother might rank high with your lifetime list of dramatic actions. The family kept the notes, two pieces of paper with similar wording, preserved as a happy record of Herman's dramatic homecoming. As I said, perhaps many years later Augusta gave Kate Gansevoort, Uncle Peter's daughter, the note that was in her papers when they went to the New York Public Library.

I knew that since Herman had told Allan not to tell their mother, he must also have told anyone he met in Boston not to write to Lansingburgh. He was at a disadvantage because he did not know when the authority to discharge him would arrive from Washington. He had to keep everyone from writing during an indefinite period. Now, who in Boston was likely to have learned that he had returned on the *United States* and to have written his mother announcing that remarkable fact? First, Guert Gansevoort, Melville's first cousin.

I knew that Melville had to ask Guert not to write his aunt Maria in Lansingburgh or his own mother in Watertown (across the Hudson). Every sailor on the *United States* knew the name Guert Gansevoort because of the tragic, mysterious story of the "mutiny" on the *Somers* late in 1842. Not discharged but not held incommunicado below decks, Melville probably learned right away that his cousin Guert was there in the Navy Yard, on the receiving ship *Ohio.* Some people would have shunned him, but Herman would have regarded him with sympathy and likely with some sense of awe, as he tended to regard survivors of great human dramas. I had to assume that Herman acted naturally, and a cousin seeking out another cousin was only acting naturally. Before he left Boston Herman certainly knew where Guert was: Allan told him so. My assumption is that Melville saw Guert, probably more than once, learned a good deal from him about Helen's visits to Boston and Guert's visits to Lansingburgh, talked Pacific adventures with him even if they avoided much talk of the *Somers,* and swore him to secrecy so he could surprise his mother.

Guert would have had the best possible news—that Maria Gansevoort Melville and her other children were all alive and in generally good health. He may have known that Allan was not robust, but he knew that Gansevoort, physically powerful but vulnerable, had not been bedridden for any long period during Herman's absence. Guert had a budget overflowing with stories, since he had visited, more than once, the house in Lansingburgh in Herman's absence. On one particular visit, in 1841, everyone had been struck by Guert's resemblance to Herman. Then Augusta wrote to Allan (in a letter now in the Berkshire Athenaeum): "he looks very much like Herman, we all noticed it." At that time Guert himself had expressed his own concern, born of long nautical experience ("oh how he blames Herman for going to sea"). Guert must have heard from Helen and perhaps Elizabeth also that Gansevoort Melville had escorted Helen to Lenox, Massachusetts, in September 1841 to see her former teacher, Elizabeth Sedgwick, whose husband was the clerk at the court (headed by Shaw) which met there in that month. There Gansevoort and Helen had encountered Judge Shaw, his wife, Hope, and his daughter, Elizabeth (as I knew from the Augusta Papers). Helen had written Augusta about how amazed she had been at the interest the Shaws manifested toward her:

> I could scarcely credit that persons comparatively strangers should take such a warm interest in Gan & myself. Gan staid at the Hotel, but spent all his evenings with us, and made all together the most delightful coterie, what with the judges, judges ladies, Miss S. & Mr [Henry] Inman the portrait painter, who was on a professional visit there. Mrs Shaw insists upon my making her a long visit this winter in Boston; both herself & husband gave me the most pressing & earnest invitations, & Mama says I may go, if there is any way for me to reach there short of Gan's taking me, which of course should not be thought of.

As Guert knew, this fortunate, and possibly even fortuitous encounter in Lenox (I credit Gansevoort with a high degree of calculating forethought) had brought Helen into the same household with "Miss S.," Elizabeth Shaw, with the result that the two young women (for all the five years' difference in their ages) had spent many months of the last years in the same household, either in Boston or Lansingburgh.

From very early Guert was a party to this new intimacy of the young women, for a letter in the Augusta Papers (January 24, 1842) shows that Helen was regarding Guert as her potential escort back to Lansingburgh. Leon Howard could not have known of the Lenox meeting (whether it was Gansevoort's ambush or a simple coincidence), but he knew from the *Log* that Helen had spent many months visiting Chief Justice Lemuel Shaw's daughter, Elizabeth, beginning late in 1841, and that Elizabeth had visited in Lansingburgh and wrote regularly to Helen. Howard did not know what I knew from a letter in the Augusta Papers—that in November 1843, eleven months before Herman returned (a year after the tragic events on the *Somers*), Guert gallantly had dispatched a longboat to carry Helen with her host, Judge Lemuel Shaw, and his daughter, Elizabeth, for a tour of the *Ohio*. Helen and Elizabeth had been entertained by Helen's Gansevoort cousin there in the Navy Yard, where Guert and Herman were talking! Herman surely learned from Guert, I decided, that the one person in all of Boston who had recent letters from Lansingburgh was Elizabeth Shaw, since he knew she corresponded with Helen and may have known she corresponded also with Augusta. If Herman saw Guert first, before seeing his aunts or the Shaws, Guert would have said something like, "You know who you have to go see, it's Elizabeth Shaw. She gets a letter from Lansingburgh every week or so."

I knew that Herman had to ask Elizabeth Shaw not to write to his sisters. I see this as indisputable. If he were to surprise his mother, Herman had to call on Elizabeth Shaw once he had talked to Guert, if indeed he did not see her at her father's house first. This is the way real people behave. Once Guert knew he was on the *United States* any number of other people acquainted with the Shaws might have heard of his arrival. If Herman did not call on Elizabeth promptly she might learn of his return from some friend of Guert's or one of the aunts and then write excitedly to Helen. Can I prove this? I can't be sure whether Herman saw the Shaws first or Guert first, but I will convince you that Herman spent time at the Shaw house. In the course of talking to Elizabeth Shaw in October 1844 Herman learned that she had known of his sailing for the Pacific on the *Acushnet* almost before he left, since in the first days of January 1841 Gansevoort had given the Shaw family an account which emphasized how comfortable he had made Herman for his four-year voyage. As Gansevoort wrote Allan a few days later, on the fourteenth: "It is a great consolation to me that I have done my duty towards him, thoroughly & conscientiously in this his last cruise upon land"—that is, the cruise from Manhattan to New Bedford and Fairhaven.[4] Later, Gansevoort had informed Shaw in July 1842 that the family had received news of Herman, a letter mailed from the coast of Peru. At the Shaw house Herman gained a rough sense of just how much visiting had occurred, even during that time when traveling for young women was contingent upon finding suitable male escorts, and how much Elizabeth had learned about him.

On her last visit to Lansingburgh Elizabeth had learned the contents of his letters written from Honolulu. That is, she knew already whatever Herman had told the family about his experiences in Nukuheva, in the Typee valley, in Tahiti, and much else. I emphasize this: *She knew more, before seeing him, than any biographer has known of episodes of his life, such as his first experiences on the coast of South America and the Galápagos as well*

*as his experiences in the Marquesas and Tahiti, whatever episodes were strik-
ing enough for him to have described in his letters from Peru and Honolulu.*
Through occasional bulletins, such as his rare letters or the irregular newspaper accounts of sightings of the *Acushnet*, and especially through her
conversations with Helen and later with all the Melvilles (except Allan, perhaps), Elizabeth inevitably had come to share the anxiety all the Melvilles
felt about the fate of the sailor, last heard from when he was in the Sandwich
Islands. Once Helen's visits had begun, Elizabeth would have joined her in
watching in the Boston papers for reports that the *Acushnet* had been spoken, such as those in the *Atlas* of November 29, 1842. Elizabeth knew some
characteristics Herman may not have been proudest of, such as a tendency
to tease his sisters, for she had read Helen's letter about his taunting the girls
with the witches' gross rhymes from *Macbeth*—had held that letter and even
added her own note to it.

Now Herman must have listened to her with more avidity than anyone had
ever done, simply because never in his life had any stranger to him possessed
so much intimate information about him and possessed as well so much new
information about his family and particularly about how his letters had been
read and shared. And she must have hung on his words, whether about his
captivity among the Typees or other adventures. He may have called on one
or both of his Boston aunts first, or even his Dorchester or Hingham aunts; if
not, at some point the conversation must have come round to those women.
Since Elizabeth knew all about Helen's habit of making morning calls on
her aunt Priscilla, the most natural thing in the world, if she was consulted
by Herman, was to walk him over to Priscilla's, assuming he had not already
begun his dutiful calls upon his aunts. The aunt to call on first was Priscilla
because, as Elizabeth knew, she had done the unthinkable—she had gone to
visit his family in Lansingburgh the previous summer.

*I knew that Herman had to ask at least his aunt Priscilla and his aunt Jean
not to write to his mother.* These two Melvill aunts lived in Boston. Another,
Mary, the wife of the great adventurer Captain John D'Wolf, was a ferry ride
away in Dorchester, and Helen Melvill Souther was a fairly long drive away,
in Hingham. (The fifth living Melvill aunt, Lucy Melvill Clark Nourse, was
in Hallowell, Maine, where Elizabeth Shaw had vacationed with her.) Before
he arrived at Boston in October 1844, Herman would not have thought there
was much danger that his Melvill aunts, if they heard of his return, would
hastily send word of his arrival to their sister-in-law, Maria Melville. When
he sailed on the *Acushnet*, six or seven years had passed without the aunts
having communicated with his mother, and he and the other children felt

his mother's profound grievances against her sisters-in-law. Money was the problem: Maria's husband had squandered all of his enormous share of old Major Melvill's fortune and the sisters wanted to protect their own enormous shares against Allan's creditors. Herman may have known that after their farewells at New Bedford or Fairhaven Gansevoort intended to go on to Boston in January 1841 to present himself to Lemuel Shaw and some of his Boston relatives. On his return to New York Gansevoort wrote Shaw (January 11, 1841): "None of them made anything more than the most general possible enquiries regarding the situation of my Mother, myself or any of the family" (*Log*, 114). Herman would not have known this (even if it had been mentioned in letters to him, none of the letters addressed to him in the Pacific ever reached him), but it fit perfectly with what he knew when he and Gansevoort parted. Now in 1844 Guert had the surprising news that his sister Helen had endured, and even more or less enjoyed, a good deal of contact with the aunts, especially the two who lived in Boston, and that correspondence between at least one of the aunts and Maria at last had been initiated. Maria had been invited to visit them, at least through messages sent by Helen. Guert may have known (for his and Herman's uncle Peter Gansevoort in Albany knew) remarkable news—that Aunt Priscilla had spent part of the previous summer (July? early August?) with Maria in Lansingburgh.

Elizabeth Shaw had specific news to balance Guert's. She could tell Herman that during Helen's first stay in Boston, from December 22, 1841, until March 30, 1842, his sister had not sought out her Melvill-Scollay relatives, or at least had not sought out all of them. Some learned of her presence from others, apparently. On February 16, 1842, Helen wrote to Augusta: "Tell dear Mother, that yesterday while I was out calling, Miss Scollay called upon me and left her mothers card, she said that they seldom went out, and had not heard of my being in town until last week." On the same day she wrote:

> Aunt Jean and Aunt Priscilla seem to "set the most by me," and call me "diamond," "jewel," and all sorts of endearing epithets. Mrs Shaw was so kind as to ask Aunt P. to spend a day here, and I know it was purely on my account, for some reason or other, she does not appear to have kept her stand in society, and Aunt Jean says that none of the old friends of the family visit her, not even "Aunt Scollay." But this is no business of mine, she always treats me with affection, and as she is the only aunt within walking reach, and my visits seem to give her so much delight, I often run down to see her right after breakfast, and return [in] time enough for the morning campaign, whether it is to pay or receive calls.

Aunt Jean was a compulsive talker, Helen had concluded, and the whole Wright household was hopelessly "uncongenial." Aunt Mary D'Wolf was "supremely selfish," Helen thought, and Aunt Helen Souther lived much too far away in bleak Hingham. Nevertheless, Helen had behaved with proper deference to them all. If Herman had not planned to call on his aunts, Guert's news, reinforced by Elizabeth's news, made calling on them urgent. Even an unfriendly aunt could seize the pleasure of being a busybody and wreck Herman's surprise.

The strongest reason for thinking Herman saw some of his aunts in October 1844 is that early in 1846, when *Typee* was published in New York, he went to great trouble to obtain copies of the book for all of his Melvill aunts. He was on easy, familiar terms with them, judging from the way he wrote Priscilla, at least, to assure her that copies would be forthcoming. We have no record of Herman's going to Boston in 1845, but he was there from March 4 through March 12, 1846, almost a year and a half after his return from the Pacific. In March 1846, a surviving label shows, Aunt Priscilla gave some sort of gift to him; he kept it, presumably with the label.[5] Perhaps then, perhaps another time in 1846, Aunt Jean gave him a copy of the New Testament and Psalms which he made much use of. *When was this intimacy established?* Conceivably, Herman could have first paid his respects to his aunts on the early March 1846 visit, mere days before *Typee* would be in his hands. Given what we know now, including the language in which he expressed himself to Shaw on March 19, 1846, I conclude still that he saw some of his Melvill aunts in October 1844. Otherwise, unless there are visits to Boston we do not know about (and what would the motive for them be, if not courtship?), he would not have been on such good terms with them when *Typee* was published.

I knew that Herman had to ask Lemuel Shaw and any other old friends of Allan Melvill not to ruin his surprise. Perhaps even before he learned of Elizabeth's intimacy with his family, Herman had Judge Shaw much on his mind because of the case of the purser's slave. Paying his respects to Shaw would have seemed appealing to the soon to be freed, or newly freed, young man who might, if his aunt Nancy had not died, have called Shaw his uncle just as he called John D'Wolf his uncle. As Herman knew from his uncle Thomas, Shaw had remained in close contact with all the actual Melvill heirs (Allan's brother and sisters), since he was the executor who doled out to them their portions of income from the estate while D'Wolf, nominally the co-executor, let Shaw do the work. Melville knew that Shaw had written to Maria on February 12, 1834, assuring her of the "deep interest & solicitude" he felt for her

children, who were also the children of one of his "oldest & best friends."
Shaw had made a promise: "I shall at all times & under all circumstances,
do all in my power, to promote their best interests." He had done nothing
during the years of Maria's grimmest poverty, but Herman almost certainly
knew before he sailed for the Pacific that Gansevoort had planned to seek
Shaw out as an advisor and sponsor after seeing him off. Shaw must have
felt something very much like guilt, however unjustified, or he would not
have been quite so generous to Maria's oldest son, Gansevoort, in January
1841, when, having seen Herman off to the South Seas, he arrived in Boston
soliciting funds to take a therapeutic voyage in the Caribbean, and later in
the year appealed for another grant. Without old loyalty and some sense of
guilt, Shaw might not have been so receptive when Gansevoort and Helen
appeared in Lenox in the fall of 1841 at precisely the time Shaw was holding
court there. Helen, of course, was there to visit her old schoolteacher Elizabeth Sedgwick, and Gansevoort was escorting her, as a reliable male had
to do. In Lenox, Shaw proved quite eager "to promote their best interests."
Shaw had not felt himself able to help the Melvilles when they most needed
his help, but as they came into his ken as young adults, he would do what he
could, and he could do much.

   In the intervening years of his executorship Shaw had demonstrated a
great deal of forbearance with the grandchildren of Thomas and Priscilla
Melvill. On March 15, 1842, Thomas Melvill, Jr., lamented to Shaw "any
circumstances have occurred w[hi]ch induce you to think less favorably of
[Thomas's son] Robert."[6] Repeatedly, Robert aggrieved Shaw in his misman-
agement of the Homestead Farm south of Pittsfield, which was owned by
the estate of old Thomas and Priscilla, not by Robert's father. Thomas, Jr.'s
sailor son, Thomas Wilson Melvill, was an alcoholic drummed out of the
navy and, now a whaleman, had been seen ashore at times, always swearing
again that he had left off "his habit of drinking" and always drinking. Shaw
received reports about Thomas Wilson but was spared seeing him. Much
more intrusively, Lucy Melvill Nourse's stepson, John Nourse, by 1841
was, as Amos Nourse said to Shaw, making "head quarters of your house,"
where there were small bedrooms enough to put up undemanding young
men, now that the oldest son, Oakes, was absent. Shaw had been frustrated
but forgiving when Gansevoort repeatedly ignored his good advice to build
up his reputation as a lawyer instead of polishing his oratory on the hare-
brained cause of the repeal of the union between England and Ireland or,
worse, the championing of Democratic candidates for high office. (Nothing
Gansevoort had been saying in the West was more objectionable to a Whig
like Shaw, formerly a Federalist, than his widely reported tribute to Jackson

on March 15, 1844, at the Jackson Jubilee.) Having established this pattern of guardianship to those who might have been his nieces and nephews (or even step-nephews), if he learned of Herman's presence in Boston in October 1844, Shaw would have made overtures to him. Shaw would have invited Herman to make his own "head quarters" on Mount Vernon Street, just as he had allowed John Nourse (then dying in Hallowell) to do.

Shaw already knew of Herman's captivity in the Marquesas, from Helen and his daughter, before he knew of Herman's return, and he had many friends with ears ready to hear such stories. He knew, also, the astonishing success of the book by his young acquaintance, Richard Henry Dana, Jr., on a far less promising subject than Herman would have. Besides, he also had to have known, again from Helen and his daughter, that Herman had been in Maui before going to Honolulu, and therefore might have news of his cousin who had married a native woman and still lived there. Captain John Percival on November 12, 1840, had written from Dorchester to tell Shaw that John Shaw on the island of "Mowhee" had married "a native female & had several children."[7]

Until he called at the Shaw house Herman would have had no idea that Shaw already knew stories of his adventures in the South Seas, but he would have had good reason to think of calling on him, if only with the pretext of congratulating him on his decision in the Lucas case. His reporting on the behavior of the purser, in particular, would have been certain to gratify the chief justice. If he had called on Shaw before he knew of Helen's intimacy in the household, he might have arrived expecting Shaw to put him in touch with other surviving intimates of Allan Melvill, notably Daniel P. Parker, owner of ships in the China trade, who lived nearby in the magnificent house at 40 Beacon Street, facing the Common. In New York City in 1828 Parker had been entrusted by Allan Melvill with two of his sons, and had safely left off Herman at the D'Wolf house in Bristol and escorted Gansevoort on to the old Major Melvill's house in Boston. Around the first of June 1848 Melville, who disliked asking favors of anyone, unhesitatingly wrote Parker hoping he could get Tom to sea right away. Merchants and shipowners were numbered among Shaw's closest friends, as Percival certainly was, and Parker was an old and dear friend. Melville met, pretty early, or heard specific stories about some shipowners and captains, such as one of the owners of Dana's ship, the *Pilgrim*, whom he cited in the *Literary World* (March 6, 1847). Captain Percival, who had already charmed Helen, was at sea, but Shaw saw to it that he and Herman met, later, and they became friends. Shaw would naturally have introduced Herman around, as he did in March 1846, when the great Amos Lawrence gave Herman a book on the Bunker

Hill battle and monument with his "kind regards." At some point before he began to write "Melville" instead of "Melvill" when addressing Maria or her children, or his own daughter, Shaw presented Herman with a book or perhaps a published speech or other sort of pamphlet from which someone has torn off the inscription: "Mr Herman Melvill/from his friend/Lemuel Shaw."[8] It could be plausibly suggested that "Mr" marks a degree of formality, "Melvill" marks a newness in the connection (since Shaw was accustomed to writing "Melvill"), and "friend" marks a distance perhaps greater than father-in-law (though "friends" still meant "relations"). No document yet discovered shows indisputably that Herman met Shaw in October 1844, much less Parker or other friends of his father, but at some point between October 1844 and the summer of 1845 (or at the latest in a letter to Gansevoort late in 1845) Herman decided to dedicate *Typee* to Shaw, "affectionately" (as the English dedication said) or "gratefully" (as the American said). How did Herman become so affectionate toward him, or so grateful? From a brief encounter in Lansingburgh in May 1845? The reasonable thing to assume is that Lemuel Shaw in October 1844 heard Herman's tales from his own mouth and encouraged him to write them down. If a local lawyer, young Dana, the son of a poet, could become a famous writer, so could Herman, the grandson of the Hero of the Tea Party, Thomas Melvill.

What Made the Most Sense to Me

At the outset I was baffled by the fact that Melville lingered in Boston a day or two even after his discharge: why would a young man, eager to reunite with his mother and brothers and sisters, delay for a moment taking the new Western Railroad across Massachusetts to the nearest stop east of the Hudson, Greenbush, where he had taught school? A desire to surprise his mother and sisters is one powerful motive for not writing home, but that does not account for his lingering any longer than he had to. At last, on Sunday, October 13, Herman wrote a letter—not to his mother or to his older brother (whom he knew to be somewhere in the West, on his way home) but to his brother Allan in New York. Even then Herman did not mail the letter promptly. Having already learned that the family was alive and well, he was, uncharacteristically, biding his time for reasons of his own. Practically speaking, he was not yet discharged, not until the fourteenth. Then he could have mailed his letter, but he waited until the sixteenth.

Herman's letter is not known to be extant, so its contents must be inferred from Allan's reply. As I said, Herman had made it clear to Allan that he had not written to anyone at Lansingburgh: he wanted his surprise. Therefore Allan promised that he would wait for a reply from Herman before writing home. Furthermore, Allan wanted Herman to go to New York City before going home so "they" could "rig" him out with clothes (he did not expect Gansevoort back until the twenty-third although Gansevoort himself, on October 16, told his friend William Cramer that he "must be in the city of New York" on the morning of the twenty-first). Herman had explained that "'the circumstances connected with the ship'" (his words) had prevented his "immediate presence" (Allan's words) among the family. Herman's failure to specify just what "the circumstances" were caused Allan to feel vague alarm mingled with specific exasperation: not even home yet, his brother was causing unnecessary concern by his thoughtless failure to convey all the requisite information when he had the chance. He had given no address, so Allan simply sent the letter to "Herman Melville / Boston," which was good enough.[9]

One way or another, what with reiterated news from his Gansevoort cousin and his Melvill aunts and the newspapers, in the days before his discharge Melville had much to mull over, some of which he could share with his friends, from whom he was preparing to part. He said good-bye to them, in small groups or one at a time, probably last of all to Jack Chase, that "great heart" whom he never forgot, and to whom he dedicated *Billy Budd*, the book he was working on when he died. Another sort of sailor, as I suggested in the biography, might have made his way with shipmates to the nearest doggery and there have drunk himself blind until his companions hoisted him upon a train for the first leg of his journey to New York (for I knew from Allan's letter that Melville had gone there from Boston, not Lansingburgh). I did not for a moment believe that Herman had disappeared for days or even a day or two into the netherworld of the Boston waterside. He behaved, I judged from documents (including several from subsequent years), like a responsible grandson of the Hero of the Tea Party. He saw Guert Gansevoort, he saw his aunts, he saw Lemuel Shaw and Elizabeth Shaw. In the transition from ordinary seaman to scion of great Boston families, Herman was detained there by forces that were, day by day, shaping his future. Even while he was being encouraged to write out his adventures, his telling of those adventures, I decided, was compelling the attention of Elizabeth Shaw. He was, we know, charismatic, "incomparable in dramatic storytelling," young Dana said on March 18, 1849 (*Log*, 293). He was handsome, later photographs show, and bearded, as he probably was, still (Gansevoort wanted him to shave before seeing their mother), and at some point was fitted out with shore clothing, perhaps from Oakes's old clothes, which might have gotten him from Boston to New York, at least, where his brothers could rig him out. He was the wanderer all of his family had longed to see again, and feared they would never see, and now Elizabeth was the one to welcome him.

Once I had weighed all the new evidence intermixed with the old, I felt this as a powerful situation. I was moved by what I knew, and in the biography I treated the meeting of Herman and Elizabeth, perhaps, too much with the brush of a writer of a present-day Harlequin romance. Here is a bit of it:

> However he was rigged out, most likely in sailor's gear still, as Allan assumed, he [Herman] must have made a sensational impression, especially on Elizabeth Shaw. Like most of the Melvilles, he was handsome, and he was young—twenty-five. Just now darkly tanned, he was in all likelihood the most athletic young man she had ever seen in her house, and one who more or less unconsciously combined athleticism with eroticism in his gait, since he could not have gained his land legs yet. Sailors liked to exaggerate the roll, knowing it was perceived as erotic and knowing that they could protest, in all innocent indignation, that they were merely walking as they had to walk. (Richard Henry Dana, Jr., liked to affect it, long after he had stopped involuntarily compensating for the pitch of a ship.) Elizabeth Shaw had shared the concern of Helen and the whole Lansingburgh family about his fate until his letters from Honolulu arrived. Then she had become party to whatever he had written his family about his stay among the Typees and his subsequent adventures in Tahiti and Eimeo, besides his whaling experiences. It had been impossible not to be caught up in his family's feelings about the wanderer. . . .
>
> In exchange for her stories of his family, Herman told her some of his wondrous adventures, and judicious testimony is clear that he was a remarkable talker, once his lips were opened. Lizzie was not the greatest belle of Boston, but she was one of the most privileged— the only young woman that October to hear from the bearded lips of a brilliant, dark, muscular, handsome young man enthralling accounts of his adventures, foremost of which was a wondrous tale of his indulgent captivity among a cannibal tribe in the Marquesas—by now, after so much practice, a far better story than he had told in his letters from Hawaii, which she knew all about. Herman must have conveyed, as well, amazing incidental insights and observations about great whales and other beasts of the sea and about peoples and places she could never hope to know. Their meeting

had a Shakespearean precedent: Othello-like, he told her of "moving accidents" by flood and field (or Typee vale) and of "hair-breadth
'scapes"; Desdemona-like, she loved him for the dangers he had
passed, and he loved her that she did pity them. (1:306, 311)

(I did not mention that reviewers of *Typee* very naturally turned to *Othello*
for the phrase "hair-breadth 'scapes.") This strikes me now as more attentive
than imaginative, but I could have doctored it with perhapses, and should
have, perhaps.

Realistically speaking, if Herman and Elizabeth did not meet in 1844, the
first time they met as adults was when she visited at Lansingburgh from May
25, 1845, to June 8, 1845. Her father brought her there and may have stayed
briefly. It is not known if anyone escorted her home or if (this is unlikely) she
took the train at Greenbush and went across the stretch of New York and all
of Massachusetts alone. Shaw seems to have gone on to Chicago to see his
oldest son, Oakes, and his wife and child, and then returned, and, perplexingly soon, accompanied Elizabeth to Chicago starting on June 23, 1845. The
next known contact between the families is that on December 3, 1845, Helen
arrived at the Shaw house for a visit, escorted from New York City by Allan,
not Herman.

Once Herman had finished *Typee* in the early summer of 1845, he offered
it to the Harpers, who brusquely rejected it. Vulnerable rather than resilient
and aggressive, he took the rejection as final. So crushed, he was in no position to pursue Elizabeth Shaw or any other young woman. The remarkable
American Thomas Low Nichols (politician, reformer, lawyer, doctor, sexolo-
gist) by reading the manuscript left in Gansevoort's and Allan's office may
have determined Melville's career when he recommended that Gansevoort
carry the manuscript to London when he left to become secretary of the
American legation there. In the fall of 1845 Gansevoort offered it to John
Murray, and when word reached home in Gansevoort's letter of November
3, Herman could begin to hope again that the book would be printed. It was
December 3, 1845, before Murray informed Gansevoort that he would publish *Typee*, so it was toward the end of the year that Herman learned his book
was being prepared for the press. Yet when Gansevoort packed up the manuscript at the end of July 1845 it may already have been dedicated to Shaw.
"Gratefully" (in the American edition) might apply better to Gansevoort
than Herman, but there is absolutely no reason to think that the dedication
was supplied by the admittedly officious older brother. Gansevoort was going
out of his way, in London, to make sure that whatever was important to the
author was carried out, including the placing of belated pieces of prose.

What this means is that by July 1845 or by the late fall of 1845, at the latest, Herman had decided to dedicate the book to Shaw. On February 28, 1846, Herman wrote Gansevoort that the news of the book was "gratifying enough." Since Gansevoort promised soon to "venture to make some suggestions" about Herman's "next book," it was already certain that he would follow up *Typee* with another adventure story. Herman on the twenty-eighth had brought up (as Gansevoort again quoted back to him) "a subject &c &c 'on which I intended to write but will defer it.' What do you allude to?" One strong possibility was that he intended to go to Boston in a very few days to see Judge Shaw—and to pursue his acquaintance with Lizzie. On March 19, 1846, sending Shaw a copy of *Typee*, Herman spoke of Shaw's "knowing the author so well." Knowing the Melvill family so well, knowing Allan Melvill so well, knowing Gansevoort Melville well, knowing Helen very well—all that is readily documented. Shaw's knowing Herman so well is *not* documented. He had met the boy on his visits to the aged Melvills; he had met him in May 1845. This does not add up when you look at the March 19, 1846, letter—you need a renewed acquaintance of some days in October 1844, I believe.

This is a fuller version of what Herman wrote Shaw on March 19, 1846: "Herewith you have one of the first bound copies of 'Typee' I have been able to procure.—The dedication is very simple, for the world would hardly have sympathized to the full extent of those feelings with which I regard my father's friend and the constant friend of all his family. I hope that the perusal of this little narrative of mine will afford you some entertainment, even if it should not possess much other merit. Your knowing the author so well, will impart some interest to it." This was Melville's formal inscription in the book: "Chief Justice Shaw/With the sincere respects/of the author." Frugally, Melville enclosed a letter for Shaw to deliver to Priscilla Melvill, with word that she and her sisters would receive copies as soon as he could procure them. Then he added: "Remember me most warmly to Mrs Shaw & Miss Elizabeth, & to all your family, & tell them I shall not soon forget that agreeable visit to Boston." By "agreeable visit" Herman was referring to the March 4, 1846, visit to the Shaws—long after he had written the dedication, but while it was still a secret from the Shaws; Melville liked to surprise people he cared for. When did Shaw come to know "the author so well"? In late May 1845? The day or so that Shaw was there before going on to Chicago? Well, not likely. In early March 1846 the dedication was already in type in two countries. No. October 1844 looks better and better, and to carry two young lovers through the bitter disappointment of 1845, when the dream of authorship seemed to vanish, you need, I still think, a powerful early attraction.

Consider the picture if Herman and Elizabeth did not talk for hours in October 1844. What if they first met in late May 1845 when she visited at Lansingburgh for two weeks? Herman was probably there in his mother's house, and blue sheets of paper may have been strewn around his mother's desk, a pile enough to make a book, if he could find a publisher. Perhaps everyone in the house was confident that the book would be published. But soon after Elizabeth left, Herman took the manuscript to New York City and offered it to the publisher of *Two Years Before the Mast*, the Harpers, only to have it dismissed as a fabrication. The psychological toll on Herman was devastating, embittering him against the Harpers—and why not?[10] Rejected insultingly, he did not go knocking on the doors of other publishers. In that small publishing circle in extreme downtown Manhattan, the other publishers would likely know the manuscript had been rejected as worthless. He did not possess, at this time, the stamina or the driving motivation that could force him, against his nature, to persist in trying to find a publisher. If Herman looked like a promising author at the end of May, all through the summer and far into the fall, even to the start of winter, he looked like a sailor who had overreached himself in hoping to publish a book like the Harvard man, Dana. Herman was not marriageable material in 1845, and as far as we know he did not go to Boston all that year. Early in December it was Allan who took Helen to New York City, then escorted her to the Shaws.

If Herman and Elizabeth first met in May 1845, she knew a good deal about him, as we have seen. However appealingly adventurous he had been, he was not to be thought of as a husband, living as he was with his mother and sisters or else dependent on his brothers in New York City, and gambling on starting a career as a writer. She heard from Helen in the next months after May 1845, in Chicago or home from Chicago, but what she heard may have concerned Gansevoort much more than Herman: one brother was embittered by being passed over for political appointments for months even before the younger one became embittered by his treatment at the hands of the Harpers. All in all, 1845 was not a good year for the Melville family until Gansevoort's appointment came through at the end of July, and even then the rest of the year was almost gone before Herman could be sure that his manuscript would be printed. Herman was not in a position to pursue a courtship, and if he and Elizabeth first met as grownups in May 1845 there was no budding courtship to pursue.

Then the question arises as to why Herman went to Boston in early 1846. He did not go to tell Lemuel Shaw that he was dedicating *Typee* to him: he was a writer who liked to surprise his dedicatees. He did not go to see his aunts, though he did see them. He went as a suitor to Lizzie. He went as a suitor on the basis of the presumed meeting in late May and early June 1845? I think not. He can't have gone as a suitor unless he and Lizzie had shared many memorable hours of telling each other stories in the comfort of the great house on Mount Vernon Street in Boston, in October 1844. If you admit that Herman saw Guert or saw either of his aunts, then you know that Herman knew Elizabeth Shaw had up-to-date news from his family and that he would have been foolish not to seek her out and ask her not to write to Lansingburgh. Then all the objections unravel and you have Herman Melville and Elizabeth Shaw meeting at 49 Mount Vernon Street. Then it becomes plausible that they became engaged as soon as she arrived for the long 1846 visit, on August 31. On May 30, 1847, Maria Melville wrote about Elizabeth to Augusta: "In July she will have been engage'd eleven months, a long time now a days." That means that she was engaged in August, on the last day of the month. I take "eleven months" seriously. A person can say "four months" meaning, "Oh, about four or five months," and a person can be approximate with eight when the accurate number of months is nine, but when Maria says eleven she has to add only one to reach a full year. It is much harder to make a mistake, that is, when you say "eleven" than it is when you say "four" or "eight." Eleven months is a specific number, one shy of a year. Maria could have said "about a year" but she specified eleven months. I believe her. To anyone who reads the Augusta Papers her record for accuracy speaks for itself.

Turn the argument around: To insist that Herman and Elizabeth did *not* meet in October 1844 you have to buy into not *one* improbability but a *string* of improbabilities. You have to believe that Herman did not learn that his first cousin Guert Gansevoort, whose name was known to every sailor in the fleet because of the *Somers* tragedy, was there in the Navy Yard, and that he did not talk to him, as he would have done belatedly, if somehow he had not known about Guert's being there on the *Ohio* until Allan told him. You have to believe that Herman did not go to see either his aunt Priscilla or his aunt Jean, though he would have wanted to caution them not to let his family know he was there, just in case they were in communication with Maria or were moved to get in touch of her with news they may have heard of his return. You have to believe that Herman's intimacy with his aunts in mid-March 1846 occurred from one or more encounters in early March 1846, not from an earlier contact. You have to believe that Herman stayed on in Boston in October 1844, delaying his departure for New York a day or two with no good reason—perhaps in order to carouse with some of his ship-mates—something quite unlike him. You have to believe that Herman's intimacy with Shaw and Elizabeth after one brief encounter in late May

1845 was sufficient to account for his dedicating *Typee* to Shaw that summer or fall (for he wrote the dedication long before his visit to Boston early in March 1846) and to account for his making that trip to Boston early in March, and to account for his speaking of Shaw's knowing him so well in his letter accompanying a copy of the American edition of *Typee* later in March. You have to believe that Herman and Lizzie could hardly have become engaged as early as the end of August 1846, the date Maria gave. You have to think Maria was wrong, something I know better than to do. Sometimes, it makes sense to think that the people you are writing about behaved the way normal people behave. Sometimes, young people meet and are powerfully drawn toward each other and cherish that attraction during long months of separation before circumstances make it possible to declare their love. For Herman and Elizabeth to become engaged on August 31, 1846, or in the next days afterward, they need to have spent time together in October 1844. I was not a Harlequin romancer when I quoted the Moor: "She loved me for the dangers I had passed and I loved her that she did pity them."

Chapter 15

MELVILLE'S SHORT RUN
OF GOOD LUCK (1845–1850)

Fool's Paradise Without International Copyright

In the June 2007 *Nineteenth-Century Literature* I challenged Raymond Weaver's 1921 pronouncement that "after *Pierre,* any further writing from Melville was both an impertinence and an irrelevancy" (343). This view was more baldly stated by William Braswell in 1936: "Melville expected *Pierre* to be his final publication. In this novel he was having his last fling" (427). (If he was having a reckless fling, I would say, it was not when he wrote the original version of *Pierre* but in early and later in January 1852, after he had agreed to the Harper terms for the contract.) As I have said, I also deplored Nina Baym's updating of this theory in her arrestingly titled 1979 "Melville's Quarrel with Fiction," particularly since she had ignored previous scholarship that flatly disproved her assertions. Rather than renouncing fiction, Melville had completed a new book, *The Isle of the Cross,* in the spring of 1853. Melville "never had a quarrel with fiction," I said in the *Nineteenth-Century Literature* piece, "his quarrel was with the marketplace—publishers and reviewers" (41). I might have stressed that the reviewers who most actively worked to end Melville's career were representatives of what we would call the religious right, zealots determined to use their power to crush any writer who (once fairly warned) would not conform to their notions of Christian piety. More important, I ought to have stressed that to a very great extent Melville's career as a novelist was truncated by the lack of an international copyright law. I had stressed in the second volume of my biography that the Harpers had been almost unbelievably mercenary toward Melville after their December 1853 fire, charging him again for costs he had already paid, but I did not understand just how brutally they had behaved in 1852 when they profited immensely while using the current status of the copyright situation to grind Melville down.

It is old news that the lack of an international copyright law had some impact on Melville's career. Doing his best to decipher Melville's London journal (reading "Colbour" for "Colburn"), Weaver sketched some of Melville's calls on publishers in London. Weaver understood that the succession of "publishers continued to chasten" Melville "with reflections on the state of the copyright laws," but he did not show that he knew what the issues were. He made the quest for a publisher of *White-Jacket* into a triumph at the high cost of ignoring the intensity of Melville's passion to "see Rome" during a several-month Grand Tour. Emphasizing Melville's "Hurray and three cheers!" for a belated sale, Weaver portrayed a successful Melville who in fact had been both deeply disappointed at his failure to get enough money soon enough and deeply grateful to get what he belatedly got, so he could return home with at least a part of his mission accomplished. Lewis Mumford in 1929 was downright flippant about Melville's attempts to sell *White-Jacket* in London (126):

> One meets the publishers one by one, Bentley, who did Mardi, Murray, who published Typee and Omoo, Mr. Longmans [that is, Longman], Mr. Chapman, Mr. Bohn, Mr. Moxon, who was Charles Lamb's crony; and when one can't make the deal one had hoped for, one goes down the line; but the answer is always the same: the copyright is unsatisfactory. . . . The prospects are not too pleasant; but if the matter could be settled at once one wouldn't have the excuse and the opportunity to visit the Dulwich Gallery, remote from London, but full of splendid treasures. . . .

For Mumford, the chance to sightsee a little canceled the disappointment at not selling *White-Jacket* right away for a high price.

Biographers learned over the decades. The index to my first volume lists fifteen pages where copyright is discussed, including one particular British court case, and the second volume cites two pages. Here I do not try to rival the researches of Catherine Seville, the author of *The Internationalisation of Copyright Law: Books, Buccaneers and the Black Flag in the Nineteenth Century*, and Ronan Deazley, the author of *Rethinking Copyright: History, Theory, Language*, historians of the struggle to pass an international copyright law, or the great digital archive "Primary Sources on Copyright (1450–1900)" created by the Universities of Cambridge and Bournemouth. What scholars and critics have said about the effect of the lack of an international copyright law on the career of Herman Melville has been impressionistic. Indeed, the topic has remained the elephant in the room during all discussions of Melville's career, acknowledged in passing but intimidatingly formidable. In what follows I try to keep the focus on what Melville himself would have learned and what he said and did, as well as what was said about him and done to him. He was much more central to the debate than we had thought.[1]

1842: Dickens Damages the Cause of International Copyright

Gansevoort Melville's placing his younger brother Herman's first book with the great London publisher John Murray late in 1845 for a hundred pounds was a personal triumph with international implications. All Americans still winced at Sydney Smith's declaration in his 1818 *Edinburgh Review* article on "America": "Literature the Americans have none—no native literature, we mean. It is all imported." There were, Smith acknowledged "some pieces of pleasantry by Mr. Irving. But why should the Americans write books, when a six weeks' passage brings them, in their own tongue, our sense, science and genius, in bales and hogsheads?" Two years later, in another *Edinburgh Review* article also entitled "America," Smith asked the devastating question which every educated American could soon recite: "In the four quarters of the globe, who reads an American book?" As a youth Melville profited at the Albany Young Men's Association and at the Lansingburgh Academy from books shipped over "in bales and hogsheads," but more often he profited directly from reprintings of some of those foreign books by Americans in the coastal cities, especially Philadelphia and New York, and also in Albany (where printers were sustained by the business of the state capital), and many much smaller towns.

Melville read American reprints of British books all his life. Indeed, his working copies of English poets more often than not were American reprints. The family Spenser, a 1787 London set, was a turn-of-the-century gift to his father, and other foreign books were passed around in the family, but his Shakespeare, his Milton, and his Wordsworth were American-made, based on British editorial and biographical work. The Wordsworth editor had devoted years to studying his poet for the James Kay edition (Philadelphia, 1839), but the Hilliard, Gray headnote to their Boston set of Shakespeare was disingenuous in explaining why there would have been no "propriety" in acknowledging S. W. Singer as editor, and the Milton by the same firm did not even bother to justify its use of the work of British scholars. When he was buying on credit from Putnam and Harper, Melville often bought

their imprints, often of foreign books. Beginning in the 1850s he bought
many Boston editions of Tennyson, the Brownings, Arnold, and other poets,
cheaply printed but in legible type. Melville passionately loved old books as
artifacts especially if they contained rich, challenging thought and language,
but with exceptions (such as some treasured rarities he bought in London in
1849, the Thomas Beale that Putnam imported especially for him in 1850,
secondhand foreign books first owned by other family members, or those
he picked up in book-bins and shops) his books were most often American-
made, although their content was most often foreign. There was a reason: in
the absence of an international copyright law, American publishers did not
need to pay anything to reprint foreign books, so good books by foreign writers were almost always much cheaper than any desirable books by American
writers.

While Melville was on whaleships and a man-of-war in 1841–44, Gansevoort became a lawyer (as did their younger brother Allan). At the same
time, several of Gansevoort's instant-retrieval *Index Rerum* entries suggest,
he was thinking of making a parallel career as an author. In 1842 he paid
close attention to Charles Dickens's tour of the United States, as did the other
Melvilles. In Boston early that year Helen Maria Melville (the sister born
after Gansevoort and before Herman) looked at Francis Alexander's portrait
of Dickens more than once as the artist worked on it. On February 16, she
wrote her mother about the reward she might give their cousin Augustus Peebles if he escorted her home to Lansingburgh: "in requital I will allow him to
shake hands with my *right* hand, a thing which I have not permitted to any
one, since that useful member was immortalized by the pressure of the right
hand of Boz." Dickens had a massive personal financial grievance, since as
things stood American publishers were reprinting many thousands of copies
of his writings without paying him anything. At the outset of his tour he was
charged by "all the best American writers," starting with Washington Irving,
to deliver their petition for an international copyright law to Senator Henry
Clay, as he wrote to John Forster on February 27, 1842 (Forster, 328). The
petition explained that the English parliament had decided that copyright
was a privilege of Great Britain and that only "by courtesy alone" should British publishers pay American writers for their books. The American petitioners
deplored the present lack of international copyright "as fatally subversive
of the interests of our youthful literature, and as unjust and ungenerous
towards foreign authors." The signers did not criticize the chief opponents
of international copyright (book publishers and owners of a-novel-in-an-issue
newspapers) other than to say that publishers could not be expected to "pay
an adequate price for native works, when they can obtain their supply of new

books (a supply often far beyond the demand) from English authors *for nothing*" (Houtchens, 20). As the months passed it became clear that Dickens had been a poor choice as front man for the cause. By his relentless complaints about what the lack of a copyright law had cost him he surprised many Americans into the conviction that he was a mercenary ingrate.

In the June 18, 1842, *New World*, after the initial frenzy had died, Gansevoort enjoyed "Duggin's Impressions of America"—"a most amusing caricature sketch of Dickens (as also of *Willis, Bryant, & Halleck*)—with a capital travesty a/c of the Grand Ball given to Dickens at the Park Theatre to which he is represented as going in the character of Jim Crow" (that is, shoe-polished up as a black man). ("Duggin's" in the title was an error for "Duggins," the spelling in the text which broadened the hint that the subject was Dickens.) This was a brilliant piece from *Tait's Magazine* signed by Bon Gaultier, the pseudonym of William Edmonstoune Aytoun and Sir Theodore Martin, as outrageous a backwoods story as anything Mark Twain later shocked an audience with, but it was not about Dickens's support of copyright. As the "travesty" showed, word had gotten round New York City in the "flash press" (such as the *Whip and Satirist of New-York and Brooklyn*, March 12, 1842) of Dickens's presence at late nocturnal escapades in Five Points months before he described the "Nigger Ball" in *American Notes*. The article was indeed "most amusing," as Gansevoort said, and it reflected what the British had already learned about Dickens's hardening view of the United States and, in particular, its great literary men.

In his *Index Rerum* Gansevoort Melville also made note of an article he had read the next week, in the June 25, 1842, *New World*—"Copyright, Domestic and International," reprinted from the London *Spectator*. What he read he would have retained and, in his semipaternal way, would very likely have passed on to Herman early in 1845, when the sailor began writing. This angry article criticized both Dickens ("who has constituted himself the apostle of an international copyright in America") and "his coadjutors." The most conspicuous coadjutor was "a Mr. CORNELIUS MATTHEWS" (that is, "Mathews"), who had dared to send copies of his "fustian" speech on copyright to editors of British journals. Mathews had described the frenzy, the "state of desperate anarchy" in which "violent hands" laid hold on copies of new English books and magazines (especially pieces by Dickens) as they were unloaded from ships in New York and other ports and rushed into multiple competing editions. The *Spectator* ended the quotation with mockery of Mathews for having lamented, "What hope is there here for the native author?" Mathews was bad, according to the *Spectator*, but Dickens's own extravagance in his speeches on copyright was "second only" to Mathews's:

"The straining after effect in all these orations betrays the want of a real feeling; and the want of real feeling is the fruitful parent of overpiled hyperbole, burlesque, and pathos."

What Dickens and Mathews were doing was still worse, declared the *Spectator*. They were social and political incendiaries:

> There is something more than bad taste in this: there is a display of lamentable ignorance. The litterateurs who make these orations display errors as gross as the mechanics who brawl for short-time bills, a legislative minimum of wages, and similar panaceas of the quack-doctors of the social system. Mr. MATTHEWS opines that a system of international copyright will procure an audience for the "writer of merit," whose "popularity," being "a degree less" than that of him who now engrosses the public ear, is "not listened to." The "Popular writer" (Boz, for example) will continue to carry it over the "man of merit" (Mr. MATTHEWS, we will suppose) though there were fifty international copyrights. Mr. MATTHEWS' mistake is exactly the mistake of the working-classes when they fancy that laws of political economy are dependent upon legislation.

The *Spectator* explained ruthlessly: "the trade of literature is a poor one; but there is just as little doubt that, for the great mass of those who pursue it, an intern[ation]al copyright would not in the smallest degree mend the matter." Literary geniuses, the *Spectator* was sure, do not need to be protected by copyright because they are so rare, there scarce being one Homer, Shakespeare, or Dante in a century, and, besides, "it is questionable whether great geniuses need its assistance." All this Gansevoort read and reflected on two and a half years before his brother Herman (no Homer, Shakespeare, or Dante) began writing *Typee*.

Fed by outrage toward the ungrateful visitor, American publishers led the fight against international copyright, but often obliquely, as in the letter in the *Boston Courier* (April 14, 1842). This letter (signed "P.") attacked the advocacy of international copyright in *Arcturus*, the short-lived New York City magazine edited by Evert A. Duyckinck and Cornelius Mathews. *Arcturus* was "anti-national" and a copyright law would be "unpatriotic" and worse, "suicidal." If the law were adopted, there would be "no originality, no independence, no patriotism, no raciness, no domestic flavor," but only pallid imitation of British authors. The "poor man and the poor woman" in the United States could afford to buy no books at all, only "the yearly almanac and the village newspaper." Worst of all, many of the six hundred paper mills and their fifty thousand employees would be idled because books would enter the country already printed and bound on British paper and other materials by British labor, while our "own numerous artisans connected with the manufacture of books will be ruined." In this carefully misleading article, P. said not a word about American publishers' no longer being able to appropriate British works for free, if there were an international copyright law.

It was not only American *book* publishers who opposed a copyright law. Park Benjamin's mammoth newspaper the *New World* in 1842 printed Bulwer's *Zanoni* "entire in one extra *World* of 33 quarto pages," all for one bit (twelve and one-half cents, referred to as a "shilling"), as advertised in its June 25, 1842, issue. In that issue, the one where he printed the article Gansevoort noted on "Copyright, Domestic and International," Benjamin printed a rant on "Copyright" from Thomas Hood's June issue of *Colburn's New Monthly Magazine*, a mockery of a speech given by Cornelius Mathews. The speech, it said, "fearlessly denounces the unjust practices of the Literary Loafers on the other side of the Atlantic; and forcibly points out the serious evils that must result from the trading system of the great DEALERS IN TRANS-MARINE STORES, in Cliff-street and the Broadway." (The Harpers were the great publishers of Cliff Street and Wiley & Putnam of Broadway, both later publishers of Herman Melville.) *Colburn's* summarized Mathews sardonically: "Amongst these ill consequences stands foremost the impossibility that America can ever possess a National Literature" without international copyright. It scoffed at Mathews's argument that even American geniuses would be driven to renounce authorship unless they were "blest with a competency."

The writer in the *New World* in commenting on this article portrayed himself as the enemy of American book publishers and the friend of American authors: "We are the best friends of the American authors; because, by breaking up the monopoly of republication which has too long existed here, we force the booksellers into paying for manuscripts if they would enjoy any exclusive privilege." Talent, the *New World* declared, "is wholly independent of legislation; it never entreats but always commands success." Cruelly, borrowing from the article in the London *Spectator* printed earlier in the same issue, Benjamin or his minion in the *New World* declared that "fifty International Copyright Bills" would never make the American people "purchase the 'Works of Cornelius Matthews.'" Real geniuses would thrive because "the American people will take good care of their men of genius." From this time on it became impossible to exaggerate the power of the arguments that proponents of an international copyright law were unpatriotic and that true geniuses would never be silenced.

Having already harmed the cause of copyright while in the United States, on July 7, 1842, back in his home in Regent's Park, Dickens wrote to the editor of the London *Spectator* an intemperate letter in which he denounced the Boston publishers who had sabotaged his international copyright campaign. Quite rightly, he declared that they were deliberately misleading the American public because they had "a strong interest in the existing system of piracy and plunder." He announced a solemn resolution (to which he did not adhere): "For myself, I have resolved that I will never from this time enter into negotiation with any person for the transmission across the Atlantic of early proofs of any thing I may write, and that I will forego all profit derivable from such a source." He singled out newspaper editors, not book publishers, for his vitriol: "They are for the most part men of very low attainments, and of more than indifferent reputation; and I have frequently seen them, in the same sheet in which they boast of the rapid sale of many thousand copies of an English reprint, coarsely and insolently attacking the author of that very book, and heaping scurrility and slander upon his head."

American newspaper editors, offending or innocent, reacted as one. The *Boston Atlas* on August 6, 1842, announced that it had suspected that Dickens's American visit was "prompted by mercenary and less worthy motives than were generally imagined" and now his letter confirmed that suspicion. With this letter, Dickens had, in fact, alienated many Americans by his mercenary talk in the United States even before his *American Notes* (published that October, and promptly serialized in American newspapers such as *Brother Jonathan*) and *Martin Chuzzlewit* (serialized 1843–44) further outraged many Americans with long memories, among them William Cullen Bryant (as became clear late in 1849 when Dickens exposed the English forger and thief Thomas Powell).[2] The *Hartford New England Weekly Review* on August 20, 1842, hooted at the idea of Bulwer coming over with a second "dose": "Yankees don't love to be reviled at their own firesides; and, an Englishman who should worry us about copyrights, at the dinner table, would be apt to find his head and shoulders in the dock, before morning." If Dickens was in favor of an international copyright law, American newspaper editors decidedly were not.

Thus it was partly Dickens's fault when John L. O'Sullivan in the February 1843 *Democratic Review* recanted his support of a copyright bill:

> The International Copyright so eagerly clamored for is all a humbug. We desire to speak both prudently and politely,—with a due fear of the Lord and Mr. Dickens . . . that we were ourselves once seduced even into signing an International Copyright petition to Congress,

before we had matured that riper wisdom on the subject. . . . We are
constrained to say to him, as was once said to his own immortal Pick-
wick, that though in so many other points of view a most glorious
fellow, yet in this particular aspect, *pro tanto* [insofar] and *quoad hoc*
[to this extent], "Sir, you are a Humbug!"

Journalists felt free to rejoice in the absence of such a law, as in this piece
which the *Washington Daily Intelligencer* on May 27, 1847, quoted from
the *New York Mirror*: "The new edition, the *first* American one we believe,
of Izaak Walton's Complete Angler, is on the eve of publication, with abundant annotations from the pen of the Rev. Dr. [George W.] Bethune. It will
contain contributions from [Henry William] Herbert, [Charles] Lanman,
and others. The opportunity of drawing freely from the copyright labors of
English editors, gives the publishers a means of rendering this the most comprehensive edition published." What patriotic American would not want his
or her fellow country-people to have the most comprehensive and cut-rate
edition of *any* favorite British classic? How else could even men and women
on the frontiers become part of the most literate, well-informed, not to say
learned populace in the world? With the national interests in mind, what
American genius would be so selfish as to deny his fellow citizens the best
editions of great books?

1845–1846: The Publishing World Melville Entered

Herman Melville started writing *Typee* in New York City at the end of
1844 or early 1845 while Gansevoort was waiting for James K. Polk to be
inaugurated in March and then to reward him for his spectacular service
as a Democratic campaigner in the election of 1844. As the months passed
Gansevoort's reward was slow in coming, and Herman was also profoundly
frustrated, for after finishing the book in Lansingburgh he had offered it to
the Harpers only to be told that it was obviously fiction and not fit to publish. The Harpers were the obvious choice as the biggest publisher and the
one which had put out young Richard Henry Dana's *Two Years Before the
Mast* in 1839, a book Melville had read just before he sailed as a whaler. Just
possibly, Melville knew that the Harpers had made Dana world famous but
without royalties from the vast annual sales, since they had bought the book
outright for $250. Herman's hope of a career gone, even as Gansevoort's hope
of a political reward seemed futile, he stashed the manuscript in a drawer at
Gansevoort's and the younger brother Allan's law office and perhaps went

back to Lansingburgh for a time. What happened next was purely fortuitous, Thomas Low Nichols's reading the manuscript and advising Gansevoort to try to sell it in England. Gansevoort's mind had been on his own career more than his brother's, but he knew from his reading in 1842, if not later, that Nichols's recommendation was wise.

Strategically or naively, Gansevoort peddled Herman's manuscript as if he were oblivious to the fact that British copyright law was still unsettled. In *Chappell v. Purday* Chief Baron Pollock, after reserving judgment on the case since January 1845, had decided on June 12, 1845, that a foreign author residing abroad who composed and published his work abroad could not copyright it in Britain, but he left it possible that an author residing abroad might acquire a copyright on a book if it were published first in England. Late in 1845, a generous British publisher could act on the assumption that he could safely purchase a book by an American, living in the United States, if it had not been published previously. Gansevoort succeeded.

Gansevoort and Herman understood that if Herman were to have a literary career he needed to secure copyright for his book in both England and the United States. Luck was with them early in the new year. On January 13, 1846, Washington Irving, in London on his return from his time as minister to Spain, made much of Gansevoort, then holding the secretary of legation post he himself had once held. The minister, Louis McLane, was out of the office for the crucial days after Irving's arrival in London. Had he gained Irving's ear, he would have poisoned his old friend against Gansevoort, who had gotten the position over McLane's choice and whom he regarded as a firebrand. Gansevoort was indeed fiery, and febrile, and just then pushing himself to fulfill his duties to the country and his family even as he was dying, though no one suspected how seriously he was ill (McLane viciously reported to Washington that he was malingering). As it was, Irving read some of the proofs of *Typee* and intervened on behalf of the book with his young publisher George P. Putnam, who also happened to be in London. Putnam wrote Gansevoort: "In reply to your proposal respecting a new work by your brother entitled 'A residence in the Marquesas' we beg to say that if you will secure the Copyright in New York . . . we [can] publish the work in New York as soon as it is proposed to publish it here." As Herman's "atty and agent with full power," Gansevoort made a formal acceptance to Wiley & Putnam, specifying their responsibility on copyright: "I depend upon you to secure the copy right in the U S, and hereby authorize you to take it out in my brothers name, Herman Melville."

Late in February, as I have told in another chapter, the third brother, Allan, left in charge of the law office in New York, wrote a hasty, confusing letter which panicked the family in Lansingburgh. On February 23, the day before Gansevoort had his first copies of *Typee* in London, Herman left Lansingburgh, as Maria Melville wrote to her daughter Augusta on February 28 in something of a panic, fearful that the book was not to come out in Wiley & Putnam's Library of Choice Reading and fearful that no copies of the English edition had arrived. If the book were not published in the United States by March 1, Maria explained, Herman would lose the copyright in America. The "copy right was all to Herman," she wrote, as well it should have been. From New York on February 28, while waiting for *Typee* to arrive, Herman wrote to Gansevoort. From the reply it is clear that Gansevoort assumed, as surely Herman did, that his literary career had begun, for he promised that in one of his next letters he would "venture to make some suggestions" about his next book. At this stage any topic deferred meant a message never communicated, for Gansevoort died on May 12, 1846.

Already in 1842 and 1843, when Gansevoort was following the copyright agitation in New York, the cast of characters and the arguments about international copyright were settling into place as Herman would know them. Despite the revulsion against international copyright after Dickens's visit and his next books, Cornelius Mathews and other Americans persisted, as the *Philadelphia North American and Daily Advertiser* reported on August 31, 1843:

> A Copyright Club has been formed in New York. The object of the club, as expressed in its circular, is "to procure the enactment of such law or laws as shall place the literary relations of the United States and foreign countries, in reference to copy-right, on just, equitable, and proper grounds. The first meeting of the club was held at the Athenæum Hotel, on the 23d inst., at which the following gentlemen were elected members; Wm. Cullen Bryant, President, Gulian C. Verplanck, Vice President; Cornelius Matthews, Corresponding Secretary, Evert A. Duyckinck, Recording d[itt]o, A. W. Bradford, Treasurer; Charles F. Hoffman, C. F. Briggs, Parke Godwin, John Keese, Robert Tomes, and C. J. Raymond, Executive Committee.

Verplanck, the Dutch New York state and national legislator, was popularly remembered for his indignation at the Scottish Irving's disrespect for the colonial Dutch in his Knickerbocker's *History*. Keese was famous for the felicitous rhymes he dropped into his book auctioneer's chants. Two years later, in October 1844, Gansevoort ridiculed the poet-editor of the *New York Evening Post* after Bryant ineptly sent around a "secret circular" opposing the annexation of Texas. "Give us Polk and Dallas," cried Gansevoort, "and we shall have Texas in spite of all the protests of all the conspirators, and thousands more like them." Never forgiving Gansevoort for calling him a conspirator any more than he forgave Dickens for insulting newspapermen, Bryant remained aloof from Herman Melville also. Godwin was already Bryant's son-in-law. Later, in 1852 Henry J. Raymond (the initial "C" was a misprint) as editor of the Harper-controlled *New York Times* reversed himself and argued against international copyright in a way cruelly damaging to Herman Melville. Gansevoort Melville had been an intimate friend and traveling companion of Alexander W. Bradford, his mentor from Albany days, and knew some of the others and knew about the rest.

Most of the 1843 signers were much on the scene four years later along with others who had been abroad. Early in 1846 as secretary of the American legation in London, after "a long, friendly & I may almost say intimate conversation" Gansevoort became friends with Nathaniel Parker Willis, once chatting "till midnight over a bowl of hot rum punch" (*Gansevoort Melville's 1846 London Journal*, 18). Herman and Willis became friendly, a few years later, in New York City. The great Washington Irving himself, the author of those "pieces of pleasantry" Sydney Smith had alluded to, after walking and talking with Gansevoort in London and recommending *Typee* to Putnam, would surely have become Herman's patron in the United States if the Gansevoort-hating Minister Louis McLane had not gotten to him. Consummate old-boy that he was, Irving never spoke Melville's name again, as far as we know, although they were frequently linked in articles as fellow sufferers or fellow profiteers from the copyright situation.[3]

On February 10, a week after he had delivered to Putnam all the proof sheets to be transmitted to the United States, Gansevoort went to an entertainment where he "met many Americans," including Putnam and his wife, and also saw "Dickens & his wife—both coarse & vulgar in appearance." Like all Americans, Gansevoort remembered 1842. At Wiley & Putnam, the editor of the Library of American Books, into which *Typee* was placed, was Evert Duyckinck, formerly the co-editor of the short-lived copyright-championing *Arcturus* (and with its other editor, Cornelius Mathews, the principal contributor). Wiley rushed *Typee* into print before realizing how strongly it criticized the Protestant missionaries in the South Seas, and when, after a few months, he demanded that such criticism and sexual indecencies be removed, Duyckinck was delegated to supervise the expurgation. To know Duyckinck was to meet his inseparable companion Mathews. Herman was easily absorbed into the small world Gansevoort had been part of, where he had to take things as they came, unexpected friendships (as from Nathaniel Parker Willis, who remembered Gansevoort's kindnesses) and sometimes aloofness that might or might not have been baffling. Herman had known Bradford before he went to the Pacific and later became more or less intimate co-workers or friends with not just Duyckinck and Mathews (his chosen companions for many months) but also with Hoffman, Briggs, and Tomes. It was a small world.

1847–1848: Melville — Oblivious to Financial Reality

When Melville began his career a fellow American could still coolly assert in the *Broadway Journal* (February 8, 1845), that "a national literature cannot flourish in the United States of North America." Even some literary Americans could not rid themselves of a sense of cultural inferiority: as late as 1877, Oliver Wendell Holmes confessed to feeling sometimes that "aesthetically speaking, America is but a penal colony [of England]" (Morse, 2:222). The hope that there could be a great American literature written by members of a permanent literary class was necessarily linked to the achievement of international copyright. There were salaried Harvard professors like Henry Wadsworth Longfellow who wrote poetry and history books (and the second Mrs. Longfellow brought with her the Appleton wealth) and there were wealthy newspaper editors like William Cullen Bryant who had written poetry. Ralph Waldo Emerson lectured for pay, but lived on what he inherited from his first wife. Nathaniel Hawthorne lived hand to mouth until his college friend Franklin Pierce gave him the plum post of American consul at Liverpool. Henry David Thoreau simplified his wants and died with the bulk of his writing unpublished. Walt Whitman was a carpenter, a newspaper editor, and later a government clerk, who lived cheaply.

On December 18, 1846, the Harpers eagerly signed a contract for *Omoo*, having missed out on *Typee*, but on Christmas Day Melville's mother explained to her daughter Augusta: "Herman is very busy correcting Omoo — and, at the same time endeavoring to procure employment in the C[ustom] H[ouse]." On December 30, 1846, Melville wrote Murray that he had arranged with Harper & Brothers to stereotype and publish the new book: "But it is an express condition that after furnishing me with a complete proof, they shall defer publication until I have time to make arrangements to bring out the book in England. They are not to publish until I notify them so to do. Thus the English copyright can be secured." Gansevoort's successor as secretary of the legation, John Brodhead, handled the sale for Herman, a fairly easy task since John Murray declared himself "much pleased with Omoo — Herman Melvilles new work. Though it has not the novelty of the former, it is full of talent & interest." Murray wrote Brodhead: "I shall be happy to give, for the copyright of it in this country, the Sum of One Hundred & Fifty Pounds." Plainly, Murray was working still on the benign interpretation of Chief Baron Pollock's comments in *Chappell v. Purday* (1845). With *Omoo* finished but not published, and anticipating that he would have to supplement his literary income, Melville went to Washington early in 1847 to try to gain a Custom House job. The family all understood that Melville could expect his income as a writer only to supplement what he made from a real job, not to support himself and his dependents. He failed to get the job but when the early reviews of *Omoo* were almost all enthusiastic (despite attacks from American Protestants with missionaries in the South Seas, and belated criticism of *Typee*), he was able to convince himself that he could succeed as a writer even without having a real job. To understand the reality of life without international copyright was one thing and to act on that understanding was another.

Even without a job in the Custom House, Melville still hoped to marry Elizabeth Shaw. Maria Melville thought Lizzie and Herman could live with her and her four daughters in the rented Lansingburgh house. After all, Lizzie had spent many months there in the last several years. In her cool, deferential way Lizzie resisted until her father came up with a solution. He would advance two thousand dollars against Lizzie's inheritance. According to an ante-nuptial agreement John Gretchko discovered, Allan Melville's fiancée Sophia Thurston would loan five thousand dollars to Herman Melville upon a bond and mortgage for a house and lot in Leyden Place (Fourth Avenue) in New York City for the joint residence of Herman and Allan with the loan to be simultaneous with the assignment of the lease to Herman Melville. This house acquired by "indenture of lease" (not purchase) was on a good street, Fourth Avenue, near Twelfth Street, in the vicinity of Broadway and Union Square, where Herman and Lizzie would live with Maria and her four daughters as well as Allan and *his* bride, Sophia Thurston, and, whenever he was in port, the youngest son, the sailor, Tom. Nothing is known as of now about how expenses, including taxes, were managed. As I have said, we now know, thanks to my discovering 1850 and 1851 advertisements in newspaper databases, that this was a substantial dwelling, a "full sized," fourteen-room three-story house with an attic. According to the 1850 census, four servants (all foreign) lived in, perhaps sleeping in the attic. The married couples seem to have had a little more personal space than the others, although Herman worked in part of his and Lizzie's private area. According to Lizzie's letter to her stepmother on December 23, 1847, Herman had "his room" with his writing desk; she had "her own room," where their bed was, but she seems also to refer to it as "our room," where they have their private time after dinner. Later, after his walk (when he might visit a well-lighted reading room), they all would "collect" in the parlor and one of the family (not Herman, whose eyes were not good enough) would read aloud until ten.

In this very pleasant Manhattan house Melville finished *Mardi* in late April or early May 1848. His wife on May 5 wrote her stepmother: "The book is done now, in fact (you need not mention it) and the copy for the press is in far progress, but where it is published on both sides of the water a great deal of delay is unavoidable and though Herman will have some spare time after sending the proof sheets to London which will be next month sometime probably he will not want to leave New York till the book is actually on the booksellers shelves." As Merrell Davis summarized in 1952, "the whole series of chapters describing the voyage of the Narrator and his companions to the countries of the known geographical world could not have been written until some time after the book was said to be done and 'the copy for the press . . . in progress'" (82). A more cautious man would have tidied up the book as it stood—without the allegorical tour of Revolutionary Europe and a United States in social and political uproar over slavery. Murray would probably have rejected it since it would have been, after the opening, plainly a work of fiction, but another publisher, probably Richard Bentley, who had made overtures to him, would have taken it, and it would surely have been better received than the engorged book which Bentley published in 1849. Then Melville would have shown his gratitude toward his father-in-law for subsidizing his move to New York City, and with a more or less successful third book behind him he could have turned to another book in the summer of 1848 and might well have finished that fourth book while the 1848 *Cocks v. Purday* ruling was encouraging British publishers to believe that they could hold secure copyright on a book by an American if they had first published it in England.

Mardi is easy to defend as the declaration of the literary independence which Melville was to secure in *Moby-Dick*, if not already in *White-Jacket*. It is not easy to defend on practical grounds. As a son-in-law, as a husband, as a man who wanted to have a secure literary career, Melville ought to have finished off *Mardi* early in May 1848 and published it as soon as he could manage. He did not, and *Mardi* cost him his relationship with his first publisher, Murray: who knows? Murray conceivably could have been so taken with the early non-allegorical version that he might have overcome his strong prejudices against fiction. When the time came, Richard Bentley's reader recommended against the book, but Bentley accepted it anyway and published the book to perturbing reviews and disappointing sales. Melville had endangered his reputation to the point that he had to abandon the thought

of doing something yet more ambitious than *Mardi*. Ignorant, of course, of
the reader's report, Melville in his June 5, 1849, letter to Bentley acknowledged but dismissed the reviews: "The critics on your side of the water seem
to have fired quite a broadside into 'Mardi'; but it was not altogether unexpected." He continued recklessly:

> You may think, in your own mind that a man is unwise,—indiscreet,
> to write a work of that kind, when he might have written one per-
> haps, calculated merely to please the general reader, & not provoke
> attack, however masqued in an affectation of indifference or con-
> tempt. But some of us scribblers, My Dear Sir, always have a certain
> something unmanageable in us, that bids us do this or that, and be
> done it must—hit or miss.

Yet in the new book he was just beginning, *Redburn*, Melville intended to
heed the *manageable* something in him, and in fact did so, albeit imperfectly
in that book and more nearly perfectly in the next one, his second of the
summer, *White-Jacket*.

Melville used the term "broadside" to describe the London critics of
Mardi, but he might have argued that he had convinced some London
critics that there was more to him than they had assumed from *Typee* and
Omoo. Sales were bad, but the reviews were not denunciations. Here are
phrases from some major reviews. The *Athenæum*: "this strange book . . . the
affectation of its style . . . many madnesses. . . . Among the hundred people
who will take it up, lured by their remembrances of 'Typee,' ninety readers
will drop off at the end of the first volume." The *Atlas*: "a remarkable book.
When a man essays a continual series of lofty flights, some of his tumbles
will be sufficiently absurd; but we must not be thus hindered from admiring his success when he achieves it." The *Literary Gazette*: "We never saw a
book so like a kaleidoscope. As for giving any idea of it, we have none ourselves." The *Examiner*: "an outrageous fiction; a transcendental *Gulliver*, or
Robinson Crusoe run mad. A heap of fanciful speculations, vivid descriptions, satirical insinuations, and allegorical typifications, are flung together
with little order or connexion; and the result is a book of which the interest is
curiously disproportioned to the amount of cleverness and ability employed
in it." *Bentley's* pronounced Melville "a man intoxicated with imagination."
The *New Monthly Magazine and Humorist* quoted "enough to show that this
is a very remarkable work," then continued: "The style is, unfortunately, too
frequently objectionable, and there is a want of consecutiveness in the narrative, and of decided purpose at the end; but there is a mixture of quaintness

and shrewdness, and of learning and fancy, which imparts a charm to every page, however desultory." The *Critic:* "a production of extraordinary talent." The *Weekly Chronicle:* "we have turned the book over, like a dog might a jellyfish, without being able to make it out, for the life of us. . . . Our readers should get this book, if merely for the curiosity of the thing; strange works come under our paper-knife at times, but a stranger production than 'Mardi' we never met with." The *Home News:* "It is lamentable to see the author of 'Typee and Omoo' so grossly abuse his talents; and it is scarcely honest to avail himself of the reputation which he has established by his former writings to entrap his admirers into the purchase of an unintelligible rhapsody." When Melville presented himself in London in November 1849 many people recalled reading (and even writing) such reviews and some of them even recalled reading *Mardi.*

1849–1851: Too Late, Melville Takes Action

The timing of Melville's offering the new book, *Redburn,* to Bentley, could not have been worse. Days earlier the *Boosey v. Purday* case had been decided. Suddenly there was a flat ruling that a foreigner could not hold copyright in England even if the book was first published there. By this ruling, John Murray did not own copyright to *Typee* and *Omoo* and Richard Bentley did not own the copyright to *Mardi.* Under the circumstances, Bentley on June 20 was magnanimous: "I am willing to give you £100 secured to you on account of half profits. More than this, surrounded as I am with the want of success of Mardi and the stupid decision, at present with regard to copyright, it will not be in my power to give." He went on to appeal to American self-respect: "Why do not you a people, with the grand literature the United States now has, why not at once with dignity come into the International Copyright Act. Surely your literary men have power to accomplish this, and now is the time to do it & shame, our miserable, paltry, shabby lawgivers, & settle the matter beyond question." This did not spur Melville to any public action such as his friends Duyckinck and Mathews had been taking, but the dangers were real enough to make him work harder than he had ever done. Being responsible at last, after being self-indulgent for almost two years on *Mardi,* Melville wrote *Redburn* in two months, then immediately in the next two months wrote a second book of the summer of 1849, *White-Jacket.* Now he thought he deserved a reward. He would take the proofs to England and sell them in person and on part of the proceeds he would make a year-long Grand Tour of Europe, making notes all along the way to put into profitable new books.

We tend to disregard contemporary information which flies in the face of what we know actually happened. Knowing that three months after he left home Melville was on his way back, we assumed that newspaper reports of his planning to be abroad for a year were erroneous, as any newspaper report is apt to be. In my biography I took seriously the reports that Melville was intending to make a Grand Tour of Europe because they jibed with Melville's journal entries on October 15 and 18 about enthusiastic, even ecstatic planning of possible itineraries while on shipboard on his way there, and a more cautious entry on October 26. In 1996 I did not have the November 10, 1849, letter to Richard Bentley, now in the Reese Collection, the one in which Melville refers to his plan to return to London around April or May, in the spring, after his travels on the Continent or perhaps the Levant. When he wrote Bentley, Melville was so full of his plans for travel that he did not even mention the possibility of being paid for *Redburn*; as it turned out, on the twelfth Bentley gave him his note for "£100 at 60 days," saying he "Could'nt do better," and expressing "much anxiety & vexation at the state of the Copyright question." The best Bentley could offer at that time for the sheets of *White-Jacket*: two hundred pounds for publishing a thousand copies. As Melville noted in his journal on November 12, "A liberal offer. But he could make no advance."

If Melville were to make his Grand Tour, he needed an advance. Thereupon he embarked on his quest for a publisher, starting next with Murray, who "was very civil—much vexed about copyright matter" (November 14). Then Henry Colburn rejected *White-Jacket* "on the ground, principally, of the cursed state of the copyright matter" (November 17). At that point Melville acknowledged, "Bad news enough—I shall not see Rome—I'm floored," but began putting the best face on the situation ("appetite unimpaired however—so down to the Edinburgh Castle & paid my compliments to a chop"). Nevertheless, he was bitterly disappointed. He had seldom if ever wanted anything as much as he had wanted to make a Grand Tour, and if the decision on *Boosey v. Purday* in June had gone the other way, he might gotten enough money to finance his trip. Had he spent several months in Europe just at this juncture he might have returned to write a succession of books based on his new travels.

Now trying only to get the best price for *White-Jacket* before returning home, Melville called on Longman in Paternoster Row; on Moxon in Dover Street, Piccadilly, behind Murray's Albemarle Street offices; on David Bogue in Fleet Street, far over on the East End; on Dickens's publishers, Chapman & Hall, on Piccadilly, just before they moved to the Strand; on Bohn at York Street, Covent Garden. The reviews of *Mardi* earlier in 1849, as well as the current reviews of *Redburn*, affected the way the London literary community responded to Melville's making the rounds of publishers late in 1849 trying to sell *White-Jacket*. Gossipers who remembered *Mardi*, especially, mocked him in a way they would not have mocked the author of *Typee*, *Omoo*, and, to take one of Melville's own self-satirizing titles, *Hullabaloo*. While gaining some respect as an eccentric genius, he had lost some of the cachet he had gained so easily in 1846. Melville was hearing from New York, also, for Allan was sending him newspapers.

Melville may have seen news from home about copyright in letters Allan sent, or in the London *Daily News* report (December 13) from its New York correspondent about Putnam's generosity to the Swedish novelist Frederika Bremer. The correspondent gushed that "the feeling in favour of international copyright is growing stronger every day." Many American writers had "been so disgusted with the meanness of the great American publishers, that they have abandoned the pursuit of literature altogether." Others could not support themselves by their writing:

> Mr. Halleck is a mere clerk; Mr. Hoffman occupies a stool in a department in Washington; Mr. Bryant labours daily as an editor; Mr. Sparks is a professor in a college; Mr. Bancroft was obliged to turn his attention to politics; Mr. Street is a sort of deputy-librarian, with a small salary; even Mr. Cooper had to dip a little into cotton, for lack of early success in novel-writing; and Mr. Herman Melville receives more from an English publisher for a single work than all he ever has received, or will receive, from any American. You may now perceive that the shoe which has pinched us so long is very likely to be cast away.

In London, the British publishers who had rejected *White-Jacket* could reflect that if the claim in the London *Daily News* about Melville were true, he would not be receiving so extravagant a reward again, and Melville could reflect on his failure, early in 1847, to gain a Custom House appointment, an outdoor job so much preferable to being "a mere clerk" or occupying a stool in a department.

All unwillingly, Melville was entering into public commentary on the lack of international copyright. Part of it he brought on himself, for on January 12, 1850, in his *Home Journal* N. P. Willis reported on a personal letter Melville had written him from London:

> Our friend Herman Melville is one of the first and most signal realizers of the effect of the recent English repudiation of copyright.

As our readers probably know, it has been a rule among publishers abroad that an agreement of prior publication, between one of their number and an American author, should be as valid as the legal copyright of an English author. To punish us for our wholesale thieving of English books, they have broken up this protection, by mutual consent, and, now, an American author can no more sell a book in England than Dickens can sell one here—justly enough! Melville went abroad, about the time that this retaliatory system came first into action—but knowing nothing of it, and relying on the proceeds of the English editions of his books, for the means of prolonged travel. He writes us that he has abandoned his more extended plans, with this disappointment, and will return sooner than he expected.

Willis then undercut his depiction by echoing the standard piety about genius finding its way: "A man of genius has comparatively no need of money. . . . Poverty sits gracefully on him. With his finer senses, he enjoys ten times as much of everything he sees, hears, tastes, touches and loves." Melville had been familiar with poverty, and on him it had never sat gracefully.

1850: Mockery of Melville's Treks "from Piccadilly to Whitechapel"

On January 15, 1850, while Melville was on his protracted voyage home, almost the six weeks Sydney Smith had gibed about, the *Times* of London printed a letter from "an importer of foreign books" who protested against the Custom House authorities who had begun to seize "all copies of books written by foreign authors which happen to be reprinted in this country upon the plea that such importation is an infringement of the copyright laws." This had happened to the sheets of *Omoo*, early in 1847. Now, said the *Times*, "if you wanted a copy of the original American edition, say of Prescott's *History of Ferdinand and Isabella*, you could not import it, because, forsooth, Mr. Bentley has reprinted (I will not say pirated) it." On the nineteenth the *Times* printed the lament of "An Importer of Foreign Books" protesting against recent seizures by British Customs officials of bound copies of American books he was trying to bring into the country. The Importer commented:

> In times past, Fenimore Cooper could obtain as much as 700£ for the fancied "right" in this country, but his new novel, *The Ways of the Hour*, is in the market for 300£, but no one has the temerity to bid. This could not be, if the "right" asserted by the "Custom-house

Officer" really existed. Let me ask him how it happens that the author of *Typee*, &c., who recently made a voyage to this country on purpose to sell the "right" of his unpublished *White Jacket*, wearily hawked this book from Piccadilly to Whitechapel, calling upon every publisher in his way, and could find no one rash enough to buy his "protected right."

On the twenty-fifth Bentley responded disingenuously in a letter I quote below: Melville had offered the book to him first and he had bought it.

At the end of January, in New York, the English forger Thomas Powell in *Living Authors of America* (buried in the chapter on Poe) viciously called Irving and Melville (who had sailed in October on good terms with Powell) the two worst enemies of the American mind. Their sin, he said, was monopolizing the money English publishers paid to Americans. Melville had been hospitable to Powell at the Fourth Avenue house after the unscrupulous Englishman had insinuated himself into the literary circle headed by Evert A. Duyckinck. Melville, who had deferentially filed away Powell's cautionary parting advice on how not to let landlords cheat him, seems to have been as effectively duped as Duyckinck and his brother George.[4] Seeing this latest treachery of their rotund protégé of the previous summer, the Duyckincks in the *Literary World* of February 2, 1850, printed a quotation with Powell's damning "ENEMIES OF THE NATIONAL MIND" as their title but tried to mock him by adding a parenthetical subtitle: "A dead lift for the copyright question." The idiom "dead lift" may mean a hoisting machine that misfunctions, thereby sinking something instead of raising it, or maybe just a "dead weight":

> It is a curious fact that the worst enemies of the national mind have been a few of her own sons. These are authors who till lately have entirely enjoyed the monopoly of the English market; now they will be obliged to join the body of native authors, and hurry to the rescue. So long as they could trespass on the mistaken courtesy of the British publishers, and get four thousand guineas for this Life of Columbus, and two hundred guineas for that Typee, there was no occasion for any interference; in fact, they were materially benefited by this crying injustice to the great body of authors. Now their own rights are in jeopardy, and they must join the ranks of International Copyright.

This malice, with its blatant lie about what Murray paid for *Typee* and a lie about Melville's previous stance on copyright, was what welcomed Melville home, in Powell's book and in the *Literary World*.

On February 5, 1850, Bryant's *New York Evening Post* printed a long letter from Cornelius Mathews, "International Copyright. Another Prop Knocked Away," a summary of the judgment on the appeal of *Boosey v. Purday*, as passed on to Mathews by George P. Putnam. Then on February 6 Powell seized Willis's affectionately rueful article in the *Home Journal* for use in a complicated piece of chicanery. James Gordon Bennett had been duped into forming an alliance with Powell late in 1849 while most of the newspapers were reveling in Dickens's exposure of Powell as a forger and a thief. Now Bennett printed in the *Herald* a long article entitled "Fruits of Literary Appropriation" in which Powell quoted and slightly embroidered his own "Enemies of the National Mind" passage from *Living Authors of America*, without identifying himself as the author of the book or of the newspaper article: "It is a very curious fact, that while the American publishers have hitherto robbed the authors of the old world of the fruits of their intellectual labors, and grown rich upon the spoils, English publishers have been in the habit of paying liberal sums to our own writers." Powell denounced Irving for coolly appropriating the work of "Navarete, a Spanish historian, of great talents and learned research, who had just then brought out the 'Life and Voyages of Columbus.'" Irving's own "Life and Voyages of Christopher Columbus," he asserted "never cost him one hour's research, and was a little more than a free and fanciful paraphrase of the great work of the Spaniard. Navarete deserved all the credit, but Irving got it, throughout the English world." Powell continued with a claim about how much Irving had been paid (fifteen thousand dollars by Putnam, more by Murray in London) and the assurance that Cooper also had "received immense sums" at home and in England, and other American writers, including Prescott and Bancroft, had been "richly remunerated" by the London publishers.

Melville was chief among the other "enemies" Powell was accusing: "Even the flippant, kaleidoscope, polka-dancing Melville has been enabled to line his pockets pretty substantially by the revenues accruing from his English editions. Hitherto our American writers have been almost as generously rewarded, by the publishers of London, for the works they have brought out, as they would have been if their books had been covered by the shield of a copyright." (The "polka-dancing" remains unexplained.) Now, Powell declared, the "publishers of Great Britain" had "suddenly turned the tables," and "the golden streams which were flowing from the great London houses into the pockets of our popular American authors, have been suddenly checked":

> Mr. Melville started, we are told, some time ago, for England, with
> the early proof sheets of his last book, intending, on the avails of it,

to make the fashionable tour over the continent, and luxuriate in the capitals of Europe, upon the fruit of his labors. The revulsion came on. He was coolly informed, by his former London publisher, that he could pay no more copyrights; and the aforesaid intellect quits the great metropolis in despair, with empty pockets, and turns his face once more towards his native land.

Powell of course had not been "told" by gossips about Melville's plans, which he reported accurately, except for his tone and his charge that Melville would have been anything but frugal. Powell had discussed those plans with Melville, sharing his ripe friendly wisdom with the younger man, who he thought would be more at a loss in London than in the South Seas. Now in the *Herald* Powell shamelessly repeated his own insulting words, giving them much more currency than they had enjoyed in his book: "It is a curious fact, that the worst enemies of the national mind, have been a few of her own sons. These are the authors who, till lately, have entirely enjoyed the monopoly of the English market. Now they will be obliged to join the body of native authors, and hurry to the rescue. Now their own rights are in jeopardy, and they must join the ranks of international copyright." (Six years later, on April 14, 1856, in the *New York Daily News*, Powell announced that Murray had paid Melville $1,000 for the copyright to *Typee*—not so far off, if you count both the original £100 and £50 for a sequel about Toby, the rough equivalent of $750.)

In the *Literary World* of February 9, 1850, Duyckinck announced Melville's return and tried to set things straight without directly confronting Powell again: "Notwithstanding the unsettled state of the International Copyright Question, he was met in a spirit of liberality by Mr. Bentley, who is at present largely engaged in the publication of American books, with whom he entered into a satisfactory arrangement for his next work. It is a romance entitled 'White Jacket; or, the World in a Man-of-War.'" Commentary on Melville continued on February 14, 1850, in a letter from "P." (dated January 25, 1850), the London correspondent of the *North American and United States Gazette* (Philadelphia). The news was bad:

> It is now said that, through a perverted meaning of the English copyright act, Americans have for years enjoyed privileges which they have denied to British subjects in their own country. It is declared that neither Prescott, Cooper, Irving, Bancroft, Sparks, Bryant, or any other American author, is entitled to a copyright for any of his works in England, under any circumstances. These gentlemen believe that their works, or their publishers, are protected, but in a

recent important case the Lord Chief Baron decided that *"no alien can either hold or assign a copyright in this country."* Prescott, Bancroft, and others, will soon hear of new and cheap English editions of their works on every book stall in London. Cooper's novels are already reprinted, and sold at one shilling sterling each. A beautiful edition of Bryant's Poems is sold for two shillings. Channing's works are all reprinted. Cooper could always obtain seven or eight hundred pounds for a new novel, but his last work, *"Ways of the Hour,"* is handed about from one shop to another, and not even three hundred is offered. Melville's *"White Jacket"* was carried by the author from the West-end to the East-end, and from thence back to Bentley, who finally took it at a trifling sum. It will be seen that an international copyright treaty is now all-important to both England and America.

By this time Bentley had given notice that he would sue anyone who reprinted any American work he had paid for, not so much to recover damages as to get a ruling which would "settle the question, which is still a matter in dispute, whether an alien can hold or assign copyright in England." In this letter by "P." the conventional phrase "West-end to East-end" accurately traced the terrain Melville had covered with his bundle of proofs, although its tone may be elusive. Later comments seem more obviously sardonic and even contemptuous.

On February 23, 1850, while Melville was at home in New York City waiting for *White-Jacket* to be published, and almost certainly after he had started writing *Moby-Dick,* the *New York Albion* reprinted from the *Times* of London the lament of "An Importer of Foreign Books," including the lines about Melville's wearily hawking *White-Jacket* "from Piccadilly to Whitechapel, calling upon every publisher in his way, and could find no one rash enough to buy his 'protected right.'" "From Piccadilly to Whitechapel," like "from the West-end to the East-end," was a common phrase meaning from one end of London to the other, from the elegant West End around Piccadilly to the increasingly squalid area near Fleet Street, where in fact Melville had called on David Bogue. On February 23 the *Literary World* also printed a long article on "International Copyright" which also quoted the news that Melville had "wearily hawked this book from Piccadilly to Whitechapel." There was no escaping the slurs.

In the *Times* on January 25, 1850, Bentley had tried to set straight the "Importer" as far as he was concerned, and on March 2, 1850, the *Literary World* reprinted the publisher's letter under the heading "MR. MELVILLE AND COPYRIGHT IN ENGLAND":

> Your anonymous correspondent avers that the author of *Typee* could find no one rash enough to buy the "protected right" of his unpublished *White Jacket*, after "wearily hawking this book from Piccadilly to Whitechapel." My answer to this is, that the work was in the first instance offered to me by the author himself, and I have become the purchaser of what I firmly believe to be the copyright, for a considerable sum; quite sufficient to make me in earnest to defend that right, should the "Importer," or any of his friends, attempt to invade it.

The Duyckincks followed this with a letter from an unidentified American ("K.") defending Melville against the charge of peddling his wares in ungentleman-like fashion:

> GENT.—Without going into the question of International Copyright raised by the correspondence in the London Times, and copied into your journal of the 23d inst., I believe injustice may be done Mr. Melville as well as his publisher, by allowing the statement that the former "wearily hawked his unpublished *White Jacket* from Piccadilly to Whitechapel, calling upon every publisher in his way," &c., to pass uncontradicted. It is simply untrue. But that is not all. Mr. Melville had not the slightest difficulty in making an arrangement for the publication of *White Jacket* with Mr. Bentley, the publisher of Mr. Melville's previous work, and what is more, such arrangement was concluded promptly, without impediment or finesse. Mr. Melville is not the man to "hawk" his wares in any market, and Mr. Bentley not the publisher to allow so capital a book to escape him. One word, by the way, of the latter. His liberality to authors is proverbial. To Washington Irving for his *Alhambra*, Mr. Bentley paid one thousand guineas . . . .

Who K. could be is unknown, but presumably someone near the Melville family who wanted to portray him as above mere commercial concerns. (Augustus Kinsey Gardner?) Following K.'s letter (as part of the whole "Mr. Melville and Copyright in England"), the *Literary World* under the subheading "Assumed copyright in foreign authors" reprinted the "short-hand report" of the *Boosey v. Purday* case of June 5, 1849, which Bentley had bitterly cited to Melville just after the decision had been reached. Here, with Melville as the example at hand, Americans (including the Harpers and other publishers) could read the Lord Chief Baron's lengthy pronouncement that foreign writers could hold no copyright in England.

Chapter 16

Melville Without International Copyright (1850–1854)

A Harper "Sacrifice" for the "Public Good"

In late March 1850 (according to the *Boston Daily Evening Transcript* on April 8) a "modest paragraph" began to be "adroitly insinuated in the editorial columns of some of our most respectable newspapers." This referred to the Boston publisher Frederick Gleason's notice that he had so admired a story by a young novelist, Waldo Howard, that he had pressed into his hands "some $3000.00 in payment for the manuscript of *The Mistake of a Lifetime; or, the Robber of the Rhine Valley*, while promising also the happy Mr. Howard a share of the profits." This item was widely reprinted, with slight updatings. Before the publicity died down the *Transcript* led a campaign mocking Gleason and his prize, so that on June 7 the *Burlington (Vt.) Centinel* called attention to the Boston papers which had been poking fun at "Waldo Howard, Esq." with "uncommonly sharp sticks." Midway during this high-spirited gossip, on April 8, the *Transcript* gave editors something else to copy besides Gleason's promotional paragraphs—the news that the editors of *Yankee Nation* were claiming to have paid considerably upwards of five thousand dollars for an original novel, beating Gleason:

> Most refreshing it is to see our authors so liberally remunerated. If the young and the obscure derive such sums from the sale of their manuscripts, what may be expected of those, whose fame is already established? May we not soon hope to see Hawthorne riding in his carriage—Whipple building a chateau—Benjamin giving princely entertainments at Newport—Longfellow making a Lawrence-like

donation to Harvard University—Melville keeping his yacht—and
our lady writers (the unmarried ones) all run after as heiresses?

Perhaps playing on the lyrics of the new song by Charles Mackay ("There's a
Good Time Coming"), the writer concluded that it was "evident, that a good
time for authors is coming." This article also was reprinted widely, as is plain
from the reprintings in the relatively few papers available in recent newspaper databases. Here was much better news than stories about Melville's
hawking *White-Jacket* from Piccadilly to Whitechapel. American writers
were doing extremely well without an international copyright law, just as the
opponents had been saying for years. In early March 1850 Americans had
already been assured that the proud, self-respecting Melville was "not the
man to 'hawk' his wares in any market," and now they were assured that Melville was in no financial trouble at all.

In late May 1850, while papers were still telling their readers tardily that
Melville might soon be "keeping his yacht," the Harpers issued a prospectus
for "Harpers' New Monthly Magazine" (the actual magazine had the apostrophe before the *s*). Focused on his whaling manuscript (halfway through,
he estimated), Melville may have thought casually that *Harper's* might be a
good a place to publish, sometime. There was no reason he should guess just
how big a threat to his career the magazine would be, but in fact the Harpers
had been clear enough. Their editors, they declared, would scan British and
French "Reviews, Magazines and Newspapers" for pieces by "the best writers" ("Lamartine, Dickens, Alison, Lever, Bulwer, Croly, and Macaulay").
Even better for the American public, *Harper's* promised to reprint fiction
only a few weeks later than it was first serialized in London: "The Magazine
will transfer to its pages, as rapidly as they may be issued, the continuous tales
of Dickens, Bulwer, Croly, Lever, Warren, and other distinguished contributors to British periodicals." All this Americans could have for three dollars a
year or twenty-five cents an issue.

On June 27, 1850, with *Harper's New Monthly Magazine* already a reality, Melville began trying to sell his new book to Richard Bentley: "In the
latter part of the coming autumn I shall have ready a new work and I write
you now to propose its publication in England." It would be, he said, "a
romance of adventure founded upon certain wild legends in the Southern
Sperm Whale Fisheries, and illustrated by the author's own personal experience, of two years & more, as a harpooneer." He was optimistic, since
Bentley had paid him for *White-Jacket* even under the present ruling on
copyright:

> Should you be inclined to undertake the book, I think that it will be worth to you £200. Could you be positively put in possession of the copyright, it might be worth to you a larger sum—considering its great novelty; for I do not know that the subject treated of has ever been worked up by a romancer; or, indeed, by any writer, in any adequate manner.

Even looking that far ahead, he saw that it would be "indispensable" that Bentley on the day of sale give him a note for the two hundred pounds, which he could then discount for cash.

In his sales pitch Melville was asking Bentley to risk two hundred pounds even under the Lord Chief Baron's decision of June 5, 1849, and to pay Melville more than that if the law changed so as to allow Bentley to possess the copyright. On August 2, 1850, Thomas Delf, the bookseller Melville had twice called on but missed when in London, wrote his friend George Duyckinck of a strange new complication: "Murray has just applied in the Court of Chancery for an injunction against H G Bohn, Routledge and others, for pirating W. Irving's & Melville's [works] on the plea that these gentlemen are not aliens in England. How they will like to be claimed as Britishers I know not, but Mr [Thomas] Powell must put them in his next Edition of the Living Authors of England." Delf continued sardonically: "We may require W. Irving's certificate of baptism and H. Melville's pedigree, really this new start is very amusing. What marvelous ingenuity is there in the Law!"

On August 10, 1850, the London *Examiner* reported on a case in the Vice Chancellor's Court: "Copyright in the Works of American Authors.—Murray *v.* Bohn.—Murray *v.* Routledge":

> On Thursday the case of Murray *v.* Routledge, affecting the copyright of "Melville's Marquesas Islands," was brought forward. The plaintiff claimed the copyright, by purchase, of Mr Herman Melville, of New York, of the work in question, which was first published in England by him in 1846, as well as "Omoo," in 1847. The plaintiff complained of a violation of his copyright by the publication of those works in "The Popular Library," by Mr George Routledge, of Soho square. The case made by the defendant's affidavit was, that these works had been previously published before appearing in this country, and that as in Mr Irving's case, the author was an alien at the time of that publication in this country, and was not domiciled in England.

It was decided that this case should "stand over" until *Murray v. Bohn* was tried.

The situation gave great delight to London satirists. *Punch* on August 24, 1850, demanded of Americans, "How Do You Like It?" For years "Literary Jonathan made a piratical war on Literary John Bull. An English book was an American book—in all but the profit it brought in to its author." Meanwhile, *Punch* went on, the British had been magnanimous: "Washington Irving received his well-earned £10,000 from Mr. Murray. Mr. Melville pocketted the (equally well-earned) price of his *Typee* and *Omoo* and *White Jacket*. So Mr. Cooper made his honest market with Mr. Bentley, and touched the proceeds, but *nous avons changé tout cela!*" After this reminder of Molière's memorable retort, *Punch* declared Murray's and Bentley's copyrights for American works to be "good for nothing," all "open to the pirates of this side the water." Finally, *Punch* demanded: "How will the Washington Irvings, the Prescotts, the Coopers, the Melvilles of America like this? Will they agitate for an International Copyright, now that their brains are exposed to the same gratis picking, as our poor English ones have been so long subjected to?"

On September 14, 1850, the *Literary World* reported on Murray's attempts to "enjoin Bohn and Routledge," who had "issued cheap editions of the works, from the publication of the books of Washington Irving and Herman Melville." The *Athenæum* had confirmed what Thomas Delf had reported, that Murray was so concerned to protect his valuable Irving copyrights that he was claiming that Irving was not an American after all, "his father having been a native of the Orkneys, and his mother a native of Falmouth, and that though he himself was born in New York, he is the son of British born subjects and therefore no alien." Routledge had been equally reckless, professing to believe that *Typee* and *Omoo* were not first published in England. On September 21, 1850, *John Bull* in the "Value of American Copyrights" reported that Murray had paid Irving, all told, nearly "£10,000 for copyrights." Not to be outdone, Bentley reported that he had paid nearly £16,000 "to three other eminent American authors for their copyrights in this country, these being Mr. Prescott, Mr. Fenimore Cooper, and Mr. Hermann Melville." Casual readers could divide sixteen by three and come up with a quotient which was several times higher than Melville's actual earnings from Bentley. On October 12, 1850, the *Literary World* quoted the London *Athenæum* on the nearly £10,000 that Murray had paid Irving and quoted Bentley as saying he had paid "Mr. Prescott, Mr. J. Fenimore Cooper, and Mr. Melville between £15,000 and £16,000." The *Boston Daily Evening Transcript* on November 14 gave the same report for all of Melville's Boston family to read. In the middle of this Melville tried to cooperate, on September 25, 1850, signing an indenture conveying to John Murray the copyright of *Typee* and *Omoo* in consideration of previous payments made by Murray "and in consideration of ten shillings of lawful British money in hand also paid . . . for and during the term of Forty two years from the several days of the first publication thereof."

In September, ready to abandon New York City, Melville prevailed upon his father-in-law to advance three thousand dollars toward the purchase of a farm in Pittsfield adjacent to the Melvill place to the east, and early in October with his wife, his mother, and, at that time, three of his sisters, Melville moved there, soon naming the farm Arrowhead. There, after many interruptions, he settled back to work on *Moby-Dick*. While he worked, much was happening. Copying from the London *Chronicle* of December 12, 1850, the *Albion* on January 4, 1851, reported "The Copy-Right Law Still Unsettled," but that a new ruling seemed to overturn *Boosey v. Purday*, the decision which so distressed the publishers Melville visited late in 1849.

Melville must have heard what seemed like good news from England, but he was obsessed with his whaling book. Others were more alert to the damage *Harper's* might do to American writers, for the January 1851 *Whig Review* printed "Puny Poets and Piratical Publishers," nominally a review of N. P. Willis's new edition of his *Poems*, which the reviewer found both popular and unworthy. The gist of the review was a denunciation of American publishers as "selfish and unpatriotic" and in particular the publishers of any unspecified monthly magazine "gotten up by influential and wealthy houses, which will overmatch American productions, as well in quantity as quality of matter." It was obvious what he was talking about even before he accused the editors at *Harper's New Monthly Magazine* of being unconcerned that American writers were "generally too poor to write and work for nothing," which they would be doing, now that they were competing with the best of British and French writing. The reviewer perceived the diabolical sweep of the Harper scheme: "Hence, a large publishing house like that of the Harpers, wealthy, influential, and anti-American in feeling as concerns literary development and encouragement, may easily swell their enormous gains by pampering British writers who are legally debarred from copyright in this country." Meanwhile, an American-hearted publisher, if there was such a creature, one "devoted to the culture of home literature, and forced to pay high for good writers," would be "crowded out of the market."

Early in 1851 the Harpers were caught doing a dirty trick. George Putnam paid John Murray for the right to publish George Borrow's *Lavengro* in what he made into a handsome edition. Copies were for sale at one dollar around the country in late February 1851. Three days later copies were for sale at two shillings (twenty-five cents) in the "Harpers' Cheap Reading" series, set from a stolen copy—supplied by a bribed Putnam clerk. The story took a satisfying turn which made the rapacity of the Harpers news for months, in the United States and even abroad. Lewis Gaylord Clark apparently regaled Dickens with the story, and Thomas Powell had the story in his April 26, 1851, *Figaro!* from the London *Punch*, which he quoted at some length, taking delight in the "monster, in the human form," who had delivered the defective copy to the Harpers. "Who is the monster?" Powell asked, in a way that may have pointed toward his own experience with a Putnam clerk, the Duyckinck brother-in-law Henry Panton. On May 17, 1851, the *Tallahassee Floridian and Journal* reprinted more of the indictment of Harpers from *Punch*. The writer singled out one Harper brother, James, the Nativist (anti-Catholic, anti-immigrant) mayor of New York in 1844–45:

> The house of book-taker and book-seller Harper, of New York, is a house built of the skulls of English authors. Never did Philip, the terrible red man, take so many scalps as have fallen to the lot of the Ex-Mayor of New York. He is a man all brains—the brains of other people. Harper makes his daily four meals off the bones of British penmen. A joint of Bulwer decks his breakfast table; at luncheon he has a snack of Tennyson, at dinner, Dickens and Macaulay, with Mrs. Somerville and Mrs. Howitt as side-dishes; and at supper—for Harper has a wondrous digestion—James and Mrs. Trollope.

Yet in New York "a knave's trick" had been played upon the Harpers. Putnam's, the writer explained, had paid John Murray for Borrow's *Lavengro* "much to the virtuous ire of the house of Harper." "Harper" (James, standing in for the whole firm) had received a copy from the clerk and, "jocund and smiling, rubbing his hands," had "set an army of compositors to work" and produced their *Lavengro* simultaneously with Putnam's. The thief, doubly treacherous, had betrayed the Harpers, giving them "an imperfect, a maimed, a crippled *Lavengro*," missing whole pages. The harp of these Harpers, said *Punch*, was "not strung with common cat gut; but with the literary heart-strings of scribbling Britishers!" This kind of gossip made the rounds in New York City with knowledgeable embellishments while the Harpers were trying to present themselves as both patriotic and moral.

No one rented the empty Fourth Avenue Melville house during the months it was advertised, November through March, but the indenture of lease finally sold in the late winter of 1851, for less than Melville had hoped. Much of the money must have gone back to Sophia Thurston Melville.

Some of it went to the previous owner of Arrowhead, who was carrying the mortgage and had been waiting months for a portion of the promised down payment. Some of it went to out-of-season construction, refurbishing the old farmhouse and building a piazza. When Melville asked the Harpers for a substantial advance in April 1851, Fletcher Harper poor-mouthed: "The requirements of our business have compelled us to make an extensive and expensive addition to our establishment: one which will demand all our resources. We feel unable, therefore, to make the advance desired, especially as, on making up your account, a copy of which we send you, we find there is a balance due us of nearly seven hundred dollars." The amount they cited was, in fact, $695.65. Frantic, Melville made his own "Mistake of a Life-time." Keeping it confidential, a friendly loan, he borrowed $2,050 from a man he knew from Lansingburgh and New York City, Tertullus D. Stewart. The terms were five years at nine percent interest, Melville to pay $92.25 every November 1 and May 1 and to repay the $2,050 on May 1,1856. (He made the November 1, 1851, interest payment and defaulted twice a year from then on.) Once the Harpers had refused his request for an advance, Melville had hopes of leaving them for a more supportive publisher, so he used some of Stewart's money to pay Richard Craighead to set and stereotype what he was calling *The Whale*, so that he could lease or sell the plates to any publisher he came to terms with, if he could rouse himself to hawk the work from Ann Street to Cliff Street.

All through 1851 news from England on copyright seemed good. On June 12, 1851, the *Boston Daily Evening Transcript* printed "Foreign Copyright in England," a secondhand report from the *Washington Republic* on the May 1851 decision by Lord Campbell "under which American and other foreign authors are admitted to the privilege of enjoying a copyright for their publications in England." On June 14, 1851, the *Literary World* reported at length on that "Boosey vs. Jeffereys" (properly "Jeffreys") decision: "From this it would appear that the present interpretation of the law is, that a foreign author may secure the copyright of his work in England by first publishing it there, and that he may assign his right to do so." The London *Morning Chronicle* of July 1, 1851, printed a notice of "Infringement of Copyright" signed by "John Murray" and dated 50, Albemarle Street, June 1851: "I hereby give notice, that if any bookseller, or other person, shall sell, or expose for sale, any copy, or copies, of any pirated editions, whether published by George Routledge, or others, of the works of Washington Irving and Herman Melville, or in any way infringe my copyright in them, I shall immediately take legal proceedings to protect my rights." Several American newspapers reported on a July 1, 1851, meeting of "distinguished authors and well-known London publishers" in the Hanover Square Rooms to discuss "the anomalous state of the English copyright laws," Sir Edward Lytton Bulwer chairing.[1] According to these reports, Bulwer announced that "Boosey vs. Purday," which had so perturbed Bentley in June 1849, had "lately been reversed by Lord Campbell, who has decided that foreigners, by sending their works to this country for first or simultaneous publication, have the same privileges as English authors." John Murray announced that he had "recently commenced proceedings against Mr. George Routledge, a publisher of cheap books, for reprinting the works of Washington Irving and Herman Melville, the copyrights of which were purchased by Mr. Murray." Following Lord Campbell's decision, Murray continued, "Routledge has compromised the case with Mr. Murray, by withdrawing from circulation and delivering to Mr. Murray all copies of these reprints, and has agreed not to infringe further on Mr. Murray's rights in these works." Murray was emboldened to give public notice to all booksellers that if they offered for sale any copies of these "pirated editions" legal proceedings would be taken against them. Bentley and other London publishers who had purchased works of American authors gave similar notices.

Lord Campbell's decision was well timed for Melville to approach Bentley on July 20, 1851, a year after his first writing about the whaling book. Accepting Bentley's offer of £150 "at three & six months," Melville then made his longest surviving comments on international copyright:

> And here let me say to you,—since you are peculiarly interested in the matter—that in all reasonable probability no International Copyright will ever be obtained—in our time, at least—if you Englishmen wait at all for the first step to be taken in this country. Who have any motive in this country to bestir themselves in this thing? Only the authors.—Who are the authors?—A handful. And what influence have they to bring to bear upon any question whose settlement must necessarily assume a political form?—They can bring scarcely any influence whatever. This country & nearly all its affairs are governed by sturdy backswoodsmen—noble fellows enough, but not at all literary, & who care not a fig for any authors except those who write those most saleable of all books nowadays—i e—the newspapers, & magazines. And tho' the number of cultivated, catholic men, who may be supposed to feel an interest in a national literature, is large & every day growing larger; yet they are nothing in comparison with the overwhelming majority who care nothing about it. This country is at present engaged in furnishing material for future authors; not in encouraging its living ones.

Wishfully, more than a little fatuously, he suggested that if England would "come out magnanimously, & protect a foreign author" then Americans would eagerly reciprocate: "For, be assured, that my countrymen will never be outdone in generosity.—Therefore, if you desire an International Copyright—hoist your flag on your side of the water, & the signal will be answered; but look for no flag on this side till then."

1851–1852: The Harpers Grind Melville Down

Henry Raymond had been in the pockets of the Harpers as early as 1847, when he was writing for the *Courier and Enquirer*. In the abolitionist *Washington National Era* (May 27, 1847) the New York correspondent "John Smith the Younger" (J. A. Houston) gave his view of the situation: "Mr Raymond, the writer in the *Courier*, is connected with the Harpers, the great American publishers, and therefore speaks by the card." (As in Hamlet's words to Horatio, "We must speak by the card, or equivocation will undo us," to speak by the card meant to speak reliably, by the shipman's card, or the face of a mariner's compass.) Formerly a founding member of the Copyright Club, Raymond already in 1847 was speaking for his masters, the Harper brothers. It was his job to spread news in the *Courier and Enquirer* of how rich authors were getting *without* the protection of an international copyright law. As Houston said, Raymond was maintaining that "the present order of things is just as advantageous to authors as the system for which the advocates of an international copyright law so strenuously contend. All authors of celebrity, he says, in both countries, receive large sums for 'advance' copies of their works." Raymond was a happy and soon-to-be very well recompensed tool of the Harpers.

Having succeeded with *Harper's New Monthly Magazine* in 1850, in mid-1851 the Harpers found a way of extending their influence through a New York City paper that would champion the best interests of Harper & Brothers, now that James Watson Webb, the proprietor of the *Courier and Enquirer*, had soured on Henry J. Raymond. The new journal was the *New York Times*, of which the founding editor was the Harpers' loyal helper, Raymond. On May 9, 1851, the *North American and United States Gazette* (Philadelphia) announced that Raymond was said to have retired from the *Courier and Enquirer* and would "shortly sail for Europe, to recruit his health. The rumor is, that certain parties in New York have offered Mr. Raymond very abundant means to establish another paper in that city, and that the overture will probably be accepted." On July 31, 1851, the *Trenton State*

Gazette quoted the *New York Day Book* as saying that sixty thousand dollars had been raised to start the paper, ten thousand of which came from James and John Harper. Other reports had Fletcher Harper holding ten thousand dollars of stock. The Harpers issued a blanket denial. The *Boston Daily Evening Transcript* on August 18 quoted the *New York Journal of Commerce* as having been "requested to state that there is no truth in the reports that any member of the firm of Harper & Brothers is to be interested, directly or indirectly, by contribution or otherwise, in any newspaper about to be started in the city of New York or elsewhere." Nevertheless, on November 9 the *Philadelphia Sunday Dispatch* announced that the "Times enjoys the reputation of a heavy, advanced capital, and is owned in shares, by several leading houses: Harper & Bros, they say, have $10,000 in it." The early rumors probably had a high proportion of truth in them, for the Harpers soon were exercising control over the *Times*. Every year New York City dailies were founded and foundered, but the Harpers were immensely wealthy, and a paper they backed, even one with a pedestrian title like the *Times*, had a good chance of lasting a year or two, at least until their investment had turned a profit.

Melville in the summer of 1851 thought his career was progressing. With the publication of *The Whale* his high literary stature would be secured. He thought he had new choices because he owned the plates of the whaling book, and Duyckinck a little officiously was pushing him to consider J. S. Redfield as the publisher. Melville settled with the Harpers in September at the usual rate of half profits after costs. Perhaps inertia was to blame. When he had been mocked for hawking *White-Jacket* from one end of London to the other he may have remembered what it had been like as a young man to go out on foot looking for work, fruitlessly. Now he was profoundly reluctant to go out peddling the Craighead proofs around lower Manhattan. He still had some of Stewart's $2,050 left (enough to repay Stewart $92.25 interest on the first of November). Early in the fall he had every reason to think that *The Whale* (the later title, *Moby-Dick*, having reached Bentley too late) would be a handsome book brilliantly reviewed, and the Harper edition would be eagerly awaited, since it had been heralded by "The Town-Ho's Story" in the October *Harper's New Monthly Magazine*.

Yet within weeks of the publication of the American edition in mid-November Melville's mood had changed. His wife's illness after the birth of Stanwix late in October affected everyone, especially since she had to be taken to Boston for prolonged recuperation, leaving Melville wifeless for weeks, just when he unreasonably felt abandoned after Hawthorne left Lenox on November 21. Now writing *Pierre* as his "Kraken" book, his attempt to master the psychological romance that the Bell brothers (or Brontë sisters, as they might be) and men like Bulwer were practicing, Melville worked himself into a febrile state of mind and body that by late December 1851 was worrying his family even before his neighbor Sarah Morewood at Christmas called attention to the dangers of his obsessive work. Part of his new anxiety came from local hostility, where neighbors were gossiping that *Moby-Dick* was worse than blasphemous. Part of it came from reviews he saw, including Duyckinck's pained and paining reproach for his irreverence in the *Literary World*. What he felt about the reviews of *Moby-Dick* is recorded in inverted fashion in the praise he assigned to young Pierre's reviewers in passages he added in January 1852 to the book that he had completed at the end of December.[2]

The copyright situation was better than ever, just then, but yet another factor in Melville's anxiety came from horror at realizing late in November and early in December that *The Whale* had been bungled, printed without the epilogue, making him an object of ridicule in London. Plainly, in pushing those "E" sections into the back of the third volume ("Etymology," "Extracts") the half page of the Harper text containing the epilogue had been lost. This time, just by luck, few English reviews were reprinted in the United States, and the most conspicuous of those complained about the incompetence or downright madness of writing a story in which the narrator did not survive. The bulk of the review in the *Athenæum* was quoted in the *Boston Post* on November 20 along with scathing comments based on the British paper's denunciation of the ending, the Boston writer claiming to "have read nearly one half" of *Moby-Dick* but obviously not having read as far as the epilogue. Then the entire article was reprinted in the *Statesman*, the sister paper of the *Post*. The *Athenæum* review was then reprinted in full in the December *New York Eclectic Magazine*, and in December Rufus Griswold's *International Magazine* reprinted the *Spectator* review, which also complained about the ending in which the narrator did not survive. The *Boston Post* was determined that the Harpers would see what they had to say: "'The Whale' is not worth the money asked for it, either as a literary work or as a mass of printed paper. Few people would read it more than once, and yet it is issued at the usual cost of a standard volume. Published at *twenty five cents*, it might do to buy, but at any higher price, we think it a poor speculation." Melville's aunts and Lizzie's family, of course, saw this. Melville could conceivably have protested to the *Post* that he had written an ending for his book, truly, but there was always the chance that the editor could make fun of any comment he ventured to make.

Now, bafflingly, and certainly self-destructively, Melville kept silent in the United States and failed to write to Richard Bentley about the loss of the epilogue in the English edition. He was on friendly terms with Bentley and must have assumed that the loss of the epilogue was accidental, not deliberate. He could have suggested that the "fine old man of fifty" (as Melville had estimated) make a feature of the lost epilogue in *Bentley's Magazine*, as soon as possible, or, better, that Bentley go public with an apology to the purchasers of the three volumes and offer a leaf containing the lost passage for buyers to tip into their copies. To be sure, admitting a mistake would not have given Bentley what "The Story of Toby" gave Murray, a publicity bonanza, but a shrewd publisher could have made favorable news out of the blunder. There is no indication that Melville ever said one word to Bentley about the disaster. Indeed, there is absolutely no indication that Bentley ever knew the epilogue had been lost from his edition. The Harpers could have looked at the scathing denunciations in the *Athenæum* and the *Spectator* without noticing that the basis for the complaints was a textual blunder, the loss of something that was properly printed in their own *Moby-Dick*. Melville by early December understood what had happened, whether or not he had received his copies of *The Whale*. If Melville had apprised Bentley of the blunder, just possibly the publisher might have felt some obligation to behave somewhat differently the next spring.

When Melville arrived in town with *Pierre*, the Harpers did not need a love story in which incest was alluded to and perhaps enacted (as the contemporary printer's pun went) between the sheets. They had love stories from G. P. R. James, Bulwer, and many more. They did not need an American author against whom they had strong grievances because of the denunciations which his books, most recently *Moby-Dick*, had received from religious reviewers. At the extreme there was the all-inclusive warning in the *New York Independent* on November 20, 1851:

> The Judgment day will hold him [Melville] liable for not turning his talents to better account, when, too, both authors and publishers of injurious books will be conjointly answerable for the influence of those books upon the wide circle of immortal minds on which they have written their mark. The book-maker and the book-publisher had better do their work with a view to the trial it must undergo at the bar of God.

This was far worse than the mockery in the *Post* of *Moby-Dick* being six times overpriced—this touched the Harpers personally. They did not need *Pierre*, and they had money-making plans that would keep Melville in his place, plans which they were keeping absolutely secret.

At the Harpers' offices on Cliff Street on New Year's Day or one of the following days there probably was no casual author-publisher chat in which Melville could have pointed out that the writer in the *Post* had not read far enough into *Moby-Dick* to know what the British paper said about *The Whale* was not true of the American book. He might, in a more friendly setting, have interested the Harpers in making delightful publicity from the appalling embarrassment in one of *Harper's* back sections. In the "Editor's Easy Chair" or the "Editor's Drawer," either one, they could have inserted a clever item about Bentley's blunder in dropping the epilogue. If the Harpers had been paying attention to a valued writer, they could, on their own, have come up with a strategy for making the best of an awkward accident. They could even have exposed the ignorance of the *Boston Post.* Nothing of the sort happened. The negotiations over *Pierre* were grim. Fletcher Harper, who had rejected Melville's plea for an advance in April, perhaps had decided to punish Melville yet again for offending many Christians and embarrassing him and his brothers. Rather than setting him loose to reenact on the icy streets of Manhattan his well-publicized peregrinations about London with the sheets of *White-Jacket*, they did not reject *Pierre* outright but hit Melville in the purse, offering him only twenty cents on the dollar after their costs rather than the old terms, fifty cents on the dollar. If he had not been able to live on half profits, how could he live on twenty cents?

After the first days of 1852 Melville was no longer on speaking terms with the Duyckincks, and he seems not to have visited any of his other editorial friends, such as Willis, who might have enjoyed writing up the textual misadventure with the epilogue. Not a word has been found in newspapers or magazines or other sources about the lost epilogue, not for many decades. Judging from what happened later, as I have explained, Melville took the manuscript to Duyckinck, perhaps hoping the interest of Redfield in *Moby-Dick* would be re-aroused for the new book. Duyckinck's dismay or outright horror lies behind what Melville did late in the first week of January or the second week: he wrote a satirical attack on the Duyckincks into the completed manuscript. Duyckinck's condemnation also must lie behind Melville's brusque impersonal notes early the next year canceling his subscription to the Duyckincks' *Literary World.* Whatever happened in the first week of 1852, Melville did not embark on a door-to-door hawking of his new manuscript. And once again, as in 1848, Melville did not know when to stop with a completed manuscript. He may have felt, that month, that the contract, which he accepted within a few days, sealed the end of his career. If he ever indulged in what felt to him like a "last fling," it was in the middle of January 1852.

Melville's miserable negotiations with the Harpers lie behind his writing cold-blooded publishers into the additions to *Pierre* as the authors of this letter to Pierre (bk. 26):

> "Sir:—You are a swindler. Upon the pretense of writing a popular novel for us, you have been receiving cash advances from us, while passing through our press the sheets of a blasphemous rhapsody, filched from the vile Atheists, Lucian and Voltaire. Our great press of publication has hitherto prevented our slightest inspection of our reader's proofs of your book. Send not another sheet to us. Our bill for printing thus far, and also for our cash advances, swindled out of us by you, is now in the hands of our lawyer, who is instructed to proceed with instant rigor."

This explosive epistle is signed "Steel, Flint, & Asbestos," the steel and flint to strike the spark and the asbestos to control its spread. Melville was recalling John Wiley's fury at realizing just how much irreligion had slipped into the first American edition of *Typee* in the haste to print it so as to establish the copyright. He was also probably reliving how the Methodist Harpers had reproached him in the first days of January 1852, assuming that they laid out the protests that had come to them such as those in the December 6, 1851, *New York Churchman* ("sneers at revealed religion and the burlesquing of sacred passages of Holy Writ") and the January 1851 *Methodist Quarterly Review* ("a number of flings at religion"). He was also recalling that gossip in Pittsfield in mid-December 1851 had labeled *Moby-Dick* as "more than blasphemous." Self-reproach was inextricably mixed with rankling self-justification.

The left hand at *Harper's* did not always know what the right hand at Harpers was doing. George Ripley had written a very respectful review of *Moby-Dick* for the December *Harper's New Monthly Magazine* (out before the end of November), and the "Literary Notices" in the January issue (out a few days after Christmas) contained some brief praise from the London papers. Over the weeks in November and December nowhere near the usual number of London papers made it to the United States, apparently (another aspect of Melville's run of bad luck), but in the April issue *Harper's* printed remarkable praise of *The Whale* from the London *Leader*. From the Harpers, probably, Allan Melville obtained the full *Leader* review and at the beginning of chapter 42 of his *Moby-Dick* Allan copied out this sentence: "There is a chapter on the 'Whiteness of the Whale' which should be read at midnight alone with nothing heard but the sounds of the wind moaning without, and the embers falling into the grate within." Ironically, by that time Melville was being damaged by *Harper's New Monthly Magazine* as well as directly by the brothers Harper.

Just at the time Melville took *Pierre* to the Harpers they had a great scheme going, in secret. Still denying having any hand in the infant *New York Times* (although everyone knew better), they absolutely depended on no one's finding out about their coup against Griswold's *International Magazine*, their brilliant new way of turning the lack of an international copyright law to their profit. Starting well before *Moby-Dick* was published and all during the interim between coming to terms on the contract for *Pierre* early in January and the actual signing of the contract on February 20 and all during the interim between the signing of the contract and the setting of the manuscript and the production of proofs in April, which necessitated Melville's settling in for a time at Allan's house, the Harpers were engaged in a high-stakes campaign designed to enhance their prestige—a campaign that had the collateral effect of grinding Melville further into the dust.

The Harpers had found a way to profit hugely while demonstrating that English authors did not need an international copyright law. Their behavior was perfectly in character. They were so notorious for meanness and self-promotion that on Frederika Bremer's arrival in October 1849 James Gordon Bennett in his *Herald* had happily made an announcement which would "be read with delight by thousands":

> It is rumored that the mammoth house of Harper Brothers, the Napoleons of cheap literature, particularly of the romance school, are preparing to present the celebrated Swedish novelist with a costly and superb memorial in the form of a massive silver vase (with $10,000 in California gold dust inside) on one side of which is to be engraved her own portrait, crowned with a wreath of laurel, and surrounded with exquisitely wrought scenes from her works. On the other side, much less conspicuously (with that modesty which so conspicuously characterizes that great house) will be grouped the portraits of the illustrious brothers, John, Jim, Fletch and Wesley.

Citing as his imaginary source "the industrious sweep at the crossing," the boy hired to sweep up horse droppings, Bennett made clear just how ungenerously the Harpers were known to treat "the authors whose works they print." Bennett's satire worked because the Harpers were in fact masters of grand gestures that did not cost them very much.

The Harpers' bargain-priced 1852 coup, still secret until the first of March (secret even when the contract for *Pierre* was signed on February 20), came about because the greedy, choleric Rufus Griswold began glorying, in the summer of 1851, in the possibility that his new *International Magazine*, published by Stringer and Townsend, could overtake in popularity *Harper's New Monthly Magazine*. Griswold had a brainstorm. Charles Dickens had been lamenting for nine very long years about being robbed by American publishers. Griswold would offer Dickens big money for the right to serialize his next novel from advance sheets sent only to him. Foolishly, Griswold rushed to William Cullen Bryant, who obligingly printed this in the *Evening Post* for August 29, 1851: "We understand that Messrs. Stringer & Townsend, publishers of the *International Magazine*, have entered into an arrangement with Charles Dickens, Esq., for advance sheets of his new novel, for the *International*. The price fixed is $4,000. This is creditable alike to the enterprise of the publishers and the sagacity of Dr. Griswold, its accomplished editor." The publicity campaign for the *International* seemed to be paying off. On September 1, 1851, the *Boston Daily Evening Transcript* happily paraphrased this item and elaborated it:

> LITERARY INTELLIGENCE. The New York Evening Post states that Messrs Stringer & Townsend, publishers of the International Magazine, have contracted with Charles Dickens for the proof sheets of his forthcoming novel. The price paid by the publishers is $4000; and the novel will appear simultaneously in England and this country. This is a good hit on the part of the enterprising publishers of the "International." It was prompted probably by their wide-awake editor, Mr Rufus W. Griswold.

On September 7 the *St. Louis Sunday Morning Republican* echoed the news from the *Evening Post*. On December 12 the *Brattleboro (Vt.) Semi-Weekly Eagle* quoted the December issue of the *International* as announcing improvements but stating a policy of not serializing any long works "except Dickens' new novel." The *Eagle* was curious about the race between the two magazines: "How it will end we cannot predict, but we incline to the opinion that the Internation[al] will not come out second best." In the January 1852 number "the indefatigable" Griswold again announced as forthcoming "the new Novel of Charles Dickens." Newspaper editors continued to anticipate the novel from Griswold's magazine. As the *Barre (Mass.) Patriot* declared on March 5, 1852, after receiving that month's *International Magazine*, "In the next number the publishers promise to commence Dickens' new story called *The Bleak House*. Stringer & Townsend, N. Y. Publishers." Shamelessly, or forgetfully, the *Patriot* on April 2 declared that what especially distinguished the April *Harper's* was the start of its serialization "of Dickens' new tale, the *Bleak House*."

The Harpers were good Methodists when fellow Methodists complained about Melville's irreligion. They were, day in and day out, shrewd Yankee masters of the main chance and sharp "practice." They were, in a word, unscrupulous.[3] Seeing Griswold's foolish paragraph in the *Evening Post*, they immediately acted. The story emerged in the *Nation* in 1867, in the 1870 *Charles Dickens: The Story of His Life* (published by the Harpers), in Griswold's son's 1898 *Passages from the Correspondence and Other Papers of Rufus W. Griswold*, and in the April 9, 1899, *Brooklyn Daily Eagle* account of the career of the recently dead William Adee Townsend, the long-lived Stringer & Townsend partner. The *Daily Eagle* account quoted the *Nation*, which credited the idea to Townsend as a way of surpassing *Harper's New Monthly Magazine*. James Stringer, an Englishman by birth, then going abroad, was armed with letters of introduction from Irving, Bryant, and others, and authorized to offer Dickens two thousand dollars (said the *Daily Eagle*) for advance sheets of his next novel, but Griswold was reckless:

> The steamer on which he sailed had hardly got out of sight before Dr.
> Rufus W. Griswold of the International had given the Evening Post a
> sensational paragraph, stating that Mr. Dickens had been engaged to
> write for the International Magazine a new novel. . . . The watchful
> Harpers dispatched post haste a messenger in the next boat.

Stringer went formally to Dickens's publishers, Chapman & Hall, where he was made to feel uncomfortable, if not actually rebuffed. Diffident, awkward, he set off on his Continental tour without sending word of his failure back to New York. The Harpers' ambassador in defiance of decorum went right to Dickens's house and sealed the deal, and kept closed-mouthed about it for months while Griswold continued to promote the deal he thought Stringer had concluded.

The bombshell exploded on the last days of February, in the March issue of *Harper's*. Copies were for sale in Albany on March 1 and in Boston by March 2. On the ninth a "large supply" was for sale in Milwaukee. As if taking their marketing clue from Gleason's promotion of *The Mistake of a Lifetime*, on March 1, 1852, the Harpers gloated in the *New York Times*, the young newspaper over which they claimed to have absolutely no influence:

> The HARPERS announce that they have purchased the proof-sheets
> of Dickens's new novel, to be received in advance of its appearance
> in London, for the sum of *two thousand dollars*. It is to be called

"BLEAK HOUSE, or the East Wind," and will be completed in twenty numbers. The first part will appear in the April number of Harper's Magazine. The sum mentioned above is certainly a very large remuneration—nearly as much as even Dickens could make upon any one of his novels in this country, if all the profits were secured by an international copyright.

With their eye fixed on profits the Harpers on March 9, 1852, sent flyers to many newspapers. The announcement made it very clear how much more they valued Dickens than any American author:

> The publishers of Harper's New Monthly Magazine are happy to announce that they have completed an arrangement by which they will receive regularly, in advance of its publication in England, the sheets of the new Novel of Mr. Charles Dickens, to be entitled "Bleak House, or the East Wind." The first number of this work will be published in the April number of this Magazine in an attractive and popular form. For the privilege of thus laying this new and important work of the greatest of living novelists before the readers of Harper's New Monthly Magazine, in advance of its appearance in any other form in the United States, the publishers have paid the sum of two thousand dollars. They refer to this fact simply as indicating their purpose to spare no expense necessary to render their Magazine in every respect deserving of the unparalleled success it has achieved. Mr. Dickens stands confessedly at the head of living authors, and his writings surpass those of all others, not more in the genius they display, and the absorbing interest by which they are marked, than in the steady and consistent devotion to the interests of morality and of the great masses of the people of every country.

Two thousand dollars for Dickens and twenty cents on the dollar after costs for Melville. Quoting the *New York Mirror*, on February 19 the *Pittsfield Sun* declared that the demand for the magazine was increasing "at the rate of 10,000 a month, and that, too, without the aid of a single travelling agent in the U. States." (One hundred thousand copies, said the *Portsmouth Journal* on September 18, 1852.) The loss of the Dickens novel killed the *International Magazine*. On March 24, 1852, the *Boston Daily Atlas* reported that the Harpers had bought the *International Magazine* and had devoured it by merging its puny eleven thousand or so subscribers into the mammoth Harper's list. They not only gained thousands of subscribers, they profited month by month: Boston had copies of the first part of *Bleak House* in "a neat pamphlet of 48 pages" by March 20, 1852.

February 19, 1852, when the local *Sun* celebrated the great growth of *Harper's*, was the day before Allan Melville, as Herman's lawyer, signed the contract for *Pierre* just as it was drafted early in January (the parties having decided that the original contingency clauses obviated the alterations Allan had suggested to the Harpers on January 21). Harper and Brothers paid Melville five hundred dollars, partly earnings from earlier books, partly an advance on *Pierre*. "Twenty cents per copy" for each copy sold at one dollar was specified for Melville, after the Harpers recouped their costs with "the proceeds of 1190 copies." Melville did not have to leave Pittsfield. After turning the manuscript over to Allan, Melville seems to have passed into a long phase of denial that he, by plopping into the book a last-minute satire of the American literary scene and then a bleak portrayal of his own unraveled career, had irrevocably damaged what he had thought of as a "Kraken" book. It might, of course, have already been damned by the theme of incest, for that was present in the original version. Allan had signed the impossible contract from the Harpers before Bentley's clerk blunderingly mailed Melville an unfinished letter, which Bentley followed up with an apology on March 4, but with the unpleasant news that so far Bentley had lost more than £453 on Melville, a number that would be reduced by any subsequent sales. Nevertheless, Bentley was willing to consider publishing *Pierre* on half profits, without an advance, after seeing it.

The relevance of all this to Melville is that by paying Dickens two thousand dollars the Harpers had gained what they could pass off as moral authority in their renewed campaign against international copyright. Dickens had already been enriching them year by year. A writer in the *New York Spectator* (November 12, 1842) described the one-bit sale of *American Notes*:

> We happened to be in Cliff street yesterday just as the first copies of the Harper edition, well-printed and neatly bound, were given out to a swarm of boys, whose clamor and crowding to be early served made up a very fair representation of Babel on a reduced scale. The little [v]enders were as eager as though there had not been a copy out, notwithstanding the issue of two large editions from the offices of the *New World* and *Brother Jonathan*.

For a few examples, the Harpers in 1843 published *Martin Chuzzlewit*; in 1849 *The Haunted Man and The Ghost's Bargain. A Fancy for Christmas Time*; in January 1852 Dickens's *Child's History of England*; and as late as

August 1852, while they were serializing *Bleak House*, they printed *Dombey & Son*.

In order to profiteer, the Harpers had to rehabilitate the national villain of 1842. Wasting no time, on March 16 they printed in the *Times* a long eloquent tribute redefining their star author as "Dickens—the Reformer." The purpose of this new book by Dickens, to be serialized in *Harper's New Monthly Magazine* through 1852 and through October 1853, would be "the demolition of abuses and the reform of institutions which impede the progress and crush the energies of the race." Dickens now exerted "an influence upon the national mind superior to that of any other man." The *Times* hailed him as "a stalwart champion of Democracy, of the rights of the People." Charles Dickens was "one of the means by which God works, to bring about the equality of man, and level all distinctions, but those with which He has chosen to diversify our race." Some distinctions, of course, were God-given, like the Mark of Cain. Reprinted, in part (the *Trenton Gazette*) and whole (the *Philadelphia Freeman*), this ecstatic praise went far toward rehabilitating the national pariah of late 1842.

Horace Greeley took on the Harpers in the March 17, 1852, *Tribune* piece on "International Copyright," his response to "the pleasant announcement of a new tale of Dickens." The Harpers and their fellow publishers were "pirates upon the sea of mind," buccaneers roaming "with the black flag of absolute confiscation." By appearing to be generous to Dickens, the Harpers were thwarting any consideration of a legal obligation to pay for *Bleak House*. Melville was brought into the fray:

> England shames us in this matter. Her position is more than generous; it is just. By the decision of last spring [May 1851], and by the recent convention with France, the British nation nobly recognizes the right which we ignominiously scorn. Do the Messrs. Harpers pay Dickens for his book? But they could print it, if they would, without paying, whereas Mr. Bentley pays Bancroft, Melville, and the biographers of Margaret Fuller, under the sanction of the British Law, which protects them, and secures them their rights.

The *Tribune* concluded with a question: "Do we mean always to submit to this world-notorious brand of meanness—to recognize every right but that of genius?" (In Boston the Shaws saw the mention of Melville in the approving reprint of the article in the March 18, 1852, *Boston Daily Evening Transcript*.) This battle was going on when Melville arrived in New York to proofread the new book, for once accompanied by Lizzie. The Arrowhead

Melvilles were expected on March 18, but, Allan wrote Augusta, he was afraid a storm might detain them. They apparently stayed there an exceptionally long time, Melville dealing with the proofs of *Pierre*, and did not return until April 16, when Lizzie found her sons "well & improving" under their grandmother Melville's supervision.

Having rehabilitated Dickens and now seizing for themselves the high ground of "virtuous ire," the Harpers were ready for the next step in their campaign, launching an all-out attack on international copyright through the newspaper they still professed not to control, the *New York Times*. While Melville was still in New York, where his brother Allan skimmed all the major papers, the April 13, 1852, *Times* exalted "Society" and the "public good" over the "private rights" of authors. Acknowledging the argument "that Society has no right, even for its own good, to rob authors of their property," it asserted the "established principle, essential to the welfare of individuals as well as of Society, that private interests must be held subordinate to the public welfare." Besides, the existing laws of copyright afforded "to authors perhaps quite as large remuneration as would be consistent with the general interests of Society." And always greed could be disguised as patriotism: Americans are superior in general intelligence to the English and people of other countries because books are cheap: "Every American reads, because he can get books." The next day the *Times* printed a letter from "READER": "There is one class of persons whose interests are usually overlooked by the opponents of international copyright, viz., American authors. They will never be adequately remunerated, as long as publishers can have foreign books gratis. If there is to be protection, why are not the brains of the country as much entitled to it as the hands?" Why indeed, Melville would have asked, looking ahead two weeks to the time his second installment of interest to Stewart was due, $92.25, money he no longer had.

As Melville was leaving New York on April 16 he wrote Bentley what I called in my biography "a long, maundering, specious, self-justifying, begging, try-anything letter" (2:106). To save time he was sending proofs from type instead of waiting for proofs from the stereotype plates. He could not accept publication on the basis of half profits, yet he hoped that their connection would continue "on the new field of productions" on which he had embarked, the outright romance. *Pierre*, after all, possessed "unquestionable novelty" since it treated of "utterly new scenes & characters" and was "very much more calculated for popularity" than his earlier books, "being a regular romance, with a mysterious plot to it, & stirring passions at work, and withall, representing a new & elevated aspect of American life." Desperately, he suggested suppressing his damaged name: "I have thought that, on several accounts, (one of which is, the rapid succession in which my works have lately been published) it might not prove unadvisable to publish this present book anonymously, or under an assumed name:—'By a Vermonter' say"— or, he added in a postscript, "By Guy Winthrop." After the train ride home Melville confronted new issues of the *Literary World* and again instructed its "editors" (whom he could not bear to address by name) to discontinue his subscription.

The April 13 *Times* had contented itself with saying "that society is so dependent upon books for its welfare that the individual must be sacrificed. This is, of course, the elemental principle of Society. The point to be resolved is, always, *how much* he is to be sacrificed." The *Tribune* on April 20 rephrased the *Times* just slightly in order to make clear that the Harpers believed in sacrificing the author. Two days later, the *Times* argued at length that "the obvious requirements of the public good" were more important than "the claims of authors." The *Tribune* began its April 23 reply with the comparison of American publishers to pickpockets "appropriating the fruits of the author's labor without recompense." Horace Greeley[4] mocked the Harper-*Times* position, quoting what they might say to a Harper author: "'My dear fellow! your works are so valuable, precious, inestimable, indispensable, that we cannot afford to pay you their market value . . . . Rejoice that you are deemed of such invaluable use to us that we shall do our utmost to starve you to death.'" In the conclusion the *Tribune* hinted at the deception involved in a newspaper's arguing for a book publisher who owned a controlling interest in it. The *Times* "while declaiming lustily against Monopoly, is simply seeking to uphold the gigantic monopoly of one great publishing house which now nearly engrosses the issue of cheap reprints."

On April 24, Raymond in the *Times* replied that successful writers receive "a very abundant reward for their labors" and that no one had "proposed to 'rob' them of any portion of their earnings." The Harpers, just then, were preparing to print *Pierre*, on which they were going to pay Melville less than half what they had previously been paying him after deducting their carefully calculated costs. Melville could have refuted Raymond.

On April 26, the *Tribune* at once put the argument on moral grounds. American publishers were stealing from British writers. Furthermore, the lack of an international copyright kept any writer in trepidation if not terror at the possibility of concerted onslaughts from any special interest quarter, as Melville knew from the attacks on him by the religious right:

> The author is tempted to humor the prejudices and pander to the conceit of the little public next him, because his bread must depend on its favor; when, if all who use his work were held responsible to

him therefor, he would be impelled to look fearlessly over the heads of this little band into the broad empyrean of Truth, seeing all he might and proclaiming all he saw.

Melville's refusal to listen to those who told him "to humor the prejudices" had led to Bentley's censoring *The Whale* and to Duyckinck's reproaching him for irreverence in *White-Jacket* and particularly for the irreligion in *Moby-Dick*. It led Bentley to reproach him, gently but honestly, in a letter written a few days later.

The *Tribune* on April 26 concluded with the fact that the Harpers were "intensely hostile to International Copyright" and "that the Editor of *The Times* has for years maintained intimate and profitable business relations with that house; and we add the expression of our confident belief that *The Times's* foray on International Copyright was impelled by considerations hereby indicated." The *Times* was assailing international copyright "by considerations of personal interest." Raymond on the twenty-seventh claimed to lose some self-respect when he stooped to deny "such aspersions," then offered a distraction, accusing Greeley of being "a large stockholder in a New-Jersey *Zinc Mining* Company" even while trying to convince the public "that all other paints except *zinc* paints" (particularly "White Lead" paints, Greeley explained on the twenty-eighth) "are injurious and poisonous in the highest degree." Besides, Raymond continued, Greeley had a stake in gold mines in California and copper mines on Lake Superior and was promoting those companies in the *Tribune*.

On the first of May Melville defaulted on the $92.25 he owed T. D. Stewart for his loan of $2,050. On May 5 Bentley wrote him a frank, almost paternal letter in which he did not mention copyright, the situation had so deteriorated. If Melville would allow him "to make or have made by a judicious literary friend such alterations as are absolutely necessary to 'Pierre' being properly appreciated" in England, he would still publish it, on half profits. Melville received that letter about mid-May. Broken, he again acted suicidally in passing up this chance to have *Pierre* published in England. He seems not to have responded to the letter at all, despite Bentley's great generosity and courtesy to him. At some point in May or June he had to tell or let Allan tell the Harpers to go ahead and publish, since for the first time he had no English publisher with a release date to consider.

Ironically, in mid-May, about the time Melville received Bentley's letter, a new phase of the *Times-Tribune* controversy began, this time involving him by name. The *Troy Budget* inadvertently started the trouble with a squib on the prosperity of New York City publishers, starting with the Harpers, who "print a hundred thousand monthly of their magazine, including the demand for back numbers." In its own squib on May 17, the *Tribune* quoted the *Budget*, then commented: "Very good. Now will *The Budget* inquire as to the state and prospects of our *Authors*? We haven't heard of any of *them* moving into free-stone edifices very lately." (Freestone is a stone like limestone, soft enough to cut and chisel.) This was just the opening Raymond and the Harpers needed. The next day, Raymond quoted both the *Budget* and the *Tribune* comment, then counterattacked:

> The Tribune is badly posted. "Our Authors" have been for the last two or three years building themselves substantial edifices as a very encouraging rate. BANCROFT, besides buying a "free-stone" house in the city, has built a fine country-seat at Newport. HEADLEY has built a splendid mansion at Newburgh. MELVILLE has bought a farm at Stockbridge. IRVING and PAULDING have splendid seats on the Hudson. PRESCOTT has received from the Harpers not less than $40,000 for his books. MORSE has been paid more than $20,000 from the sale of his books. ALBERT BARNES has received from his Commentaries over $20,000. Prof. ANTHON has made over $60,000 — STEPHENS over $40,000, — the ABBOTTS over $15,000, &c., &c., &c.

Stockbridge? Stockbridge? Then Raymond added a few more names and figures before declaring " 'Our Authors' are the last persons in the world on whose behalf a plea of poverty should be made. . . . The fact is, that authors generally, who *deserve* success, meet with an abundant reward for their labor. Those who fail, owe their failure mainly to the fact that their books are not such as the public wants."

Raymond, I would think, knew where Melville lived, outside Pittsfield, and knew from the Harpers that they had reduced his after-costs share for *Pierre* to an absolutely impossible twenty cents on the dollar instead of the old fifty cents, terms under which he had, a year and a few weeks earlier, been denied an advance because he was so far in debt to the Harpers. Raymond would have known that Melville had been in town, and in Cliff Street, in April 1852, during his own daily interchanges with Greeley, and he might have heard that (now that *Pierre* was being stereotyped) the only hitch was that Harpers needed to be told that it was free to publish, as far as any British connection was concerned.

The other writers named in the *Times* were indeed wealthy, and to name Melville among Prescott, Barnes, Anthon, Stephens — all Harpers authors — may well have been deliberate sadism. The more quotable section of the

Times column was picked up, so that, for a few examples (those on search-able databases in 2010), on May 19 Philadelphians knew about the "Profits of Authorship," including that farm at Stockbridge. On the twenty-first Boston read the *Times* article, without the headline, in the *Atlas*. The Shaws probably knew better already from Lemuel Shaw, Jr.'s letters from England, where he had talked to people at Bentley's, but they got to read the assurance: "Our authors are the last persons in the world on whose behalf a plea of poverty should be made." On the twenty-first, with the headline "Profits of Authorship," Trenton knew, and on the twenty-fifth, with the same heading, Baltimore knew. Under the headline "Literary Pay" the *Bellows Falls (Vt.) Chronicle* reprinted the story on June 1, and on June 4 the *Natchez Courier* picked up the same version from one place or another. On September 11, 1852, with the heading *"Profits of Authorship,"* even Tallahassee knew. Melville's prosperous farm in Stockbridge was by then as well known, almost, as his farm outside Pittsfield. This is the sort of thing Allan would have sent Herman, even knowing that it would be excruciating to someone whose profits from authorship were disappearing.

Someone who had followed the debates in the *Tribune* and the *Times* published in the July 1852 *American Whig Review* a long article, "A Letter to the Proprietors of Harpers' Magazine," an indictment of the juggernaut tactics of the Harpers. I would bet that Cornelius Mathews wrote it. Not naming names, he identified men like Melville who were "irresistibly driven to authorship by their own mental constitution," yet "totally helpless in the more material departments of human endeavor." Americans could choose: "We have it in our option to keep them under and to better their only hopes of success, or to allow them the rewards of diligent service in the calling for which they are fitted." The writer went on to accuse Raymond:

> The amount of income which he derives from condensing the current intelligence of each month into your pages is very considerable. His devotion to your periodical is, therefore, very easily accounted for. It could not be expected that the editor of the Times, even if he were disposed to take the national side of the copyright question, should, under existing circumstances, speak his mind with sincerity or boldness; but the position he has undertaken to defend leads me to believe that he is very far gone in his reverence for the profitable schemes of literary pillage by which he is nourished; and that the dictates of his soul, habituated to this moral obliquity, no less than policy, prompt him to lend his aid to the perpetuation of the present injustice with which American authors are obliged to contend.

In a footnote the writer declared that Raymond's "pocket" would not let him uphold international copyright, and that pecuniary greed lay behind his insulting American writers "by informing them that it is their own lack of brains that make their books unable to "compete with English books." Mathews (if my guess as to the author is right) reminded everyone of those men who formed the "International Copyright Club" in 1843, among whom was Raymond. In another footnote the writer spoke sarcastically of "rich authors, those who have built freestone houses out of their literary earnings," knowing that some of those authors existed only in the imaginations of the Harpers and Raymond.

When the *Boston To-Day* objected "to the tone" of the letter in the *Whig Review*, Raymond solemnly quoted it while piously portraying *Harper's* as encouraging American literature. The author of the letter in the *Whig Review* had lamented that *Harper's* had not only killed the *International Magazine* but had weakened the Philadelphia magazines. Now Raymond cruelly and accurately observed that the *Whig* was only another "decaying rival" to *Harper's*. Early in 1853, when it seemed again that Congress would pass an international copyright law, Raymond rose to battle the *Tribune* and to defend "his relations with the house of HARPER & BROTHERS." The Harpers, he wanted it known, had never "attempted to exert" any influence upon him in regard to the copyright controversy "or any other subject." Never. By that time Melville was in deepest pain, crushed by the savagely insulting reviews of *Pierre*.

Sheer bad luck plagued Melville late in 1851 and early in 1852, and to the series of his own mistakes must be added his failure to respond to Bentley's generous offer to publish *Pierre* on half profits; having *Pierre* published, in a somewhat less outraging form, would have kept Melville's name alive in England. Before that, Bentley should have kept him supplied with notices of *The Whale*. Had Melville known just how enthusiastic some of the London reviews of *The Whale* had been, he might have done many things differently, beginning in November 1851. Still earlier, if Melville had rejected the Harper offer for *Pierre* and found another New York publisher for it, in its original shorter form, he might have gotten half profits after costs, as he had been doing with Harpers. Then he might not have made the reckless additions—although, judging from the reviews, which seldom mentioned the section on Pierre as an author, the condemnation would have been about the same. Such are some of the possibilities that seem clear in long retrospect. As it was, Melville in his last letter to Bentley was self-annihilating, as we saw, willing to publish anonymously or under a pseudonym.

On May 22, 1852, several members of the family ("The Author, his mother, & wife & sister Augusta") took a long drive which Augusta recorded in "The Excursions of /52." Using "The Author" made it clear that Augusta thought nothing had changed. In the next weeks she recorded a great season of family outings, in all of which Melville must have been inwardly tormented. There was the humiliation of having authorized Harpers to proceed with the publication of *Pierre* (which meant telling them there would be no foreign publication), then waiting for the book to be reviewed. For their part, the Harpers began passing the word around New York that they thought Melville was slightly crazy—not crazy enough that people should stop buying *Typee* and *Omoo* from them, but crazy—unlike Charles Dickens, the great British novelist whom they were serializing month by month in *Harper's New Monthly Magazine*. Elizabeth Stoddard, a cousin of Hawthorne's and the wife of the young poet Richard Stoddard, passed on the news bluntly on August 23 ("the Harpers think Melville is a little crazy"), as surely other favored recipients did. Her husband about this time dined with the Hawthornes in Concord and after half a century (in his 1903 *Recollections*) could not remember the topics of conversation but (remembering the Liverpool section of Hawthorne's posthumous *Passages from the English Note-Books*) was certain that they did not talk "of fate, free-will, foreknowledge absolute," a topic of Melville's conversations in Southport with Hawthorne in 1856, as he knew from Julian Hawthorne's biography of his parents.

Early in July Melville made an excursion with his father-in-law to Nantucket. They kept things pleasant, Shaw already knowing the situation at Bentley's from his son Lem's visit but saying nothing to Herman, while Herman said nothing to him about the loan from Stewart and his having already defaulted on it. The treasure from the trip was Attorney General Clifford's story of an abandoned Falmouth woman, Agatha Hatch. When Melville returned from Nantucket he found an invitation from Hawthorne, and replied on July 17, 1852: "I am sorry, but I can not at present come to see you at Concord as you propose.—I am but just returned from a two weeks' absence; and for the last three months & more I have been an utter idler and a savage—out of doors all the time. So, the hour has come for me to sit down again." He could not think of doing anything but sitting down to write, but after the denunciations of *Pierre* he could not write, and for months he kept offering the story of Agatha Hatch to Hawthorne. After the election of the Democrat Pierce in November he refused his mother's appeals to begin seeking a Custom House job or a foreign consulship. He should have known that Pierce's classmate Hawthorne would receive the plum appointment, to Liverpool, but he still hoped until his visit to Hawthorne early in December that his friend would write the story, and only decided to write it himself in mid-month. He worked obsessively on it during the time he might have been mustering support for a consulship, and agreed to stand for one too late to have any hope of gaining a post. He finished his book, *The Isle of the Cross*, in late May 1853 and took it to New York early in June. The Harpers refused to publish it. He kept it a while, and referred to it in November as being in existence. In December came the great Harpers fire in which many of Melville's books and unbound sheets were destroyed, although the stereotype plates were saved. The Harpers with almost unimaginable greed charged their losses off against him, charging him all over again for the costs of printing and binding, to a total of about $1,000, as Melville confessed to his father-in-law in 1856, when the time came for Stewart to collect the $2,050 and the unpaid interest and probably interest on the unpaid interest.

Late in August 1854 the American papers announced that the law of copyright in England had finally been settled on August 8 by the House of Lords on the appeal case of *Jeffreys v. Boosey*. The decision, as the *Washington National Intelligencer* said on August 26, "having been made by the highest tribunal, is not subject to review." After a little reflection the *Boston Daily Evening Transcript* summed matters up: "This decision will render useless the measures hitherto adopted by Americans, to secure the benefit of English copyright, by first publication in Great Britain." Melville had lost his second English publisher in May 1852 and, although some of his books were later pirated in England, and although Longman published *The Confidence-Man* at his wish, he never made a penny from England after Bentley paid him for *The Whale*. From May 1852 until May 1856 Melville wrote the now-lost book *The Isle of the Cross*, wrote many stories, wrote *Israel Potter* (previously serialized), collected some of the stories in *The Piazza Tales* with a new prefatory piece, and wrote *The Confidence-Man* (probably almost done in May 1856). During this time he defaulted once or twice on his mortgage payments to Dr. Brewster, the previous owner of Arrowhead, and defaulted every six months on his interest payments to Stewart. He was living in deepest denial, waiting for the inevitable collapse of his attempt to earn a living for his family as a writer in America. The collapse came in May 1856, when his friend Stewart was ready to seize Arrowhead. Melville confessed his plight to his father-in-law, sold half of the farm, and, with Shaw's help, left on a therapeutic journey to Europe and the Levant in 1856–57. Thereafter, except during some long intervals, he continued to write, but besides writing and traveling about with three annual lectures starting in late 1857 what he wrote, most of the time for the rest of his life, was poetry, and none of it made him any money. He took no consolation at having been sacrificed for the public good.

✢ *Chapter 17* ✢

MELVILLE AND HAWTHORNE'S DINNER
AT THE HOTEL IN LENOX

Harrison Hayford's "Melville and Hawthorne: A Biographical and Critical Study" (1945) was one of the great Yale dissertations on Melville directed by Stanley T. Williams. For "Melville and Hawthorne" Hayford assembled all the known factual information about the two writers (including the most basic, a fresh list of their meetings), and in his investigations discovered unknown letters and other documents now so familiar that few people remember who found them. Hayford's diffidence about being a noncombatant in World War II (because of tuberculosis) and Leon Howard's advice kept him from publishing the dissertation in the elegant, unpretentious Yale Studies in English where Merrell R. Davis's dissertation on *Mardi* found such an appropriate home. Besides some letters of Sophia Hawthorne published by Eleanor Thomas Metcalf in *Herman Melville: Cycle and Epicycle* (1953) so few new documents emerged in the next decades that Hayford's dissertation could have been published any year up through the 1970s with only minimal updating.[1]

In 1945 the last meeting of Melville and Hawthorne in the Berkshires which Hayford could document was on August 8, 1851, the expedition to see the Shakers at Hancock Village, but he speculated (244) about a final meeting:

> Very likely, however, in the three months before Hawthorne moved away from Lenox there were further visits. At least one meeting seems probable, on November 7, when Melville may have presented Hawthorne a copy of *Moby Dick*, fresh from the press, while Hawthorne gave young Malcolm Melville a copy of *The Wonder Book*, also just printed.

411

(The full title is *A Wonder-Book for Girls and Boys.*) Here Hayford placed this
footnote:

> This episode is purely conjectural, and may be substantiated or dis-
> proved by the inscription in the presentation copy of *Moby Dick* now
> in the possession of Dr. A. S. W. Rosenbach. . . . [In the Houghton
> Library] there is a copy of the *Wonder Book* inscribed by Hawthorne,
> "Malcolm Melville/from Mr Hawthorne/Nov. 7th 1851." *The Won-
> der Book* was not published until November 15 . . . ; hence this was
> an advance copy. My conjecture is that Melville at the same time
> presented Hawthorne an advance copy of *Moby Dick*, which was
> published, apparently, about the same day as *The Wonder Book.*

The Rosenbach *Moby-Dick* turned out to be a copy the Hawthornes acquired
to replace the earlier one they had presumably lost in their mid-1850s peregrinations. Hayford had the dates a little wrong but he had the unacademic
good sense to know that Melville would have wanted to present a copy of
Moby-Dick to its dedicatee.

More than four decades passed before I discovered fresh evidence about
early November 1851 in the Augusta Papers and published it in the first
volume of my biography. There I explained that a meeting took place on
November 4, 1851, at the home in Lenox of Charles and Elizabeth Sedgwick, he the clerk of the Massachusetts Supreme Court, she the mistress
of the notable school which Melville's sister Helen had attended in 1835.
As the time neared for Hawthorne to leave the little red cottage to go to a
rented house in West Newton, Massachusetts, Sedgwick, who had tried to
bring Hawthorne together with the English novelist G. P. R. James (inter-
nationally famous as the "solitary horseman" novelist, then oddly living at
Stockbridge), decided that the only thing to do was to throw a party midweek
(on November 4, a Tuesday), with only a couple of days' notice, so he could
at least gather James, Hawthorne, and Melville at his hearth one time. This
gathering was a farewell party for the Hawthornes.

The next day after the party, November 5, 1851, Maria Melville wrote a
full account to her daughter Augusta, then visiting Allan in New York City
(Parker, 1:876):

> On monday morning [November 3] immediately after breakfast we
> drove to town. At the post office was a note directed to Mrs Melville
> of course I opened it, it contained an invitation for me to come to
> tea on tuesday Eveg. wishing me to extend the invitation to M^r & M^rs

Herman Melville & my daughters, or any friend or friends we might
have with us, from Mrs Sedgwick as an inducement to come so far we
were to meet the James' from Stockbridge & a few friends. Herman
said he would take us at once and seem'd pleased. As we were to be
there at seven or lose our tea, we started from home at half past five.
It was very *cold—muffs were brought down & Buffaloes.*

Although "a few flakes of snow fell," they "had a pleasant drive to Lenox
Herman being in excellent spirits." His excellent spirits may indicate that
he knew nothing yet of Hawthorne's plans to leave Lenox. As it turned out,
they did not meet Sophia Hawthorne there and did not meet the great English novelist (Parker, 1:877). Hawthorne came alone, explaining that he and
his wife "went out alternate" so one would be with the children. Mrs. James
explained that her husband had commenced a new book that day and "could
not break out on any account." Melville was the attraction for Hawthorne,
not James: he had been "induced to come to meet Herman." Whether or
not Melville knew already that Hawthorne was planning to leave Lenox, he
must have been playing out in his mind a scene he would enact any week
now—an exultant ride or drive over to the little red cottage with a presentation copy of *Moby-Dick.*

Whatever else Melville and Hawthorne talked about on this occasion,
they must have expressed frustration that their new books had not arrived. I
say "must have": these were real human beings who were apt to act much the
way normal men act. Each man knew that the other was awaiting a new book,
and each also had a long-cherished surprise for the other in his book. Do I
know that each had a surprise, that they had not blabbed to each other previously? Well, I know the reticence of the men, and the pleasure of delayed
gratification. Hawthorne had dated his preface to *The Snow-Image* three days
earlier, but a different work, *A Wonder-Book for Girls and Boys,* was due to
be published any day. Months earlier, he had written into a late chapter of *A
Wonder-Book* a tribute to his friend's struggle to shape out "the gigantic conception of his 'White Whale,' while the gigantic shape of Graylock looms
upon him from his study-window." (This was the first time the title of the
book, in any form—*The White Whale, The Whale, Moby-Dick*—had been
mentioned in any other book.) Any day, also, Melville was expecting copies of his book, now retitled *Moby-Dick.* James's absence, as well as Sophia's,
meant that it was easier for the two men to confer a little over Hawthorne's
plans and Melville's responses to them.

Melville had a seriously sick wife (left at home) and a new book on the
brain and probably partly on the page, but before the evening was out he

must have (another reasonable "must have") conveyed his sense that they had to say good-bye properly, not in a moment's public chat at someone else's tea party. Hawthorne would have told him how much he wanted to get the new book—to Malcolm, he might have said. Melville would have confessed to Hawthorne how frustrated he would feel if his book came out just too late for him to carry a presentation copy to Hawthorne. Both the men could talk openly about their eagerness to see their books without mentioning the compliment buried deep inside of the one and the greater compliment blazoned on the dedication page of the other.

A day or two later Hawthorne received his first copies of A *Wonder-Book* and inscribed one, on November 7, to Malcolm, knowing that before long the father would see the pre-publication compliment to the "White Whale." Hayford in 1945 had visualized a scene, not located in a town or house, in which Hawthorne presented the volume in person, but Hawthorne would not have made his way to Pittsfield. More likely, according to his frugal habit, he found someone to carry the book to Pittsfield. According to Hayford's speculation, on that same day, November 7, Hawthorne entrusted a copy of A *Wonder-Book* to Melville and Melville gave him in exchange a copy of *Moby-Dick*. When I focused on the timetable in the late 1980s I knew that was a little off. From my years of review hunting I knew that the *Albany Evening Journal* and the *Boston Daily Evening Transcript* each had printed reviews on November 12 and the *Boston Courier* and the *Troy Daily Whig* noticed the book on November 13, the *Troy Budget* on November 14. I knew when books were first available, and suspected also that the Harpers would not have been much concerned with getting advance copies of *Moby-Dick* to Melville, though they would willingly pass sheets to the *Literary World* at Allan's behest. If Allan and the Harpers were alert, Melville should have received copies on or a couple of days before the official publication date of November 14 (a Friday). The arrival of the whaling book a week or so after Hawthorne inscribed a copy of his book for Malcolm, was, after all, providential: if copies had been delayed a week longer Melville would not have been able to hand a presentation copy to the man to whom he had dedicated it in token of admiration of his genius.

Here the information might have stood, at least until valuable (but limited) newspaper databases became available in the twenty-first century, had I not spent June 24 and 25, 1987, in the Boston Public Library bent into microfilm readers scanning Lowell and Lawrence newspapers for reviews of *Moby-Dick* and other Melville books and information about Melville's brother-in-law, John Hoadley. Something else struck me—in the *Lowell*

Weekly Journal and Courier for December 19, 1851, an article on the Hawthorne cottage outside Lenox, reprinted from a longer article in the *Windsor (Vt.) Journal.* (By 2010 this Lowell paper was available on a database.) The author, no name or pen name given, newly moved from Vermont to Lenox, was acting as a special correspondent to his hometown newspaper, since the natural scenery and the local celebrities (dead ones like Jonathan Edwards as well as living) were of general interest, even in Vermont. As partially reprinted in the Lowell paper, the author seemed not to know that he was describing a cottage that not only looked deserted but *was* deserted:

> A correspondent of the Windsor, Vt., Journal, at Lenox, writes that in a spot of unrivalled loveliness on the Northern shore of the Mountain Mirror [Stockbridge Bowl] stands a small, uninviting, insignificant, red house, with green window blinds, and one single pine tree before it. One might pass it at almost any time of the day, and think it vacant; the doors would all be shut, the blinds all closed, and the single pine tree would look as sullen as if it were conscious of its loneliness. There would be no path to the gate, and no knocker on the door, and one would immediately conclude that the red house of the two gables was shut against the resort of men—and he would not be far from right, for there lives Nathaniel Hawthorne.

According to Hawthorne's notebook in the Ohio State University Edition (313), "We left Lenox, Friday morning, November 21st (I think) 1851, in a storm of snow and sleet; took the cars at Pittsfield, and arrived at West Newton that evening." This meant, I assumed, that the letter-writer may have observed the cottage later in November or even in December, not knowing that the author was no longer in residence. Nevertheless, the cottage could not have changed much in a week or two, so the description was still applicable to what Hawthorne had known.

   That was interesting enough, but the editor of the *Weekly Journal and Courier* tantalized me with what he acknowledged omitting: "The writer, after giving a brief description of Mr H's personal appearance, proceeds as follows . . . ." I needed that brief description of Hawthorne's personal appearance which (I knew) no Hawthorne scholar had ever seen. I could be the first to plunder it, for my biography, if I had the space. I determined to find the *Windsor (Vt.) Journal,* knowing that literary-minded people, like this writer, often took on the job of special correspondent, offering reports from the hinterlands to the metropolis or the metropolis to the hinterlands, or from one metropolis to another.

I had, in fact, an intense interest in special correspondents. I had hopes of devoting myself, some day, to a study of American special correspondents for American newspapers, including a few who wrote letters to or from European capitals. I knew that the greatest untouched or scarcely touched resource for politics, public construction works, economics, literary history, architectural history, theatrical history, musical history, and much more of value lay in the disappearing files of American newspapers in the letters of special correspondents who distilled the day's or week's or month's news for people in other cities. In 1988, the next year after finding the quotation from the *Windsor Journal,* I found in the *New Orleans Commercial Bulletin* a big book's worth of weekly letters from the young lawyer Oakey Hall (later district attorney and mayor), an intimate of the Duyckinck circle, who casually sprinkled his pages with little gems about Melville. Who would have guessed that Melville wrote *White-Jacket* in "a score of sittings"? That was the gossip current among the New York literati at the time. Now, well into the new millennium, the digitizing of many American newspapers may make it easier for others to fulfill my dream of a library of books consisting of these contemporary letters, even if the great majority of newspaper files already have been destroyed, Southern files by Grant and Sherman, files from all the rest of the country by space-needing librarians in the twentieth century. Very few biographers of nineteenth-century American writers have availed themselves of the rich resource of these letters of special correspondents.

That dream now beckons me still, but in 1987 and the next years my time and travel funds were not limitless. I was teaching full time, and I had hundreds of documents to transcribe into the ever-expanding *Melville Log,* starting with the Augusta Papers. I added the Lowell item to the *Log* on August 11, 1990. Every few months when I had to divide my files because I kept inserting so many new documents into late 1851, I conscientiously moved the note up to the top of a new file containing November and December 1851: "MUST FIND WINDSOR VT. JOURNAL." I went to the Library of Congress where I was told that the *Windsor (Vt.) Journal* was not extant anywhere. Hoping still, I prevailed upon a student from New England to look in Vermont libraries, reimbursing his expenses. My diary for April 24, 1990: "Chris off to NH—called to leave message about that Windsor VT Journal paper on NH." Later, I asked Richard E. Winslow III, the Portsmouth librarian and naval historian, if he would put it on his hunting list, since he was beginning to specialize in hunting for Melville and Thoreau reviews in regional New England newspapers. In August 1992 Winslow found a file of the *Journal.* Comparatively few special correspondents, even the unpaid amateurs, contented themselves with one attempt to enlighten and amuse friends at home while establishing their own reputations as competent amateur writers. Winslow knew to keep looking, and of course more was in the *Windsor Journal* than the article condensed in the Lowell paper. The Lowell paper had omitted a reference by the writer to his description of the Mountain Mirror in an earlier letter.

The December 12, 1851, *Windsor Journal* article signed by "Maherbal" had indeed contained a physical description of Hawthorne omitted in the Lowell paper:

> If, however, on a closer inspection you observed a wreath of smoke curling up from the chimney of the house of the two gables, and had curiosity enough to saunter around the precincts in hopes of seeing signs of life, until about four o'clock, you would finally hear the door creak, and there would stand before you a middling-sized, thick set man, with a large and vigorous, though not unpleasant face, and lying under a profusion of coarse black hair, a head of massive development. There would be nothing very striking in his countenance, except it were his dark and intelligent eye, arched by a very black eye-brow, yet you would gather from the *tout ensemble* of the expression that it betokened an intensely-working and thorough-going intellect.—Were it not that the countenance is relieved and heightened by the vigor and intensity of mental activity that beams through it, you would think there was something in it very heavy and sombre. If you ever had any hint that there was a vein of rancor and acrimony in his character, you would look in vain for any indications of it in his face, unless you commenced to imagine what expression that black eye, would take, and that heavy eye-brow, and that firmly drawn mouth, when he was belaboring the Custom House officials, or spurring his bitterness against some Puritan hypocrite. But while you were making these observations, your hero would raise his eyes from the ground long enough to give you one of those modest but expressive glances which mark the man of seclusion and reflection, and then with a kind of swinging gait which would assure you that he was not used to bustle among the crowds of business or fashion, would wend his way up to the village Post office.

This was valuable, but in the end I found I just could not work it into the space I was allotting the chapter of the biography.

There was a bigger surprise, for the Vermont paper had concluded with a paragraph on the Hawthornes' removal from the cottage: "Within a few days

past Mr. Hawthorne has left our goodly village, to spend the winter in Newton. Strange that he should encamp so near Salem! Lenox was a great way
off, but not far enough to dispel the lurid gleams that were reflected from
'Gallows Hill,' upon the House of the Seven Gables!" I would guess that this
is a postscript, perhaps added to the letter when the writer learned belatedly
that the cottage was now quite unoccupied.

All this was valuable and interesting, but Maherbal had tardily written
another report which was dated January 10, 1852, and printed in the *Windsor
Journal* on January 16, 1852: "*G. P. R. JAMES—HERMAN MELVILLE.*"
Here was news indeed:

> HERMAN MELVILLE, another distingué [like G. P. R. James] in the lit-
> erature of fiction, is a resident of Pittsfield. Although he has been for
> some time favorably known to a certain class of readers as a novelist,
> he is yet comparatively a young man—not above thirty-five years of
> age. The Melville family have long been known in Pittsfield as rank-
> ing among the upright and respectable members of society, though
> by no means of the so-called highest class. Herman Melville him-
> self is a son-in-law of the celebrated Chief Justice Shaw of Boston. As
> may be gathered from the fact that Melville dedicated his book lately
> published to Nathaniel Hawthorne, "in admiration of his genius," the
> two distinguished writers of fiction are personal friends—not however
> familiar, intimate friends by any means—for if the complaints on the
> part of the Pittsfield people with regard to the exclusiveness of the one,
> and the representations of Maherbal in the *Journal* concerning the
> social character of the other, are to be taken as conclusive in the mat-
> ter, they seem to be alike strangers to any thing like familiarity of social
> intercourse. Not very long ago, the author of the "Scarlet Letter" and
> the author of "Typee," having, in some unaccountable way, gotten a
> mutual desire to see one another, as if neither had a home to which he
> could invite the other, made arrangements in a very formal manner to
> dine together at a hotel in this village. What a solemn time they must
> have had, those mighty conjurors in the domain of the imagination,
> all alone in the dining-room of a hotel! In the small talk of the flippant
> beaux and light-headed belles of Berkshire, the solemn attempt of two
> of the greatest characters of which the county could boast, towards an
> acquaintance, was made a subject of infinite merriment.

Winslow's packet containing Maherbal's letters was in my mail on August
29, 1992.

My hands still shaking as I held the photocopies, I went to the computer and deleted the note I had copied and recopied from one expanding file to the next several times a year: "MUST FIND WINDSOR VT. JOURNAL." Jay Leyda was four and a half years dead but I told him—the only dead scholar I talked to. As I mentioned in chapter 4, on July 7, 1988, five months after his death, doped with antibiotics and stoked by the thrill of discovery, I hallucinated him in New Orleans, a city of ghosts for me from the early 1950s. As I stood before the newspaper rack pulling out plum after plum of Oakey Hall's intimate revelations about Melville, there on my right was Jay in his faded blue raincoat, but he did not stay long. Yards of brittle Scotch tape (the paper-rotting kind) had been slathered, years earlier, to the pages of the *Commercial Bulletin* and no matter how cautiously I turned the pages the dried tape fell off onto the floor, not taking the high-rag-content paper with it. Members of the Tulane staff were intent on their holiday, wheeling carts of alcohol by to fete the throng of visiting rare book and manuscript librarians, so they ignored me as I shifted my feet for two days in what sounded more and more like a fast-breeding nest of rattlesnakes. That was 1988, the only time I hallucinated.

In 1992 I telephoned Hayford. We had been on the phone already, my diary shows, talking about Cornelius Mathews's audacious toast about "bloomers" (see Parker, 1: 852):

> At 2 pm mail & all hell broke loose. Winslow had found not only the Windsor VT NH article I wanted but also one on HM—abt his dining with Hawthorne at a Hotel—the day he gave him a copy of MD—Jesus *my mind is wild*. Harry had called. Called him bk—

Hayford, who in 1945 had listed Melville's known meetings with Hawthorne, now listened to me read to him Maherbal's account. It was obvious to him, as to me, what the occasion was, although he had not yet read my account of the previous (November 4) meeting. The discovery was the good goddess's bonus, above and beyond anything any of us could have imagined. It was time for celebration. "Wanted a drink," I jotted down honestly. This was six years after dropping Jay Leyda off after his last research trip. Back then, on Amtrak, weighing the odds of my having the strength to finish both the *Log* and a biography, I had decided that anything reducing my alertness had to go until *The New Melville Log* was published, so I had stopped drinking anything alcoholic. (In 1986, of course, I had no notion that such a resolve would endure for a quarter century or more, awaiting the publication of *The New Melville Log*.) Now, in 1992, I celebrated by talking to Hayford. Then I telephoned Maurice Sendak and read the whole account of the meeting to him, a man with a well-documented visual imagination, and went back to work.

The discovery sent our minds in several directions, one toward self-reproach. At least Hayford had imagined a meeting in which Melville handed Hawthorne *Moby-Dick*, and the book-dealer and collector William Reese had mused about the high monetary and emotional value of the copy inscribed to Hawthorne. As Reese said to the Grolier Club (published in its *Gazette* in 1993), "one can always contemplate something really big—the actual dedication copy to Hawthorne of *Moby-Dick*." Unquestioning inmates of the Ivory Towers, the great lot of us academics aside from Hayford never once thought that what you do when you dedicate a book to a friend who lives nearby is take him a copy and watch his face when he reads the dedication and your inscription.

What is wrong with academics in general? Well, we are good at erecting ramparts against thought. If we acknowledge the value of documents at all, we fixate on documents we are familiar with and think we understand. The long-known letter Melville wrote to Hawthorne on November 17 (that date seems certain enough) has proved such a rampart. It is so passionately confessional, so ecstatic, that we fixated on it almost to the exclusion of what we can infer about Hawthorne's letter that prompted it. We know from Melville's reply that, unwontedly reckless in his emotional and intellectual response to the power of the book that gave the dedication its true significance, Hawthorne had offered in his letter to review *Moby-Dick*, repayment in kind for Melville's momentous essay on *Mosses from an Old Manse*.

We can also make other reasonable inferences about the content of Hawthorne's letter, especially if you know that a dramatic meeting with Melville preceded Hawthorne's reading the book. We fixated on that letter apart from its place in all that is known of the nature of the conversations Melville and Hawthorne had enjoyed since August 1850 and their surviving comments about each other, and the surviving material evidence in journals, books, and letters. We should have recognized that Hawthorne had been eagerly awaiting the appearance of his friend's book, the book he had hailed in his own *Wonder-Book*.

For many years we fixated on Melville's letter to the near-total exclusion of any questioning of how Hawthorne got a copy of *Moby-Dick* so soon. Except for Hayford's vague depiction, did *any* academic ever wonder, when there was no other copy in Lenox that we know of and when the book was not yet in the Pittsfield bookstore, not until mid-December? We slap our heads the way I slapped mine when I realized that Melville himself had written the note announcing that he could be expected home from the Pacific at any moment. *Every Melville scholar must feel chagrined at not having realized that, in order for Hawthorne to have had the copy of* Moby-Dick *so soon, Melville must have carried a copy to him.* What fools we academics be! Melville liked to surprise people, the way he surprised his mother and sisters in 1844. He wanted to see Hawthorne's face as he first saw the dedication page. We ought to have known this sort of thing happened, even before we had the documentation of the meeting in the Lenox hotel. Shame on us for not thinking of writers as real people with normal needs.

In August 1992 I had other things to do besides trying to do justice to the scene. I had just pushed into 1856 in my draft of the latter portion of my biography. I had started at the publication of *Moby-Dick* rather than Melville's birth because what I was adding to the *Log* made me question whether I would have the strength to write about the last four decades of Melville's life after exhausting myself on the first decades. Would I succumb to the heartache of the later decades, I worried, and leave the second half of the book unwritten (I was still thinking of it as one volume), as William Manchester would later leave his biography of Churchill uncompleted? Better to draft the second half first, so I did. When it became clear that the biography would have to be broken in two because I had found so many new episodes and that each volume would be longer than the whole was originally envisioned, the question of where to break it became urgent. The first volume had to end on a high dramatic note. I don't remember all the talk back and forth, but at some point John Wenke said, "You don't have any choice. You have to end it in the hotel."

What I wrote about that meeting of Hawthorne and Melville proved as controversial as anything in the whole first volume. Philip Weiss in the *New York Times Magazine* for December 15, 1996, recalled my lecture at the 92nd Street Y: "The high point of the lecture would also be the high point of Parker's book: a largely imagined description of a sacred moment, a meeting that Parker discovered took place between Melville and Hawthorne in 1851." The scene, as I will show, was not really "largely imagined," but the words "largely imagined" had grim consequences such as this 1999 item on the Internet signed Sara Smollett:[2]

> Parker says that Hawthorne and Melville agreed to meet as soon as Melville published *Moby-Dick*. He says that Melville drove to Hawthorne's to invite him to a formal farewell dinner and/or publishing celebration at Curtis's hotel in Lenox. I don't know where he got this from since he quotes no sources nor have any other sources referred to this meeting. He also says that Lenoxites were curious about the

two local recluses in the hotel. This seems to me to be pure fabrication on the part of Parker in order to present a more dramatic story. (Okay, so ten out of ten for style, but minus several million for credibility.) He concludes this volume of his biography with a description of their meeting. Where is he getting this from? He's clearly just making up details and is not at all reliable.

Smollett piled contempt on contempt: "I also think Hershel Parker sacrifices his biographical integrity by ending his book with a charming and fabricated story. This is just one example of Parker speculating without offering any evidence to back up his opinions." More temperate critics still reflexively push the accusation forward, as Erica Da Costa does (2000): "Where there were no facts to rely on, Parker necessarily imagined plausible scenarios."

Then came this annihilating early review, nominally of my second volume. In the *Nation* (May 20, 2002) Brenda Wineapple rather than reviewing my second volume declared that the final scene from the first volume was fantasized, even worse than "largely imagined": "Parker's fine sleuthing turned up a newspaper article, printed in the 1852 Windsor, Vermont, *Journal*, that recounts Melville meeting Hawthorne for dinner at a hotel in Lenox, Massachusetts, conveniently situated between Pittsfield and the small house the Hawthornes were occupying on the border of what today is known as Tanglewood" (38–39). Wineapple continued (39): "And on the basis of this gossip column" (of course, it was not a gossip column), "Parker speculates that the dinner took place circa November 14 and that as the two friends lingered, alone in the dining room, Melville handed *Moby-Dick* to Hawthorne. ('In no other way could Hawthorne have had a copy so soon,' Parker explains.)" She was building toward this demolition of my integrity as a biographer (39):

> As Hawthorne held *Moby-Dick* in his hand, "he could open the book in his nervous way (more nervous even than normally)," writes Parker, "and get from his friend a guided tour of the organization of the thing now in print, and even sample a few paragraphs that caught his eye or that the author eagerly pointed out to him." He could indeed. Whether he *did* is another matter, though not for Parker, as secure in his fantasy as Edmund Morris is in his imaginary *Dutch: A Memoir of Ronald Reagan*. "Take it all in all," Parker concludes, "this was the happiest day of Melville's life."

Not for Wineapple the high spiritual mood in which Stanton Garner read the last pages, his awe "that there never was, nor ever will be, such another moment." Not for Wineapple the ecstasy that the old-time Melville-Hawthorne scholar Harrison Hayford felt at the ending of the full printout of the first volume, as I quote later in this chapter: "It breaks into SONG—a Song of Jubilation & Praise." You can't write a biography or write a conscientious review of one without revealing your own character.

At some point I learned that the sharply dressed woman sitting in the front row as I gave talks about my discoveries, Laurie Robertson-Lorant, was writing a biography of her own, and I knew in the late 1990s that my ferocious reviewer, Andrew Delbanco, was planning his own biography of Melville. I had not heard anything about Wineapple except that she was planning a biography of Hawthorne, but on reading this scathing comparison of me to Edmund Morris it was apparent to me that she regarded herself as a rival. If I got a Pulitzer for the second volume instead of just being one of two finalists, as in 1997, would the Pulitzer committee be willing to consider her for a Pulitzer in only another year or two, when her Hawthorne biography was published? Two Pulitzers on Melville and Hawthorne in close proximity? Knocking me out of competition would clear the field for her biography of Hawthorne. If this was her strategy, wittingly or not, it seems to be the same one Andrew Delbanco had been employing for years and employed devastatingly in 2002, when he said because of my unsubstantiated surmises about *The Isle of the Cross* and *Poems* readers had to use me with caution throughout both volumes.

Here is Wineapple's own version of this scene, in her 2003 biography of Hawthorne (243):

> In the fall, they [the Hawthornes] sold much of their furniture at auction, including Hawthorne's mahogany writing desk, and gathered the remaining household goods, leaving behind their five cats and a sorrowful Melville. There was nothing to be done about Melville, of course; he had a family of his own. Early in November, Hawthorne met Melville for dinner at the Lenox hotel, and that night Melville presumably gave Hawthorne his inscribed copy of *Moby-Dick*, cooked, Melville hinted, partly at Hawthorne's fire. "I have written a wicked book," Melville was to tell him, "and feel spotless as a lamb." The letter (lost) that Hawthorne wrote in praise of *Moby-Dick* drove the younger author to rapture: "Your heart beat in my ribs and mine in yours, and both in God's," Melville surged with hopeful intimacy, demanding in the next breath, "Whence come you, Hawthorne? By what right do you drink from my flagon of life?"

The cats had indeed been abandoned, according to Julian, and Melville could have been sorrowing, despite the exultant tone of his letter to Hawthorne. Whether he *was* sorrowful is another matter, though not for Wineapple, who (this is a devastating thing to say, but true) is as secure in her fantasy as Edmund Morris is in his imaginary *Dutch: A Memoir of Ronald Reagan*. This is cheeky, vulgar writing about sacred days in the lives of two momentous men who deserve a full measure of respect.

But this is far worse than vulgar writing. Appallingly, all but unbelievably, Wineapple misquoted what Melville wrote Hawthorne three days or so later, his claiming to "feel spotless as the [*not* a] lamb." We are dependent on Rose Hawthorne Lathrop's transcription, but this daughter of Hawthorne's knew a biblical reference when she saw one. Melville felt then, after writing *Moby-Dick* (a wicked book, he said), and after reading Hawthorne's letter—anyone who knows the Bible or falteringly consults a biblical concordance would have recognized—as spotless as Jesus, the Lamb of God. He was telling Hawthorne that he felt as spotless as Jesus when John the Baptist espied him approaching to be baptized, in John 1:29: "The next day John seeth Jesus coming unto him, and saith, Behold the Lamb of God, which taketh away the sin of the world." Did Wineapple visualize Melville as the Pittsfield farmer who milked his own cow and had been around sheep, so he would naturally say he felt like a Berkshire County sheep—all of which are known to be at all times spotless? The way Wineapple misquoted the text desecrates Melville's exalted comparison of himself to Jesus presenting himself for baptism and trivializes the whole of the last encounter in the Berkshires of these two momentous men. Would you trust anything she wrote about Melville and theology? More important, would you trust her to describe any moment or any passage in literature involving grandeur of spirit? Could she rise to any high occasion? Dennis Donoghue did not think so.

Wineapple, said Donoghue in the *Los Angeles Times Book Review* (September 28, 2003), depicted Hawthorne as "a miserable, whining man, aloof, self-obsessed, determined to be unhappy. . . . Wineapple seems to have wearied of her subject and become exasperated with his debility" (R16). Donoghue saves for the ending his unhappiness about Wineapple's vulgarities of style:

> I don't think Wineapple is secure in her interpretation of Hawthorne. This may account for the strange mixture of styles in her writing. Much of the book is ordinary, decent standard English, as in the passages I've quoted. But a lot of it is in the style of romantic fiction. "The Eternal City huddled in January's icy glare," meaning

that it was cold in Rome that January: "Head bent, the Reverend
Bentley wears his broad-brimmed hat, he usually does, and raises
his skirts as if to dodge temptation, passing whorehouses and ware-
houses hunkered near the water's edge." Nonsense: no evidence for
any of this, except maybe the hat. "Perhaps he took her hand then,
warm and small in her wintry glove." Perhaps, perhaps not. "Age
clasped his throat." It what? "Liverpool loomed on the shore, ware-
houses standing like upended coffins in an overcast dawn." Maybe:
I doubt it. Hawthorne wrote romances, but that doesn't justify his
biographer in writing romantic sentences. And then, presumably to
enrich the mixture, Wineapple uses demotic American, pretending
that the past tense of "tread" is "tread," not "trod," and that "like" has
wiped out "as" just as "that" has displaced "who" and "whom": "like
Hawthorne does," "like Dickens or Balzac do," and "the man that he
kills."

So much for Donoghue on Wineapple. He was not smitten with her biography of Hawthorne.[3]
    What Wineapple purveyed about me in the *Nation* was romantic fiction,
indeed, and inaccurate as biography. Had she walked the Berkshire terrain without realizing that the Curtis Hotel is not conveniently equidistant
or nearly equidistant from the little red cottage and from Arrowhead? Melville could not have telephoned Hawthorne, in any case, and asked him to
meet part way, in Lenox, so being convenient is irrelevant. "Convenient"
would have meant Hawthorne was between Melville and the hotel so Melville could drop him off on his way home. Wineapple is wrong in saying the
meeting I described was in early November (243), and she erred in the endnotes when she cited me as authority for "Early in November" (439). In my
biography, I *did* reveal an early November meeting—the November 4 meeting at Charles and Elizabeth Sedgwick's in Lenox, but Wineapple ignored
this new information. Then, she mis-imagined the new meeting I discovered, taking it as nocturnal. In the Melvilles' usage, family dinner ended by
one thirty or so and the afternoon could be taken up with work for several
hours. Gansevoort could haul skins to Schenectady after dinner in the winter and get back after dark. Redburn could have dinner ashore in Liverpool
and resume work at one thirty. Under extreme pressure young Allan could
be forced to work through the day and take dinner as late as four or even five,
although later in New York City the large household dined at four. Dinner at
a western Massachusetts hotel, as in North Adams, was noon or shortly afterward. That such was the case in the summer of 1851 is clear from the driver's

attempt to deliver the Morewood-Melville party to the North Adams hotel at dinner hour—for after the showdown with the cunning driver and the local constabulary and the trip back to Pittsfield, Mrs. Morewood proposed a fishing party for the afternoon, and planned a midnight supper (Parker, 1:862). Midnight suppers at gala parties were not uncommon. Yes, on occasion Melville could go to Lenox at night, even in November, but he took Hawthorne to the hotel for dinner, presumably after the guests had dined, for he booked the dining room for himself. This would have been after any guests at the hotel had finished dinner, the midday meal, perhaps two in the afternoon. A biographer needs to visualize the whole scene.

Was what I wrote so irresponsible in its misguided loftiness that Wineapple could honestly compare my biography to the notoriously fictionalized *Dutch*? Let's see how secure I was in my "fantasy." What, factually, could I glean from the letter from Maherbal? Well, a very great deal indeed!

1. The writer knew that Melville had dedicated *Moby-Dick* to Hawthorne and could accurately quote from the dedication.

2. Melville and Hawthorne met each other "not very long" before January 10, 1852, and therefore fairly soon before November 21, 1851, when Hawthorne left Lenox, as Maherbal knew.

3. The two men met in a Lenox hotel, for dinner.

4. Observers, possibly a good many, looked into the dining room where the men sat at a table alone together. At the least, Lenoxites learned of the meeting. In the biography I read Maherbal as indicating that some of the Lenoxites peeked in at the two writers. That, I see now, was visualizing too eagerly so that I pushed the evidence somewhat.

5. Any observers, like the rest of Berkshire County, had confirmed Maherbal in the belief that the writers were acquainted already but had not become intimate friends.

6. Pittsfield people had complained about Melville's exclusiveness.

7. Lenox people had complained about Hawthorne's exclusiveness.

8. Melville and Hawthorne both seemed to be "strangers to any thing like familiarity of social intercourse" with each other and presumably with other people. The populace had not known of their intimacy.

9. Maherbal thought of Melville as the author of *Typee* and Hawthorne as the writer of *The Scarlet Letter*, which implies that he was thinking of the sensualist vs. the Puritan moralist—a comical pairing. In the chapter on Melville as a heterosexual sex symbol (13) I quote Maherbal's testimony that Melville's name "often lingers now in terms of adulation upon many rosy lips," a fair indication of how he and many others saw Melville.

10. "Not very long ago," the two writers had "in some unaccountable way, gotten a mutual desire to see one another." Maherbal had no idea of a purpose for the meeting.

11. The men should have met in either Melville's house or Hawthorne's house, Maherbal thought (not taking account of Hawthorne's lack of mobility and not realizing that the Little Red House would have been in disarray, from packing).

12. Instead, the writers violated local custom by making "arrangements in a very formal manner to dine together at a hotel in this village," thereby baffling if not outraging the conventional standards of those who learned what they had done. Men could have dinner at the Astor House in New York or the Parker House in Boston but in Lenox local men absolutely did not *do dinner* in the hotel.

13. Maherbal reflected in something like awe or disbelief at what had occurred in the local hotel: "What a solemn time they must have had, those mighty conjurors in the domain of the imagination, all alone in the dining-room of a hotel!"

14. Flippant young men and light-headed young women of Lenox and indeed in all of Berkshire may have witnessed and certainly heard stories of this "solemn attempt of two of the greatest characters of which the county could boast, towards an acquaintance."

15. These Berkshire County beaux and belles made this meeting "a subject of infinite merriment."

16. The meeting was in a very public place. (There was in 1851 another hotel, the Ives Hotel, but the Berkshire Coffee-House, later called "the Red Inn" and by 1851 the Wilson Hotel, still later to be the Curtis Hotel, was the only famous hotel in Lenox. Melville's brother had stayed there and his father-in-law always stayed to hold court. Both Melville and Hawthorne had prior connections with the Wilson Hotel [at least according to Curtis, Hawthorne did] and Melville had later connections.)[4]

17. The meeting lasted a good long time, time enough for the men to get to know each other, time enough to justify making the formal arrangement for the use of the dining room. Two hours? Three hours?

In the light of all this factual detail, what had I invented or fantasized? I made a conscious decision to treat the golden gift of this unknown meeting in a style appropriately heightened to describe Melville's giving an inscribed copy of *Moby-Dick* to Hawthorne and watching his face as he read the dedication. Given what we know of their meeting on November 4 and Hawthorne's signing a book for Malcolm on the seventh and Melville's having to give *Moby-Dick* to Hawthorne in order for him to read it and write to him about it, I take it as pretty well proven. (You can imagine the Harpers sending Hawthorne an advance copy of the book, but that is fantasy. Fields sent copies out to Hawthorne's friends, to be sure.) Melville had an urgent need to meet Hawthorne, did in fact meet him, and thereafter Hawthorne possessed a copy of *Moby-Dick*, and wrote Melville about it very soon thereafter, and from Maherbal we know of a private meeting in a public place which the Lenoxites found very strange.

In the final pages of the first volume of my biography I attempted to show how Lenox and Pittsfield felt about the two authors in their county who had never made themselves frequent worshippers in their churches or familiar guests at their dinner tables. I needed to remind the reader that the jail where Uncle Thomas had been confined was cheek-by-jowl with the courthouse where Shaw presided—in a row with the Wilson Hotel. I needed to remind the reader of how resentful many in the Berkshires were that Hawthorne had proved so maddeningly reclusive and that Melville had almost never attended church with his sisters and mother and had rebuffed the ministerial advances. I wanted to recall Melville's late account of his youthful impression of the awe in which the Pittsfield men regarded the courtesies of Uncle Thomas and the rich man of the village, Edward Newton: "To the ensuing conversation, also, they listened with the look of steers astonished in the pasture at the camel of the menagerie passing by on the road."[5] I wanted to play up, throughout the ending, the mingled admiration, irritation, frustration, and envy of the local inhabitants, playing that off against the easy intimacy and conspicuous distinction of the two men in the dining room, however they were dressed. These two men, I did not venture to say, were striking looking, Melville very handsome and Hawthorne grizzled now but displaying much of the facial gorgeousness that had marked the decades of his early maturity. They were, however people responded to their looks, genuine national and international celebrities, and well worth staring at or hearing about. I was happy to use a bit of Melville's markings, a decade later, of Hazlitt's railing about the narrowness and viciousness of country people and his enthusiastic seconding of Hazlitt's opinions.

To flesh out the scene I conscientiously looked at reliable accounts of Hawthorne's characteristic mannerisms, which I knew less well than Melville's. His legs (longer than Melville's) would have been under the table, but what about his hands? Witnesses testified to his nervous gestures. Would Hawthorne then put the book down and not look at it again and proceed to talk about his plans for life in West Newton? That would not have been

polite. The only polite thing to do is to look through the book a little, not
neglecting your host, but getting a sense of what goes on in the book.[6] What
does Melville do when you are holding the book? Could he resist pointing
out the compliment to Salem women? In ordinary human behavior they
would have picked the book up many times and passed it back and forth.
And they talked of their achievements and their plans, Melville, perhaps,
of what he had already done on *Pierre*. Is this wild fantasy in the manner of
Edmund Morris's *Dutch*?

   This is my final paragraph in the July 14, 1995, printout Hayford read and
marked:

> There were onlookers aplenty, but no eavesdroppers to record their
> conversation. Decades later Melville wrote into the manuscript a
> closeted interview between Captain Vere and Billy Budd—an inter-
> view the secrets of which the narrator does not reveal. At some well
> chosen moment Melville took out the book they had been awaiting
> and handed his friend an autographed copy of *Moby-Dick*, the first
> presentation copy. How else would Hawthorne have had a copy so
> soon, one that he had read by the 15th or 16th? Here, in the dining
> room, Hawthorne for the first time saw the extraordinary dedica-
> tion—the first time a book had ever been dedicated to him. Never
> demonstrative, he was profoundly moved. Alone with the author, he
> could open the book, get a guided tour of the organization of the
> thing in print, and even sample a few paragraphs that caught his eye
> or that the author particularly wanted him to see, perhaps some pas-
> sages he had seen in March in Melville's study. Hawthorne could see
> enough, in that period of sampling, to be profoundly impressed by
> the genius of the author of this book queerly named for an enormous
> sperm whale, *Moby-Dick*. The flippant beaux and the light-headed
> belles were witnessing a sacred occasion in American literary life as
> the men lingered at the table, drinking, soothed into ineffable soci-
> alities, obscured at times from view by their tobacco smoke. They
> lingered long after the dining-room had emptied, each reverential
> toward the other's genius, each aware that when they met again, in
> West Newton, in Boston, or wherever their Fates might bring them
> together, they would not fall at once into these present terms of inti-
> macy. Inevitably, Hawthorne, the one who was leaving, was looking
> forward, and Melville at moments was looking back at his decision
> to finish his book near this older writer, but at other moments he
> was living intensely in the present, a moment he might have been

robbed of if the book had been delayed, the time when his friend held in his hand his farewell gift, the printed and bound book, a tangible token of Melville's admiration for his genius. Take it all in all, it was the happiest day of Melville's life.

In the book as printed in 1996 this paragraph became, by Hayford's direction, two long paragraphs and a very short final one, the two longer ones incorporating Hayford's suggestions for strengthening the prose. My last line was changed a little, not by Hayford's advice, to "Take it all in all, this was the happiest day of Melville's life." I indignantly rejected someone else's correction of "Take" to "Taken": I was an Okie who had worked to acquire a prose voice, and I was challenging and alluring the reader into complicity with me. Besides, "take him all in all" had been good enough for Hamlet.

"A real DIAMOND of a find," Hayford wrote in his minute criticism on the printout of that scene, as he pushed for clearer visualizing of Hawthorne and Melville at the table. Hayford then filled the back of the last page of the printout, starting a third of the way down the left and raying out east, north, and south, here transcribed in order of inscription:

> 1:15 a.m. 17 July 95 Reader (HH) at end of book after the past 10 days' day & night sessions. Surpassingly GOOD!—this whole last Chapter (A WOWZER—even & esp. to us old Shipmate Melvilleans)—THAR SHE BREACHES (to high heaven) etc etc
>
> But do labor, up to the moment when you surrender the last page proofs, to polish the whole passage and this [final] ¶ to its full shining climactic peak.
>
> *Every word counts*—as in a lyric *poem*, which this *is* (it breaks into SONG—a Song of Jubilation & Praise)—(I'm carried away—as I've been all week in this HOUSE and the presence of the author of this stunningly magnificent biography.)

I print this here as a memorable record of the lifelong response to new details about Melville and Hawthorne by the man who had pioneered the recovery of documentary records of their acquaintance and had striven to capture the essential qualities of their relationship. I print it, also, as an illustration of how great lifelong scholarship, like Hayford's work on Hawthorne and Melville, can become part of an ongoing collaboration of scholars, as when Hawthorne surprised both Hayford and me by coming back onstage so often in the first draft of the second half of my biography, which Hayford read before reading the earlier chapters that became the first volume. *Herman*

Melville: A Biography, Hayford knew very well, would not have been written without his own "Melville and Hawthorne."

The attacks on my integrity as a biographer by New York critics in 2002 were devastating to my health and peace of mind. Expecting thanks, I was helpless against the onslaught from Wineapple. I was shattered by the lies in the later reviews by Richard H. Brodhead, Andrew Delbanco, and Elizabeth Schultz, all of whom said or implied that I had made up two lost books, *The Isle of the Cross* which Melville completed in 1853, *Poems* which he completed in 1860. Everything I wrote was suspect, Delbanco said, in the light of my fantasy about these two lost books. In 2002 all the New York reviewers, led by Wineapple, formed a united front which a Pulitzer committee could not ignore. The 1997 committee had given the prize to an early fictional "misery memoir" and named me as one of the two finalists. The 2003 committee did not have to consider the second volume at all, despite my pretensions to doing fresh archival research—had not the best New York City reviewers deplored my writing a fantasy biography? I did not speak out about Brodhead, Delbanco, and Schultz until 2007. It is time now that I also speak out about Brenda Wineapple. How much, I challenge her or you, how much about the final scene in my first volume is fantasized? Did I deserve to have my biography denounced as a companion fantasy to Edmund Morris's *Dutch*? Whom do you trust, Wineapple, the desecrator of Melville's reference to the Lamb of God, or Harrison Hayford, the great Melville scholar? Or me, the patient Melville biographer?

⁘ Chapter 18 ⁘

WHY MELVILLE TOOK
HAWTHORNE TO THE HOLY LAND

Biography Enhanced by Databases and an Amateur Blogger

THIS CHAPTER DRAWS ON MY decades of work in American newspapers as supplemented by new resources—newspapers and magazines in databases. A quantum leap in accessibility occurs every time new files enter the databases. Even a database which includes only two newspapers from Boston and two from New York is far more useful than anyone might at first expect, because any two papers would print articles from dozens of other cities, while papers from other cities in the database such as Milwaukee, San Francisco, Detroit, and New Orleans will regularly reprint items from not just the two but also other Boston and New York papers. My tracing of Hawthorne's reputation in this chapter is solidly grounded on my old archival research but made richer and more precise by what I have found in the latest databases available. It also draws gratefully on a young blogger who in a matter of sources outdid all the academics of half a century, including Walter E. Bezanson and me. With the new evidence from databases I strengthen and somewhat shift the chapter in the second volume of my biography, "The Man Who Had Known Hawthorne: 1869." The evidence for one major argument in this chapter cannot be conclusive, but convinces me. You will decide.

In his 1960 Hendricks House edition of *Clarel,* a reworking of his 1943 Yale dissertation, Walter E. Bezanson, having mustered evidence that the character Vine was very much like Hawthorne, triumphantly declared that one action of Vine's "is not only Hawthornesque; it is Hawthorne's" (xciv). Quoting the passage in which Vine tosses stones "into valley down" or "pelted his own shadow there," Bezanson cited as source this section of Hawthorne's 1868 *Passages from the American Note-Books:* "An idle man's pleasures and occupations and thoughts during a day spent by the sea-shore; among them, that of sitting on the top of a cliff, and throwing stones at his own shadow, far below" (xcv). The image, Bezanson asserted, "is too precise to be coinciden-tal." Bezanson summarized his findings: "It seems likely that Melville used the composition of *Clarel* as an opportunity to brood privately and at length over the man who had meant most in his own life" (xcii).

In a talk at the May 29, 1976, Pittsfield centennial of *Clarel* (published a whole decade later in 1986, then frugally salvaged and elaborated in the second volume of my biography), I accepted Bezanson's argument that the character Vine is based on Hawthorne and I endorsed part of his reading of Vine: "Bezanson finely says that Melville's depiction of Vine shows that he had decided that 'beneath his shy and opulent serenity Hawthorne was scared'" ("The Character of Vine in Melville's *Clarel*," 113). Acknowledg-ing his insight that a "tournament of merits" was played out in the poem between Rolfe, standing for Melville, and Vine, standing for Hawthorne, I went a little further, in a different direction (113):

> The implications of the longer speeches and thoughts of Vine are that Melville had decided Hawthorne was not merely burnt-out as an artist at an early age—he had also decided that in later life Haw-thorne was coasting on an unmerited reputation for mental force, not to say profound intelligence. In reality he had none of Melville's own "strange power to reach the sinuosities of a thought" (the won-derful phrasing of the reviewer of *Moby-Dick* in the Washington *National Intelligencer*—William A. Butler?) let alone the ability to move cogently from one gnarled thought to another.

On the basis of a detailed analysis of gestures and speeches I was con-vinced that "Vine's deeds often reveal an erratic staginess and contempt for himself and others, and his words, however prettily melancholy they are, reflect the shallowness and discontinuity of his mind—the mind of a man 'Whose race of thought long since was run—/For whom the spots enlarge that blot the golden sun'" (113). In the audience a new reader of *Clarel*, Helen Vendler, I was told, kept saying, "He's right, he's right," but a dangerously florid middle-aged man sprang up and shouted for several minutes, actually foaming at the mouth, about my affront to Hawthorne's intellectual stature. He was so out of control as to be unanswerable, only to be soothed. Curiously, no critic or scholar in 1986 or later has mounted even a temperate rejection of my argument about Vine, as far as I know.

For the 1991 Northwestern-Newberry *Clarel* we reprinted Bezanson's great 1960 introduction to the Hendricks House edition. Bezanson did not want to rewrite it to include new information because he had come to think of it as a historical literary artifact which should not be altered, although he could not resist slipping in an anachronistic reference to Melville's recently discovered Dante. To take account of new discoveries, I wrote a "Historical Supplement" to his essay. It became clear to me that in his dissertation, in the 1960 edition, and in 1990 and 1991 Bezanson was focused on the aesthetic structure of his monograph, not on the chronology of Melville's life. Conspicuously, he placed his momentous identification climactically, toward the end of the monograph, where it would leave the patient reader of the long essay dazzled by this delayed revelation. Bezanson's very understandable aesthetic choice to place the identification where he did had deterred him from perceiving its full significance.

By 1990 I had worked enough with Melville's life in the late 1860s to offer a suggestion: "the portrayal of Vine needs to be seen in relation to the attention paid by the press to Hawthorne's posthumous writings . . . and to Melville's known reading and re-reading of Hawthorne in the late 1860s and early 1870s and his acquisition of Hawthorne books" ("Historical Supplement," 652). A diary entry for March 31, 1990: "Serious cleaning up—adding & moving about of marginalia. Before getting out of bed the fine idea of saying '*one* "*decision*"' was to take NH along on the journey." In the "Historical Supplement" I offered the tentative suggestion that Hawthorne did not merely give Melville a chance to brood for years in private and at length over their relationship (during the long composition) but may have had something to do with Melville's being able to conceive or reconceive and finally undertake the poem: "For all we know, a decision to dramatize (and fantasize) a 'tournament of merits' between a character like himself and one like Hawthorne could have been a factor (perhaps even a precipitating one) in his ability to begin at last to make use of his experiences in the Holy Land" (652).

I had not speculated on what event or events might have caused Melville to decide to undertake the poem when he did, but I accepted Jay Leyda's suggestion that Melville started work on *Clarel* in January 1870, his evidence being Melville's first known purchases of source books for the poem. Leon Howard, following Leyda, had thought work on it had not "actually begun in any systematic way until at some time in 1870" (298). Bezanson (xxxiii) thought Melville may have begun the poem earlier: "At some definite point between the end of the War and 1870, when he began to purchase books for his work, he made the crucial decisions which enabled him to go ahead with *Clarel*." He continued, "there is speculative evidence that

Melville had written something like a quarter or third of his poem by 1870. The best hypothesis would seem to be that Melville began his poem about 1867" (xxxiii). The obvious problem with this is that "some definite point" is tantalizingly *indefinite*. Withholding the Hawthorne identification for maximum artistic effect, making it the climax of his monograph, Bezanson did not focus on the *Passages from the American Note-Books* as possible evidence for the earliest date Melville could have thought of putting Hawthorne in the poem, 1868, and did not attempt to reconcile that date with his casual suggestion of "about 1867." Hilton Obenzinger (ix) in his 1999 *American Palestine: Melville, Twain, and the Holy Land Mania* was, by contrast, amazingly specific, although amazingly casual: "In 1866, at the start of his long tenure as an inspector for the New York Customs House, he began *Clarel: A Poem and Pilgrimage in the Holy Land*, composing the narrative poem intermittently during his first ten years on the waterfront." No evidence has been produced for either 1866 or 1867. It seemed to me that Leyda's dating was the soundest, since Melville habitually assembled source books before or soon after beginning to write.

I and all other commentators had accepted Bezanson's identification of the source of the passage in *Clarel*, but as it turns out, this universally acknowledged source is not necessarily the true one. In February 2011 I came across Nicole Perrin's blog, www.bibliographing.com, in which she described her recent marathon reading of Melville, including *Clarel*. There she called attention to a section of "Foot-prints on the Sea-shore" in *Twice-Told Tales* in which Hawthorne climbs to the precipice and looks down into the water: "There lies my shadow in the departing sunshine with its head upon the sea. I will pelt it with pebbles. A hit! A hit!" (324). Details in this sketch, based on Hawthorne's manuscript notebook, are arguably closer to the lines in *Clarel* than the lines Bezanson quoted. In any case, they form a quite sufficient source for Melville since the sketch was available to him in the 1842 Munroe edition of *Twice-Told Tales* which Hawthorne gave him in January 1851 and which he had in his possession the rest of his life (and now is in the Houghton Library).[1]

Perrin's discovery makes us pay attention to something we had all ignored, the time Melville started work on *Clarel*. Bezanson did not use Melville's reading the section of the *Note-Books* about Hawthorne's pelting his shadow as a possible way of dating the composition of the book and canto in which the pelting occurs. That is, Bezanson did not look at the early-published sections of the *Note-Books* to be sure this section did not appear there, and he did not look at the evidence which seems to show that although the American volume had been out since 1868 Melville did not buy it until the day he bought the new *Passages from the English Note-Books* in 1870, although he may have read it earlier. Accepting Bezanson's assertion that the words from the *Note-Books* had been Melville's source for the line in which Vine pelts his own shadow, it did not occur to me, either, that the availability of the pelting image in the *Passages from the American Note-Books* gave a terminus post quem for the composition of that passage, if it were the source. We were all blinded by the stunning resemblance Bezanson had pointed out between the passage in Hawthorne and the lines in Melville's poem, blinded by the fact that Melville's use occurred in the third book of *Clarel*, not near the outset, and blinded by Bezanson's artfully delayed revelation of his identification of Vine and Hawthorne. Knowing of "Foot-prints on the Sea-shore," we have no need to worry about when Melville could have read a passage in the *American Note-Books* before writing this scene about Vine: he had "the" source or a perfectly good source with him all along. *American Note-Books* remains important as one of many reminders of Hawthorne during Melville's composition of *Clarel*, not as a source for the characterization of Vine.

The Northwestern-Newberry *Clarel* was published early in 1991, before I knew of Melville's last meeting with Hawthorne in the Berkshires. By the time I wrote the second volume of my biography (2002) I was willing to speculate that as 1870 approached, "in the barrenness of his life, a failure as a writer, a failure as a husband, a tragic failure as a father," Melville "would not have to go on the pilgrimage alone: he could take Hawthorne with him and reevaluate their friendship at leisure" (2:683–84). In the poem, I suggested, Melville "would not announce what he thought about his friendship with Hawthorne: in the course of writing the poem he would *discover* what Hawthorne had meant to him" (2:684). Now I was ready to strengthen Bezanson's claim and my own earlier claims: a powerful psychological experience in late August 1869 led to the exhilarating idea of taking Hawthorne along on his pilgrimage to the Holy Land, an idea which liberated Melville from his long intermittent broodings over his time in the Holy Land and precipitated his being able to plan *Clarel* late in 1869 and to begin serious work on it around January 1870. If I was right, Vine was not merely one of several characters Melville lined up, over an indefinite period of more or less vague planning, to be worked into the poem: the challenge of an ongoing epic-long exploration of his honest mature conclusions about Hawthorne may have been what precipitated Melville's beginning to write *Clarel*.

My argument requires going forward from Hawthorne's departure from Lenox late in November 1851. In the natural course of things when an intimate friend moves away you think about him often at first. After Hawthorne left Lenox Melville was writing obsessively on *Pierre* for weeks, apparently thinking of it as a "Kraken" book in its psychological complexity, greater than *The Whale* (his title for *Moby-Dick* until the last minute). Then some days after Christmas he took the manuscript to New York. After devastating negotiations with the Harpers he accepted an impossible contract and within days began introducing a new satirical autobiographical section which became dangerously self-destructive as the hero himself attempts to write a great book. About the time he started the enlargements, Melville wrote politely to Sophia Hawthorne, thanking her for praising *Moby-Dick* and of course concealing all his anxiety about the punitive contract he had just accepted for *Pierre*. Soon after he returned to Arrowhead he answered a letter from Julian Hawthorne (in his best boyish printing) in which he countered Julian's story about the depth of snow in West Newton with a description of the depth of the snowdrifts among his own big hemlocks and maples, and concluded by remembrances to Julian's father and this futile hope: "[M]ay Heaven always bless you, & may you be a good boy and become a great good man." (Well after Melville's death Julian served prison time for mail fraud.) In the next months of 1852 Melville was in suspense, living at times in a fool's paradise, hoping for Bentley to publish *Pierre* but never authorizing him to alter it for British sensibilities, irrationally hopeful for praise in the United States once the Harpers published *Pierre* but unable to design a fast backup book like *Redburn*. Three weeks before *Pierre* came out in August, Melville visited eastern Massachusetts and vacationed with his father-in-law. In Nantucket with Shaw and John H. Clifford, the attorney general of the commonwealth, the conversation turned to the "great patience, & endurance, & resignedness of the women of the island" (as Melville wrote to Hawthorne on August 13), a theme which led Clifford to tell a story from one of his cases, about a Pembroke and Falmouth woman, Agatha Hatch, a deserted wife.[2]

The story of Agatha Hatch came to be associated in Melville's mind with Hawthorne, partly because Hawthorne had written the classic romance of an isolated woman and a short tale about a vanished husband, partly because he received the author's gift of *The Blithedale Romance* just before receiving in the mail from Clifford legal documents setting forth the Agatha Hatch story. The early reviews of *Pierre*, coming at almost the same time, were so brutal that Melville could not at once think about starting a new literary work. He apparently did not fully understand that Hawthorne's writing a campaign biography for Franklin Pierce meant that his friend would be thinking of a prosperous future, abroad, once Pierce became president. Brooding over the story Clifford had told, and over the documents, Melville formed the idea that Hawthorne should write the story of Agatha Hatch (perhaps knowing that Hawthorne had given Longfellow the plot of *Evangeline*),

and initiated a prolonged discussion by letter in which he offered suggestions for Hawthorne's treatment of the story. The persuasion continued even
in person, in Concord, on December 2, 1852, after which Melville finally
accepted the fact that Hawthorne could not write it, and began it himself, in
mid-December.

Melville completed the book on or around May 22, 1853, as *The Isle of
the Cross*. After its rejection by the Harpers he began writing in what he
thought of as Hawthorne's most successful genre, the short story. In the
next several years, Hawthorne and some of his shorter tales (what Melville
called "minor," according to the publishing convention) were in his mind
as he wrote some of his own stories. Everyone agrees on the Poesque and
Hawthornesque elements in "The Bell-Tower," for example. "The Piazza,"
written as an introduction to the *Putnam's Magazine* pieces he collected
as *The Piazza Tales*, may well mark Melville's beginning to think beyond
the simplistic aesthetic ideas Hawthorne had expressed in "The Artist of the
Beautiful"—ideas which Melville had taken as authoritative when he first
read that story in 1850. In parts of *The Confidence-Man*, finished in 1856,
Melville recalled such Hawthorne tales as "The Celestial Railroad" and
"The Seven Vagabonds." Between Melville and Hawthorne's hours together
in Southport and Liverpool late in 1856 and their final brief meeting in April
or May 1857, Hawthorne helped Allan Melville place *The Confidence-Man*
with a London publisher. There is a report of a now-lost Christmas greeting
from the Hawthornes in 1857 (one of the newfangled Christmas "cards"),
but almost nothing more, except that on March 6, 1863, Sophia Hawthorne
was trying to track down a copy of *Moby-Dick* which ought to have reached
them several weeks earlier, presumably the copy now at the Rosenbach,
which replaced the inscribed one that was apparently lost in their travels and
may yet make some lucky rummager in Liverpool, Southport, or Rome very
wealthy indeed. As Melville began making himself into a poet in 1857 and
1858, he thought less of Hawthorne and more about English poets, and as
he began to make himself into a serious student of aesthetics he moved far
beyond the lessons of "The Artist of the Beautiful." Chances are that during
the first years of the Civil War Melville seldom had Hawthorne on his mind
for long at a time.

In the 1850s and early 1860s Melville's name occasionally had been
linked with Hawthorne's in a curious genre which began a little before they
met, then absorbed them both among the principal players—articles on the
Massachusetts Berkshires as the haunt of celebrities, mainly literary men
and women. Evert Duyckinck helped fix the formula in the *Literary World*
for September 27, 1851, the third of his articles on "Glimpses of Berkshire

Scenery": "Miss Sedgwick, as is well known to all readers of American literature, is there, and near by arose for the world, doubtless, first painted on the mists of the valley, the vision of The House with the Seven Gables. Herman Melville, in the vistas of his wood and the long prospective glance from his meadows to the mountains, blends the past and the future on his fancy-sprinkled page." Norton's *Literary Gazette* in September 1852 printed "Homes of Literary Men in Berkshire, Mass." mentioning both Melville and Hawthorne. The *Great Barrington Courier* on September 22, 1853, gave excerpts from the *New York Herald*'s "Berkshire County," mentioning both men. Many such articles followed. During the Civil War, naturally enough, fewer were published, a notable exception being Henry T. Tuckerman's "Authors in Berkshire," written in Lenox during October 1863, just before the Melvilles moved to New York, and printed on November 16 in the *American Literary Gazette*. In the "soft radiance of a brilliant autumn sunset" Tuckerman had lingered around the "little red house" where Hawthorne had "dwelt during his novitiate as an author" and decided that it would be hard to find a spot in New England "better fitted to inspire and content a poetical mind." G. W. Curtis in the *Harper's* "Editor's Easy Chair" in October 1867 contributed to the revivified genre, declaring that neither Bryant, Hawthorne, Miss Sedgwick, nor Melville "had too warmly praised the beauty or described the character" of the landscape of the Berkshires. After the war several years passed before the little genre found new contributors, but thereafter it quickly entered into its durable phase, so that even today one looks for an annual article in the *New York Times* on vacationing in the literary Berkshires in the footsteps of Melville and Hawthorne.

In April 1864 tragic news brought Hawthorne to Melville's attention. All the papers (and there were still a dozen or more important daily papers in Manhattan) reported that on April 10 William D. Ticknor, the co-owner of Ticknor & Fields, had died while on a trip with Hawthorne. The most startling part of the news was that, according to the widely copied *Philadelphia Press*, the trip had been for *Hawthorne*'s benefit, and the younger Ticknor had "been enjoying rude health." The writer (whom the travelers had called upon together, there in Philadelphia—perhaps George William Childs) explained that Ticknor's family had been summoned by telegraph, but arrived too late: "Mr. HAWTHORNE, who never left him from the time he was taken ill, held his hand at the moment he breathed his last, and is deeply affected by the severe blow which has deprived him of a friend, counsellor, and man of business." The *New York Times* reprinted this account, as other papers did, while Melville was in Washington and northern Virginia, going on a scout against John Mosby's guerrilla forces.

The news of Hawthorne's attendance at Ticknor's deathbed may have been delayed in getting to Melville, but he learned it, and it stirred him. The next month, May 24, his sister Fanny (in Gansevoort, New York) wrote to their cousin Kate Gansevoort, in Albany, "You may have noticed in the papers a few weeks ago, in the account of Mr Ticknor's death in Philadelphia, that Mr Hawthorne was the friend that was with him." This was Fanny's preamble to still more upsetting news: "We were quite shocked yesterday upon looking over the morning paper, to see the notice of Nathaniel Hawthorne's sudden death." Also from the house in Gansevoort, Maria Melville wrote the same day to Kate's father, her brother Peter, echoing the newspaper accounts of the circumstances of Ticknor's death the month before (Parker, 2:576):

> I was quite shocked to see the sudden death of Nathaniel Hawthorne, in New Hampshire where he was on a visit, & was found dead in his bed, he had left home for the benefit of his health. A few weeks, since he visited Philadelphia with his friend W. D. Ticknor, the Boston publisher, who was taken sick & died, Mr Hawthorne never leaving him from the time he was taken sick, & was holding his hand at the moment he was breathing his last. Mr Hawthorne was deeply affected at his death, & not being well; then travelling for his health. It is very probable the sudden shock was too much for him. Herman was much attached to him & will mourn his loss. He staid with him a few days in Liverpool, & I beleive has not seen him since. We have just received a letter from Lizzie, she writes that Herman was much shocked at hearing of Mr Hawthornes sudden death. Thacker[a]y also died very suddenly being found dead in his bed.

"Herman was much shocked." He had indeed been "much attached to him." In his grief he was reminded that Hawthorne was very much his senior even while he acknowledged that his own recent scout against Aldie, however valuable to him for varying reasons, had been evidence, if evidence was needed, that he was not the vigorous young man he had been in 1850 and 1851, the time of his intimacy with his now dead friend.

Hawthorne's Boston publisher, James Fields (he who in 1850 had worn his citified patent leather shoes in the climb up Monument Mountain the day Hawthorne and Melville met), speedily undertook what grew into the single most sustained and successful publicity campaign ever waged on behalf of a nineteenth-century American author. One early obstacle was lingering resentment among abolitionists and their sympathizers for what was widely seen as Hawthorne's sympathy with the views of Southerners. The *Tribune*, edited by Horace Greeley, who had so strongly pressured Lincoln to eman- cipate the slaves, on October 4, 1865, recalled the "unfortunate" campaign biography of Franklin Pierce where Hawthorne "could see in the anti-Slavery movement only 'the mistiness of a philanthropic theory,' and in Abolition only 'the ruin of two races.'" Rather than defending Hawthorne from such criticisms, Fields's strategy was to distract readers first by putting out new edi- tions of Hawthorne's books and then by serializing new works posthumously in his *Atlantic Monthly*. Late in 1864 and early in 1865 the new *Twice-Told Tales* was widely reviewed. The January 1865 *Godey's* review of *Twice-Told Tales* referred to Hawthorne's "rapidly increasing body of readers"—rapidly increasing since his death. By January 1865 the early volumes of *The Works of Nathaniel Hawthorne* (planned for fourteen volumes) were reviewed in the *Christian Examiner*, which made special mention of the romance which Fields had offered a foretaste of in the *Atlantic Monthly*: "The little that has been published of 'The Dolliver Romance' makes it more evident than it was before, if that were necessary, that, when Hawthorne died, American litera- ture sustained the greatest loss that has ever befallen it." (The writer was sure that only Abraham Lincoln was a more important American.)

After the twin shocks of 1864 and after Fields had mustered his formi- dable publicity campaign, ignoring Hawthorne had become impossible for anyone, especially anyone who had known him at all well. Hard as he was working on his Civil War poems "after the fall of Richmond" (as he states in the preface to *Battle-Pieces*), Melville in May 1865 was rereading in Hawthorne's *Mosses from an Old Manse*, the book which had triggered and channeled his explosion of admiration in August 1850. Now he was struck by the early thoughts on fame and death which Hawthorne had written into "Monsieur du Miroir." "What a revelation," Melville wrote on the passage about the narrator's staking much "to win a name." The narrator says that when he no longer can look in the mirror the man in the mirror "will pass to the dark realm of Nothingness, but will not find me there." This, Melville decided, "trenches upon the uncertain and the terrible" (*Log*, 674). He was reliving his admiration for Hawthorne, and reviving the curiosity that had attached to Hawthorne for him from the beginning, curiosity springing from his sense that Hawthorne had a secret like some of his characters, as Julian later thought Melville believed.

In an immediate response to the death the *Round Table* on May 28, 1864, had declared: "The greatest loss that American literature has ever sustained is the death of Nathaniel Hawthorne." Others were challenging Melville to reappraise the stature of the man. James Russell Lowell sounded a new level of praise in the October 1865 *North American Review,* a periodical recently acquired by Fields: Hawthorne had been "the rarest creative imagination of the century, the rarest in some ideal respects since Shakespeare." Surveying seven volumes of the new Ticknor & Fields uniform edition, the January 1866 *Methodist Quarterly Review* mildly reproached Hawthorne for saying no word against slavery but was clear on his stature: "At the head of romance-writers in the English tongue, stands Nathaniel Hawthorne." All through 1866 there was no escaping Hawthorne and praise of him, for each month all year long Fields printed excerpts in the *Atlantic* from Hawthorne's American diaries. Melville had good reason to expect that he might be mentioned in a late excerpt (he was not). Every month many newspapers mentioned the ongoing series, so escaping the *Atlantic* was impossible for a literary man, even a man getting a book of poetry into print. All that year the consensus was growing that Hawthorne was a great writer. On October 6, 1866, the *San Francisco Bulletin* in a review of *Miscellaneous Papers* by Washington Irving concluded that Irving's style was "surpassed by no modern writer, if we except Hawthorne," and on October 15 for the *Galaxy,* "Brockden Brown and Hawthorne" were "the two most eminent American writers of the subjective school." On November 3, 1866, the *Tribune* in a review of Irving's *Spanish Papers* declared: "He and Hawthorne are our wells of English undefiled."

During this early surging of Hawthorne's fame Melville's name was almost never mentioned in connection with Hawthorne's, since even the articles on literary pilgrimages to the Berkshires were pretty much in abeyance still, in the first years after the war. Databases now allow me to be more precise than I was in the biography. I said it wrong. In the comments of the reading public in the late 1860s Melville was *not* the man who had known Hawthorne in the Berkshires. That *was* true of the 1870s, when it became clear to Julian Hawthorne and to Rose Hawthorne's husband George Lathrop that Melville's letters were essential to Hawthorne biography for the Lenox episode and that his recollections might also be valuable, if he could be persuaded to talk. In the late 1860s, in reality, Melville was in a more pathetic situation as the man who *thought* he had known Hawthorne. At times Melville must almost have thought that he had *not* known him, after all, since he was part neither of the public mourning nor the early posthumous fame.

Melville was of course totally excluded from a new and increasingly popular competitive journalistic genre, the literary pilgrimage to Concord, in which other names were associated with Hawthorne's. The *New York Times* on November 10, 1867, was condescending about the "gossiping correspondent" who contributed "A Visit to Concord, Mass.—Its Celebrities" to the

Chicago Tribune, but it quoted the whole article, even its disparagement of Hawthorne's Wayside ("a curious jumble of cheap buildings of various sorts, as if built a piece at a time by some man whose means and tastes were equally deficient"). On December 9, 1865, the *Lowell Daily Citizen* printed an article on "Old Concord" in which R. W. Ball asked, "Why is it that this same town of Concord is to be so famous in the annals of American genius?" and "Why has it been the favorite haunt of the best American thinkers and writers?" In a tiny note taken from the *Boston Evening Post* (relating just to Hawthorne), the *Milwaukee Daily Sentinel* on April 15, 1867, pointed to "Signs of Hawthorn's Popularity," varying the spelling: "Hawthorn's man-uscripts are to be copied for publication. The present tenant of 'The Old Manse' says that every day last season there were tourists who called to see it. In England, too, travellers are going over the country he has described with such pictorial skill in 'Our Old Home.' John Bright said that those places were almost unknown before Hawthorne explored them." The *Cin-cinnati Daily Gazette* on April 29, 1869, picked up from the *New York Times* a literary pilgrimage, "Concord and Its Celebrities." The June 1869 *Over-land Monthly* contained "A Day in Hawthorne's Haunts," which was widely reprinted. On February 18, 1871, the *San Francisco Bulletin* reported that pil-grims were coming from England to stand at Hawthorne's grave. (The writer of "A New England Village" in the November 1871 *Harper's New Monthly Magazine* declared that the "house in which Hawthorne lived at Stockbridge is every year visited by hundreds of people from all parts of the world—from England especially." The writer added, "Herman Melville had a residence within an easy drive of Hawthorne.") After Bronson Alcott himself tried the genre in *Concord Days,* the *New York Tribune* (September 2, 1872) noted his "portraiture of certain eminent men among the author's acquaintance, Emerson, Hawthorne, Wendell Phillips, Garrison, and Thoreau" occupied "the foreground of the personal gallery." Typical of the continued interest was "Concord, Mass. An Intellectual Atmosphere and a Home of Authors— The Alcotts and the Hawthornes" in the *Chicago Inter-Ocean* (October 27, 1874). The distinction between the two literary-geographic genres was not quite "Concord genius" versus "Berkshire scenery," but in the temporary decline of articles on the literary inhabitants of western Massachusetts James Fields had deftly moved the focus to the Concord-Boston axis.

Praise of Hawthorne became more and more weighty. On April 4, 1867, the *New York Tribune* in a review of W. R. Alger's *The Solitudes of Nature* pointed out Alger's "passing allusion to the greatest American mas-ter of English prose, showing a just insight into the character of that unique genius"—that is, Hawthorne. In a much-copied article in the *Nation,* "The

Great American Novel" (January 9, 1868), John W. DeForest said that "Hawthorne, the greatest of American imaginations, staggered under the load of the American novel." In its January 23 reprint, for example, the *Cincinnati Daily Gazette* spread this high ranking of Hawthorne through the Ohio Valley. The adulatory "The Genius of Hawthorne" in the *Atlantic* (attributed to his sister-in-law Elizabeth Palmer Peabody) went very far indeed: "Hawthorne takes rank with the highest order of artists." On October 10, 1868, *Every Saturday* questioned whether among American geniuses "there is any one of higher rank than Nathaniel Hawthorne,—if, indeed, his equal." Lowell in his review of the *American Note-Books* in the *North American Review* for January 1869 called Hawthorne "the most profoundly artistic genius of these latter days"; if you were to add "a little to him, and he would have been the greatest poet since Shakespeare." The January 21, 1869, *Independent* quoted the London *Spectator* of December 21, 1868, as doubting whether "any English writer now living" wrote such "pure and classical English as was written by Nathaniel Hawthorne," and the February 6, 1869, *Littell's* quoted the same passage.

In November 1868, knowing that he was not a character in the 1866 serialized portions of the American diaries, Melville would have seen substantial reviews of the book version, *Passages from the American Note-Books*, all around him—in the *Tribune* (the thirteenth), the *Round Table* (the fourteenth), the *Albion* (the twenty-first), then on December 3 the *Independent* and December 15 the *New York Times*, to name only a few. He must have handled the volumes in a bookstore long enough to see that he was in the book as a very minor character indeed. Here were Hawthorne's laconic notes on August 5, 1850: "Drove with Fields and his wife to Stockbridge, being thereto invited by Mr. Field of Stockbridge, in order to ascend Monument Mountain. Found at Mr. Field's Dr. Holmes and Mr Duyckinck of New York; also Mr. Cornelius Matthews and Herman Melville. Ascended the mountain . . . and were caught in a shower." Melville would have found this entry for August 7, 1850: "Messrs. Duyckinck, Matthews, Melville, and Melville, junior, called in the forenoon. Gave them a couple of bottles of Mr. Mansfield's champagne, and walked down to the lake with them." "Junior" was Allan Melville, named for his father; both of Herman Melville's difficult names were spelled correctly (unlike the surname of Cornelius Mathews), but there was nothing more about him. Had he imagined being part of Hawthorne's life? Perhaps, and the way he was all but ignored in the book version of the notebooks made it less than urgent to lay out a day's pay for a copy.

In early 1869 reviews of the *American Note-Books* continued. Then *Putnam's Magazine* in September 1869 printed Sophia Hawthorne's "English

Show-Places—Newstead Abbey" and the next month "Old Boston and St Botholph's." That year, also, Julian was published in *Putnam's*. George Putnam was a cousin of Sophia Hawthorne's, but he was not merely doing a favor: both Sophia and Julian were marketable personages. Julian, the lad who had loved him in 1850 and 1851, was alive and making a reputation for himself, in contrast to Melville's own son Malcolm who had shot himself to death in September 1867. Would it have been possible for Melville to think of Julian without thinking of Malcolm, who had been one and a half when Melville met the Hawthornes? In October 1869 the death of Franklin Pierce occasioned many articles among which were several printings of Pierce's account of Hawthorne's death, and then by the third of November 1869 the papers were conveying the news that Pierce had left five hundred dollars to each of the three Hawthorne children. On November 5, 1869, the *Tribune* listed Sophia's *Notes in England and Italy* ("worth reading") in the "Books of the Week." The *Independent* reviewed it on November 18. Everyone was respectful. Then in 1871, 1872, 1873 and later years Julian was in *Harper's*, sometimes with short stories, sometimes with serials.

During these first years after Hawthorne's death Melville read a great deal about Hawthorne and many words written by Hawthorne, most of those words unfamiliar to him. He must have seen the passages from *The Dolliver Romance* in the *Atlantic* in 1864 and 1871. Besides rereading stories in *Twice-Told Tales* in 1865, he surely read some of the *Atlantic's* excerpts from the American notebooks in 1866. On January 8, 1868, presumably having just read Hawthorne on the "Boston Custom House" in the January 1868 *Atlantic* (out in December), Melville bought the 1863 edition of *Our Old Home: A Series of English Sketches*. On June 8, 1870, he apparently bought the 1868 *Passages from the American Note-Books* as well as the just-published *Passages from the English Note-Books*. Using some tantalizing ellipsis dots, Sophia had put in the account of his talk with Hawthorne in the dunes at Southport and their excursion to Chester. In the English book, at least, there was enough recognition to justify his buying the book, and picking up the American book at the same time. Defensive, perhaps, cack-handed after seeing the ellipsis dots, he dated his purchase only in the one already two years old, not in the *English Note-Books*. In July 1870 Melville acquired a copy (a replacement copy?) of *The Scarlet Letter*.

Having already seen that Sophia had given space to his 1856 visit, Melville would have been still more reassured the next year by Fields's own depiction of Hawthorne on the climb up Monument Mountain and into the Icy Glen, part of his recollections in the February *Atlantic*. Here the world could learn at last that Melville had performed athletic feats on Monument Mountain:

"We scrambled to the top with great spirit, and when we arrived, Melville, I remember, bestrode a peaked rock, which ran out like a bowsprit, and pulled and hauled imaginary ropes for our delectation." At the Ice-Glen (commonly "Icy Glen"), Fields said, "Hawthorne was among the most enterprising of the merry-makers; and, being in the dark much of the time, he ventured to call out lustily, and pretend that certain destruction was inevitable to all of us." At dinner, "Hawthorne rayed out in a sparkling and unwonted manner," so that Fields concluded that the "5th of August was a happy day throughout, and I never saw Hawthorne in better spirits." There was still nothing in print about Melville and Hawthorne's having time alone together to get acquainted (not until J. E. A. Smith's articles in the *Pittsfield Evening Journal* weeks after Melville's death), but this caught the mood of the day, even Hawthorne's excitement. Melville had his own memories, freshly evoked by Fields's account. The February *Atlantic* came out early enough for Fields's recollections to be reprinted in the *New York Tribune* on January 18, 1871, so that Melville's fellow New Yorkers, perhaps including some of his fellow workers in the Custom House, saw this remarkable account, perhaps startling in its treatment of Melville as literary celebrity. Later it was picked up by the *San Francisco Bulletin* and probably other papers. At last Melville was certified as having known Hawthorne in 1850 in Massachusetts as well as having visited him in England in 1856.

Melville bought the 1865 printing of *The Snow-Image* on January 6, 1871, just before Fields's article appeared, and he bought the *Passages from the French and Italian Note-Books*, signing it on March 23, 1872. His wife gave him the 1872 *Septimius Felton* for his birthday, August 1, 1872. As Julian Hawthorne wrote in the *Literary Digest International Book Review* (August 1926), recalling his visit to Melville in 1883, Melville seemed "to have pondered much over his brief intercourse with Hawthorne, conjecturing some baffling problem in his life." Certainly in the years after Hawthorne's death Melville had pondered much over their relationship. It had been brief, to be sure, but the most important relationship with any man not blood kin to him, more important, it seems, than even the relationship with Jack Chase, his mentor on the *United States*.

In forming his chronological *Log*, Jay Leyda had plundered the late-published Hawthorne notebooks and memoirs for their information about Melville in 1850 and the next few years. After a time I tumbled to the fact that Leyda had not taken account of the way these publications affected Melville as they came out, beginning a few years after Hawthorne's death. By contrast, I determined to use the *Note-Books* and other publications as events in Melville's present life in the 1860s, 1870s, and afterward. Looking at what

I could find about the growth of Hawthorne's reputation, I saw the exquisite agony Melville suffered as fragments appeared from Hawthorne's uncompleted projects and he thought of the loss of his own career, the loss of the completed *The Isle of the Cross* and the completed *Poems*, and the failure of *Battle-Pieces*. At some point in the fall of 1869, I decided in 1990, while we were preparing the Northwestern-Newberry *Clarel*, Melville could work his new obsession into any old plans if he took Hawthorne along with him on the pilgrimage. In January 1870, familiar by now with his routines at the Custom House, sure that he could work out his self-analysis at a bearable pace, whatever new was published about Hawthorne (and his own minor role in his life), Melville started buying source books for *Clarel*. Others were making pilgrimages, already, to Hawthorne's grave in Sleepy Hollow, but he would take Hawthorne along with him on his long pilgrimage in the Holy Land—he would take the living Hawthorne along, it must almost have felt.

Melville had been very slow to use his experiences in the Holy Land. Judging by notations in one of his 1856–57 journal notebooks he may have thought about writing something about his European experiences. The notations suggest that he contemplated a work to be called *Frescoes of Travel by Three Brothers*, whether to be in prose or in poetry is unknown.[3] It might have been planned to have Greece and Italy as some of the settings, and England. In it Melville may have thought of the old genre of parallel lives, portraying Rousseau, Cicero, Byron, and Haydon, the four associated with, or weighed against (his heavily drawn bow-shaped brace suggested) Venice, Olympus, Parthenon, and Leonardo, although his notation left unclear whether Cicero was to be played off against or paralleled with Olympus, or Haydon put against not a place but a great man, Leonardo. Hawthorne had no role in *Frescoes*; he was alive, and Melville's own mood was then retrospective only in historical terms, not personal. In the biography I mustered evidence that Melville was reading epic poems and commentary on the poetic epic on the *Meteor* on his voyage to San Francisco in 1860 when he assumed that his *Poems* would be waiting for him upon disembarking, shipped by Panama, and that, having established his credentials as a poet, he could begin his own poetic epic on his epic voyage to Calcutta. News that *Poems* had been rejected and was unpublished was devastating, and as far as we know Melville showed no more interest in writing an epic poem for almost a decade. Had Melville's rekindled ambition to write an epic poem been growing since the publication and failure of *Battle-Pieces* in 1866, especially after he gained a place in the Custom House late that year? Possibly—yet 1867 was a terrible year of marital crisis and Malcolm's suicide, not a good year to master a demanding new job and to begin to think high epic thoughts. Nevertheless,

WHY MELVILLE TOOK HAWTHORNE TO THE HOLY LAND

the old urge to prove himself by writing a poetic epic must have been grown gradually during the years he was seeing Hawthorne's name at every turn.

The idea of making a version of Hawthorne a character in an otherwise fictional troop could have occurred to him casually and then come back to him naggingly as a possibility. In the biography I advanced the theory that the idea came to him more as a lightning bolt. I had drafted the 1869 section before I learned of Melville's last meeting with Hawthorne in the Berkshires in a Lenox hotel, that private meeting in the general dining room. I knew this had to be the Curtis Hotel, an assumption verified now from articles in the new databases, although those databases show that the owner in the years Hawthorne was there visiting or in residence, 1849–51, was M. S. Wilson, and that in November 1851 the hotel was known either as "the Lenox Hotel" or "Wilson's Hotel." William O. Curtis acquired the old guest ledgers when he bought the hotel and in yarns spun over the years made it seem as if he had been the owner in 1849–51, when Hawthorne was in Lenox. Clark W. Bryan in *The Book of Berkshire* (1886) declared that Hawthorne's name was on the register of Curtis's Hotel, meaning the time when it was Wilson's Hotel. Curtis's obituary in the *New York Times* (February 21, 1895) also declared that Hawthorne's name was on the register of the Curtis Hotel. The obvious times for Hawthorne to have stayed there were his scouting expedition in 1849, his arrival in 1850, and his departure in 1851, but other documents seem to show that he stayed in private houses the first two times and left directly from the Little Red House in 1851. In any case, Curtis as the ticket and express agent on the Housatonic Railroad in 1851, while still running his stagecoaches and his livery and boarding stable, was in a position to know the comings and goings, even if no one has verified his claim that Henry Wadsworth Longfellow visited Hawthorne at Lenox and even if his claim that Melville knew Fanny Kemble in the Berkshires is almost surely wrong.

Now, thanks to newspaper databases, I have the names of the hotel straight. What Fanny Kemble in the late 1830s called the Old Red Inn was the brick Berkshire Coffee-House. Melville had been familiar with the corner from his youth. The Town Hall was across the street to the south. On a good day you could look that way and see Mount Washington. The three-story Berkshire Coffee-House (by the mid-1840s Wilson's Hotel) was on the corner, the Court House next to the north, then a public house (Ives's) with the jail attached—the jail where Melville's uncle Thomas had languished months for debt in the 1830s. Melville's brother Gansevoort and sister Helen stayed in the Berkshire Coffee-House in 1843 when his future father-in-law Lemuel Shaw was there with his daughter and wife—the occasion of Helen's all-important meeting with Lizzie Shaw. By, at latest, the mid-1840s until 1853 it was owned by M. S. Wilson. Melville visited there when Judge Shaw came for his regular court dates.[4] In 1853 the buyer at auction was Oliver P. Tanner, and the obituary in the *New York Times* on February 21, 1895, may have been right in saying Curtis acquired it in 1858.

The hotel went through occasional renovations. The *Boston Daily Advertiser* said on October 21, 1885, that it had received "addition upon addition," but still looked like "an ordinary rural tavern, with its unpainted brick walls and wooden gable." For his triumphant dinner with Hawthorne, his chance to present him with a copy of *Moby-Dick* just before he left the Berkshires, Melville wanted the nearest he could get to the Astor House or the Parker House. If he truly thought he had written a wicked book (as he wrote to Hawthorne a few days later, November 17, 1851), he may even have been ready to toast his friend in golden goblets seized from the Temple in Jerusalem, for Belshazzar was on his mind, as *Moby-Dick* showed. In sober fact, as he wrote a few days later, he would happily sit down and dine with Hawthorne "and all the gods in old Rome's Pantheon." In Lenox, that meant arranging with an innkeeper you knew to let you have the dining room for your private banquet all through the too-short afternoon, after any out-of-season guests had taken their midday meal. In some jocular byplay, could M. S. Wilson have said to Melville something like, "Fine, you get the dining room all afternoon and I get a signature on the register from your reclusive friend we have never laid eyes on all these months"? Or had Hawthorne really been a guest there in 1849 or 1850, as was later asserted? Perhaps the guest register will yet be located, intact, for it was known to be valuable even in the nineteenth century. I have, over the years, tried to persuade enterprising locals to run it down. In any case, Hawthorne might, like Melville, have been as comfortable at Wilson's Hotel as he could be anywhere in Lenox.

On July 24, 1994, after I knew of Melville's last dinner with Hawthorne in Lenox, I visited the Curtis Hotel and saw that some of it was the actual building where Melville and Hawthorne had dined and was stirred at realizing that although modified the room still exists where Melville gave Hawthorne his presentation copy of *Moby-Dick*. Following Melville's footsteps, I measured the distance to the Little Red House, 1.7 miles one way and back 2 miles another way. Then, remembering that Melville had been exiled from Arrowhead in 1869 to the distant Curtis Hotel, I began realizing how Melville must have felt being back in that room eighteen years after he had been there alone with Hawthorne. "Thrilled at recreating memories," I said in my diary, and "what painful memories, connected with *Clarel*." I added in the diary: "Importance it gives HM: a MEMORY for 1869 when he is at the

Curtis—thinking about NH and *MD*." I had become "very excited, emotional."[5] I realized then that I needed the full *Springfield Republican* piece Jay Leyda had abbreviated in the 1969 "Supplement" as a Lenox item and had placed before August 30, 1869: "Among the notabilities who have been summering at Curtis's hotel in Lenox . . . Herman Melville of New York." On January 27, 1995, I entered into the *Log* the full *Springfield Republican* item:

> Among the notabilities who have been summering at Curtis's hotel in Lenox are Mr Bille, the Danish minister, Capt H. Stockton of Newport, R. I., Mr and Mrs W. H. Phillips of Washington, R. S. Oliver of the United States army, Judge Skinner of Chicago, Herman Melville of New York, Col Schuyler Crosby, United States army, R. Rangabe, charge d'affairs for Greece, Henry Cram of New York, Gen John A. Dix and family of New York, William A. Neil and family of Ohio, C. C. Harrison and E. E. Connor of Philadelphia, and S. B. Schlesinger and Col C. P. Horton of Boston.

According to the *Pittsfield Sun* on August 26, 1869, the interior of Curtis's hotel had "recently been greatly improved," but the grand expansions of the Berkshire Coffee-House/Wilson's Hotel/Curtis's Hotel had not taken place yet. The dining room was not greatly altered until 1884. In August 1869 the hotel was far more crowded than in November 1851 but it was architecturally pretty much as it had been, although it was a much brighter place in August than it had been in any November. This was still the room where Melville had presented Hawthorne with *Moby-Dick*. Almost eighteen years earlier Melville had sat here with Hawthorne absolutely certain that his secret ambitions for the whaling book would be met, in the next week, with public acclaim and phenomenal sales. His career would be on an entirely new footing. No longer merely the American DeFoe, he would be recognized as a great American writer. After all, he had just published the greatest book yet written by an American. None of that had happened, and early in December 1851 the Harpers had given him a contract for *Pierre* so punitive that it foreshadowed the end of his career. Now he was a customs inspector, his first son almost two years dead, his career over so long ago that some reviewers of *Battle-Pieces* in 1866 had been surprised to hear from him.

For July 11, 2000, my diary says "Heart-breaking 1869 Chapter—the new generation filling Arrowhead & the Curtis Hotel." My new anguish came first from the fact that Melville was crowded out of Arrowhead by other, younger guests, pushed into the next town—not into a *Pittsfield* hotel, given his aloofness and the townspeople's hostility. When I made my diary entry in 1994 about understanding the psychological importance of Melville's going back to the Curtis Hotel in 1869 I had focused on "recreating memories." My point was that I was not working from a document but from a reasoned certainty about what Melville most likely would have thought in 1869, given his characteristic pattern of brooding over the past when he was revisiting a place of significance to him. Believing that he had to have remembered the time when he had hired the dining room all for himself and a single guest, I worked into the 1869 chapter something for which not a scrap of documentary evidence survives, the assumption that Melville in 1869 remembered 1851 and was powerfully affected by the contrast between the two times. Tony Kushner in a June 2005 interview with Frederic Tuten said, "There's a terrifyingly sad moment in Hershel Parker's biography of Melville where he's completely forgotten and he's seen Hawthorne become the great American writer." One reader, at least, understood the poignancy of my story: any biographer will identify with my glorying in knowing that the greatest American playwright of his generation was moved by what I depicted.

Already by the early 1990s I had focused on Melville's fascination with the feelings evoked when disparate places are juxtaposed, as in what he said to Evert Duyckinck on July 3, 1846: "[T]his strange bringing together of two such places as Typee & Buffalo, is really curious." In chapter 27 of *Omoo* (in a passage I take as autobiographical) Melville described his inspection of the wreck of "an American whaler, a very old craft," on the beach in Tahiti: "What were my emotions, when I saw upon her stern the name of a small town on the river Hudson! She was from the noble stream on whose banks I was born; in whose waters I had a hundred times bathed. In an instant, palm-trees and elms — canoes and skiffs — church spires and bamboos — all mingled in one vision of the present and the past." The first example is simple; the second, more complex, is already moving toward his recognizing incongruous similarities in which disparate people, objects, and times tended to blur and merge into other people, objects, and times, and merge back — a process we would call morphing. Melville repeatedly described powerful, even hallucinatory, experiences when memories clashed with the present, catching him off-guard, unready to confront the past. We have records of some powerful experiences which involve Melville's revisiting a place where something momentous happened to him years before.

I am convinced that a downright hallucinatory experience occurred in late May 1849. Melville had planned to write a book still more ambitious than *Mardi* until the reviews began to make it plain that could not be so self-indulgent. Just then, as I set out in chapter 5, his youngest brother, Tom, signed on the *Navigator*, bound for China. Herman went aboard his ship and saw him off, reenacting the scene in Manhattan ten years earlier, when his now-dead brother Gansevoort had seen him off on his own first voyage. In those ten years Melville had gone to the Pacific and returned and become a published writer with the help of Gansevoort—who had died launching *Typee* in England and in New York. Now Tom, ten years his junior, looked uncannily the way Herman himself had looked, and Herman, ten years later, was playing the role of the older brother. In Melville's mind at the end of May 1849, I decided, two New York wharf scenes glided into one and fused, and the bewilderingly similar sets of brothers glided across each other and fused in his mind. Demonstrably, within days Melville was reliving his first voyage in *Redburn* (which he dedicated to Tom). Demonstrably, the decision to write this semi-autobiographical book was sudden. This practical, straightforward book was also reckless, as far as the psychological consequences for Melville were concerned. He must naively have thought he could draw on his own memories to write a short book very fast and be done with it. He did not think of repercussions, of the dangers of dropping an angle into the well of childhood (*Pierre*, bk. 21.1). Writing the book, I decided, had unleashed memories that propelled him into sudden psychological growth that continued through the next years.

On November 4, 1849, Melville wrote in his journal: "This time tomorrow I shall be on land, & press English earth after the lapse of ten years—*then* a sailor, *now* H.M. author of 'Peedee' 'Hullabaloo' & 'Pog-Dog.'" Here the place is general, "English earth," and the dramatic change is from nonentity to celebrity. In London one night during that trip (November 24), a little drunk, horribly strung out on caffeine, he could not sleep: "No doubt, two years ago, or three, Gansevoort was writing here in London, about the same hour as this—alone in his chamber, in profound silence—as I am now. This silence is a strange thing. No wonder, the old Greeks deemed it the vestibule to the higher mysteries." He was supplanting, replacing Gansevoort as the Melville brother in London, as he had supplanted Gansevoort a few months earlier as the one seeing a nineteen-year-old brother off to sea as a sailor. Memories were working on him as they had been working for the last half year, since Tom sailed and he began writing *Redburn*.

Albert Rothenberg in *The Emerging Goddess* identifies what he calls "homospatial thinking" as operating throughout the creative process. "The conception of two or more entities occupying the same space is an abstraction from nature," Rothenberg says, "not a form of concretion or a concrete mode of thinking" (71). Whether or not most creative artists are conscious of this process I do not know. However much went on unconsciously with him,

Melville was one creator who was exquisitely conscious of this particular phenomenon in his life-experiences even as he employed it in his writings, starting with *Omoo*. In *Pierre* Melville made profound use of the psychological phenomenon of hallucinatory overlapping of experiences:

> And now, by irresistible intuitions, all that had been inexplicably mysterious to him in the portrait [the chair portrait of Pierre's father], and all that had been inexplicably familiar in the face [the face of Isabel], most magically these now coincided; the merriness of the one not inharmonious with the mournfulness of the other, but by some ineffable correlativeness, they reciprocally identified each other, and, as it were, melted into each other, and thus interpenetratingly uniting, presented lineaments of an added supernaturalness.
>
> On all sides, the physical world of solid objects now slidingly displaced itself from around him, and he floated into an ether of visions . . . . (bk. 4.5)

Here Melville's immediate model is Dante's depiction in the *Inferno* (canto 25) of the way the bodies of two Florentine thieves fuse together: "Agnello! See! thou art not double now, / Nor only one!"

In *Israel Potter* the hero after leaving Squire Woodcock's house in Brentford dressed in the dead squire's clothing comes upon a strangely familiar landscape:

> The whole scene magically reproduced to our adventurer the aspect of Bunker Hill, Charles River, and Boston town, on the well-remembered night of the 16th of June. The same season; the same moon; the same new-mown hay on the shaven sward; hay which was scraped together during the night to help pack into the redoubt so hurriedly thrown up. (chap. 13)

Years later, in London, glimpses of a garden produce memories, "rural returns of his boyhood's sweeter days," so that memories of home would "overpower him for a time to a sort of hallucination" (chap. 25). On one of these occasions, in St. James's Park, Israel hears "some hob-shoe" which he takes to be the hoof of his mother's favorite old pillion horse, "Old Huckleberry." He confuses the sounds of cattle driven to Smithfield with cattle on the farm and tries to head them to the barnyard: "Israel, now an old man, was bewitched by the mirage of vapors; he had dreamed himself home into the mists of the Housatonic mountains; ruddy boy on the upland pastures again."

In "The Paradise of Bachelors and the Tartarus of Maids" (an uncollected piece published in *Harper's*) Melville plays off the second half of the diptych against the first. The speaker in the Woedolor Mountain in New England winds down into the Mad Maid's Bellows'-pipe and sees the grim Black Notch beyond, then says: "[S]omething latent, as well as something obvious in the time and scene, strangely brought back to my mind my first sight of dark and grimy Temple-Bar," scene of the earlier story. As Black, his horse, darts through the Notch, he remembers "being in a runaway London omnibus" which had "dashed through the ancient arch of Wren." Melville analyzes: "Though the two objects did by no means completely correspond, yet this partial inadequacy but served to tinge the similitude not less with the vividness than the disorder of a dream." Under the spell of "this mysterious mountain nook," the narrator says, "what memory lacked, all tributary imagination furnished, and I said to myself, 'This is the very counterpart of the Paradise of Bachelors, but snowed upon, and frost-painted to a sepulchre.'" The "inverted similitude" recurs as the narrator is reminded of the "sweet, tranquil Temple garden."

Melville's November 8, 1856, diary entry in Liverpool is specific, if terse: "After dinner went to Exchange. Looked at Nelson's statue, with peculiar emotion, mindful of 20 years ago." Melville did not analyze, but the peculiar emotion owed something to his greater aesthetic sophistication, having seen statues in London and Paris in 1849. In 1839 this had been the finest large sculpture group he had ever seen, and on a nautical subject powerful to him. He was a young man, healthy but all too conscious of the disparity between the way his father had moved in high circles in Liverpool seventeen years earlier and his own abject situation. In 1856 the image of Nelson dying even as he is crowned with victory meant something different to a man whose career had been destroyed within weeks of his publishing his masterpiece, *Moby-Dick*. There are other examples, but these are enough to show that one of the characteristics of Melville's mature depiction of psychological processes in himself and in his writings was an outgrowth of perceptions he had been experiencing at least as early as 1846 and had written into *Omoo*, the portrayal of images from different times and places which alternate rapidly in the mind, merge with each other, and (in some examples) disentangle again.

In the first book of *Clarel*, "Jerusalem," canto 41, Melville makes use of the evocation of old memories. Reading some half-effaced writing on the wall of his room triggers in Clarel complex memories, introduced by the narrator's generalization: "In one's nervous trance / Things near will distant things recall, / And common ones suggest romance: / He thought of her built up in wall, / Cristina of Coll'alto; yes, / The verse here breaking from recess—." As Scott Norsworthy noticed in 2009, Clarel is recalling "Coll'alto" from Samuel Rogers's *Italy* (1.10), a previously unidentified source, although we knew Melville's defense of the poem against Hazlitt's strictures (Parker, 2:495). In the final book, "Bethlehem," in the canto called "The Prodigal" (4.26), the title applies to a sensual, joyous young man of Clarel's age but of a wholly opposite set of experiences. In their conversation Clarel is stiff, prissy, and the Lyonese bursts out, indicting Clarel and his likes, "You can't enjoy." Clarel, aroused by the young man's sensuality and beginning to suspect that he is Jewish, and therefore even more exotic than he had realized, unwillingly gazes at him until he hallucinates the Lyonese's hair as resembling the hair of a Polynesian girl who, "inland eloping with her lover" and feeding on berries and on love, had been recovered and chastised by deacon-magistrates. They sleep in the same room, and Clarel dreams of the Lyonese as lord of Persia and another character, the ascetic monk Salvaterre, as lord of the desert, a contrast between sensualist and "pale pure monk." In the dream, "A Zephyr fanned; / It vanished, and he felt the strain / Of clasping arms which would detain / His heart from such ascetic range." Rather than reflexively dismissing the dream, Clarel recognizes organic change in himself, a statement the narrator then qualifies slightly: Clarel "felt, at least, that change was working— / A subtle innovator lurking."

In 1869 Melville was in the same dining room where something momentous had happened in 1851, surely the most exalted hours of his life, *Moby-Dick* published and a copy in the hands of the man he had dedicated it to. Reliving those hours was so powerful that it pushed Melville to a decision that allowed him, a few months later, to begin writing *Clarel*. Whether or not he "saw" Hawthorne in the dining room at the Curtis Hotel in 1869, his grand aging head morphing, for instance, into the head of his uncle Peter's friend General Dix, to whom Melville inscribed a copy of *Battle-Pieces*, or Colonel Crosby (from the same family as the Van Rensselaer in-law?), or the head of whoever sat where Hawthorne had sat, he remembered. Eighteen years later, again in the Curtis Hotel, reliving his dinner with Hawthorne was the catalyst that allowed him to start writing *Clarel*, just as the power of the memory of Gansevoort's seeing him aboard his first ship propelled him into the composition of *Redburn*. A difference is the amount of thought he might already have given to a poem about travelers in the Holy Land; with *Redburn*, he just started writing, without planning, while he may have been thinking about his poem on the Holy Land for months or years. For years, perhaps, he had been planning to put his experiences in the Holy Land into a modern poetic pilgrimage where man-made structures and demonic terrain would be the backdrops to hours and hours of some of the best talk anyone had ever heard on all the great topics of the century. Steven Olsen-Smith has found that Melville had ensconced himself in the "Eastern Travels" alcove of the Astor Library on February 1, 1869—a fair indication that he was thinking about the big project that was to follow *Battle-Pieces*, perhaps involving the Holy Land. An "alcove" was just right for absorbing and reflecting: Melville always loved snug places, even those where you kept your eyes open, although in *Moby-Dick* he had explained that "no man can ever feel his own identity aright except his eyes be closed" (chap. 11). Melville had a project, inchoate, maybe, sketched out in some detail, maybe. But after his vacation, he was haunted by something not connected to Jerusalem and the desert—haunted by the collision of November 1851 and August 1869, and the strange transformation of the two men who had been, at that moment, the two greatest writers in America. Melville brooded through September, October, November, and December 1869 over how he could come to terms with the utter failure of his own career while Hawthorne, dead five years, was exalted to the highest American literary empyrean. The solution was to take Hawthorne along with him to the Holy Land.

❧ Chapter 19 ❧

MELVILLE AS A TITAN OF LITERATURE AMONG HIGH-MINDED BRITISH ADMIRERS

The Kory-Kory and Queequeg Component

IN 1988 I AMASSED a nine-inch-high stack of biographical information about the admirers, mainly British, who first made Herman Melville a cult figure, then gradually celebrated him as one of the world's titanic writers. Thanks to Professor George Worth's extended loan of microfilm of the James Hannay papers, I was able to trace a continuous line from London around 1850 on through the Leicester admirers in the 1880s and the accumulation of tributes after Melville's death and on into the twentieth century.[1] Early in the next century I came upon an extraordinary, not yet verified, claim for an exalted passing of the torch of admiration for *Moby-Dick* from one great writer to another. This Galway affidavit I print at the end of this chapter. In the nineteenth century newspaper editors would insert items with the prefix "INTERESTING IF TRUE": the Galway document might be labeled "AMAZING IF TRUE." It embodies the purpose of this chapter, to challenge a new generation to rethink episodes in Melville's life and, specifically, to tell a new and infinitely more detailed story of how his reputation burgeoned in Great Britain during his life and after his death. Within a few years of my discovering the Galway document an old way, through a clipping in a presentation copy of Raymond Weaver's biography, anyone can find it in a periodical database. The question is who will try to verify it.

Back in 1988, turning through biographical accounts of dozens of British poets, artists, and novelists, I wished aloud for a database daisy-chain, not quite visualizing what either term meant or what databases could mean but liking the alliteration and knowing that a high proportion of the admirers merged their aesthetic admiration with sexual stirrings. There was nothing surprising about this: I had read Albert Rothenberg's *The Emerging Goddess* carefully, and I knew from Melville's association of literary and sexual sensuality in *Pierre* that he had intuited what Rothenberg brilliantly deduced. I revive this chapter from its resting place as part of the "Historical Note" in the Northwestern-Newberry *Moby-Dick* (1988) only because no one has taken up the challenge to carry the whole topic farther. As I have pointed out, Andrew Delbanco in his "Melville in the '80s" ignored the "Historical Note" altogether: he showed then no interest in the composition of *Moby-Dick*, the reviews of it, or the "Melville Revival." Some scholarship has continued, notably Frederick J. Kennedy and Joyce Deveau Kennedy's 1999 history of the influence in America of the Canadian admirer Archibald Mac-Mechan. Among much else, they showed that Henry Salt had republished MacMechan's pioneering article on *Moby-Dick* in his *Humane Review* where British admirers of Melville certainly saw it, although MacMechan's great but previously almost unexplored influence was mainly on the revival in the United States (and Canada). Much remains unexplored.

In other chapters such as those on copyright I have mustered new evidence from the electronic databases now commonly available to researchers. As a challenge, I have refrained from doing so on this chapter. The chapter remains valid enough as I wrote it, a reliable preliminary survey, but dozens of supplementary biographies of British literary people and other studies published since 1988 have contributed items that could be used to fill out the picture of the Melville Revival in England. I wager now that someone can use this chapter as a test of just how many more, and more intricate, literary connections have been made since 1988 and can yet be made between and among these known admirers of Melville and still others to be identified. A young researcher or middle-aged computer geek or simply one of the ineffable crew I think of as "divine amateurs" of any age who would exploit the Internet and spend a year or two in manuscript archives of British literary men and women (wherever these documents rest, even in Texas) could write a valuable scholarly tome. Perhaps better, such a person could write a best-selling account, for in this densely peopled little world of early Melville enthusiasts even the walk-on characters glow with star quality.

Because of the peculiar truncation of Melville's career and the long period of neglect before the revival of *Moby-Dick*, at the expense of *Typee* and *Omoo*, most twentieth-century Melville lovers (at least after the revival in the 1920s) have taken him as the man who plundered seventeenth-century prose and dramatic poetry in a work which challenged man's treatment by the gods — the man who wrote a book without women (as some say, a little inexactly), a book notoriously (as some early British reviewers complained) without a love story. Until recently critics have talked about Melville's later career without realizing that in the sexually teasing portions of his first book, *Typee* (1846), he had started something which quickly passed out of his control. As I show in the earlier chapter paired with this, he had become the first American literary sex symbol (heterosexual), and he lived the next forty-five years with the image he had created. By contrast, much recent criticism like that of Elizabeth Hardwick has emphasized Melville as a persistent portrayer of masturbatory and homosexual situations and has taken him as a homosexual icon without bothering to enlighten the world as to the precise relationship of masturbation to homosexuality. Renewed interest in the history of colonialism and ethnology has recently pushed homosexual readings of Melville back beyond *Moby-Dick* to *Typee* and *Omoo*, retrieving Charles W. Stoddard's 1860s fascination with the tayo relationship.[2] So strong is the interest in homosexuality that some of the recent writing on *Typee* has involved lubricious sleights-of-hand where words of the surviving sixteen leaves of the first draft are mistranscribed so as to import homosexual implications into the text, according to a rhetorical agenda rather than a determination to transcribe what Melville wrote. All in all, the recent well-nigh obsessive interest in sexuality in Melville has been disproportionately focused on homosexuality, sometimes with extreme Marxist ramifications, as in Laurie Robertson-Lorant's inclusion of Ishmael and Queequeg among "same-sex interracial homosocial couples" who represent "transgressive paradigms of homosocial brotherhood and male intimacy that challenge and seek to subvert the soulless, misogynistic competitive construction of masculinity dictated by the new market capitalism and industrialization" (620). Whew! Not one of the British admirers of Melville I memorialize in this chapter could write like that.

I started in 1988 with puzzles. At some time before 1900—no one had shown precisely when—Melville gained the status of sex symbol among some homosexual readers, primarily in England. This reputation was based on his portrayal of the tayo relationship and on his mentions of the Areoi fraternity in *Typee* (1846) and *Omoo* (1847) even more than on his portrayal of Ishmael and Queequeg. That last point seems the stronger because in *The Whale* (1851), which for a long time was what the British read instead of *Moby-Dick*, there was no bridegroom clasp of the two men, no matrimonial hug, no heart's honeymoon, and no free and easy affectionate throwing of Queequeg's brown tattooed legs over Ishmael's and drawing them back. By the 1920s Melville held international cult status among literary homosexuals, a status he still holds. The first homosexuals to idolize Melville were not all British, but how important was the influence in England of the American homosexual admirer, Charles Warren Stoddard? The earliest known evidence involves Stoddard, who, two years after he wrote a fan letter to Melville, printed in the *Overland Monthly* "A South Sea Idyl" (1869), in which the male narrator has a fervid affair with a young Polynesian tayo reminiscent of Kory-Kory, the narrator's male attendant in *Typee*. Stoddard also wrote fan letters to Whitman and still later wrote ardently to Robert Buchanan, the earnest British champion of Melville, who, never having met him, appended a rhapsodic dedicatory essay to him in the strange, neglected poetic tribute to Melville, *The Outcast* (which I discovered was available in New York the week of Melville's death).

For a decade after 1988, when I first tried to identify Melville's late-nineteenth-century English admirers, I repeatedly challenged students to establish just when homosexuals (American, British, international) began to share with each other a sense that Melville meant them to take Kory-Kory and other characters as a signal of his own sexual orientation or at least of his openness to their orientation. No one rose to the challenge, but now with the help of the Internet and electronic databases it would be feasible to build a real database daisy-chain. I speak lightly still of the alliterative assignment, but anyone pursuing the subject will learn how little Melville's nineteenth-century British admirers pursued his writings for pornographic satisfaction, however much sexual satisfaction they found with other men, sometimes satisfaction enhanced by their sharing *Moby-Dick*. In this chapter I write about notably high-minded literary men (and a few women), lovers of Melville's language and compulsive quoters of phrases and sentences, among whom were idealistic sexual reformers who drew encouragement from Melville. Some of the admirers I write about in this chapter were cranks and eccentrics, but I see them as momentous men, distinguished from modern critics of Melville by a profound and loving knowledge of world literature and an excited perception that Melville deserved a high rank in it.

In London after the mid-1850s Melville's achievement in *The Whale* seemed to be forgotten. Perhaps people who read the book in 1851 cherished it and brought it to the attention of their friends during the next decade (perhaps some of the remarkable artists, literary men, and travelers who dined with Melville so jovially in 1849 did so), but indications that any such continuity existed are scant, such as the 1922 recollection of J. St. Loe Strachey that in 1893, during the "boom" following Melville's death, a "lady of letters" expressed her delight that people were reading Melville again, and added: "I can't tell you how enthusiastic we all were, young and old, at the end of the 'forties and beginning of the 'fifties, over *Typee*, *Omoo*, and *Moby-Dick*. There was quite a furore over Melville in those days. All the young people worshipped him" (559–60). This remains tantalizing but unverified.

For the decade and a half following 1853 there was (as far as we know, even from new databases I have not been resolute enough to resist) near-total silence about *The Whale* in the London periodicals, yet a change in British attitudes toward American literature was in progress. There had been previous changes since 1820, when Sydney Smith posed his scornful rhetorical question, "In the four quarters of the globe, who reads an American book?" The height of the new midcentury respect for American literature is well represented by the concluding compliment the London *Morning Advertiser* paid to *The Whale* on October 24, 1851: three volumes "more honourable to American literature, albeit issued in London, have not yet reflected credit on the country of Washington Irving, Fenimore Cooper, Dana, Sigourney, Bryant, Longfellow, and Prescott." In the next phase, beginning around the midcentury and overlapping with the previous phase, some British critics concluded that Irving and Cooper were not validly American in spirit but were imitation English writers (precisely the conclusion Melville had come to about Irving, at least, in his essay on Hawthorne). This phase is well represented by the way the *Leader* on November 8, 1851, cleared the field before commencing to talk about *The Whale*:

> Want of originality has long been the just and standing reproach to American literature; the best of its writers were but second-hand Englishmen. Of late some have given evidence of originality; not *absolute* originality, but such genuine outcoming of the American intellect as can be safely called national. Edgar Poe, Nathaniel Hawthorne, Herman Melville are assuredly no British offshoots; nor is Emerson—the *German* American that he is!

George H. Lewes may have written these words, or possibly the author was the young Scottish sailor James Hannay, then just crashing into London life as a bohemian and professional critic and novelist. Hannay wrote for the *Leader* (July 3, 1852) a review of James Russell Lowell's *Poems* in which he paid tribute to the "breath of genius" that swept through all of Melville's books, and the same distinction between generations of American writers as promulgated in the *Leader* informs Hannay's brief preface (dated November 1852) to his 1853 edition of Poe's poems. There Hannay spoke kindly of Irving and Cooper as essentially British, both founding their work "on our own classical models" (xi). Now, however, the British public was getting "acquainted with writers amongst the Americans who are really national" (xii)—Emerson, Lowell, Hawthorne, Poe—and Melville, whom he extolled for *The Whale*, "such a fresh, daring book—wild, and yet true,—with its quaint, spiritual portraits looking ancient and also fresh,—Puritanism, I may say, *kept fresh* in the salt water over there and looking out living upon us once more!" (xii). Even though the less discriminating attitude of the *Morning Advertiser* continued to be dominant, a new opinion was forming. While the effects of *The Whale* were still reverberating in London, a few readers (mainly young people) were pondering their way toward a further stage in their sense of what was of value in American literature.

They were in the minority. George Eliot (less radical and less well read on the subject than her companion Lewes), in the January 1856 *Westminster Review* (290) praised *Hiawatha* and *The Scarlet Letter* as the "two most indigenous and masterly productions in American literature." (To her credit, in the same article she praised *Walden* for "plenty of sturdy sense" mingled with "unworldliness.") By the 1860s the British reading public and the British literary establishment were seeing Henry Wadsworth Longfellow as a poet almost if not quite the equal of Alfred Tennyson and (especially after his death in 1864) seeing Nathaniel Hawthorne as equal or superior to most living British novelists. In *American Literature: An Historical Sketch 1620–1880* (1882) John Nichol, a professor of English literature at the University of Glasgow, praised *The Scarlet Letter* as the most important romance written in the English language during the century. To most English readers Hawthorne felt, as Irving had felt, unthreatening, indeed, downright *English*. It took time for an anti-establishment evaluation of American writers to crystallize. It took the publication of *Walden* in 1854 and *Leaves of Grass* in 1855, then more years, for only a few copies of these books reached England in the mid-fifties (among them the one that reached George Eliot). *Walden* was first published in England in 1884 and first actually printed there in 1886, while part of *Leaves of Grass* was first printed there, without "Song of Myself" and otherwise sanitized, in W. M. Rossetti's *Poems of Walt Whitman* of 1868. It took time for young radical writers to have the evidence with which to conduct their shakedown of the American canon, but by the 1860s and 1870s a remarkable number of the brightest, most vigorous British lovers of literature and art, men (the available evidence is almost exclusively about men) who shared idealistic and iconoclastic social views as well as aesthetic values, were deciding that great literature had come from one or another of three American writers (or perhaps two of them or all three) who at the time were practically unknown in Great Britain and were marginal figures in their own country: Melville, Whitman, Thoreau.

Although it is clear that a quarter century or so after the publication of *The Whale* a number of British artists and writers saw Melville in a new way, how the change occurred has not been documented in any detail. What follows here is a suggestive and impressionist survey of some connections among Melville's admirers and the admirers of Whitman and Thoreau. More evidence for how Melville's reputation grew in Great Britain during this period may be found by searching out published comments on Melville which I did not locate and discovering new documentary evidence in archives. Any young scholar may now verify, challenge, and correct this account by using all the modern tools, starting, I assume, with newspaper and magazine databases, Google Books, and Google searches. Then the scholar would extend my work here in correlating that information with study of who attended the same public schools and the universities together, who lived near each other (or shared quarters with each other), who belonged to the same clubs, who wrote for the same newspapers and magazines, who shared a publisher, who were bound by mutual acquaintances, by family connections, and by personal affection for each other.

Subject to challenge and correction this much can be ventured still, early in the twenty-first century: the younger members of the British literary world who constituted the admirers of Melville, Whitman, and Thoreau belonged for the most part to three or four overlapping groups. They were members of the Pre-Raphaelite Brotherhood of artist-writers or their associates; they were adherents of the working-men's movement (which is datable from 1854, when F. D. Maurice, the Christian Socialist, founded the Working Men's College in London); they were (a little later) Fabian Socialists; or they were themselves sea-writers or writers about remote countries. To belong in any of the first three of these groups was to be politically and socially radical, never far from the revolutionary spirit of Shelley (or from the aging but still formidable physical shapes of men and women who had seen "Shelley plain," including Trelawny and Peacock). To belong to the last group almost always meant to have done one's own fieldwork in comparative anthropology and to have learned (often under Southern constellations) to think untraditionally and independently and therefore to look at European society unconventionally.

One link between these writers and the *Leader* of the early 1850s was certainly young James Hannay, who made an almost instant transition from sailor to London journalist connected with Lewes's paper, which was especially influential (as Francis Espinasse recalled in *Literary Recollections and Sketches*) "among the younger and more thoughtful members of the 'advanced' party in politics and religion"—and in literature (293). From unpublished entries in Hannay's diaries we learn that in late 1852 he began a conscientious reading or rereading of Melville, who was already "a favourite writer" of his. While he was reading Melville he was also seeing the Rossetti family, although he moved in a faster, "bohemian" set and drank a great deal more alcohol (W. M. Rossetti remembered) than most members of the Pre-Raphaelite Brotherhood did. Between reading *White-Jacket* and *Mardi* he spent Sunday evening, December 5, 1852, at Dante Gabriel Rossetti's, slept over, and breakfasted the next morning with "Gabriel" (the name the family used). The evidence stops there: Hannay does not record that he discussed Melville with D. G. or his brother W. M. (who earlier in the year read a little Tacitus with Hannay and spent the night at his place). Hannay was still intimate with the Rossettis in the 1860s when W. M. Rossetti was preparing his selection from *Leaves of Grass*. (In the preface Rossetti recalled that one of the few reviews which did not sneer at the 1855 *Leaves of Grass* had appeared in the *Leader*, and in his *Recollections* he made it clear that he assumed the reviewer was Lewes.) On Christmas Day of 1870 D. G. Rossetti put *Pierre* on his list of "high-class" book orders, saying, with offhand authority, that he believed it was "not easily met with like others of his [Melville's], as it has not been republished in England" (*Log*, 716).

The Hannay-Rossetti connection is suggestive but not quite conclusive, and other links are also tenuous. We know that in 1855 the painter William Bell Scott, master of a school of design in Newcastle on Tyne, sent a copy of the first American edition of *Leaves of Grass* to W. M. Rossetti, who was powerfully drawn toward the American and toward others, including Algernon Swinburne, who shared his sense of the importance of the American poet. (Swinburne lived with D. G. Rossetti for a time in the mid-1860s at Cheyne Walk.) W. M. Rossetti was affected by the literary-social workingmen's movement centered in the Working Men's College, at which D. G. Rossetti was a part-time staff member. The poet James Thomson ("B. V." the "B." for Bysshe, in tribute to Shelley), who displayed his knowledge of *Mardi* in 1865 in the scruffily radical *National Reformer* edited by his friend the freethinker Charles Bradlaugh, became a friend of W. M. Rossetti's in 1871 and in a second article on Whitman in Bradlaugh's journal in 1874 became the first, as far as we know, to compare Melville and Whitman in print in England, describing Melville as the only living American writer who approached Whitman "in his sympathy with all ordinary life and vulgar occupations, in his feeling of brotherhood for all rough workers." This claim (reprinted in the posthumous 1892 *Poems, Essays and Fragments*, 86) could have been made from a reading of Melville's early books or even from the Bentley edition of *The Whale*, although it omitted from chapter 26 "The great God absolute! The centre and circumference of all democracy! His omnipresence, our divine equality!" and tamed "thou great democratic God!" to "thou great God!" Had Thomson brought a copy of *Moby-Dick* home from his trip to America in 1873?

Early in 1881 Thomson went to Leicester for the opening of a new Secularist hall and formed a friendship with J. W. Barrs, who lived nearby. During his visits that year he introduced some of Melville's works to Barrs and (directly or through Barrs) to James Billson, a young solicitor who for years regularly taught classes in Latin and Greek at the Working Men's College there. In class Billson gave rein to "his strong and racy sense of humour" as he taught artisans "enough Greek to enjoy Aristophanes" (*The Leicestershire Archæological Society/The 78th Annual Report*, xx–xxi). Two years after Thomson's death in 1882 from dipsomania, young Billson, spurred by the enthusiasm he now shared with Barrs and other friends, wrote Melville an admiring letter (August 21, 1884) in which he made clear that in his provincial experience (unlike D. G. Rossetti's) Melville's books were scarce, and "in great request." Billson added: "as soon as one is discovered (for that is what it really is with us) it is eagerly read & passed round a rapidly increasing knot of 'Melville readers.'" Barrs, who in 1886 sent gifts of Thomson's books to Melville, introduced Thomson's friend the blind poet Philip Bourke Marston to *Mardi* in the 1880s. (Thomson seems not to have done so himself, although he is the link between Barrs and Marston, and his last alcoholic collapse was in Marston's room in D. G. Rossetti's house on Cheyne Walk.) Marston subsequently obtained all of Melville's books that were "accessible to him" presumably to have read aloud to him. Marston knew the Pre-Raphaelites Madox Brown and the short-lived Oliver Madox Brown as well as Swinburne; he was especially intimate with W. M. Rossetti (who in 1874 married Lucy Brown, Madox Brown's daughter) and with D. G. Rossetti. In the 1870s the Rossettis and Swinburne knew John Payne, who in 1903 published a sonnet on "Herman Melville" in which he praised the five earlier books but valued *The Whale* over Melville's "idylls of the life afloat."[3]

In the early 1880s the English sea-writer W. Clark Russell tried to revive Melville's reputation, apparently unaware of fellow admirers. In the London *Contemporary Review* (September 1884) he claimed first rank for Melville among "the poets of the deep":

> Whoever has read the writings of Melville must I think feel disposed to consider "Moby Dick" as his finest work. It is indeed all about the sea, whilst "Typee" and "Omoo," are chiefly famous for their lovely descriptions of the South Sea Islands, and of the wild and curious inhabitants of those coral strands; but though the action of the story is altogether on shipboard, the narrative is not in the least degree nautical in the sense that Cooper's and Marryat's novels are. . . .

"Moby Dick" is not a sea-story—one could not read it as such—it is
a medley of noble impassioned thoughts born of the deep, pervaded
by a grotesque human interest, owing to the contrast it suggests
between the rough realities of the cabin and the forecastle, and the
phantasms of men conversing in rich poetry, and strangely moving
and acting in that dim weather-worn Nantucket whaler.

The speeches in "Midnight—Forecastle" (chap. 40—which William Allen
Butler in a review in the *Washington National Intelligencer* had found so dis-
gusting) "might truly be thought to have come down to us from some giant
mind of the Shakespearean era." *Moby-Dick* as a whole was "like a drawing
by William Blake" or "of the 'Ancient Mariner.'" Russell was early in preferring *Moby-Dick* to Melville's other works and also early in admiring it not
simply as a superb nautical tale but as a work of poetic imagination set in a
nautical frame.

After publishing his article Russell wrote to the American writer A. A.
Hayes in Washington, D. C., who showed the letter to W. A. Croffut. On
December 14, 1884, Croffut published this badly printed piece in his regu-
lar feature in the *New York World*, "Important Trifles":

In Washington the other day I met A. A. Hayes, a well-known writer
of short stories for the magazines. He showed me a letter from
W. Clark Russell, the Englishman, whose sea stories are having such
a run. "Russell is an American by birth," he said, "though I suppose
there are few who know it. He is the son of Henry Russell, who, some
thirty-five years ago, was a popular ballad singer, travelling in this
country, singing 'A Life on the Ocean Wave,' 'A Fine Old English
Gentleman,' &c. Clark was born in New York at that time." The
letter said: "If my life is spared I hope some day to visit New York
and muse, if musing be possible on Broadway, on the site of the old
Carleton Hotel, in which I emitted my first cry of suffering—my first
illustration of my theory of life. . . . I feel that the best sea stories ever
written are those of Henry Melville and Richard H. Dana, jr. If you
know that fine writer, Melville, why not write his life? Why not let
the world know as much as can be gathered of the seafaring experiences and personal story of the greatest genius your country has
produced—leagues ahead of Longfellow and Bryant as a poet. . . .
There are no people of old who equal the Americans in their peculiar love [of] ocean and in their methods of expressing a sense of its
sublimity."

("Henry" was probably not Russell's error but Croffut's or the compositor's recollection of "Henry Russell." The Melvilles saved the clipping, undated; Jay Leyda put it in the *Log* at the end of 1873, ascribed to the wrong newspaper; Dennis Marnon identified it in 2011.) As I showed in my second volume and in chapter 5 of this book, on March 26, 1885, Elizabeth Shaw Melville and Melville's cousin Kate Gansevoort Lansing went out to Brentano's, where Kate ordered the back copy of the *Contemporary Review* containing Russell's article. Some of the family may already have read the article, some only after the issue arrived. Clark's essay changed the family's attitude toward Melville's literary genius.

The playwright and novelist Charles Reade, older than and apparently independent of the circle of the Pre-Raphaelites and friends of "B. V.," not only read *The Whale* (perhaps after encountering it at the publisher's, for he became a Bentley novelist late in 1852) but annotated it in a way that suggested to Michael Sadleir (who saw his copy decades later) that he had thought of making an abridgment of it. In 1885, the year after Reade's death, his friend the dramatist and poet Robert Buchanan visited Whitman while staging one of his own plays in Philadelphia and on his return to London published in the *Academy* (August 15, 1885) "Socrates in Camden, with a Look Round," a poem on Whitman that included a tribute to the power of Melville as the

> sea-compelling man,
> Before whose wand Leviathan
> Rose hoary white upon the Deep,
> With awful sounds that stirred its sleep.

Melville, he continued, "Sits all forgotten or ignored,/While haberdashers are adored!" In a footnote Buchanan said he had "sought everywhere for this Triton, who is still living somewhere in New York. No one seemed to know anything of the one great imaginative writer fit to stand shoulder to shoulder with Whitman on that continent." The praise of Melville was extraordinary, and the other comment is puzzling. In New York City Buchanan had visited E. C. Stedman, a neighbor of Melville's, who in corresponding with British writers while preparing his book on Victorian poetry had formed a notable Swinburne archive, and who then was or soon afterward became an adherent of *Moby-Dick*, "its tale often on his lips, and the recommendation by all odds to read it at once to nearly every young writer who sought his counsel" (see Sealts, *Early Lives of Melville*). Whatever the reason Buchanan did not locate Melville, his footnote may have roused Stedman to make polite overtures to Melville, for Stedman's son Arthur soon made Melville's acquaintance and later became in effect his literary executor, in consultation with Mrs. Melville. Buchanan's fascination with Melville grew, and his *The Outcast*, the poem I mentioned as going on sale in New York a week or so before Melville died, was a strange homage to him through a mixing of the Flying Dutchman legend with a *Typee*-like romance. The volume concluded with an open letter on the state of his own career and the deplorable state of English publishing, part confessional, part apologia, addressed to an American he had never met, Charles Warren Stoddard, who not only corresponded with both Whitman and Melville but also introduced Melville's works to Robert Louis Stevenson. Buchanan's connection with the Pre-Raphaelites was intense but adversarial, for his "The Fleshly School of Poetry," first published in the *Contemporary Review* (October 1871), so grieved D. G. Rossetti that W. M. Rossetti recalled it as precipitating his breakdown and early death. In so small a literary society mutual enthusiasms among enemies are perhaps inevitable, and no one has shown that there was anything like two sets of rival Whitman or Melville admirers in London.

At some time before 1889 Henry S. Salt, the all-round humanitarian as well as Fabian Socialist, learned of Melville from the bookseller and publisher Bertram Dobell, the friend of Thomson's who arranged the book publication of *The City of Dreadful Night* (1880); Salt in turn brought *The Whale* to the notice of William Morris, and a week or two afterward heard Morris quoting it "with huge gusto and delight" (Salt, *Company I Have Kept*, 109). Writing his biography of Thomson apparently led Salt into acquaintance with the Leicester admirers of both Thomson and Melville, then into writing an essay on Melville in 1889 and another in 1892. In the second essay Salt said he had been told "of instances in which English working-men became his [Melville's] hearty admirers." Perhaps Billson had communicated to his artisan students a love of Melville as well as of Aristophanes. In 1889, Salt wrote to Melville just after his first essay on him appeared in the *Scottish Art Review*. Knowing that Barrs was sending Melville a copy of the essay, he sent Melville his own recent book on Thomson, thereby reaffirming the confluence of interests Salt and the Leicester admirers shared.

Born at midcentury (in India), Salt could not remember Melville's reception in the 1840s and 1850s, so he pulled down old periodicals to see what contemporary reviewers had said—an act that makes him the first recorded "Melville scholar," as distinguished from reviewer or simple enthusiast. Always high-minded, he looked hard through Melville's early books for signs of "direct ethical teaching" and had to settle for praising Melville's "strong and genuine feeling" on the rather vague subject of humanity as well as a few specific positions such as his opposition to modern warfare. In 1892, after Melville's death, Salt's second Melville article, in *Gentleman's Magazine*, showed that he had come to delight in Melville's language, especially in *The Whale*, which he now praised as a work of "ambitious conception and colossal proportions," the "crown and glory" of Melville's later phase (253, 252). Here he made good use of Melville's private letters to Billson, and in a footnote listed some competent judges who numbered among Melville admirers: William Morris, Theodore Watts, R. L. Stevenson, Robert Buchanan, and W. Clark Russell. The least well remembered of these admirers, the solicitor Walter Theodore Watts, had become intimate with D. G. Rossetti and helped W. M. Rossetti with legal matters after his brother's death. Later, as Theodore Watts-Dunton, he was Swinburne's protector for three decades, and on one occasion talked to George Bernard Shaw and Salt about George Meredith and Melville on the way to see Swinburne, "taking it for granted that they had never heard of them, though Salt was a friend of both" (Winsten, 82). (Meredith, as it happened, had reviewed *The Confidence-Man* in the *Westminster and Foreign Quarterly Review*.) Shaw himself recorded in a posthumously published preface to Stephen Winsten's *Salt and His Circle* (1951) that he agreed with Salt on the subject of *Moby-Dick*. Among more radical British literary people, interest in Whitman, Melville, and Thoreau converged, so that in 1894 Salt could write scathingly not only of a "recent unhappy defamation of Walt Whitman" but specifically of "Lowell's malicious misrepresentations of Thoreau" (*Richard Jefferies*, 115), that effort of a member of the American literary establishment to suppress a better writer—and better man—than himself. Salt and his friends stood ready to defend the writers they felt were not properly esteemed at home but were known in England among a widening circle of devotees.

Unquestionably Salt was at the center of that circle. In the 1880s and 1890s he initiated correspondence not only with Melville but with other Americans, among them acquaintances of Thoreau and the early Thoreau collector Dr. Samuel A. Jones, and John Burroughs, the admirer of both Whitman and Thoreau, and in 1890 he published his biography of Thoreau, the product of intense and judicious research by transatlantic correspondence. Soon after Melville's death he began a correspondence with Arthur Stedman and was kept informed of the slow progress toward a selected edition of Melville's works. He wrote Dr. Jones on June 9, 1892, after his second article on Melville had been reprinted in the United States: "Did you see my art. on Melville in the *Eclectic* for April? I wonder whether you are a Melville enthusiast? You *ought* to be. He was one of the very greatest of American writers" (Oehlschlaeger and Hendrick, 158). Jones's lack of alacrity evoked a further recommendation on November 11, 1892:

> I can't help thinking that you would greatly enjoy Herman Melville's works, if you once got started off on them, especially *Typee* and *The Whale*. They are so full of profound reflection & earnest human-ity—I do not know any literature I more heartily enjoy reading. He is undoubtedly one of the great brotherhood of nature-writers. (Oehlschlaeger and Hendrick, 166)

Dr. Jones had in fact seen Melville years before in a Manhattan bookstore without knowing who he was and without knowing his writings. After Salt's insistence he looked for Melville's books and had the good fortune to become the first major Melville collector we know of outside of the Melville family. Extended comments on Thoreau and on Whitman, as well as on Melville, run through many of Salt's writings, such as his 1894 *Richard Jefferies: A Study*, in which Salt quoted from a manuscript on Jefferies by Dr. Jones, whom he identified as "a well-known student of Thoreau" (115). In the months before and after Melville's death in September 1891, Salt found that the "literateurs" of the British publishing world, aloof from issues of human nature and society, were threatened by his proposed collection of essays on "the whole *Nature* subject," to be called *The Return to Nature* and to con-sist of his articles on "Jefferies, Carpenter, Burroughs, Thoreau, Melville, &c, &c." Had Salt found a publisher for *The Return to Nature*, or had he set himself to write a biography of Melville instead of Thoreau, the course of Melville's reputation would have been incalculably but powerfully altered. As it was, he promoted Melville's reputation for decades more, living long enough to give letters Arthur Stedman wrote him to Willard Thorp, the first great academic Melville scholar. Thorp, of course, lived to encourage many Melville students, including, for two decades, me.

Edward Carpenter, who had been curate for F. D. Maurice, broke with the church, remaining a Socialist and becoming a champion of homosexual love. He was a worshipper first of Shelley, then Whitman, and he knew *Typee* and *Omoo*, but also *The Whale*. Several of his close acquaintances, nota-bly Salt, were Melville admirers. After reading W. M. Rossetti's edition of Whitman he initiated a correspondence with the American poet and made a pilgrimage in 1877 to see Whitman at Camden (he "stayed in the house with him for a week"), then went to Concord to learn about Thoreau (Tsuzuki, 34). Emerson put him up. Having bathed in Walden Pond, Carpenter on his return sent a copy of *Walden* to William Morris, who thought it presented a one-sided view of life; more important for Thoreau's reputation, he also introduced *Walden* to his Socialist friend Salt. Carpenter's *Towards Democracy* was a Whitmanesque plea for equality of mankind infused with his ideal of love, which he specified elsewhere as "a powerful, strongly built man, of my own age or rather younger—preferably of the working class" (Tsuzuki, 42). There is no reason to question Chushichi Tsuzuki's observation that an "element of sexual attraction" was present for Carpenter and others "in the fellowship of Socialism, and sustained its moral fervour" (151). Such a sexual element infused the earlier working-men's movement as well. Carpenter, who soon became a spokesman for an idealized notion of homosexuality in works such as *Homogenic Love* (1895), was in the thick of Melville admirers. Havelock Ellis asked Melville for information about his ancestry at about the time he was using Carpenter as a major case study of homosexuality. Ellis's intimate friend Salt resorted to chapter 3 of *Moby-Dick* in describing an occasion when Carpenter was left looking "a sort of diabolically funny" ("Sage at Close Quarters," 199); Augustine Birrell, mentioned below, was a friend from Carpenter's Cambridge years. In *Iölaus* (1902) Carpenter used Melville's "reliable" first two books to illustrate male friendship customs in the pagan world, quoting first the account of the Polynesian habit "of making bosom friends at the shortest possible notice" (from *Omoo*, chap. 39), then the description of the "Polynesian Apollo" Marnoo (from *Typee*, chap. 18). Carpenter had enormous influence not only on his contemporaries at home and abroad but also on at least two younger writers who were also profoundly influenced by Melville—D. H. Lawrence and E. M. Forster.

Melville had endured many jests in the press about his fickleness in abandoning the charming Fayaway and marrying the daughter of Judge Lemuel Shaw. Jonathan Katz in *Gay American History* (1976) describes Stoddard's debt to Melville in "A South Sea Idyl." In *Gay/Lesbian Almanac* (1983) Katz shows that Carpenter's *Homogenic Love* was read in the canyons of Northern California in the 1890s by men who were corresponding with Carpenter. It may well turn out that in the nineteenth century Stoddard was far from the only man who responded to Kory-Kory more than to Fayaway.

Undeniably, for many readers, male or female, the appeal of *The Whale* or *Moby-Dick* during its gradual discovery was grounded in part on the fact that by style and subject matter it could nurture a class-bridging philanthropic idealism not without an element of seductive eroticism. The late-nineteenth-century British admirers of Whitman, Melville, and Thoreau were driven by industrialization, urban poverty, and repressive moral codes to look afresh at all human institutions (conspicuously including Christianity) and at man's relationship with nature. Hawthorne in *The Scarlet Letter* (chap. 18) had made his position clear on the lawless thoughts that visited Hester Prynne. When she looked from an "estranged point of view at human institutions" she showed that in her suffering she had been taught "much amiss" (chap. 18). That conservatism marked Hawthorne as irrelevant to most of the early British admirers of Melville, Whitman, and Thoreau. In their social idealism they were willing to experiment with ways of establishing on a surer ground of mutual happiness not only what Hawthorne called "the whole relation between man and woman" (chap. 24) but also the whole relation between man and man. To be true to their principled radicalism these British admirers excluded no aspect of life from idealistic experimentation: being social idealists led logically to their being sexual idealists and sexual explorers. To be sure, some of them drank heavily. One was court-martialed for a tantalizingly vague offense which apparently occurred while swimming with other men. They included some celibates (temporary or long-term), some male homosexuals and bisexuals, apparently a fetishist or two, more than one man who although heterosexual (or possibly either homosexual or celibate by preference) married lesbians. (Carpenter gave Kate Salt a name for her sexual status—"an Urning," thereby arming her in her refusal to consummate her marriage.) Some of them strained or violated social and sexual conventions in various ways—tolerating a ménage à trois out of respect for the principle of another's freedom, living more or less communally for extended periods, displaying an unusual intensity in male-male relationships, keeping a mistress or living so as to be suspected of keeping one, cohabiting with a divorced woman, marrying a divorced woman. There was not a libertine among them.

Concurrent with the enthusiasm about Melville among survivors of or connections of the Pre-Raphaelite writer-artists and adherents of the workingmen's movement and Fabian Socialism, and to some extent independently, a reevaluation of Melville was going on among other British writers—seawriters like W. Clark Russell, travelers and out-of-doors men, men who had been to the far reaches of the Empire, where *Typee* and *Omoo*, standard works in John Murray's Colonial and Home Library, had also penetrated decade after decade, *Typee* in the unexpurgated text. (Rudyard Kipling, a nephew of the wife of the Pre-Raphaelite Edward Burne-Jones, appropriately put some books by Melville on his reading list for the Empire League.) In regions remote from London *The Whale* was sometimes passed hand to hand under strange circumstances, as when in the early 1870s "a sweet, dainty little English lady" came aboard a small trading schooner in Apia, in the Samoas, and gave the "grizzled old captain" some books, offering the three volumes of *The Whale* as "the strangest, wildest, and saddest story I have ever read." The captain read the entire three volumes aloud to the crew, which included the sea-writer-to-be Louis Becke, who told the story as the introduction to Putnam's 1901 London issue of *Moby-Dick*. In the 1970s at my request Richard Colles Johnson acquired a photocopy from the holder of the only known copy, the British Library. No one is on record as having been moved by Becke's remarkable account until I read it then and put it in *"Moby-Dick" as Doubloon*. One of the greatest tributes to Melville could have been lost. But it might have been found, later on, for on December 4, 2011, Nigel Cross g-mailed me that he owned a nice copy of the 1901 Putnam's edition "inscribed from J. H. Barrie to Arthur Quiller Couch [known as "Q"] with the latter's book plate." Something of a decent association copy indeed, and proving the point of this chapter about how literary people passed Melville around by hand. Barrie, of course, used *Typee* and *Moby-Dick* in *Peter Pan*. What did Q say about Melville in print or in private?

By the 1890s Hannay was dead, but Russell and the young Becke were far from the only living voyager-authors or authors-to-be who cherished a love of *Moby-Dick*. In the summer of 1896, as a teenage laborer in a Yonkers carpet mill, John Masefield made up a short list of sea-authors he had not read and bought some Melvilles (including *Moby-Dick*) from a Sixth Avenue book dealer. He appreciated the "masterly account" of New Bedford, and his love of Melville grew. During the 1890s W. H. Hudson introduced Morley Roberts to *Moby-Dick* (and they also talked together about Richard Jefferies). Afterward Roberts recalled that he and Hudson often "wondered how it was that the Americans still looked forward to some great American book when all they had to do was to cast their eyes backward and find it." By the first years of the twentieth century Hudson had also talked about the book with Joseph Conrad, whose fulminations against *The Whale* on January 15, 1907 ("a rather strained rhapsody with whaling for a subject and not a single sincere line in the 3 vols of it") are so excessive as to arouse suspicions that he was denying a rival he saw as powerful, if not denying an influence on his own work (see Parker and Hayford, *"Moby-Dick" as Doubloon*, 123). The American artist Peter Toft (whom Melville dispatched in 1886 with greetings to Russell, who had not been sure that Melville was still alive) introduced *Moby-Dick* to the sea-novelist Frank T. Bullen; later Bullen in turn talked about the book with J. St. Loe Strachey (whose cousin John Addington Symonds was obsessed with the poetry and the life-example of Walt Whitman). Hudson in 1917 predicted that in time Thoreau would be regarded as "one without master or mate," in the "foremost ranks of the prophets"—evidence that some of these travel-writer and nautical-writer admirers of Melville shared either Buchanan's dual enthusiasm for Whitman and Melville or the frequent enthusiasm of the Pre-Raphaelites and the supporters of the working-men's movement and the Fabian Socialists for Whitman or Thoreau (or both) as well as Melville.[4]

These lovers of *The Whale* or *Moby-Dick* in the decades before the centennial of Melville's birth sometimes declared their love for it publicly, and sometimes treated it as a self-identifying and other-identifying token. H. M. Tomlinson in the *Nation and Athenæum* in 1922 reported what he had learned about the work as a talisman:

> That book, indeed, appears to have been a wonder treasured as a sort of secret for years by some select readers who had chanced upon it. They said little about it. We gather that they had been in the habit of hinting the book to friends they could trust, so that "Moby Dick" became a sort of cunning test by which genuineness of another man's response to literature could be proved. If he was not startled by "Moby Dick," then his opinion on literature was of little account. It should be observed, however, that the victim was never told this, because this test was made by those who seemed scared by the intensity of their own feelings aroused by the strange, subliminal potency of the monster called the White Whale. (857)

Some lovers of the book had taken greater risks than handing someone else a book: in the year of Melville's death a young teacher in Baltimore, Edward Lucas White, invited another young man, Frank Jewett Mather, to his rooms and read to him from *Moby-Dick*, thereby initiating one of the most important American enthusiasms for Melville. If Houghton Mifflin had not refused in 1906 to give him the five-hundred-dollar advance he needed, Mather would have proceeded with a biography of Melville, with the cooperation of Melville's daughter Bessie.

Such sharing of the book, even between heterosexual men, was not without the component of ritual bonding, for reading aloud usually occurred in companionable seclusion and required from the uninitiate the intense intimacy of becoming alive to Melville's words not through his own eyes but through the voice of the reader. To say the least, in this sort of sharing more was at stake than the possible validation of the reader's own advanced literary judgment. And in discussing the appeal of Melville to the British admirers from the last decades of his life through the 1920s it is essential also to remember the way William Morris read the book and immediately began quoting it with "huge gusto and delight." The "bold and nervous lofty language" that Melville had created in the book, and the humbler but equally memorable quaintnesses of phrasings, took rank in his admirers' minds with phrases from Shakespeare and were irresistibly sharable.

In the next generation Melville's most famous admirers would include men (D. H. Lawrence and T. E. Lawrence—Lawrence of Arabia—are obvious examples) who devoted about as much passionate writing to male-male relationships as to male-female relationships, as well as bisexual women, most notably Virginia Woolf. Even though Melville did not come, as Whitman and Thoreau did, with social program in hand, the British admirers saw him as having learned to think the way they wanted to think, "untraditionally and independently." Equally appealing to these writers was his intense awareness of his own "moods of thought," his phrase in *Pierre* (bk. 24.1), and his capacity for analyzing and evoking complicated moods of body-and-mind, often in relationship to the physical universe and to the fellowship of all human beings (among whom, as many of his admirers were keenly aware, were well-muscled men whose appeal was not diminished by their not always being of the white race and not always being altogether fluent in the English language). Part of Melville's special appeal to his British admirers came from specific scenes of male bonding as well as from his more general underlying feeling of brotherhood with all men. A substantial set of Melvilleans from late in his own time to the present has consisted of male (and some female) homosexuals or bisexuals, men and women who can become influential out of proportion to their absolute numbers (however high those numbers are) in artistic and literary circles—journalistic critics, academic critics, editors, bibliographers, rare book dealers, publishers, and writers as diverse as Carl Van Vechten, Lawrence of Arabia, E. M. Forster, W. H. Auden, Malcolm Lowry, and Angus Wilson. I issue a challenge to queer theory and gay studies professors to abandon the Eve Kosofsky Sedgwick stereotypes and look at American and English admirers of Melville in their full family, societal, and cultural contexts.

Little enough is known about the relationship between sexual orientation and the cherishing and sharing of literary works (certainly not in relation to Melville). Little was said until recently about the much larger topic of the relationship between aesthetic responses, sexual stimulation, and social and cosmic questionings—a topic that must form a part of any history of the reputation of *The Whale* and *Moby-Dick*. In his supercharged psychological, aesthetic, and intellectual unfolding which culminated in 1851 and early 1852, Melville recognized something very like what modern French literary theorists call the pleasures of the text and devised a style which he thought would allow him to write about such a forbidden topic. Very likely the first literary writing he did after finishing *Moby-Dick* was the opening of *Pierre* as we know it, where Pierre simultaneously thrills from the onset of puberty and the effect of imaginative eroticism in literature, *The Faerie Queene* recognized as pornographic.

The Melville Revival which began in nineteenth-century London simmered there until the centennial of Melville's birth, 1919. The term was justifiably used in the *New York Times Saturday Review of Books* on July 22, 1899, where "T. B. F." reported in "Book News in London" on "a conspicuous revival of interest in America's sea author," the result of W. Clark Russell's "repeated glowing tributes." Russell deserves such credit, but it took dozens of men and women over the course of four decades to bring about the rediscovery of Melville and *Moby-Dick*. In the first two decades of the twentieth century John Masefield repeatedly praised *Moby-Dick* in his books and in interviews. Not all his early tributes to Melville have been located, but in *A Mainsail Haul* (1905) he put an evocative prose fantasy into the mouth of an old sailor named Blair. In this "Port of Many Ships" the "great white whale, old Moby Dick, the king of all the whales," leads all the other whales of the world in raising all the sunken ships and drowned sailors and towing them "to where the sun is." Then "the red ball will swing open like a door, and Moby Dick, and all the whales, and all the ships will rush through it into a grand anchorage in Kingdom Come" (24–26). During this time W. H. Hudson was as loyal an admirer as Masefield, and, as I have mentioned, Melville's influence was plain in the writings of James Barrie. Many of the admirers from the 1890s survived for decades—G. B. Shaw, H. S. Salt, and other Fabians spanned literary generations—but did they talk much about Melville to younger friends in the 1910s? There were living links between the Pre-Raphaelite admirers of Melville and the Bloomsbury crowd (around 1915 Ford Madox Hueffer encouraged D. H. Lawrence and introduced him to Edward Garnett, who had corresponded with Melville—but did they mention Melville to each other?). Little evidence has yet been brought forth, but a surprising number of Lady Ottaline Morrell's friends came to know *The Whale* or *Moby-Dick*. Among them were Augustine Birrell (born like Salt in midcentury) and younger literary people—Walter de la Mare, D. H. Lawrence, J. D. Beresford (in whose Cornwall cottage Lawrence first read *The Whale*, in 1916), later Virginia Woolf, Leonard Woolf, Lytton Strachey, and Aldous Huxley. De la Mare knew Alice Meynell (mother of Viola Meynell, who emerged as an enthusiast in 1920) and John Freeman, who in 1926 became the first Englishman to write a book on Melville. We know that some of these people were among the secret sharers of *The Whale* or *Moby-Dick* in the 1910s, but the proof is yet fragmentary and elusive.

That proof will come in large part from the Internet, but sometimes old-fashioned book searching will produce surprises. I buy copies of Raymond

Weaver's biography when I can. After all, he never returned Melville's drawing of Arrowhead to his granddaughter Eleanor Metcalf, so the nearest thing to it is the reproduction in *Herman Melville: Mariner and Mystic*. Maybe, just maybe, Melville's original drawing is stuck in some copy. I bought a copy on eBay around 2002, one Weaver had inscribed to Thomas Monro, who had stashed clippings in it. Among the discolored and torn clippings was an article entitled "Passing on the Torch," a partial reprint from the "Gossip Shop" in *The Bookman* of February 1922, presumably by John Farrar. (Now you can easily find it online.) Here is the full text, italicized to emphasize the extraordinary claims set forth in it:

> *The history of "Moby Dick", Melville's titanic dramatization of human fortitude and implacable resolve, has been the history of a book's laudation by literary artists who recognized in Melville an artist who transcended all that they themselves could do in words. The most interesting genealogy of "book recommending," the passing on of a torch from one hand to another, was supplied one day recently by James Stephens, the wizard who wrote "The Crock of Gold," "Mary, Mary," and "The Demi-Gods." Reveling over "Moby-Dick" with Samuel McCoy, who has just returned from Ireland, Stephens said:*
>
> *"Did I ever tell you how I first heard of the book? George Meredith, who was about twenty years old when 'Moby Dick' was first published, read it, recognized a master in Melville, and passed the book on to Watts-Dunton. Watts-Dunton, equally enthralled, urged Dante Gabriel Rossetti to read it. Rossetti ran with it to Swinburne, crying out that Swinburne must read it. Swinburne, finding in it the roar of the sea described as he himself could not, with all his music, silently passed it on to Oscar Wilde, then the most glittering star among the literary lights of London. Wilde, a Dubliner, handed the book on to another Irishman, young William Butler Yeats, making, as he did so, an epigram on Melville's greatness that would be worth repeating— if I could remember it. Yeats, coming back from London to Dublin, brought a copy of the book with him and presented it to George Russell, 'A.E.,' essayist, poet, painter, and seer, commanding him by all the ancient gods of Eire to read it at once. And 'A.E.,' chanting solemn rhapsodies through his beard, handed it on to us, his disciples. I pass it on to all I know, as the greatest prose work in the English tongue.*
>
> *"Melville," added Stephens thoughtfully, "was the last of the bards. He was wider than Shakespeare."*

*Pronounced on the afternoon of August 7, 1921, in the dingy little
dining room of the hotel in Galway town on the west coast of Ireland,
where bearded sailors from all the ports of the world once drank Spanish wine in the Galway inns.*

I knew the 1922 *Nation and Athenæum* article quoted above. I knew the
story of how around the turn of the last century Sir Alfred Lyall had casually passed *The Whale* to friends along with other books, making no special
mention of it. If they returned it with perfunctory thanks, he had taken their
measure. If they came back raving, they were to be clasped as lifelong friends.
I had made many connections already, identifying those who were known to
have passed *The Whale* or *Moby-Dick* on to a friend, and the Kennedys had
made others. This account in the *Bookman* is so wonderfully specific that I
want to believe the whole of it. I want to know how much truth there is in
the story of what was sworn to in the dingy little dining room of the hotel in
Galway town on the west coast of Ireland. Who will go to the archives and
to the databases and expose it as a fabrication or triumphantly verify it in the
course of writing a fine book on what the Melville Revival owes to such loving readers?

Chapter 20

DAMNED BY DOLLARS

Moby-Dick *and the Price of Genius*

ONE OF MELVILLE'S younger granddaughters told her children that the price of genius was too high for a family to pay. This chapter is about the price of genius, the price of beauty—what it cost Melville and his family for him to give us *Moby-Dick.*

In early May 1851, when he had finished almost all of *Moby-Dick* except the concluding chapters and late insertions, Melville wrote Hawthorne about "the silent grass-growing mood in which a man *ought* always to compose," a mood that could seldom be his: "Dollars damn me; and the malicious Devil is forever grinning in upon me, holding the door ajar." Critics have tended to take these words as a playful commentary on the strains of authorship: the printer's devil, the boy who runs with copy from author to compositor, is peering into the writer's study, hands outstretched for new pages to carry to the print shop; the harassed author never has enough time quite to perfect his prose before surrendering it to the printer.

Melville went on to say that because dollars damned him, because he was so rushed, "the product is a final hash," and all his books were botches. We have not taken Melville's own judgment seriously, partly because for a long time we have seen him as a great writer and *Moby-Dick* as a great book, not a botch. *Moby-Dick* was seldom taught in American colleges before 1950. Indeed, there were very few professors of American literature until a few years after the war, when for the first time American literature programs or departments became common. Before that, in the 1920s and 1930s, most teachers who loved *Moby-Dick* had to wait twenty or thirty years to teach it, as the late Robert Spiller told me ruefully. The wide teaching of *Moby-Dick* in colleges after World War II coincided with the triumph of a theory of literature, the New Criticism, which dictated a method of classroom teaching

appropriate to a period when new colleges were being founded to accommodate the returning GIs, colleges that had to start their libraries from
scratch, competing with many other new colleges doing the same thing. Old
books and newspaper files were hard to buy (even as other libraries were
recklessly trashing their bulky bound newspapers) and major manuscript collections for the nineteenth century were seldom on the market. The New
Criticism required that its practitioners ignore biographical evidence as irrelevant to criticism and to see any poem or novel as a perfect work of art. This
made the life of a teacher simple. Even a work which any commonsensical
reader would regard as obviously the product of disparate and unresolved
impulses—such as Melville's *Pierre*—could be celebrated cleverly in articles
demonstrating its unity. Far more intensely did critics celebrate the unity of
Moby-Dick. Decade after decade, critics resolutely ignored Melville's own
words, and often ignored also even obvious anomalies in the text such as the
momentous introduction and sudden removal of Bulkington. Of course, critics proclaimed, *Moby-Dick* was a unified work of art, not a botch.

Likewise, critics could not take seriously the possibility that dollars had
really damned Melville. How could he say he was damned? Why, he had
the rare satisfaction of knowing for the rest of his life that he had written a
great book! Why, within three decades after his death he had ascended into
the highest literary realms, compared not to J. Ross Browne the American
whaler but to Sir Thomas Browne the Restoration physician and moralist,
compared not to William Scoresby the whaling authority but to William
Shakespeare! Almost no one celebrated *Moby-Dick* as a great book which
nevertheless contained elements that the harried author had not harmonized
to his own satisfaction. The conspicuous exception, Harrison Hayford, was as
late as 1978 in publishing his "Unnecessary Duplicates" (now available in
the 2001 Norton Critical Edition of *Moby-Dick*). The New Criticism is still
dominant in the study of American literature, however disguised over the last
decades as Phenomenology, as Structuralism, as Deconstruction, as the New
Historicism. Here I use long-forbidden evidence, biographical evidence, in
looking at Melville's gamble that he could write a great book which would
be immensely popular, and at the human consequences of that gamble. In
order to do this story justice I retread briskly some ground already covered in
this book.

After his return from the Pacific in 1844, Melville began the semi-
autobiographical *Typee* in New York City and finished it in 1845 while living
with his mother, four sisters, and a younger brother in a rented house in
Lansingburgh, New York, now part of Troy, across the river from Albany.
In 1845 the Harpers rejected his story of living with South Sea natives in

the Marquesas as impossible to be true, perhaps thinking no uneducated sailor could have such experiences and later write such a story. Later the Harpers rued that hasty decision. Delayed a year, Melville's career began with that book, *Typee* (London: John Murray; New York: Wiley & Putnam, 1846). Relying on George Putnam's judgment, Wiley had rushed *Typee* into print without reading it, then promptly made Melville expurgate sexual passages along with all the criticisms of Protestant missionaries. By late 1846 the newspapers and magazines published by the lower Protestant churches had united against him, and for the rest of his active career Melville was hounded by what we would classify as right-wing Christians. (Presbyterians, a notably missionary-minded denomination, were particularly hard on Melville; that was why he provocatively made Ishmael claim to be a good Presbyterian.) Melville's career was consolidated by *Omoo* (London: John Murray; New York: Harper & Brothers, 1847), a semi-autobiographical account of his experiences on his second whaleship and in the islands of Tahiti and Eimeo. Once he found he could run up a tab at the Wiley & Putnam and then at the Harpers' bookstore, Melville began buying books that he needed if he were to write his own books, regardless of the fact that he was eating up his profits in advance. On the strength of the popularity of *Omoo*, Elizabeth Shaw and her father, Lemuel Shaw, the chief justice of the Massachusetts Supreme Court, decided that her eleven-month engagement to Melville could be followed, in August 1847, by marriage.

Melville did not have enough money to get married, especially with his mother and four sisters at least partially dependent upon him. Heddy Richter, who read and indexed the two volumes of my biography and has read *Melville Biography: An Inside Narrative*, argues that Augusta Melville in the mid 1840s should have relieved the strain on the family. She was engaged at least briefly to her second cousin John Van Schaick (the one who shopped in Troy for Maria's party for Herman and Lizzie) and she had come very close to marriage with another second cousin, Augustus Peebles. Young Augustus had some annoying mannerisms if not minor character flaws, but he was wealthy, and could have sheltered Maria and another daughter or two, if not all of them, albeit perhaps in a house where Maria's first cousin Maria Van Schaick Peebles was mistress. Did an impoverished Victorian woman have the duty to lift up the status of her entire family by an opportune marriage? As it was, by choosing not to marry, Augusta added to the financial burdens on her brother Herman all through the next decade.

John Gretchko has discovered an ante-nuptial document which provides that Sophia Thurston, from a wealthy Bond Street family, upon her marriage to Melville's lawyer brother Allan, will loan Herman Melville five thousand dollars for purchase of the indenture of lease on a house on Fourth Avenue priced at six thousand dollars. Melville's father-in-law advanced him two thousand dollars, a thousand of which apparently went as part payment on the twenty-one-year indenture of lease. That left a thousand dollars for Melville to use in moving himself, his bride, his mother, and his four sisters from Lansingburgh to Manhattan, setting up housekeeping there, and living on until it ran out. Maria and her daughters and Herman, Allan, and their wives moved in at the same time. The house, as I explain in chapter 6 on the basis of newspaper advertisements, was commodious if not downright luxurious, with furnace, water closets, and hot water to the third floor. By 1850 there were four live-in servants. It is not yet clear what the payments listed as "rent" amounted to or who paid them, and it is not clear how the brothers divided the living expenses, including the payment to servants. No one has done a good job with equivalents, not even the U.S. government with its inflation charts, which would suggest that two thousand dollars in 1847 would equal fifty-some thousand now. But in terms of comparable New York City property values, two thousand dollars in 1847 would buy something roughly like five million dollars now: you have to multiply not by twenty-five or thirty but by a thousand or more. Everyone acknowledges that a million dollars is not what it used to be, and the cost of six thousand dollars was very serious money—four years' income for an average Manhattan family, or more.

Melville had made a start on his third book, *Mardi*, before his marriage. After the move to New York he apparently took stock and admitted that he had been spending his profits in advance. Instead, he began systematically borrowing books whenever he could restrain himself from buying his own, but he indulged himself another way, taking more than a year and a half to write that book, the first in which he dared to be ambitious of literary greatness. All this time he was counting on the English copyright ruling remaining favorable to American writers who published books first in England. The Melvilles' first child, Malcolm, was born early in 1849, shortly before *Mardi* (London: Richard Bentley; New York: Harper, 1849) was published and widely attacked—having already lost Melville his first English publisher, John Murray, who read it and rejected it. At this time, in April 1849, Melville paid Wiley about forty dollars for the plates of *Typee* so the Harpers could print from them, without having to buy them, and become Melville's sole U.S. publisher. Abandoning his hopes to turn at once to another ambitious book, Melville instead wrote a book designed to be popular, *Redburn* (London: Bentley; New York: Harper, 1849), and then immediately wrote another one, *White-Jacket* (again Bentley and the Harpers, 1850). Hurt by a new London ruling that held that Americans could not obtain copyright in Great Britain, Melville managed to sell *White-Jacket* in England only because he went there and charmed Bentley into taking a chance on it after several other publishers had rejected it outright. Melville's heart was set on a Wanderjahr, a footloose exploration of Italy, the Holy Land—the Grand Tour, justified, for a thirty-year-old husband and father, by the fact that he would be gathering material for popular new books. Melville did not get enough from Bentley for *White-Jacket* for him to fulfill that desire. On the especially long voyage home, in January 1850, frustrated, ambivalent, aspiring, he began planning a book that would be popular as well as ambitious—a book about whaling.

Melville worked hard on it, probably writing at first without much reference to source books. After three months, he described it to the younger Richard Henry Dana as half done—not unrealistic, because the previous summer he had written *Redburn* in two months then had written *White-Jacket* in the next two months. Melville's first break from work seems to have been a hurried excursion to West Point. At some point (about this time?), he came upon the passages on Tupai Cupa in George Lillie Craik's *The New Zealanders* (London, 1830) and, as Geoffrey Sanborn discovered, promptly introduced Queequeg into the manuscript, endowing him with aspects of Tupai Cupa's appearance and history. Melville needed some basic books about whales as well as books about whaling, but one important book was not easy to get: Putnam had to order Thomas Beale's *Natural History of the Sperm Whale* (1839) from England. By the time it arrived, on July 10, 1850, Melville needed vigorous outdoor exercise, more than he may have gotten by that possible expedition to West Point.

His visit to Pittsfield, Massachusetts, began merely as a vacation at his late uncle's farm (technically, it had been owned by the estate of Melville's late Boston grandfather), but he brought the whaling manuscript with him, and for at least a few days in the second half of August he worked on it there, in the old mansion. The widow and children (or technically the trustees of the estate) had sold the great old house, in need of repairs—moldering, but a mansion—and the land (250 acres) for $6,500; the purchasers, the Morewoods, would not take possession for several months. Melville had not known the farm was for sale. Once he found that he had just missed the chance to buy the farm (which one of his cousins in 1848 had called his "first love"), he may have been seized by an absolutely unreasonable jealousy. Then once he had made friends with Nathaniel Hawthorne, who for several months had been living outside nearby Lenox, Melville knew that if he were to do justice to his book he had to live in the Berkshires, starting immediately. Melville's behavior makes some sense if you calculate the power the Berkshires held in his memory from the times he had visited his uncle Thomas Melvill and later from the summer of 1837, when he had worked the farm before teaching at a rural school in the nearby mountains. His behavior also makes emotional sense if you take account of his disillusion at the way his friends among the New York literati were viciously sniping at each other, and particularly if you consider his exaltation at the possibility of finishing his book with Mount Greylock in view to the north and his new friend Nathaniel Hawthorne a few miles away to the south. If he remained in Manhattan, he could not make the book as good as it could be. Besides, he had been amazingly responsible several months before: he had cut short his stay in London just as he was meeting marvelous literary men and artists, and he had sacrificed the year-long Grand Tour that surely would have proved of such high economic benefit to his family, in the long run. Now the most important thing in his life was that he make the whole book as great as the part he had already written.

Melville was not being rational, but he was persuasive. His father-in-law, after already advancing him the $2,000 in 1847, advanced him $3,000 more toward the purchase of Dr. John Brewster's farm adjoining the old Melvill property. For a total of $6,500—exactly the price of the Melvill farm—he bought a much smaller farm (160 acres) and a decrepit old farmhouse— a house that had never been grand, as his uncle's had been and would be again. This might seem barely rational of Shaw. But for his money Shaw got the assurance that as long as he paid his annual September visit to hold court in Lenox he could see his daughter and her family in Pittsfield, and during the rest of the year she would be only a direct ride away on the new railroad that ran right across Massachusetts.

In mid-September 1850 Melville probably turned over to Brewster the $3,000 that Shaw had just advanced him. He arranged at the same time that Brewster would hold a mortgage of $1,500 on the property. That leaves a discrepancy of $2,000. The best I can figure it, Brewster agreed, orally, to wait a while for the $2,000, say a month or two, until the indenture of lease on the highly desirable Fourth Avenue house could be sold at a tidy profit and Melville could pay Sophia Thurston what she had advanced him and turn over $2,000 more of the proceeds to him. When Melville returned to New York, Tertullus D. Stewart (a friend from Lansingburgh) offered to loan him whatever he needed to tide him over, but Melville refused: he would not need the loan. In October 1850 Melville and his wife along with his mother and three of his sisters moved to the farm, which he promptly named Arrowhead. Perhaps his brother Allan had already purchased his new house on Thirty-first Street, for he and *his* wife and two children, one a new baby, along with one Melville sister, were preparing to move out of the Fourth Avenue house within a few weeks. By Christmas the Fourth Avenue house was empty but unsold. In January 1851 Allan talked about buying it himself, because he and his wife were unhappy being so far uptown (that far uptown was out of town, remote from everything, they had found), but that proved to be just talk. Meantime, Melville had not gotten settled in a writing room until well into November, and then he had to be dispossessed for the family Thanksgiving (including the aunt and cousins) to be held there because there was no room on the first floor big enough for the tables. His wife had taken the baby and fled the chaos to Boston, the only place you could celebrate Thanksgiving properly, and did not return until New Year's Day, 1851. The older sister also fled, hurt as she left by Herman's irritation at having to drive her to the station during his writing hours, and his mother and two remaining sisters spent December in frustration, imprisoned: he would not trust them to drive the horse, Charlie, and he hated taking time off from writing to drive them where they wanted to go and wait to bring them back, or drive home and return for them. In January, he was so desperate for concentrated writing time that he suddenly let them test-drive Charlie and thereafter trusted them to go where they wanted.

The discomforts and inadequacies of the farmhouse became more apparent all the time, and by the end of February 1851 it was clear that the cooking facilities were too primitive for the cook (they always had a cook or else were actively recruiting one), the outdoor well was inconvenient, they needed an inside kitchen pump, the parlor walls were soiled, some of the upholstered furniture looked worse after the move, certain rooms needed painting, and the barn in particular required painting. Melville hired men to start the renovations in the dead of winter, maybe before the first of March. The first order of business was grotesquely impractical, digging foundations in the still-frozen ground, and not just for a kitchen and a wood-house but also for a narrow piazza on the cold north side of the house. This piazza, too small for a whole family to use, would be Herman's vantage point for viewing Greylock from the first floor, just below his small window for viewing it in his writing room before starting his day's task.

In March the lease on the house in town was sold at last, the buyer paying $7,000, of which $5,000 must have gone to Sophia Melville. That left $2,000 for Melville, minus any fees that he may have owed. In any case, as he admitted five years later, on May 12, 1856, the sum received had fallen "short of the amount expected to have been realized." Instead of having $2,000 to turn over to Dr. Brewster, six months late, perhaps with no interest being charged on it, he had somewhat less than $2,000, and he had workmen to pay as well as Dr. Brewster. He would need more money, just to pay Dr. Brewster the remainder of the purchase money, not counting the $1,500 mortgage. In March Melville began thinking of taking Mr. Stewart up on his generous offer to help a friend in need, but as a last resort. First, on April 25, Melville wrote to Fletcher Harper asking for an advance on his whaling manuscript. A clerk at the Harpers brought Melville's account up to date on April 29, and on April 30 the Harpers sent their refusal, citing their "extensive and expensive addition" to their plant and pointing out that Melville was already in debt to them for "nearly seven hundred dollars." At once, on May 1, Melville borrowed $2,050 from Stewart, for five years, at nine percent interest. Some of the money, maybe a good deal of it, went to make up the $2,000 Melville had to pay Dr. Brewster, some of it went for the workmen at Arrowhead. Some of it was earmarked to pay a compositor in New York City, for in his anger at the Harpers Melville decided to pay for the setting and plating of the book himself in the hope of selling the plates to another publisher for a better deal than the Harpers would give him. In early May, not later, as we had thought, Melville carried the bulk of the manuscript to town, and left it with Richard Craighead, the man who had stereotyped *Typee* for Wiley and Putnam. *Moby-Dick* had to be a great financial success, and there was some hope that it would be. On the basis of a new copyright ruling, Richard Bentley, Melville's British publisher, gave Melville a note for £150 (about $700, after Melville took a penalty for cashing the note early). Melville had the money to make the $90 annual mortgage payment to Dr. Brewster in September and to pay Stewart his semi-annual interest of $92.50 on November 1, 1851, more than a month after the three-volume *The Whale* was published in London, a week after the Melvilles' second child, Stanwix, was born, and two weeks before the publication of the Harper *Moby-Dick*. (The American title, a last-minute substitution, reached London too late to be given to the book there.)

Some of the London reviews were full of extravagant praise. On October 24, 1851, the London *Morning Advertiser* concluded that the three volumes reflected more credit on America and were "more honourable to American literature" than any other works it could name. On October 25 *John Bull* called this the most extraordinary of Melville's books: "Who would have looked for philosophy in whales, or for poetry in blubber? Yet few books which professedly deal in metaphysics, or claim the parentage of the muses, contain as much true philosophy and as much genuine poetry as the tale of the *Pequod*'s whaling expedition." The *Leader* on November 8 said that *The Whale* was "a strange, wild, weird book, full of poetry and full of interest." The *Morning Post* on November 14 said that "despite its occasional extravagancies, it is a book of extraordinary merit, and one which will do great things for the literary reputation of the author." The *Weekly News and Chronicle* on November 29 echoed the *Leader*: it was "a wild, weird book, full of strange power and irresistible fascination for those who love to read of the wonders of the deep."

Normally, many British reviews of Melville's books had been reprinted in the United States. This time, for crucial weeks, the only reviews of the three-volume *The Whale* known in the United States were two hostile ones published in London on the same day, October 25, in the *Athenæum* and the *Spectator*. They were hostile largely because there was no epilogue in the English edition to explain just how Ishmael survived. Most likely, Bentley had told his compositors to shove all the etymology and extracts, all that distracting "e" junk, into the back of the third volume, and in the process of shifting things around the single sheet containing the epilogue (half a page of type, scrunched, very likely, from being on the bottom of the tall stack shipped across the Atlantic) had gotten lost. One of the rewards in carefully rereading the book is the chance to see just how early and how deftly Melville began preparing for Ishmael's survival, but without the epilogue any reviewer reading fast could be excused for assuming that Melville had violated the basic contract between writer and reader: if you create a first-person narrator, you make sure he or she lives to record the story somehow. The loss of the epilogue tainted the whole British reception, freeing hostile reviewers to write scathingly of Melville, and forcing friendly reviewers to find ways of praising the book despite such an obvious flaw. The fact that only the *Athenæum* and the *Spectator* reviews were reprinted in the United States anytime soon was worse than bad luck—it was disastrous for Melville.

Here I glance back at my account in chapter 16. On November 20, 1851, the reviewer in the *Boston Post* saved himself work by constructing his long review mainly from the *Athenæum*, which had declared that the style of Melville's tale was "in places disfigured by mad (rather than bad) English; and its catastrophe is hastily, weakly, and obscurely managed." As it happened, the *Athenæum* did not spell out just what was wrong with the "catastrophe" it condemned. The reviewer in the *Post* confessed not to have read quite halfway through the book, and so had no notion of what the ending was like. Any Bostonian might have laid aside the *Post* knowing that the London paper had been contemptuous of *Moby-Dick* but having no idea why the reviewer thought the catastrophe was so bad. In case anyone in Boston had missed the review in the *Post*, the sister paper the *Statesman* reprinted it in full, long quotations from the *Athenæum* intact, two days later, on November 22. The *Spectator* review was reprinted in the *New York International Magazine* for

December, and not reprinted again, as far as is known. The *Spectator* gave
a clearer indication what was wrong with the ending of the London edition,
saying that the *Pequod* "sinks with all on board into the depths of the illimit-
able ocean," narrator presumably included, but the complaint was muffled
by the different charge that Melville continually violated another rule, "by
beginning in the autobiographical form and changing ad libitum into the
narrative"—something that any reader halfway into the book might have
agreed with.

Long before he saw a set of *The Whale*, Melville saw at least what the *Post*
reprinted from the *Athenæum*, but unless he saw the *International Magazine*
he did not know for sure that the epilogue had been omitted from *The Whale*.
He made no protest to Bentley, it is clear, and no American reviewer read the
International Magazine and seized the chance to challenge the Londoners:
"Aren't these Brits odd? They are saying Ishmael does not survive, but right
here in my copy Ishmael is rescued by the *Rachel*." Later Melville saw a
handful of some of the short quotations from a few reviews besides those in
the *Athenæum* and the *Spectator*, including the ones in *John Bull* and the
Leader, but he never, in all the rest of his life, ever had any idea that despite
the loss of the epilogue many British reviewers had showered honor on him
as a great prose stylist.

In the United States Melville's friend Evert Duyckinck reviewed the book
promptly in two successive weeks in the *New York Literary World*, an influential, tone-setting paper. The first installment was devoted to belaboring
the coincidence that the book was published just as news was arriving of the
sinking of the *Ann Alexander* by a whale off Chile. In the second, November
22, Duyckinck complained about Melville's irreverence toward religion, the
"piratical running down of creeds and opinions." He had warned Melville
politely in his review of *White-Jacket* early in 1850 that he would not countenance irreverence. There was strong praise from some reviewers in the
United States, but it did not last long, and it was submerged by the ferocious
religious reviews, such as the one in the *New York Independent* (quoted in
chapter 16) on the trial which the book-maker and the book-publisher must
undergo at the bar of God. The low-church religious press would have leapt
on Melville anyhow, but Duyckinck lent intellectual and literary respectability to such pious denunciations.

In the first two weeks after publication the Harpers sold 1,535 copies of
Moby-Dick, but in the next two months or so they sold only 471 more, and
after that sales dwindled rapidly. Meanwhile, Melville was writing a new
book, a psychological novel based on what he had learned about his own
mind in the last years and in which he played off Dutch Calvinist Christianity

against Bostonian—and British—feel-good Unitarianism. Self-analysis had begun in earnest two and a half years earlier, after Melville had written *Redburn* as a fast, easy book because much of it was autobiographical. In early June of 1849, as he wrote his story, he had done a reckless thing, to use his later words: he had dipped an angle into the well of childhood, gone fishing in his own memory, where who knew what monstrous creatures might be brought up. Melville had been psychologically naive still in planning a fast and easy expedition into his childhood. The intense psychological unfolding that began in the act of writing *Redburn* (or the aftermath of having written it) had allowed Melville to write *Moby-Dick* and *Pierre*—the first version of *Pierre*.

What happened to *Pierre* I have told in the HarperCollins Kraken Edition (1995), illustrated by Maurice Sendak, in volume 2 of my biography (2002), and earlier in this book. Melville was, in the eyes of the Harpers at the start of 1852, a liability because of his unpopularity with the religious press and disposable since he was merely an American writer. They did not need to nurture their American writers. Already they were betting correctly that their secret acquisition of Charles Dickens's *Bleak House* as a serial in their magazine would be like striking gold in California, and they may already have let Henry J. Raymond know the hard line against American authors they wanted him to take in the *Times*. Melville had no leverage, for *Moby-Dick* was not going to be as popular as *Typee*, not even as popular as *Redburn*, sales figures already showed. What was he to do? What he did, after a few days, was reckless to the point of being suicidal. He began enlarging the manuscript with pages about Pierre as a juvenile author (a wholly new turn in an already completed manuscript), then with pages about Pierre's immaturely attempting a great book. In some of these pages he maligned Pierre's publishers. The Harpers honored their contract to publish *Pierre*, on such ruinous terms to the author, but, as I have said, by the next summer, after the ferocious reviews of *Pierre* began to appear, they quietly began letting literary people know that they thought Melville was crazy—"a little crazy," to be exact—not too crazy to keep people from buying *Redburn* and *White-Jacket*.

Pierre lost Melville his English publisher, Bentley, who figured if he continued to sell copies of the books he had in print he would eventually lose only £350 ($1,650) or thereabouts by publishing Melville, somewhat short of $50,000 in present purchasing power. Bentley would have printed *Pierre*, expurgated (as he had silently expurgated *The Whale*, without consulting Melville at all), if Melville had taken his generous offer to publish it without an advance and to divide any profits it made. During most of 1851 Melville had felt little guilt about his secretly borrowing $2,050 from Stewart: after all, the whaling book was so good that it had to succeed, and he could pay Stewart back before his wife and father-in-law found out about the loan. After January 1852, when he knew the Harper contract was disastrous, he may have hoped against hope for three or four months that all would work out, that Bentley would like *Pierre* and offer a handsome advance, or even that against all odds *Pierre* might sell so well in the United States that he would make money—even at twenty cents for every dollar the Harpers took in (after recouping their expenses) rather than fifty cents. Melville may have tried to deny again in January 1852 and in April and May 1852 that his career was over, however long he might try to postpone the death gasps. He may not have realized what he was relinquishing when he did not take up Bentley's offer of half profits, but by late August 1854, as explained in chapter 16, Melville knew that the copyright ruling on *Jeffreys v. Boosey* meant that he would never again earn money from publishing books in England.

When *Pierre* was published in the summer of 1852 it was savaged as no significant American book had ever been savaged. "Herman Melville Crazy," read a headline I discovered decades ago. Reviewers already had called Melville crazy for writing *Moby-Dick*, and accusations that he was insane recurred, still more strongly, in the reviews of *Pierre*, confirming in the minds of his mother-in-law and his wife's brother and two half-brothers the possibility that Melville was insane as well as a failure. That fall Melville tried to interest Hawthorne in writing a story he had heard that summer about a woman on the coast of Massachusetts who had nursed a shipwrecked sailor and married him, only to have him desert her. Starting mid-December 1852 Melville wrote the story himself, finishing it on or around May 22, 1853, the day his first daughter, Elizabeth, was born. The fate of *Moby-Dick* and *Pierre*, and his new labors on the book about the abandoned woman, *The Isle of the Cross*, had taken their toll on his health. As a sailor, Melville had been an athlete, and late in 1849, on the voyage to England, could still climb "up to the mast-head, by way of gymnastics" (*Journals*, October 13). In the summer of 1851 he fearlessly climbed high in a tree on an expedition to Greylock. That vigor disappeared. In a memorandum made after his death (Sealts, *Early Lives*, 169), Melville's widow recalled: "We all felt anxious about the strain on his health in Spring of 1853"—perhaps as early as April, when his mother was so concerned that she wrote her brother Peter Gansevoort hoping he could persuade his political friends to gain Herman a foreign consulship from the new president, Hawthorne's college friend Franklin Pierce: "The constant in-door confinement with little intermission to which Hermans occupation as author compels him, does not agree with him. This constant working of the brain, & excitement of the imagination, is wearing

Herman out." The year before, on May 1, 1852, Melville had defaulted on the semi-annual interest payment of $92.50 that he owed his friend Stewart, and he had defaulted on it that November. His mother's letter was written a week before he defaulted for the third time on his interest payments to Stewart. Elizabeth Shaw Melville may have recalled this period in early spring as the time when the family was most concerned about Melville, but the worst came at the end of spring, in June, when he carried *The Isle of the Cross* to New York City only to have the Harpers refuse to publish it, just at the time when it was quite clear that he had no hope of gaining a foreign consulship.

Melville was thoroughly whipped, but bravely he started writing short stories within weeks or even days of returning home with the manuscript of *The Isle of the Cross*, which he retained for some months, at least, and possibly some years, before presumably destroying it. When a single letter of his has sold for much more than $100,000, the value of that manuscript, if it emerged today, might rival that of a very expensive painting. But in September 1853, with the manuscript in his possession still, Melville defaulted on the payment of $90 due to Dr. Brewster. The money went for preparations for the wedding of his sister Kate to John C. Hoadley. Several weeks later, he defaulted, as he did every six months now, on the interest he owed Stewart.

Melville wrote to the Harpers late in November 1853 that he had "in hand, and pretty well towards completion," a book, "partly of nautical adventure"; then he qualified himself: "or rather, chiefly, of Tortoise Hunting Adventure." At that time he promised it for "some time in the coming January," and asked for and received the advance—a dollar for each of the three hundred estimated pages. He had specified that he was expecting "the old basis—half profits"—not the punitive terms he had accepted for *Pierre*. Now he paid Dr. Brewster the $90 he should have paid in September. This slight relief was followed by catastrophe. On December 10, 1853, much of the Harper stock of printed books and sheets was destroyed by fire, and the brothers charged Melville all over again for their costs before giving him royalties on his books—in effect, hanging on to the next $1,000 or so he earned. That is, to emphasize the unconscionable nature of their behavior, the Harpers recouped their losses in the fire by charging their expenses against him not once but twice.

If in mid-December Melville thought that after their disaster the Harpers could not possibly publish any book right away, then he could have written them and asked in so many words if they would be able to publish the book they had just given him the advance for. If they had replied that they could not be back in business for six months, he could not have returned their advance because he had already spent much or most of it, but he could have asked their permission to try to place the tortoise manuscript elsewhere and to turn over to them $300 if he got that sum from another source or, more reasonably, turn over to them $300 worth of articles for their magazines. Instead, he seems to have made an expedient, emotional decision that does not look wholly defensible. He decided to get more money from another publisher for the tortoise story, or for *part* of the tortoise material — or at least for material also dealing with tortoises. The batch of pages Melville sent to George Putnam on February 6, 1854, seems to be what was published in the March *Putnam's* as the first four sketches of "The Encantadas," the second of which was "Two Sides to a Tortoise."

In mid-February 1854 Melville endured a "horrid week" of pain in his eyes (words Allan Melville quoted back to their sister Augusta on March 1). Melville had been crowding Augusta with pages to copy for him, overworking her and overworking himself. He was suffering from public shame brought on him by *Pierre*, private shame at having been late with a payment to Brewster, and shame at his continually defaulting on the interest he owed Stewart, compounded by shame at doing something with the tortoise material that looks less than straightforward, no matter that the Harpers were themselves behaving abominably. No wonder he was sick.

In the next two years Melville wrote a full-length book, *Israel Potter*; several stories; and "Benito Cereno," which proved substantial enough to be serialized in three installments at the end of 1855. Early that year, with "Benito Cereno" far along, if not quite finished, he collapsed. In her memoir his widow recorded: "In Feb 1855 he had his first attack of severe rheumatism in his back — so that he was helpless." How long he was helpless is not clear. The timing of the attack suggests the possibility of couvade, because his wife gave birth to her fourth child, Frances, on March 2, 1855. This pregnancy had proceeded in pace with the monthly installments of *Israel Potter*, the last of which appeared in March, before book publication. Melville knew that his sister Kate Hoadley was also pregnant (she bore her daughter on May 30, 1855). In "The Tartarus of Maids" Melville made the narrator say: "But what made the thing I saw so specially terrible to me was the metallic necessity, the unbudging fatality which governed it." The unbudging fatality of the gestation process was a reminder to him, during each of the last two of his wife's pregnancies, of the passing of months, including the Mays and Novembers in which he missed interest payments to Stewart and the September in which he had missed a payment to Brewster. (He missed the September 1855 payment, too.) The day of reckoning was approaching remorselessly — May 1, 1856 — and Melville was progressively less able even to hope to avert the disaster. Malcolm's life had begun

in triumph; Stanwix's life had begun in distress—with Lizzie's horribly painful breast infection and the doctor-enforced early weaning of the baby, while
Melville was reading reviews of *Moby-Dick* and writing *Pierre*. Melville's
daughters' lives began when his state was even more miserable. After Bessie's
birth Melville had failed to get *The Isle of the Cross* into print and had failed
to obtain a consulship; before Frances's birth he had become helpless from
rheumatism.

According to his widow, Melville's first attack of severe rheumatism in
February 1855 was followed in June by an attack of sciatica, which lasted
through August, according to some comments made in September 1855.
Nevertheless, later that year Melville began a satire on American optimism,
The Confidence-Man, and continued to work on it during the early months
of 1856; during all this time, apparently, Tertullus D. Stewart was threatening to seize the farm—the same property already mortgaged to Dr. Brewster.
Melville wrote his plight into the manuscript in the story of China Aster
(chap. 40). In April 1856, just before the entire loan of $2,050 and back
interest (and probably interest on the interest) became due, after living with
the literally crippling secret of his debt since the first of May 1851, Melville had to confess his folly to his father-in-law and throw himself on Shaw's
mercy. For once, luck favored Melville, and he managed to sell off half the
farm swiftly. Yet the sale was not simple (as Lion G. Miles recently discovered): the buyer paid for the property in three annual installments, nothing
up front in 1856. Shaw must have advanced the money himself to pay off
Stewart then recouped it out of the buyer's 1857 and 1858 payments. Loving
and magnanimous still, Shaw recognized how ill Herman was and advanced
him still more money for a trip abroad in hopes of restoring his health.
Before he sailed, Melville had completed *The Confidence-Man*, which on its
publication in 1857 earned him not a penny, so he was out for the paper and
ink in which he wrote it, and the paper and ink with which his sister Augusta
copied it, and Augusta had copied it for nothing. At least she could see it in
print, unlike *The Isle of the Cross*, which she had also copied.

After his return from his journey to the Holy Land and Europe in 1856–
57, the next word of Melville's health is in 1858, as his widow recalled in her
memoir (Sealts, *Early Lives*, 169): "A severe attack of what he called crick in
the back laid him up at his mothers in Gansevoort in March 1858—and he
never regained his former vigor & strength." The next year on November 21,
1859, his neighbor Sarah Morewood, mistress of his uncle's grand old house,
wrote to a friend: "Herman Melville is not well—do not call him moody,
he is ill" (*Log*, 609). The back pain recurred: Melville's mother at Christmas 1867 described Herman as then finally able to go out: "his trouble was

a 'Kink in his back'" (*Log*, 693). In 1882 he suffered again what his wife on September 8 described to Kate Gansevoort Lansing as "one of the attacks of 'crick in the back.'"[1]

In the late 1850s Melville may not have put enough food on the table. At least one year, his father-in-law sent money for winter provisions. Melville earned a little money from lecturing for three seasons, late 1857 to early 1860. In early 1860 he completed a book he called *Poems*. At least two publishers rejected it and it was never published, though some of the poems he published in *Timoleon* (1891) may have been in the 1860 collection. In 1861 Judge Shaw died and Elizabeth Melville inherited enough money to support herself, her four children, and her husband for a few years. Melville's old debt to the Harpers was finally erased by sales in 1865, and he published a poorly received book of Civil War poems, *Battle-Pieces*, in the summer of 1866. The Harpers did not pay Melville for the war poems they printed in *Harper's Monthly* and the book made him no money. Melville did not have regular earnings until late in 1866, when he took a four-dollars-a-day job as a custom officer in New York City, a job he held nineteen years. We know now that there was a terrible marital crisis in early 1867. Elizabeth's brothers encouraged her to believe Melville was insane and with her minister, Henry Bellows, explored the possibility that she might leave him. Her strength of character emerged in verses she wrote to commemorate her prayerful decision to stay with her husband. That fall the Melville's oldest child, Malcolm, shot himself to death at age eighteen. Melville's life contracted even more tightly after 1869, when he began secretly working on a new poem that grew to eighteen thousand lines. He paid to have *Clarel* printed in 1876, using money his uncle Peter Gansevoort had left for that purpose; it was contemptuously reviewed, and in 1879 the publisher made him authorize the destruction of the remaining bound copies and sheets, which were cluttering up the office.

In the decades after its publication *Moby-Dick* was seldom mentioned in print. Melville's loyal friend Henry T. Tuckerman praised it in the November 16, 1863, *American Literary Gazette* as having "the rare fault of redundant power," redundant in the Miltonic sense of overflowing. In 1884, the English sea-novelist W. Clark Russell said the sailors' talk in the forecastle scene in *Moby-Dick* "might truly be thought to have come down to us from some giant mind of the Shakespearean era." Kate Gansevoort Lansing acquired a copy of Russell's article and thereafter some in the family began to understand that Herman Melville had been an important writer. Even before Melville's death in September 1891, and abundantly thereafter, Elizabeth Shaw knew that her husband was being recognized as one of the greatest American writers, and she proudly guarded his reputation as best she could. In this endeavor she was assisted by her older daughter, Bessie, who was born on or about the day *The Isle of the Cross* was completed. Mrs. Melville died in 1906, Bessie in 1908—late enough to have met with a would-be biographer, Frank Jewett Mather, whose plans fell through because Houghton Mifflin would not advance him five hundred dollars for the project. In the centennial of Melville's birth and in the next few years, first in England and then in the United States, Melville was at last saluted as belonging with Shakespeare and other great writers of the world.

None of this extraordinary fame impressed Melville's surviving daughter, Frances. Until her death in 1938 she blamed him for her sister Bessie's arthritis (caused by insufficient food, she thought), blamed him for her brother Malcolm's suicide in 1867, blamed him for innumerable acts, such as rousting her and her older sister out of bed at least one night early in 1876 to help him proofread *Clarel*, blamed him for her brother Stanwix's wasted life and early death (in 1886). She alone remembered that her father's in-laws (always excepting Judge Shaw) had believed every newspaper and magazine assertion that Melville was insane; she alone remembered that for some time in the 1860s her mother may also have thought him insane, on the basis of his behavior, presumably, as well as on the full authority of many unimpeachable writers in the press; and she alone knew that her Bostonian uncle and half uncles had tried to devise a way her mother could separate from her father without creating a scandal. Frances Melville Thomas told her oldest daughter that she did not know "H.M." in the new light of world fame: her resentments were so strong that his new reputation was a disparagement of her own memories and her own feelings. Two of her daughters were old enough to remember Melville well and to have known Mrs. Melville intimately, as young women, so they were able to correct Frances's views by their own memories, but the two younger daughters, born near the time of Melville's death, remembered Mrs. Melville less clearly and were more dependent on Frances for information about their grandfather. At least one of them absorbed Frances's lesson that the price of genius was too high for any family to pay. Early in the twenty-first century, the few surviving great-grandchildren felt entitled to whatever simple or complex pleasures they could find in being descended from Herman Melville. By the time the last of the great-grandchildren died in 2011, the high price of genius had at last been paid, in full.

Notes

Preface

1. In 1984 Ira Bruce Nadel in his *Biography: Fiction, Fact, and Form* declared that "the biographer is akin more to the creative writer than the historian" (11) and that "in biography language alters fact and draws on fiction to clarify its form" (209). Factual biographers still dominate the field, Nadel regrets in his introduction, even though "contemporary theories of fictional form and narrative technique have clarified our awareness of order and belief, presentation and authenticity, in biographical writing" (5) so that we should be redefining "the role of the biographer, transforming him from a journeyman or manufacturer of lives into a creative writer of non-fiction" (11); the biographer should be "akin more to the creative writer than the historian" (11). Grant Webster in *Biography* (Summer 1986) reviewed Nadel's book very hostilely: "Nadel's central point is that biography ought to be more fictional . . . . Put another way, factual biographies are bad in the sense that they are dated, and so do not reflect our current understanding of reality" (277). Victoria Glendinning in "Lies and Silences" in *The Troubled Face of Biography* (1988) could not restrain her outrage (54): "Nadel . . . asks: 'To what extent is fact necessary in a biography? To what extent does it hinder the artistic and literary impulse of the biographer? To what degree does the biographer alter fact to fit his theme and pattern?' His view is that the biographer has every right to change facts in order to make a psychological or artistic point. This makes me shiver. He also believes in what I would see as the intrusion of the biographer, suggesting that 'discovery in biography now exists equally in what the biographer reveals about himself as well as what he uncovers about his subject.' It is probably true that compulsive biographers immerse themselves in other people's lives as a way of obliquely investigating their own; but this is the biographer's own business. Nadel's ego-trip is at one remove. If [Richard Holmes's] *Footsteps* were to become a model for all biographers, we should have to find a new word for the genre." Elizabeth Longford offers "Reflections of a Biographer": "Today in certain quarters biography has become theory without life. . . . Biography is too important to become a playground for fantasies, however ingenious; I believe its future is safe with the reading public, who will keep it human, not too solemn" (148).

Nadel's arguments may be recognized in twenty-first-century pronouncements. In a carefully hypothetical scenario in "The Biographer as Archaeologist" (2002), William St Clair's speaker, more or less not speaking for St Clair, still frets trendily (222): "I cannot allow my narrative to be imprisoned within the confines of so-called biographical facts." The sturdy Frederick R. Karl in his 2005 *Art into Life* (x) declares unambiguously: "The thread that binds most of my pieces is my belief that biography is not 'fixed' or set, but a contingent, almost random genre. More akin to fiction than

499

to history, it is less than a novel, but sometimes more than history. It is linked to auto-biography (of the writer), frequently full of sound and fury, but signifying significant information." In 2009 Michael Benton made what looks like a last-ditch attempt to oppose biography and history by claiming that biography is a hybrid: "It is the veri-fiable facts of history crossed with the conventions of narrative" (35). I demur: the facts of history can be presented in verifiable chronological form in annals, without narrative, but otherwise the "conventions of narrative" are at play in most history just as in biography. I would write a biography of Abraham Lincoln employing precisely the conventions of narrative I employed in writing on Melville. In the last few para-graphs of chapter 8 I look at an attack on biography from within, attempts to define archives out of any resemblance to storehouses of public and private documents.

2. In Spartanburg, South Carolina, Professor John B. Edmunds, Jr., acting for his mother, Helen Edmunds, entrusted Joyce Deveau Kennedy with a big shoebox full of papers. Kennedy was alone in a motel room late at night when she found Mel-ville's letter to Sam Savage (August 24, 1851). She immediately called her husband, Frederick Kennedy, then, sleeping very little, she read and reread the letter many times, waiting for morning so she could spring her find on the owner. Scholars live for such moments. E-mail from Joyce Deveau Kennedy, August 26, 2011.

Unless otherwise noted, quotations of letters to and from Melville follow the Northwestern-Newberry *Correspondence* volume (1993). Information from Jay Ley-da's *The Melville Log* (1951, 1969) is cited as "*Log*"; information from my two-volume biography, *Herman Melville* (1996, 2002) is cited simply as "Parker." Quotations from other family documents are my transcriptions unless otherwise noted.

Introduction to Part I

1. It takes very little to drive one toward sympathy with Ted Hughes's outrage at people's reading his thoughts; see Martin Stannard's discussion in "The Necrophiliac Art?" (36–37) on Germaine Greer, Ted Kennedy, and Ted Hughes as living authors persecuted (as he says particularly of Greer) by parasites rooting about in their private lives. As I show later, even in a catch-all article Andrew Delbanco assumes that he can read my mind ("Melville in the '80s," 709–10).

Chapter 1

1. Unless otherwise specified, all quotations from Melville's works and correspon-dence follow the Northwestern-Newberry Editions. I cite chapters from Melville's published book-length works rather than page numbers so that readers can locate passages in other editions (Melville's chapters are usually short).

2. *Frank Leslie's Sunday Magazine* 11 (1882): 249–50, the fourth installment (of five) in the series "Reminiscences of an Old New Yorker" by "An Old Fogy."

3. I identified with Melville only in a handful of quotidian ways. I reject Frederick R. Karl's prescriptions (215–16): "The biographer creates or designs several scenarios for himself, using of course as many of the facts of the subject's life as he possesses. But these are usually few, combed from the subject's own musings, or letters, or dia-ries, and, therefore, unreliable, more fiction than fact perhaps. . . . And very often the biographer's choice [of scenario] depends on elements of his, or her, own childhood, or development, or more mature outlook: he 'uses' his subject to confirm aspects of life meaningful to him, the biographer, in a kind of countertransference, while all the

while posing as an independent or neutral observer." After reading Karl's *The Craft of Literary Biography* I can't imagine reading his book on William Faulkner. However, after-the-fact empathy with the trashing of Melville's masterpieces is another matter: how could I not recognize living reviewers as specters of the religious fanatic W. O. Bourne, the sexually twisted psychotic alcoholic G. W. Peck, and the self-righteous E. A. Duyckinck?

4. Without my conditional "just might," Stephen B. Oates in *Biography as High Adventure* reports on his visit to John Brown's farm in upstate New York: "No wonder the old man felt at home in the Adirondacks. Up here in the mountains, as though suspended between heaven and earth, he could feel closer to his God" (130).

5. Unlike the way Hermione Lee treated Edith Wharton in "A Great House Full of Rooms" (2004), I never patted my author on the head for his budding aesthetic awareness. Lee, following in Wharton's footsteps in Italy, quoted her as saying "quite rightly" (of the Portinari chapel) that "the whole chapel has a mood of 'blitheness.'" Added Lee, "And so it does" (34). Lee also reassured her readers that Wharton was acute in her descriptions of Palladian villas: "And always, Wharton gets the tone of the place exactly right" (35). Lee, of course, "could see exactly" what Wharton meant "by the combination of 'logic and beauty' in the best Italian garden design" (35). I never once felt tempted to reveal that my aesthetic sensibilities were as fine as or finer than Melville's. Jeffrey Meyers ("Reflections of a Book Reviewer," 59) is blunt in finding Lee's *Edith Wharton* "too long and too boring to finish"—and I would say bullying as to the stature of her author and her treatment of her.

6. Melville's likely source is *Isabel; or, Sicily: A Pilgrimage* (Philadelphia: Lea and Blanchard, 1839), 74–75. See the footnote on page 155 in a recent printing of the 2001 Norton Critical Edition of *Moby-Dick*. Late in 1861 and early in 1862 Melville and Tuckerman, both ailing, made failed attempts to see one another in New York, but, whether or not they met then, Tuckerman in October 1863 was ignorant of Melville's latest plans: "Impaired health induced him to retire to this beautiful region [the Berkshires], and in the care of his fruits and flowers, and the repose of a domestic life, he seems to have forsworn the ambition of authorship, but we trust only for a time" ("Authors in Berkshire," *American Literary Gazette and Publisher's Circular* [Philadelphia], written in October, published on November 16, 1863). This passage is quoted in Parker, 2:555; the attempts to meet each other in late 1861 and early 1862 are in Parker, 2:481 and 2:484.

7. See Melville's letter of March 7, 1850, to Evert A. Duyckinck.

Chapter 2

1. I found easy access to materials everywhere. At the New-York Historical Society there were unpublished scathing comments on Melville's brother Gansevoort in Philip Hone's diaries, just as I thought there ought to be. Four decades later a clerk was outraged when I asked to check something in the diaries. The idea of expecting to handle the original diaries! She brusquely told me to fill out forms for the microfilms.

2. As I tell in another book, *Ornery People*, the green room had triggered a late 1930s memory of a green room in San Antonio where I had been dimly aware of someone's suffering; long afterward, I learned what trauma had occurred there and realized that I may not have judged Bowers fairly in 1962.

3. Boswell, *Journal of a Tour to the Hebrides* (Dublin: White, Byrne, and Cash, 1785), 257.

4. Likely spots for Tanselle to have mentioned the category of conjectural emendations would have been 55 n. 23, and especially 65, in the last several lines of the text.

5. Very belatedly, in 2012, while lamenting the need to stow away my papers and books for one uncompleted project, once again, to make room for the next, thereby ensuring that I will have difficulty (some month or year later) regaining control of all the papers I had put away, I focused on the title of chapter 98 in *Moby-Dick*, "Stowing Down and Clearing Up." I must never have been easy with the title, for, I now see, in my biography I referred to "cleaning up," but it had not occurred to me to suggest that "Clearing" is simply a misreading of Melville's "Cleaning." You read the chapter and see if "clearing" is not duplicative of "stowing" and that what is going on in the two-part chapter is first stowing and then *cleaning*. Test also a reading I introduced into the 2001 Norton Critical Edition of *Moby-Dick* a few years ago (regardless of the fact that the 2001 edition was using the Northwestern-Newberry variation of the 1967 Norton text): in "A Bosom Friend" surely Melville meant Queequeg to be astonished at so many fifty pages being "bound" together, not "found" together. All of us, textual editors and greenest amateurs, are credulous readers.

6. In fairness to Samuels, after telling this I will give an only slightly mangled version of a story he told his colleagues. Early in his long career at Northwestern he received a $200 annual raise (or was it $250?) and at the next family gathering in Chicago happily told his lawyer-brothers the news. They spoke simultaneously, one asking him if that was per week and the other if it was per month. I got the story from Hayford, who, I believe, always made considerably less than Samuels.

7. The *Chronicle of Higher Education* is listed online as the sponsor of a subsidiary website called "Brainstorm" (chronicle.com/blogs/brainstorm/) where it seems that anyone can say anything. Marc Bousquet, acting as a latter-day Edmund Wilson, on January 5, 2011, recklessly accused me of gorging at the public trough: "Consider the work of textual scholar Hershel Parker, whose romantic theory of editing has been applied under the imprimatur of many distinguished grant-funded projects. . . . We give Parker millions to reconstruct what Melville would have published if his editor or friends hadn't interfered." It is easy enough on the Internet to identify rogue posters and ignore them, but the innocent may take seriously lawless accusations on a site sponsored by the esteemed *Chronicle*. This Parker never saw those "millions." While I was being paid in part from a federal program, I made $9,000 in 1965–66, $10,000 the next year, and $10,500 in 1967–68. I served hard time for the money those years! Later, I never had even a National Endowment for the Humanities grant, working as I was on a dead white man just at the wrong time. As I see it, in the interests of trendiness the *Chronicle of Higher Education* has given license to its "Brainstorm" bloggers. After the role of the Internet and the social media in the well-publicized conviction of Dharun Ravi for a hate crime at Rutgers University in March 2012, will free-and-easy pontificators on the Internet think twice before tweeting, posting, e-mailing, texting, blogging, and aiming their spycams at others?

Chapter 3

1. This review like hundreds of others is reprinted in *Herman Melville: The Contemporary Reviews*, edited by Brian Higgins and Hershel Parker (1995); reviews of Melville's works are quoted from this collection unless otherwise indicated.

2. I could do with three or four more documents from January 1852. In the chapter "Walking the Boundaries" of his *The Art of Biography* (1965), Paul Murray Kendall says, "When biographers talk shop among themselves, you will hear animated discussions of a problem rarely mentioned by reviewers, the problem of gaps. That paper trail, extending from the birth certificate to the death certificate, is never continuous or complete" (18). He adds: "There are no rules for handling gaps. Each paper trail is unlike any other paper trail. Each biographer is unlike any other biographer. The right way to fill gaps is unknown, the wrong ways are legion." Kenneth Silverman in "Mather, Poe, Houdini" comes out for honesty: "For the sake of coherence, the temptation is to pretend the gaps don't exist. . . . But if the biographer means to grant the subject its own life and respect its otherness, the facts do the bossing. When important information is missing, the reader should be told, awkward as that may be" (115). Sara Wheeler in "Polar Gap" asks (88): "How is one to fill the gaps? You can't make it up; you can't invite the reader to take his choice; you can't do nothing."

Hilary Spurling in "Neither Morbid nor Ordinary" (1988) does worse than nothing—she surrenders the field: "In order to convey this factual material, the biographer will generally, and I think inevitably, be forced to stoop to fiction. . . . Any reconstruction which is not to be purely external, and therefore superficial, must be quite largely made up. . . . The biographer is stuck with such facts as he has managed to scrape together: generally a job lot, much too full in places, hardly there at all in others, nearly always with pitiful gaps and crucial explanations missing" (116). Faced with most gaps, I went first to the newspapers, as local as possible (but which meant Hawaiian papers, in 1841–44, as well as ship sightings as reported in Boston, New York, and other cities), and worked outward. Melville's voyage on the *Lucy Ann* was short and well documented, but for the months at sea on the *Acushnet* or the *Charles and Henry* or the *United States*, or for Melville's stay in Hawaii, like Kendall, I tried to "reconstruct the probable pattern" of the days the best I could. Some periods I finessed as best I could: I would pay a year's book-buying budget for a dozen records of life in the Melville house from early February through May 1850. Were any of the German maids writing home to their families? If so, have any of those letters survived?

3. "What Quentin Saw 'Out There,'" *Mississippi Quarterly* 27, no. 3 (1974): 323–26, revised for *Critical Essays on William Faulkner: The Sutpen Family*, ed. Arthur F. Kinney (New York: G. K. Hall, 1996), 275–78. Cleanth Brooks wrote me on July 10, 1974, apologizing for his delay in commenting on the piece: "I'm sorry to have been so long. But I found that I was forced to review the whole book in order to see where I stood. (I'm most grateful that your article forced me to do that.)"

4. Roschelle says that "a learner's prior knowledge often confounds an educator's best efforts to deliver ideas accurately. . . . Prior knowledge can be at odds with the presented material, and consequently, learners will distort presented material" (1). He continues: "Prior knowledge determines what we learn from experience. Prior knowledge also forces a theoretical shift to viewing learning as 'conceptual change'" (2). Roschelle cites K. A. Strike and G. J. Posner, "A Conceptual Change View of Learning and Understanding," in *Cognitive Structure and Conceptual Change*, ed. L. H. T. West and A. L. Pines, 211–31 (New York: Academic Press, 1985).

5. In chapter 9 on 233–34 I quote Mark Kinkead-Weekes's 2002 account of how the Cambridge biographers of D. H. Lawrence started in small time-spans "with nothing but space ahead." He almost precisely describes how in the early 1990s I would read for the first time stretches of my vastly expanded *Log* until I reached the

point of saying, "Here's my story for this part—now stop and tell it." Kinkead-Weekes and I both try to suppress our "prior knowledge" (which never turns out to be precisely accurate) while we encounter old information (however corrected) amid new information in a fresh chronology. The ideal reader of a biography based on old and new archival evidence would know nothing about the subject, for adjusting to a new twist on a more or less familiar story, still more to a new episode, is indeed a test of intelligence (as I say on 234), one that all of us sometimes fail. A cognitive scientist like Jeremy Roschelle might profitably investigate the way literary critics respond to biographies that contain massive admixtures of old and new information.

Ann Thwaite in "Writing Lives" (1988) innocently tells of hiring someone to make a chronology for her (26), but when you make the chronology yourself you discover discrepancies and perceive connections no "intelligent typist" could find. A biographer also profits by holding to a chronology after creating it. Kinkead-Weekes (248) points out a consequence of Hermione Lee's violating chronology in her life of Virginia Woolf: "Lee seems oddly infected with the intellectual snobbery which is as problematic as VW's social snobberies. A strictly chronological method might not have tended so to identify biographer with subject."

6. Wells, "A Checklist of Melville Allusions in Duyckinck's *Literary World:* A Supplement to the Mailloux-Parker *Checklist,*" *Extracts* 29 (January 1977): 14–17. The *Literary World* is not in the Cornell online file of American magazines, although its literary and cultural significance is very high. As late as the 1990s I was still gleaning after the earlier harvesters, and finding sheaves of glistening wheat, such as the February 2, 1850, article on Powell's calling Irving and Melville the two worst enemies of the American mind.

7. "Hershel Parker, who for some years now has been publishing authoritative pieces on Melville, has recently offered an educated guess as to what happened next," Lynn began (4), then continued with an accurate version of my argument.

Chapter 4

1. See Clare Spark's *Hunting Captain Ahab* (501) for a poignant letter from Gilman to Leyda (September 13, 1947) after Zoltán Haraszti had ripped off some of his and Merrell Davis's work: "The dog-eat-dog aspect of academic life is despicable, but it can't be wished away." It took a long time for Leyda to understand that academics were under hard pressure not to share their discoveries before they published them; Hayford, characteristically, was generous with Leyda to a fault. What remained incomprehensible to Leyda, and to me, is why people would want to sit indefinitely on unique documents. Nowadays, anything discovered on an Internet database by a searcher in Athens, Georgia, may be discovered independently half an hour later by a searcher in Athens, Greece: find it, share it, as I did in 2011 when I put new Philo Logos documents on my blog (fragmentsfromawritingdesk.blogspot.com).

2. Paul Lauter's account of the transition from Williams to Feidelson is in "Society and the Profession, 1958–83" (1984): "A measure of how far the course moved away from traditional literary history toward the content of symbolism and American Literature were the incredibly low grades earned by students who did not come to class but relied on the old cribs to prepare for the first exam" (425). In the early 1980s, just as Feidelson's views were enjoying a late efflorescence (see Barbara Foley's article, discussed in chap. 8), Lauter was leading some professors, primarily younger ones,

in what might have been an embarrassing urge to undertake an enterprise which sounded downright scholarly—the reexamination of the American literary canon. This being one of my own concerns, I sought Lauter out while his group was creating *Reconstructing American Literature* (1983) and was his only companion in the bowels of the Americana (now the Sheraton) when boxes arrived with the first copies. I possess the first presentation copy, inscribed on December 29, 1983—"To Hershel: To continue and develop the debate."

After careful examination, I decided the syllabi sometimes brought good previously neglected writers into the classroom but in ways that were often sexist—biased against men. I also thought them biased against regions of the country, particularly the South, but also the West and the Midwest, including Chicago; biased against even women regional writers unless they happened to be from New England; biased against stories about fundamental Protestantism; biased against any writer who did not have leftist leanings, or leanings that could be construed as leftist. As part Choctaw and part Cherokee I felt condescended to by contributors who, I thought, were assuaging their cultural guilt by teaching what purported to be American Indian literature but was textually suspect and anyhow was anomalous, since it was in translation. The creators of the syllabi had been taught well by people who told them to neglect literary history and biography. The New Criticism eats away at your ability to look at historical evidence. Lauter's group wanted to expand the canon but they had no intention of reading widely to see what works of high literary value were lying neglected in the broad field of literature. They were creating interest in neglected writers on political grounds but were not willing to or competent to reevaluate the whole range of American literature on literary grounds. Lauter's impact on the American academy was profound and remains so. Without his influence, the profession would not have turned so far into neo-Marxism and, I believe, *American Literature* would never have published the concerted attack on Melville scholarship in the March 1994 "New Melville" issue.

3. It is strangely ironic that Leon Howard was so disdainfully abused by Professor Charles N. Feidelson, Jr. When Leon Howard first saw Feidelson, half a generation younger than he was, at an MLA meeting, he suffered an attack of something close to what was called the heebie jeebies—frantic, inarticulate distress. Early in Howard's life, about the year Charles N. Feidelson, Jr., was born, the senior Charles N. Feidelson had treated the teenage Leon abusively at a Birmingham, Alabama, newspaper office. Leon first saw the Yale Feidelson at about the age the newspaper man had been when Leon knew him, and according to Leon, Feidelson Junior looked enough like his father had looked in the late 1910s that the sight of him reduced Leon to helpless terror. Professor Feidelson, I feel sure, was never told of his effect on Leon. While Feidelson Junior was serving in the military, Feidelson Senior, long recognized as a powerful journalist, was selectively commenting in a Birmingham newspaper on Nazi Germany and ultimately on the liberation of concentration camps. A clear photograph of Feidelson Senior at work is in Dan J. Puckett's "Reporting on the Holocaust: The View from Jim Crow Alabama" (*Holocaust and Genocide Studies* 25, no. 2 [Fall 2011]: 219–51).

Beyond the scope of this inside narrative is speculation about a newspaperman's selective denial or suppression and a professor's repudiation of biographical evidence, but materials exist for a remarkable father-son exploration.

4. Feidelson was in line with some of the first founders of the New Criticism. Malcolm Bradbury in "The Telling Life" (1988) quotes, "No biographical evidence can change or influence critical evaluation" (136), from the chapter on "Literature and Biography" in René Wellek and Austin Warren's *Theory of Literature* (New York: Harcourt Brace, 1949), reprinted in paperback in 1956 and 1962. *My Flawed Texts and Verbal Icons* (1984) describes many literary works where biographical evidence (including evidence of composition and revision) absolutely invalidates some critical evaluations and suggests useful ways other evaluations might proceed. There can be no doubt, however, that many academics writing today still function under internalized formulations like this one of Wellek and Warren or similar ones by Feidelson and others. There can be no doubt, either, that Feidelson's powerful exaltation of himself and his best students as high-flying (archangelic? or merely angelic?) readers led many of those students over the next decades to express contempt for scholarship and to treat scholars not only as "earth-bound" but actually from nether regions, as when the Yale professor Richard H. Brodhead in 2002 called me a "demon researcher."

The most extreme New Critical reaction to *Flawed Texts and Verbal Icons* was Gary Davenport's in *Sewanee Review*, where he said it was a good thing I was wrong because if I were right all Western Civilization would crumble because it was built on the sanctity of texts. My arguments were "inimical to the higher values of literary culture that have survived, somehow, from the beginnings of literacy to our Age of Information" (504). At the other extreme, G. Thomas Tanselle in Bowers's *Studies in Bibliography* (1986) pronounced that the book was of only practical, not theoretical, importance (34). So much for my career as a metatextualist! In the *New York Times Book Review* (April 6, 2003) Judith Shulevitz resurrected it in "The Close Reader; Get Me Rewrite," using it to explain "why original versions often do seem so superior" (31). But more than a quarter century after its publication, after I thought it was long forgotten by all besides Shulevitz, I find that the reputation of *Flawed Texts and Verbal Icons* is high among an astonishing range of scholars, among them editors of the Bible! classicists! medievalists! Shakespeareans! musicologists! conservationists! specialists in the modern British novel! and even literary theorists. The book shows up in wholly unexpected places such *The Katrina Papers: A Journal of Trauma and Recovery* (2008) by Jerry W. Ward, Jr. After losing his library to "the Storm" a copy of *Flawed Texts and Verbal Icons* is one of the books that allows him to plan a course in "Introduction to Scholarship" (204). For Ward, he and I are "essentialists in radically different ways" (205). Of me he says (205), "As I read his critique of theory, I am amazed by similarities between his position and mine." What counts is living long enough to see manifestations of surprising afterlife for what Ward calls "already an old book if not a forgotten book or a condemned book" (204).

5. Lyndall Gordon in "The Death Mask" (1) tells of arriving at Harvard when batches of unpublished James letters still wore "their 4-year ban: 'Reserved for Mr Edel'" after the ban had been lifted. Pierre A. Walker in the *Henry James Review* (2000) tells the miserable story of Edel's hold on the James letters and his treatment of, in Edel's revealing term, "a woman named Millicent Bell" (282).

6. In "The Biographer as Archaeologist" William St Clair asks, more or less ironically (221), "What are we to make of a form of historical writing which by its nature is narrowly limited to a specific historical context, where the discovery by the biographer of some previously unnoticed letters is thought to require that the biographical

edifice previously constructed by others should have to be redesigned and rebuilt? Where the latest biographer, faced with much the same corpus of primary materials as his or her predecessors, decides that a particular event in the subject's life was far more determinative, more of a turning-point, or more telling as a vignette of the operation of character in action, than had previously been appreciated, and then goes on to construct the whole written life in a different shape?" The Augusta Papers comprise an entirely different order of archival material than St Clair envisions, one which requires the rewriting or fresh writing of dozens of episodes of Melville's life.

7. I had forsaken my thousand-dollar Osborne with its minnow-sized appetite for a $20,000 Wang in the Marine Studies department to which I had access by special permission. The word-processing program allowed me to make "super-moves"—to move a sentence, say, from one file to another! Glory be, that Wang could move a paragraph *from one chapter to another!* Nothing can dim my awe at that machine, or my gratitude for using it. Understand: I wrote my first college correspondence course papers on an all-capitals typewriter in the Kansas City Southern depot at Singer, Louisiana, in 1953.

8. In September 1986 Leyda and I were told sternly that we *had* to walk down from the eleventh floor of the New York State Library during a fire drill. I said, "Not possible," and we made friends with a great librarian, James Corsaro, as we waited for an emergency elevator that never came. Corsaro told us about Civil War papers available in Gettysburg but Leyda didn't get to see any of them.

9. Some biographers are able to avoid such labors. I marvel at the story Jeremy Lewis tells in "Pantherine" of how Barbara Skelton offered him a bargain: "She would allow me to read his [Cyril Connolly's] letters on the condition that I typed them out at the same time." Well, no: that "seemed a dotty idea"—it seemed like work, in other words (47). Luck was with Lewis: "Some time later, I was presented with a complete transcript of those troublesome letters by a mutual friend who knew how much I wanted to read them, could decipher Connolly's spidery scrawl, was a far quicker typist than I could ever be, and—miraculously—had managed to put them in some kind of order after much quizzing of postmarks and the like" (48). Oh, that William M. Murphy ("John Butler Yeats") and I could have sat together with Lewis's account, moaning and laughing and commiserating with each other as we passed it back and forth.

10. Now as this book is finished the first of three print volumes of *The New Melville Log* is in the works, thanks to the help of Robert Sandberg with layout and design.

11. Published as "Textual Criticism and Hemingway," *Hemingway: Essays of Reassessment*, ed. Frank Scafella, 17–31 (New York: Oxford University Press, 1991). In the learned and friendly Hemingway crowd were some two-fisted smokers (the most aggressive of whom is long dead from lung cancer), but toward Vandans was a green rivulet I ran along—one of the most beautiful places I have ever run.

12. Two decades and more later, the first division point is Melville's beginning to write *Redburn* in early June 1849.

13. I did not anticipate evoking so many members of Melville's family from near oblivion and bringing them into intimacy with people I thought I had known all along. In "Reassembling the Dust" Paul Mariani recalls aiming from the start to achieve such a populated book (108): "When I was younger it was Richard Ellmann's biographical example in dealing with Joyce which had held me, and I see

now that what I wanted to give American audiences in particular was a book about Williams peopled with his friends and enemies which would be a counterpart in every way except in tone to what Ellmann had offered in his homage to Joyce. I make no secrets about it. Call it hubris." As the previous paragraphs make clear, I dismiss the argument of Frederick R. Karl in *Art into Life* that "letters are notoriously *unreliable*; they are as fictional as autobiography, with which they share the subject's perception of himself. They are not history, they are not *the* truth, they are not even honest memory. They must be read as fictions of a sort, not as documents or data. . . . They must be handled not as documentation but as part of the 'fiction' the subject [the letter writer] has made of his life" (22). A few times members of the Melville family and their correspondents set out to deceive the recipients of their letters. Cousin Julia Maria Melvill was such a budding humorist and satirist that I was careful to report and not endorse what she said, and to verify when I could. In his letter of June 26, 1840, Thomas Melvill, Jr., had good reasons for misleading Lemuel Shaw on how he lost his job in Galena. Herman Melville in writing to his English publishers vacillated between absolute candor and wishful thinking. In any letter by Melville's mother I would take her word for a thousand pounds.

14. Leon Edel in "The Figure Under the Carpet" reflects on such archives as modern presidential papers: "Can a biographer afford to spend his lifetime wading through such great masses of paper, Himalayas of photographs, microfilms, kinescopes, and still emerge, if not suffocated, with any sense of a face or a personality? What comes out of these archives are books too heavy and too long" (23). That may well be, and in comparison the Augusta Papers is a small batch, yet it yielded precious evidence of human personalities day after day as I transcribed the documents. And how can a biographer discover new episodes and not tell them?

15. There is a period of days or weeks or possibly longer during which a biographer may be torn between the need to look longer at the evidence and a new, increasingly urgent need to begin making sense of it by starting to write. For me it was a period of intense anxiety. If your research has revealed new stories, the stories are not quite real until you write them down, so at some point, if the biographer's engagement with the material in the gathering phase has been prolonged and intense, the conflict between the need to keep on gathering material and the need to start writing becomes excruciating. Then the biographer has to yield, and begin writing. In Walt Whitman's "When Lilacs Last in the Dooryard Bloom'd," as early as section 9 the poet is tempted to begin to write the poem but knows he has to prolong the looking, listening, gathering phase: "I hear—I come presently—I understand you;/But a moment I linger—for the lustrous star has detain'd me;/The star, my comrade, departing, holds and detains me." In section 13 the conflict between the need to look longer and the need to sing is almost overwhelming, the star holding the poet and "the lilac with mastering odor" holding him only a little longer ("Sequel to *Drum-Taps*" [1865–66] in "The Walt Whitman Archive," ed. Ed Folsom and Kenneth M. Price, www.whitmanarchive.org). Is there anywhere a more compelling account of the tension between the urgency to get relief by writing and the necessity to hold back until the preparatory tasks are far enough along, so that the writing can be worthy? By far the best scholarly account of arousal and anxiety once one has yielded to the need to start writing is in chapter 13 of Albert Rothenberg's *The Emerging Goddess: The Creative Process in Art, Science, and Other Fields.*

In "Writing Lives" Ann Thwaite describes the phase after she has "stopped gathering material" but before she has quite "steeled" herself to write, a longish interval of "'reactivating'" during which she looks over and sorts the material she has "gathered over many years" (25). She adds, "I never write a word of the final narrative until I have stopped research" (26). Wary of her account insofar as she seems to make starting to write an overly rational process, I am relieved when she goes on to say that biographers "share with the creative writer the need for a *compulsion* to write" (27). But high psychological and physiological disturbance is lacking in her account. In "The Art of Biography," also in the *Troubled Face* collection with Thwaite's piece, Robert Blake comments (92): "A certain moment comes when one should write." Then he says (93): "It is important to bear in mind that in historical research as in other things there is a law of diminishing returns, that a moment comes when commonsense or one's 'hunch' tells one that, however much you go on you will not really do more than dot 'i's' and cross 't's'." I wonder that some biographers can write so calmly about ending the gathering phase and starting to write.

16. I never had what Graham Robb (in "A Narcissist's Wedding," 11–14) calls the "fantasy of a real relationship" with Melville, and I bridled when Philip Weiss in the *New York Times Magazine* called him my "hero." Melville never talked to me, but I talked to him very frequently, often reinforcing what his mother told him, and he never once heeded me. I *was* haunted, nights at a time, by the Melville family, particularly the women, after spending many hours transcribing their letters, listening to their voices, imagining the responses as Helen, say, read what Augusta was writing.

17. In "The Art of Biography" Robert Blake (93) quotes from Samuel Johnson's life of Alexander Pope, where Johnson explains why it took Pope so long to translate the *Iliad*: "According to this calculation, the progress of Pope may seem to have been slow; but the distance is commonly very great between actual performance and speculative possibility. It is natural to suppose, that as much as has been done to-day may be done to-morrow — but on the morrow some difficulty emerges, or some external impediment obstructs. Indolence, interruption, business, and pleasure, all take their turns of retardation; and every long work is lengthened by a thousand causes that can, and ten thousand that cannot, be recounted. Perhaps no extensive and multifarious performance was ever effected within the term originally fixed in the undertaker's mind. He that runs against Time, has an antagonist not subject to casualties." I think Johnson would have approved the way I described Melville's work on *Clarel* across four chapters (with an interrupting chapter in the middle), mixing narrative of family life with description of likely progress on the poem.

18. Have any biographers been able blithely to juggle all the normal professional obligations even while dedicating themselves to an intimidating project that turns out to be all but overwhelming? I needed time off, but I received only two routine half sabbaticals, such as every professor received, regardless of how much or how little he or she had published. The rest of the time, I taught my usual load with, I swear, at least my usual measure of passion. At the start of my work on the biography, I carried on my usual professional life — long enough to write the eulogy for Merton M. Sealts, Jr., and present the Hubbell Medal to him at the American Literature Section luncheon, at the New York City MLA, 1992. As early as 1990 I had begun retrenching. I never attended another Melville Society meeting except the one in Cancun. I announced in Toronto in 1993 that attending MLA had become an

ethical issue, and after 1993 I dropped my membership. Smoke-filled meetings filled with old New Critics and new New Historicists were easy enough to avoid. Giving up membership on editorial boards was harder, but I did resign from them, even my beloved *Nineteenth-Century Literature*. After reviewing books in *Nineteenth-Century Literature*, *Resources for American Literary Study*, *D. H. Lawrence Review*, and *Modern Language Quarterly*, I stopped short: I could not write reviews and write a biography.

I kept giving talks for several years. In 1988 talked at CUNY, at Providence, and at Schruns on Hemingway. With Harrison Hayford I made a three-week tour of Japanese colleges and universities in October 1989, giving six talks, then talked on textual theory, jet-lagged, in Washington, D.C. In 1990 I talked in Albuquerque and twice at the Chicago MLA. In 1991 I talked at Fairhaven; at Morris Library of the University of Delaware; in New York on Henry James; and took part in a "Panel on Melville Biography" at the Melville Society Centenary Meeting in Pittsfield, 1991. In 1992 I talked in Buffalo; Clemson, S.C.; talked along with Maurice Sendak at the Berkshire County Historical Society; talked in the Great Hall of the Nantucket Athenaeum; and in New York City. In 1993 I talked in Philadelphia and in Toronto. I talked at Salisbury, Maryland, in 1993; at State College, Pennsylvania; at the University of Delaware Library again. In 1994 I talked again at Salisbury State University and at the University of Delaware Library. In 1995 I gave a joint lecture with Maurice Sendak at the Philadelphia Academy of Vocal Arts; and talked on Stephen Crane at the USAF Academy, Colorado Springs. In 1996 I gave a big talk at the 92nd Street Y Unterberg Poetry Center and later another in Toronto, at the publication of the first volume of my biography.

I had committed myself to many projects before undertaking the biography and taking over *The New Melville Log*. Any academic who writes a biography can tell you about a downside to focusing your efforts on one project: you don't get raises without regular publications. Unless you publish sections of your biography piecemeal, you don't get credit even if you have drafted several hundred pages in a given year. If you publish your biography piecemeal, or talk about it too much, you risk getting scooped. And of course when you do publish your biography you get (if you are lucky) credit for one book, that one year, and it will weigh equally with a colleague's new book on symbolism in James's "The Pupil." As a matter of self-preservation I met my old commitments, albeit slowly. I published *Reading "Billy Budd"* (1990; my first copy was January 1991); the *Checklist of Melville Reviews*, by Kevin J. Hayes and Hershel Parker (1991); *Critical Essays on Herman Melville's "Moby-Dick,"* edited by Brian Higgins and Hershel Parker (1992). Four volumes in the Northwestern-Newberry Edition appeared: *Moby-Dick* (1988); *Journals* (1989); *Clarel* (1991); and *Correspondence* (1993). My contribution to the *Moby-Dick* "Historical Note" was monograph length, and I wrote a long "Historical Supplement" for *Clarel*. I edited my 1820–65 section of the third edition of *The Norton Anthology of American Literature* (1989). I wrote for *Review* (1988); *Melville Society Extracts* (November 1988); for *College Literature* (1990); for *American Literature* (1990 — on *The Isle of the Cross*); for *Modern Language Studies* (1990); again for *Melville Society Extracts* (1990); for *Documentary Editing* (1990); for *Hemingway: Essays of Reassessment* (1991); for *American History Illustrated* 26 (1991); for *College Literature* (1991); for *Editors' Notes* (1991, an essay suppressed for several years because it exposed Bowers as having chosen the wrong copy-text for William James's *Pragmatism*); an essay for *Critical Essays on Herman Melville's "Moby-Dick"* (1992); for *Analytical & Enumerative Bibliography* (1992, a note correcting a false statement by Bowers and advertising the essay on Stephen Crane's *Maggie* suppressed for two decades); an article for *Suicidology: Essays in Honor of Edwin S. Shneidman* (1993); for *Melville Society Extracts* (1993); for the *Henry James Review* (1993); for *Profils américains* (1993).

I did the fourth edition of *The Norton Anthology of American Literature* (1994), writing a new author headnote for Emily Dickinson and including for the first time in any anthology Whitman's first group of homosexual poems, "Live Oak, with Moss," treating it frankly as a gay manifesto, and published an article on it in *Nineteenth-Century Literature*. Anthologizing the sequence where thousands could read it every year was the single most important thing I ever did in my career, being confident that it has saved lives. The article on James's prefaces was so important to me that I put it (and the article on "Live Oak, with Moss") ahead of the first volume of the biography. So far, the strongest admirer of the James essay has been the novelist David Morrell, who found it interesting, informative, and ennobling. It is neglected, even in uncritical reprintings of R. P. Blackmur's edition of *The Art of the Novel* where no thought is given to the order in which James wrote the prefaces, but it's in print and in the best journal it could be in. I would not risk dying before I published those two pieces: that's how I thought about them. "The Flawed Grandeur of Melville's *Pierre*" was reprinted in *Herman Melville: A Collection of Critical Essays* (1994). I published in *Melville Society Extracts* (1994); *Resources for American Literary Study* (1995); published *Herman Melville: The Contemporary Reviews*, edited by Brian Higgins and Hershel Parker (1995); in *Melville Society Extracts* (1995); *Pierre: or, The Ambiguities*, edited by Hershel Parker, pictures by Maurice Sendak (1995); in *Bulletin of the Bibliographical Society of Australia and New Zealand* (1995—the essay on Bowers's *Maggie*, bravely printed at last); in *Studies in the Novel* (1995); in *Critical Essays on William Faulkner: The Sutpen Family* (1996); and in *Sut Lovingood's Nat'ral Born Yarnspinner: Essays on George Washington Harris* (1996). The first volume of my biography, *Herman Melville: A Biography, 1819–1851*, came out in October 1996. After that I retrenched still further, focusing on the second volume and other books that were not complete. Other academic biographers must have comparable stories of being torn between retrenching in order to focus on the biography and the need to produce tangible (published) evidence of scholarly and critical activity. You don't make up an unusually small annual raise—as part of your base salary on which percentage raises are figured it is the department's gift that goes on taking away.

19. In July 1990 Brian Higgins warned in *American Literary Scholarship* (55) that Neal Tolchin's transcriptions from family letters in *Mourning, Gender, and Creativity in the Art of Herman Melville* were not to be trusted, citing me for his authority specifying a particularly disastrous misreading of a letter Melville's mother wrote in February 1846. In December 1990 the Melville Society meeting was packed with new New Historicists, second-generation New Leftists (who had fervor but less purpose than the first), and a large group of second- and third-generation New Critics who had never done archival research and had certainly not been taught to do responsible research. I misread the atmosphere in the room as one of free-floating political correctness, not sharply focused, but the mood of the audience was hostile from the start. When Wai-chee Dimock resurrected Lewis Mumford's long-refuted

claim that Hawthorne had based Ethan Brand on Melville (before he met him or read anything but *Typee*), Hayford mildly reproved her, saying that if she thought it was acceptable to bring forth the Ethan Brand claim as a serious possibility, she was using a different standard for evidence than he used. At that, there was a subterranean murmur of anger in the audience like the incipient rebellion in *Billy Budd*, the mood hardening into fury that anyone's idea could be considered invalid on grounds of biographical evidence. In the new post-scholarly climate to point out errors was to violate the playground rules: one should always enhance one's playmate's self-esteem. The audience was further incited when an onlooker described by Robert K. Wallace in *Melville and Turner* (611) as "the petulant stranger in the doorway" kept crying out, with regard to Melville and history, 'THE FACTS DON'T MATTER.'" Accepting reality, I never attended another Melville Society meeting in the United States, although I went in 1997 to Cancun so we could climb the pyramids at Chichen Itza. Partly because of the hostile takeover of the Melville Society, I decided, as I said from the platform of a program on F. Scott Fitzgerald in Toronto in 1993, that attending the annual Modern Language Association convention had become a moral issue. The issue was settled right after that meeting when a Melvillean some years my senior proposed that we adjourn to his hotel room where we could "strip to the waist" and I could "go at him one to one" over *Tender Is the Night*.

20. In "Mather, Poe, Houdini," Kenneth Silverman says eloquently: "Secondary characters should be brought no less physically alive. In some biographies, the subject's friends and acquaintances exist as names instead of presences. But to serve dramatically, the attendants too need dirty fingernails, whispery voices, and bulging pockets, individualizing features that hard digging usually turns up" (112). In the Augusta Papers Melville's sister Fanny's essay on an assigned topic, a portrait of herself, gave me sufficient insight; without it I would have been helpless. I knew already that Hoadley, hard of hearing, leaned forward to speak to anyone. The clipping described Kate's obsessive compulsion that the corners of a tablecloth be just so. I already knew from Eleanor Melville Metcalf's 1953 book (28) that Kate was of "an anxious make," but this was deeper and darker.

21. In "Reassembling the Dust" Paul Mariani asks (109) how the biographer is to transfer all his notes "into a readable narrative which shall do justice to the subject? What tone shall he or she take toward the material, what distance assume in relation to the subject, what language employ?" Having risked being honest in the last line of the first volume ("Take it all in all, this was the happiest day of Melville's life"), for the second volume I had to find a tone humanly decent enough, pleasant enough without being egregiously chipper, to carry me and the reader through four decades spotted with previously unrevealed agonies. Tony Kushner in an interview with Frederick Tuten made it clear that he understood, and the late Allan Casson, a colleague from the University of Southern California, wrote me: "I enjoyed and admired your Melville biography. It's a magnificent work—though perhaps the most heartbreaking biography I've ever read."

22. I sympathize with Robert Skidelsky in "Confessions of a Long-Distance Biographer": "My original 1970 contract with Macmillan publishers was to write a single-volume 150,000-word biography to be delivered 'not later than 31 December 1972'. This must rank high in the annals of contractual fantasy" (15).

23. See my *Melville: The Making of the Poet* (159).

24. With Sealts and Hayford unable to comment on what I was writing, Maurice Sendak was the one who encouraged me, as on April 25, 2000: "He had read 1st 5 chapters & was full of praise—chewy—tone tougher than V1, strength, purpose—'bloody story [but you are going to] hear it my way'—wonderful—speed is different—moving like a great ice floe—e/t more threatening. Not depressing book but a frightening book. [In his picture for cover he] may give HM look of inexpressible pain—stunned—can't even blink.' And Sendak was appreciative of [my memo,] 'How I Taught Song of Myself.' So, great encouragement from Maurice."

25. Dexter Filkins, "Ailing Churchill Biographer Says He Can't Finish Trilogy" (*New York Times*, August 14, 2001): "Felled by two strokes after the death of his wife in 1998, Mr. Manchester, who is 79, says he has tried several times to kick-start the writing of the final Churchill book, of which he has completed 237 pages. He is skeptical of his publisher's suggestion that he finish the book with a collaborator, and he says he has finally surrendered to the conclusion that his body is too feeble and his mind too diminished to carry on with the project" (C1). "He says his memory is no longer the vast storehouse that it once was. And he says he can no longer summon the energy, mental or physical, to engage in the . . . strenuous activity of writing" (C17).

Chapter 5

1. In "The Art of Biography," Robert Blake comments on the sort of Victorian biography in which the writers tried "to make the facts speak for themselves, or to tell itself without the interpolation of the author." No, he says: "In reality the facts do not speak for themselves. A biographer who tries to avoid interpreting them is abdicating from his central task. It may be difficult to make such an interpretation. It may be the case that two (or even more) interpretations are possible. What is sure to kill a biography is to make no interpretation at all" (77). In *Writing Lives Is the Devil!* (1993), Gale E. Christianson scoffs at any biographer who would claim that the characters in the narrative " 'have been allowed to speak for themselves' ": "Someone, presumably the author, decided which lines to quote or to omit, which gestures to play up or to play down, which descriptive details to retain or to cut" (14). Equally blunt is Robert D. Hume in "The Aims and Limits of Historical Scholarship": "Facts do not speak for themselves: the historian not only collects and selects facts but interprets them" (405). In that essay all of Hume's section on "Problems of Evidence and the Interpretation of 'Facts' " (405–10) is relevant to this chapter.

2. Oddly, the legend has been retold as unhistorical fantasy in Brenda Wineapple's *Hawthorne: A Life*: "The date was set for Monday, August 5, a day soon to be promoted as an American *Déjeuner sur l'Herbe* (without the scandal): Hawthorne, fully clothed, pursues the Great Carbuncle while Herman Melville, Mr. Neptune, rapturously pursues Mr. Noble Melancholy. It's a good story" (222). But Wineapple tells an inaccurate story, beginning with the word "soon."

3. Many times a biographer will echo Sergeant Cuff in Wilkie Collins's *The Moonstone*: "In all my experience along the dirtiest ways of this dirty little world I have never met with such a thing as a trifle yet" (New York and London: Harper and Brothers, 1874), 114.

4. I discussed my correction to "wildly" in "Melville and Hawthorne in the Berkshires," in *Aspects of Melville*, ed. David Scribner (Pittsfield: Berkshire County Historical Society at Arrowhead, 2001), 24.

5. A classic analysis of this topic is J. A. Downie's 2007 "Marlowe, May 1583, and the 'Must-Have' Theory of Biography," *Review of English Studies*, n.s. 58, no. 235 (June 2007): 245–67.

6. I sent Philip Young printouts because I had heard him talk about Hemingway once long before and knew that he had a voice of his own. He was a professor but nevertheless alive, as so few professors are. There is more to the story. Asked to read Young's posthumous *The Private Melville* before its publication, I saw that the juvenile copy editor had systematically, I thought ruthlessly, eliminated everything free, dashing, and personal about the style, everything that made Phil Young unique. After I alerted the director of the press, Katherine Young restored her husband's prose. For the dust jacket I wrote a careful blurb: "*The Private Melville* is personal, even private (as the topic mandates), and idiosyncratic; it is opinionated and provocative. It contains no trace of fashionable jargon: where are the *Poetics of Privacy*? Instead, it proceeds from manuscript evidence and from texts of literary works. Young addresses a broad audience that will be eager to follow the seemingly random, indirect probings of a fine intellect in intense pursuit of disparate phases of Melvillean experience." Hayford never quite got over being annoyed with me for seeming to egg Young on by giving him my transcriptions of those letters and for writing this blurb, no matter that I left open whether the "intense pursuit" was successful or not. Young's chapter "The Last Good-Bye: 'Daniel Orme'" was the weakest: "'Daniel, or me' is a rude offense against a writer who was clever with puns" (155). Not until 2002 did I discover, by reading a gift from Mark Wojnar, Colin White's *The Nelson Companion* (Bridgend: Bramley Books, 1997), that Melville knew famous images of Lord Nelson by the engraver Daniel Orme.

Ah, in my copy of *The Private Melville*, a grateful note from Phil Young starting, "You are a prince." I don't regret writing the blurb for *The Private Melville*.

7. In making this book *An Inside Narrative* I draw on my diaries and other personal documents more than letters to me from scholars and critics. Clare L. Spark in *Hunting Captain Ahab* (2001) has published masses of behind-the-scenes correspondence among Melvilleans, and Hayford includes some in his very long *tour de force*, "Melville's Imaginary Sister," published posthumously in *Melville's Prisoners* (2003), 132–83.

8. Garner, "The Picaresque Career of Thomas Melvill, Junior: Part II" (8). Good researchers sooner or later experience the high excitement of discovering unknown episodes of their subject's lives. That excitement does not necessarily make the biographers the best narrators of what they discover, although it does almost guarantee that they will make a more comprehensive and sensitive narrator than anyone else could do, at least in the first telling. Stanton Garner told a good story about Uncle Thomas's being caught stealing in the store in Galena while Melville was in the Pacific. I told a truer story, and one directly involving Melville, since I had discovered that the theft and the firing had occurred shortly before Melville showed up unannounced in Galena. (I say "unannounced" confidently not just because I remember how young men behave but because Herman is not mentioned in his uncle's letters to Lemuel Shaw of late June and early July 1840, the last dated just before Herman must have arrived.) When I wrote the episode I was in a wrought-up state because for many months I alone had known and sympathized with *what I foresaw* would be Melville's disappointment at finding his uncle jobless and unable to help him.

(That sounds peculiar but you can know you are going to have to describe something previously unknown but not focus on it in acute pain until you actually describe it.) Ishmael understood about foreseeing what he would achieve: "Oh, Ahab! what *shall be grand in thee*, it must needs be plucked at from the skies, and dived for in the deep, and featured in the unbodied air" (chap. 33, my italics). The first teller of a new story gets the privilege of choosing, but to a great degree the manner of telling should be controlled by the amount and the nature of the documentary evidence available. I see now that I chose to tell this story about Galena pretty baldly despite my strong emotions, perhaps *because* I was leery of over-coloring the story with my emotions. Garner, as I show elsewhere, behaved just the way a fine scholar should behave upon being corrected.

9. A sidelight on method: how was I to avoid writing parts of my biography from Melville's more or less autobiographical books? I resolved on extreme measures. I set myself the goal of creating a full draft of the part of 1842 which Melville described in *Typee* and *Omoo* by working solely from other surviving documents (some authentic, some plainly skewed), never quoting those two books. A 1976 discovery by Rita K. Gollin helped, and I had a valuable typescript from Wilson Heflin that I much later handed over to Mary K. Bercaw Edwards and Thomas Farel Heffernan for their edition of Heflin's masterpiece (2004). That salutary exercise helped me break the 1920s reliance on Melville's books as straight biography. Breaking that reliance, I emphasize, requires heroic discipline, and disciplined judgment of another sort is required in acknowledging that *Typee* and others of Melville's books are in fact, in passages, something like straight autobiography. I guessed right about Melville's teaching school after he got home from Galena just because I allowed for the possibility that something in "Loomings" could be straight (or something very close to straight) autobiography. You have to be imaginative, alert, subtle, and supplied with a kit of phrases like "as far as we know" and "it just might be" or my offhand favorite, "for all we know."

10. It is astonishing how many times reviewers expose themselves as having absolutely no sensitivity to tone and absolutely no sense of humor about such evidence as laundry lists and shopping lists; just possibly, they check their sense of tone and humor at the door of the solemn archives along with their cupcakes and ballpoint pens. Laundry lists can be telling and shopping lists can be charming.

11. Other critics plume themselves on their superiority by accusing a biographer of inventing an episode (such as Melville's completion of *Poems* in 1860) for which there had long been a mass of documentation. Who is to challenge the reviewers hired as Melville experts by the *New York Times* or the *New Republic*? A critic decried my citing the poetic meter and some of the subject matter of *Snow-Bound* as a likely influence on *Clarel*. Where, he demanded, was the documentary proof that Melville ever heard of *Snow-Bound*? Sometimes you have to assume that writers are human beings like the rest of us: a New York City poet publishing a book of poetry in 1866 *will* read the most famous poem published in the country in that very year, 1866. I had collected three dozen reviews of the poem, mainly from New York City papers and magazines available to Melville, and offered to show them to the critic. He retorted sadly and more than a little smugly that I had just revealed how lax my standards of evidence were. Such high-minded critics will insist that I wait until we have a letter in which Kate Gansevoort Lansing bemoans Herman's reading aloud

from the *New York World* a tedious passage from *Snow-Bound* on the crazy Queen of Lebanon.

Chapter 6

1. In the editors' preface to the posthumous publication of Wilson Heflin's *Herman Melville's Whaling Years*, Thomas Farel Heffernan explained the shock both men felt: "'We almost had a fist fight over it,' Heflin said" (xv).

2. A problem for me as a biographer was that Melville, unlike me, *did* tell sexual stories, and to this hour I cannot determine what language he would use, say among male literary friends in New York City. I simply cannot tell how explicit he could be in entertaining the pious Evert Duyckinck with stories of Hawaii or years later with recounting the goings-on in Sing Sing, that "orgie of indecency and blasphemy" (*Log*, 523). I have no way of knowing how he adapted his stories to various male audiences. What stories did he tell when he was warmed-up at Dr. Francis's on a Sunday evening, "capitally racy and pungent" (as discussed later in this chapter)? And what sort of vocabulary did he use? There ought to be records in extant diaries and letters.

Chances are that Melville's stories were always told with great masculine gusto, if we read backward from the one specific witness we have, the Houghton Mifflin editor Ferris Greenslet, who wrote to Willard Thorp on November 22, 1946, about his encounter with Melville in a barbershop in Glens Falls in 1885 or 1886. There the barber, familiar with Melville, drew him out by asking about "girls" in the South Sea island (Parker, 2:890):

"'My God!' said the whiskerando, 'I'll say there were! I went back to the island a couple of years after I left there on board a man-of-war and the first thing I saw when I went ashore was my own little son about a year and a half old running around naked in the sun on the beach.'

"'How did you know it was your son?' asked the barber.

"'He had to be,' said the story teller. 'He carried his bowsprit to starboard!'"

To explicate the story is to wax laborious and stupid, because the point is that in a real narrative of the South Seas the boy would have been naked, not in pantaloons, whether with his bowsprit dressed to starboard or larboard. The bragging old man exposes himself as a great tease, undercutting his entire story as the auditors realize that the "son" would not have worn tailor-made pantaloons in which his genitals were pushed to the same side, presumably, as Melville's own, the right side. Even earlier than *Typee* and all through his life Melville liked to tease his auditors. He stirred up sexual feelings in many of his readers, some of whom by their own words are convicted of being randy and strutting. But did he, early in his life, employ comical euphemisms such as the aptly nautical "bowsprit" he used in the boy's hearing at Glens Falls? That's racy and pungent enough without being crude.

3. Letter in the New York Public Library, Gansevoort-Lansing Additions.

4. The recent discovery of these leaves from the first draft of *Typee* presented a problem for me. Plainly I had to treat them in some detail, even though nowhere else in the first volume was I dealing with such evidence. In the chapter "The Sailor at the Writing-Desk: 1844–1845" I tried to make sparkling narrative out of a highly detailed description of Melville at work on the surviving draft leaves and presumably the rest of the draft. I see some provocative sentences in that chapter: "As he wrote the draft, Melville was forced to grapple with some basic problems in narratology. . . .

To judge from the discrepancies between the draft pages and the printed book, Melville's most pressing difficulty had nothing to do with how to construct a narrative and get it down on paper in an intelligible way. His problem was how to present himself as author in proper relationship to his presumed readers" (1:362). One biographer who understands this difficulty of making narrative from unlikely material is Kenneth Silverman in "Mather, Poe, Houdini": "The works to be discussed can be not only so many but also so complex that interpretation displaces the narrative by overwhelming it" (109). Silverman happily reveals his strategy for writing about Poe's "The Poetic Principle": "The important essay demanded discussion, yet that meant rupturing a thirty-page narrative of the main romantic affair in his [Poe's] life. I took advantage of the fact that he gave 'The Poetic Principle' as a lecture, with [Sarah Helen] Whitman seated before him in the audience. In a few hybrid paragraphs that mix exposition and narration I tried to present the essay as at once something Poe wrote and something he did." This he calls, with evident relief and pride, an example of a work "smuggled into the flow of the writer's life by making exposition simulate narrative" (109).

5. Academics can be so learned that they overlook the obvious. Hennig Cohen in his erudite article " 'Why Talk of Jaffa'?: Melville's *Israel Potter*, Baron Gros, Zummo, and the Plague" fails to consider Melville's experience of epidemics in the United States.

6. "Herman Melville, 1972," 166. Leyda's point with the odd wording was that the tooth was there for anyone to see. I was the one who happened to see it among the Revolutionary carriages and then told him about it.

7. How often do biographers and other researchers discover something important while looking for something else? Dennis Marnon in an e-mail on June 11, 2011, described how he located A. A. Hayes's report of W. Clark Russell's praise of Melville which had been misdated in the *Log* (784) and assigned to the wrong newspaper: "I was searching for something else and saw those oddly configured three asterisks separating brief chat-type items, and then all that was left was slogging through the individual issues." An ironical phrase like Marnon's "all that was left," of course, may cover hours of slogging. Why did Steven Olsen-Smith and Todd Richardson spend many hours looking in the *New York World* for a little notice by Melville? A cynic would say the reason is that the job of looking through many years of a newspaper is, after all, finite, but scholars know that the reason is simply that we need to know.

8. My cautious wording about Google (giving the date I searched) reflects my failure now and then to find something which I had readily found earlier: not everything on Google stays on Google, although we assume it does. With only the clues from the words in the last chapter of *The Confidence-Man* (Napoleon, outlined, tree) I instantly found the "hidden art" engraving of the ghost of Napoleon gazing at his tomb in St. Helena's. The next day I couldn't, and was happy I had recorded the title and year of the engraving. Catch when you can.

9. "A Novelist in the Custom House," *San Francisco Bulletin*, July 17, 1879; "President Arthur: What George Alfred Townsend Thinks of Him," *Helena (Mont.) Independent*, October 7, 1881.

10. Much later, Elizabeth Hardwick and Andrew Delbanco acquired some of the same disdain—perplexing because it has so little basis. Are they fixated on Hawthorne's notebook observation on November 11, 1856 (*Log*, 528), about Melville's

· short supply of underwear while traveling, his being "a little heterodox in the matter of clean linen"?

11. Paul Murray Kendall in his *The Art of Biography* (1965) best understands my frustration: "An apparently documented fact collided head-on with my concept of Warwick himself and of his friend Louis XI of France, the famous 'spider King'" (10). The information "was false alike to the character of Warwick . . . and to the character of King Louis. . . . One document, a very solid-seeming document, was forcing the two men to behave as if they had fallen into trauma and lost their identities. The truth of fact simply did not square with psychological truth, as I saw it. Since I could neither accept nor ignore the former, I could only desperately scrabble for evidences to undermine it." At last, Kendall "dug out a series of counterfacts" (11) and congratulated himself. In "Shaping the Truth" Miranda Seymour says of a somewhat more serious offense, "I can't let myself off the hook" (257). That's how I feel.

Introduction to Part II

1. As it turned out, for Emerson and Thoreau, in particular, great discoveries came not in new caches of letters and other documents so much as in intensive study of documents long housed in libraries. In the 1960s a band of scholars studying Emerson's journals and notebooks was able to show for the first time what went into the creation of great essays like "Experience." Their archival work proved unexpectedly controversial, for in 1968 the fledgling *New York Review of Books* assigned Lewis Mumford, the author of the 1929 critical biography of Melville, space for a ferocious attack on "Emerson and the Pedants" (according to the cover) or "Emerson Behind Barbed Wire" (3). What offended him were the elaborate symbols used to guide the reader through the stages of composition. Thereafter critics of Emerson's creative processes and stylistic development were slow to use the new treasures laid at their feet.

2. Frances Wilson, Claire Tomalin, and Jane Ridley will sympathize when I confess that, initially baffled by the reduplicative name of the rival in the front row of my lectures, on the analogy of Kory-Kory in *Typee* I began to think of the note-taker as "Lory-Lory." In "A Love Triangle" (2004) Frances Wilson describes the horror of discovering that she had not one but two rivals working on Harriette Wilson: "Every biographer has a tale to tell about being haunted by a rival. But if one rival gives the effect a turn of the screw, what do you say to *two* rivals?" (38–39). Then the tables turn. On a new book, *she* becomes the Rival, and the Other Biographer warns her off: "She asked me not to ruin her life" (41). (In the same letter [at UCLA] in which he sent a small check Henry A. Murray lamented to Jay Leyda that Leyda had destroyed his hopes of writing a biography of Melville. A *four-aspirin* headache after reading that, in the 1970s, I noted in my diary. Murray left sufficient evidence that he had minimal competence with handling documentary evidence.) Claire Tomalin in "Starting Over" records her "rather nasty shock" at learning of a rival book on Pepys (90). Jane Ridley in "Tarts" recalls her "publishing race with the prolific American biographer Stanley Weintraub" (188); "prolific" of course means *fast*—faster than the complex story deserved to be packaged up for sale. When biographers talk about "rivals" nothing quite compares with Mark Holloway's discovery of "six rivals, only two of whom were potentially dangerous" ("Norman Douglas," 97).

A longtime archival researcher becomes downright petty: did I really want to talk about Melville's last meeting with Hawthorne in the Berkshires with a still-youthful, still-energetic rival in the front row, taking notes? Was it really fair that she had access to everything I had ever published? Of course it was fair, but feelings can get hurt. I cited *Correspondence* (379) for a letter Ruth Blair had found so recently that her article was still forthcoming when the Northwestern-Newberry note was written. That seemed iffy, but, after all, any letter found ten years before would have been in the volume, and I would have cited only *Correspondence* without a second thought. *Finders are not keepers*, unless they sit on their discoveries, but I wish I had cited Ruth Blair, her discovery was so new.

Chapter 7

1. In an endnote attached to this sentence Grenberg refers to me: "A definitive apologia for biographical-historical-textual criticism is found in Hershel Parker, *Flawed Texts and Verbal Icons* . . . . I simply do not share Parker's absolute faith in biographical-historical 'facts'—which in my view are as 'flawed,' partial, and subject to question and ambiguity as the flawed literary texts he rightfully abhors" (215). If I quite understood what Grenberg was not quite saying I would probably disagree with it.

2. Perhaps Brodhead remembered that footnote in my 1984 *Flawed Texts and Verbal Icons* protesting against his breezy good cheer that Melville had written more and still more additions to *Pierre*—prose on which he could practice his formulaic New Criticism (28–29 n. 17). My diary for the 1991 conference says harshly "idiotic Brodhead" out of context. We must have met, for in a photograph of me and Sendak I see him standing off to the side. Surely I was too polite to remind him that he had been blind to human agony in what he said of *Pierre*.

3. Four years later, in 2006, it was astonishing how many people, starting with Duke University lacrosse players, the lacrosse coach and his family, and parents of lacrosse players at Duke, said just what I had said in 1984, almost as if character that revealed itself in one's literary criticism could really carry over into a person's behavior in real life. I refer to one of the ugliest episodes in the history of any American university. A corrupt district attorney (subsequently disbarred) for political gain charged three innocent Duke students, members of the lacrosse team, with raping and sodomizing a black stripper. Of the books published so far on this upside-down Scottsboro case, the best is Stuart Taylor, Jr., and KC Johnson's 2007 *Until Proven Innocent: Political Correctness and the Shameful Injustices of the Duke Lacrosse Rape Case*. There was no rape, only a trumped-up rape case that could have sent three (or more) young men to jail for thirty years. As Taylor and Johnson's subtitle says, the most vocal professors at Duke responded to the accusations in a frenzy of political correctness which targeted all members of the lacrosse team. A group of professors, soon dubbed the Group of 88 or Gang of 88, issued a full-page ad in the Duke *Chronicle* now commonly referred to as the "Listening Statement." It was designed to turn "up the volume" of accusations against the already endangered lacrosse players.

One of the signers, Cathy Davidson, on January 5, 2007, in the *Durham News & Observer* performed a dazzling deconstruction of the "Listening Statement." Taylor and Johnson were stunned by this literary hocus-pocus, for Davidson "contended that, before the ad appeared, 'many black students at Duke disappeared into humiliation and rage as the lacrosse players were being elevated to the status of martyrs, innocent victims of reverse racism.' This Orwellian exercise in lying or lunacy—it was hard to be sure which predominated—turned history on its head. In fact, the lacrosse players had been viciously savaged during that period and for weeks thereafter by the likes of Cathy Davidson on campus and by the media across the country. The protesters to whom the Group of 88 ad had said thank you held signs reading CASTRATE; SUNDAY MORNING; TIME TO CONFESS; and REAL MEN DON'T DEFEND RAPISTS" (325). As all this unfolded I remembered March 1994 when I first held Davidson's special "New Melville" issue of *American Literature:* "Consternation, loss of breath . . . . Intense pain, shame, rage. The most vicious personal attack ever to appear in *AL* without doubt." Nine months after the "Listening Statement" Davidson had "turned history on its head." Well, her politically correct "New Melville" had turned Melville scholarship on its head: how could I forget the thunderous announcement in 1994 that we already had "full-scale biographies of Melville"? Her "New Melville" issue of 1994 had dehumanized me, just as in 2002 Brodhead had dehumanized me as a demonic researcher. One of the Group of 88, Houston Baker, literally dehumanized the Duke lacrosse players. In an e-mail to Patricia Dowd, the mother of a member of the lacrosse team who was frantic about the threats against her son, Baker savagely told her that the lacrosse players lived like a bunch of "farm animals" and declared that Dowd herself was the "mother of a 'farm animal'" (Stuart and Johnson, 106). In "Selective Moral Disengagement in the Exercise of Moral Agency," Albert Bandura is clear on the psychological consequence of gang attacks on a victim either when all attack as a mob or when the attacks are spaced out: "Combining diffused responsibility with dehumanization greatly escalates the level of punitiveness" (109). In the lacrosse case as with several of my reviewers, even though we are dealing with university professors we cannot modify Bandura's word "greatly" to read "subtly": nothing was restrained about the pronouncements and actions of the Group of 88.

As I had so presciently said in 1984, Brodhead had been blind to human agony in his 1976 book and was still selectively blind to human agony in 2006 as president of Duke University. At his meeting with the lacrosse captains his concern seemed to be for himself, the lawyer Robert Ekstrand told Stuart and Johnson: "Brodhead's eyes filled with tears. He said that the captains should think of how difficult it had been for him. They needed to be held accountable for their actions, which had put him in a terrible situation. Ekstrand felt his blood starting to boil. Here, he thought, is a comfortable university professor wallowing in self-pity in front of four students who are in grave danger of being falsely indicted on charges of gang rape, punishable by decades in prison" (92). "Confronted with a crisis of epic proportions, with Duke's hard-won reputation at risk," Stuart and Johnson say (137), Brodhead "faced his ultimate test of courage. And in an extraordinary moral meltdown, he threw in his lot with the mob." He fired the altogether admirable coach Michael Pressler and canceled the lacrosse season. "Let them lay by their helmets," did Brodhead say to himself, reveling in the chance to play another Richard? Brodhead's condemnations of the men's lacrosse team ("Whatever they did is bad enough"—Stuart and Johnson, 190) and his subsequent post-settlement slurs against Coach Michael Pressler (which resulted in payment of damages) are well known. "The facts kept changing," Brodhead said to Ed Bradley on *60 Minutes* (October 15, 2006), excusing himself for not defending the lacrosse players. Here he revealed a New Critical view of "facts" as insubstantial, irrelevant, not real, precisely Charles Feidelson's attitude in his review of *The Melville Log*. The facts had not changed: Brodhead had refused to look at exculpatory facts. Sometimes you pay when you dehumanize others. Duke has paid out tens of millions because the administration did not act with concern for its students, but the story goes on. In the law's long delay the discovery process is under way in 2012 in two lawsuits against Brodhead stemming from his behavior toward the lacrosse players, one for "constructive fraud" and one for "obstruction of justice."

The definition of "constructive fraud" would be relevant to literary reviewing if only a reviewer were expected under law to reveal his or her incompetence to pronounce judgment on the book being reviewed. Constructive knowledge is information that a person is presumed by law to have, regardless of whether he or she actually does, when such knowledge is obtainable by the exercise of reasonable care. By extension, a reviewer of a major biography in the *New York Times* would be presumed to have such knowledge as is obtainable by the exercise of reasonable care in reading the book being reviewed even if the reviewer had not known about such things before accepting the job and taking pay for reviewing a book. By this definition Richard H. Brodhead had constructive knowledge of the facts which he then misrepresented since he did not acknowledge the evidence on the pages presumably open before him in my biography before saying that I alone surmised that Melville finished a book called *Poems* in 1860. A dean at Yale represents himself to the *New York Times* as being competent to review a biography based on archival research. When he is not so competent or else deceitfully behaves as if he were incompetent, that dean at Yale is breaching the newspaper's trust and confidence in him by failing to do his duty to write a competent review. You are guilty of constructive fraud if you gain an unfair advantage over another as in damaging his reputation by deceitful or unfair methods. Is there not a connection between Brodhead's behavior toward his duty as a book reviewer and his behavior toward his duty to students when he was president at Duke? Would that reviewers could legally be held to standards that presidents of universities can be held to!

4. I quote Rollyson's comments in chapter 9. In "Reassembling the Dust" (1986) Paul Mariani quotes Leon Edel's protest in "The Figure Under the Carpet" against reviewers who "fall into the easy trap of writing pieces about the life that was lived, when their business is to discuss how the life was told." Mariani has ironical fun with what he learned from the reviews of his biography of William Carlos Williams: "It is as though, in the case of biography, the reader somehow believed that the life the biographer has assembled for us existed prior to the writing itself" (104). Of course the reviewer knew all along the account which he or she inaccurately purveys at length in the review.

5. Weiss began his "Herman-Neutics" this way (60): "Hershel Parker, a professor of English at the University of Delaware, is the dean of Melville scholars, legendary for his staggering precision and his devotion to his hero. For years, he has woken up in the middle of the night to put in extra hours deciphering the author's letters." Well, Melville was not my hero; most of the letters were by members of Melville's family, not Melville himself; and Hayford would not have liked being shunted away from his deanship. Weiss continued: "I first met Parker in March, at a biographer's brunch at the Unterberg Poetry Center of the 92d Street Y. He is a tall, handsome man of 61, with a raw-boned face and a shock of white hair. He wore a sling on his right arm because of a rotator cuff injury—like the object of his obsession, Parker is a high-strung man who experiences his stresses in physical ways. His speech that Sunday

in Manhattan was punctuated with anger. He lashed out at the journal American Literature for an issue it had done on the New Melville, an issue full of accusations that Melville scholars had hidden evidence that Melville was a misogynist, a scoundrel. Parker viewed the issue as a personal attack. 'They wanted to stop the biography because it's about a dead white male,' he said. 'It was a pre-emptive strike to silence me before I come out with it, just because of the mere fact that I celebrate and magnify Melville and regard him as great. For that, obviously, I should be shot.'"

The contempt for archival Melville scholarship in Cathy Davidson's "New Melville" was evident in the gleeful way she later gloried in the publicity Weiss gave her. In the September 1998 American Literature she rejoiced that because of Weiss's article her special issue was "national news—not just in the Chronicle of Higher Education but even in the New York Times Magazine. . . . The Times doesn't usually devote its pages to Melville" (457–58). The preface to Davidson's and Jessamyn Hatcher's No More Separate Spheres! (2002) used the word "brushfire": "These essays speak for themselves. However, we wish to look at one of these essays precisely because of the brushfire of attention caused when first published in American Literature in 1994, a reaction that went all the way to the New York Times Magazine" (18). Davidson's "No! In Thunder!" in American Literature (December 2004) revisited the glory of "national news" and "the brushfire of attention" as a "ruckus": "The ruckus surrounding that issue revealed an interesting truth. As much as expanding the canon may raise ire, nothing upsets people more than messing with Great Authors. The Melville issue garnered a flood of mail, positive and negative. It was the subject of myriad editorials and articles, including some in the Chronicle of Higher Education. Eventually, it was even the jumping-off place for a long article in the New York Times Magazine" (673). Davidson remains unrepentant about the shoddiness of evidence in the "New Melville" issue but has made no further public comment on there being no need in 1994 or afterward for a new biography of Melville.

6. In an interview Dominic Hibberd, biographer of Wilfred Owen, said, "You can't just leave the reader with a nothingness to jump over; you've got to suggest something that might have happened, at any rate. Maybe I have imposed my own views on things rather more than I realised, but no . . . , I think I really was honest as far as one possibly could be. But then on some matters you do have to use some kind of instinct" (Benton, 155; ellipsis in original).

7. Sutherland, Last Drink to LA (London: Faber and Faber, 2001), quoted from the online extract in the Manchester Guardian, August 13, 2001.

8. Leon Edel in "The Figure Under the Carpet" comments on biographies that "are mere compendiums" (18–19): "A compendium is like a family album: a series of pictures, selections from an archive. The biographer producing such a work often pretends that he is allowing the character to speak for himself or herself. This is an ingenuous way of avoiding biographical responsibility. That responsibility involves not only accumulating and offering facts: it entails the ability to interpret these facts in the light of all that the biographer has learned about his subject." Others who have thought about the problem have come to the same conclusion in much the same wording. In The Biographer's Gift Ronald Steel responds to Frank E. Vandiver's "Biography as an Agent of Humanism": Ultimately the biographer "must bring his creative imagination into play. There must be an imaginative leap into the unknown to capture the psychological reality underlying the statistical 'facts.' This leap into the unknown is

the element that the greatest biographies share with fiction. What separates them from fiction is that they operate within an objective reality that must be respected" (29).

9. Ian Hamilton in his 2008 *How to Do Biography: A Primer* (333) commented on Goodwin's feeling "compelled to resign from the Pulitzer Prize Committee in 2002" after being exposed for plagiarism.

10. I was already exhausted and undergoing a series of surgeries I had postponed so I would not have to interrupt progress on the biography. I did not have the strength even to try to get corrections printed. I had always blamed Melville for not going public about the "Epilogue" missing from *The Whale*, even if only to say he couldn't quite make sense of what the American papers were reporting about what the British reviewers were saying. In 2002 I was persuaded that the *New York Times* would find a way of mocking any letter of protest against the review, such as letting Brodhead write a snide put-down. Besides, I was confident the next review after Brodhead's in the *Times* would correct him. I was not expecting the would-be biographer Delbanco to echo Brodhead and then Schultz to echo both Brodhead and Delbanco. The reviewers' lies remained blazoned on the Internet along with Alan Helms's "slippery fish" slur derived from Delbanco.That particular slur is in Helms's "Commentary" in the December 1997 *Nineteenth-Century Literature* (52, no. 3, 413–15), where he defends his printing of Whitman's "Live Oak" poems from the texts revised and reordered in *Calamus*: "But Parker is a slippery fish, as anyone familiar with the new first volume of his two-volume biography of Melville can attest—an exhaustive, exhausting book in which conjecture repeatedly turns into 'fact' without so much as a nod to evidence of any kind. In a recent review of that book in *The New York Review* (15 May 1997) Andrew Delbanco takes Parker to task for this misleading habit" (414–15). My reply to Helms in this "Commentary" appears on pages 415–16 of that issue, but rather than defending myself from this accusation I wrote something that demands to be repeated in the new century: "Whitman matters too much to let a spurious text drive out the real 'Live Oak, with Moss,' particularly a nonauthorial text that (judging from Helms's essay and his new defense of it) asks to be read as a document dealing with 'homophobic oppression.' It would, as I said, be tragic 'if even one young person' coming to terms with his or her homosexuality encountered Alan Helms's text, 'Live Oak with Moss,' instead of Whitman's real text" (415).

11. See "Out of Rushmore's Shadow: The Artistic Development of Gutzon Borglum," Stamford Museum and Nature Center, Stamford, Conn., online exhibit information from February 2000 (http://www.tfaoi.com/newsm1/n1m582.htm).

12. In "Very Like a Whale: Parker's *Melville*" Robert Milder complained about my ignoring Melville's marginalia (6): "When so few primary materials exist for knowing the man, it is odd that Parker should neglect this richly provocative resource, which others have explored with important results." In my index "Marginalia" takes up more than half a column in small type. Not only did I use Melville's marginalia throughout, including many words of Melville's never published before, such as that in his Spenser and in his Hazlitt's *Lectures*. Daringly, I thought, I had constructed an entire dramatic chapter from marginalia, "A Humble Quest for an Aesthetic Credo: January–April 1862." Why are reviewers unwilling to read the book but quick to accuse the author of something he is innocent of?

Since this is an inside narrative, I confess that the slurs and outright lies in the reviews of my second volume in 2002 made me feel "hounded to death" and came

close to breaking my spirit. My diary for November 3: "Maurice had been in Phila—
came bk late & called at 11 s/t his time. *Helped* greatly by reminding me again that
the critics are ticks & lice." The next day: "Letting this go only after tying it up. Mumford, Wilson, Kazin & the Suck-ups—the 'New York Intellectuals' *aren't.*" Aren't
intellectuals, I meant, and don't behave intelligently. I inveighed a little longer about
"the decades-long worship of mediocre pseudo Marxists" and then stopped working
for the first time in my life. Instead, for two months I played on the Internet to see if
any written record survived of any of my American ancestors. Within a week I knew
that my white ancestors had all been here by the mid 1700s at the latest. I could
see "the deranged haters" for what they were: "I *belong* here despite their attempts
to silence me." I was, I discovered, a representative Southerner, able by year's end
to see my way toward writing *Ornery People: What Was a Depression Okie?*, stories
about my astonishingly well-documented ancestors. Then I was ready to go back to
work, stronger, but still not able to sleep peacefully because the lies were all out there
in print and on the Internet. As I said on page 191, suffering in silence is a killer.
Starting to speak out in June 2007 did not purge lies from paper pages and monitor
screens, but it brought me peace.

Chapter 8

1. Robert Blake again speaks sanely of the biographer: "He must never write as if
there was a pre-ordained fate for his hero, and never try to explain his actions as if
they were steps towards the fulfillment of a manifest destiny" (89). Yet stretching or
shoving a writer to fit into a manifest destiny according to a historical or biographical design seems somewhat kinder to me than Milder's relentlessly crushing Melville
into a leaden box built by fanatical New Critical theorists.

In "Necessary Ignorance of a Biographer" (1995), John Worthen holds up for
examination Leon Edel's theory that the biographer should seek out the "essence"
of his subject so that all the random detail the biographer discovers "must flow from
his pen in an orderly fashion . . . must be fitted into a narrative calm and measured
and judicial" (231). He also examines the practice of biographers who, like Edel,
"comprehend all sides, command all points of view, know all there is to be known."
His example is D. H. Lawrence's meeting with Frieda Weekley, which biographers
had read as foreordained (Harry T. Moore: "He was unconsciously preparing himself for the woman"; Jeffrey Meyers: "He . . . was ready, at last, for Frieda Weekley").
Worthen quotes other examples of biographers who ignore their own ignorance and
head "blithely towards understanding" (234). Quoting the opening of Peter Ackroyd's
Dickens, in which the novelist lies dead in the house which his father had pointed
out to him "as a suitable object of his ambitions," Worthen says that this method
sanctions "the vision of a life seen as inevitable progress to that final point; it informs
us that this life is to be comprehended in terms of its ironically achieved ambitions,
and of the power of the father" (235). Far more extreme is Milder's imposing upon
Melville's life not a theory of biography like Edel's but a theory of criticism like
Wellek and Warren's and Feidelson's—all the more strange because the New Criticism notoriously rules biographical evidence out of order. Milder seems so to have
internalized the New Criticism that he cannot refrain from drawing on it even when
the subject is Melville's life.

By contrast, I see in my biography just how open I was to the random, as in making a connection between Melville's seeing his brother Thomas off for China and his immediately starting *Redburn*, having been reminded of his brother Gansevoort's seeing him off for Liverpool almost exactly ten years earlier. I knew also of Tom's remarkable physical similarity to Herman and that Melville was susceptible to strong emotions whenever he experienced striking juxtapositions of people, places, and events. I decided that Melville started the book with no idea that self-exploration would be profoundly disturbing and finished it without knowing the dangers he had run; only in the next months, in *White-Jacket* and *Moby-Dick*, did he make high literary profit from his new psychological depths, and only in a late addition to *Pierre*, a year and a half after writing *Redburn*, did he acknowledge the psychological dangers of dipping an angle into the "well of childhood" (bk. 21.1). None of this would have fit into a preconceived scheme to demonstrate throughout the biography the "essence" of Melville. Dependent upon the fortuitous survival and recovery of Tom's start of a diary written as he lay in the New York harbor, I responded to the revelations that followed the moment I dated the diary to late May 1849. When I reflect on the momentous ramifications of my routine redating of this "1860?" diary I wonder when a researcher in the paper archives or the Internet databases will next stumble upon a document in which such far-reaching revelations are packed. I wager now that Melville's last three decades will yet be enlightened by at least one such seemingly trivial discovery.

2. How far this is from 1965 and Paul Murray Kendall's *The Art of Biography*: "The force of science has exerted a wide range of pressures on life-writing. It has, in general, stimulated the researcher . . . to higher standards of precision and thoroughness than have hitherto been observed. . . . Serious biographers have been spurred by the prevailing reverence for 'the scientific approach' to seek out their evidence with dogged persistence, to eschew second-hand materials and concentrate upon the original document, the actual letter, to view with skepticism all doubtful information however attractive, and to interpret their findings with a rigorous regard for the elusiveness of truth" (118). Robert D. Hume sets out his principles for what he calls "Archaeo-Historicism" in *Reconstructing Contexts* (1999). The name he chose was not as catchy as "New Criticism" or "Reader Response Criticism," but the program itself is wholly admirable: "I stress in particular the degree to which its results rest on the existence of hard evidence and the testability of that evidence. A method that does not have built into it serious provision for validation and invalidation of its results can be no more than an elaborate game played for the self-glorification of the participants. Because of gaps and limitations in evidence we often cannot be certain whether an archaeo-historicist interpretation is correct or not, and we may never know. One of the virtues of the method, however, is that one strives to be right and is always in danger of being proved wrong" (190). This is a very valuable scholarly and theoretical manifesto that deserves a wide, thoughtful audience despite what Oxford is charging for it.

3. Brodhead was not alone in his carelessness: look on page ix at the names of some of those who read and approved this bassackwards reading before the book was published. Harold Bloom reprinted the chapter, uncorrected, in his "Period Studies" series, *American Renaissance*.

4. Richard B. Schwartz in his *After the Death of Literature* (1997) described these "crises" proclaimed by literary critics as factitious battles "between straw men, carefully constructed by the combatants to sustain a pattern of polarization that could be exploited to provide continuing professional advancement" (1). Every university press ought to have been testing newly submitted manuscripts on crises by Schwartz's incisive analysis.

5. Until I challenged him in 1984 Richard H. Brodhead's blindness to Melville's agony in his 1976 book had gone unremarked. The New Criticism had kept readers' eyes diverted from the reality of author, whose sufferings had no place in elegant literary criticism. As it had been under the New Criticism, so it was under Deconstruction. What grieves Jay Martin here is the fact that a brilliant young critic has willfully blinded himself so that he had wasted his time and wasted much of his readers' time: "What a book he might have written had he followed his authorities less and favored his insights more!" (655). Martin and I seem instinctively to use the imagery of sight and blindness in making sense of intelligent critics who seal themselves into programmatic ignorance.

6. Oddly, Robertson-Lorant makes the same error of dating this letter 1839 (77).

7. It is an indication of just how blind criticism has kept itself to work on creativity, perception, and memory that I can cite my 1984 preface to *Flawed Texts and Verbal Icons* (xiii–xiv) as still an adequate introduction despite more recent work by some of those I name there, and by others. Albert Rothenberg (*Emerging Goddess*, 1979) and the Cornell school cognitive psychologists (especially James J. and Eleanor Gibson) and students of memory (notably Ulrich Neisser) still stand ready to challenge and enlighten literary critics and biographical scholars.

8. Hume in *Reconstructing Contexts* explicitly describes the New Historicism of Dimock's time (6): "The 1980s practitioners of New Historicism . . . have always struck me as carrying out a text-based form of close reading, not as engaging in a serious attempt to investigate original contexts. I agree with Howard Felperin that 'American new historicism . . . is not genuinely *historical* or seriously political either.' From my point of view, a basic tenet of historicism must be that it rejects arbitrary selection and demands investigation of a wide range of background materials—or at the very least, rigorous justification of selectivity. The critical results of New Historicism have often been valuable, but essentially as a kind of comparatist New Criticism, with some New Left ideological trimmings and notions of subversion borrowed from deconstruction. Most such studies have little to do with systematic contextual scholarship." (Hume's citation is to Felperin's *The Uses of the Canon: Elizabethan Literature and Contemporary Theory* [Oxford: Clarendon Press, 1990], 155.)

In *New Readings in Theatre History* Jacqueline S. Bratton flippantly treats Hume as antediluvian (3): "Spats take place. Despite many years of the digestion of Foucault and Derrida . . . it was still possible in 1999 for the respected theatre historian Robert D. Hume to refer to New Historicism as 'an unfortunate complication' and to assert a version of the credo of the positivist which he calls 'Archeo-historicism' in the face of the widely held consensus about the non-neutrality of facts. Robert Hume is by no means alone in maintaining an antiquarian interest in the stage. At the opening of the twenty-first century many disparate, sometimes mutually discrediting, activities are going on." Bratton's superficiality is evident in her glib "widely held consensus"—as opposed to a "narrowly held consensus"? It is common for critics to take aggressive stands on essentially biographical and historical issues without first acquiring biographical and historical information.

In 2000 Anne D. Neal, Jerry Martin, Mashad Moses, and other members of the staff of the American Council of Trustees and Alumni issued a saddening report, *Losing America's Memory: Historical Illiteracy in the 21st Century* (Washington, D.C.: American Council of Trustees and Alumni, 2000; available at http://www.eric .ed.gov/). People with fine academic credentials had been practicing historicism successfully without knowing much about history.

9. Barbara W. Tuchman's "In Search of History," in her *Practicing History* (1981), points out what used to be known to anyone writing a term paper: "Selection is what determines the ultimate product, and that is why I use material from primary sources only. My feeling about secondary sources is that they are helpful but pernicious. I use them as guides at the start of a project to find out the general scheme of what happened, but I do not take notes from them because I do not want to end up simply rewriting someone else's book. Furthermore, the facts in a secondary source have already been pre-selected, so that in using them one misses the opportunity of selecting one's own." Ironically, I quote this from a Google Books preview which does not give page numbers.

10. Cohen and Yannella silently corrected the extra *s* in "Toms's qualifications." The word that gave them trouble before "Hon. John T. Hoffman" is simply "the." The "three words" after "sailors" are really only a single word, "in" — "by his knowledge of sailors in twenty years experience of the sea." The third "undeciphered word" is "unless" ("and unless offered are seldom obtained without the asking").

11. I was baffled when I first read Wineapple's depiction of my attitude toward Nathaniel Hawthorne in her 2002 review: "Parker focuses on Melville's relationship to Hawthorne. But it's one of his book's more contradictory themes, since Parker is irritated by the pairing. Neighbors only for eighteen months, the two authors afterward saw one another about three more times but in the nineteenth-century eye were yoked forevermore, Melville in the background and remembered, 'if remembered at all,' snaps Parker 'as a man who had known Hawthorne, the literary man who had known Hawthorne during the Lenox months'" (39). In continuing to quote her I do not pause to correct factual errors in her reporting: "Of course, Parker isn't the first biographer implicitly to lay the blame for Melville's neglect at Hawthorne's feet" (40). I never do that. Strangely, it is Wineapple who blames Hawthorne for taking "Melville literally" (40; "at face value" in her 2003 Hawthorne biography, 244) and not writing about *Moby-Dick*. Then Wineapple went on with what looks (at first glance) like a wholly irrelevant comment on another biographer: "Laurie Robertson-Lorant, whose earnest *Melville: A Biography* appeared the same year as the first installment of Parker's biography, doesn't much like Hawthorne" (40). What does that comment tell us about Wineapple's focus? She goes on: "Despite Melville's capaciousness, Parker is convinced that envy preoccupies Melville, though the evidence suggests Parker is the envious one, so riled is he by Hawthorne's posthumous reputation and Melville's sinking one. Parker closely identifies with Melville, at times too closely, and will cross swords with anyone who ignored, outsold, criticized or just plain didn't like Melville" (40). Earlier I "snapped" and now I am "riled"? No. Envious? Riled "by Hawthorne's posthumous reputation"? No. This makes no sense to me at all. I do mention jealousy in a particular context, Melville's returning in 1869

to the Curtis Hotel, where he had last seen Hawthorne before he left Lenox: Melville, I say, "began to reflect (jealously, skeptically, judiciously, and still lovingly) on the mental, aesthetic, and physical characteristics of the man who had so bewitched him and now so outshone him" (2:683). See how far those words are from the vulgar words Wineapple uses to describe my attitude.

I remained baffled until Dennis Donoghue's review of Wineapple's biography in the *Los Angeles Times* (September 28, 2003) made her psychology clear: "Wineapple seems to have wearied of her subject and become exasperated with his debility" (R16; I quote his comments at more length in chap. 17). Growing contemptuous of Hawthorne herself the longer she worked on her book, she seems to have projected her own disdain for him onto me so she could punish me for the feelings she could admit in herself. Melville was never my hero, but I loved him the more I learned about him. Other biographers admit to becoming irritated at their subjects, and everyone holds up the horrific example of Lawrance Thompson, who so radically changed his opinion of Robert Frost. Wineapple, meet Thompson. Writing biography can bring out the best in you, or not.

12. The only "agenda" I bring to transcribing is an intention to recover what the writer wrote or meant to write. Frequently enough scholars mistranscribe a word because of what they expect to see, but those are just blunders. I confess to mistranscribing Catharine Sedgwick's "Linwoods" as "Lintons," but that was clearly because of the power over me of *Wuthering Heights*.

A word in Maria Melville's May 30, 1847, letter to Augusta (in the Augusta Papers) baffled me—an important passage on Herman's going to Boston to try to persuade Elizabeth Shaw to set a date for their wedding: "He is very restless and ill at ease very lonely here without his intended, I can see no reason why it should be postponed any longer, if Lizzie loves Herman as I think she does with her whole heart & soul why, she will consent to live here for the present, and she can be happy too—all the elements of happiness are thick around us if we only will hold them to us, and not wantonly leave them un[seized]." The word had to be something like "ungathered" but I could not do better than the over-dramatic "unseized"; by a blunder the square brackets marking the undeciphered word were lost from the printing in my biography so that the sentence ended with "leave them" (Parker, 1:522). In July 2011 Dennis Marnon received from the New York Public Library an image of the passage shot at high resolution so that a word could be enlarged clearly beyond four hundred percent. With that new clarity and his own highly evolved skills, Marnon read the word as "unsecured," which instantly satisfied me and my fellow-puzzler over the word, Scott Norsworthy. Sometimes you need all the help you can get on the *whole* of a letter, as with John Hoadley's description (vivid, detailed, we could see that much) of the celebration Melville witnessed in Pittsfield in 1863 when word came of the Northern victories at Vicksburg and Gettysburg. In *The Civil War World of Herman Melville* Stanton Garner (490) summed up our efforts, as I quote elsewhere: "I am indebted to the late Jay Leyda and to Hershel Parker for their aid in reading this almost illegible letter." How painful it would have been to have possessed the letter and not have been able to use much of it in our books, but by pooling our efforts Garner, Leyda, and I read it all, I believe. The Northwestern-Newberry editors did not know who wrote the draft preface for *White-Jacket* when we published our edition. When Dennis Marnon gave me an early private tour through his Houghton Library exhibition for the centennial of Melville's death I said, "Oh, that's Helen's hand," and he corrected the label before the evening ceremony. By then, of course, I had transcribed many of Helen's letters in the Augusta Papers.

13. Mark Allen Greene in a review of Burton's *Archive Stories* (*Biography*, Summer 2007) points out that some of Burton's postmodern contributors "evince an overwrought effort to expand the concept of archive so far beyond narrow traditional boundaries that it is expanded beyond recognition; anything—a life, a novel, published histories—becomes an archive. There is also a naivete by many authors about things archival, whether the 'discovery' that government archivists serve the state (rather than having some abstract allegiance to truth and justice), or surprise that court files contain documentary evidence created by the arrested" (398).

14. Greene is far from being a reactionary. See his inaugural address as president of the Society of American Archivists on the SAA website, December 17, 2010. The nearest he comes to being pugnacious toward those assaulting the traditional idea of archives is this passage: "During the 1990s our profession witnessed an assault on the cultural purpose of archives and their material, in favor of an argument that our most important purpose was maintaining evidence of transactions for institutions. It seemed to me then, and still today, that this was a legalistic vision of archives that excluded the very value that our institutions and society most often identified and cherished about our profession."

15. Linda Ferreira-Buckley expresses ideas like Burton's in a review of Gesa E. Kirsch and Liz Rohan, eds., *Beyond the Archives: Research as a Lived Process*. Ferreira-Buckley approvingly describes the seventeen essays: "All are first-person narratives that recount parts of an author's archival research, from exploring a subject to honing focus, and from recalling early insecurity about one's training or even one's abilities to gaining confidence about method and object, often the result of casting off objectivist standards of truth in favor of modes of interpretation that embrace a range of aptitudes. Indeed, the authors generally celebrate the insights made possible by emotion and intuition, which is not to say that evidentiary standards are not in place" (868). Ferreira-Buckley's offhand assurance about the retention of the "evidentiary standards" may satisfy some skeptics. It is hard to believe that Barbara C. Tuchman would be heartened by Christine Mason Sutherland's caution in "Getting to Know Them" (in the Kirsch and Rohan collection): "I think it is important to read early works in editions that would have been familiar to the authors [being studied]. This physical contact with the books of the period is part of sharing their experience" (31).

Chapter 9

1. N. John Hall takes for granted that he and rival biographers of Anthony Trollope "were all working from the same materials" (23). Claire Tomalin coolly explains her situation: "I'm in that agreeable phase of preparing myself to write. Organizationally, it's utterly different from Pepys. Hardy's letters are, more or less, all published; Pepys's weren't. I don't expect to discover anything new, rather to see Hardy from a new perspective" (94–95).

2. "What work it was is not clear," Hayford says of Maria Melville's letter about a new work. See also Harrison Hayford and Merrell Davis, "Herman Melville as Office-Seeker," in which Hayford and Davis quote Maria Melville's April 20, 1853,

letter (174–75) without commenting on her saying Herman had become "so completely absorbed by this new work, now nearly ready for the press."

3. In his biography Leon Howard did not take Maria Melville's April 20, 1853, letter altogether seriously, but he did assume it meant that Melville had been trying to write the Agatha story: "He probably did not become 'so completely absorbed by his new work' as to worry his family seriously until after March 21" (when the Harpers account came). "Herman himself may have realized by this time that the Agatha story . . . was not instinct with enough narrative continuity to lend itself to his customary method of writing" (202). "Whether he bogged down or simply gave out in his efforts, the 'new work' seems not to have been 'made ready for the press'" (203).

4. In Dettlaff, see especially 647–48. Baym's title was a play on Lawrance Thompson's controversial 1952 Princeton University Press book, *Melville's Quarrel with God*.

5. Sara Wheeler says: "Most biographers are familiar with the agony of the declining decades—that yawning phase about which one longs to write, 'And so the years passed'" (87).

6. In *Cannibal Old Me* (2009) Mary K. Bercaw Edwards played Devil's advocate with the suggestion that Melville may not have stayed with the Typees at all.

7. See chapter 4, n. 19 above.

8. Since Jeffrey Meyers thought it his duty to correct factual errors in books he reviewed ("Reflections of a Book Reviewer," 59), I point out that the name of the "persistent jackal" of a reviewer who lay in wait for him in the *New Criterion* (63) book after book was not William Tuttleton but James Tuttleton. The phenomenon of "persistent jackal" I treat elsewhere in this book without naming it with Meyers's vivid precision.

In an interview published in his *Literary Biography*, Michael Benton asked Dominic Hibberd about his giving the previous Wilfred Owen biographer Jon Stallworthy only one index reference. Hibberd replied: "Yes. I ignored him completely but, when I had written a chapter on, say, Dunsden, I then read his chapter on Dunsden just to make sure that I hadn't missed anything out. Every time I did that I couldn't help noticing how inaccurate he was. All sorts of little things weren't right, and large areas of Wilfred's activities and experiences he had nothing to say about at all . . . so that I became more and more confident as I went on that I was really writing a new account of Wilfred's life" (169). I'm a little surprised Hibberd did not stop turning through Stallworthy after the first couple of episodes, to avoid an ongoing risk of infection, since no one else is likely to stick within the same chronology you are holding to.

Susan J. Owen in *Restoration Theatre and Crisis* (25) quotes Robert Hume's "Texts within Contexts": "Few of us would recommend ignoring predecessors or eschewing the courtesies of scholarly discourse. But *deference* seems the wrong attitude. If we accept our predecessors' conclusions, what can we change? If we do not ask new questions then we consign ourselves to crumbs and bickering . . . even the most historicist of scholars needs to adopt a rigorously skeptical attitude toward the facts, questions, logic, and conclusions of even the most respected predecessor." Owen comments: "Precisely. To engage critically with other critics' work is a compliment, a sign that one regards that work as serious."

9. In my case, there was such an overwhelming mass of new evidence (for dating of events, in particular) that correcting anyone else was impossible. Other biographers

handle cases their own way. Declan Kiberd in a review of Gordon Bowker's *James Joyce: A Biography* says: "Ellmann was a brilliant biographer and skilful interviewer, early enough on the scene to talk with many of Joyce's acquaintances, some of whom told him untruths. Bowker, without fuss, fixes mistaken details" ("A Fine, Unfussy Biography of James Joyce," Manchester *Guardian*, August 5, 2011).

10. After compiling the great bulk of my chronology I became concerned that some well-known episode might have dropped out of my computerized files, so before starting to write I quickly flipped through biographies of Melville (up through Miller's). I found nothing, but at least I looked.

11. I disagree with Kathryn Hughes's contemptuous comments (556) in her review of *Literary Biography*: "In his final chapter Michael Benton brings his study of biography right up to date by looking at some of the most successful innovations from recent works, ones which have sidestepped the chronological cradle-to-grave plod in favor of a more selective, nimble, and self-conscious approach to the business of telling a life story." There is not necessarily anything plodding about a chronological telling of a story.

12. Inaugural program, "Crafting an Eloquent Beginning," Leon Levy Center for Biography at the City University of New York, December 2008 (http://www1.cuny.edu/mu/podcasts/2008/12/10/crafting-an-eloquent-beginning/).

13. In fairness to reviewers I cite Jeffrey Meyers's hilarious "Reflections of a Book Reviewer." Any reader of my "inside narrative" will rejoice at Meyers's tell-anything tell-all devil-take-the-hindmost account of his brilliant but bumpy career as a reviewer, for several of the magazines, reviewers, and biographers I discuss also figure in his animadversions. Meyers is amusingly blunt in commenting on such luminaries as Hermione Lee and Jay Parini (59) and Edward Said (65). He locates himself as poised at the historical turning point I treat at the end of chapter 7: "I have not tried to review online, which seems still less real to me than print, but reviewing has recently become more difficult as venues disappear" (61).

14. In August 2011 I wanted information about the book *Higher Education?* and was pleased to see a review on Amazon by Richard A. Schwartz, the author of *After the Death of Literature*. I posted a comment, slightly trimmed here: "Hurrah for Amazon for allowing real scholarly academic critics a place where they can have a large audience for a review and not have to wait a year or two to get into print in an academic journal. Is Schwartz retired? If he is still working, will he get credit for a scholarly review posted on Amazon, where almost anyone can post? If universities and colleges *don't* credit something like this as a publication, they ought to." Schwartz replied: "I'm not yet retired. I do list in my c.v. that I do reviews for Amazon. I believe Amazon reviews to be very worthwhile because, as you note, they reach so many people. They also invite instant dialogue." HP: "At best, Amazon is a great force for democratic intellectual exchange. I tumbled to this when I wrote a review of Sally Bushell's *Text as Process* [Charlottesville: University of Virginia Press, 2009] for a Wordsworthian journal only to have it rejected as not the laudatory review that was required. It was not hostile at all, just honest. I had taken time off serious work to review it because the topic was so important and because Bushell cited me as one of the two American theorists she was engaging, but then did not engage my ideas. Ten minutes later I had it up for all the world to see, not just the 300 subscribers of the Wordsworthian journal. It is great not to be suppressed, but it is also great just to write

a review on your own, as you did, and post it on Amazon." Even if dishonest publishers hire people to write positive reviews, honest reviewers can still do what Schwartz and I do, sign our real names to anything we post as an Amazon review. Along with literary bloggers and litblogs, reviewing in Amazon or any future similar sites will go far to make up for the decline in number and quality of print reviewing.

15. "Smitten" is not the only example of Wineapple's indelicate diction. In wholly inappropriate contexts Sophia guffaws (210) and Melville bellows (237).

16. *The Emerging Goddess*, chapter 13 (the great chapter for literary critics): "Sexual impulses aroused during the creative process might induce conflictual anxiety because they are forbidden or because they require discharge. Or the alert, moderately tense state connected to creating gives rise to feelings of attraction and the need for sexual discharge" (372). Ideally, it seems, artists, male or female, would prefer to achieve sexual discharge without much in the way of distracting conversation: they want to keep thinking about where they are in the work. On the morning of Friday, August 9, 1850, Melville was sexually aroused by writing about Hawthorne but did not have the self-awareness, I assumed, that might have let him realize what was happening to him. Not knowing why he was aroused, I thought, he acted out that arousal by kidnapping a bride. I called it deflected sexuality because it *was* deflected from a homosexual manifestation to a comically excessive heterosexual one. (Later, in *Clarel*, I think, Melville understood this mood quite well, and was greatly amused by what he came to understand about his 1850 self.)

17. Idolatrous worshippers of Sedgwick, Martin and Person described me as panicking when I was the one who understood the situation and conveyed it on the page of my biography. They outright accused me of not knowing what I was writing. Sedgwick in *Epistemology of the Closet* (19) cites the "forensic use of the 'homosexual panic' defense for gay-bashing." "Homosexual panic" in Sedgwick is "a defense strategy that is commonly used to prevent conviction or to lighten sentencing" for gay-bashers. In *Between Men* (162), she defines her term: "'Homosexual panic'—that modern, intra-psychic, potentially almost universal extension of the secularization of homosexual anathema." (That, incidentally, is a better-than-average specimen of Sedgwick prose.) If a male manifests "homosexual panic" he is partly just being male but he is also by definition a very bad sort who justifies his gay-bashing. When Martin and Person accuse me of "homosexual panic" they are making a very ugly charge, and a wholly unwarranted one. In their zeal to apply Sedgwick they did not pay attention to what I wrote. I was funny: if only they had read the passage aloud to each other, they surely would have understood. Over the years I have thought a good deal about sexuality and literary composition and have taken pains to apply what Albert Rothenberg says in chapter 13 of his *The Emerging Goddess*.

18. In "Melville, Three Ways" Hester Blum disagrees: "Scholars . . . can certainly come to their own conclusions about how best to use or adopt" research (372). Blum means "critics," not scholars, apparently, and leaves wide open the likelihood that critics will decide to *ignore* altogether the discoveries of scholars. Her comments come in the context of defending Sacvan Bercovitch from the Higgins-Parker charge that he ignored biographical evidence. In *Rites of Assent: Transformations in the Symbolic Construction of America* (245–50), Bercovitch claimed that "textual scholarship" had shown that when writing *Pierre* "Melville was in complete command of his materials from the start"—that is, he described Robert Milder's 1974 New Critical article as an

example of "textual scholarship," this in a decade when genuine textual scholarship, history of the composition, revision, expansion, truncation, publication, and republication of American texts had burgeoned as never before. Bercovitch here was acting as critic, not scholar. In volume 2 of the *Cambridge History of American Literature* he led a group of critics writing as historicists, not a group of literary historians, biographers, and textual scholars. Blum, like Bercovitch, makes no distinction between an argument on the basis of a New Critical close reading and arguments on the basis of documentary evidence, some of which, at least, I believe every critic has the duty to assimilate before publishing anything on the topic, even if the critic chooses to argue about the significance of the evidence. Critics who write without taking account of scholarly evidence are filling the world with empty words.

19. Weinstein's "Melville, Labor, and the Discourses of Reception" is trendily not "about Melville's reception" but about "the discourses constituting that reception" (202).

20. As Egan's almost even-handed contrast of "theoretical, speculative investigations" and old-fashioned scholarship suggests (623), American reviewers (despite William H. Epstein and others) have not yet quite caught up with the haughty disdain with which many British critics (even those long resident in the United States) reproach scholars who do not parrot postmodern shibboleths. See Greg Clingham's put-down (in *Biography*, Fall 2007) of Howard D. Weinbrot for not rising to "the subtle, nuanced forms of reading and attention that go beyond the formal and the empirical" (647). Yet Egan palpably thrills to the "remarkable" results in the speculative articles on Douglass and Melville in the book edited by Levine and Otter: "A sense of heightened critical possibilities is tempered by a theoretical self-consciousness about the effects of studying these two canonical figures 'in relation'" (625).

21. Milder does not fit into my chapters on the New York Intellectuals, despite Jason Epstein's rapturous praise of his *Exiled Royalties* as "exigent," but you see in Milder a non–New York City reviewer who also slavishly follows Arvin and Arvin's followers in minimizing Melville's 1849 trip and in reducing the 1856–57 trip to the first meeting with Hawthorne and a bit on Palestine and a bunch of statues ("Brief Biography," 30, 40–41). (Epstein's praise of Milder is quoted from James Atlas, "The Ma and Pa of the Intelligentsia," September 21, 2006, mydigest.espacioblog.com.)

22. In Bryan C. Short's *Cast by Means of Figures: The Rhetorical Development of Herman Melville* the subtitle is clear enough: the book will trace Melville's works so as to demonstrate that one phase of Melville's career (in practice, usually one book) grows out of the previous one and grows into the next, successively, while all the time Melville's rhetorical skills are presumably enlarging and being enhanced. Omitted, it would seem, would be the treatment of any "rhetorical degeneration" in Melville's prose or poetry. Short calls this book a "rhetorical biography" (8), thereby emphasizing chronological development. He will "describe Herman Melville's development in a way which dovetails literary biography with rhetorical theory" (8). "As a rhetorical biography" the book will analyze "tropological structures which cut across the boundary between Melville's works and the documents of his life" (9). Yet this is not what happens in Short's book. Like Milder and Delbanco, Short cannot take into account the most intriguing evidence about Melville's development between *Pierre* and the short stories such as "Bartleby." In the absence of the completed *The Isle of the Cross*, that evidence lies, of course, in Melville's letters to Nathaniel Hawthorne

in which he tried to persuade his friend to write the story of Agatha Hatch, the abandoned wife. Those letters contain some of the Melville's aesthetic ideas couched as practical hints to another romancer—ideas as important, I would think, as those in his lecture "Statues in Rome" or in his annotations and markings in Hazlitt's lectures. Fixated on Melville's published books, Short triumphantly delivers this shockingly unimaginative declaration: "The rhetoric of Melville's magazine fiction builds on that of *Pierre* as *Omoo* builds on *Typee*" (125). No! it builds upon Melville's hints to Hawthorne, which we can read, and upon however he developed his rhetorical strategies in the lost *The Isle of the Cross*. Can a critic ever be sensitive enough to speculate intelligently about what writing the lost book might have contributed to Melville's rhetorical development?

23. William Epstein for a short time made a strong effort to take over biography for postmodernism. His preface to *Contesting the Subject: Essays in the Postmodern Theory and Practice of Biography and Biographical Criticism* (1991) begins, "This is the inaugural volume in a new series of books on the theory and practice of biography and biographical criticism," and continues with a full description of the range of the series (xi). On August 1, 2011, Becki Corbin of Purdue University Press assured me that this 1991 first volume was also the last. In his "Recognizing the Life-Course" chapter in *Recognizing Biography* (1987) Epstein manages to call on Eve Kosofsky Sedgwick, Michel Foucault, and Jacques Derrida (166) before making all things clear (166–67): "One of the consequences of the general theory of relativity is what philosophers of science refer to as the 'world-line' thesis, which tries to describe the trajectories in space-time of individual moving bodies. In a sense, the general theory of relativity problematizes the classical understanding of the 'world-line' in much the same way that our post-modern approach (informed by Derridean and Foucauldian perspectives) calls into question the traditional recognition of the 'life-course,' which is concerned with the trajectories in cultural space-time of individual human bodies." Strikingly, for all his modish problematizing, Epstein never denies the relevance of perceiving the trajectory of an author's life, even when he says "a narrative of the biographer's course of research is competing with (as it is complementing) a narrative of the biographical subject's life-course" (170).

Ira Bruce Nadel in a slashing review in *Biography* of Backscheider's *Reflections on Biography* attacked particularly her "skepticism toward new approaches, and her persistent belief in a unified trajectory of a life" (767). In truth, she romanticizes the parallels between fictional heroes of popular fiction and figures in popular biographies, ending with this (106): "Richard Ellman[n]'s 'facing the task of getting the evidence to yield what information it will' extends to experiencing the 'subject's life as forcing its coherence upon' the biographer's mind." Here Backscheider fails to consider the possibility that the known evidence for a subject's life may be incoherent and that critics speaking biographically will not see beyond a broken, gap-filled outline of a writer's life. (Backscheider explains that she is quoting two sources, "Ellmann described by Park Honan [*Authors' Lives*, New York: St. Martin's, 1990], p. 68, and Jay Martin, 'Historical Truth and Narrative Reliability,' *Biography and Source Studies* [1994], 72.") Professor Martin was kind enough to send me a photocopy of this piece.

24. Long at work on his biography of John Butler Yeats before Leyda wrote these words, William M. Murphy in "John Butler Yeats" remarked on legal records that

"nobody had ever bothered looking into before" (44). He continued (44–45): "That led me to a conclusion about the Yeats industry: so many people were concerned with WBY's writings directly, with critical analyses of his poetry and prose, that factual information about him and his family had been systematically disregarded."

Chapter 10

1. "Presentism – Historical Time, Concerns of History, Bibliography" (http://science.jrank.org/pages/7999/Presentism.html).

2. In this May 2004 review Shedd quotes Lynn Hunt's "Against Presentism" and agrees with her that presentism "robs history of any chance of objectivity, since presentists invariably judge the past in terms of the present" (paragraph 1).

3. The catachresis here in Delbanco's "chilling prescience" calls attention to his habitual refusal to see the past in anything like its own terms. He regularly tries to understand the nineteenth century as he can relate it to contemporary America and relate contemporary America to it, not to understand it as writers like Melville experienced it.

4. Milder discounts Robertson-Lorant's book without comment on her reliability. Delbanco, unabashed at his ignorance of archival research, in his May 15, 1997, *New York Review of Books* review of my first volume (22 n. 3) rather too hastily assured his readers that her book "is carefully researched and vividly written." How would he know whether or not it was carefully researched? Had he checked three hundred of her quotations against letters in the Melville archives? As I said very discreetly in the preface to my first volume, not focusing on her errors, Robertson-Lorant "made vigorous forays into much the same archival material I have used, but she was sporadic rather than exhaustive in her study of the family letters" (xiv). Her errors pervade the book, but, nevertheless, she worked at writing a biography from the archives, as Delbanco did not, and deserves credit for doing so.

5. Quotations from "The Encantadas" in the next several paragraphs follow the Northwestern-Newberry Edition, in *"The Piazza Tales" and Other Prose Pieces, 1839–1860*, Sketch Eighth (151–62) and Sketch Ninth (162–70).

6. Quotations from "Benito Cereno" are also from *"The Piazza Tales" and Other Prose Pieces, 1839–1860*, 46–117.

7. In publicizing *Melville: His World and Work* Delbanco fashioned an opinion piece for newspaper circulation. It appeared in, for instance, the October 17, 2005, *Los Angeles Times*. It was a curious piece, "anti-American" in its claim that America lumbered through the world creating enemies, perhaps a valid assertion in 2005 but a misreading of Melville's story; "anti-Bush" in its reading of the invasion of Iraq; and distinctly "presentist," promoting even in newspapers the idea that Melville was presciently describing the America of 2005, the era of Bush II.

8. Page citations here are to the widely available *"Moby-Dick" as Doubloon* so readers can easily sample the three articles by Weathers, Foster, and Heimert together; full references appear in the Works Cited.

9. At the end of 2010 the Johns Hopkins University Press chose to announce aggressively a new presentist work by William V. Spanos. Here are the "publisher's comments" on Spanos's *The Exceptionalist State and the State of Exception: Herman Melville's "Billy Budd, Sailor"*: "Critics predominantly view Herman Melville's *Billy Budd, Sailor* as a 'testament of acceptance,' the work of a man who had become

politically conservative in his last years. William V. Spanos disagrees, arguing that the novella was not only a politically radical critique of American exceptionalism but also an eerie preview of the state of exception employed, most recently, by the George W. Bush administration in the post-9/11 War on Terror. . . . Spanos demonstrates . . . that Melville's uncanny attunement to the dark side of the American exceptionalism myth enabled him to foresee its threat to the very core of democracy in the twentieth and twenty-first centuries. This view, Spanos believes, anticipates the state of exception theory that has emerged in the recent work of Giorgio Agamben, Alain Badiou, Judith Butler, and Jacques Ranciere, among other critical theorists." The book as published early in 2011 is indeed overtly presentist. It also contains a multipart rabid screed against Hayford and Sealts's 1962 edition of *Billy Budd, Sailor,* and against me in particular as a supporter of Hayford and Sealts in *Reading "Billy Budd"* (1990). He claims that my "real criticism is directed against critical perspectives, emerging in the context of the protest movement during the Vietnam War—and theoretically emanating from Europe (the 'Old World')—that was [*sic*] politicizing Melville's text, indeed, reading it (and his earlier fiction) as a radical political critique of a conservative society" (60). My stance, he trumpets, "like Hayford's and Sealts's, is everywhere, in fact, informed by a conservative ideology" (61). I shuddered at Andrew Delbanco's ascribing prurient thoughts to me and I am not pleased by Spanos's triumphant assertions that I hold political views which are alien to me. Already in the 1960s and still more so in 1988 when I wrote the book on *Billy Budd* I was informed by "a conservative ideology" only in regard to shoddy literary criticism and incompetent scholarship. In reading masses of literary criticism and what passes for scholarship while writing *Melville Biography: An Inside Narrative* I have not encountered much in the way of great criticism based on accurate textual, historical, and biographical scholarship. Instead, I see missed opportunities—in the 1970s, for instance, a myriad of opportunities to write fresh literary criticism based on new textual scholarship, in the 1980s a myriad of opportunities to write fresh literary history based on new historical and biographical research, and in the early twenty-first century a myriad of opportunities to explore episodes in Melville's life using my two-volume biography and other tools as signals toward insufficiently explored archival material on Melville and on hundreds of people who came in contact with him—people such as those who attended Dr. John Wakefield Francis's Sunday evenings with Melville.

As far as presentism goes, my approach is opposite to Robertson-Lorant's, Delbanco's, and Spanos's. My focus was so firmly on understanding Melville in relation to his own circumstances that I think I made not one comparison of anything in the narrative to anything in the twentieth century. Stephen B. Oates in "Biography as High Adventure" (originally published in *Timeline* [1985]; collected in his 1986 *Biography as High Adventure*) identifies a position I share when he says the biographer "must keep his own voice out of the story so that the subject and his times can live again" (125).

Chapter 11

1. See, alas, Richard Hauer Costa, in *Edmund Wilson: Our Neighbor from Talcottville:* "Rereading *The Fruits of the MLA* after a decade, I still chuckled over many of Wilson's examples of elephantine academic marshalling to the picking up of peas. . . . *The Fruits of the MLA* is as amusing for the haters of the proliferation that

passes for scholarship among some English academics as *The Cold War and the Income Tax* is reinforcing for some enemies of the IRS" (86).

2. Determined not to rely only on *Redburn*, I went to Liverpool and read the *Mercury* day by day for the period Melville was there as well as a little earlier and later. (Signs said, "If you leave anything it will be pinched." The microfilm reader knob had been pinched, and I shortened my right little finger in cranking the reels.)

3. See the Northwestern-Newberry *Journals*, 233–34. I could have avoided this note, but like any under-appreciated transcriber of difficult manuscripts I want to honor Gerald M. Crona.

4. Clare L. Spark in her 2001 *Hunting Captain Ahab* describes Weaver's attempt to block Trilling's appointment (227) and their reconciliation (624).

5. In "Arvin's Melville, Martin's Arvin," Eric Savoy stresses Arvin's importance to Robert K. Martin and indeed insists that "Arvin *matters* supremely to Americanists" (611); he does not mention Arvin's continuing importance to the New York Intellectuals writing on Melville.

6. My momentous "shopping expedition" of Cousin Kate Gansevoort Lansing was yet to come, in the 2002 volume—and was yet unknown to me. In "The Figure Under the Carpet" Leon Edel says, "I agree with T. S. Eliot that one never knows what a laundry list will reveal" (24).

7. According to Heinz Dietrich Fischer and Erika Fischer in *The Pulitzer Prize Archive* (2003): "After the jurors of 1997 had considered one hundred and sixteen books in the biography or autobiography category, they nominated these three finalists: *In the Wilderness*, by Kim Barnes; *Angela's Ashes*, by Frank McCourt; and *Herman Melville, Vol. 1, 1819–1851*, by Hershel Parker. . . . The biography of Herman Melville by Hershel Parker, as the jury report states, contains 'great passages of exciting writing and his biography will be the one that scholars and Melville fans will be reading and referring to for the next fifty years. . . . This biography is a stunning achievement.' [Biography Jury Report, 2 January 1997.] The Pulitzer Prize Board bestowed the award on Frank McCourt's *Angela's Ashes—a Memoir*."

Chapter 12

1. After the world celebrated Y2K a year early as if it had begun the new millennium, I may be forgiven for edging Elizabeth Hardwick's 2000 book over into this chapter. Barbara Epstein printed a shamelessly long sample of the book in the June 15, 2000, *New York Review of Books* (15–16, 18, 20) under the title "Melville in Love," presumably in love with Harry Bolton, a character in *Redburn*. In the piece is Hardwick's strange twisting of my comments on the Come-Outers, discussed below. With my agreement, Maurice Sendak allowed Epstein to decorate the piece with what was printed as a too-purply reproduction of his cover picture for the first volume of my biography of Melville.

2. This was February 25, 1997. Kazin was not at his mature best, judging from one of the milder comments in my diary: "knows a little rumor & thinks it is truth." I added: "M's 'sideline' of poetry—So I had to straighten him out. Paul was fine." Later I copied down Kazin's words from a videotape so I could quote them correctly in *Melville: The Making of the Poet* (8).

3. Toronto being far enough removed from Manhattan, Lawrie Cherniack on July 8, 2000, complained in the *Globe and Mail* without known repercussions:

Hardwick's book showed "poor editing, poor writing, and lack of insight into Melville the writer." Hardwick, said Cherniack, treated Melville's writing "as autobiographical when it suits her, and twists the writings when they don't suit her."

4. Now the Internet makes simultaneous discoveries commonplace. As it happened, Gary Scharnhorst (the only other American researcher with a nerve in the right shoulder pinched from turning the handles of microfilm readers) answered my appeal in *American Literature* (October 1989) by sending in this news for the March 1990 issue: "The *Springfield Republican* of 11 June 1853 under 'Pittsfield Items' noted that 'Herman Melville has gone to New York to superintend the issue of a new work'" (101). As the *American Literature* editor Louis Budd said, Scharnhorst's information could fit into the text of my article in that issue (at p. 12 n. 47). Later, Scott Norsworthy found a similar announcement in a Boston paper.

5. White's description of Helms appears in a dust-cover blurb on Helms's 1995 *Young Man from the Provinces: Gay Life Before Stonewall.*

6. Perhaps we should see Delbanco's taking words from a secondary source, as in his taking phrases from the Augusta Papers as "quoted in" my biography, as a token of his general remove from actual scholarship. Perhaps even more often than he plunders me for words from manuscripts, he lifts phrases from books or articles by those he admires so that he may savor and share among friends their excellent phrasing or clever insight. His eye is on his contemporaries.

Chapter 13

1. John Lardas Modern in *Secularism in Antebellum America* (2011) happily describes Bourne's "choice to riff on Melville's more voluptuous phrasings and narrative threads" (57)—a riff in which Bourne assumes "the voice of Tommo as he succumbs to the 'beauteous nymph Fayaway'" (58).

2. To keep clear what I knew and did not know while writing my biography, I leave "Maherbal" unidentified in chapter 17. The imaginative Scott Norsworthy (2011) discovered that he was the nineteen-year-old Matthew Henry Buckham, a new graduate of the University of Vermont and from 1851 to 1853 principal of the Lenox Academy. Later he had a distinguished career as a professor at the University of Vermont.

3. Homosexual readings of the "tayo" (male friend) relationship as described in *Typee* go back to Charles W. Stoddard, who wrote Melville a fan letter sometime before January 20, 1867, and who remembered Kory-Kory as he wrote "Chumming with a Savage" in *South Sea Idyls* (Boston: James R. Osgood, 1873). The *Hartford Daily Courant* (October 18, 1873), wearing the sexual blinders common at the time, saw Stoddard's Polynesian romance as purer than Melville's: "Since Herman Melville enchanted the world with the revelations of Typee, there has been nothing written so saturated with the dreaminess of the South Sea as these loungings of Mr. Stoddard in Tahiti. And against the love of the maiden Fayaway, we may place as a purer picture the passion of the little heathen Kana-ana for his friend the author."

Chapter 14

1. In 1999 I also had letters Paul Metcalf had found in a liquor box when he was moving. This "Metcalf Donation" to the Berkshire Athenaeum consisted of letters Agnes Morewood had loaned Metcalf's mother, her second cousin Eleanor Metcalf,

in the 1940s and which had not been returned by the time the Morewoods donated most of their papers to the Berkshire Athenaeum in the 1950s.

2. In order to muster evidence when none was apparent, I asked myself questions. What did Melville have in his possession as he took a train or a ship, for instance on his way to see Allan in New York in 1844 or on his return from seeing Richard Tobias Greene in Rochester in 1846. If he had papers in his possession, were they to be dealt with when he reached his destination? Would he inevitably read them or finger them? In 1846 did he carry a copy of *Typee* all the way to Westport just he could bestow one on Tom's captain?

3. The 1951 *Log* contains documentation of such background information as this about Lucas. The Chart of Correspondents in the first volume of my biography (900–906) lists the repositories which hold the letters I quote. In this chapter family letters not quoted from the *Log* are from the Augusta Papers unless otherwise specified.

4. This letter is in the 1999 Metcalf donation to the Berkshire Athenaeum.

5. The label appears in the November 2005 Swann Gallery auction catalogue.

6. This is in the Massachusetts Historical Society, Lemuel Shaw Collection (MHS-S).

7. Again, MHS-S.

8. This inscription is on a scrap of paper now in the possession of David Shneidman.

9. This letter, which Henry A. Murray owned for many years (since the 1930s?), is now in the Reese Collection.

10. We know how the Harpers' rejection affected Melville from Charlotte Hoadley's February 14, 1944, letter to Victor Paltsits in the New-York Historical Society—where Leyda sent me from his hospital bed. I took her seriously when she said, "One thing I do know, the Harpers refusing it calling it a second 'Robinson Crusoe' embittered his whole life" (Parker, 1:376). For many years Charlotte was witness to conversations of Melville's sisters and even his mother. At that time, pitchers had ears.

Chapter 15

1. Some of the evidence I present here I gathered at the Colindale Branch of the British Library in 1997 and at the old New York Public Library Annex (where access to paper and microfilm was easy). I pulled together much of the evidence in this chapter in a week or so with the help of Gale databases of English newspapers and magazines, America's Historical Newspapers, the *New York Times* database, fultonhistory.com, and the databases available with a subscription to the New England Historic Genealogical Society. I draw here on much old work in the Melville archives, such as Gansevoort Melville's *Index Rerum*, but I offer this chapter and some later ones as the sort of studies which can be expedited and enriched by recently available databases.

2. See my *The Powell Papers: A Confidence Man Amok Among the Anglo-American Literati*, especially section 6, "The Furor over Charles Dickens's Accusations" (111–54).

3. Melville's anonymous derogatory comments in his essay on Hawthorne's *Mosses from an Old Manse* in 1850 hurt Irving deeply. He could easily have learned who the author was but whether or not he did is not known. See *The Powell Papers*, 213–14.

4. Melville's hospitality, *Powell Papers*, 37–39; Powell's cautions, 76. In Powell's *Living Writers of America* the "worst enemies of the national mind" passage is on 112–13, printed by the Duyckincks in the *Literary World*, February 2, 1850; the passage is printed in *The Powell Papers*, 180.

Chapter 16

1. Quotations in this paragraph are from an article in the *North American and United States Gazette* (July 17, 1851); the *Baltimore Sun* of July 19 had all the same information.

2. In chapter 3 I quote only a bit from the hyperbolic praise Melville has "the high and mighty Campbell clan of editors of all sorts" heap upon young Pierre's adolescent literary efforts (in bk. 17.1)—just the sort of panegyrics the reviewers and the "editors of various moral and religious periodicals" had *not* lavished upon Melville himself. "'He is blameless in morals, and harmless throughout,'" says one; another critic "had no reserve in saying, that the predominant end and aim of this author was evangelical piety." In this passage Melville's anger would have been tonic irony, if he had been writing for separate publication rather than starting what grew into his lengthy and increasingly painful Pierre-as-author insertions into the manuscript already completed and contracted for in a short form. (By "Campbell" Melville meant "Scottish," or Scotch, as he would say, one of the formidable Edinburgh pack that Bryon satirized in "English Bards and Scotch Reviewers"—not a slur on the poet Thomas Campbell, whom Byron and Melville both respected.)

3. Prima facie evidence is the twenty cents on the dollar contract the Harpers gave Melville for *Pierre* and their careful gossiping in the summer of 1852 that he was a little crazy. Strong evidence, as explained below, lies in the far-advanced secret Harper plans for Dickens's *Bleak House* at the time Melville offered them *Pierre* and their subsequent publicity campaign in exaltation of Dickens—a campaign which succeeded in refurbishing Dickens's reputation in the United States. In early 1852 the Harpers waged this campaign in their public announcements and by having Henry J. Raymond write ferocious attacks in the *New York Times* on international copyright—attacks in which Raymond advocated sacrificing American authors for the public good, as explained later. Throughout late 1851 and the early months of 1852 the mendacious Harpers denied backing the *Times* or owning it and controlling its position on copyright.

4. I say "Greeley" rather than crediting also his co-editor Thomas McElrath because it was clear to contemporaries which editor was writing these articles attacking the Harper-Raymond articles in the *Times*. In the small world of New York journalism, Raymond had worked for Greeley and McElrath (the managing editor) at the *Tribune* and later, in 1846–47, as many readers would have remembered, Raymond in the *Courier* and Greeley in the *Tribune* had conducted a public debate over Fourierism (espoused by Greeley) which ended, according to Greeley's biographer James Parton, in the vanquishing of Fourierism in America (*Life of Horace Greeley* [New York: Mason Brothers, 1855], 216). Harper and Brothers printed the debate in a double-columned pamphlet in 1847: *Association Discussed:, Or, The Socialism of the Tribune Examined. Being a Controversy Between the New York Tribune and the Courier and Enquirer by H. Greeley and H. J. Raymond*. Thinking that the *Times* was founded in the fall of 1852 instead of in 1851 (382), Parton missed out on the whole early 1852 exchange over copyright.

Chapter 17

1. Withholding distinguished work from publication became habitual with Hayford; only in 2003 did Northwestern University Press publish posthumously his *Melville's Prisoners*, a collection of essays and speeches authorized by his son Charles Hayford and seen into print by Alma MacDougall Reising, with a foreword by me.

2. Available at http://www.yellowpigs.net/classes/hawmel/.

3. "Smitten" was how Wineapple described Melville's feelings for Hawthorne. See also chapter 9, n. 15.

4. With the aid of databases in 2010 I learned that in the biography I should have used the 1851 name, the Wilson Hotel, instead of the later name, the Curtis Hotel. William O. Curtis in his later years (so much a hotelier that he could be referred to simply as "Boniface Curtis") talked as if he had been the owner of the hotel from the late 1840s, and in fact he was much on the scene because of his and his brother's livery stable and a stage route as well as a boarding house nearby.

5. This sketch, now known to be by Melville, appeared in the 1876 *History of Pittsfield* (see Sealts, "Thomas Melvill, Jr., in *The History of Pittsfield*," 214).

6. In "Biography as an Agent of Humanism" Frank E. Vandiver says (18): "All historians strive for verisimilitude, and one of the best ways to achieve it is to mix the sounds and sights of a place with action. This kind of art is at its best lost in its craft. Garrett Mattingly's classic *The Armada* is a good case study. He may assume, and use without fear of critic's horror, the sounds of the sea and ships, the sounds of wind and sail, the smells of powder and cordage. . . . All these devices will be true to subject and circumstance—hence to art." Hence my depiction of Hawthorne's commonly remarked-on nervous gestures with his fingers as I described him at the table in the hotel in Lenox in November 1851. I did not anticipate a "critic's horror" at my being as self-indulgent as Edmund Morris in *Dutch*!

Chapter 18

1. Since a theme of this book is the burgeoning significance of Internet blogging I quote some of the blog comments which followed after I discovered the part of Perrin's blog entitled " 'Let us keep each other's secrets,' " probably by receiving a Google "Scholar Alert."

HP, February 15, 2011: "Nicole, all hail! [I did not then know Nicole's surname.] It looks to me as if you found something very important that Bezanson missed and that none of the rest of us saw. Bezanson pointed out the passage in *American Note-Books* about an idle man's sitting on a cliff throwing stones at his own shadow, far below, but he did not point out the passage in "Foot-prints on the Sea-Shore," which is much closer to HM's passage in *Clarel*. Congratulations! Nicole, I have a new chapter on Melville and Hawthorne in the nearly complete *Melville Biography: An Inside Narrative*. In it I deal with the slow stages of learning about *Clarel*. I want to cite you in the neatest most professional way, the URL, the blog title, exactly. I am not surprised at all that an Internet blogger would come up with something the professionals missed. It will happen more and more often, and everyone will be grateful, I trust. Knowing what you know now, do read my *Clarel* chapters in the biography and let me know if you see anything else you can help with."

NP, February 15, 2011: "Wow, this is amazing! . . . Certainly the most thrilling thing to happen here at *bibliographing*."

HP, February 16, 2011: "Thank you, Nicole. Last night I drafted a new paragraph for my chapter on *Why Melville Took Hawthorne Along on the Pilgrimage* [working title]. The academic failure to think! Bezanson did not think to check the timing of the availability of that passage of the *American Note-Books* (or whether [it was] in a pre-publication form in the *Atlantic* or [was] not available till the book came out in 1868) and it never occurred to me that its availability had anything to do with the dating of [Melville's] work on *Clarel*. Of course the fact that the description of Vine's pelting his shadow comes in the third book seems to make knowing about the availability less important. Nevertheless, we all goofed, as we so often do, blinded by the obvious relevance of the words in the *Note-Books*. Now simply by reading more of Hawthorne's minor pieces Nicole discovers that "Foot-prints" is very likely the true source and that the *Note-Books* may or may not have been a supplementary source! And of course Melville had owned "Foot-prints" in his 1842 Munroe *Twice-Told Tales* which Hawthorne gave him in 1851. So the publication of *Passages from the American Note-Books* has no significance at all in dating Melville's work on *Clarel*.

"Academics do the dumbest things. It occurred to only one academic, I think [Harrison Hayford], that Melville might have given NH the copy of *Moby-Dick* which he wrote to him about on 17 November 1851. It also occurred to a man in the real world, Bill Reese, the New Haven book dealer! What do you do when you dedicate a book to a friend who is about to leave the area? When you get copies you rush off to give him a copy before he goes! And we never knew until we had the account of the meeting at what became the Curtis Hotel, in Lenox. Long live responsible bloggers! May they continue to live in the real world."

2. See *Correspondence*, 231–42, and Parker, 2:114–20, 136–45.

3. See *Journals*, 154–55, 539–41.

4. Wilson's politics were not Judge Shaw's. The *Boston Atlas* on November 3, 1849, reported that the innkeeper at a Democratic convention had offered a resolution opposing slavery in any form, and had been voted down, decisively.

5. Frank E. Vandiver in "Biography as an Agent of Humanism" asks, "How dare a biographer assume a thought, a bias, a prejudice of a subject unless some letter, some speech, some reliable source speaks?" (18). If I had not had many examples of Melville's homospatial visions of different times at the same place as detailed in this chapter I would not have been so daring.

Chapter 19

1. The starting point for my research in 1988 was Brian Higgins's *Herman Melville: An Annotated Bibliography*, and Higgins provided some articles he copied from his hometown publications, *Transactions of the Leicestershire Archæological Society* (now, of course, available online) and the Leicester *Wyvern*. Books on Pre-Raphaelites, Fabian Socialists, and others which I surveyed by the yard (books such as are on the open shelves of all university libraries), would require many pages to list, and any such listing would thwart the purpose of encouraging others to elaborate or challenge the hypotheses advanced here.

2. Stoddard is discussed further in the next paragraph; see also chapter 13, n. 3 above. In chapter 39 of *Omoo*, Melville sketches the way the old Polynesian bosom-friend relations ("extravagant friendships, unsurpassed by the story of Damon and Pythias") had in modern Tahiti degenerated "into a mere mercenary relation."

Melville professes to have had his own tayo there, Poky, "a handsome youth," who never could "do enough" for him.

3. At this point I all but abandon citing sources: anyone checking my quotations and assertions on an Internet browser should find them fast and then be led into further connections between and among the British admirers of Melville.

4. Hudson made these comments at a Humanitarian League meeting in 1917; quoted on page 3 in John F. C. Pontin, "Henry David Thoreau / Henry S. Salt," *Thoreau Journal Quarterly* 7, no. 3 (July 1975): 3–11, available at http://www.henrysalt .co.uk/studies/essays/henry-david-thoreau-henry-stephens-salt.

Chapter 20

1. Letter in the New York Public Library, Gansevoort-Lansing Collection, Box 311. See also Parker, 2:851.

Works Cited

Allen, Gay Wilson. *The Solitary Singer: A Critical Biography of Walt Whitman.* New York: New York University Press, 1967.

Ames, Mary Clemmer. *A Memorial of Alice and Phœbe Cary, with Some of Their Later Poems.* New York: Hurd and Houghton, 1873.

Arvin, Newton. *Herman Melville.* New York: William Sloan Associates, 1950.

Backscheider, Paula. *Reflections on Biography.* Oxford: Oxford University Press, 2001.

Baker, Carlos. Review of *The Melville Log*, by Jay Leyda. *American Quarterly* 5, no. 1 (Spring 1953): 77–82.

Balaam, Peter. *Misery's Mathematics: Mourning, Compensation, and Reality in Antebellum American Literature.* New York: Routledge, 2009.

Bandura, Albert. "Moral Disengagement in the Perpetration of Inhumanities." Special issue, "Evil and Violence." *Personality and Social Psychology Review* 3, no. 3 (1999): 193–209.

———. "Selective Moral Disengagement in the Exercise of Moral Agency." *Journal of Moral Education* 31, no. 2 (2002): 101–19.

Banting, Pamela. "The Archive as a Literary Genre: Some Theoretical Speculations." *Archivaria* 23 (Winter 1986–87): 119–22.

Barbarow, George. "Leyda's Melville—A Reconsideration." *Hudson Review* 7, no. 1 (Winter 1955): 585–93.

Batchelor, John, ed. *The Art of Literary Biography.* Oxford: Clarendon Press, 1995.

Baym, Nina. "Melville's Quarrel with Fiction." *PMLA* 94 (October 1979): 909–23.

Beaver, Harold. "Ishmael and His Clan." Review of *Herman Melville: A Biography, 1819–1851*, by Hershel Parker. *TLS*, January 10, 1997, 3–4.

———, ed. *Moby-Dick.* Harmondsworth, Middlesex, Eng.: Penguin, 1972.

Benton, Michael. *Literary Biography: An Introduction.* Chichester, West Sussex, Eng.: Wiley-Blackwell, 2009.

Bercaw Edwards, Mary K. *Cannibal Old Me: Spoken Sources in Melville's Early Works.* Kent, Ohio: Kent State University Press, 2009.

Bercovitch, Sacvan, ed. *Cambridge History of American Literature.* Vol. 2, *Prose Writing, 1820–1865.* New York: Cambridge University Press, 1995.

———. Review of *American Romanticism and the Marketplace*, by Michael T. Gilmore. *TLS*, January 9, 1987, 40.

———. *Rites of Assent: Transformations in the Symbolic Construction of America.* New York: Routledge, 1993.

Berman, Paul. "Into the Deep." Review of *Melville: A Biography*, by Laurie Robertson-Lorant. *Slate*, July 10, 1996, http://www.slate.com/articles/arts/books/1996/07/into_the_deep.html.

———. "Spirits from the Vasty Deep." Review of *Herman Melville: A Biography, 1819–1851*, by Hershel Parker. *New York Times Book Review*, December 22, 1996, 12–13.

———. "Wilson and Our Non-Wilsonian Age." In *Edmund Wilson: Centennial Reflections*, edited by Lewis M. Dabney, 266–75. Princeton: The Mercantile Library of New York in Association with Princeton University Press, 1997.

Bezanson, Walter, ed. *Clarel*. New York: Hendricks House, 1960.

———. "Historical and Critical Note." In *Clarel*, by Herman Melville, edited by Harrison Hayford, Alma A. MacDougall, Hershel Parker, and G. Thomas Tanselle, 505–637. Evanston and Chicago: Northwestern University Press and the Newberry Library, 1991.

Blake, Robert. "The Art of Biography." In Homberger and Charmley, 75–93.

Blum, Hester. "Melville, Three Ways." *Studies in the Novel* 41, no. 3 (Fall 2009): 368–75.

Bostridge, Mark, ed. *Lives for Sale: Biographers' Tales*. London: Continuum, 2004.

Bousquet, Marc. Brainstorm (*Chronicle of Higher Education* blog), January 5, 2011, chronicle.com/blogs/brainstorm/.

Bradbury, Malcolm. "The Telling Life: Some Thoughts on Literary Biography." In Homberger and Charmley, 131–40.

Braswell, William. Review of *The Melville Log*, by Jay Leyda, and *Herman Melville*, by Leon Howard. *American Literature* 24, no. 2 (May 1952): 245–47.

———. "The Satirical Temper of Melville's *Pierre*." *American Literature* 7, no. 4 (January 1936): 424–38.

Bratton, Jacqueline S. *New Readings in Theatre History*. Cambridge: Cambridge University Press, 2003.

Brill, A. A. "Introduction." In *Leonardo da Vinci: A Study in Psychosexuality*, by Sigmund Freud, translated by A. A. Brill, 24–25. New York: Random House, 1947.

Brodhead, Richard H. "All in the Family." Review of *Herman Melville: A Biography*, by Hershel Parker. *New York Times Book Review*, June 23, 2002, 13–14.

———. "Bookend: The Book That Ruined Melville." *New York Times Book Review*, January 7, 1996, 35.

———. *Hawthorne, Melville, and the Novel*. Chicago: University of Chicago Press, 1976.

———. *The School of Hawthorne*. New Haven, Conn.: Yale University Press, 1986. Chap. 2, "Hawthorne, Melville, and the Fiction of Prophecy," 17–47, reprinted in *American Renaissance*, edited by Harold Bloom, 201–40. New York: Chelsea House, 2004.

Bryant, John, ed. *A Companion to Melville Studies*. Westport, Conn.: Greenwood Press, 1986.

———. *The Fluid Text: A Theory of Revision and Editing for Book and Screen*. Ann Arbor: University of Michigan Press, 2002.

———. Review of *Melville: His World and Work*, by Andrew Delbanco. *New England Quarterly* 79, no. 2 (June 2006): 333–36.

Bryant, John, and Robert Milder, eds. *Melville's Evermoving Dawn: Centennial Essays*. Kent, Ohio: Kent State University Press, 1997.

Burton, Antoinette. *Archive Stories: Facts, Fictions, and the Writing of History*. Durham, N.C.: Duke University Press, 2005.

Butterworth, Trevor. "Slouching Towards Begorrah." *NewsWatch*, October 28, 1999.

Charvat, William. *The Profession of Authorship in America: 1800–1870*. Edited by Matthew J. Bruccoli. Columbus: Ohio State University Press, 1968.

Cherniack, Lawrie. Review of *Herman Melville*, by Elizabeth Hardwick. *Globe and Mail* (Toronto), July 8, 2000.

Christianson, Gale E. *Writing Lives Is the Devil! Essays of a Biographer at Work*. Hamden, Conn.: Archon, 1993.

Clingham, Greg. Review of *Aspects of Samuel Johnson*, by Howard D. Weinbrot. *Biography* 30, no. 4 (Fall 2007): 645–49.

Cluff, Randall. "'Thou Man of the Evangelist': Henry Cheever's Review of *Typee*." *Leviathan* 3, no. 1 (March 2001): 61–71.

Cohen, Hennig. "'Why Talk of Jaffa'?: Melville's *Israel Potter*, Baron Gros, Zummo, and the Plague." In Sten, 162–78.

Cohen, Hennig, and Donald Yannella. *Herman Melville's Malcolm Letter: "Man's Final Lore."* New York: Fordham University Press and the New York Public Library, 1992.

Costa, Richard Hauer. *Edmund Wilson: Our Neighbor from Talcottville*. Syracuse, N.Y.: Syracuse University Press, 1980.

Cowen, Walker. "Melville's Marginalia: Hawthorne." *Studies in the American Renaissance* (1978): 279–302.

Crews, Frederick C. "Melville the Great." Review of *Melville: His World and Work*, by Andrew Delbanco. *New York Review of Books*, December 1, 2005.

Da Costa, Erica. Review of *Herman Melville*, by Elizabeth Hardwick. *New York Times*, July 30, 2000.

Davenport, Gary. "Necessary Fictions." Review of *Flawed Texts and Verbal Icons*, by Hershel Parker. *Sewanee Review* 93, no. 3 (July–September 1985): 499–504.

Davey, Michael J. *A Routledge Literary Sourcebook on Herman Melville's "Moby-Dick."* London: Routledge, 2003.

Davidson, Cathy, ed. Special issue, "New Melville." *American Literature* 66, no. 1 (March 1994).

———. "No! In Thunder!" *American Literature* 76, no. 4 (December 2004): 665–75.

———. Preface. Special issue, "No More Separate Spheres!" *American Literature* 70, no. 3 (September 1998): 443–63.

Davidson, Cathy, and Jessamyn Hatcher. Preface. *No More Separate Spheres!* Edited by Davidson and Hatcher, 1–6. Durham, N.C.: Duke University Press, 2002.

Davis, Merrell R. *Melville's "Mardi": A Chartless Voyage*. New Haven, Conn.: Yale University Press, 1952.

Davis, Merrell R., and William H. Gilman. *The Letters of Herman Melville*. New Haven, Conn.: Yale University Press, 1960.

Delbanco, Andrew. "The Great Leviathan." Review of *Herman Melville: A Biography: 1819–1851*, by Hershel Parker. *New York Review of Books*, May 15, 1997, 18–23.

———. "The Great White Male." Review of *Herman Melville: A Biography, 1851–1891*, by Hershel Parker. *New Republic* 227, no. 14 (September 30, 2002): 33–37.

———. *Melville: His World and Work*. New York: Knopf, 2005.

———. "Melville in the '80s." *American Literary History* 4, no. 4 (Winter 1992): 709–25.

———. "Melville's Fever." Review of *Pierre, or the Ambiguities*, by Herman Melville, edited by Hershel Parker, pictures by Maurice Sendak, and *Pierre, or the Ambiguities*, edited by Harrison Hayford, Hershel Parker, and G. Thomas Tanselle, with Historical Note by Leon Howard and Hershel Parker. *New York Review of Books*, April 4, 1996, 42–45.

Dettlaff, Shirley M. "Melville's Aesthetics." In Bryant, *Companion to Melville Studies*, 625–65.

Dimock, Wai-chee. *Empire for Liberty*. Princeton: Princeton University Press, 1989.

Donoghue, Dennis. "Contempt Bred of Familiarity." Review of *Hawthorne: A Life*, by Brenda Wineapple. *Los Angeles Times Book Review*, December 28, 2003, R16.

Dryden, Edgar A. *Monumental Melville: The Formation of a Literary Career*. Stanford, Calif.: Stanford University Press, 2004.

Duff, Wendy M., and Verne Harris. "Stories and Names: Archival Description as Narrating Records and Constructing Meanings." *Archival Science* 2 (2002): 263–85.

Edel, Leon. "The Figure Under the Carpet." In Pachter, 16–34. (Also in Oates, 18-31.)

Egan, Hugh. Review of *Melville: The Making of the Poet*, by Hershel Parker, and *Frederick Douglass and Herman Melville*, edited by Robert S. Levine and Samuel Otter. *American Literature* 81, no. 3 (September 2009): 623–25.

Eliot, George. "Belles Lettres." *Westminster Review* 65, no. 127 (January 1856): 290–312.

Elliott, Emory, ed. *Columbia Literary History of the United States*. New York: Columbia University Press, 1988.

Epstein, William H., ed. *Contesting the Subject: Essays in the Postmodern Theory and Practice of Biography and Biographical Criticism*. West Lafayette, Ind.: Purdue University Press, 1991.

———. *Recognizing Biography*. Philadelphia: University of Pennsylvania Press, 1987.

Espinasse, Francis. *Literary Recollections and Sketches*. London: Hodder and Stoughton, 1893.

Esposito, Scott. "Litblogs Provide a New Alternative for Readers." *Rain Taxi* (Summer 2005), http://www.raintaxi.com/online/2005summer/blogs.shtml.

Faggen, Robert. "Beyond Melville the Literary Legend." Review of *Melville: His World and Works*, by Andrew Delbanco. *Los Angeles Times*, October 16, 2005.

———. "A Genius of Concealment." Review of *Herman Melville: A Biography, 1819–1851*, by Hershel Parker. *Los Angeles Times*, December 15, 1996, 8.

Feidelson, Charles. "Melville Chronicled." Review of *The Melville Log*, by Jay Leyda; *Herman Melville: A Biography*, by Leon Howard; and *Melville's Early Life and "Redburn,"* by William H. Gilman. *Yale Review* 41 (December 1951): 297–300.

———. *Symbolism and American Literature*. Chicago: University of Chicago Press, 1953.

Ferreira-Buckley, Linda. "Beyond the Archives: Research as a Lived Process." Review of *Beyond the Archives: Research as a Lived Process*, edited by Gesa E. Kirsch and Liz Rohan. *Biography* 32, no. 4 (Fall 2009): 867–70.

Feyerabend, Paul. "Creativity—A Dangerous Myth." *Critical Inquiry* 13, no. 4 (Summer 1987): 700–711.

Field, Maunsell B. *Memories of Many Men and of Some Women*. New York: Harper and Brothers, 1874.

Fields, James. "Our Whispering Gallery II." *Atlantic Monthly* 27, no. 160 (February 1871): 246–58.

Fischer, Heinz-Dietrich, and Erika Fischer. *The Pulitzer Prize Archive.* Farmington Hills, Mich.: Thomson Gale, 2002.

Foley, Barbara. "From New Criticism to Deconstruction: The Example of Charles Feidelson's *Symbolism and American Literature.*" *American Quarterly* 36, no. 1 (Spring 1984): 44–64.

Forster, John, *The Life of Charles Dickens.* Philadelphia: J. B. Lippincott, 1872.

Foster, Charles H. "'Something in Emblems': A Reinterpretation of *Moby-Dick.*" *New England Quarterly* 34, no. 1 (March 1961): 3–35. Excerpted in Hayford and Parker, "*Moby-Dick*" *as Doubloon,* 277–84.

France, Peter, and William St Clair, eds. *Mapping Lives: The Uses of Biography.* Oxford: Oxford University Press, 2002.

Fraser, Antonia. "Optical Research." In Bostridge, 113–17.

Garner, Stanton. *The Civil War World of Herman Melville.* Lawrence: University Press of Kansas, 1993.

———. "The Picaresque Career of Thomas Melvill, Junior: Part II." *Melville Society Extracts* 62 (May 1985): 1, 4–10.

———. Review of *Herman Melville: A Biography, 1819–1851,* by Hershel Parker. *Melville Society Extracts* 112 (March 1998): 27–29.

Gibson, James J. *The Senses Considered as Perceptual Systems.* Boston: Houghton Mifflin, 1966.

Gilman, William H. *Melville's Early Life and "Redburn."* New York: New York University Press, 1951.

Glendinning, Victoria. "Lies and Silences." In Homberger and Charmley, 49–62.

Gollin, Rita K. "The Quondam Sailor and Melville's *Omoo.*" *American Literature* 48 (March 1976): 75–79.

Gordon, Lyndall. "The Death Mask." In Bostridge, 1–6.

Gornick, Vivian. "The Scrivener and the Whale." Review of *Melville: His World and Work,* by Andrew Delbanco. *Nation,* December 5, 2005, 43–46.

Green, Dan. "Problems in the Story Line." The Reading Experience 2.0, October 23, 2007, http://noggs.typepad.com/the_reading_experience_al/page/10/.

Greene, Mark Allen. "The Power of Archives: Archivists' Values and Value in the Post-Modern Age." Inaugural address as president of the Society of American Archivists, December 17, 2010. Available at http://www2.archivists.org/sites/all/files/GreeneAddressAug08.pdf.

———. "The Power of Meaning: The Archival Mission in the Postmodern Age." *American Archivist* 65, no. 1 (Spring–Summer 2002): 42–55.

———. Review of *Archive Stories,* by Antoinette Burton. *Biography* 30, no. 3 (Summer 2007): 397–99.

Greg, W. W. "The Rationale of Copy-Text." *Studies in Bibliography* 3 (1950–51): 19–36. Reprinted in his *Collected Papers,* edited by J. C. Maxwell, 374–91. Oxford: Clarendon Press, 1966.

Grenberg, Bruce L. *Some Other World to Find: Quest and Negation in the Works of Herman Melville.* Urbana: University of Illinois Press, 1989.

Grey, Robin, and Douglas Robillard with Hershel Parker. "Melville's Milton: A Transcription of Melville's Marginalia in His Copy of *The Poetical Works of*

John Milton." *Leviathan* 4 (March and October 2002): 117–204. Reprinted in *Melville and Milton,* edited by Robin Grey, 115–203. Pittsburgh: Duquesne University Press, 2004.

Grimes, William. Review of *Melville: His World and Work,* by Andrew Delbanco. *New York Times,* October 5, 2005.

Gunn, Giles, ed. *A Historical Guide to Herman Melville.* New York: Oxford University Press, 2005.

Hall, N. John. "Those Wonderful Youths and Maidens, My Reviewers." In Salwak, 22–31.

Halttunen, Karen. Review of *Mourning, Gender, and Creativity in the Art of Herman Melville,* by Neal L. Tolchin. *American Historical Review* 95, no. 2 (April 1990): 576–77.

Hamilton, Ian. *How to Do Biography: A Primer.* Cambridge: Harvard University Press, 2008.

Hannay, James, ed. *The Poetical Works of Edgar Allan Poe with a Notice of His Life and Genius.* London: Addey and Co., 1853.

Hardwick, Elizabeth. "The Decline of Book Reviewing." *Harper's Magazine,* October 1959, 139–43.

———. *Herman Melville.* New York: Penguin, 2000.

Hawthorne, Nathaniel. *The American Notebooks.* Edited by Claude M. Simpson. Columbus: Ohio State University Press, 1972.

———. *Passages from the American Note-Books.* Boston: Ticknor and Fields, 1868.

———. *Passages from the English Note-Books.* Boston: Fields, Osgood, 1870.

———. *Twice-Told Tales.* Boston: Munroe, 1842.

Hayford, Harrison. "Melville and Hawthorne: A Biographical and Critical Study." Ph.D. diss., Yale University, 1945.

———. *Melville's Prisoners.* Evanston, Ill.: Northwestern University Press, 2003.

———. "The Significance of Melville's 'Agatha' Letters." *ELH, A Journal of English Literary History* 13 (December 1946): 299–310.

Hayford, Harrison, and Merrell Davis. "Herman Melville as Office-Seeker." *Modern Language Quarterly* 10, nos. 2 and 3 (June and September 1949): 168–83, 377–88.

Hayford, Harrison, and Hershel Parker, eds. *"Moby-Dick" as Doubloon.* New York: Norton, 1970.

Heflin, Wilson. *Herman Melville's Whaling Years.* Edited by Mary K. Bercaw Edwards and Thomas Farel Heffernan. Nashville: Vanderbilt University Press, 2004.

———. "New Light on Herman Melville's Cruise in the *Charles and Henry.*" *Historic Nantucket* 22 (October 1974): 6–27.

Heimert, Alan. "*Moby-Dick* and American Political Symbolism." *American Quarterly* 15, no. 4 (Winter 1963): 498–534. Excerpted in Hayford and Parker, *"Moby-Dick" as Doubloon,* 306–18.

Helms, Alan. "Commentary." *Nineteenth-Century Literature* 52, no. 3 (December 1997): 413–16. Exchange between Helms and Hershel Parker on Whitman's "Live Oak, with Moss," available at http://www.classroomelectric.org/volume3/price/lowm.php?inc=helmsparker.

Hemstreet, Charles. *Literary New York: Its Landmarks and Associations.* New York: G. P. Putnam's Sons, 1903.

Higgins, Brian. "Melville." *American Literary Scholarship* (1988): 53–66.

Higgins, Brian, and Hershel Parker, eds. *Herman Melville: The Contemporary Reviews.* New York and Cambridge: Cambridge University Press, 1995.

Higgins, Brian, and Hershel Parker. *Reading Melville's "Pierre; or, The Ambiguities."* Baton Rouge: Louisiana State University Press, 2006.

Holloway, Mark. "Norman Douglas." In Meyers, 89–105.

Holmes, Richard. *Footsteps: Adventures of a Romantic Biographer.* London: Hodder and Stoughton, 1985.

Homberger, Eric, and John Charmley, eds. *The Troubled Face of Biography.* New York: St. Martin's, 1988.

Houtchens, Lawrence H. "Charles Dickens and International Copyright." *American Literature* 13, no. 1 (March 1941): 18–28.

Howard, Leon. *Herman Melville: A Biography.* Berkeley and Los Angeles: University of California Press, 1951.

Howard, Leon, and Hershel Parker. "Historical Note." In *Pierre; or, The Ambiguities,* edited by Harrison Hayford, Hershel Parker, and G. Thomas Tanselle, 365–79. Evanston and Chicago: Northwestern University Press and the Newberry Library, 1971.

Hughes, Kathryn. Review of *Literary Biography,* by Michael Benton. *Biography* 33, no. 3 (Summer 2010): 552–56.

Hume, Robert D. "The Aims and Limits of Historical Scholarship." *Review of English Studies,* n.s., 53, no. 211 (2002): 399–422.

———. *Reconstructing Contexts: The Aims and Principles of Archaeo-Historicism.* Oxford: Oxford University Press, 1999.

———. "Texts Within Contexts: Notes Toward a Historical Method." *Philological Quarterly* 71, no. 1 (Winter 1992): 69–100.

Hunt, Lynn. "Against Presentism." *Perspectives on History,* May 2002, http://www.historians.org/perspectives/issues/2002/0205/0205pre1.cfm.

Irving, Pierre M. *The Life and Letters of Washington Irving.* New York: G. P. Putnam, 1864.

Karl, Frederick R. *Art into Life: The Craft of Literary Biography.* Youngstown, Ohio: Etruscan Press, 2005.

Katz, Jonathan. *Gay American History.* New York: Avon, 1976.

———. *Gay/Lesbian Almanac.* New York: Carroll and Graf, 1983.

Kendall, Paul Murray. *The Art of Biography.* New York: Norton, 1965.

Kennedy, Frederick, and Joyce Deveau. "Archibald MacMechan and the Melville Revival." *Leviathan* 1, no. 2 (October 1999): 5–37.

Kiernan, Brian. "A Tale of a Tale." Review of *Herman Melville: A Biography, 1819–1851,* by Hershel Parker. *Sydney Morning Herald,* June 14, 1997.

Kinkead-Weekes, Mark. "Writing Lives Forwards: A Case for Strictly Chronological Biography." In France and St Clair, 235–52.

Kushner, Tony. *The Art of Maurice Sendak: 1980 to the Present.* New York: Harry N. Abrams, 2003.

———. "Writing the Playwright." Interview with Frederick Tuten. *Guernica,* June 2005, http://www.guernicamag.com/interviews/71/writing_the_playwright_1/.

Lal, Vinay. Review of *Dwelling in the Archive: Women Writing House, Home, and History in Late Colonial India,* by Antoinette Burton. *Biography* 27, no. 3 (Summer 2004): 673–76.

Lauter, Paul. *Canons and Contexts.* Oxford: Oxford University Press, 1991.

———. *Reconstructing American Literature: Courses, Syllabi, Issues.* Old Westbury, N.Y.: Feminist Press, 1983.

———. "Society and the Profession, 1958–83." *PMLA* 99, no. 3 (May 1984): 414–26.

Lee, Hermione. "A Great House Full of Rooms." In Bostridge, 31–37.

Lee, Maurice S. "Melville's Subversive Political Philosophy: 'Benito Cereno' and the Fate of Speech." *American Literature* 72, no. 3 (September 2000): 495–519.

———. *Slavery, Philosophy, and American Literature, 1830–1860.* Cambridge: Cambridge University Press, 2005.

Leonard, John, "The Wise Woman and the Whale." Review of *Herman Melville*, by Elizabeth Hardwick. *New York Review of Books* 47, no. 12 (July 20, 2000): 4–6.

Levine, Robert S., ed. *The Cambridge Companion to Herman Melville.* Cambridge: Cambridge University Press, 1998.

———. "Introduction." In Levine, 1–11.

Lewis, Jeremy. "Pantherine." In Bostridge, 43–51.

Leyda, Jay. "Herman Melville, 1972." In *The Chief Glory of Every People: Essays on Classic American Writers*, edited by Matthew J. Bruccoli, 161–71. Carbondale: Southern Illinois University Press, 1973.

———. *The Melville Log: A Documentary Life of Herman Melville, 1819–1891.* 2 vols. New York: Harcourt, Brace, 1951. Reprinted with "Supplement," New York: Gordian Press, 1969.

———. *The Portable Melville.* New York: Viking, 1952.

Longford, Elizabeth. "Reflections of a Biographer." In Salwak, 146–48.

Lowe, Matthew Forrest. Review of *Melville: His World and Work*, by Andrew Delbanco. *Literature and Theology* 20, no. 3 (September 2006): 335–38.

Lundin, Roger. "Orphan in the Storm." Review of *Melville: His World and Work*, by Andrew Delbanco. *Books & Culture: A Christian Review*, September 1, 2005.

Lynn, Kenneth S. "Melville's Rage." Review of *Correspondence*, by Herman Melville, edited by Lynn Horth, and *Herman Melville's Malcolm Letter*, by Hennig Cohen and Donald Yannella. *TLS*, December 31, 1993, 3–4.

Mansfield, Luther S., and Howard P. Vincent, eds. *Moby-Dick.* New York: Hendricks House, 1952.

Mariani, Paul. "Reassembling the Dust." In Oates, 104–23.

Marrs, Cody. "A Wayward Art: *Battle-Pieces* and Melville's Poetic Turn." *American Literature* 82, no. 1 (March 2010): 91–119.

Martin, Jay. Review of *Home as Found: Authority and Genealogy in Nineteenth-Century American Literature*, by Eric J. Sundquist. *American Literature* 52, no. 4 (January 1981): 654–55.

Martin, Robert K., and Leland S. Person. "Missing Letters: Hawthorne, Melville, and Scholarly Desire." *ESQ: A Journal of the American Renaissance* 46, nos. 178 and 179 (First and Second Quarters 2000): 99–122.

Masefield, John. *A Mainsail Haul.* London: Elkin Mathews, 1905.

Maugham, W. Somerset. "Herman Melville and *Moby Dick*." In his *Great Novelists and Their Novels*, 211–32. Philadelphia: John C. Winston, 1948.

McFedries, Paul. "Presentism." Word Spy, November 3, 1997, http://www.wordspy.com/words/presentism.asp.

Melville, Gansevoort. *Gansevoort Melville's 1846 London Journal and Letters from England, 1845*. Edited by Hershel Parker. New York: New York Public Library, 1966.

Melville, Herman. *Billy Budd, Sailor (An Inside Narrative)*. Edited by Harrison Hayford and Merton M. Sealts, Jr. Chicago: University of Chicago Press, 1962.

———. *Clarel: A Poem and Pilgrimage in the Holy Land*. Edited by Harrison Hayford, Alma A. MacDougall, Hershel Parker, and G. Thomas Tanselle. Vol. 12 of *The Writings of Herman Melville*. Evanston and Chicago: Northwestern University Press and the Newberry Library, 1991.

———. *The Confidence-Man: His Masquerade*. Edited by Harrison Hayford, Hershel Parker, and G. Thomas Tanselle. Vol. 10 of *The Writings of Herman Melville*. Evanston and Chicago: Northwestern University Press and the Newberry Library, 1984.

———. *Correspondence*. Edited by Lynn Horth. Vol. 14 of *The Writings of Herman Melville*. Evanston and Chicago: Northwestern University Press and the Newberry Library, 1993.

———. *Israel Potter: His Fifty Years of Exile*. Edited by Harrison Hayford, Hershel Parker, and G. Thomas Tanselle. Vol. 8 of *The Writings of Herman Melville*. Evanston and Chicago: Northwestern University Press and the Newberry Library, 1982.

———. *Journals*. Edited by Howard C. Horsford with Lynn Horth. Vol. 15 of *The Writings of Herman Melville*. Evanston and Chicago: Northwestern University Press and the Newberry Library, 1989.

———. *Mardi; and, A Voyage Thither*. Edited by Harrison Hayford, Hershel Parker, and G. Thomas Tanselle. Vol. 3 of *The Writings of Herman Melville*. Evanston and Chicago: Northwestern University Press and the Newberry Library, 1970.

———. *Moby-Dick; or, The Whale*. Edited by Harrison Hayford, Hershel Parker, and G. Thomas Tanselle. Vol. 6 of *The Writings of Herman Melville*. Evanston and Chicago: Northwestern University Press and the Newberry Library, 1988.

———. *Omoo: A Narrative of Adventures in the South Seas*. Ed. Harrison Hayford, Hershel Parker, and G. Thomas Tanselle. Vol. 2 of *The Writings of Herman Melville*. Evanston and Chicago: Northwestern University Press and the Newberry Library, 1968.

———. *"The Piazza Tales" and Other Prose Pieces, 1839–1860*. Ed. Harrison Hayford, Alma A. MacDougall, G. Thomas Tanselle, et al. Vol. 9 of *The Writings of Herman Melville*. Evanston and Chicago: Northwestern University Press and the Newberry Library, 1987.

———. *Pierre; or, The Ambiguities*. Ed. Harrison Hayford, Hershel Parker, and G. Thomas Tanselle. Vol. 7 of *The Writings of Herman Melville*. Evanston and Chicago: Northwestern University Press and the Newberry Library, 1971.

———. *Published Poems: "Battle-Pieces," "John Marr," and "Timoleon."* Edited by Robert C. Ryan, Harrison Hayford, Alma MacDougall Reising, and G. Thomas Tanselle, with Historical Note by Hershel Parker. Vol. 11 of *The Writings of Herman Melville*. Evanston and Chicago: Northwestern University Press and the Newberry Library, 2009.

———. *Redburn: His First Voyage*. Edited by Harrison Hayford, Hershel Parker, and G. Thomas Tanselle. Vol. 4 of *The Writings of Herman Melville*. Evanston and Chicago: Northwestern University Press and the Newberry Library, 1969.

———. ["Thomas Melvill, Jr."]. In *The History of Pittsfield (Berkshire County), Massachusetts, from the Year 1800 to the Year 1876*, compiled and edited by J. E. A. Smith, 398–400. Springfield, Mass.: C. W. Bryan, 1876.

———. *Typee: A Peep at Polynesian Life*. Edited by Harrison Hayford, Hershel Parker, and G. Thomas Tanselle. Vol. 1 of *The Writings of Herman Melville*. Evanston and Chicago: Northwestern University Press and the Newberry Library, 1968.

———. *White-Jacket; or, The World in a Man-of-War*. Edited by Harrison Hayford, Hershel Parker, and G. Thomas Tanselle. Vol. 5 of *The Writings of Herman Melville*. Evanston and Chicago: Northwestern University Press and the Newberry Library, 1970.

Metcalf, Eleanor Melville. *Herman Melville: Cycle and Epicycle*. Cambridge, Mass.: Harvard University Press, 1953.

Meyers, Jeffrey, ed. *The Craft of Literary Biography*. New York: Schocken, 1985.

———. "Reflections of a Book Reviewer." *Antioch Review* 70, no. 1 (Winter 2012): 57–68.

Milder, Robert. "Circling Melville." Review of *Herman Melville: A Biography, 1851–1891*, by Hershel Parker; *Melville: A Biography*, by Laurie Robertson-Lorant; and *Melville and His Circle: The Last Years*, by William B. Dillingham. *Nineteenth-Century Literature* 52, no. 4 (March 1998): 529–43.

———. *Exiled Royalties: Melville and the Life We Imagine*. Oxford: Oxford University Press, 2006.

———. "Herman Melville 1819–1891: A Brief Biography." In *A Historical Guide to Herman Melville*, edited by Giles Gunn, 17–58. New York: Oxford University Press, 2005.

———. "Melville's 'Intentions' in *Pierre*." *Studies in the Novel* 6 (Summer 1974): 186–99.

———. "Very Like a Whale: Parker's *Melville*." Review of *Herman Melville: A Biography, 1851–1891*, by Hershel Parker. *Belles Lettres: A Literary Review* 2, no. 1 (September–October 2002): 5–6.

Miles, Edwin A. "The Forty-second Meeting." *Journal of Southern History* 43, no. 1 (February 1977): 73–102.

Miller, Cheryl. "The One That Got Away." Review of *Melville: His World and Work*, by Andrew Delbanco. *Claremont Review of Books* 6, no. 2 (Spring 2006): 29–31.

Miller, Donald L. *Lewis Mumford: A Life*. Pittsburgh: University of Pittsburgh Press, 1989.

Miller, Edwin Haviland. *Melville: A Biography*. New York: George Braziller, 1975.

Miller, Perry. *The Raven and the Whale: The War of Words and Wits in the Era of Poe and Melville*. New York: Harcourt, Brace, 1956.

Minnigerode, Meade. *Some Personal Letters of Herman Melville and a Bibliography*. New York: The Brick Row Bookshop, 1922.

Modern, John Lardas. *Secularism in Antebellum America*. Chicago: University of Chicago Press, 2011.

Monk, Ray. "Life Without Theory: Biography as an Exemplar of Philosophical Understanding." *Poetics Today* 28, no. 3 (Fall 2007): 527–70. Available at http://poeticstoday.dukejournals.org.

Morse, John Torrey, Jr. *Life and Letters of Oliver Wendell Holmes*. 2 vols. Boston: Houghton Mifflin, 1896.

Mumford, Lewis. *Herman Melville.* New York: Harcourt, Brace, 1929.

———. "Emerson Behind Barbed Wire." Review of *The Journals and Miscellaneous Notebooks of Ralph Waldo Emerson,* edited by William H. Gilman, Alfred R. Ferguson, Merrell R. Davis, Merton M. Sealts, Jr., and Harrison Hayford, and *The Early Lectures of Ralph Waldo Emerson,* edited by Robert E. Spiller and Stephen E. Whicher. *New York Review of Books,* January 18, 1968, 3–5.

Murphy, William M. "John Butler Yeats." In Meyers, 33–54.

Murray, Henry A. "Introduction" and "Explanatory Notes." In *Pierre; or, The Ambiguities,* edited by Murray, xiii–ciii, 429–504. New York: Hendricks House, 1949.

Murray, Henry A., with Harvey Myerson and Eugene Taylor. "Allan Melvill's By-blow." *Melville Society Extracts* 61 (February 1985): 1–6.

Myerson, Joel. "Editing and Politics." *Text* 6 (1993): 111–16.

Nadel, Ira Bruce. *Biography: Fiction, Fact, and Form.* New York: St. Martin's, 1984.

———. Review of *Reflections on Biography,* by Paula Backscheider. *Biography* 23, no. 4 (Fall 2000): 762–67.

Neisser, Ulrich. *Memory Observed.* San Francisco: W. H. Freeman, 1982.

Nichols, Dr. Thomas L. *Forty Years of American Life.* London: John Maxwell, 1864.

Norsworthy, Scott. "Matthew Henry Buckham, a.k.a. 'Maherbal.'" http://melvilliana.blogspot.com/2011/11/matthew-henry-buckham-aka-maherbal.html.

Oates, Stephen B., ed. *Biography as High Adventure: Life-Writers Speak on Their Art.* Amherst: University of Massachusetts Press, 1986.

Obenzinger, Hilton. *American Palestine: Melville, Twain, and the Holy Land Mania.* Princeton: Princeton University Press, 1999.

Oehlschlaeger, Fritz, and George Hendrick, eds. *Toward the Making of Thoreau's Modern Reputation: Selected Correspondence of S. A. Jones, A. W. Hosmer, H. S. Salt, H. G. O. Blake, and D. Ricketson.* Urbana: University of Illinois Press, 1979.

Olsen-Smith, Steven, and Merton M. Sealts, Jr. "A Cumulative Supplement to *Melville's Reading.*" *Leviathan* 6 (March 2004): 55–77.

Olsen-Smith, Steven, Peter Norberg, and Dennis C. Marnon, eds. "Online Catalog of Books and Documents Owned, Borrowed and Consulted by Herman Melville." Melville's Marginalia Online, http://melvillesmarginalia.org.

Otter, Samuel. *Melville's Anatomies.* Berkeley: University of California Press, 1999.

Owen, Susan J. *Restoration Theatre and Crisis.* Oxford: Clarendon Press, 1996.

Pachter, Marc, ed. *Telling Lives: The Biographer's Art.* Washington, D. C.: New Republic Books, 1979.

Parini, Jay. "The Hunting of Herman Melville." Review of *Melville: His World and Work,* by Andrew Delbanco. *Guardian* (London), November 4, 2005. Available at http://www.guardian.co.uk/books/2005/nov/05/highereducation.biography.

Parker, Hershel. "The Character of Vine in Melville's *Clarel.*" *Essays in Arts and Sciences* 15 (June 1986): 91–113.

———, ed. *The Confidence-Man: His Masquerade.* Second Norton Critical Edition. New York: Norton, 2006.

———. *Flawed Texts and Verbal Icons.* Evanston, Ill.: Northwestern University Press, 1984.

———. "Further Notices of *Pierre.*" *Extracts* 12 (October 1972): 4–5.

——. *Herman Melville: A Biography, 1819–1851* and *Herman Melville: A Biography, 1851–1891.* 2 vols. Baltimore: Johns Hopkins University Press, 1996, 2002.

——. "Herman Melville Crazy." *Extracts* (January 1973): 7.

——. "Herman Melville's *The Isle of the Cross*." *American Literature* 62 (March 1990): 1–16.

——. "Historical Supplement." In *Clarel: A Poem and Pilgrimage in the Holy Land,* edited by Harrison Hayford, Alma A. MacDougall, Hershel Parker, and G. Thomas Tanselle, 639–73. Evanston and Chicago: Northwestern University Press and the Newberry Library, 1991.

——. "Introduction." In *Melville's Prisoners,* by Harrison Hayford, vii–xi. Evanston, Ill.: Northwestern University Press, 2003.

——. "*The Isle of the Cross* and *Poems*: Lost Melville Books and the Indefinite Afterlife of Error." *Nineteenth-Century Literature* 62 (June 2007): 29–47.

——. "Melville and Hawthorne in the Berkshires." In *Aspects of Melville,* edited by David Scribner, 21–27. Pittsfield, Mass.: Berkshire County Historical Society at Arrowhead, 2001.

——. *Melville: The Making of the Poet.* Evanston, Ill.: Northwestern University Press, 2008.

——. "The Metaphysics of Indian-hating." *Nineteenth-Century Fiction* 18 (September 1963): 165–73.

——. "New Evidence on the Reception of *Pierre*." *Extracts* 13 (January 1973): 7.

——. "*The New Melville Log*: A Progress Report and An Appeal." *Modern Language Studies* 20, no. 1 (Winter 1990): 53–66.

——, ed., with pictures by Maurice Sendak. *Pierre; or, The Ambiguities: The Kraken Edition.* New York: HarperCollins, 1995.

——. *The Powell Papers: A Confidence Man Amok Among the Anglo-American Literati.* Evanston, Ill.: Northwestern University Press, 2011.

——. *Reading "Billy Budd."* Evanston, Ill.: Northwestern University Press, 1993.

——. "The Real 'Live Oak, with Moss': Straight Talk about Whitman's 'Gay Manifesto.'" *Nineteenth-Century Literature* 51, no. 22 (September 1996): 145–60.

——. "Walter E. Bezanson: A Memorial." *Leviathan* 17, no. 5 (March 2012): 37–42.

Parker, Hershel, and Harrison Hayford, eds. *Moby-Dick.* Second Norton Critical Edition. New York: Norton, 2001.

Parks Daloz, Laurent A., Cheryl H. Keen, James P. Keen, and Sharon Daloz Parks, eds. *Common Fire: Lives of Commitment in a Complex World.* Boston: Beacon Press, 1996.

Poirier, Richard. "The Monster in the Milk Bowl." Review of *Pierre; or, The Ambiguities: The Kraken Edition,* edited by Hershel Parker with pictures by Maurice Sendak. *London Review of Books,* October 3, 1996, 19–22.

Reiff, Raychel Haugrud. *Herman Melville: "Moby-Dick" and Other Works.* Tarrytown, N.Y.: Marshall Cavendish Benchmark, 2008.

Reynolds, David. *Beneath the American Renaissance.* New York: Alfred A. Knopf, 1988.

Ridley, Jane. "Tarts." In Bostridge, 186–90.

Robb, Graham. "A Narcissist's Wedding." In Bostridge, 11–14.

Robertson-Lorant, Laurie. *Melville: A Biography.* New York: Clarkson Potter, 1996.

Rollyson, Carl. *Biography: An Annotated Bibliography.* Lincoln, Neb.: iUniverse, 2007.

———. *Biography: A User's Guide*. Chicago: Ivan R. Dee, 2008.

———. "'Fascinating Fascism' Revisited: An Exercise in Biographical Criticism." *Journal of Historical Biography* 5 (Spring 2009): 1–22. Available at http://www.ufv.ca/jhb/.

Rollyson, Carl, and Lisa Paddock. *Herman Melville A to Z: The Essential Reference to His Life and Work*. New York: Facts On File, 2001.

Roschelle, Jeremy. "Learning in Interactive Environments: Prior Knowledge and New Experience." In "Public Institutions for Personal Learning: Establishing a Research Agenda," edited by J. H. Falk and L. D. Dierking, 37–51. Washington, D.C.: American Association of Museums, 1995. Available at http://ctl.sri.com/publications/displayPublication.jsp?ID=116.

Rosenthal, Tom. Review of *Melville: His World and Work*, by Andrew Delbanco. *Independent* (London), January 15, 2006.

Rothenberg, Albert. *The Emerging Goddess: The Creative Process in Art, Science, and Other Fields*. Chicago: University of Chicago Press, 1979.

Russo, Maria. Review of *Herman Melville*, by Elizabeth Hardwick. *Salon*, July 26, 2000, http://www.salon.com/2000/07/26/hardwick/.

Salt, Henry S. *Company I Have Kept*. London: George Allen and Unwin, 1930.

———. "Herman Melville." *Scottish Art Review* 2 (November 1889): 186–90.

———. "Marquesan Melville." *Gentleman's Magazine* 272 (March 1892): 248–57.

———. *Richard Jefferies: A Study*. London: Swan Sonnenschein, 1894.

———. "A Sage at Close Quarters." In *Edward Carpenter: In Appreciation*, edited by G. Beith, 180–99. London: George Allen and Unwin, 1933.

Salwak, Dale, ed. *The Literary Biography: Problems and Solutions*. Iowa City: University of Iowa Press, 1996.

Sanborn, Geoffrey. "Whence Come You, Queequeg?" *American Literature* 77, no. 3 (June 2005): 227–57.

Sandberg, Robert A. "'The Adjustment of Screens': Putative Narrators, Authors, and Editors in Melville's Unfinished *Burgundy Club* Book." *Texas Studies in Literature and Language* 31 (Fall 1989): 426–50.

Savoy, Eric. "Arvin's Melville, Martin's Arvin." *GLQ: A Journal of Lesbian and Gay Studies* 14, no. 4 (2008): 609–14.

Scharnhorst, Gary. "Melville Information Response." *American Literature* 62, no. 1 (March 1990): 101.

Schonberger, Howard. "Purposes and Ends in History: Presentism and the New Left." *History Teacher* 7, no. 3 (May 1974): 448–58.

Schultz, Elizabeth. "Melville's Agony: After the Whale." Review of *Herman Melville: A Biography, 1851–1891*, by Hershel Parker. *Common Review* 2 (Winter 2002): 40–46.

Schwartz, Richard B. *After the Death of Literature*. Carbondale: Southern Illinois University Press, 1997.

Sealts, Merton M., Jr., *The Early Lives of Melville: Nineteenth-Century Biographical Sketches and Their Authors*. Madison: University of Wisconsin Press, 1974.

———. *Melville's Reading: Revised and Enlarged Edition*. Columbia: University of South Carolina Press, 1988.

———, ed. "Thomas Melvill, Jr., in *The History of Pittsfield*." *Harvard Library Bulletin* 35, no. 3 (Spring 1987): 201–17.

Sealy, Douglas. Review of *Herman Melville: A Biography, 1819–1851*, by Hershel Parker. *Irish Times*, February 8, 1997.

Sedgwick, Eve Kosofsky. *Between Men: English Literature and Male Homosocial Desire*. New York: Columbia University Press, 1985.

———. *Epistemology of the Closet*. Berkeley: University of California Press, 1990.

Selby, Nick. *Herman Melville, "Moby-Dick."* New York: Columbia University Press, 1999.

Sethi, Aniti. Review of *Melville: His World and Work*, by Andrew Delbanco. *Observer* (London), November 13, 2005.

Seymour, Miranda. "Shaping the Truth." In French and St Clair, 253–66.

Shedd, John. Review of *History in the Present Tense: Engaging Students through Inquiry and Action*, by Douglas Selwyn and Jan Maher. *History Teacher* 37, no. 3 (May 2004): paragraphs 1–6.

Short, Bryan Collier. *Cast by Means of Figures: Herman Melville's Rhetorical Development*. Amherst: University of Massachusetts Press, 1992.

Shulevitz, Judith. "The Close Reader; Get Me Rewrite." *New York Times Book Review*, April 6, 2003, 31.

Silverman, Kenneth. "Mather, Poe, Houdini." In Salwak, 107–16.

Skidelsky, Robert. "Confessions of a Long-Distance Biographer." In Bostridge, 15–30.

Smith, David Livingston. *Less Than Human: Why We Demean, Enslave, and Exterminate Others*. New York: St. Martin's, 2011.

Smith, Sidonie. "Presidential Address: Narrating Lives and Contemporary Imaginaries." *PMLA* 126, no. 3 (May 2011): 564–74.

Smollett, Sara. "Inquiry Log." May 11, 1999. http://www.yellowpigs.net/classes/hawmel.

Smythe, Karen Elizabeth. *Figuring Grief: Gallant, Munro, and the Poetics of Elegy*. Montreal: McGill-Queen's Press, 1992.

Spanos, William V. *The Exceptionalist State and the State of Exception: Herman Melville's "Billy Budd, Sailor."* Baltimore: Johns Hopkins University Press, 2010.

———. "Modern Literary Criticism and the Spatialization of Time: An Existential Critique." *Journal of Aesthetics and Art Criticism* 29, no. 1 (Autumn 1970): 87–104.

Spark, Clare L. *Hunting Captain Ahab: Psychological Warfare and the Melville Revival*. Kent, Ohio: Kent State University Press, 2001.

Spurling, Hilary. "Neither Morbid nor Ordinary." In Homberger and Charmley, 113–22.

Stannard, Martin. "The Necrophiliac Art?" In Salwak, 32–40.

Starr, William W. "Biography Explores Man Behind Classic 'Moby-Dick.'" Review of *Herman Melville: A Biography, 1819–1851*, by Hershel Parker. *The State* (Columbia, S.C.), January 26, 1997.

St Clair, William. "The Biographer as Archaeologist." In France and St Clair, 219–34.

Steel, Ronald. "Responses." In Veninga, 26–29.

Sten, Christopher, ed. *The Savage Eye: Melville and the Visual Arts*. Kent, Ohio: Kent State University Press, 1991.

Stern, Julia A. *The Plight of Feeling: Sympathy and Dissent in the Early American Novel*. Chicago: University of Chicago Press, 1997.

559

Strachey, J. St. Loe. Review of *Herman Melville: Mariner and Mystic*, by Raymond Weaver. *Spectator* 128 (May 6, 1922): 559–60.

Sturrock, John. "The New Model Autobiographer." *New Literary History* 9, no. 1 (Autumn 1977): 51–63.

Sussman, Henry. "The Deconstructor as Politician: Melville's *Confidence-Man.*" *Glyph* 4 (1978): 32–56.

Sutherland, Christine Mason. "Getting to Know Them: Concerning Research into Four Early Women Writers." In *Beyond the Archives: Research as a Lived Process*, edited by Gesa E. Kirsch and Liz Rohan, 28–36. Carbondale: Southern Illinois University Press, 2008.

Sutherland, John. *Last Drink to LA*. London: Faber and Faber, 2001.

———. Review of *Herman Melville: A Biography, 1819–1851*, by Hershel Parker. *Sunday Times* (London), January 5, 1997.

Tanselle, G. Thomas. "Historicism and Critical Editing." *Studies in Bibliography* 39 (1986): 1–46.

———. "Some Principles for Editorial Apparatus." *Studies in Bibliography* 25 (1972): 41–88.

———. "Textual Study and Literary Judgment." *PBSA* 24 (1971): 109–22.

Taylor, Stuart, Jr., and KC Johnson. *Until Proven Innocent: Political Correctness and the Shameful Injustices of the Duke Lacrosse Rape Case*. New York: St. Martin's, 2007.

Taylor, Welford D. Review of *Herman Melville: A Biography: 1819–1851*, by Hershel Parker. *Richmond (Va.) Times-Dispatch*, September 14, 1997.

Thomson, James. *Poems, Essays and Fragments*. London: B. Dobell, 1892.

Thwaite, Ann. "Writing Lives." In Homberger and Charmley, 17–32.

Tolchin, Neal L. *Mourning, Gender, and Creativity in the Art of Herman Melville*. New Haven, Conn.: Yale University Press, 1988.

Tomalin, Claire. "Starting Over." In Bostridge, 90–95.

Tomlinson, H. M. "The Vogue of Herman Melville." *Nation and Athenæum* 31 (September 30, 1922): 857–58.

Tsuzuki, Chushichi. *Edward Carpenter, 1844–1929: Prophet of Human Fellowship*. Cambridge: Cambridge University Press, 1980.

Tuchman, Barbara W. "Biography as a Prism of History." In Oates, 93–103.

———. *Practicing History*. New York: Random House, 1981.

Tuckerman, Henry T. *Book of the Artists. American Artist Life*. New York: G. P. Putnam and Son, 1867.

———, ed. *Old New York; or, Reminiscences of the Past Sixty Years*, by John W. Francis. Revised edition, "With a Memoir of the Author" by Tuckerman. New York: W. J. Widdleton, 1866.

Tuttleton, James W. "Melville in the Try-Pots." Review of *Herman Melville: A Biography: 1819–1851*, by Hershel Parker. *New Criterion* (December 1996): 23–30.

Updike, John. "Melville's Withdrawal." *New Yorker*, May 10, 1982, 120–47.

Vandiver, Frank E. "Biography as an Agent of Humanism." In Veninga, 3–20.

Veninga, James F., ed. *The Biographer's Gift: Life Histories and Humanism*. College Station: Texas A&M University Press, 1983.

Vincent, Howard P., and Luther S. Mansfield, eds., *Moby-Dick*. New York: Hendricks House, 1952.

Walker, Pierre A. "Leon Edel and the 'Policing' of the Henry James Letters." *Henry James Review* (Fall 2000): 279–89.

Wallace, Robert K. *Melville and Turner: Spheres of Love and Fright.* Athens: University of Georgia Press, 1992.

———. "Melville's Prints and Engravings at the Berkshire Athenaeum." *Essays in Arts and Sciences* 15 (June 1986): 59–90.

———. " 'Unlike Things Must Meet and Mate': Melville and the Visual Arts." In *A Companion to Herman Melville,* edited by Wyn Kelley, 342–61. Malden, Mass.: Blackwell, 2006.

Ward, Jerry W., Jr. *The Katrina Papers: A Journal of Trauma and Recovery.* New Orleans: University of New Orleans Publishing, 2008.

Weathers, Willie T. "*Moby-Dick* and the Nineteenth-Century Scene." *University of Texas Studies in Literature and Language* 1, no. 4 (Winter 1960): 477–501. Excerpted in Hayford and Parker, "*Moby-Dick*" *as Doubloon,* 272–77.

Weaver, Raymond. *Herman Melville: Mariner and Mystic.* New York: Doran, 1921.

Webster, Grant. Review of *Biography: Fiction, Fact, and Form,* by Ira Bruce Nadel. *Biography* 9, no. 3 (Summer 1986): 277–79.

Weinstein, Cindy. "Melville, Labor, and the Discourses of Reception." In Levine, 202–23.

Weiss, Philip. "Herman-Neutics." *New York Times Magazine,* December 15, 1996, 60–65, 70, 72.

———. "Melville Mystery Cannot Be Stifled By New Biography." *New York Observer,* June 17, 2002, 1.

———. "Where's the Jewish Visionary of Western Integration?" *Mondoweiss* (June 17, 2009), http://mondoweiss.net/2009/06/one-of-the-most-liberating-things-updike-ever-said-was-at-the-beginning-of-an-essay-on-melville-when-he-said-all-melville-sc.html

Werth, Barry. *The Scarlet Professor: Newton Arvin: A Literary Life Shattered by Scandal.* New York: Doubleday, 2001.

Wheeler, Sara. "Polar Gap." In Bostridge, 86–89.

Widmer, Ted. Review of *Melville: His World and Work,* by Andrew Delbanco. *New York Observer,* September 26, 2005.

Wilson, Edmund. "Fruits of the MLA: I. 'Their Wedding Journey.'" Review of *Their Wedding Journey,* by W. D. Howells, edited by John K. Reeves, and *Typee,* by Herman Melville, edited by Harrison Hayford, Hershel Parker, and G. Thomas Tanselle. *New York Review of Books* 11, no. 5 (September 26, 1968): 7–10. Reprinted in Wilson, *Fruits of the MLA,* 3–47. New York: The New York Review, 1968.

Wilson, Frances. "A Love Triangle." In Bostridge, 38–42.

Wineapple, Brenda. *Hawthorne: A Life.* New York: Knopf, 2003.

———. "Melville at Sea." Review of *Herman Melville: A Biography, 1819–1851,* by Hershel Parker. *Nation* 274, no. 19 (May 20, 2002): 38–42.

Winsten, Stephen. *Salt and His Circle.* London: Hutchinson, 1951.

Wood, James. "The All of the If." Review of *Herman Melville: A Biography, 1819–1851,* by Hershel Parker. *New Republic* 216, no. 11 (March 17, 1997): 29–36.

———. "God's Dictionary." Review of *Melville: His World and Work,* by Andrew Delbanco. *New Republic* 233, nos. 26–28 (December 26, 2005–January 9, 2006): 25–29.

Worthen, John. "The Necessary Ignorance of a Biographer." In Batchelor, 227–44.

Yannella, Donald, and Kathleen Malone Yannella. "Evert A. Duyckinck's 'Diary: May 29–November 8, 1847.'" *Studies in the American Renaissance* (1978): 207–58.

Young, Philip. *The Private Melville.* College Station: Pennsylvania State University Press, 1993.

Index

Most subentries are listed alphabetically, but some historical subjects are in chronological order. Fictional characters are listed by first names. Writings are listed under authors' names, where known. Periodicals are indexed under the city of publication. Relatives of Herman Melville are identified parenthetically, e.g., D'Wolf, Mary (aunt).

About the Author

Hershel Parker is General Editor for the final volumes of the Northwestern-Newberry Edition of *The Writings of Herman Melville* (Northwestern University Press) and the author of the two-volume *Herman Melville: A Biography*.